Theoretical and Numerical Combustion

Third Edition

Thierry Poinsot
Institut de Mécanique des Fluides de Toulouse, CNRS

Denis Veynante
Ecole Centrale Paris, CNRS

Printed by Aquaprint, Bordeaux, France

First edition: R.T. Edwards 2001
Second edition: R.T Edwards 2005
Third edition by the authors

Cover photo credits:

- Cover picture: Dr Vincent Moureau. CORIA Rouen. LES and DNS of a lean premixed swirl flame (Moureau et al. [458]).

- Bottom picture: Dr Anthony Ruiz, CERFACS and SNECMA DMF Vernon. DNS of hydrogen / oxygen combustion in a rocket engine (Ruiz and Selle [575]).

- Back cover right: Dr Felix Jaegle. CERFACS. LES of evaporating fuel spray in an aeronautical multipoint injector (Jaegle et al. [306]).

- Back cover left: Dr Pierre Wolf and Dr Gabriel Staffelbach, CERFACS. Large Eddy Simulation of azimuthal instabilities in an helicopter gas turbine chamber [713, 626].

Special thanks to Juliette Poinsot for the design of the cover pages and to Dr Jean Francois Parmentier for the Elearning web site associated to the book.

This book will be printed and updated every three months. If you find typos, mistakes or things which should be clarified, please send a mail to poinsot@imft.fr and we will modify the following versions.

Theoretical and numerical combustion / Thierry Poinsot, Denis Veynante.
Third Edition, 603 pages.
Includes bibliographical references and index
ISBN: 978-2-7466-3990-4

Contents

3 Laminar diffusion flames

Preface

Introduction

Combustion is the heart of our society where it produces approximately ninety percent of the total energy generated on earth[i] . Despite the growth of renewable energies, combustion will remain the main energy source for a long time and combustion science must allow this without wasting fossil fuels, increasing pollution levels or modifying climate. These challenges can not be met without simulation. Since its first two editions in 2001 and 2005, *Theoretical and Numerical Combustion* has been used by students and researchers interested in numerical simulation of reacting flows but also in the theory required to understand these simulations. This new edition has been improved in various places to clarify various sections (many pointed out by readers) and to incorporate the most significant results of the last five years.

The most important difference for readers is that the book is now coupled to a web site called *elearning.cerfacs.fr* where multiple additional resources are available. For example, many of the chapters are accompanied by videos of the corresponding courses which correspond almost exactly to the first chapters of the book (*elearning.cerfacs.fr/combustion*). At the same address, various tools are available to illustrate the book contents. They can be used by PhD students and engineers for their research work; illustrations based on CFD animations or simple tutorials are also available to simplify the description of phenomena which are much more easily understood by watching a movie than by reading a long written explanation.

Combustion is a field where advances occur rapidly and our primary objectives in preparing this third Edition were:

- to capture the most recent advances in combustion studies so that students and researchers alike can (hopefully) find the essential information in this text;

- to simplify, as much as possible, a complex subject so as to provide a reasonable starting point for combustion beginners, especially those involved in numerical simulations; and

- to build a formation tool based on the present book but also on web possibilities to speed up the learning process of students and researchers. This global tool will be updated on

---

[i]A general introduction to the challenges of combustion science to meet present societal needs in terms of pollution control, climate change, efficiency, fuel availability, technology... is available as a video at *elearning.cerfacs.fr/combustion/n7masterCourses/introduction* or *on youtube: watch?v=JK-K-QTSOqY*.

a regular basis in the future.

Obviously, numerical techniques for combustion are essential tools for both engineers and research specialists. This evolution toward more simulations is dangerous if it is not accompanied by a minimum expertise in combustion theory. Obtaining expertise in combustion theory and modeling is much more difficult than simply being able to run "off-the-shelf" codes for combustion. Yet, considering the enormous stakes associated with the design of combustion devices in terms of both economy and human safety, it is imperative that this deep understanding not be shortcut. To accomplish this we have maintained our presentation of the basic combustion theories, and have sought to establish necessary connections and interrelationships in a logical and comprehensible way. A major evolution of numerical combustion of the past few years is the development of methods and tools to study *unsteady* reacting flows. Two combined influences explain this trend; namely,

- Many of the present challenges in the combustion industry are due to intrinsically unsteady mechanisms: autoignition or cycle-to-cycle variations in piston engines, ignition of rocket engines, combustion instabilities in industrial furnaces and gas turbines, flashback and ignition in aero gas turbines... All these problems can be studied numerically, thus partially explaining the rapid growth of the field.

- Even for stationary combustion, research on classical turbulent combustion models (herein called RANS for Reynolds Averaged Navier Stokes) is being replaced by unsteady approaches (herein called LES for Large Eddy Simulations) because computers allow for the computation of the unsteady motions of the flames. However, these unsteady methods also raise new problems: for example, how are numerical results compared with experimental data, and what explains the deviations?

This book can be read with no previous knowledge of combustion, but it cannot replace many existing books on combustion (Kuo [361], Lewis and Von Elbe [383], Williams [710], Glassman [245], Linan and Williams [399], Borghi and Destriau [73], Peters [502]) and numerical combustion (Oran and Boris [483]). We concentrate on what is not in these books: i.e. giving to readers who know about fluid mechanics all the information necessary to move on to a solid understanding of numerical combustion. We also avoid concentrating on numerical methods for fluid mechanics[ii]. Information on Computational Fluid Dynamics (CFD) may be found in classical textbooks (Roache [559], Anderson [10], Hirsch [294], Tannehill et al. [640], Oran and Boris [483], Ferziger and Perić [210], Sengupta [606]). This text discusses which equations to solve and not on how to solve them.

Two important topics are also absent from the present edition:

- The presentation is limited to deflagrations, i.e. to flames with low speed. Detonations are not considered here (Oran and Boris [483]).

[ii]Even though this book is not on CFD, readers might find interesting to read this short manual (3 pages...) on things to do to make sure your CFD work will fail (or not): *elearning.cerfacs.fr/advices/poinsot/cfd*.

- The chemistry of combustion is also a topic which requires many books in itself. This text does not try to address this issue: the construction of chemical schemes and their reduction and validation are not discussed here. The impact of chemical schemes on reacting flow computations, however, is discussed, especially in the field of turbulent combustion. Recent progress in this field, both at the fundamental level and for practical applications, has changed the way industrial combustion systems are being designed today. The important numerical tools needed to understand this evolution are presented.

The book is organized as follows:

- Chapter 1 first describes the conservation equations needed for reacting flows and reviews different issues which are specific to the numerical resolution of the Navier Stokes equations for a multi-species reacting flow. Tables summarizing the main conservation forms used in numerical combustion codes are provided. Specific difficulties associated with reacting flows are also discussed: models for diffusion velocities, possible simplifications for low-speed flames and simple chemistry approximations. Compared to previous editions, the discussion about diffusion velocities was revised, clearly stating exact formulations and usual approximations (§1.1.4).

- Chapter 2 describes numerical methods for laminar premixed flames. It includes a summary of many significant theoretical results which are useful for numerical combustion: these results provide an understanding of the results and limitations of numerical combustion codes, but also give insight into how to initialize them, determine necessary grid resolutions, and how to verify their results. Extended definitions and examples of flame speeds, flame thicknesses and flame stretch are discussed.

- Chapter 3 introduces laminar diffusion flames and two specific concepts associated with such flames: mixture fraction and scalar dissipation. Asymptotic results and the structure of the "ideal" diffusion flame are used to provide an accurate picture of the phenomenology of these flames before computation.

- Chapter 4 introduces the basic concepts used to study turbulent combustion. Elementary concepts of turbulence and flame/turbulence interaction are described. Averaging and filtering procedures are discussed. A classification of the different methods (RANS: Reynolds Averaged Navier Stokes, LES: Large Eddy Simulation, DNS: Direct Numerical Simulation) used in numerical combustion for turbulent flames is given. This chapter also discusses the incorporation of complex chemistry features in turbulent flame computations (§4.8), the classification of physical approaches to model turbulent combustion (§4.5.5), and the comparison between LES and experimental data (§4.7.8).

- Chapter 5 presents turbulent premixed flames. After a description of the main phenomena characterizing these flames, a review of recent results and theories is presented for RANS, LES and DNS approaches. Implications for turbulent combustion computations are discussed. The close relations between all numerical techniques used in the last ten years (especially DNS results used to develop RANS or LES models) are emphasized.

- Chapter 6 presents turbulent diffusion flames. These flames present even more complexities than premixed flames and numerical investigations have recently helped to uncover many of their specificities. Models are also very diverse. The topology of diffusion flames is first described and RANS methods used for turbulent non premixed combustion are classified for CFD users. Recent advances in the field of LES and DNS are described.

- Chapter 7 addresses the problem of flame/wall interaction which is a critical issue in all combustors: walls must be able to sustain the high flame temperatures. Asymptotic results and DNS studies are used to illustrate the main characteristics of this interaction. Models describing flame/wall effects codes are described. Since the presence of a flame strongly modifies the turbulence as well as the density and the viscosity near walls, models for wall friction and heat transfer in reacting flows are also discussed.

- Chapter 8 describes theoretical and numerical tools used to study the coupling phenomena between combustion and acoustics. This coupling is the source of not only noise, but also of combustion instabilities which can modify the performances of combustors and sometimes lead to their destruction. Basic elements of acoustics in non reacting flows are described before extending acoustic theory to reacting flows. This chapter then focuses on three numerical tools for combustion instability studies: (1) one-dimensional acoustic models to predict the global behavior of a system submitted to longitudinal waves, (2) three-dimensional Helmholtz codes to identify all acoustic modes in a burner and (3) multi-dimensional LES codes to investigate the response of the combustion chamber itself which is a critical building block for acoustic models. Examples of applications of these methods in complex geometries are given in Chapter 10.

- Chapter 9 presents recent techniques to specify boundary conditions for compressible viscous reacting flows. Modern simulation techniques (LES or DNS) as well as recent applications of CFD (such as combustion instabilities described in Chapter 8) require elaborate boundary conditions to handle unsteady combustion and acoustic waves as well as to adjust for numerical schemes which do not provide large levels of dissipation. This chapter provides an overview of such methods and offers a list of test cases for steady and unsteady flows which can be used in any code.

- Chapter 10 describes applications of LES to complex-geometry swirled combustors to predict the mean flow structure and to analyze unsteady hydrodynamic and acoustic phenomena. These examples provide information on the flow physics of these combustors while also demonstrating how recent numerical tools can be applied today.

Thierry POINSOT

Institut de Mécanique des Fluides
UMR CNRS/INP/UPS 5502
Institut National Polytechnique
de Toulouse/ENSEEIHT

Denis VEYNANTE

Laboratoire E.M2.C.
UPR CNRS 288
Ecole Centrale Paris

List of web resources associated to this book

The web site *elearning.cerfacs.fr* contains various types of files which readers may find useful:

Videos

These 90 minutes videos correspond to essential elements of the first three chapters of the book but also to more general combustion material. They cannot replace reading the corresponding chapters but they usually make this reading faster and easier.

- A general introduction to combustion challenges: the place of combustion in the world's energy, climate change and pollution issues, combustion systems optimization, various examples of combustion applications and difficulties, combustion instabilities, pollutants, basics of thermodynamics and kinetics:
  elearning.cerfacs.fr/combustion/n7masterCourses/introduction

- Definition of state variables, the state equation, conservation of enthalpy, how to evaluate flame temperatures, effects of dissociations (chapter 1):
  elearning.cerfacs.fr/combustion/n7masterCourses/adiabaticflametemperature

- The conservation equations for combustion (chapter 1): which equations must be solved in general for a multi species reacting gas ? Continuity, momentum, species equations, diffusion velocities, kinetics, Arrhenius forms, the multiple forms of energy, enthalpy, temperature equations. Simplifications in low-speed flames:
  elearning.cerfacs.fr/combustion/n7masterCourses/conservationequations and
  elearning.cerfacs.fr/combustion/n7masterCourses/conservationequationsP2

- Autoignition times in a fully premixed gas (zero dimensional problem depending only on time). Link between ignition time and activation energy. Effects of heat losses on autoignition. Crossover temperature:
  elearning.cerfacs.fr/combustion/n7masterCourses/autoignition

- Canonical premixed flames (1- chapter 2): the one-dimensional premixed flame. Equations, assumptions, unity Lewis number lean flame analysis, front structure, simple matched expansion asymptotics analysis:
  elearning.cerfacs.fr/combustion/premixedlaminarflamesP1

- Canonical premixed flames (2 - chapter 2): complete resolution of the premixed flame equations using a simplified rate model (Echekki Ferziger), the eigenvalue problem, final form for the flame speed. Consumption and displacement speed, spherical flames. Physical interpretation of flame speeds, flammability limits:
  elearning.cerfacs.fr/combustion/n7masterCourses/premixedlaminarflamesP2

- Canonical diffusion flames (1 - chapter 3): non-premixed regimes, passive scalars and mixture fraction, pure mixing, mixing lines, infinitely fast chemistry, flame structure in

z-space, application to simple laminar flames:
elearning.cerfacs.fr/combustion/n7masterCourses/diffusionflamesP1

- Canonical diffusion flames (2 - chapter 3): what is the integrated reaction rate, what controls a non-premixed flame, complete solution for the unsteady unstrained 1D and the steady strained planar diffusion flame under constant density assumption: *elearning.cerfacs.fr/combustion/n7masterCourses/diffusionflamesP2*

Illustrations

For many combustion examples, short presentations and movies are more useful than a long discussion. Throughout the third edition, links are given to various illustrative resources available on the Elearning web site.

On-line tools and exercices with corrections

Multiple on-line tools and exercices are available on the web site:

- Comparison of methods to compute the burnt gas temperature. From analytical techniques to numerical codes (Cantera, Cosilab, Chemkin). Application to CH_4/air flames: *elearning.cerfacs.fr/combustion/n7masterCourses/adiabaticflametemperature.* A simple calculator for adiabatic flame temperatures based on Cantera. Specify fuel type, pressure and initial temperature, oxygen dilution and obtain the final temperature on line: *elearning.cerfacs.fr/combustion/tools/adiabaticflametemperature.*

- Fast Fourier Transforms: a simple tool to compute the FFT of a signal. Paste the time variations of a signal, the time step and obtain the FFT on line: *elearning.cerfacs.fr/numerical/signal/fourieranalysis.* Tutorial on Fourier analysis: *elearning.cerfacs.fr/numerical/signal/tutorialSpec*

- Combustor modes computations: eigenmodes calculation for combustors containing various 1D ducts and flames. Specify ducts lengths and temperatures, inlet and outlet coefficient reflections and obtain the frequencies and structure of the acoustic eigenmodes: *elearning.cerfacs.fr/combustion/tools/soundtube*

- Dispersion and dissipation of numerical schemes in CFD: a simple tutorial in dispersion and dissipation effects in CFD and a simulation tool are available at: *elearning.cerfacs.fr/numerical/schemes/1Dscheme.*

- Basic notions on discretization of flow equations: a tutorial on discretization methods used in recent CFD codes is available at: *elearning.cerfacs.fr/numerical/schemes/mesh.*

Chapter 1

Conservation equations for reacting flows

1.1   General forms

Analytical and numerical resolutions of the equations of combustion are the main topic of this book. The numerical methods used for combustor designs are key issues in present and future combustion science[i]. The first step is to derive these equations and this section[ii] presents the conservation equations for reacting flows and highlights the differences between these equations and the usual Navier-Stokes equations for non-reacting cases:

- a reacting gas is a non-isothermal mixture of multiple species (hydrocarbons, oxygen, water, carbon dioxyde, etc.) which must be tracked individually. Thermodynamic data are also more complex than in classical aerodynamics because heat capacities in a reacting gas change significantly with temperature and composition,

- species react chemically and the rate at which these reactions take place requires specific modeling,

- since the gas is a mixture of gases, transport coefficients (heat diffusivity, species diffusion, viscosity, etc.) require specific attention.

The derivation of these equations from mass, species or energy balances may be found in such standard books (Williams [710], Kuo [361], Candel [104]). This chapter concentrates on the various forms used in combustion codes and on their implications for numerical techniques.

---

[i]See a general introduction on general combustion issues and impact on society: *elearning.cerfacs.fr/combustion/n7masterCourses/introduction* or *on youtube: watch?v=JK-K-QTSOqY*.

[ii]This section is available on line in two courses: the first one focuses on thermochemistry, state equation and adiabatic flame temperature computations: *elearning.cerfacs.fr/combustion/n7masterCourses/adiabaticflametemperature*. The second one describes conservation equations for reacting flows: *elearning.cerfacs.fr/combustion/n7masterCourses/conservationequations*.

1.1.1   Choice of primitive variables

Combustion involves multiple species reacting through multiple chemical reactions. The Navier-Stokes equations apply for such a multi-species multi-reaction gas but they require some additional terms.

First, species are characterized through their mass fractions Y_k for $k = 1$ to N where N is the number of species in the reacting mixture. The mass fractions Y_k are defined by:

$$\boxed{Y_k = m_k/m} \tag{1.1}$$

where m_k is the mass of species k present in a given volume V and m is the total mass of gas in this volume. The primitive variables for a three-dimensional compressible reacting flow are:

- the density $\rho = m/V$,

- the three dimensional velocity field u_i,

- one variable for energy (or pressure or enthalpy or temperature T),

- and the mass fractions Y_k of the N reacting species.

Going from non reacting flow to combustion requires solving for $N + 5$ variables instead of 5. Knowing that most chemical schemes involve a large number of species (N is larger than 50 for most simple hydrocarbon fuels), this is the first significant effort needed to compute reacting flows: increase the number of conservation equations to solve.

Thermochemistry

For a mixture of N perfect gases, total pressure is the sum of partial pressures:

$$p = \sum_{k=1}^{N} p_k \quad \text{where} \quad p_k = \rho_k \frac{R}{W_k} T \tag{1.2}$$

where T is the temperature, $R = 8.314 \, J/(mole K)$ is the perfect gas constant, $\rho_k = \rho Y_K$ and W_k are respectively the density and the atomic weight of species k. Since the density ρ of the multi-species gas is:

$$\boxed{\rho = \sum_{k=1}^{N} \rho_k} \tag{1.3}$$

the state equation is:

$$\boxed{p = \rho \frac{R}{W} T} \tag{1.4}$$

where W is the mean molecular weight of the mixture given by:

$$\frac{1}{W} = \sum_{k=1}^{N} \frac{Y_k}{W_k} \qquad (1.5)$$

Mass fractions are used in most combustion codes, but other quantities are also commonly introduced to measure concentrations of species (see Table 1.1):

- the mole fraction X_k is the ratio of the number of moles of species k in a volume V to the total number of moles in the same volume.

- the molar concentration $[X_k]$ is the number of moles of species k per unit volume. It is the quantity used to evaluate kinetic rates of chemical reactions (see Eq. (1.24)).

Quantity	Definition	Useful relations
Mass fraction Y_k	Mass of species k / Total Mass	Y_k
Mole fraction X_k	Moles of species k / Total moles	$X_k = \frac{W}{W_k} Y_k$
Molar concentration $[X_k]$	Moles of species k / Unit volume	$[X_k] = \rho \frac{Y_k}{W_k} = \rho \frac{X_k}{W}$
Mean molecular weight W	$\frac{1}{W} = \sum_{k=1}^{N} \frac{Y_k}{W_k}$ and $W = \sum_{k=1}^{N} X_k W_k$	

Table 1.1: Definitions of mass fractions, mole fractions, molar concentrations and useful relations.

For a reacting flow, there are multiple possible variables to represent energy or enthalpy: Table 1.2 gives definitions for energy (e_k), enthalpy (h_k), sensible energy (e_{sk}) and sensible enthalpy (h_{sk}) for one species.

Form	Energy		Enthalpy	
Sensible	e_{sk}	$= \int_{T_0}^{T} C_{vk} dT - RT_0/W_k$	h_{sk}	$= \int_{T_0}^{T} C_{pk} dT$
Sensible+Chemical	e_k	$= e_{sk} + \Delta h_{f,k}^o$	h_k	$= h_{sk} + \Delta h_{f,k}^o$

Table 1.2: Enthalpy and energy forms for species k. Enthalpies and energies are related by $e_{sk} = h_{sk} - p_k/\rho_k$ and $e_k = h_k - p_k/\rho_k$.

The mass enthalpy of formation of species k at temperature T_0 is written $\Delta h_{f,k}^o$. In principle, any value could be assigned to the reference temperature T_0. $T_0 = 0$ would have been a logical choice (Reynolds and Perkins [552]) but gathering experimental information on formation enthalpies at 0 K is difficult so that the standard reference state used to tabulate formation enthalpies is usually set to $T_0 = 298.15\,K$.

In addition to the reference temperature T_0, a reference enthalpy (or energy) value must also be chosen. This level is set up by assuming that the enthalpy h_k is such that:

$$h_k = \underbrace{\int_{T_0}^{T} C_{pk} dT}_{\text{sensible}} + \underbrace{\Delta h_{f,k}^o}_{\text{chemical}} \qquad (1.6)$$

so that the sensible enthalpy h_{sk} is zero at $T = T_0$ for all substances (even though the enthalpy at $T = T_0$ ($h_k = \Delta h_{f,k}^o$) is not). Furthermore, sensible energies are defined to satisfy $h_{sk} = e_{sk} + p_k/\rho_k$. This choice requires the introduction of the RT_0/W_k term in e_{sk}: the sensible enthalpy h_{sk} is zero at $T = T_0$ but the sensible energy e_{sk} is not: $e_{sk}(T_0) = -RT_0/W_k$.[iii]

In all these forms, energies and enthalpies are *mass* quantities: for example, the formation enthalpies $\Delta h_{f,k}^o$ are the enthalpies needed to form 1 kg of species k at the reference temperature $T_0 = 298.15\,K$. These values are linked to molar values $\Delta h_{f,k}^{o,m}$ (which are often the values given in textbooks) by:

$$\Delta h_{f,k}^o = \Delta h_{f,k}^{o,m}/W_k \qquad (1.7)$$

For example, the mass formation enthalpy of CH_4 is -4675 kJ/kg while its molar formation enthalpy $\Delta h_{f,k}^{o,m}$ is -74.8 kJ/mole. Table 1.3 gives reference values of $\Delta h_{f,k}^o$ and $\Delta h_{f,k}^{o,m}$ for some typical fuels and products used for examples in this book.

Substance	Molecular weight W_k (kg/mole)	Mass formation enthalpy $\Delta h_{f,k}^o$ (kJ/kg)	Molar formation enthalpy $\Delta h_{f,k}^{o,m}$ (kJ/mole)
CH_4	0.016	-4675	-74.8
C_3H_8	0.044	-2360	-103.8
C_8H_{18}	0.114	-1829	-208.5
CO_2	0.044	-8943	-393.5
H_2O	0.018	-13435	-241.8
O_2	0.032	0	0
H_2	0.002	0	0
N_2	0.028	0	0

Table 1.3: Formation enthalpies (gaseous substances) at $T_0 = 298.15\,K$.

[iii] Another solution would be to define $e_{sk} = \int_{T_0}^{T} C_{vk} dT$ and $e_k = e_{sk} + \Delta h_{f,k}^o - RT_0/W_k$ where $\Delta e_{f,k}^o = \Delta h_{f,k}^o - RT_0/W_k$ would be a formation energy at constant volume. In this case e_{sk} and $h_{sk} - p_k/\rho_k$ would be different. The final equations are equivalent.

The heat capacities at constant pressure of species k (C_{pk}) are mass heat capacities related to molar capacities C_{pk}^m by $C_{pk} = C_{pk}^m/W_k$. For a perfect diatomic gas:

$$C_{pk}^m = 3.5R \quad \text{and} \quad C_{pk} = 3.5R/W_k \tag{1.8}$$

In practice, the changes of C_{pk}^m with temperature are large in combusting flows and C_{pk}^m values are usually tabulated as temperature functions using polynomials (Stull and Prophet [632], Heywood [284]). Fig. 1.1 shows heat capacities C_{pk}^m (divided by the perfect gas constant R) as a function of temperature. While N_2 and H_2 heat capacities are of the order of $3.5R$ at low temperatures, they deviate rapidly from this value at high temperature.

The mass heat capacities C_{pk} of usual gases are displayed in Fig. 1.2. CO_2, CO and N_2 have very similar values of C_{pk}. Water has a higher capacity (2000 to 3000 J/(kgK)) and H_2 mass heat capacities are much higher (of the order of 16000 J/(kgK)).

The mass heat capacities C_{vk} at constant volume are related to the C_{pk} by:

$$C_{pk} - C_{vk} = R/W_k \tag{1.9}$$

For a mixture of N species, Table 1.4 summarizes the different forms used for energy and enthalpy (eight because of the possible combinations between sensible, kinetic and chemical parts). The enthalpy h is defined by:

$$h = \sum_{k=1}^{N} h_k Y_k = \sum_{k=1}^{N} \left(\int_{T_0}^{T} C_{pk} dT + \Delta h_{f,k}^o \right) Y_k = \int_{T_0}^{T} C_p dT + \sum_{k=1}^{N} \Delta h_{f,k}^o Y_k \tag{1.10}$$

while the energy $e = h - p/\rho$ is given by, using Eq. (1.4), (1.5) and (1.9):

$$e = \sum_{k=1}^{N} \left(\int_{T_0}^{T} C_{pk} dT - RT/W_k + \Delta h_{f,k}^o \right) Y_k = \sum_{k=1}^{N} \left(\int_{T_0}^{T} C_{vk} dT - RT_0/W_k + \Delta h_{f,k}^o \right) Y_k$$

$$= \int_{T_0}^{T} C_v dT - RT_0/W + \sum_{k=1}^{N} \Delta h_{f,k}^o Y_k = \sum_{k=1}^{N} e_k Y_k \tag{1.11}$$

Most compressible codes use the total non chemical energy (E) and enthalpy (H) forms for non reacting flows.

The heat capacity at constant pressure of the mixture, C_p, is:

$$\boxed{C_p = \sum_{k=1}^{N} C_{pk} Y_k = \sum_{k=1}^{N} C_{pk}^m \frac{Y_k}{W_k}} \tag{1.12}$$

Eq. (1.12) shows that the mixture heat capacity C_p is a function both of temperature (T) and composition (Y_k). It may change significantly from one point to another. However, in most hydrocarbon/air flames, the properties of nitrogen dominate and the mass heat capacity

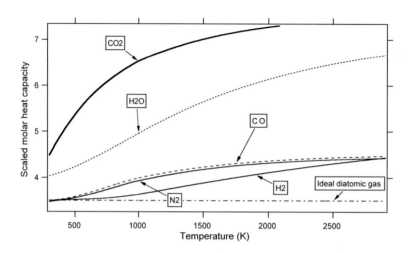

Figure 1.1: Scaled molar heat capacities at constant pressure C_{pk}^m/R of CO_2, CO, H_2O, H_2 and N_2.

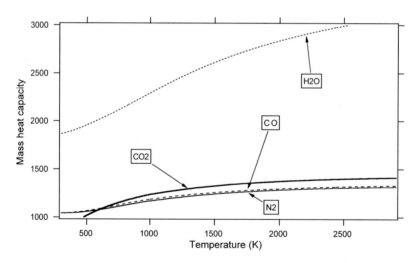

Figure 1.2: Mass heat capacities (J/(kgK)) at constant pressure C_{pk} of CO_2, CO, H_2O and N_2.

Form	Energy	Enthalpy
Sensible	$e_s = \int_{T_0}^{T} C_v dT - RT_0/W$	$h_s = \int_{T_0}^{T} C_p dT$
Sensible+Chemical	$e = e_s + \sum_{k=1}^{N} \Delta h_{f,k}^o Y_k$	$h = h_s + \sum_{k=1}^{N} \Delta h_{f,k}^o Y_k$
Total Chemical	$e_t = e + \frac{1}{2} u_i u_i$	$h_t = h + \frac{1}{2} u_i u_i$
Total non Chemical	$E = e_s + \frac{1}{2} u_i u_i$	$H = h_s + \frac{1}{2} u_i u_i$

Table 1.4: Enthalpy and energy forms used in conservation equations.

of the mixture is very close to that of nitrogen. Furthermore, this value changes only from 1000 to 1300 J/(kg K) when temperature goes from 300 K to 3000 K so that C_p is often assumed to be constant in many theoretical approaches (§ 2 and 3) and some combustion codes.

The heat capacity of the mixture at constant volume, C_v, is defined as:

$$C_v = \sum_{k=1}^{N} C_{vk} Y_k = \sum_{k=1}^{N} C_{vk}^m \frac{Y_k}{W_k} \qquad (1.13)$$

where the heat capacities C_{vk} of individual species are obtained by: $C_{vk} = C_{pk} - R/W_k$ for mass values or $C_{vk}^m = C_{pk}^m - R$ for molar values.

Viscous tensor

The velocity components are called u_i for $i = 1$ to 3. The viscous tensor τ_{ij} is defined by:

$$\tau_{ij} = -\frac{2}{3}\mu \frac{\partial u_k}{\partial x_k}\delta_{ij} + \mu\left(\frac{\partial u_i}{\partial x_j} + \frac{\partial u_j}{\partial x_i}\right) \qquad (1.14)$$

where p is the static pressure and μ is the dynamic viscosity. The kinematic viscosity is $\nu = \mu/\rho$. The bulk viscosity is supposed to be zero (Kuo [361]). δ_{ij} is the Kronecker symbol: $\delta_{ij} = 1$ if $i = j$, 0 otherwise.

Viscous and pressure tensors are often combined into the σ_{ij} tensor defined by:

$$\sigma_{ij} = \tau_{ij} - p\delta_{ij} = -p\delta_{ij} - \frac{2}{3}\mu\frac{\partial u_k}{\partial x_k}\delta_{ij} + \mu\left(\frac{\partial u_i}{\partial x_j} + \frac{\partial u_j}{\partial x_i}\right) \qquad (1.15)$$

Molecular transport of species and heat

The heat diffusion coefficient is called λ. The diffusion coefficient of species k in the rest of the mixture (used in Fick's law, see below) is called D_k. Diffusion processes involve binary diffusion coefficients (D_{kj}) and require the resolution of a system giving diffusion velocities. This is not done in most combustion codes (Ern and Giovangigli [201]): solving the diffusion problem in a multi-species gas is a problem in itself. Simplified diffusion laws (usually Fick's law) are used in a majority of combustion codes and this text is restricted to this case. The D_k coefficients are often characterized in terms of Lewis number defined by:

$$Le_k = \frac{\lambda}{\rho C_p D_k} = \frac{D_{th}}{D_k} \qquad (1.16)$$

where $D_{th} = \lambda/(\rho C_p)$ is the heat diffusivity coefficient. The Lewis number Le_k compares the diffusion speeds of heat and species k. Section 2.4 shows that this parameter is important in laminar flames. Le_k is a local quantity but, in most gases, it changes very little from one point to another. The kinetic theory of gases (Hirschfelder et al. [295]) shows that λ changes roughly like $T^{0.7}$, ρ like $1/T$ and D_k like $T^{1.7}$ so that Le_k is changing only by a few percents in a flame. This property is used in § 1.1.3.

The Prandtl number, Pr, compares momentum and heat transport:

$$Pr = \frac{\nu}{\lambda/(\rho C_p)} = \frac{\rho \nu C_p}{\lambda} = \frac{\mu C_p}{\lambda} \qquad (1.17)$$

The Schmidt number, Sc_k, compares momentum and species k molecular diffusion:

$$Sc_k = \frac{\nu}{D_k} = Pr\, Le_k \qquad (1.18)$$

Soret (molecular species diffusion due to temperature gradients) and Dufour (heat flux due to species mass fraction gradients) effects are neglected for this presentation (Ern and Giovangigli [201], Giovangigli [237]).

Chemical kinetics

Consider a chemical system of N species reacting through M reactions:

$$\sum_{k=1}^{N} \nu'_{kj} \mathcal{M}_k \rightleftharpoons \sum_{k=1}^{N} \nu''_{kj} \mathcal{M}_k \quad \text{for} \quad j = 1, M \qquad (1.19)$$

where $\mathcal{M}_k$ is a symbol for species k, ν'_{kj} and ν''_{kj} are the molar stoichiometric coefficients of species k in reaction j. Mass conservation enforces:

$$\sum_{k=1}^{N} \nu'_{kj} W_k = \sum_{k=1}^{N} \nu''_{kj} W_k \quad \text{or} \quad \sum_{k=1}^{N} \nu_{kj} W_k = 0 \qquad \text{for} \quad j = 1, M \qquad (1.20)$$

where

$$\nu_{kj} = \nu''_{kj} - \nu'_{kj} \qquad (1.21)$$

For simplicity, only mass reaction rates are used. For species k, this rate $\dot{\omega}_k$ is the sum of rates $\dot{\omega}_{kj}$ produced by all M reactions:

$$\dot{\omega}_k = \sum_{j=1}^{M} \dot{\omega}_{kj} = W_k \sum_{j=1}^{M} \nu_{kj} \mathcal{Q}_j \quad \text{with} \quad \frac{\dot{\omega}_{kj}}{W_k \nu_{kj}} = \mathcal{Q}_j \qquad (1.22)$$

where $\mathcal{Q}_j$ is the rate of progress of reaction j.

Summing all reaction rates $\dot{\omega}_k$ and using Eq. (1.20), one obtains:

$$\sum_{k=1}^{N} \dot{\omega}_k = \sum_{j=1}^{M} \left(\mathcal{Q}_j \sum_{k=1}^{N} W_k \nu_{kj} \right) = 0 \qquad (1.23)$$

showing that total mass is conserved.

The progress rate $\mathcal{Q}_j$ of reaction j is written:

$$\mathcal{Q}_j = K_{fj} \prod_{k=1}^{N} [X_k]^{\nu'_{kj}} - K_{rj} \prod_{k=1}^{N} [X_k]^{\nu''_{kj}} \qquad (1.24)$$

where K_{fj} and K_{rj} are the forward and reverse rates of reaction j. Note that kinetic rates are expressed using molar concentrations $[X_k] = \rho Y_k / W_k = \rho_k / W_k$ (see Table 1.1).

The rate constants K_{fj} and K_{rj} constitute a central problem of combustion modeling. They are usually modeled using the empirical Arrhenius law:

$$K_{fj} = A_{fj} T^{\beta_j} \exp\left(-\frac{E_j}{RT}\right) = A_{fj} T^{\beta_j} \exp\left(-\frac{T_{aj}}{T}\right) \qquad (1.25)$$

Expressing the individual progress rates $\mathcal{Q}_j$ for each reaction means providing data for the preexponential constant A_{fj}, the temperature exponent β_j and the activation temperature T_{aj} (or equivalently the activation energy $E_j = RT_{aj}$). Before giving these constants, even identifying which species and which reactions should or should not be kept in a given scheme is the challenge of chemical kinetics. Describing the construction of chemical schemes and their validation is beyond the scope of this text. In most numerical approaches for reacting flows, the chemical scheme is one of the data elements which must be available for the computation. Certain properties of the kinetics data have a crucial effect on the success of the computation (as discussed in Section 2) so numerical combustion users cannot avoid considering the characteristics of these schemes. An example of a kinetic scheme for H_2 - O_2 combustion (Miller et al. [442]) is given in Table 1.5 in standard CHEMKIN format (Kee et al. [331]). First, elements and species which have been retained for the scheme are listed. For each reaction, the table then gives A_{fj} in cgs units, β_j and E_j in cal/mole. The backwards rates K_{rj} are computed from the forward rates through the equilibrium constants:

$$K_{rj} = \frac{K_{fj}}{\left(\dfrac{p_a}{RT}\right)^{\sum_{k=1}^{N} \nu_{kj}} \exp\left(\dfrac{\Delta S_j^0}{R} - \dfrac{\Delta H_j^0}{RT}\right)} \tag{1.26}$$

where $p_a = 1$ bar. The Δ symbols refer to changes occurring when passing from reactants to products in the jth reaction: ΔH_j^0 and ΔS_j^0 are respectively enthalpy and entropy changes for reaction j. These quantities are obtained from tabulations.

```
ELEMENTS
  H    O    N
END
SPECIES
H2 O2 OH O H H2O HO2 H2O2 N2
END
REACTIONS
H2+O2=OH+OH                          1.700E13     0.0      47780.
H2+OH=H2O+H                          1.170E09     1.30      3626.
H+O2=OH+O                            5.130E16    -0.816    16507.
O+H2=OH+H                            1.800E10     1.0       8826.
H+O2+M=HO2+M                         2.100E18    -1.0         0.
  H2/3.3/ O2/0./ N2/0./  H2O/21.0/
H+O2+O2=HO2+O2                       6.700E19    -1.42        0.
H+O2+N2=HO2+N2                       6.700E19    -1.42        0.
OH+HO2=H2O+O2                        5.000E13     0.0      1000.
H+HO2=OH+OH                          2.500E14     0.0      1900.
O+HO2=O2+OH                          4.800E13     0.0      1000.
OH+OH=O+H2O                          6.000E08     1.3         0.
H2+M=H+H+M                           2.230E12     0.5     92600.
  H2/3./ H/2./  H2O/6.0/
O2+M=O+O+M                           1.850E11     0.5     95560.
H+OH+M=H2O+M                         7.500E23    -2.6         0.
  H2O/20.0/
HO2+H=H2+O2                          2.500E13     0.0       700.
HO2+HO2=H2O2+O2                      2.000E12     0.0         0.
H2O2+M=OH+OH+M                       1.300E17     0.0     45500.
H2O2+H=H2+HO2                        1.600E12     0.0      3800.
H2O2+OH=H2O+HO2                      1.000E13     0.0      1800.
END
```

Table 1.5: 9 species / 19 reactions chemical scheme for H_2 - O_2 combustion (Miller et al. [442]). For each reaction, the table provides respectively A_{fj} (cgs units), β_j and E_j (cal/mole).

At this point, for numerical combustion users, it is important to mention that data on Q_j correspond to models: except for certain reactions, these data are obtained experimentally and values of kinetic parameters are often disputed in the kinetics community (Just [318], Westbrook et al. [703]). For many flames, very different schemes are found in the literature with very comparable accuracy and the choice of a scheme is a difficult and controversial task.

Unfortunately, the values of the parameters used to compute $\mathcal{Q}_j$ and the stiffness associated with the determination of $\mathcal{Q}_j$ create a central difficulty for numerical combustion: the space and time scales corresponding to the $\mathcal{Q}_j$ terms are usually very small and require meshes and time steps which can be orders of magnitude smaller than in non reacting flows. Particular attention must be paid to the activation energy E_j (usually measured in kcal/mole in the combustion community): the exponential dependence of rates to E_j leads to considerable difficulties when E_j takes large values (typically more than 60 kcal/mole). A code for laminar flames may work perfectly with a given mesh when E_j is small but will require many more points to resolve the flame structure when E_j is increased even by a small amount (see § 2.4.4).

Stoichiometry in premixed flames

Even though multiple radicals may be involved in a flame, certain species are more important to characterize the combustion regime. The equivalence ratio (the ratio between fuel and oxidizer mass fractions) is the first parameter used to characterize a flame. Its definition depends on the configuration of the burner (premixed or non premixed: Fig. 1.3).

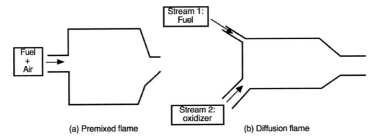

Figure 1.3: Premixed and diffusion flames configurations.

In a premixed combustor (Fig. 1.3a), fuel and oxidizer are mixed before they enter the combustion chamber. If ν'_F and ν'_O are the coefficients corresponding to fuel and oxidizer when considering an overall unique reaction of the type

$$\nu'_F F + \nu'_O O \rightarrow Products \tag{1.27}$$

(for example $CH_4 + 2O_2 \rightarrow CO_2 + 2H_2O$), the mass fractions of fuel and oxidizer correspond to stoichiometric conditions when:

$$\boxed{\left(\frac{Y_O}{Y_F}\right)_{st} = \frac{\nu'_O W_O}{\nu'_F W_F} = s} \tag{1.28}$$

This ratio s is called the mass stoichiometric ratio. The equivalence ratio of a given mixture is then:

$$\boxed{\phi = s\frac{Y_F}{Y_O} = \left(\frac{Y_F}{Y_O}\right) \bigg/ \left(\frac{Y_F}{Y_O}\right)_{st}}$$ (1.29)

It can also be recast as:

$$\phi = s\dot{m}_F/\dot{m}_O$$ (1.30)

where $\dot{m}_F$ and $\dot{m}_O$ are respectively the mass flow rates of fuel and oxidizer.

The equivalence ratio controls premixed combustion: rich combustion is obtained for $\phi > 1$ (the fuel is in excess) while lean regimes are achieved when $\phi < 1$ (the oxidizer is in excess). Most practical burners operate at or below stoichiometry. In hydrocarbon/air flames, the fresh gases contain Fuel, O_2 and N_2 with typically 3.76 moles of nitrogen for 1 mole of oxygen. Since the sum of mass fractions must be unity, the fuel mass fraction is:

$$\boxed{Y_F = \frac{1}{1 + (1 + 3.76 W_{N_2}/W_{O_2})\,s/\phi}}$$ (1.31)

Table 1.6 shows typical values of the stoichiometric ratio s and of corresponding fuel mass fractions for stoichiometric mixtures ($\phi = 1$) with air.

Global reaction		s	Y_F^{st}
$CH_4 + 2(O_2 + 3.76N_2)$	$\rightarrow \quad CO_2 + 2H_2O + 7.52N_2$	4.00	0.055
$C_3H_8 + 5(O_2 + 3.76N_2)$	$\rightarrow \quad 3CO_2 + 4H_2O + 18.8N_2$	3.63	0.060
$2C_8H_{18} + 25(O_2 + 3.76N_2)$	$\rightarrow \quad 16CO_2 + 18H_2O + 94N_2$	3.51	0.062
$2H_2 + (O_2 + 3.76N_2)$	$\rightarrow \quad 2H_2O + 3.76N_2$	8.00	0.028

Table 1.6: Stoichiometric ratio s and fuel mass fraction for stoichiometric combustion ($\phi = 1$) in air given by Eq. (1.31).

Values of the fuel mass fraction at stoichiometry are very small (Table 1.6) so that the premixed gas entering the chamber contains mostly air: adding fuel to air to obtain a reacting mixture does not significantly modify the properties of air in terms of molecular weights, transport properties and heat capacities compared to pure air. This is used in many theories of premixed flames and in certain codes to simplify the evaluation of transport and thermodynamic properties.

Stoichiometry in diffusion flames

For a diffusion flame, fuel and oxidizer are introduced separately into the combustion chamber through two (or more) inlets where flow rates and mass fractions are controlled separately. For the combustor of Fig. 1.3b with only two inlets (one for the fuel stream with a fuel mass fraction Y_F^1 and the other for the oxidizer stream with an oxidizer mass fraction Y_O^2), a first definition of equivalence ratio is:

$$\boxed{\phi = sY_F^1/Y_O^2}$$ (1.32)

This ratio characterizes the local structure of the flames formed when the two streams (fuel and oxidizer) interact. However, it does not represent the overall behavior of the combustor for which a global equivalence ratio ϕ_g must be introduced:

$$\phi_g = s\dot{m}_F^1/\dot{m}_O^2$$

(1.33)

where $\dot{m}_F^1$ and $\dot{m}_O^2$ are the flow rates of fuel in the first inlet and of oxidizer in the second respectively. The global (ϕ_g) and the local (ϕ) equivalence ratios are linked by:

$$\phi_g = \phi\dot{m}^1/\dot{m}^2$$

(1.34)

where $\dot{m}^1$ and $\dot{m}^2$ are the total flow rates entering inlet 1 and 2 respectively. For premixed combustors, fuel and oxidizer are carried by the same stream and $\dot{m}^1 = \dot{m}^2$ so that $\phi_g = \phi$. For non premixed systems, these two quantities may differ significantly.[iv]

1.1.2 Conservation of momentum

The equation of momentum is the same in reacting and non-reacting flows[v]

$$\frac{\partial}{\partial t}\rho u_j + \frac{\partial}{\partial x_i}\rho u_i u_j = -\frac{\partial p}{\partial x_j} + \frac{\partial \tau_{ij}}{\partial x_i} + \rho \sum_{k=1}^{N} Y_k f_{k,j} = \frac{\partial \sigma_{ij}}{\partial x_i} + \rho \sum_{k=1}^{N} Y_k f_{k,j}$$

(1.35)

where $f_{k,j}$ is the volume force acting on species k in direction j. Even though this equation does not include explicit reaction terms, the flow is modified by combustion: the dynamic viscosity μ strongly changes because temperature varies in a ratio from 1:8 or 1:10. Density also changes in the same ratio and dilatation through the flame front increases all speeds by the same ratio. As a consequence, the local Reynolds number varies much more than in a non reacting flow: even though the momentum equations are the same with and without combustion, the flow behavior is very different. A typical example is found in jets: turbulent non reacting jets may become laminar once they are ignited (Lewis and Von Elbe [383]).

1.1.3 Conservation of mass and species

The total mass conservation equation is unchanged compared to non reacting flows (combustion does not generate mass):

$$\frac{\partial \rho}{\partial t} + \frac{\partial \rho u_i}{\partial x_i} = 0$$

(1.36)

[iv]The excess air, defined by $e = 100(1 - \phi_g)/\phi_g$, is also used to characterize the overall mixture. It gives the percentage of air in excess of the flow rate required to consume all the fuel injected into the burner.

[v]In this book, two notations are used for gradients: either ∇f or $\frac{\partial f}{\partial x_i}$.

The mass conservation equation for species k is written:

$$\boxed{\frac{\partial \rho Y_k}{\partial t} + \frac{\partial}{\partial x_i}(\rho(u_i + V_{k,i})Y_k) = \dot{\omega}_k} \quad \text{for} \quad k = 1, N \qquad (1.37)$$

where $V_{k,i}$ is the i-component of the diffusion velocity V_k of species k and $\dot{\omega}_k$ its reaction rate. Summing all species equations (1.37) and using Eq. (1.23) ($\sum_{k=1}^{N} \dot{\omega}_k = 0$) gives:

$$\frac{\partial \rho}{\partial t} + \frac{\partial \rho u_i}{\partial x_i} = -\frac{\partial}{\partial x_i}\left(\rho \sum_{k=1}^{N} Y_k V_{k,i}\right) + \sum_{k=1}^{N} \dot{\omega}_k = -\frac{\partial}{\partial x_i}\left(\rho \sum_{k=1}^{N} Y_k V_{k,i}\right) \qquad (1.38)$$

which must lead to the total mass conservation (1.36) so that a necessary condition is:

$$\boxed{\sum_{k=1}^{N} Y_k V_{k,i} = 0} \qquad (1.39)$$

1.1.4   Diffusion velocities: full equations and approximations

The diffusion velocities V_k are obtained by solving the system (Williams [710]):

$$\nabla X_p = \sum_{k=1}^{N} \frac{X_p X_k}{\mathcal{D}_{pk}}(V_k - V_p) + (Y_p - X_p)\frac{\nabla P}{P} + \frac{\rho}{p}\sum_{k=1}^{N} Y_p Y_k (f_p - f_k) \quad \text{for} \quad p = 1, N \quad (1.40)$$

where $\mathcal{D}_{pk} = \mathcal{D}_{kp}$ is the binary mass diffusion coefficient of species p into species k and X_k is the mole fraction of species k: $X_k = Y_k W/W_k$. The Soret effect (the diffusion of mass due to temperature gradients) is neglected. The system (1.40) is a linear system of size N^2 which must be solved in each direction at each point and at each instant for unsteady flows. Mathematically, this task is difficult and costly (Ern and Giovangigli [201]). Two simplifications are common: the Fick's law for theoretical and analytical flame studies and Hirschfelder and Curtiss approximation in most numerical tools. These two methods are discussed below.

Fick's law

If pressure gradients are small and volume forces are neglected, system (1.40) can be solved exactly in two cases. First, if the mixture contains only two species ($N = 2$), the system (1.40) reduces to a scalar equation where the unknown are the two diffusion velocities V_1 and V_2:

$$\nabla X_1 = \frac{X_1 X_2}{\mathcal{D}_{12}}(V_2 - V_1) \qquad (1.41)$$

Starting from $Y_1 = W_1 X_1/W$, it is simple to show that $\nabla X_1 = W^2/(W_1 W_2)\nabla Y_1$. Substituting ∇X_1 into Eq. (1.41) and using $Y_1 V_1 + Y_2 V_2 = 0$ (from Eq. (1.39)) leads to:

$$V_1 X_1 = -\mathcal{D}_{12}\frac{Y_2}{X_2}\nabla X_1 \quad \text{and} \quad V_1 Y_1 = -\mathcal{D}_{12}\nabla Y_1 \quad \text{or} \quad \boxed{V_1 = -\mathcal{D}_{12}\nabla ln(Y_1)} \tag{1.42}$$

which is Fick's law (Kuo [361]). This expression is exact. A second case where Fick's law is exact is multispecies diffusion ($N > 2$) when all binary diffusion coefficients are equal (Williams [710]): $\mathcal{D}_{ij} = D$. In this situation, system (1.40) is written:

$$X_p V_p = X_p \sum_{k=1}^{N} X_k V_k - D\nabla X_p \quad p = 1, N \tag{1.43}$$

Following Williams [710], Eq. 1.43 can be multiplied by Y_p/X_p and summed over all p's using Eq. (1.39) to obtain an expression for $\sum_{k=1}^{N} X_k V_k$:

$$\sum_{k=1}^{N} X_k V_k = D\sum_{p=1}^{N} Y_p \nabla ln(X_p)$$

Substituting this expression back into Eq. (1.43) leads again to Fick's law:

$$V_p = D\sum_{j=1}^{N} Y_j \nabla ln(X_j) - D\nabla ln(X_p) = D\sum_{j=1}^{N} Y_j \nabla ln(Y_j W) - D\nabla ln(Y_p W) = -D\nabla ln(Y_p)$$

using the expression of molar fractions: $X_p = Y_p W/W_p$. Most flame theories (see Chapters 2 and 3) assume that all species have identical diffusion coefficients so that Fick's law is a common choice in theoretical flame studies. As soon as a more detailed description of transport is required (typically to describe more complex kinetics), Fick's law should not be used and in most codes, it is replaced by the Hirschfelder and Curtiss approximation.

Hirschfelder and Curtiss approximation

When Fick's law can not be used, the rigorous inversion of system (1.40) in a multispecies gas is often replaced by the Hirschfelder and Curtiss approximation (Hirschfelder et al. [295]) which is the best first-order approximation to the exact resolution of system (1.40) (Ern and Giovangigli [201], Giovangigli [237]):

$$\boxed{V_k X_k = -D_k \nabla X_k} \quad \text{with} \quad D_k = \frac{1 - Y_k}{\Sigma_{j\neq k} X_j/\mathcal{D}_{jk}} \tag{1.44}$$

The coefficient D_k is not a binary diffusion but an equivalent diffusion coefficient of species k into the rest of the mixture. Eq. 1.44 leads to the following species equation[vi]:

$$\boxed{\frac{\partial \rho Y_k}{\partial t} + \frac{\partial \rho u_i Y_k}{\partial x_i} = \frac{\partial}{\partial x_i}\left(\rho D_k \frac{W_k}{W}\frac{\partial X_k}{\partial x_i}\right) + \dot{\omega}_k} \tag{1.45}$$

[vi]Note the W_k/W factor in the RHS diffusion term of Eq. (1.45), missing in Fick's law (1.42).

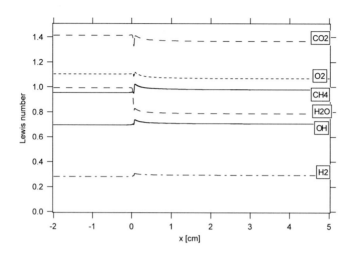

Figure 1.4: Variations of Lewis numbers (defined by Eq. (1.16)) of the main species in a stoichiometric laminar methane air flame (B. Bedat, private communication, 1999).

The Hirschfelder and Curtiss approximation is a convenient approximation because the diffusion coefficients D_k can be simply linked to the heat diffusivity D_{th} in many flames: the Lewis numbers of individual species $Le_k = D_{th}/D_k$ are usually varying by small amounts in flame fronts. Fig. 1.4 shows a computation of Lewis numbers of main species for a premixed stoichiometric methane/air flame plotted versus spatial coordinate through the flame front. Lewis numbers change through the flame front (located at $x = 0$) but these changes are small.

Global mass conservation and correction velocity

Mass conservation is a specific issue when dealing with reacting flows. Obviously, the sum of mass fractions must be unity: $\sum_{k=1}^{N} Y_k = 1$. This equation adds to the N equations (1.37) while there are only N unknowns (the Y_k's): the system is over determined and there are only N independent equations. Any one of the N species equations (1.37) or the mass conservation equation (1.36) may be eliminated: this apparent problem is not a difficulty when exact expressions for diffusion velocities are used. However, this is no longer the case when Hirschfelder's law is used. In this case, the RHS term of Eq. (1.38) becomes $\frac{\partial}{\partial x_i}(\rho \sum_{k=1}^{N} D_k \frac{W_k}{W} \frac{\partial X_k}{\partial x_i})$ which is not zero: global mass is not conserved. Despite this drawback, most codes in the combustion community use Hirschfelder's law (or even Fick's law) because solving for the diffusion velocities is too complex. Two methods can be used to implement such laws and still maintain global mass conservation:

- The first and simplest method is to solve the global mass conservation equation (1.36) and only $N-1$ species equations using directly Eq. (1.44) to express diffusion velocities.

The last species mass fraction (usually a diluent such as N_2) is obtained by writing $Y_N = 1 - \sum_{k=1}^{N-1} Y_k$ and absorbs all inconsistencies introduced by Eq. (1.44). This simplification is dangerous and should be used only when flames are strongly diluted (for example in air so that Y_{N_2} is large).

- The second method is more accurate and introduces a correction velocity V^c in the expression of the diffusion velocity in Eq. (1.44):

$$V_k = -D_k \frac{\nabla X_k}{X_k} + V_c \tag{1.46}$$

so that the species equations (1.45) becomes:

$$\boxed{\frac{\partial}{\partial t} \rho Y_k + \frac{\partial}{\partial x_i} \rho(u_i + V_i^c)Y_k = \frac{\partial}{\partial x_i}\left(\rho D_k \frac{W_k}{W} \frac{\partial X_k}{\partial x_i}\right) + \dot\omega_k} \tag{1.47}$$

The correction velocity V^c must be chosen to ensure global mass conservation. If all species equations (1.47) are summed, the mass conservation equation must be recovered:

$$\frac{\partial \rho}{\partial t} + \frac{\partial \rho u_i}{\partial x_i} = \frac{\partial}{\partial x_i}\left(\rho \sum_{k=1}^{N} D_k \frac{W_k}{W}\frac{\partial X_k}{\partial x_i} - \rho V_i^c\right) = 0 \tag{1.48}$$

so that the proper expression for the correction velocity is:

$$V_i^c = \sum_{k=1}^{N} D_k \frac{W_k}{W}\frac{\partial X_k}{\partial x_i} \tag{1.49}$$

At each time step, the correction velocity is computed and added to the convecting field u_i to ensure the compatibility of species and mass conservation equations. In this case, it is still possible to solve for (N-1) species and for the total mass but, unlike for the first method, the result for Y_N is correct. The final expression for the diffusion velocity is:

$$\boxed{V_k = -D_k \frac{\nabla X_k}{X_k} + V_c = -D_k \frac{\nabla X_k}{X_k} + \frac{1}{W}\sum_{k=1}^{N} D_k W_k \nabla X_k} \tag{1.50}$$

The Hirschfelder and Curtiss approximation with a correction velocity degenerates to the Fick's law in the two limiting cases presented in the previous section: binary diffusion[vii] or equal diffusivities for all species. This can be verified by first expressing ∇X_k as a function of ∇Y_k in the general case, starting from $X_K = Y_k W/W_k$ and $W = \sum X_k W_k$:

$$\nabla X_k = \frac{W}{W_k}\nabla Y_k + \frac{Y_k}{W_k}\sum_{j=1}^{N} W_j \nabla X_j \tag{1.51}$$

[vii]Binary diffusion is actually only a special case of the 'equal diffusivity' approximation since $D_{12} = D_{21}$.

If all species diffusivities are equal ($D_k = D$), using the Hirschfelder and Curtiss approximation (1.50) with a correction velocity V_c leads to Fick's law again:

$$V_k = -D\frac{\nabla X_k}{X_k} + V_c = -\frac{D}{X_k}\left(\nabla X_k - \frac{X_k}{W}\sum_{j=1}^{N} W_j \nabla X_j\right) = -D\frac{\nabla Y_k}{Y_k} \qquad (1.52)$$

after replacing ∇X_k using Eq. (1.51). Note that this property is obtained only when the Hirschfelder approximation is used with a correction velocity given by Eq. (1.50).

1.1.5   Conservation of energy

Multiple forms of energy conservation equation can be written. To construct them, it is convenient to use the following relation (which may be used in all left hand sides of enthalpy, energy or temperature equations) for any quantity f:

$$\rho\frac{Df}{Dt} = \rho\left(\frac{\partial f}{\partial t} + u_i\frac{\partial f}{\partial x_i}\right) = \frac{\partial \rho f}{\partial t} + \frac{\partial \rho u_i f}{\partial x_i} \qquad (1.53)$$

using continuity (Eq. 1.36). The last form of Eq. (1.53) is called conservative. Starting from the conservation equation for total energy e_t (Kuo [361]):

$$\rho\frac{De_t}{Dt} = \frac{\partial \rho e_t}{\partial t} + \frac{\partial}{\partial x_i}(\rho u_i e_t) = -\frac{\partial q_i}{\partial x_i} + \frac{\partial}{\partial x_j}(\sigma_{ij}u_i) + \dot{Q} + \rho\sum_{k=1}^{N} Y_k f_{k,i}(u_i + V_{k,i}) \qquad (1.54)$$

where $\dot{Q}$ is the heat source term (due for example to an electric spark, a laser or a radiative flux), not to be confused with the heat released by combustion. $\rho\sum_{k=1}^{N} Y_k f_{k,i}(u_i + V_{k,i})$ is the power produced by volume forces f_k on species k. The energy flux q_i is:

$$q_i = -\lambda\frac{\partial T}{\partial x_i} + \rho\sum_{k=1}^{N} h_k Y_k V_{k,i} \qquad (1.55)$$

This flux includes a heat diffusion term expressed by Fourier's Law ($\lambda\partial T/\partial x_i$) and a second term associated with the diffusion of species with different enthalpies which is specific of multi-species gas. Using the relation between energy and enthalpy: $h_t = e_t + p/\rho$ and the continuity equation (1.36) yields:

$$\rho\frac{De_t}{Dt} = \rho\frac{Dh_t}{Dt} - \frac{Dp}{Dt} - p\frac{\partial u_i}{\partial x_i} \quad \text{and} \quad \rho\frac{De}{Dt} = \rho\frac{Dh}{Dt} - \frac{Dp}{Dt} - p\frac{\partial u_i}{\partial x_i} \qquad (1.56)$$

Using Eq. (1.56) to eliminate e_t in Eq. (1.54) gives the conservation equation for h_t:

$$\rho\frac{Dh_t}{Dt} = \frac{\partial \rho h_t}{\partial t} + \frac{\partial}{\partial x_i}(\rho u_i h_t) = \frac{\partial p}{\partial t} - \frac{\partial q_i}{\partial x_i} + \frac{\partial}{\partial x_j}(\tau_{ij}u_i) + \dot{Q} + \rho\sum_{k=1}^{N} Y_k f_{k,i}(u_i + V_{k,i}) \qquad (1.57)$$

The equation for the sum of sensible and chemical energy (e) is obtained by writing first the kinetic energy equation $u_j u_j / 2$. Multiplying the momentum equation (1.35) by u_j:

$$\frac{\partial}{\partial t}\left(\frac{1}{2}\rho u_j u_j\right) + \frac{\partial}{\partial x_i}\left(\frac{1}{2}\rho u_i u_j u_j\right) = u_j \frac{\partial \sigma_{ij}}{\partial x_i} + \rho \sum_{k=1}^{N} Y_k f_{k,j} u_j \qquad (1.58)$$

Subtracting this equation from Eq. (1.54) gives a balance equation for e:

$$\rho \frac{De}{Dt} = \frac{\partial \rho e}{\partial t} + \frac{\partial}{\partial x_i}(\rho u_i e) = -\frac{\partial q_i}{\partial x_i} + \sigma_{ij}\frac{\partial u_i}{\partial x_j} + \dot{Q} + \rho \sum_{k=1}^{N} Y_k f_{k,i} V_{k,i} \qquad (1.59)$$

The conservation equation for the enthalpy h is then deduced from Eq. (1.59) and (1.56):

$$\rho \frac{Dh}{Dt} = \frac{\partial \rho h}{\partial t} + \frac{\partial}{\partial x_i}(\rho u_i h) = \frac{Dp}{Dt} - \frac{\partial q_i}{\partial x_i} + \tau_{ij}\frac{\partial u_i}{\partial x_j} + \dot{Q} + \rho \sum_{k=1}^{N} Y_k f_{k,i} V_{k,i} \qquad (1.60)$$

where $\Phi = \tau_{ij}\partial u_i / \partial x_j$ is the viscous heating source term.

The above expressions are not always easy to implement in classical CFD codes because they use expressions for energy and enthalpy including chemical terms ($\sum_{k=1}^{N} \Delta h_{f,k}^{o} Y_k$) in addition to sensible energy or enthalpy and because the heat flux q also includes new transport terms ($\rho \sum_{k=1}^{N} h_k Y_k V_{k,i}$). Sensible energies or enthalpies are sometimes preferred. From the definition of h_s ($h_s = h - \sum_{k=1}^{N} \Delta h_{f,k}^{o} Y_k$), substituting h_s for h in Eq. (1.60) and using the species equation (1.37) leads to:

$$\rho \frac{Dh_s}{Dt} = \dot{\omega}_T + \frac{Dp}{Dt} + \frac{\partial}{\partial x_i}\left(\lambda \frac{\partial T}{\partial x_i}\right) - \frac{\partial}{\partial x_i}\left(\rho \sum_{k=1}^{N} h_{s,k} Y_k V_{k,i}\right) + \tau_{ij}\frac{\partial u_i}{\partial x_j}$$
$$+ \dot{Q} + \rho \sum_{k=1}^{N} Y_k f_{k,i} V_{k,i} \qquad (1.61)$$

where $\dot{\omega}_T$ is the heat release due to combustion:

$$\dot{\omega}_T = -\sum_{k=1}^{N} \Delta h_{f,k}^{o} \dot{\omega}_k \qquad (1.62)$$

The sensible enthalpies of species k, $h_{s,k} = \int_{T_0}^{T} C_{p,k} dT$ appear on the RHS of Eq. (1.61). The corresponding term $\frac{\partial}{\partial x_i}(\rho \sum_{k=1}^{N} h_{s,k} Y_k V_{k,i})$ is zero:

- if the mixture contains only one species or

- if all species have the same sensible enthalpy: $\sum_{k=1}^{N} h_{s,k} Y_k V_{k,i} = h_s \sum_{k=1}^{N} Y_k V_{k,i} = 0$.

In all other cases, this term does not vanish even though it is sometimes set to zero because it is usually negligible compared to $\dot{\omega}_T$.

The equation for the sensible energy e_s may be deduced from Eq. (1.61) and (1.56):[viii]

$$\rho \frac{De_s}{Dt} = \frac{\partial \rho e_s}{\partial t} + \frac{\partial}{\partial x_i}(\rho u_i e_s) = \dot{\omega}_T + \frac{\partial}{\partial x_i}\left(\lambda \frac{\partial T}{\partial x_i}\right)$$
$$-\frac{\partial}{\partial x_i}\left(\rho \sum_{k=1}^{N} h_{s,k} Y_k V_{k,i}\right) + \sigma_{ij}\frac{\partial u_i}{\partial x_j} + \dot{Q} + \rho \sum_{k=1}^{N} Y_k f_{k,i} V_{k,i} \tag{1.63}$$

Another way is to work with the sum of sensible and kinetic energies (the "total non-chemical" energy in Table 1.4). Adding Eq. (1.63) and (1.58) leads to the equation for $E = e_s + \frac{1}{2}u_i u_i$:

$$\rho \frac{DE}{Dt} = \frac{\partial \rho E}{\partial t} + \frac{\partial}{\partial x_i}(\rho u_i E) = \dot{\omega}_T + \frac{\partial}{\partial x_i}\left(\lambda \frac{\partial T}{\partial x_i}\right)$$
$$-\frac{\partial}{\partial x_i}\left(\rho \sum_{k=1}^{N} h_{s,k} Y_k V_{k,i}\right) + \frac{\partial}{\partial x_j}(\sigma_{ij} u_i) + \dot{Q} + \rho \sum_{k=1}^{N} Y_k f_{k,i}(u_i + V_{k,i}) \tag{1.64}$$

In the same way, the equation for $H = h_s + u_i u_i/2$ is obtained by adding Eq. (1.61) and (1.58):

$$\rho \frac{DH}{Dt} = \frac{\partial \rho H}{\partial t} + \frac{\partial}{\partial x_i}(\rho u_i H) = \dot{\omega}_T + \frac{\partial}{\partial x_i}\left(\lambda \frac{\partial T}{\partial x_i}\right)$$
$$+\frac{\partial p}{\partial t} - \frac{\partial}{\partial x_i}\left(\rho \sum_{k=1}^{N} h_{s,k} Y_k V_{k,i}\right) + \frac{\partial}{\partial x_j}(\tau_{ij} u_i) + \dot{Q} + \rho \sum_{k=1}^{N} Y_k f_{k,i}(u_i + V_{k,i}) \tag{1.65}$$

In some codes (low-Mach number or incompressible formulations), an equation for temperature is used. Starting from $h_s = \sum_{k=1}^{N} h_{s,k} Y_k$ where $h_{s,k}$ is the sensible enthalpy of species k (Giovangigli [236], Giovangigli and Smooke [238]), the derivative of h_s is:

$$\rho \frac{Dh_s}{Dt} = \sum_{k=1}^{N} h_{sk} \rho \frac{DY_k}{Dt} + \rho C_p \frac{DT}{Dt} \tag{1.66}$$

[viii]Note that the sensible energy is defined here by $e_s = \int_{T_0}^{T} C_v dT - RT_0/W$ (Table 1.4). A different equation would be found if the sensible energy is defined by $e_s' = \int_{T_0}^{T} C_v dT$:

$$\rho \frac{De_s'}{Dt} = -\sum_{k=1}^{N} \Delta e_{f,k}^o \dot{\omega}_k + \frac{\partial}{\partial x_i}\left(\lambda \frac{\partial T}{\partial x_i}\right) - \frac{\partial}{\partial x_i}\left(\rho \sum_{k=1}^{N} (h_{s,k} + RT_0/W_k) Y_k V_{k,i}\right) + \sigma_{ij}\frac{\partial u_i}{\partial x_j} + \dot{Q} + \rho \sum_{k=1}^{N} Y_k f_{k,i} V_{k,i}$$

where $\Delta e_{f,k}^o$ is the formation energy at T_O: $\Delta e_{f,k}^o = \Delta h_{f,k}^o - RT_0/W_k$.

Replacing this derivative in Eq. (1.61) gives:

$$
\begin{aligned}
\rho C_p \frac{DT}{Dt} = \dot{\omega}'_T + \frac{Dp}{Dt} &+ \frac{\partial}{\partial x_i}\left(\lambda \frac{\partial T}{\partial x_i}\right) - \left(\rho \sum_{k=1}^{N} C_{p,k} Y_k V_{k,i}\right)\frac{\partial T}{\partial x_i} + \tau_{ij}\frac{\partial u_i}{\partial x_j} \\
&+ \dot{Q} + \rho \sum_{k=1}^{N} Y_k f_{k,i} V_{k,i}
\end{aligned}
\tag{1.67}
$$

The reaction term $\dot{\omega}'_T$ is not equal to $\dot{\omega}_T$, the reaction term in the equation for e_s or h_s:

$$
\dot{\omega}_T = -\sum_{k=1}^{N} \Delta h^o_{f,k} \dot{\omega}_k \quad ; \quad \dot{\omega}'_T = -\sum_{k=1}^{N} h_k \dot{\omega}_k = -\sum_{k=1}^{N} h_{sk} \dot{\omega}_k - \sum_{k=1}^{N} \Delta h^o_{f,k} \dot{\omega}_k
\tag{1.68}
$$

These two terms are both called heat release so that different authors use the same term for different quantities. They differ by a small amount due to the contribution of sensible enthalpy terms h_{sk}. Section 1.2.2 shows that they are equal when the heat capacities $C_{p,k}$'s are supposed equal for all species.

An equivalent form may be written with C_v, starting from the definition of e_s to have:

$$
\rho \frac{De_s}{Dt} = \sum_{k=1}^{N} e_{sk} \rho \frac{DY_k}{Dt} + \rho C_v \frac{DT}{Dt}
\tag{1.69}
$$

so that replacing the time derivative of e_s in Eq. (1.63) leads to:

$$
\begin{aligned}
\rho C_v \frac{DT}{Dt} = \dot{\omega}''_T &+ \frac{\partial}{\partial x_i}\left(\lambda \frac{\partial T}{\partial x_i}\right) - RT\frac{\partial}{\partial x_i}\left(\rho \sum_{k=1}^{N} Y_k V_{k,i}/W_k\right) \\
&- \rho \frac{\partial T}{\partial x_i}\sum_{k=1}^{N}(Y_k V_{k,i} C_{p,k}) + \sigma_{ij}\frac{\partial u_i}{\partial x_j} + \dot{Q} + \rho \sum_{k=1}^{N} Y_k f_{k,i} V_{k,i}
\end{aligned}
\tag{1.70}
$$

where $\dot{\omega}''_T = -\sum_{k=1}^{N} e_k \dot{\omega}_k$ is another reaction rate (equal to $\dot{\omega}_T$ when all heat capacities C_{pk} are equal).

Table 1.7 summarizes the different forms of energy equations.

Form	Energy	Enthalpy
Sensible	$e_s = h_s - p/\rho = \int_{T_0}^{T} C_v dT - RT_0/W$	$h_s = \int_{T_0}^{T} C_p dT$
Sensible+Chemical	$e = h - p/\rho = e_s + \sum_{k=1}^{N} \Delta h_{f,k}^{o} Y_k$	$h = h_s + \sum_{k=1}^{N} \Delta h_{f,k}^{o} Y_k$
Total Chemical	$e_t = h_t - p/\rho = e_s + \sum_{k=1}^{N} \Delta h_{f,k}^{o} Y_k + \frac{1}{2} u_i u_i$	$h_t = h_s + \sum_{k=1}^{N} \Delta h_{f,k}^{o} Y_k + \frac{1}{2} u_i u_i$
Total non Chemical	$E = H - p/\rho = e_s + \frac{1}{2} u_i u_i$	$H = h_s + \frac{1}{2} u_i u_i$

e_t	$\rho \dfrac{De_t}{Dt} = -\dfrac{\partial q_i}{\partial x_i} + \dfrac{\partial}{\partial x_j}(\sigma_{ij} u_i) + \dot{Q} + \rho \sum_{k=1}^{N} Y_k f_{k,i}(u_i + V_{k,i})$
h_t	$\rho \dfrac{Dh_t}{Dt} = \dfrac{\partial p}{\partial t} - \dfrac{\partial q_i}{\partial x_i} + \dfrac{\partial}{\partial x_j}(\tau_{ij} u_i) + \dot{Q} + \rho \sum_{k=1}^{N} Y_k f_{k,i}(u_i + V_{k,i})$
e	$\rho \dfrac{De}{Dt} = -\dfrac{\partial q_i}{\partial x_i} + \sigma_{ij} \dfrac{\partial u_i}{\partial x_j} + \dot{Q} + \rho \sum_{k=1}^{N} Y_k f_{k,i} V_{k,i}$
h	$\rho \dfrac{Dh}{Dt} = \dfrac{Dp}{Dt} - \dfrac{\partial q_i}{\partial x_i} + \tau_{ij} \dfrac{\partial u_i}{\partial x_j} + \dot{Q} + \rho \sum_{k=1}^{N} Y_k f_{k,i} V_{k,i}$
e_s	$\rho \dfrac{De_s}{Dt} = \dot{\omega}_T + \dfrac{\partial}{\partial x_i}(\lambda \dfrac{\partial T}{\partial x_i}) - \dfrac{\partial}{\partial x_i}(\rho \sum_{k=1}^{N} h_{s,k} Y_k V_{k,i}) + \sigma_{ij} \dfrac{\partial u_i}{\partial x_j} + \dot{Q} + \rho \sum_{k=1}^{N} Y_k f_{k,i} V_{k,i}$
h_s	$\rho \dfrac{Dh_s}{Dt} = \dot{\omega}_T + \dfrac{Dp}{Dt} + \dfrac{\partial}{\partial x_i}(\lambda \dfrac{\partial T}{\partial x_i}) - \dfrac{\partial}{\partial x_i}(\rho \sum_{k=1}^{N} h_{s,k} Y_k V_{k,i}) + \tau_{ij} \dfrac{\partial u_i}{\partial x_j} + \dot{Q} + \rho \sum_{k=1}^{N} Y_k f_{k,i} V_{k,i}$
E	$\rho \dfrac{DE}{Dt} = \dot{\omega}_T + \dfrac{\partial}{\partial x_i}(\lambda \dfrac{\partial T}{\partial x_i}) - \dfrac{\partial}{\partial x_i}(\rho \sum_{k=1}^{N} h_{s,k} Y_k V_{k,i}) + \dfrac{\partial}{\partial x_j}(\sigma_{ij} u_i) + \dot{Q} + \rho \sum_{k=1}^{N} Y_k f_{k,i}(u_i + V_{k,i})$
H	$\rho \dfrac{DH}{Dt} = \dot{\omega}_T + \dfrac{\partial p}{\partial t} + \dfrac{\partial}{\partial x_i}(\lambda \dfrac{\partial T}{\partial x_i}) - \dfrac{\partial}{\partial x_i}(\rho \sum_{k=1}^{N} h_{s,k} Y_k V_{k,i}) + \dfrac{\partial}{\partial x_j}(\tau_{ij} u_i) + \dot{Q} + \rho \sum_{k=1}^{N} Y_k f_{k,i}(u_i + V_{k,i})$

Table 1.7: Enthalpy and energy forms and corresponding balance equations. The $f_{k,i}$'s are volume forces acting on species k in direction i. $\dot{Q}$ is the volume source term. The $V_{k,i}$'s are the diffusion velocities. q_i is the enthalpy flux defined by $q_i = -\lambda \frac{\partial T}{\partial x_i} + \rho \sum_{k=1}^{N} h_k Y_k V_{k,i}$. The viscous tensors are defined by $\tau_{ij} = -2/3 \mu \frac{\partial u_k}{\partial x_k} \delta_{ij} + \mu(\frac{\partial u_i}{\partial x_j} + \frac{\partial u_j}{\partial x_i})$ and $\sigma_{ij} = \tau_{ij} - p\delta_{ij}$. The heat release $\dot{\omega}_T$ is $-\sum_{k=1}^{N} \Delta h_{f,k}^{o} \dot{\omega}_k$. For any energy or enthalpy f: $\rho \frac{Df}{Dt} = \rho(\frac{\partial f}{\partial t} + u_i \frac{\partial f}{\partial x_i}) = \frac{\partial \rho f}{\partial t} + \frac{\partial}{\partial x_i}(\rho u_i f)$.

1.2 Usual simplified forms

The complete form of the energy equation is not always needed and simplified forms are often utilized in combustion codes. The following sections present such forms.

1.2.1 Constant pressure flames

In deflagrations (Williams [710]), flame speeds are small compared to the sound speed (typical values for s_L range from 0.1 to 5 m/s while the sound speed in the fresh gases c_1 varies between 300 and 600 m/s in most combustion chambers), allowing some interesting simplifications:

- The Mach number M_a in the flow is of the order of s_L/c_1 and is small: this is sufficient to show that pressure in the state equation may be assumed to be constant. This may be checked by starting from the conservation of momentum (1.35), written here for simplicity in one dimension only with a constant viscosity μ:

$$\rho\frac{\partial u}{\partial t} + \rho u\frac{\partial u}{\partial x} = -\frac{\partial p}{\partial x} + \mu\frac{\partial}{\partial x}\frac{\partial u}{\partial x} \tag{1.71}$$

This equation may be scaled with:

$$u^+ = u/c_1 \quad x^+ = x/L \quad \rho^+ = \rho/\rho_1 \quad t^+ = c_1 t/L \quad p^+ = p/\left(\rho_1 c_1^2\right) \tag{1.72}$$

where L is a reference distance (for example the size of the burner) and c_1 is the sound speed. Index 1 refers to fresh gas quantities. Introducing the acoustic Reynolds number $R_e = \rho_1 c_1 L/\mu_1$, Eq. (1.71) becomes:

$$\frac{\partial p^+}{\partial x^+} = \underbrace{-\rho^+\frac{\partial u^+}{\partial t^+}}_{o(M_a)} \underbrace{-\rho^+ u^+\frac{\partial u^+}{\partial x^+}}_{o(M_a^2)} + \underbrace{\frac{1}{R_e}\frac{\partial}{\partial x^+}\frac{\partial u^+}{\partial x^+}}_{o(M_a/Re)}, \tag{1.73}$$

Eq. (1.73) shows that, in high Reynolds number steady flows, the changes in mean pressure are of the order of M_a^2. They are of the order of M_a in unsteady flows. For subsonic combustion with low Mach numbers, these variations are negligible and pressure can be assumed to be constant in the state equation $p = \rho R/WT$ which is replaced by $\rho R/WT = p_0 = cte$. Therefore, the density change through the flame front is directly related to the temperature change through the flame front:

$$\rho_2/\rho_1 = T_1/T_2. \tag{1.74}$$

In the energy equation, the pressure term Dp/Dt may be set to zero.

- In the same way, the viscous heating term $\Phi = \tau_{ij}(\partial u_i/\partial x_j)$ in the temperature equation is of high order in M_a and may be neglected.

The temperature equation (1.67) reduces to:

$$\rho C_p \frac{DT}{Dt} = \dot\omega_T' + \frac{\partial}{\partial x_i}\left(\lambda\frac{\partial T}{\partial x_i}\right) - \rho\frac{\partial T}{\partial x_i}\left(\sum_{k=1}^N C_{p,k}Y_k V_{k,i}\right) + \dot{Q} + \rho\sum_{k=1}^N Y_k f_{k,i}V_{k,i} \quad (1.75)$$

1.2.2 Equal heat capacities for all species

Equations for temperature may be simplified by using assumptions on the species heat capacities C_{pk}. First, assuming that all heat capacities are equal $C_{p,k} = C_p$ and $h_{s,k} = h_s$ (an assumption which is not often true in flames but is often used!), the $\sum_{k=1}^N C_{p,k}Y_k V_{k,i}$ term in the temperature equation (1.67) is $C_p\sum_{k=1}^N Y_k V_{k,i} = 0$ and the temperature equation becomes:[ix]

- for variable pressure, equal $C_{p,k}$ flames:

$$\rho C_p \frac{DT}{Dt} = \dot\omega_T' + \frac{Dp}{Dt} + \frac{\partial}{\partial x_i}\left(\lambda\frac{\partial T}{\partial x_i}\right) + \tau_{ij}\frac{\partial u_i}{\partial x_j} + \dot{Q} + \rho\sum_{k=1}^N Y_k f_{k,i}V_{k,i} \quad (1.76)$$

- for constant pressure, low speed, equal $C_{p,k}$ flames:

$$\rho C_p \frac{DT}{Dt} = \dot\omega_T' + \frac{\partial}{\partial x_i}\left(\lambda\frac{\partial T}{\partial x_i}\right) + \dot{Q} + \rho\sum_{k=1}^N Y_k f_{k,i}V_{k,i} \quad (1.77)$$

Here the two reaction rates $\dot\omega_T'$ and $\dot\omega_T$ (Eq. 1.68) are equal:

$$\dot\omega_T' = -\sum_{k=1}^N h_k\dot\omega_k = -\sum_{k=1}^N h_{s,k}\dot\omega_k - \sum_{k=1}^N \Delta h_{f,k}^o\dot\omega_k = -h_s\sum_{k=1}^N \dot\omega_k - \sum_{k=1}^N \Delta h_{f,k}^o\dot\omega_k = \dot\omega_T \quad (1.78)$$

because $\sum_{k=1}^N \dot\omega_k = 0$.

The energy and enthalpy equations also have simplified forms if all heat capacities are equal:

$$\rho\frac{DE}{Dt} = \frac{\partial\rho E}{\partial t} + \frac{\partial}{\partial x_i}(\rho u_i E) = \dot\omega_T + \frac{\partial}{\partial x_i}\left(\lambda\frac{\partial T}{\partial x_i}\right)$$

$$+ \frac{\partial}{\partial x_j}(\sigma_{ij}u_i) + \dot{Q} + \rho\sum_{k=1}^N Y_k f_{k,i}(u_i + V_{k,i}) \quad (1.79)$$

[ix]The heat capacity C_p may still be a function of temperature.

$$\rho\frac{DH}{Dt} = \frac{\partial\rho H}{\partial t} + \frac{\partial}{\partial x_i}(\rho u_i H) = \dot{\omega}_T + \frac{\partial p}{\partial t} + \frac{\partial}{\partial x_i}\left(\lambda\frac{\partial T}{\partial x_i}\right)$$

$$+ \frac{\partial}{\partial x_j}(\tau_{ij}u_i) + \dot{Q} + \rho\sum_{k=1}^{N} Y_k f_{k,i}(u_i + V_{k,i}) \tag{1.80}$$

Note that, if all heat capacities are equal but also independent of temperature, the equation for ρe_s is an equation for pressure because:

$$\rho e_s = \rho\left(\int_{T_0}^{T} C_v dT - RT_0/W\right) = \rho(C_v T - C_p T_0) = p/(\gamma - 1) - \rho C_p T_0$$

where $\gamma = C_p/C_v$. Replacing ρe_s in Eq. (1.63) gives and using the continuity equation:

$$\boxed{\frac{1}{\gamma-1}\frac{Dp}{Dt} = -\frac{\gamma p}{\gamma-1}\frac{\partial u_i}{\partial x_i} + \dot{\omega}_T + \frac{\partial}{\partial x_i}\left(\lambda\frac{\partial T}{\partial x_i}\right) + \tau_{ij}\frac{\partial u_i}{\partial x_j} + \dot{Q} + \rho\sum_{k=1}^{N} Y_k f_{k,i}V_{k,i}} \tag{1.81}$$

For most deflagrations, p is almost constant: in Eq. (1.81), the first term on the RHS (due to dilatation) compensates the other terms. When a compressible code is used for reacting flows, this equation controls pressure and explains how such codes react to perturbations. If the heat release term $\dot{\omega}_T$, for example, is too high, pressure will locally increase. If γ is not estimated correctly, the term $-\frac{\gamma p}{\gamma-1}\frac{\partial u_i}{\partial x_i}$ will also induce pressure modifications. Eq. (1.81) is a useful diagnostic tool to identify problems in codes for compressible reacting flows. It may also be used to construct a wave equation in reacting flows (see § 8.3.2).

1.2.3 Constant heat capacity for the mixture only

It is also possible to assume that the mixture heat capacity C_p is constant because one species (N_2 for example) is dominant in the mixture but that the $C_{p,k}$'s are not equal: this approximation is slightly inconsistent because $C_p = \sum_{k=1}^{N} C_{p,k}Y_k$ but it is used (Kuo [361]) for example to derive the following temperature equation by setting $Dh_s/Dt = C_p DT/Dt$ in the equation for h_s (Eq. 1.61):

$$\rho C_p\frac{DT}{Dt} = \dot{\omega}_T + \frac{Dp}{Dt} + \frac{\partial}{\partial x_i}\left(\lambda\frac{\partial T}{\partial x_i}\right) - \frac{\partial}{\partial x_i}\left(\rho T\sum_{k=1}^{N} C_{p,k}Y_k V_{k,i}\right)$$

$$+ \tau_{ij}\frac{\partial u_i}{\partial x_j} + \dot{Q} + \rho\sum_{k=1}^{N} Y_k f_{k,i}V_{k,i} \tag{1.82}$$

where $h_{s,k}$ was replaced by $C_{p,k}T$.

1.3   Summary of conservation equations

Table 1.8 summarizes the equations to solve for reacting flows.

Mass

$$\frac{\partial \rho}{\partial t} + \frac{\partial \rho u_i}{\partial x_i} = 0$$

Species: for $k = 1$ to $N - 1$ (or N if total mass is not used)

With diffusion velocities:

$$\frac{\partial \rho Y_k}{\partial t} + \frac{\partial}{\partial x_i}(\rho(u_i + V_{k,i})Y_k) = \dot{\omega}_k$$

With Hirschfelder and Curtiss approximation:

$$\frac{\partial \rho Y_k}{\partial t} + \frac{\partial}{\partial x_i}(\rho(u_i + V_i^c)Y_k) = \frac{\partial}{\partial x_i}\left(\rho D_k \frac{W_k}{W}\frac{\partial X_k}{\partial x_i}\right) + \dot{\omega}_k \text{ and } V_i^c = \sum_{k=1}^{N} D_k \frac{W_k}{W}\frac{\partial X_k}{\partial x_i}$$

Momentum

$$\frac{\partial}{\partial t}\rho u_j + \frac{\partial}{\partial x_i}\rho u_i u_j = -\frac{\partial p}{\partial x_j} + \frac{\partial \tau_{ij}}{\partial x_i} + \rho \sum_{k=1}^{N} Y_k f_{k,j}$$

Energy (sum of sensible and kinetic)

$$\frac{\partial \rho E}{\partial t} + \frac{\partial}{\partial x_i}(\rho u_i E) = \dot{\omega}_T - \frac{\partial q_i}{\partial x_i} + \frac{\partial}{\partial x_j}(\sigma_{ij}u_i) + \dot{Q} + \rho \sum_{k=1}^{N} Y_k f_{k,i}(u_i + V_{k,i})$$

with $\dot{\omega}_T = -\sum_{k=1}^{N} \Delta h_{f,k}^o \dot{\omega}_k$ and $q_i = -\lambda \frac{\partial T}{\partial x_i} + \rho \sum_{k=1}^{N} h_k Y_k V_{k,i}$

Table 1.8: Conservation equations for reacting flows: the energy equation may be replaced by any of the equations given in Table 1.7. $\dot{Q}$ is the external heat source term and f_k measures the volume forces applied on species k.

For most deflagrations, pressure is constant, body forces are zero ($f_{k,j} = 0$), viscous heating is negligible so that these equations may be simplified as shown in Table 1.9.

Mass

$$\frac{\partial \rho}{\partial t} + \frac{\partial \rho u_i}{\partial x_i} = 0$$

Species: For $k = 1$ to $N - 1$ (or N if total mass is not used)

With diffusion velocities:

$$\frac{\partial \rho Y_k}{\partial t} + \frac{\partial}{\partial x_i}(\rho(u_i + V_{k,i})Y_k) = \dot{\omega}_k$$

With Hirschfelder and Curtiss approximation:

$$\frac{\partial \rho Y_k}{\partial t} + \frac{\partial}{\partial x_i}(\rho(u_i + V_i^c)Y_k) = \frac{\partial}{\partial x_i}(\rho D_k \frac{W_k}{W}\frac{\partial X_k}{\partial x_i}) + \dot{\omega}_k \text{ and } V_i^c = \sum_{k=1}^{N} D_k \frac{W_k}{W}\frac{\partial X_k}{\partial x_i}$$

Momentum

$$\frac{\partial}{\partial t}\rho u_j + \frac{\partial}{\partial x_i}\rho u_i u_j = -\frac{\partial p}{\partial x_j} + \frac{\partial \tau_{ij}}{\partial x_i}$$

Energy (sum of sensible and kinetic)

$$\frac{\partial \rho E}{\partial t} + \frac{\partial}{\partial x_i}(\rho u_i E) = \dot{\omega}_T - \frac{\partial q_i}{\partial x_i} \text{ with } \dot{\omega}_T = -\sum_{k=1}^{N} \Delta h_{f,k}^o \dot{\omega}_k$$

Or temperature

$$\rho C_p \frac{DT}{Dt} = \dot{\omega}_T' + \frac{\partial}{\partial x_i}(\lambda \frac{\partial T}{\partial x_i}) - \rho \frac{\partial T}{\partial x_i}\left(\sum_{k=1}^{N} C_{p,k} Y_k V_{k,i}\right)$$

with $\dot{\omega}_T' = -\sum_{k=1}^{N} h_k \dot{\omega}_k$ and $q_i = -\lambda \frac{\partial T}{\partial x_i} + \rho \sum_{k=1}^{N} h_k Y_k V_{k,i}$

Table 1.9: Conservation equations for constant pressure, low Mach number flames.

1.4   Flame regimes

The equations given in the previous sections are valid for most flames (except at very high pressures) but their resolution in the most general case is impossible. To understand reacting flows, the combustion community has identified canonical situations where the combustion equations can be solved, and defined flame regimes to classify the level of complexity found in a given flame. Table 1.4 presents a first separation of flames in four categories: fully premixed vs non-premixed (also called diffusion flames) and laminar vs turbulent.

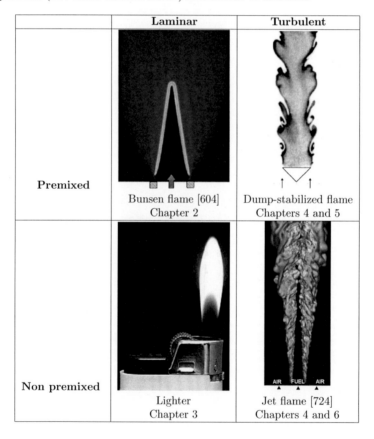

	Laminar	**Turbulent**
Premixed	Bunsen flame [604] Chapter 2	Dump-stabilized flame Chapters 4 and 5
Non premixed	Lighter Chapter 3	Jet flame [724] Chapters 4 and 6

Table 1.10: Classification of flames.

The first classification element is based on the fact that reactants are premixed or not before combustion. The form of reaction rates (Eq. 1.24) in reacting flows shows that three ingredients are required for combustion to proceed: (1) a fuel, (2) an oxidizer and (3) a high temperature. In other words, some local mixing must be achieved (to have fuel and oxidizer at the same point) in a high temperature zone before combustion can start. This property allows to separate flames into (1) cases where the mixing of fuel and oxidizer is achieved prior to combustion and (2) all other cases. The first situation corresponds to 'premixed' flames, the second one to 'non-premixed' flames (also called diffusion flames in the extreme case where fuel and oxidizer are injected in fully separated streams into the combustion chamber). Premixed and non-premixed flames have different properties: premixed flames are more intense and pollute less. They are also more dangerous because any high temperature point in a premixed gas can lead to ignition and undesired combustion. On the other hand, diffusion flames have lower burning rates, higher local maximum temperatures, leading to higher pollution levels. They are safer because reactants are stored separately and mix only within the combustion chamber. Another difference between premixed and non-premixed flames is flammability limits: non-premixed flames can burn for any flow rate of fuel and oxidizer while premixed flames are limited in terms of mixing characteristics: premixed flames which are too lean or too rich can not propagate.

Turbulence is the second classification element. Since all flows become turbulent when the Reynolds number is large enough (in other words at high speeds), flames also become 'turbulent' in most practical combustors: instead of burning reactants in a smooth flat front, the flame becomes wrinkled, unsteady and much more complicated to study. Methods (and numerical solvers) used for laminar flames have very few common elements with methods necessary for turbulent flames. Laminar flames are also quite rare when it comes to industrial applications so that most of the combustion community is working on turbulent combustion problems.

The following chapters describe first premixed (Chapter 2) and non-premixed laminar flames (Chapter 3) before considering turbulent flames (Chapters 4 to 6). In practical applications, most flames are turbulent so that studying laminar cases might be viewed as a loss of time. This is not the case: most theories for turbulent flames are based on concepts derived from laminar flame studies. Understanding turbulent combustion is impossible without a previous description of laminar flame properties as done in Chapter 2 and 3.

Chapter 2

Laminar premixed flames

2.1 Introduction

The one-dimensional laminar flame flame propagating into a premixed gas (fuel mixed with air for example) is the basic combustion configuration, both for theory and for numerical techniques[i] Numerically solving for laminar premixed flames is of interest because:

- It is one of the few configurations where detailed comparisons between experiments, theory and computations can be performed.

- It may be used to validate chemical models as discussed in Section 1.1.1.

- Many theoretical approaches may be used for laminar flames, not only to study their one dimensional structure but also the various instabilities which can develop on such fronts (Williams [710]).

- Laminar flames are viewed in many turbulent combustion models as the elementary building blocks of turbulent flames (flamelet theory: see Chapt. 5).

From the point of view of numerical techniques, computing laminar premixed flames is a first step toward more complex configurations. However, this step is not necessary to compute turbulent flames using models as shown in Chapter 5 because most turbulent combustion models essentially use completely different approaches: codes devoted to turbulent combustion can usually not be used for laminar flames.

There are many ways to compute laminar flame structure and speed depending on the complexity of the chemistry and transport descriptions (§ 2.2). With complex chemical schemes, there is no analytical solution to the problem and numerical techniques are needed (§ 2.3). However, when chemistry and transport are suitably simplified, analytical or semi-analytical

---

[i]This section is available as a video at *elearning.cerfacs.fr/combustion* under 'Master Courses': see Premixed Laminar Flames (part 1) and Premixed Laminar Flames (part 2).

solutions may be developed and these shed an essential light on the behavior of flames and on the numerical challenges to face when one tries to compute them in simple or complex situations (§ 2.4). These solutions are useful to check the precision of combustion codes and to provide initial solutions for these codes. They are also needed to determine resolution requirements for flames.

2.2   Conservation equations and numerical solutions

For laminar one-dimensional premixed flames, the conservation equations derived in Chapter 1 can be simplified starting from Table 1.9 (the index 1 corresponding to the x direction is omitted):

- Mass conservation

$$\frac{\partial \rho}{\partial t} + \frac{\partial \rho u}{\partial x} = 0 \tag{2.1}$$

- Species conservation. For $k = 1$ to $N - 1$:

$$\frac{\partial \rho Y_k}{\partial t} + \frac{\partial}{\partial x}(\rho(u + V_k)Y_k) = \dot{\omega}_k \tag{2.2}$$

- Energy

$$\rho C_p \left(\frac{\partial T}{\partial t} + u\frac{\partial T}{\partial x}\right) = \dot{\omega}_T' + \frac{\partial}{\partial x}\left(\lambda\frac{\partial T}{\partial x}\right) - \rho\frac{\partial T}{\partial x}\left(\sum_{k=1}^{N} C_{p,k} Y_k V_k\right) \tag{2.3}$$

with $\dot{\omega}_T' = -\sum_{k=1}^{N} h_k \dot{\omega}_k$

These equations describe a wave propagating from the burnt to the fresh gas at a speed which reaches a constant value s_L when transients are ignored. Solving for the structure of this flame is still a research task for complex chemistry descriptions even when the flame has reached a constant velocity. When the flame is steady, writing Eq. (2.1) to (2.3) in the reference frame of the flame (moving at speed s_L) leads to:[ii]

[ii]Note that the momentum equation is not needed anymore. It can be used to compute the pressure field after all fields have been computed by integrating (viscous terms are neglected):

$$\frac{\partial p}{\partial x} = -\rho u \frac{\partial u}{\partial x} \quad \text{or} \quad p(x) = p_1 - \rho_1 s_L(u(x) - u_1) \tag{2.4}$$

The pressure jump through a steady flame front is obtained by integrating this equation between $-\infty$ to ∞:

$$p_2 - p_1 = \rho_1 u_1^2 (1 - u_2/u_1) = \rho_1 s_L^2 (1 - T_2/T_1) \tag{2.5}$$

using the notations of Fig. 2.1. These pressure jumps through flame fronts are small: for a stoichiometric methane-air flame, with a flame speed of 0.4 ms/s and a temperature ratio T_2/T_1 close to 7, $p_2 - p_1$ is of the order of 1 Pa. Checking in compressible combustion codes whether they capture the correct pressure jump in premixed flames is a good way to verify that boundary conditions and numerical techniques are adequate.

$$\rho u = \text{constant} = \rho_1 s_L \tag{2.6}$$

$$\frac{\partial}{\partial x}(\rho(u + V_k)Y_k) = \dot{\omega}_k \tag{2.7}$$

$$\rho C_p u \frac{\partial T}{\partial x} = \dot{\omega}'_T + \frac{\partial}{\partial x}\left(\lambda \frac{\partial T}{\partial x}\right) - \frac{\partial T}{\partial x}\left(\rho \sum_{k=1}^{N} C_{p,k} Y_k V_k\right) \tag{2.8}$$

This set of equations is closed if a model is given for the reaction rate $\dot{\omega}_k$ (Arrhenius law) and for the diffusion velocities V_k (Fick's law with a correction velocity, for example) and if proper boundary conditions are provided. For premixed flames, these boundary conditions may raise some difficulties. Typical inlet conditions (at location $x = 0$) correspond to a cold premixed gas flow (Fig. 2.1): $u(x = 0) = u_1$, Y_k imposed for reactants (in proportions imposed by the code user), $T(x = 0) = T_1$ imposed.

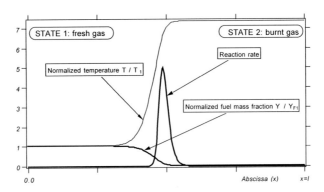

Figure 2.1: Basic configuration for computations of one-dimensional premixed flames. State 1: fresh gas quantities; State 2: burnt gas quantities.

These conditions are not enough to determine whether the flame actually exists in the computational domain:

- The temperature T_1 is usually low and most reaction terms at this temperature are almost zero. If this flow is computed in a parabolic way, i.e. by starting from $x = 0$ and updating all variables for increasing x, the mass fractions (and other quantities as well) remain constant. Reaction rates rise but so slowly that the ignition point is rejected to infinity. This is the "cold boundary" problem (Williams [710]). From a numerical point of view, this paradox is easily solved by recognizing that an additional condition must be imposed, at least in the initial conditions: the flame must have been ignited before it reaches the right side of the domain and the temperature must reach the adiabatic flame temperature at the outlet of the domain ($x = l$). Another way to express the same

point is that deflagrations are elliptic phenomena: what happens downstream controls
the flame propagation upstream. This feedback mechanism is produced by thermal and
species diffusion as shown in Section 2.4.[iii]

- Even if the flame is ignited, steady solution can exist only if the inlet velocity u_1 is equal
  to the flame speed s_L (the flame remains on a fixed position). This means that the
  problem to solve is an eigenvalue problem: the unknowns are the profiles of temperature,
  species and velocity but also the flame speed s_L which is the eigenvalue of the problem.

2.3 Steady one-dimensional laminar premixed flames

The simplest flame configuration is a planar laminar premixed flame propagating in one direction. It is a one-dimensional problem. It is also a steady problem if equations are written
in the reference frame of the flame.

2.3.1 One-dimensional flame codes

Solving Eqs. (2.6) to (2.8) is a numerical problem for which many numerical tools have been
developed in the last twenty years. These tools allow to use complex chemical schemes involving hundreds of species and thousands of reactions. When proper boundary conditions are set
up and the problem is discretized on a finite difference grid, the resulting system is a strongly
non linear boundary value problem which can be written:

$$\mathcal{L}(U_i) = 0 \qquad\qquad (2.9)$$

where $U_i = (T, Y_1, Y_2, ...Y_N, U)_i$ is the vector of unknowns at point x_i.

   This system is usually solved with Newton-type methods. There is no need to develop
such codes today because reliable tools already exist: commercial codes (PREMIX, Kee et al.
[331, 330, 329], see also *www.reactiondesign.com* or COSILAB *www.rotexo.com/cms*) as well
as open source codes (CANTERA, see *code.google.com/p/cantera*) and tools developed by
various university groups.

   Fig. 2.2 shows the output of such codes for a H_2 - O_2 flame at atmospheric pressure. The
flame speed is 32 m/s (such high deflagration speeds are obtained only for pure hydrogen -
oxygen combustion and are typical of cryogenic rocket combustion). The chemical scheme for
this computation is given in Table 1.5. For this computation, PREMIX uses an adaptive grid
and the smallest grid size is 0.001 mm while the largest one is 0.19 mm.

   PREMIX and similar one-dimensional flame codes have certain specificities. Two very
different tasks have to be performed with one-dimensional flame codes:

- for a given situation, compute a first flame or

[iii]Detonations are different: they are essentially parabolic phenomena which can be computed by time or
space marching techniques because diffusion phenomena are negligible.

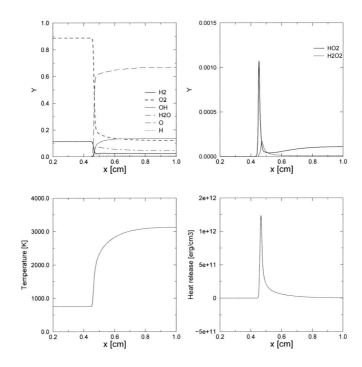

Figure 2.2: PREMIX Computation of a stoichiometric H_2 - O_2 premixed flame at 1 bar. Fresh gas temperature: 700 K. Profiles of species, temperature and heat release.

- having this first flame solution, compute other solutions for which physical parameters (equivalence ratio, temperature, pressure, etc) are varied.

Computing the first flame is always a challenge because all techniques used to solve the system (2.9) have a finite radius of convergence: if the fields given initially for T and for all species Y_k are too far from the solution, no convergence is obtained. Unfortunately, when fuels requiring 300 species must be computed, initializing these 300 profiles in a smart way is a task depending largely on the experience of the user. In many cases, other codes must be used to initialize the one-dimensional flame code. Furthermore, when new chemical schemes with new constants are introduced, the lack of convergence of the one-dimensional flame code may be due to a problem of initialization but also to an erroneous or approximate chemical model. For an M reactions scheme, $3M$ constants must be specified (see Eq. 1.25): A_j, β_j and T_{aj} for $j = 1, M$. For octane fuels, it is frequent to use up to 2000 reactions so that 6000 constants are needed. Whether these 6000 constants are well chosen and are compatible with a flame computation is a question which makes calculations of complex fuels very difficult.

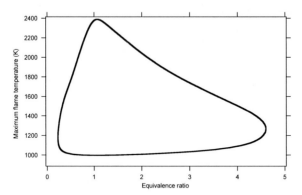

Figure 2.3: Continuation computation of twin premixed H_2 - air flames for a stretch rate of 1000 s^{-1} (Giovangigli, private communication, 1998). The maximum temperature in the flame is plotted versus equivalence ratio.

Once a solution is obtained for a given case (Case I), and another case (Case II) is studied (for example for a leaner or a richer flame), restarting the exercise from scratch is not an optimum solution: the solution obtained for Case I should be used to initialize the computation of Case II. Flame specialists have developed special continuation methods which allow the code to move in the solution domain continuously when parameters are varied (Giovangigli and Smooke [238, 239], Kalamatianos et al. [320]). These techniques are crucial when the computation is pushed close to the flammability limits: decreasing the quantity of fuel in the fresh gases, for example, eventually leads to a total quenching of the flame in which case the one-dimensional flame code should predict that the only solution is a "no flame" regime. Determining the exact limit of this extinction may be done with continuation techniques. Fig. 2.3 gives an example of a continuation computation for twin stretched premixed hydrogen/air flames in a stagnation point flow (see § 2.6 for a definition of stretched flames). The computation gives the variations of the flame temperature with equivalence ratio.

Fig. 2.3 shows that a premixed flame can not burn at all values of equivalence ratio: two 'flammability limits' (typically $\phi = 0.3$ and 4.6 for the H_2-air flame of Fig. 2.3) impose the range in which a premixed flame can burn. For other hydrocarbon-air flames (methane, propane, octane, etc), the flammability range is much smaller (typically 0.55 to 2 at atmospheric pressure and temperature). Determining flammability limits is a key issue in many combustion problems, either to make sure that the premixed gases will ignite (in piston engines for example) or to make sure that they will not ignite (in safety studies for example when fuel has been leaking inside a building). Fig. 2.3 also provides the non-physical branch going from a lean to rich condition which is unstable and is not observed experimentally.

2.3.2 Sensitivity analysis

In addition to continuation techniques, another tool has changed the way one-dimensional premixed flame codes are used today: sensitivity analysis. Being able to determine the effect of input parameters (chemical or transport parameters) is needed to understand which of these parameters control a given flame quantity.

Sensitivity to chemical parameters

Since the number of chemical parameters to introduce in a flame computation with complex chemistry can be counted in thousands, it is essential to know which of these parameters are really important for a given flame property: for example, if the activation temperature of the fourth reaction $H + O_2 \Leftrightarrow OH + O$ in the scheme given in Table 1.5 is changed, how does the flame speed change? Of course, it is possible to re-run the code and see the result. A better way is to differentiate the whole code using sensitivity analysis tools (see Lutz et al. [410], Giovangigli and Smooke [240] for a complete description) and build maps of sensitivity of all outputs versus chemical parameters (Kalamatianos et al. [320], Fotache et al. [217], Aung et al. [22]). Fig. 2.4 shows an example of sensitivity analysis of flame speeds (Aung et al. [22]) for H_2-air flames at normal temperature and a pressure of 0.35 atm. Four equivalence ratios are studied from 0.45 to 3.5. Such sensitivity analysis reveal the chain branching reaction $OH + H_2 \Leftrightarrow H + H_2O$ to be very important in the determination of the flame speed.

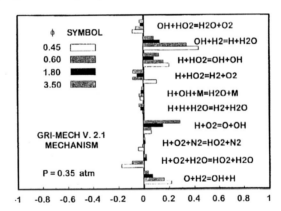

Figure 2.4: Sensitivity analysis of the laminar flame speed of hydrogen air flames. For each reaction, the figure provides the effect of a change of rate on the flame speed (Reprinted by permission of Elsevier Science from Aung et al. [22] © the Combustion Institute).

Sensitivity to transport parameters

Transport models (for diffusion coefficients, viscosity, heat diffusion coefficient) also play important roles when computing flames. The chemistry community usually works on zero-dimensional models (well stirred reactors for instance) in which space variations are ignored and only time evolutions are studied. In flames, however, the way reactants diffuse towards the place where they burn is often as important as chemistry itself (as shown by theory in the next sections) and the importance of transport on the overall results of one-dimensional flame codes has recently become an issue in many cases. As an example, Fig. 2.5 displays the variation of flame speed versus equivalence ratio for a methane/air flame for which two approaches for transport were tested in PREMIX:

- Full transport and chemistry with the GRI mechanism *www.me.berkeley.edu/gri-mech.*

- Full chemistry using the same scheme and simplified transport (Fick's law with all Lewis numbers set to unity). This assumption is used in many theoretical approaches (see § 2.4). It is true for most radicals in a flame except for very light molecules like H or H_2 which have Lewis numbers of the order of 0.11 and 0.3 respectively (see Fig. 1.4).

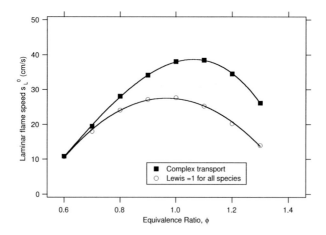

Figure 2.5: The effect of transport on premixed flames: comparison of exact transport model and simplified model (Lewis = 1 for all species) in an atmospheric methane/air flame. (B. Bedat, private communication, 1999).

Fig. 2.5 shows that assuming equal diffusivities for all species has a significant effect on flame speed. A somewhat worrying aspect of this sensitivity to transport models is that these models, even in their most refined forms, are being discussed today and that the diffusion coefficients estimated by usual packages probably exhibit larger error margins than generally expected (Paul and Warnatz [495]).

2.4 Theoretical solutions for laminar premixed flames

The computation of premixed flames with complex chemistry and transport is possible but severe restrictions prevent the use of these tools in many situations (for example, unsteady flames). Furthermore, one-dimensional planar steady premixed flames represent only one flame configuration: many more must be studied and understood for example to address the problem of turbulent combustion. Being able to tackle more complex questions on the fluid mechanics level require simplifications of chemistry and transport. This section presents some simple analytical results which have useful implications for numerical combustion.

2.4.1 Derivation of one-step chemistry conservation equations

The simplifications [iv] required to develop simple analytical solutions for laminar one-dimensional premixed flames are the following (Williams [710]):

- All species have the same molecular weight $W_k = W$ and the same constant heat capacity $C_{p,k} = C_p$. They also have the same molecular diffusion coefficient $D_k = D$ so that all Lewis numbers are equal $Le_k = \lambda/(\rho C_p D_k) = Le$. Finally species and heat diffuse in the same way so that $Le = 1$.

- Chemistry proceeds only through one irreversible reaction: $M = 1$ in Eq. (1.19).

$$\sum_{k=1}^{N} \nu'_{k1} \mathcal{M}_k \rightarrow \sum_{k=1}^{N} \nu''_{k1} \mathcal{M}_k \tag{2.10}$$

The reverse reaction rate is zero: $K_{r1} = 0$. The K_{f1} temperature dependence of the forward reaction follows an Arrhenius dependence: $K_{f1} = A_1 T^{\beta_1} e^{-T_{a1}/T}$. The reaction rates $\dot{\omega}_k$ for each species are linked to the progress rate $\mathcal{Q}_1$ at which the single reaction proceeds by Eq. (1.22):

$$\frac{\dot{\omega}_k}{W_k \nu_{k1}} = \mathcal{Q}_1 \quad \text{or} \quad \boxed{\dot{\omega}_k = W_k \nu_{k1} \mathcal{Q}_1} \tag{2.11}$$

The heat release term $\dot{\omega}_T$ in the temperature equation becomes:

$$\boxed{\dot{\omega}_T = -\sum_{k=1}^{N} \Delta h^o_{f,k} \dot{\omega}_k = -\mathcal{Q}_1 \sum_{k=1}^{N} (\Delta h^o_{f,k} W_k \nu_{k1}) = |\nu_{F1}| Q^m \mathcal{Q}_1} \tag{2.12}$$

[iv] Many of these simplifications can be removed when using more complex analytical methods. At this stage, it is simpler for readers to begin with this set of assumptions before trying to address more complex situations as studied for example in Williams [710].

where Q^m is the molar heat of reaction:

$$Q^m = -\sum_{k=1}^{N} \Delta h_{f,k}^o W_k \frac{\nu_{k1}}{|\nu_{F1}|} = -\sum_{k=1}^{N} \Delta h_{f,k}^{o,m} \frac{\nu_{k1}}{|\nu_{F1}|} = \sum_{k=1}^{N} \Delta h_{f,k}^{o,m} \frac{\nu_{k1}}{\nu_{F1}} \qquad (2.13)$$

because $\nu_{F1} = \nu_{F1}'' - \nu_{F1}'$ is negative. Q^m measures the heat released by the complete combustion of 1 mole of fuel. It is often useful to work with the heat of reaction per unit mass (the heat released by the combustion of 1 kg of fuel). There are two ways to define this quantity. The first possibility is:

$$Q' = -\frac{Q^m}{W_F} = -\sum_{k=1}^{N} \left(\Delta h_{f,k}^o \frac{W_k \nu_{k1}}{W_F \nu_{F1}} \right) \qquad (2.14)$$

The heat release source term $\dot{\omega}_T$ and the fuel source term $\dot{\omega}_F$ are then linked by:

$$\dot{\omega}_T = Q' \dot{\omega}_F \qquad (2.15)$$

Note that with this convention, Q^m is positive while Q' is negative. Some authors prefer to define Q as:

$$Q = -Q' = \frac{Q^m}{W_F} = \sum_{k=1}^{N} \left(\Delta h_{f,k}^o \frac{W_k \nu_{k1}}{W_F \nu_{F1}} \right) \qquad (2.16)$$

to have positive Q values. The link between $\dot{\omega}_T$ and $\dot{\omega}_F$ becomes:

$$\boxed{\dot{\omega}_T = -Q \dot{\omega}_F} \qquad (2.17)$$

The second convention is retained in this text. Typical values of Q^m and Q are summarized in Table 2.1. Note that the values of the heat released per unit mass of fuel Q for hydrocarbons are all very similar.

- The rate $\dot{\omega}_F$ of the reaction (2.10) is assumed to be limited by the fuel mass fraction and not by the oxidizer mass fraction. This assumption corresponds to study a very lean flame in which Y_O remains approximately constant: $Y_O = Y_O^1$. Only one species (Y_F) has then to be considered to evaluate the fuel reaction rate. This situation is obtained for

$$\nu_{F1}' = 1; \quad \nu_{F1}'' = 0; \quad \nu_{F1} = -1; \quad \nu_{O1}' = \nu_{O1}'' = \nu_{O1} = 0 \qquad (2.18)$$

so that, using Eq. (1.22) and (1.24):

$$\dot{\omega}_F = A_1 T^{\beta_1} \nu_{F1} \rho Y_F e^{-T_{a1}/T} = B_1 T^{\beta_1} \rho Y_F e^{-T_{a1}/T} \qquad (2.19)$$

where

$$B_1 = A_1 \nu_{F1} \qquad (2.20)$$

Global reaction		Q^m	Q	s	Y_F^{st}
		(kJ/mole)	(kJ/kg)		
$CH_4 + 2O_2$	$\rightarrow$ $CO_2 + 2H_2O$	802	50100	4.00	0.055
$C_3H_8 + 5O_2$	$\rightarrow$ $3CO_2 + 4H_2O$	2060	46600	3.63	0.060
$2C_8H_{18} + 25O_2$	$\rightarrow$ $16CO_2 + 18H_2O$	5225	45800	3.51	0.062
$2H_2 + O_2$	$\rightarrow$ $2H_2O$	241	120500	8.00	0.028

Table 2.1: Values of molar (Q^m) and mass (Q) heat of reactions and stoichiometric ratio $s = (\nu_O W_O)/(\nu_F W_F)$ for different irreversible reactions. The last column is the fuel mass fraction for stoichiometric combustion in air given by Eq. (1.31).

Even though these assumptions may seem strong (for example at the chemistry level), they actually preserve many essential features of flames: intense non-linear heat release, variable density and temperature.

The fuel mass fraction in the fresh gas is imposed ($Y_F = Y_F^1$). The corresponding conservation equations become (in the flame reference frame):

$$\rho u = \text{constant} = \rho_1 u_1 = \rho_1 s_L \tag{2.21}$$

$$\rho_1 s_L \frac{dY_F}{dx} = \frac{d}{dx}\left(\rho D \frac{dY_F}{dx}\right) + \dot{\omega}_F \tag{2.22}$$

$$\rho_1 C_p s_L \frac{dT}{dx} = \frac{d}{dx}\left(\lambda \frac{dT}{dx}\right) - Q\dot{\omega}_F \tag{2.23}$$

In these expressions, the fuel reaction rate $\dot{\omega}_F$ is negative.

2.4.2 Thermochemistry and chemical rates

A useful exercise is to integrate Eqs. (2.22) and (2.23) between $x = -\infty$ and $x = +\infty$ (see Fig. 2.1). Diffusive terms on both sides of the domain are zero and the inlet speed must be equal to the flame speed so that the following relations are obtained:

$$\rho_1 s_L Y_F^1 = -\int_{-\infty}^{+\infty} \dot{\omega}_F dx = \Omega_F \tag{2.24}$$

$$\rho_1 C_p s_L (T_2 - T_1) = -Q\int_{-\infty}^{+\infty} \dot{\omega}_F dx = Q\Omega_F \tag{2.25}$$

where Ω_F is the total fuel consumption in the domain.

These equations could have been written without deriving first Eqs. (2.22) and (2.23): they express simple integral properties of the flame. Eq. (2.24) shows that all fuel entering the domain ($\rho_1 Y_F^1 s_L$) is burnt downstream in the flame front by Ω_F. Eq. (2.25), on the other hand, states that the power released by the combustion of this fuel ($Q\Omega_F$) is entirely converted into sensible energy to heat up the mass flux $\rho_1 C_p s_L$ from T_1 to T_2.[v]

Now eliminating Ω_F between Eq. (2.24) and (2.25) leads to:

$$C_p(T_2 - T_1) = QY_F^1 \quad \text{so that} \quad \boxed{T_2 = T_1 + QY_F^1/C_p} \qquad (2.28)$$

which provides the adiabatic flame temperature T_2. Eq. (2.28) is a thermochemical expression which can be also directly derived from the conservation of enthalpy between fresh and burnt gas:

$$C_p(T_1 - T_0) + \sum_{k=1}^{N} \Delta h_{f,k}^o Y_k^1 = C_p(T_2 - T_0) + \sum_{k=1}^{N} \Delta h_{f,k}^o Y_k^2 \quad \text{or} \quad C_p(T_2 - T_1) = \sum_{k=1}^{N} \Delta h_{f,k}^o (Y_k^1 - Y_k^2) \tag{2.29}$$

where $T_0 = 298.15\,K$ is the reference temperature for formation enthalpies. All species involved in the summation of Eq. (2.29) are linked by Eq. (2.11) leading to:

$$\frac{Y_k^1 - Y_k^2}{Y_F^1 - 0} = \frac{W_k \nu_{k1}}{W_F \nu_{F1}} \quad \text{and} \quad C_p(T_2 - T_1) = \sum_{k=1}^{N} \Delta h_{f,k}^o \frac{W_k \nu_{k1}}{W_F \nu_{F1}} Y_F^1 = -Q' Y_F^1 = Q Y_F^1 \tag{2.30}$$

recovering Eq. (2.28).

These simple derivations have implications for combustion codes which can be summarized as follows:

- Thermochemistry (i.e. formation enthalpies $\Delta h_{f,k}^o$, heat capacities $C_{p,k}$ and reactants species mass fractions) controls *the maximum temperature* which can be reached in a premixed flame computation.

- Chemical parameters (preexponential constant A_1, activation temperature T_{a1} and exponent β_1) control *the speed of combustion*, i.e. the time or the distance needed for combustion to proceed from the fresh to the burnt state.

---

[v]This result is valid only for lean flames with one irreversible reaction. Similar expressions may be written for the general form of the combustion equations, without invoking any of the assumptions used here but their interpretation is more difficult because fuel may not be totally burnt at the exit of the domain. For example, Eq. (1.37) can be integrated from $-\infty$ to $+\infty$ for any species k in the flame reference frame to yield:

$$\rho_1(Y_k^1 - Y_k^2)s_L = -\int_{-\infty}^{+\infty} \dot{\omega}_k dx \tag{2.26}$$

where Y_k^1 and Y_k^2 are the values of Y_k at $x = -\infty$ and $+\infty$ respectively. This equation has a meaning only for species which are present on one side of the flame at least. It provides a correct estimate of the flame speed only if Y_k^2 is known. For burnt gases, for example, it yields:

$$\rho_1 Y_P^2 s_L = \int_{-\infty}^{+\infty} \dot{\omega}_P dx \tag{2.27}$$

Therefore, in a combustion code, there is no sense, for example, to increase the speed of combustion (by increasing the preexponential constant A) in order to increase the maximum temperature since these two quantities are uncorrelated. These properties, demonstrated here only for a single-step chemistry, are valid also for complex chemical schemes. It is also true for turbulent combustion models.

The adiabatic flame temperature obtained with Eq. (2.28) and Table 2.1 provides correct orders of magnitude when compared to measurements but is not a precise estimation because of two important assumptions which are not true quantitatively[vi] :

- The combustion products used in the single step reactions of Table 2.1 are not the only final products of combustion: additional reactions, especially dissociation of products like CO_2 and H_2O, take place at high temperatures. These reactions are endothermic and decrease temperature levels.

- The heat capacities C_p vary significantly with temperature and may induce errors of hundreds of degrees on the adiabatic flame temperature.

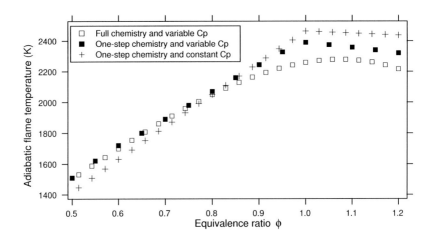

Figure 2.6: Adiabatic flame temperature for an atmospheric propane air flame ($T_1 - 300$ K) using various assumptions.

[vi]A more detailed discussion of the various methods available to compute adiabatic flame temperature is available as a corrected exercice (pdf file) at *elearning.cerfacs.fr/combustion/n7masterCourses/adiabaticflametemperature*. Moreover, a simple calculator tool giving the adiabatic flame temperature for most fuel / oxidizer combinations is also available at *elearning.cerfacs.fr/combustion/tools/adiabaticflametemperature*. This tool can provide the "full chemistry and variable C_p" curve in Fig. 2.6.

These limits may be overcome by performing equilibrium computations, by minimizing the Gibbs energy, and using special thermodynamics packages such as CHEMKIN. But Eq. (2.28) is useful to understand combustion and is used for turbulent combustion models. It is, for example, required for the derivation of the Bray Moss Libby (BML) model (Libby et al. [390], Bray et al. [89]) for turbulent premixed flames. As an example, Fig. 2.6 shows adiabatic flame temperatures for atmospheric propane/air flames computed with three different methods:

- M1: Full chemistry and variable heat capacity: both variable C_p and dissociations are accounted for.

- M2: Single-step chemistry and variable heat capacity: no dissociations are taken into account but the variations of C_p are included.

- M3: Single-step chemistry and constant heat capacity: both the dissociations and the C_p variations are neglected.

The comparison between M1 and M2 results shows the effects of dissociations (see *elearning.cerfacs.fr/combustion/n7masterCourses/adiabaticflametemperature*): at low equivalence ratio, the maximum temperature is low enough to avoid any dissociation and method M2 is precise. At higher equivalence ratio, dissociations of the products lower the temperature. For a stoichiometric flame, this effect decreases the temperature by 150 K. Method M3 is used here with $Q = 46600$ kJ/kg and $C_p = 1300$ J/(kgK). It leads to errors for all equivalence ratios which are of the order of 100 K but it still provides a correct simple evaluation of the final temperature.

2.4.3   The equivalence of temperature and fuel mass fraction

Eq. (2.22) and (2.23) may be simplified introducing reduced variables:

$$\boxed{Y = Y_F/Y_F^1} \quad \text{and} \quad \boxed{\Theta = \frac{C_p(T - T_1)}{QY_F^1} = \frac{T - T_1}{T_2 - T_1}} \tag{2.31}$$

The reduced fuel mass fraction Y goes from 1 in the fresh gases to 0 in the burnt gases while Θ goes from 0 to 1 in these zones. The equations for Y and Θ are derived from Eq. (2.22) and (2.23) using Eq. (2.28):

$$\rho_1 s_L \frac{dY}{dx} = \frac{d}{dx}\left(\rho D \frac{dY}{dx}\right) + \dot{\omega}_F/Y_F^1 \tag{2.32}$$

$$\rho_1 s_L \frac{d\Theta}{dx} = \frac{d}{dx}\left(\frac{\lambda}{C_p} \frac{d\Theta}{dx}\right) - \dot{\omega}_F/Y_F^1 \tag{2.33}$$

Summing these two equations and assuming unity Lewis number $Le = \lambda/(\rho C_p D) = 1$ gives:

$$\rho_1 s_L \frac{d}{dx}(\Theta + Y) = \frac{d}{dx}\left[\rho D \frac{d}{dx}(\Theta + Y)\right] \tag{2.34}$$

which has no source term and is a conserved (or passive) scalar equation. Since $\Theta + Y$ is 1 in the fresh gases and 1 in the burnt gases, the only solution to Eq. (2.34) is:[vii]

$$\boxed{\Theta + Y = 1} \tag{2.35}$$

This integral property of premixed flames can also be derived by stating that the total enthalpy of the mixture is constant everywhere. Temperature and fuel mass fraction are not independent quantities: when the fuel mass fraction goes down (the chemical enthalpy decreases), the temperature increases (the sensible enthalpy increases). From a numerical point of view, only one variable Θ can be solved for. The other one (Y) is obtained from Θ using Eq. (2.35). This means that the initial problem (Eq. 2.6 to 2.8) has now been reduced to the resolution of a single equation for Θ is:[viii]

$$\rho_1 s_L \frac{d\Theta}{dx} = \frac{d}{dx}\left(\frac{\lambda}{C_p}\frac{d\Theta}{dx}\right) - B_1\left(T_1 + \Theta(T_2 - T_1)\right)^{\beta_1} \rho(1-\Theta) \exp\left(-\frac{T_{a1}}{T_1 + \Theta(T_2 - T_1)}\right) \tag{2.36}$$

The reduced temperature Θ (or $1 - Y$) is also called the progress variable c.

2.4.4   The reaction rate

Even though Eq. (2.36) is a single differential equation, it is still a complex one. Furthermore, the flame speed itself remains an unknown quantity: the derivation was performed in the flame reference frame (velocity s_L) but the flame speed s_L^0 is still undetermined. The next sections show how the problem can be solved.

Before trying to solve Eq. (2.36), it is useful to understand the physics of laminar flames by analyzing its terms: flame theory has found in such flames a very open field of investigation and many of the most important results on combustion have been derived from these equations. These studies are not described here (see Williams [710, 711] for a review) but some basic results are useful for computations. To do this, some of the terminology of theoretical models for laminar premixed flames must be introduced. First, the reduced reaction rate ($\dot{\omega}_F$ in Eq. (2.33) or (2.36)) is expressed by Williams [710] in a more convenient form:

$$\frac{\dot{\omega}_F}{Y_F^1} = B_1 T^{\beta_1} e^{-\beta/\alpha} \rho(1 - \Theta) \exp\left(-\frac{\beta(1 - \Theta)}{1 - \alpha(1 - \Theta)}\right) \tag{2.37}$$

where $e^{-T_a/T}$ has been replaced by $\exp(-\beta/\alpha) \exp\left(-\frac{\beta(1-\Theta)}{1-\alpha(1-\Theta)}\right)$ and:

$$\boxed{\alpha = (T_2 - T_1)/T_2 = QY_F^1/(C_p T_2)} \quad \text{and} \quad \boxed{\beta = \alpha T_{a1}/T_2} \tag{2.38}$$

[vii]This property ($\Theta + Y = 1$) is also true in unsteady cases if the initial conditions satisfy the same property. This is a useful test for numerical algorithms applied to premixed flames: summing Θ and Y must give 1 everywhere.

[viii]Remember that B_1 is negative in this equation (see Eq. (2.20)) because ν_F is negative.

The two parameters α and β measure the heat released by the flame and the activation temperature respectively. Typical flame values are listed in Table 2.2 for a temperature $T_1 = 300K$. Flame 1 is a flame used for numerical simulations of turbulent combustion (see Chapt. 4) in which chemical parameters are modified to allow an easier computation while Flame 2 corresponds to more realistic values for hydrocarbon-air flames.

	T_2/T_1	E_{a1} (kJ/mole)	T_{a1}/T_1	α	β
Flame 1	4	110	42.7	0.75	8.0
Flame 2	7	375	150	0.86	18.4

Table 2.2: Typical values for α and β in premixed flames.

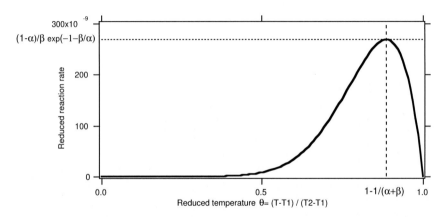

Figure 2.7: Variations of the reduced reaction rate $(\dot{\omega}_F/\rho_1 Y_F^1 B_1) = e^{-\frac{\beta}{\alpha}}\frac{\rho}{\rho_1}(1-\Theta)e^{-\frac{\beta(1-\Theta)}{1-\alpha(1-\Theta)}}$ vs Θ for $\alpha = 0.75$, $\beta = 8$ ($\beta_1 = 0$).

The density ρ is also a function of Θ if pressure is constant:

$$\rho = \rho_1 \frac{1}{1 + \alpha\Theta/(1-\alpha)} \qquad (2.39)$$

so that the reaction rate $\dot{\omega}_F$ is now a function of only one variable: Θ. Fig. 2.7 presents variations of the reduced reaction rate $\dot{\omega}_F$ for $\alpha = 0.75$ and $\beta = 8$, assuming $\beta_1 = 0$, while Fig. 2.8 gives $\dot{\omega}_F$ for increasing values of β. For each case in Fig. 2.8, the preexponential constant B_1 has been roughly adjusted to provide the same value for the total reaction rate $\int \dot{\omega}_F dx$, i.e. to provide the same flame speed. Fig. 2.8 conveys a simple idea: to compute a flame with a given flame speed, increasing β (i.e. increasing the activation temperature) leads to a stiffer problem where $\dot{\omega}_F$ is almost zero over a wide range of temperature and peaks for

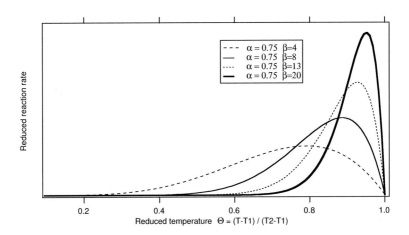

Figure 2.8: Variations of the reduced reaction rate $\dot{\omega}_F/(\rho_1 Y_F^1 B_1)$ vs Θ ($\beta_1 = 0$) for various values of β: the problem becomes stiffer when β increases (i.e. when the activation temperature increases). The preexponential constant B_1 has been adjusted to provide the same value of the total reaction rate (i.e. the same flame speed) for all flames.

Θ values very close to unity. In terms of resolution, it is already obvious that mesh points are needed to resolve the temperature (or species) profile (typically 10 to 20 grid points for $0 < \Theta < 1$) because diffusion terms are important everywhere in this zone. Fig. 2.8 shows that points are also needed in the vicinity of $\Theta = 1$ to resolve the reaction source terms. This constraint is much more demanding as shown by asymptotic analysis (Williams [710]): in general, the maximum of the reaction rate shown in Fig. 2.8 is obtained for Θ of the order of $1 - 1/\beta$. The exact value at which the reaction rate predicted by Eq. (2.37) is maximum may be calculated explicitly for this simple case, by searching for the maximum of $\dot{\omega}_F(\Theta)$ and gives:

$$\boxed{\Theta_{max} = 1 - 1/(\alpha + \beta)} \tag{2.40}$$

which is indeed close to the asymptotic estimate $1 - 1/\beta$ because β is much larger than α. The value of the maximum reduced reaction rate is (Fig. 2.7):

$$\dot{\omega}_F^{max} = \rho_1 Y_F^1 B_1 \frac{1 - \alpha}{\beta} \exp\left(-\frac{\beta}{\alpha} - 1\right) \tag{2.41}$$

The zone where the reaction rate is non-zero in a premixed flame is called the reaction zone and it is small compared to diffusion length scales. In temperature space, it roughly spans the domain $(1 - 2/\beta, 1)$ with a width of $\delta_r = 2/\beta$ (Fig. 2.9). In terms of mesh requirements, instead of adequately resolving the Θ domain from 0 to 1 (width 1), it is now necessary to resolve the $(1 - 2/\beta, 1)$ interval (width $\delta_r = 2/\beta$). In physical space, if the flame thickness is δ_L^0 (it will be defined more precisely in Section 2.5), having enough mesh points in δ_L^0 is not sufficient: the reaction zone (thickness $2\delta_L^0/\beta$) must be resolved and it is much thinner than the flame thickness.

The first implication of such a simple analysis is the following: if a mesh is sufficient, for a given Reynolds number, to resolve a non reacting flow, i.e. to resolve temperatures going from 0 to 1, the mesh density to resolve the same flow with a premixed flame must be multiplied by a factor $\beta/2$ in each direction. For typical values of β (10 to 20), this is, in most cases, a difficult task.

Asymptotic analysis also shows that there is negligible reaction in zone 1 in Fig. 2.9 (from $\Theta = 0$ to $1 - 2/\beta$): this region is dominated by convection and diffusion (phenomena already present in non-reacting flows and not bringing any new special constraint on resolution) while zone 2 (from $\Theta = 1 - 2/\beta$ to 1) is controlled by reaction and diffusion. The existence of zones where different physical mechanisms with different mesh constraints exist (coarse in zone 1, finer in zone 2 when β increases) can be handled in two ways:

- For steady or one-dimensional unsteady flame computations, a natural approach is to use adaptive meshes as done in most one-dimensional flame codes such as PREMIX. Coarse meshes may be used in the diffusion/convection zones while more refined grids are utilized in reaction/diffusion zones. Sophisticated refinement techniques may be used with efficiency for such problems as long as one-dimensional flames or multi-dimensional steady flames are studied.

- For multi-dimensional and/or unsteady flames the challenge is much more difficult. Certain authors adapt the mesh to the computation, refining the grid before the calculation takes place (Mohammed et al. [448]). Adaptive mesh techniques have also been explored (Dervieux et al. [173]) but the most successful approach to date has been to use chemical schemes with moderate stiffness (β must be low) and fine grids everywhere because unsteady flames move and can be located anywhere in the computational domain. This approach is possible only for simple chemical systems. For certain fuels, it is simply impossible to construct accurate chemical mechanisms with reasonable stiffness. The state of the art today is that while one-dimensional flame codes are able to compute almost any steady flame for arbitrarily complex chemistry data, very few of these flames can be handled in unsteady multi-dimensional flame codes.

2.4.5   Analytical solutions for flame speed

Under the previous simplifications, explicit expressions can be derived for flame speed and flame structure. There are multiple ways to do so. This section presents first the classical analysis of Zeldovich, Frank-Kamenetski and von Karman which is the basis of most asymptotic methods. A second fully analytical method is then presented.

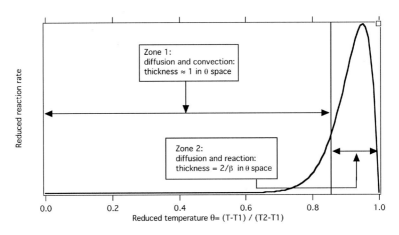

Figure 2.9: The resolution constraints due to the thickness of the reaction zone in laminar premixed flames: the reaction zone (where diffusion and convection dominate) is thinner than the preheat zone (where diffusion and reaction dominate) by a factor $\beta/2$ (Eq. 2.38).

Asymptotic analysis of Zeldovich, Frank-Kamenetski and von Karman (ZFK)

Eq. (2.36) may be further simplified by scaling the spatial variable x:

$$\xi = \int_0^x \frac{\rho_1 s_L C_p}{\lambda} dx \tag{2.42}$$

Eq. (2.36) becomes for a steady propagating laminar flame in its reference frame:

$$\frac{d\Theta}{d\xi} = \frac{d^2\Theta}{d\xi^2} - \Lambda\omega \tag{2.43}$$

where ω is a reduced reaction rate defined (Williams [710]) by:

$$\omega = (1 - \Theta)\exp\left(-\frac{\beta(1 - \Theta)}{1 - \alpha(1 - \Theta)}\right) \tag{2.44}$$

and Λ is a non dimensionalized quantity (the "flame parameter"):

$$\Lambda = \frac{\rho\lambda|B_1|T^{\beta_1}}{\rho_1^2 s_L^2 C_p}e^{-\beta/\alpha} = -\frac{\rho\lambda B_1 T^{\beta_1}}{\rho_1^2 s_L^2 C_p}e^{-\beta/\alpha} \tag{2.45}$$

as B_1 is negative.

Under the assumptions used in this section, the structure of all stationary premixed flames depends only on one parameter Λ for given α and β values. This flame parameter contains information on heat (or species) diffusion (λ) and rate constants (B_1). These two mechanisms control the flame speed: increasing the heat diffusivity or increasing rate constants increases the flame speed in the same proportion.[ix]

In expression (2.45), the numerator $\rho\lambda B_1 T^{\beta_1}$ is supposed to be constant to perform the mathematical integration. This is not a difficult assumption to satisfy: any variation of λ such that $\lambda T^{\beta_1-1} = constant$ allows this assumption to be true. Evaluating the numerator in the fresh gases gives:

$$\Lambda = \frac{D_{th}^1 \, |B_1| \, T_1^{\beta_1}}{s_L^2} e^{-\frac{\beta}{\alpha}} \tag{2.46}$$

where $D_{th}^1 = \lambda/\rho_1 C_p$ is the heat diffusivity in the fresh gas.

Various asymptotic analysis techniques have been developed in the combustion community to solve Eq. (2.43). The first one is due to Zeldovich, Frank Kamenetski and von Karman (ZFK) and gives a very simple result:

$$\Lambda = 0.5\beta^2 \tag{2.47}$$

A more precise result is developed by Williams [710]:

$$\Lambda = 0.5\beta^2 \left(1 + \frac{2}{\beta}(3\alpha - 1.344)\right) \tag{2.48}$$

In general Λ is of the order of 100 for usual flames. From values of Λ given by asymptotics and its definition (Eq. (2.45)), the flame speed may be derived leading to:

$$\boxed{s_L = \frac{1}{\beta} e^{-\frac{\beta}{2\alpha}} \left(2 \, |B_1| \, T_1^{\beta_1} D_{th}^1\right)^{1/2}} \tag{2.49}$$

for the ZFK formulation (Eq. (2.47)) or:

$$\boxed{s_L = \frac{1}{\beta} \exp\left(-\frac{\beta}{2\alpha}\right) \left(2 \, |B_1| \, T_1^{\beta_1} D_{th}^1\right)^{1/2} \left(1 + \frac{1.344 - 3\alpha}{\beta}\right)} \tag{2.50}$$

for the Williams formulation (Eq. (2.48)).

Analytical solution for a simplified reaction rate expression

Asymptotic solutions based on Arrhenius expressions such as the ZFK analysis require some work to derive the necessary mathematics. A fully explicit expression for flame structure and speed can be obtained by using another formulation for the reaction rate. The flame structure of Fig. 2.9 suggests that any reaction rate model which produces no combustion before the critical temperature $\Theta_c = 1 - 1/\beta$ and intense combustion between Θ_c and 1 should reproduce most of the flame features.

[ix] The situation is very different for diffusion flames (see § 3) where species and heat diffusivity is the primary factor controlling the overall reaction rate.

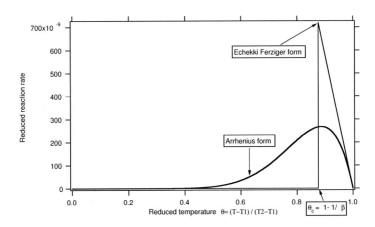

Figure 2.10: Analytical EF model (Echekki and Ferziger [197]) for premixed flame compared to the usual Arrhenius form

Among all possible forms for reaction rates, the Arrhenius form is one possibility but others are available. Some of them mimic the Arrhenius form reasonably well but offer linear forms so that the resolution of the flame equations becomes straightforward. Fig. 2.10 shows such a model proposed by Echekki and Ferziger [197] (called EF here). In the EF formulation, the reaction rate is zero before Θ_c and $\rho_1 R_r (1 - \Theta)$ when $\Theta > \Theta_c$. R_r is a model constant. From Eq. (2.21) and (2.23), the conservation equations to solve are (C_p is assumed to be constant):

$$\rho u = \rho_1 u_1 = \rho_1 s_L \tag{2.51}$$

$$\rho_1 s_L \frac{d\Theta}{dx} = \frac{d}{dx}\left(\frac{\lambda}{C_p}\frac{d\Theta}{dx}\right) + \dot\omega_{EF} \tag{2.52}$$

where

$$\dot\omega_{EF} = \rho_1 R_r (1 - \Theta) H(\Theta - \Theta_c) \tag{2.53}$$

where H is the Heaviside function and $\Theta_c = 1 - 1/\beta$. These equations may be formulated in a non dimensionalized form as with Eq. (2.43) using the flame coordinate ξ (Eq. (2.42)):

$$\frac{d\Theta}{d\xi} = \frac{d^2\Theta}{d\xi^2} - \Lambda_1 \omega_1 \tag{2.54}$$

where $\Lambda_1 = \lambda R_r / (\rho_1 s_L^2 C_p)$ and $\omega_1 = (1 - \Theta) H(\Theta - \Theta_c)$. Assuming a constant thermal conductivity $\lambda = \lambda_1$, the flame parameter Λ_1 is constant.[x] Eq. (2.52) is easier to solve than for the Arrhenius form given in Eq. (2.43): suppose that the point where the critical temperature

---

[x]Another possibility (Echekki and Ferziger [197]) is to write $\dot\omega_{EF} = \rho R_r (1 - \Theta) H(\Theta - \Theta_c)$ and later to

$\Theta_c = 1 - 1/\beta$ is reached, is fixed at $x = \xi = 0$. In this case $\xi = (\rho_1 s_L C_p)x/\lambda_1 = x/\delta$ where δ is a characteristic flame thickness given by:

$$\delta = \frac{\lambda_1}{\rho_1 C_p s_L} = \frac{D_{th}^1}{s_L} \qquad (2.55)$$

and D_{th}^1 is the thermal diffusivity of the fresh gas.

	Reaction rate $\dot{\omega}_{EF}$	Heat coefficient λ	Flame parameter Λ_1
Initial EF model	$\rho R_r (1 - \Theta) H(\Theta - \Theta_c)$	$\lambda_1 \frac{T}{T_1}$	$\frac{\rho \lambda R_r}{\rho_1^2 s_L^2 C_p} = \frac{\lambda_1 R_r}{\rho_1 s_L^2 C_p}$
Present model	$\rho_1 R_r (1 - \Theta) H(\Theta - \Theta_c)$	λ_1	$\frac{\lambda_1 R_r}{\rho_1 s_L^2 C_p}$

Table 2.3: Assumptions used by Echekki and Ferziger [197] and by this text on rate coefficients and heat diffusion coefficient. λ_1 is the value of the heat coefficient in the fresh gases.

The solution is obtained by first integrating Eq. (2.54) between $x = -\infty$ and $x = 0$ (with $\dot{\omega}_{EF} = 0$):

$$\Theta = \left(1 - \frac{1}{\beta}\right) e^{x/\delta} \qquad (2.56)$$

For $x > 0$, the solution is searched under the form $1 - \Theta = b e^{\Gamma x}$. The resolution is straightforward and gives:

$$\Gamma = \frac{1}{2\delta} \left[1 - \left(1 + 4\frac{R_r \delta}{s_L}\right)^{1/2}\right] \qquad (2.57)$$

and

$$\Theta = 1 - \frac{1}{\beta} e^{\Gamma x} \qquad (2.58)$$

By construction, the two temperature profiles of Eq. (2.58) and (2.56) are continuous at $x = 0$. However, their derivatives (the heat flux) are not if the value of the flame speed is arbitrary. This is actually the missing condition to close the problem: the true flame speed s_L^0 is the one which ensures that the heat flux is continuous at the interface between the preheat and reaction zones [xi]. By expressing this condition at $x = 0$, the value of R_r is obtained:

---

assume that $\lambda = \lambda_1 T/T_1$ so that $\rho\lambda$ is constant (see Table 2.3). In both cases, Λ_1 is constant. This derivation is given in more detail here so that the reader can understand why asymptotic or analytical techniques require assumptions on transport coefficients: in most cases, these assumptions are needed to make flame parameters such as Λ_1 constant and are therefore directly linked to the forms assumed for the reaction rates as shown in Table 2.3.

[xi]This derivation is the simplest prototype of a more general called matched expansion asymptotics (*en.wikipedia.org/wiki/Method_of_matched_asymptotic_expansions*) where two zones are solved separately and matching conditions allow to solve the eigenvalue problem.

$$R_r = \beta(\beta - 1)\frac{s_L}{\delta} = \beta(\beta - 1)\frac{s_L^2}{D_{th}^1} \tag{2.59}$$

An explicit expression for flame speed is also derived:

$$s_L = \left(\frac{1}{\beta(\beta - 1)}\frac{\lambda_1 R_r}{\rho_1 C_p}\right)^{1/2} = \frac{1}{(\beta(\beta - 1))^{1/2}}(D_{th}^1 R_r)^{1/2} \quad \text{and} \quad \Gamma = \frac{1 - \beta}{\delta} \tag{2.60}$$

This solution may be used to initialize a premixed flame propagating at speed s_L with an activation temperature corresponding to β as shown in Table 2.4. Fig. 2.10 displays profiles of reduced reaction rate $\dot{\omega}_F/(\rho_1 Y_F^1 B_1)$ versus Θ for an Arrhenius expression and for the EF model. The rate constants B (for the Arrhenius form) and R_r (for the EF model) are chosen to give the same flame speed: this is the case when $R_r = 2B/\beta \exp(-\beta/\alpha)$ (from Table 2.5). Fig. 2.11 compares the profile obtained using this model with a profile obtained from the exact integration of Eq. (2.36) for $\alpha = 0.75$ and $\beta = 8$. The agreement is satisfactory.

Comparing the expressions of flame speed for the EF model (Eq. (2.60)) and for an Arrhenius form (Eq. (2.50)) reveals similar dependences:

$$s_L \propto (D_{th}^1 R_r)^{1/2} \tag{2.61}$$

In both models, the flame speed varies like the square root of the diffusion coefficient and the square root of the reaction rate coefficient. This simple information is often useful to understand the response of flame codes to changes in transport or chemistry models.

The thickness of the reaction rate zone in Θ space for this flame is $1/\beta$ by construction. The maximum value of the reaction rate is obtained at $x = 0$ and $\Theta = \Theta_c = 1 - 1/\beta$ and is $\rho_1(\beta - 1)s_L^2/D_{th}^1$. The integral of the reaction rate ($\int_{-\infty}^{+\infty} \dot{\omega}_{EF} dx$) is $\rho_1 s_L$ as expected (see Eq. (2.24)).

Summary of simple flame speed expressions

The two previous sections have presented some basic results relating to laminar premixed flames which can be obtained by analytical means. Many more studies have been devoted to similar approaches and provide useful results for numerical combustion. Table 2.5 summarizes how asymptotic analysis may be used to predict flame speeds. In addition to the lean flame cases presented here, the results of van Kalmthout [662] for flames where the reaction rate is written as $B_1 \rho Y_F Y_O e^{-T_a/T}$ are also presented.

Choose:
Flame speed s_L, activation temperature T_a
Final temperature T_2, initial temperature T_1
Inlet velocity u_1
Estimate:
Rate parameters $\alpha = (T_2 - T_1)/T_2$ and $\beta = \alpha T_a/T_2$
Flame thickness: $\delta = D_{th}^1/s_L$
Compute reduced temperature profiles: $\Theta = \frac{T-T_1}{T_2-T_1}$
for $x < 0$: $\Theta = (1 - 1/\beta)e^{\frac{x}{\delta}}$ and for $x > 0$: $\Theta = 1 - 1/\beta e^{(1-\beta)\frac{x}{\delta}}$
Initialize temperature:
$T(x) = \Theta(T_2 - T_1) + T_1$
Initialize velocity field:
$u(x) = u_1 + s_L\alpha\Theta/(1 - \alpha) = u_1 + s_L(T/T_1 - 1)$
Fix adequate rate values:
For present model: $\dot{\omega}_F = \rho_1 R_r(1 - \Theta)H(\Theta - \Theta_c)$ with $R_r = \beta(\beta - 1)s_L^2/D_{th}^1$
For Arrhenius: $\dot{\omega}_F = B_1 T_1^\beta \rho Y_F e^{-T_a/T}$ with $|B_1|T_1^\beta = (s_L^2\beta^2 e^{\beta/\alpha})/D_{th}^1$

Table 2.4: Analytical initialization of a premixed flame using a simplified rate model. The inlet speed u_1 may differ from the flame speed s_L. The velocity field is given by Eq. (2.104).

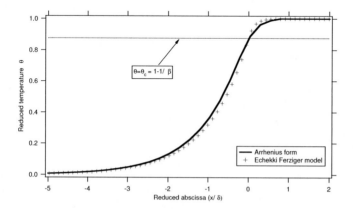

Figure 2.11: Comparison of temperature profiles obtained with Arrhenius and EF models.

Model	Fuel reaction rate $\dot{\omega}_F$ in Eq. (2.22)	Transport assumptions	Flame speed s_L
ZFK	$B_1 T^{\beta_1} \rho Y_F e^{-T_a/T}$	$\lambda = \lambda_1 (T/T_1)^{1-\beta_1}$	$\frac{1}{\beta} e^{-\frac{\beta}{2\alpha}} \left(2\,|B_1|\,T_1^{\beta_1} D_{th}^1\right)^{1/2}$
Williams	$B_1 T^{\beta_1} \rho Y_F e^{-T_a/T}$	$\lambda = \lambda_1 (T/T_1)^{1-\beta_1}$	$\frac{1}{\beta} e^{-\frac{\beta}{2\alpha}} \left(2\,|B_1|\,T_1^{\beta_1} D_{th}^1\right)^{1/2}\left(1+\frac{1.34-3\alpha}{\beta}\right)$
Van Kalmthout	$B_1 \rho Y_F Y_O e^{-T_a/T}$	$\lambda = \lambda_1 T/T_1$	$\frac{1}{\beta} e^{-\frac{\beta}{2\alpha}} \left(2\,|B_1|\,Y_O^1 D_{th}^1 \frac{2}{\beta}\right)^{1/2}$
Echekki	$\rho R_r (1-\Theta) H(\Theta - \Theta_c)$	$\lambda = \lambda_1 T/T_1$	$\left(\frac{1}{\beta(\beta-1)} D_{th}^1 R_r\right)^{1/2}$
This book	$\rho_1 R_r (1-\Theta) H(\Theta - \Theta_c)$	$\lambda = \lambda_1$	$\left(\frac{1}{\beta(\beta-1)} D_{th}^1 R_r\right)^{1/2}$

Table 2.5: Summary of assumptions and flame speed results using some simple asymptotic and analytical models for lean flames. The temperature reaction rate $\dot{\omega}_T$ is linked to $\dot{\omega}_F$ by $\dot{\omega}_T = -Q\dot{\omega}_F$ (B_1 is negative). The maximum temperature T_2 is given by $T_2 = T_1 + QY_F^1/C_p$ where Y_F^1 is the fuel mass fraction in the fresh gas. The coefficients α and β are obtained by $\alpha = (T_2 - T_1)/T_2$ and $\beta = \alpha T_a/T_2$. $\Theta_c = 1 - 1/\beta$. For the van Kalmthout results, Y_O^1 designates the oxidizer mass fraction in the fresh gases (van Kalmthout [662]).

2.4.6   Generalized expression for flame speeds

Mitani [443] also derived a more general expression for flame speeds which is not as explicit as the formulae of Table 2.5 but covers more cases (Williams [710]) and can handle non-unity Lewis number reactants. Consider a global reaction:

$$\nu'_F F + \nu'_O O \to P \tag{2.62}$$

for which the fuel consumption rate is given by:

$$\dot{\omega}_F = \nu'_F W_F B_1 T^{\beta_1} \left(\frac{\rho Y_F}{W_F} \right)^{n_F} \left(\frac{\rho Y_O}{W_O} \right)^{n_O} \exp \left(-\frac{T_a}{T} \right) \tag{2.63}$$

Where the reaction exponents n_F and n_O are not necessarily equal to ν'_F and ν'_O. The equivalence ratio is $\phi = sY_F^1/Y_O^1 = (\nu'_O W_O Y_F^1)/(\nu'_F W_F Y_O^1)$. The product $\lambda \rho B_1 T^{\beta_1}$ is assumed to be constant. This is the case for example when $\lambda = \lambda_1 (T/T_1)^{1-\beta_1}$ as in Table 2.5.

If Le_F and Le_O are respectively the fuel and the oxidizer Lewis numbers, the flame speed obtained by a first -order analysis for lean flame ($\phi < 1$) is (indices 1 correspond to fresh gases while 2 indicate burnt quantities):

$$s_L = \left[\frac{2\lambda_2 \nu'_F (\nu'_O/\nu'_F)^{n_O} \rho_2^{n_F+n_O} B_1 T_2^{\beta_1} Y_{F,1}^{n_F+n_O-1} Le_F^{n_F} Le_O^{n_O}}{\rho_1^2 C_p W_F^{n_F+n_O-1} \beta^{n_F+n_O+1}} \right]^{1/2} \cdot \\ G(n_F, n_O)^{1/2} \exp \left(-\frac{\beta}{2\alpha} \right) \tag{2.64}$$

where the G function is defined by:

$$G(n_F, n_O) = \int_0^\infty y^{n_F} \left(y + \beta \frac{\phi - 1}{Le_O} \right)^{n_O} e^{-y} dy \tag{2.65}$$

For a rich flame, this formula is still valid if indices F and O are inverted. In general, the accuracy of such expressions is reasonable for lean mixtures but poor for rich cases. An equivalent expression of Eq. (2.64) can be obtained by replacing $\lambda_2 \rho_2 B_1 T_2^{\beta_1}$ by $\lambda_1 \rho_1 B_1 T_1^{\beta_1}$:

$$s_L = \left[\frac{2D_{th}^1 \nu'_F (\nu'_O/\nu'_F)^{n_O} B_1 T_1^{\beta_1} Le_F^{n_F} Le_O^{n_O}}{\beta^{n_F+n_O+1}} \left(\frac{\rho_2 Y_{F,1}}{W_F} \right)^{n_F+n_O-1} \right]^{1/2} \cdot \\ G(n_F, n_O)^{1/2} \exp \left(-\frac{\beta}{2\alpha} \right) \tag{2.66}$$

For $n_F = 1$, $\nu'_F = 1$ and $n_O = 0$ and unity Lewis numbers, $G(n_F, n_O) = 1$ and Eq. (2.66) leads to the expression (2.49).

Choose thermodynamic data: Molecular weights of fuel (W_F) and oxidizer (W_O) Heat release per unit mass of fuel Q
Choose chemical reaction: $\nu'_F F + \nu'_O O \rightarrow P$
Choose kinetic parameters: Preexponential constant B_1, exponent β_1, activation temperature T_a Reaction exponents n_F and n_O
Choose transport parameters: Heat diffusivity in fresh gas: λ_1 Fuel and oxidizer Lewis numbers: Le_F and Le_O
Choose fresh gas characteristics: Temperature T_1, density ρ_1, equivalence ratio ϕ
Compute intermediate quantities: Stoichiometric ratio: $s = \dfrac{\nu'_O W_O}{\nu'_F W_F}$ Fresh gas fuel mass fraction: $Y_{F,1} = 1 / \left(1 + \dfrac{s}{\phi}(1 + 3.76\dfrac{W_{N_2}}{W_{O_2}})\right)$ Burnt gas temperature and density: $T_2 = T_1 + QY_{F,1}/C_p$ and $\rho_2 = \rho_1 T_1/T_2$ α and β parameters: $\alpha = QY_{F,1}/(C_p T_2)$ $\beta = \alpha T_a/T_2$ Burnt gas heat diffusivity: $\lambda_2 = \lambda_1 (T_2/T_1)^{1-\beta_1}$ Integrate G factor: $G(n_F, n_O) = \int_0^\infty y^{n_F}(y + \beta(\phi - 1)/Le_O)^{n_O})e^{-y}dy$
Compute flame speed: $s_L = \left[\dfrac{2\lambda_2 \nu'_F (\nu'_O/\nu'_F)^{n_O} \rho_2^{n_F+n_O} B_1 T_2^{\beta_1} Y_{F,1}^{n_F+n_O-1} Le_F^{n_F} Le_O^{n_O}}{\rho_1^2 C_p W_F^{n_F+n_O-1} \beta^{n_F+n_O+1}}\right]^{1/2} G(n_F, n_O)^{1/2} e^{-\frac{\beta}{2\alpha}}$

Table 2.6: Computing the speed of a lean flame in air using asymptotic results. The mixture molecular weight is supposed to be constant.

Table 2.6 shows how this expression must be used for a lean hydrocarbon/air flames. Fig. 2.12 gives an example of flame speed computations for a methane/air flame modeled by a single step reaction:

$$CH_4 + 2O_2 \rightarrow CO_2 + 2H_2O \qquad (2.67)$$

The following set of parameters was used:

$$B_1 = 1.08 \ 10^7 \ uSI; \quad \beta_1 = 0; \quad E_a = 83600 \ J/mole; \quad n_F = 1; \quad n_O = 0.5; \qquad (2.68)$$

$$\rho_1 = 1.16 \ kg/m^3; \quad \lambda_1 = 0.038 \ W/mK; \quad Q = 50100 \ kJ/kg; \quad C_p = 1450 \ J/(kgK) \quad (2.69)$$

The preexponential constant B_1 was fitted to match the flame speed measured at $\phi = 0.8$. Fig. 2.12 shows that the asymptotic formula provides a fair estimate of the flame speed with an error margin of the order of a few percent on the lean side and of 20 percent on the rich side compared to a numerical resolution of the conservation equation. When compared to

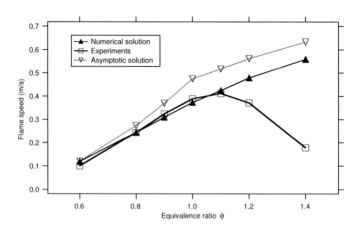

Figure 2.12: Limitations of single-step chemistry formulations: flame speeds for a methane/air mixture as a function of equivalence ratio.

experimental results (Yamaoka and Tsuji [717]), the asymptotic and the numerical solutions provide good estimates on the lean side but fail on the rich side: this is a usual limitation of single-step chemical schemes for hydrocarbon/air flames which can be suppressed by using chemical constants depending on the local equivalence ratio (Fernández-Tarrazo et al. [208], Franzelli et al. [220])[xii].

2.4.7 Stiffness of reduced schemes

Fig. 2.12 shows that using a single step reaction to describe premixed combustion provides good results in the lean regime but poor results for rich flames. This problem has been recognized for a long time and may be fixed by using other set of values for the reaction exponents n_F and n_O. Westbrook and Dryer [702] proposed reduced schemes which provide reasonable flame speeds over a wide range of equivalence ratios. From a numerical point of view, this is obtained by using small values of the reaction exponents, especially n_F. Unfortunately, such small values may lead to numerical difficulties: decreasing reaction exponents (as often done in many reduced schemes) leads to increased stiffness. This may be shown by considering a flame where $n_O = 0$ and changing n_F. Fig. 2.13 shows the variations of the reduced reaction rate of Eq. (2.37) in which a non-unity value for n_F would be used:

$$\frac{\dot{\omega}_F}{Y_F^1} = B_1 T^{\beta_1} e^{-\frac{\beta}{\alpha}} \rho (1 - \Theta)^{n_F} \exp\left(-\frac{\beta(1 - \Theta)}{1 - \alpha(1 - \Theta)}\right) \tag{2.70}$$

[xii]An important limitation of these approaches is that the local equivalence ratio must be computed at each point of the flow, something which is feasible only when all species Lewis numbers are equal.

The heat release is such that $\alpha = 0.75$ and the activation temperature corresponds to $\beta = 8$. The reduced reaction rate becomes a stiff function of the reduced temperature when small values of n_F are used. For $n_F = 0.2$ and $\beta = 8$, the chemistry formulation is stiffer than it was for $n_F = 1$ and $\beta = 20$ (see Fig. 2.8). This explains why reduced schemes often lead to numerical difficulties.

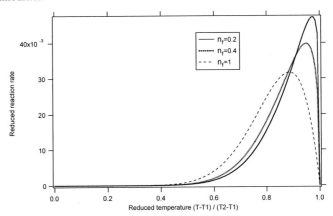

Figure 2.13: Variations of the reduced reaction rate $\dot{\omega}_F/(\rho_1 Y_F^1 B_1)$ vs Θ for various values of n_F: the problem becomes stiffer when n_F increases ($\beta_1 = 0$ and $\beta = 8$).

2.4.8 Variations of flame speed with temperature and pressure

Eq. (2.66) may also be used to evaluate the dependence of flame speed with pressure P or fresh gas temperature T_1. For example, the thermal diffusivity D_{th}^1 scales like $1/P$ while the burnt gas density ρ_2 scales like P so that, for a constant fresh gas temperature T_1, the laminar flame speed s_L at pressure P is roughly linked to its value at P_0 by:

$$s_L(P) = s_L(P^0) \left(\frac{P}{P^0}\right)^{\frac{n_F + n_O - 2}{2}} \tag{2.71}$$

Temperature changes are more difficult to anticipate because the exponential term in Eq. (2.66) is controlled by the burnt gas temperature T_2 which is not well described using simple reaction chemistry. Experimental results are usually expressed as simple polynomial functions:

$$s_L(P, T_1) = s_L(P^0, T_1^0) \left(\frac{P}{P^0}\right)^{\alpha_P} \left(\frac{T_1}{T_1^0}\right)^{\alpha_T} \tag{2.72}$$

As an example, for usual values $n_F = 0.1$ and $n_O = 1.65$, as proposed by Westbrook and Dryer [702] for lean propane/air flame, a theoretical pressure exponent $\alpha_P = -0.125$ is found from Eq. (2.71) and is consistent with the value proposed by Metghalchi and Keck [439] (Table 2.7).

Table 2.7 gives examples of values for the parameters used in Eq. (2.72) obtained for methane/air combustion (Gu et al. [255]) ($1 \leq P \leq 10$ bars, $300 \leq T_1 \leq 400$ K, $0.8 \leq \phi \leq 1.2$) and for propane/air flames by Metghalchi and Keck [439] ($0.4 \leq P \leq 50$ bars, $300 \leq T_1 \leq 700$ K, $0.8 \leq \phi \leq 1.5$, data interpolated from Metghalchi's paper).

Fuel	$s_L(P^0, T_1^0)$ (m/s)	α_T	α_P
Methane ($\phi = 0.8$)	0.259	2.105	-0.504
Methane ($\phi = 1$)	0.360	1.612	-0.374
Methane ($\phi = 1.2$)	0.314	2.000	-0.438
Propane ($\phi = 0.8$ to 1.5)	$0.34 - 1.38(\phi - 1.08)^2$	$2.18 - 0.8(\phi - 1)$	$-0.16 - 0.22(\phi - 1)$

Table 2.7: Examples of experimental correlations given by Eq. (2.72) for methane/air (Gu et al. [255]) and propane/air flames (Metghalchi and Keck [439]).

Flame speeds increase rapidly when the temperature of the fresh gases T_1 increases but decrease when pressure increases. Fig. 2.14 shows examples of flame speed variations for methane-air and propane-air flames with fresh gas temperatures for different pressures obtained with expression (2.72) and the parameters of Table 2.7.

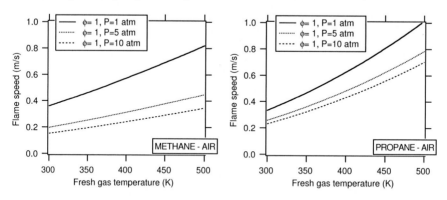

Figure 2.14: Experimental fits for speeds of stoichiometric methane/air (Gu et al. [255]), left) and propane/air flames (Metghalchi and Keck [439]), right).

2.5 Premixed flame thicknesses

Defining and estimating a flame thickness before computation is an obvious requirement for many numerical combustion problems because this thickness controls the required mesh resolution: in most combustion approaches, the flame structure must be resolved and enough points must be localized within the flame thickness. There are many ways to define thicknesses for premixed flames. Some of them require a first computation of the flame front (for example in a one-dimensional configuration) while others are based only on scaling laws and can be performed before computations start. It is also necessary to distinguish between thicknesses defined for variables such as temperature, which are useful in simple chemistry approaches (§ 2.5.1), and thicknesses corresponding to radicals, which raise very different problems (§ 2.5.2).

2.5.1 Simple chemistry

In Section 2.4.5, a flame thickness δ was introduced from scaling laws:

$$\delta = \frac{\lambda_1}{\rho_1 C_p s_L} = \frac{D_{th}^1}{s_L} \tag{2.73}$$

which can also be written as

$$Re_f = \frac{\delta s_L}{D_{th}^1} = 1 \tag{2.74}$$

where all quantities $D_{th}^1 = \lambda_1/(\rho_1 C_p)$, ρ_1, C_p and λ_1 are evaluated in the fresh gases. Re_f may be interpreted as a flame Reynolds number. The thickness δ (called here "diffusive" thickness) may be evaluated easily before any computation as soon as the flame speed is known. In practice, this thickness may be too approximate to be used for mesh determination (it is usually too small by a factor of order 5). A more useful thickness is obtained by using the temperature profile and computing:

$$\delta_L^0 = \frac{T_2 - T_1}{\max\left(\left|\frac{\partial T}{\partial x}\right|\right)} \tag{2.75}$$

Another thickness ("total thickness") δ_L^t may be constructed by defining the distance over which the reduced temperature Θ changes from 0.01 to 0.99 (see Fig. 2.15). δ_L^t is always larger than δ_L^0 and not very useful for computations: in real flames, slow reactions taking place in the burnt gases (see for example Fig. 2.2) usually create a long temperature "tail" leading to large values for δ_L^t which can be misleading if δ_L^t is used to determine the grid resolution. Since it measures temperature gradients, δ_L^0 is the most appropriate thickness to consider for mesh resolution.

The thickness δ_L^0 requires a first flame computation. Being able to evaluate it before computation is useful to determine mesh constraints. This can be achieved with correlations. For example, Blint [60] proposes the following evaluation for a flame thickness δ_L^b:

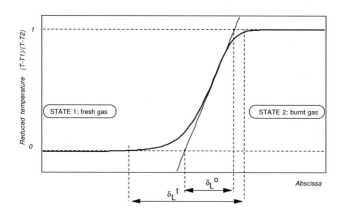

Figure 2.15: Definitions of flame thicknesses for a premixed flame.

$$\frac{\delta_L^b}{\delta} = 2\frac{(\lambda/C_p)_2}{(\lambda/C_p)_1} \tag{2.76}$$

If a Sutherland law is used for λ (supposing a constant Prandtl number (Eq. (1.17)) and a constant C_p), this relation may be simplified:

$$\frac{\delta_L^b}{\delta} = 2\left(\frac{T_2}{T_1}\right)^{0.7} \quad \text{or} \quad \boxed{\delta_L^b = 2\frac{D_{th}^1}{s_L}\left(\frac{T_2}{T_1}\right)^{0.7} = 2\delta\left(\frac{T_2}{T_1}\right)^{0.7}} \tag{2.77}$$

The thickness δ_L^b given by Eq. (2.77) does not require a flame computation and is a fairly good estimation of the flame thickness δ_L^0 as soon as the final temperature T_2 is known. This temperature T_2 is also obtained without full flame computation, simply by thermochemistry equilibrium as shown in Eq. (2.28). Note that, once a value is obtained for δ_L^0, a resolution adapted to the thickness of the reaction rate zone δ_r is still required. These two zones are roughly linked by $\delta_r = \delta_L^0/\beta$. Table 2.8 summarizes the different definitions of thicknesses and how they may be estimated before or after computation.

2.5.2   Complex chemistry

The previous section provides useful estimates of flame thicknesses when computations are performed for simple chemistry schemes ($Fuel \rightarrow Products$) in which the computation does not have to account for any intermediate radical. In real flames and in all computations using complex chemistry descriptions, many radicals are found within the flame front. These radicals may exist over distances much smaller than δ_L^0: for example, in Fig. 2.2, radicals such as H_2O_2 live in zones which are extremely thin. Defining mesh resolution in such flows is an

**From temperature profiles
(after a computation)**

Thermal thickness	δ_L^0	$(T_2 - T_1)/\max\left(\left\|\frac{\partial T}{\partial x}\right\|\right)$	Best definition
Global thickness	δ_L^t	distance from $\Theta = 0.01$ to 0.99	Not useful

**From the knowledge of s_L and of fresh gases properties
(before a computation)**

Diffusive thickness	δ	D_{th}^1/s_L	Not precise, too small
Blint thickness	δ^b	$2D_{th}^1/s_L(T_2/T_1)^{0.7} = 2\delta(T_2/T_1)^{0.7}$	Close to δ_L^0
Reaction thickness	δ_r	δ_L^0/β	Smallest thickness

Table 2.8: Flame thickness definitions and usefulness to determine the mesh size in a code.

open question at the moment for which no a priori mesh estimations may be obtained. In one-dimensional stationary flames, adaptive meshes are used and points are added in all zones where one of the species requires more resolution; but in multi-dimensional flames (typically in Direct Numerical Simulations of turbulent flames discussed in Chapters 4 to 6), a trial and error technique is still used by many researchers.

2.6 Flame stretch

Up to now, only freely propagating one-dimensional premixed flames have been considered in this chapter. Additional notions are needed to study multi-dimensional laminar flames and turbulent flames. The first one is flame stretch which is defined in this section. Extended flame speed definitions are given in Section 2.7.1.

2.6.1 Definition and expressions of stretch

A flame front propagating in a non-uniform flow is subject to strain and curvature effects which lead to changes in flame area (Williams [710]). These changes are measured by the flame stretch which is defined by the fractional rate of change of a flame surface element A (Matalon and Matkowsky [424], Candel and Poinsot [109]):

$$\kappa = \frac{1}{A}\frac{dA}{dt} \qquad (2.78)$$

A general expression of stretch may be developed from purely kinematic considerations for a thin flame sheet (Candel and Poinsot [109]):

$$\kappa = -\vec{n}\,\vec{n} : \nabla\vec{w} + \nabla \cdot \vec{w} \qquad (2.79)$$

where $\vec{\mathbf{n}}$ is the unit vector normal to the flame surface pointing towards the fresh gases and $\vec{\mathbf{w}}$ is the velocity of the flame surface (Fig. 2.16). The operator $(\vec{\mathbf{n}}\vec{\mathbf{n}} : \nabla)$ represents the gradient operator normal to the flame surface and may be written in index form as:

$$\vec{\mathbf{n}}\vec{\mathbf{n}} : \nabla\vec{\mathbf{w}} = \left[n_i n_j \frac{\partial w_i}{\partial x_j} \right] \qquad (2.80)$$

so that, in tensor notation, κ is also written:

$$\boxed{\kappa = (\delta_{ij} - n_i n_j)\frac{\partial w_i}{\partial x_j}} \qquad (2.81)$$

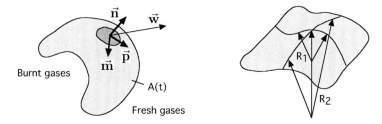

Figure 2.16: Definition of flame stretch and flame radii of curvature.

The flame propagates normally to the cold flow (wave behavior) at a displacement speed s_d (see § 2.7.1 for an exact definition of flame speeds). The flame front velocity may be written in terms of the unburned gas velocity $\vec{\mathbf{u}}$ and the displacement speed as follows:

$$\vec{\mathbf{w}} = \vec{\mathbf{u}} + s_d \, \vec{\mathbf{n}} \qquad (2.82)$$

The difference between the flame front velocity $\vec{\mathbf{w}}$ and the flow velocity $\vec{\mathbf{u}}$ is the displacement speed $s_d\vec{\mathbf{n}}$ which takes into account the effects of the flow on the flame structure itself. Substituting Eq. (2.82) into Eq. (2.79) yields:

$$\boxed{\kappa = -\vec{\mathbf{n}}\vec{\mathbf{n}} : \nabla\vec{\mathbf{u}} + \nabla \cdot \vec{\mathbf{u}} \; + \; s_d \, (\nabla \cdot \vec{\mathbf{n}})} \qquad (2.83)$$

or, in index form:

$$\boxed{\kappa = (\delta_{ij} - n_i n_j)\frac{\partial u_i}{\partial x_j} \; + \; s_d \, \frac{\partial n_i}{\partial x_i}} \qquad (2.84)$$

The term $\nabla \cdot \vec{\mathbf{n}}$ has a simple physical interpretation. It is the curvature of the flame front and is linked to the flame surface radii of curvature $\mathcal{R}_1$ and $\mathcal{R}_2$ by:[xiii]

$$\nabla \cdot \vec{\mathbf{n}} = -\left(\frac{1}{\mathcal{R}_1} + \frac{1}{\mathcal{R}_2}\right) \qquad (2.85)$$

But the notation $\nabla \cdot \vec{\mathbf{n}}$ used in Eq. (2.83) can be misleading: taking the divergence of a vector $\vec{\mathbf{n}}$ which is defined only along the flame surface requires some caution.[xiv] For a cylindrical pocket of fresh gases of radius $\mathcal{R}$ surrounded by burnt gases (Fig. 2.17a), $\nabla \cdot \vec{\mathbf{n}}$ can be evaluated in cylindrical coordinates ($n_r = -1$ and $n_\theta = 0$):

$$\nabla \cdot \vec{\mathbf{n}} = \frac{1}{r}\frac{\partial(rn_r)}{\partial r} = -1/\mathcal{R}$$

which is consistent with Eq. (2.85). The contribution of $s_d \nabla \cdot \vec{\mathbf{n}}$ to stretch in Eq. (2.83) in this case is negative: flame propagation decreases stretch and diminishes the flame surface. Similarly, for a spherical flame (Fig. 2.17b), $\nabla \cdot \vec{\mathbf{n}}$ is (in spherical coordinates):

$$\nabla \cdot \vec{\mathbf{n}} = \frac{1}{r^2}\frac{\partial(r^2 n_r)}{\partial r} = -2/\mathcal{R}$$

The first two terms on the RHS of Eq. (2.83) are often grouped to have (Candel and Poinsot [109]):

$$\kappa = (\vec{\mathbf{m}}\vec{\mathbf{m}} + \vec{\mathbf{p}}\vec{\mathbf{p}}) : \nabla\vec{\mathbf{u}} + s_d\,(\nabla \cdot \vec{\mathbf{n}}) \qquad (2.86)$$

where $\vec{\mathbf{m}}$ and $\vec{\mathbf{p}}$ are two orthonormal vectors belonging to the local tangent plane of the flame (Fig. 2.16). The term $(\vec{\mathbf{m}}\vec{\mathbf{m}} + \vec{\mathbf{p}}\vec{\mathbf{p}}) : \nabla\vec{\mathbf{u}}$ in Eq. (2.86) represents the strain in the plane locally

---

[xiii]$1/\mathcal{R}_1$ and $1/\mathcal{R}_2$ are the two main (or principal) curvatures of the flame surface. These curvatures measure respectively the highest surface curvature and the surface curvature in the perpendicular direction. For example, for a cylinder of radius $\mathcal{R}$, $\mathcal{R}_1 = \mathcal{R}$ and $\mathcal{R}_2 = \infty$ ($1/\mathcal{R}_2 = 0$); for a sphere of radius $\mathcal{R}$, $\mathcal{R}_1 = \mathcal{R}_2 = \mathcal{R}$; main curvatures for a saddle point have opposite signs.

[xiv]In two dimensions and cartesian coordinates, the vector $\vec{\mathbf{n}}$ normal to iso-levels of a field $A(x,y)$ is:

$$\vec{\mathbf{n}} = -\frac{\nabla A}{|\nabla A|} = (n_x, n_y) = \left(-\frac{\partial A}{\partial x}\left[\left(\frac{\partial A}{\partial x}\right)^2 + \left(\frac{\partial A}{\partial y}\right)^2\right]^{-1/2}, \quad -\frac{\partial A}{\partial y}\left[\left(\frac{\partial A}{\partial x}\right)^2 + \left(\frac{\partial A}{\partial y}\right)^2\right]^{-1/2}\right)$$

where $\vec{\mathbf{n}}$ is pointing towards the lower values of the A-field. Then:

$$\nabla \cdot \vec{\mathbf{n}} = \frac{\partial n_x}{\partial x} + \frac{\partial n_y}{\partial y} = -\left[\left(\frac{\partial A}{\partial x}\right)^2 + \left(\frac{\partial A}{\partial y}\right)^2\right]^{-3/2}\left[\frac{\partial^2 A}{\partial x^2}\left(\frac{\partial A}{\partial y}\right)^2 + \frac{\partial^2 A}{\partial y^2}\left(\frac{\partial A}{\partial x}\right)^2\right]$$

Along a front defined by coordinates $(x, f(x))$ (or $A(x,y) = y - f(x) = 0$):

$$\frac{\partial A}{\partial x} = -f'(x) \quad ; \quad \frac{\partial^2 A}{\partial x^2} = -f''(x) \quad ; \quad \frac{\partial A}{\partial y} = 1 \quad ; \quad \frac{\partial^2 A}{\partial y^2} = 0$$

and the local front curvature is given by $\nabla \cdot \vec{\mathbf{n}} = f''/(1 + f'^2)^{3/2}$.

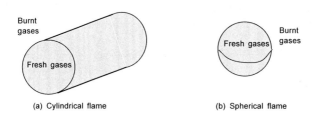

(a) Cylindrical flame   (b) Spherical flame

Figure 2.17: Pockets of fresh gases surrounded by cylindrical or spherical flames and burnt gases: in both cases, the curvature term $\nabla \cdot \vec{n}$ brings a negative contribution to stretch in Eq. (2.83).

parallel to the flame front and is sometimes written (Chung and Law [133]) as $\nabla_t \cdot \vec{u}$ where the subscript t refers to the tangential component of the ∇ operator:

$$\nabla_t \cdot \vec{u} = (\vec{m}\vec{m} + \vec{p}\vec{p}) : \nabla \vec{u} = -\vec{n}\vec{n} : \nabla \vec{u} + \nabla \cdot \vec{u} \qquad (2.87)$$

The ∇_t operator can also be used to express the second term in the RHS of Eq. (2.86):

$$
\begin{aligned}
\nabla_t \cdot \vec{n} &= (\vec{m}\vec{m} + \vec{p}\vec{p}) : \nabla \vec{n} = (\delta_{ij} - n_i n_j)\frac{\partial n_i}{\partial x_j} \\
&= \delta_{ij}\frac{\partial n_i}{\partial x_j} - n_i n_j \frac{\partial n_i}{\partial x_j} = \frac{\partial n_i}{\partial x_i} - \frac{1}{2} n_j \frac{\partial}{\partial x_j}(n_i n_i) = \nabla \cdot \vec{n} \qquad (2.88)
\end{aligned}
$$

because $\vec{n}$ is an unity vector.

From the above considerations, Eq. (2.86) is re-written as follows:

$$\boxed{\kappa = \nabla_t \cdot \vec{u} - s_d \left(\frac{1}{\mathcal{R}_1} + \frac{1}{\mathcal{R}_2}\right) = \nabla_t \cdot \vec{u} + s_d \nabla_t \cdot \vec{n}} \qquad (2.89)$$

In Eq. (2.89), the flame stretch is the sum of two terms:

- the first term, $\nabla_t \cdot \vec{u}$, is a strain term and is related to the flow non-uniformity,

- the second one, $s_d \nabla_t \cdot \vec{n} = -s_d(1/\mathcal{R}_1 + 1/\mathcal{R}_2)$, is a term due to the curvature of the reaction front.

2.6.2   Stretch of stationary flames

A flame is stationary if it does not propagate along its normal direction $\vec{n}$:

$$\vec{w}.\vec{n} = 0 \qquad (2.90)$$

This condition does not imply that the velocity $\vec{w}$ is zero: a velocity can exist in the plane tangent to the flame (see for example the single or the twin stagnation point flames in

Fig. 2.20). For a stationary flame Eq. (2.82) and (2.90) show that $\vec{u} \cdot \vec{n} = -s_d$ and the stretch factor reduces to:

$$\boxed{\kappa = \nabla_t \cdot \vec{u} + s_d \nabla_t \cdot \vec{n} = \nabla_t \cdot (\vec{u} - (\vec{u} \cdot \vec{n})\vec{n}) = \nabla_t \cdot \vec{u}_t} \tag{2.91}$$

where $\vec{u}_t$ is the tangential component of the unburned gas velocity (Chung and Law [133]).[xv]

2.6.3 Examples of flames with zero stretch

Flames can be curved or placed in velocity gradients and still be unstretched. This section presents two examples of such flames.

The steady cylindrical (or spherical) premixed flame

Consider first a steady cylindrical (or spherical) flame, fed centrally by a fresh gas injector (Fig. 2.18). After some initial displacement, this flame would stabilize itself at a fixed distance from the injectors. The absolute flame speed is zero. Obviously, the flame surface is constant and its stretch is zero even though it is curved. Actually, strain and curvature terms compensate in Eq. (2.89). For the cylindrical flame of radius $\mathcal{R}$ written in cylindrical coordinates:

$$\kappa = \nabla_t \cdot \vec{u} + s_d \nabla_t \cdot \vec{n} = -\vec{n}\vec{n} : \nabla \vec{u} + \nabla \cdot \vec{u} - \frac{s_d}{\mathcal{R}} = -\frac{\partial u_r}{\partial r} + \frac{1}{r}\frac{\partial(r u_r)}{\partial r} - \frac{s_d}{\mathcal{R}} = \frac{u_r}{r} - \frac{s_d}{\mathcal{R}} = 0 \tag{2.92}$$

because u_r is equal to s_d for this steady flame. A simpler way to check this is to use Eq. (2.91) in which $\vec{u}_t$ is zero so that κ is also zero.

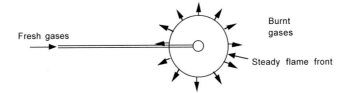

Figure 2.18: Cylindrical or spherical steady flame: the flame stretch is zero.

[xv] Eq. (2.91) is derived starting from $\nabla_t \cdot \vec{u} - \nabla_t \cdot \vec{u}_t$:

$$\nabla_t \cdot \vec{u} - \nabla_t \cdot \vec{u}_t = \nabla_t \cdot (\vec{u} - \vec{u}_t) = \nabla_t \cdot [(\vec{u} \cdot \vec{n})\vec{n}] = -(\delta_{ij} - n_i n_j)\frac{\partial}{\partial x_j}[s_d n_i]$$

$$= -s_d \left(\frac{\partial n_i}{\partial x_i} - \frac{1}{2}n_j \frac{\partial n_i n_i}{\partial x_j} \right) - n_j \frac{\partial s_d}{\partial x_j} + n_i n_i n_j \frac{\partial s_d}{\partial x_j} = -s_d \nabla \cdot \vec{n} = \frac{s_d}{\mathcal{R}}$$

because $\vec{n}$ is an unity vector.

For the spherical flame of radius $\mathcal{R}$, the same derivation leads to:

$$\kappa = \nabla_t \cdot \vec{u} + s_d \nabla_t \cdot \vec{n} = -\frac{\partial u_r}{\partial r} + \frac{1}{r^2}\frac{\partial(r^2 u_r)}{\partial r} - \frac{2s_d}{\mathcal{R}} = \frac{2}{r}u_r - \frac{2s_d}{\mathcal{R}} = 0 \qquad (2.93)$$

The planar flame in a shear flow

Another situation where flames are unstretched is displayed in Fig. 2.19. The orientation of flame fronts relative to velocity gradients is a critical parameter for flame stretch: only velocity gradients in the flame tangent plane induce flame stretch. The steady planar flame of Fig. 2.19 is submitted to a one-dimensional velocity gradient. This situation is typical of flames created in mixing layers and stabilized behind a splitter plate. For this flame, $n_1 = 0$, $n_2 = 1$, $u = (u_1(x_2), 0)$. Eq. (2.91) shows that flame strain is zero because the velocity gradient has no component in the flame plane. A usual error is to assume that flame strain in such a configuration is estimated by $\partial u_1 / \partial x_2$.

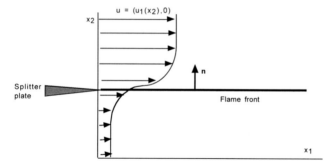

Figure 2.19: Flame stabilized in the wake of a splitter plate: the flame strain is zero.

2.6.4   Examples of stretched flames

Fig. 2.20 presents usual configurations to study laminar stretched flames experimentally or numerically. The first one (Fig. 2.20a) is the single flame in which hot combustion products (usually produced by another flame) are sent against a flow of fresh gases. In this case, the flame is stretched because the velocity in the flame tangent plane changes rapidly (first term $\nabla_t \cdot \vec{u}$ in Eq. (2.89)). For a non reacting potential flow, the stagnation point configuration has a simple analytical solution: $u = ax$ and $v = -ay$ where a is the strain rate. For a flow between two injectors, a is imposed by the flow velocities U_j^1 and U_j^2 of the two jets and the distance d between the jets. In reacting flows, it depends on the flame structure itself because of dilatation and is typically of order $(|U_j^1| + |U_j^2|)/d$. The single flame has been studied by multiple researchers (numerically for complex chemistry, with asymptotic methods for simple chemistry and experimentally). Its main drawback is that the temperature of the combustion products (stream 2) controls the solution.

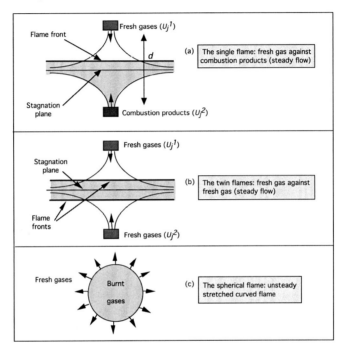

Figure 2.20: Examples of laminar stretched premixed flames.

The twin flame configuration (Fig. 2.20b) has no such drawback: by blowing fresh gas against fresh gas, two flames are established. Twin flames depend only on strain and on the fresh gas thermodynamic conditions but they are much more sensitive to strain as described below.

Finally, the spherical flame has no velocity gradient in the flame tangent plane but is curved (Fig. 2.20c): stretch is produced by the second term $\nabla_t \cdot \vec{n} = 2s_d/\mathcal{R}$ in Eq. (2.89 and is easily evaluated in such flames by measuring the changes of flame radius with time $r(t)$:

$$\kappa = \frac{1}{A}\frac{dA}{dt} = \frac{2}{r}\frac{dr}{dt} \tag{2.94}$$

Intuition is not always helpful to understand stretched flames: the spherical flame is obviously growing since its radius increases with time so that its stretch must be positive. For stagnation point flames, the flame area seems constant but stretch is indeed present: two points located in the flame plane separate from each other because their velocities in the flame plane are different; the flame element located between these two points is stretched.

Finally, flame elements can also be compressed: a spherical pocket of fresh gases consumed by an inward propagating flame has a negative stretch. In general, along a complex flame front (turbulent for example), zones of positive and negative stretch are found and the final length of a flame depends on the competition between these zones. In a turbulent flame, Chapter 5 shows that in this competition, the positive stretch zones are more frequent than the negative zones leading to a positive net growth rate for the flame front.

2.7 Flame speeds

The "speed" of a flame is a central element in combustion theory. It is also the source of many difficulties: there are multiple definitions for flame speeds and even more ways to measure them. Section 2.7.1 provides a general framework to define flame speeds while Section 2.7.2 shows how these definitions apply in a planar unstrained flame. Section 2.7.3 discusses speeds of stretched flames and points out difficulties associated to such configurations.

2.7.1 Flame speed definitions

The notion of a flame speed s_L was used up to now without further precision, by first stating that this velocity measured the speed at which the flame front was moving with respect to the fresh gases in a one-dimensional geometry. This definition is used intuitively by most researchers and corresponds to a description of the flame as an interface moving at speed s_L against the local flow. Later it was also shown (see Eq. (2.24)) that a flame speed may also be defined from the integral of the burning rate across the flame brush:

$$s_L = -\frac{1}{\rho_1 Y_F^1} \int_{-\infty}^{+\infty} \dot\omega_F dx \tag{2.95}$$

These notions, one based on kinematic properties of the flame and the other based on the integral of the reaction rate, must be connected to understand many of the recent concepts used in premixed combustion theories. This is done in the following derivation.

First, it is necessary to introduce three flame speed definitions (Poinsot et al. [524], Trouvé and Poinsot [652]) summarized in Table 2.9 and to distinguish between local and global speeds. Even though these definitions may seem equivalent or, at least, directly connected, it is not always the case and multiple differences between these definitions are evidenced below:

- Let us first consider a point on the flame surface, $\Theta = \Theta_f$ (Fig. 2.21). At any location on this surface, the local gradient of Θ defines the normal to the flame front:

$$\vec{n} = -\frac{\nabla\Theta}{|\nabla\Theta|} \tag{2.96}$$

Identification	Definition
Absolute	Flame front speed relative to a fixed reference frame
Displacement	Flame front speed relative to the flow
Consumption	Speed at which reactants are consumed

Table 2.9: Simple classification of flame speeds.

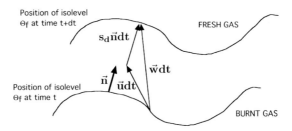

Figure 2.21: Notations for flame speed definitions.

where $\vec{\mathbf{n}}$ points into the fresh reactants. The velocity $\vec{\mathbf{w}}$ at which this point must move to remain on the surface is given by:

$$\frac{\partial \Theta}{\partial t} + \vec{\mathbf{w}}.\nabla\Theta = 0 \qquad (2.97)$$

The velocity component normal to the flame front $s_a = \vec{\mathbf{w}}.\vec{\mathbf{n}}$ is the absolute speed at which an isolevel of temperature moves relative to the laboratory frame. It depends on the value of the isolevel Θ_f where it is measured. Replacing $\nabla\Theta$ by $-|\nabla\Theta|\vec{\mathbf{n}}$ in Eq. (2.97) implies that:

$$\boxed{s_a = \vec{\mathbf{w}}.\vec{\mathbf{n}} = \frac{1}{|\nabla\Theta|}\frac{\partial\Theta}{\partial t}} \qquad (2.98)$$

The absolute speed is usually constant through the flame front if the flame is not being thickened or thinned by the flow: all Θ isolevels must move at the same speed if the thickness remains constant.

- The displacement speed measures the front speed relative to the flow i.e. the difference between the flow speed $\vec{\mathbf{u}}$ and the front speed $\vec{\mathbf{w}}$:

$$\boxed{s_d = (\vec{\mathbf{w}} - \vec{\mathbf{u}}).\vec{\mathbf{n}} = s_a - \vec{\mathbf{u}}.\vec{\mathbf{n}}} \qquad (2.99)$$

and can be obtained in simulations by:

$$s_d = \vec{\mathbf{w}}.\vec{\mathbf{n}} - \vec{\mathbf{u}}.\vec{\mathbf{n}} = \frac{1}{|\nabla\Theta|}\frac{\partial\Theta}{\partial t} + \vec{\mathbf{u}}\frac{\nabla\Theta}{|\nabla\Theta|} = \frac{1}{|\nabla\Theta|}\frac{D\Theta}{Dt} \qquad (2.100)$$

where the quantities are evaluated at the surface $\Theta = \Theta_f$. The RHS terms of Eq. (2.98) or (2.100) are easily measured in a computation as they are the terms used in the time advancement for explicit schemes. For example, using Eq. (2.3), Eq. (2.100) may be written:

$$s_d = \frac{1}{|\nabla \Theta|} \frac{D\Theta}{Dt} = \frac{1}{\nabla \Theta} \left[\dot{\omega}_T' + \frac{\partial}{\partial x} \left(\lambda \frac{\partial T}{\partial x_i} \right) - \frac{\partial T}{\partial x} \left(\rho \sum_{k=1}^{N} C_{p,k} Y_k V_k \right) \right] \qquad (2.101)$$

where all terms are available from the computation. This property is often used in DNS to evaluate flame front displacements (§ 4.6). Like the absolute speed s_a, the displacement speed is a function of the isolevel Θ_f where it is measured: by default, s_d is the displacement speed versus the fresh gases $s_d(\Theta_f = 0)$. In certain flows (spherical flames for example, §2.7.3), working with the 'burnt gas displacement speed' $s_b = s_d(\Theta_f = 1)$ is more convenient. Displacement speeds are difficult to use: since the flow accelerates through the flame front, the displacement speed changes too and depends on the position where it is measured: $s_b = s_d(\Theta = 1)$, for example, is of the order of $\frac{T_2}{T_1} s_d(\Theta = 0)$ (see § 2.7.2). However, they are useful quantities in models based for example on the G equation in which the strategy is to move the flame relative to the flow (Peters [501]).

- A third speed is the consumption speed s_c based only on reaction rates:

$$\boxed{s_c = -\frac{1}{\rho_1 Y_F^1} \int_{-\infty}^{+\infty} \dot{\omega}_F \mathbf{dn}} \qquad (2.102)$$

It measures the speed at which the flame burns the reactants.

Identification	Definition	Formula	Characteristics
Consumption		$s_c = -\frac{1}{\rho_1 Y_F^1} \int_{-\infty}^{+\infty} \dot{\omega}_F \mathbf{dn}$	Global
Displacement	$(\vec{w} - \vec{u}).\vec{n}$	$s_d = \frac{1}{|\nabla \Theta|} \frac{D\Theta}{Dt}$	Local: $s_d(\Theta_f)$
Absolute	$\vec{w}.\vec{n}$	$s_a = \frac{1}{|\nabla \Theta|} \frac{\partial \Theta}{\partial t}$	Local: $s_a(\Theta_f)$

Table 2.10: Flame speeds definitions. The normal $\vec{n}$ points into the fresh reactants.

An important difference between flame speeds is that s_d or s_a are local quantities depending on the isolevel Θ_f where they are evaluated while s_c is a quantity resulting from an integral over all Θ_f values across the flame front (Table 2.10). The speed used intuitively by experimentalists is the displacement speed measured on the fresh reactant side: $s_d(\Theta = 0)$. The following sections compare all speeds in different flames.

2.7.2   Flame speeds of laminar planar unstretched flames

The speed of a laminar planar unstretched freely propagating one-dimensional flame s_L^0 is the reference speed for all combustion studies. Even for such a flame, differences exist between speeds as demonstrated here. Fig. 2.22 presents the variations of all speeds for a planar unstretched flame where the inlet flow velocity u_1 is not equal to s_L^0: in this case, the flame moves in the laboratory frame. The consumption speed s_c is equal to s_L^0. The x axis points towards the burnt gas so that $\vec{\mathbf{n}} = -\vec{\mathbf{x}}$. The inlet speed is $\vec{\mathbf{u}}_1 = -u_1\vec{\mathbf{n}}$. All speeds are normalized by the laminar flame speed s_L^0. Because the flame propagates more slowly than the flow for this example where $u_1 > s_L^0$, the flame front goes backwards towards positive x values. The absolute speed of all isolevels is the same: the flame is convected and its thickness is constant: $\vec{\mathbf{w}} = (u_1 - s_L^0)\vec{\mathbf{x}}$. The absolute speed is $s_a = \vec{\mathbf{w}}.\vec{\mathbf{n}} = s_L^0 - u_1$ and is negative.

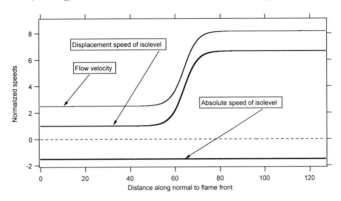

Figure 2.22: Variations of flow, displacement, absolute and consumption speeds in a one-dimensional planar laminar flame. For this example, the inlet speed u_1 is fixed to $2.5s_L^0$.

To determine the flow velocity, the continuity equation (2.21) is used. It expresses that, in the flame reference frame, the mass flow rate is conserved along $\vec{\mathbf{n}}$ and equal to the inlet flow rate.

$$\rho(\vec{\mathbf{u}} - \vec{\mathbf{w}}).\vec{\mathbf{n}} = \rho_1(\vec{\mathbf{u}}_1 - \vec{\mathbf{w}}).\vec{\mathbf{n}} \qquad (2.103)$$

so that u at each point is given by:

$$u = -\vec{\mathbf{u}}.\vec{\mathbf{n}} = -s_a + (u_1 + s_a)\frac{\rho_1}{\rho} = u_1 + s_L^0\left(\frac{\rho_1}{\rho} - 1\right) \qquad (2.104)$$

The density ratio ρ_1/ρ is also T/T_1 or $1 + \alpha\Theta/(1-\alpha)$ where Θ and α are respectively defined by Eq. (2.31) and Eq. (2.38). The flow accelerates through the flame front passing from a velocity u_1 to $u_1 + s_L^0\alpha/1 - \alpha$. The displacement speed measures the difference between the flame and the flow speeds:

$$s_d(\Theta) = s_a - \vec{\mathbf{u}}.\vec{\mathbf{n}} = s_L^0\frac{\rho_1}{\rho} = s_L^0\left(1 + \frac{\alpha\Theta}{1-\alpha}\right) \qquad (2.105)$$

It is positive because the flame propagates against the flow (even though it is moving backwards in the reference frame and s_a is negative). It reaches $s_L^0/(1-\alpha) = s_L^0 \frac{T_2}{T_1}$ in the burnt gases. Furthermore, the displacement speed is equal to the flame speed (to s_L^0 actually in this case) only when Θ_f is small, i.e. when s_d measures the displacement speed of an isolevel located close to the fresh gases. Table 2.11 summarizes these results.

Consumption speed s_c	Absolute speed $s_a(\Theta)$	Displacement speed $s_d(\Theta)$
s_L^0	$-u_1 + s_L^0$	$s_L^0(1 + \alpha\Theta/(1-\alpha))$

Table 2.11: Flame speeds in a planar unstretched flame. u_1 is the flow velocity ahead of the flame. Θ is the reduced temperature (Eq. (2.31)) and α measures the heat release (Eq. (2.38)).

2.7.3   Flame speeds of stretched flames, Markstein lengths

The planar unstretched flame constitutes one of the few flames where all speeds can be unambiguously defined and measured. If the flame is stretched (curved or strained or both), flame speeds may take different values and be more difficult to evaluate, both experimentally and numerically.

The only theoretical guide to study the speeds of stretched flames comes from asymptotic theories (Bush and Fendell [99], Buckmaster and Ludford [95], Williams [710], Pelce and Clavin [497], Clavin and Williams [141]). These studies suggest that, in the limit of small strain and curvature terms, stretch κ (defined by Eq. 2.78 and expressed as a function of flow and flame parameters by Eq. 2.79) is the unique parameter controlling the flame structure and therefore, the displacement and consumption speeds through a linear relationship:

$$\boxed{\frac{s_d(0)}{s_L^0} = 1 - \frac{L_a^d}{s_L^0}\kappa} \quad \text{and} \quad \boxed{\frac{s_c}{s_L^0} = 1 - \frac{L_a^c}{s_L^0}\kappa} \qquad (2.106)$$

where L_a^d and L_a^c are Markstein lengths. The displacement speed is defined on the fresh gas side ($\Theta = 0$). The two Markstein lengths differ, showing that the displacement speed and the consumption speed react differently to stretch.

Eq. (2.106) can also be recast as:

$$\boxed{\frac{s_d(0)}{s_L^0} = 1 - M_a^d\frac{\kappa\delta}{s_L^0}} \quad \text{and} \quad \boxed{\frac{s_c}{s_L^0} = 1 - M_a^c\frac{\kappa\delta}{s_L^0}} \qquad (2.107)$$

where δ is the unstretched flame thickness defined by Eq. (2.55):

$$\delta = \frac{\lambda_1}{\rho_1 C_p s_L^0} = \frac{D_{th}^1}{s_L^0} \qquad (2.108)$$

$M_a^d = L_a^d/\delta$ and $M_a^c = L_a^c/\delta$ are Marsktein numbers for the displacement and the consumption speeds respectively. The expression $\kappa\delta/s_L^0$ is a reduced Karlovitz number. When it reaches unity, quenching effects should appear so that the previous correlations are expected to hold only for $\kappa\delta/s_L^0 \ll 1$. Various expressions may be found for the Markstein numbers in the literature. For constant viscosity, lean, single-step flames with variable density, Clavin and Joulin [139] give:[xvi]

$$M_a^d = \frac{L_a^d}{\delta} = \frac{T_2}{T_2 - T_1} \ln\left(\frac{T_2}{T_1}\right) + \frac{1}{2}\beta(Le_F - 1)\frac{T_1}{T_2 - T_1}\int_0^{\frac{T_2 - T_1}{T_1}} \frac{\ln(1+x)}{x}dx \qquad (2.109)$$

and
$$M_a^c = \frac{L_a^c}{\delta} = \frac{1}{2}\beta(Le_F - 1)\frac{T_1}{T_2 - T_1}\int_0^{\frac{T_2 - T_1}{T_1}} \frac{\ln(1+x)}{x}dx \qquad (2.110)$$

The parameter β is given by Eq. (2.38): $\beta = (T_2 - T_1)T_a/T_2^2$. It measures the activation energy. The sign of the displacement Markstein length L_a^d controls the stability of the laminar flame fronts and may have also influence on turbulent flames: negative Markstein lengths create a natural intrinsic front instability leading to cell formation (Williams [710]).

Experimentally, Markstein lengths are determined by measuring the slope of flame speed variations versus stretch. For example, the Markstein length L_a^d can be obtained by measuring the displacement speed s_d for various stretch values and computing:

$$L_a^d = -\frac{\partial s_d}{\partial \kappa} \qquad (2.111)$$

Even though the existence of a relationship between stretch and flame speeds has been demonstrated only under restricted assumptions (single-step chemistry, high activation energy, small stretch), it is the basis of most modern flame studies. Implicitly, most experimental results are compiled assuming that flame stretch is the only parameter controlling the flame structure even though certain results suggest that this may not necessarily be true (Egolfopoulos and Law [199]). Furthermore, measuring Markstein lengths has proved to be difficult. Several techniques have been used to evaluate these lengths in various flows: spherical flames (Bradley et al. [80], Aung et al. [21, 22], Poinsot [517], Gu et al. [255], Groot and Goey [253], Kelley and Law [335], Chen [124], Halter et al. [267]), oscillating flames (Searby and Quinard [599]), stabilized V flames (Truffaut and Searby [655]), stagnation point flames (Law and Sung [370]) among other configurations. In the last ten years, discrepancies among the laminar flame speeds measured by different researchers for the same fuel have become a great concern. The uncertainties observed on Markstein lengths are even larger so that the accuracy of these techniques is often a topic of controversy and the source of many difficulties as illustrated below on three typical stretched flame cases:

[xvi]Extensions of this derivation exist for variable transport properties (Clavin and Garcia [138]) and for non adiabatic flames (Nicoli and Clavin [466]).

- stagnation point flames,

- flame tips,

- spherical flames.

Stagnation point flames

Stagnation point flames are commonly used to study laminar flames (Fig. 2.20a and b). For these flames, strain and stretch are equal since the curvature term in Eq. (2.89) is zero. Stretch has a strong influence on flame fronts. Asymptotic theory (Libby and Williams [385, 387, 388], Libby et al. [391]), measurements (Ishizuka et al. [305], Law [369]) and numerical simulations (Darabiha et al. [165], Giovangigli and Smooke [238]) provide a fairly complete description of the response of stagnation point flames to stretch effects. At low values of stretch, Markstein type behaviors are observed: flame speeds change linearly with stretch. For higher values of stretch, more sophisticated analytical theories, computations or experiments are needed.

Independently of the method used to study stagnation point flames (experiment, theory or computations), the interpretation of flame speeds in such flows must be considered with caution (Tien and Matalon [649]). Stagnation point flames are steady and therefore the absolute flame speed is zero for all isotherms:

$$s_a = 0 \quad \text{and} \quad \vec{\mathbf{w}} = 0 \tag{2.112}$$

Eq. (2.99) shows then that the displacement speed is opposite to the flow speed at every point:

$$s_d(\Theta) = -\vec{\mathbf{u}}.\vec{\mathbf{n}} \tag{2.113}$$

Fig. 2.23 shows typical velocity and temperature profiles in a stagnation point premixed flame

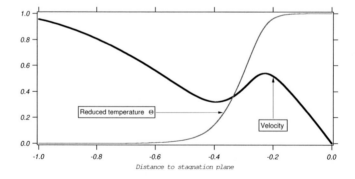

Figure 2.23: Velocity and temperature profiles in a stagnation point premixed flame.

(along the axis normal to the flame). Without flame in a potential stagnation point flow, the velocity should vary linearly with x: $u = -ax$ where a is the strain rate. In real experimental data, the u profile is not always linear versus x even far from the flame front, making the definition of strain rate difficult. More importantly, the flow speed changes rapidly and reaches zero on the stagnation plane. It exhibits a local maximum in the flame zone due to heat release. The issue is to choose at which point Eq. (2.113) must be applied to evaluate the displacement speed $s_d(0)$. Several techniques have been proposed in the literature (Deshaies and Cambray [174], Law and Sung [370]): using the minimum of the velocity in the reaction zone, extrapolating the velocity profile to the reaction zone, etc. In general, these techniques lead to ambiguous results even though they are the only possible method to use experimentally (Vagelopoulos and Egolfopoulos [660], Egolfopoulos and Law [199]). As argued by Williams [710], it is more meaningful to avoid displacement speeds in such experiments if detailed information is sought (Markstein lengths for example) and to focus on the consumption speed s_c which is unambiguously defined by the integral of the reaction rate through the front (Eq. (2.95)). Unfortunately this quantity can only be computed (and not measured) but theoretical and numerical results can be compared without ambiguity as discussed below (Table 2.12). An additional drawback of the consumption speed s_c is that it measures a flame speed only for low stretches. At large stretch values, the divergence of the streamtubes also makes s_c a dubious measurement of a true flame speed.

	Consumption speed s_c	Absolute speed $s_a(\Theta)$	Displacement speed $s_d(\Theta)$
Definition:	$-\frac{1}{\rho_1 Y_F^1} \int_{-\infty}^{+\infty} \dot{\omega}_F d\mathbf{n}$	0	$-\vec{\mathbf{u}}.\vec{\mathbf{n}}$
Experiments:	No	Yes	difficult
Computations:	Yes	Yes	difficult

Table 2.12: Flame speed expressions in a planar stagnation point flame. u is the local flow velocity. The "experiments" and "computations" lines indicate whether corresponding speeds can be obtained from measurements and/or from computations.

Stretching a flame first means feeding it with more fresh gases (because fuel mass fraction gradients are increased), but also includes cooling the flame front more intensely (because the temperature gradients are increased): since species and temperature gradients are competing in this mechanism, the Lewis number of the fuel $Le_F = \lambda/(\rho C_p D)$ which measures the ratio between heat $(\lambda/(\rho C_p))$ and species (D) diffusivities becomes a critical parameter for stretch effects. A second parameter controlling the flame response is the level of heat losses (especially radiative losses).

Figure 2.24 summarizes asymptotic results for single stagnation point flames (configuration displayed in Fig. 2.20) for $Le_F = 1$. As predicted from Eq. (2.110), the consumption speed of a flame with $Le_F = 1$ is almost insensitive to strain for low strain values: it remains constant over a wide range of strain rates because both species and temperature gradients increase in the same proportion. The only effect is that the flame becomes thinner when strain increases.

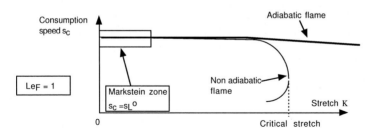

Figure 2.24: Stretch effects on a laminar flame at $Le_F = 1$: zero L_a^c Markstein length (Eq. (2.110)).

When $Le_F < 1$ (Fig. 2.25), strain effects are observed for low values of strain: the reaction rate increases when strain increases as expected from the Markstein correlation (2.110) with $M_a^c < 0$. For higher strain values, the simple linear relationship (2.107) between consumption speed s_c and stretch κ cannot be used anymore. The increase of flame speed due to strain can be quite significant: a lean hydrogen-air flame can double its speed when stretched (Egolfopoulos and Law [199]). In the absence of heat loss, quenching is obtained only at very high stretch values. When the flame is not adiabatic, sudden extinction can be observed for lower strain rate levels.

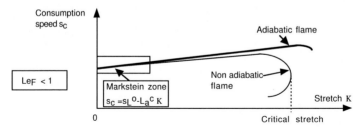

Figure 2.25: Stretch effects on a laminar flame at $Le_F < 1$: negative Markstein length (Eq. (2.110)).

For $Le_F > 1$ (Fig. 2.26), the heat release decreases with increasing strain as soon as the flame is strained ($M_a^c > 0$). Theory shows that very large values of Le_F could lead to quenching. However, usual values of Le_F are never large enough to induce quenching (Williams [710]). What happens at very large strain values depends on heat losses. Asymptotic studies reveal that heat losses control the existence of a turning point in the (s_c vs κ) curves where the flame gets suddenly quenched. The critical value where quenching occurs scales with s_L^0/δ. These sudden extinction events are also observed in experiments and constitute an excellent test of the prediction capacities of one-dimensional flame codes.

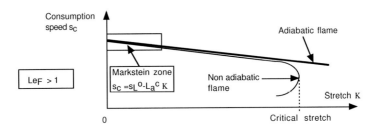

Figure 2.26: Stretch effects on a laminar flame at $Le_F > 1$: positive Markstein length (Eq. (2.110)).

Flame tips

In many flames, s_a, s_d and s_c may differ by a large amount: the best example (Fig. 2.27) is the steady laminar flame tip (Buckmaster and Crowley [94], Poinsot et al. [524]). The absolute speed s_a of all flame elements is zero. The displacement speed s_d on the flame axis must therefore compensate exactly the flow speed. Since this velocity is fixed arbitrarily and can be very large, the displacement speed must be also very large. In a flame tip, s_d can be as large as 10 times the consumption speed s_c.

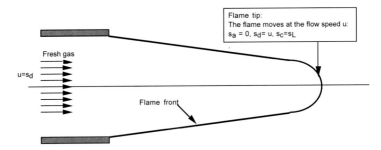

Figure 2.27: The flame tip: an illustration of displacement and consumption speeds.

A numerical simulation of a two-dimensional flame tip at $Le_F = 1$ (Poinsot et al. [524]) shows that the structure of the reaction zone is the same on the sides and at the tip of the flame (Fig. 2.28): in particular, the consumption speed s_c on the sides as well as at the tip is equal to s_L^0. However, the displacement speed $s_d = u$ on the flame axis is equal to $8s_L^0$ because the inlet velocity was fixed to $8s_L^0$.[xvii] This increase of the displacement speed on the axis is due to two mechanisms:

[xvii]This effect, obtained in a simulation at Lewis= 1 is independent of flame-tips opening and closing phenomena which may occur for non-unity Lewis numbers (Law and Sung [370]).

- as shown by the streamlines in Fig. 2.28, a stream tube centered on the flame axis is submitted to a strong expansion when passing through the flame: this induces a first decrease of the flow speed at the tip.

- the tip itself is strongly curved and diffusive mechanisms also play a role: reactants diffuse to the sides of the flame instead of entering the tip (see reactants pathlines on Fig. 2.28). On the flame axis, the fuel mass fraction decreases far upstream of the tip.

As a consequence of these two effects (flow deceleration and fuel diffusion away from the axis), the fuel flow rate entering the tip is decreased enough (by a factor 8 in this simulation) to be consumed by the reaction zone (Poinsot et al. [524]). In practice, the flame height increases until these conditions can be satisfied.

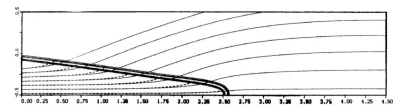

Figure 2.28: Isolevels of reaction rate, streamlines (———) and pathlines of the fuel (– – – –) in a half flame tip (Poinsot et al. [524]). ©OPA (Overseas Publishers Association) N.V. with permission from Gordon and Breach Publishers.

Such results (Table 2.13) demonstrate that flame speeds can be very different especially in curved flames. They also show that a flame can propagate against the flow at very large velocities. This is important in the framework of turbulent flames.

	Consumption speed s_c	Absolute speed $s_a(\Theta)$	Displacement speed $s_d(\Theta)$
Expression:	$-\frac{1}{\rho_1 Y_F^1}\int_{-\infty}^{+\infty}\dot{\omega}_F d\mathbf{n}=s_l^0$	0	$-\vec{u}.\vec{n} \gg s_l^0$
Experiments:	No	Yes	Yes
Computations:	Yes	Yes	Yes

Table 2.13: Flame speed expressions at the tip of bunsen-type burner at $Le_F = 1$ (Poinsot et al. [524]). The "experiments" and "computations" lines indicate whether corresponding speeds can be obtained from measurements and/or from computations.

Spherical flames

Another method to measure flame speeds and Markstein lengths is spherical deflagrations (Dowdy et al. [183], Aung et al. [21], Gu et al. [255]). Igniting a flame in a stagnant premixed vessel (Fig. 2.29) produces a spherical flame with a radius $r(t)$ which can be used to measure both flame speed and stretch. In stagnation point flames, the flow velocity can be measured everywhere to compute flame speed and stretch. This is not possible for a spherical unsteady flame and all flame information must be deduced only from the $r(t)$ data.

Flame stretch is easy to derive. Since the total flame area is $A = 4\pi r(t)^2$ and symmetry imposes zero velocity gradients in planes tangent to the flame, stretch is:

$$\kappa = \frac{1}{A}\frac{dA}{dt} = \frac{2}{r}\frac{d}{dt}r(t) \tag{2.114}$$

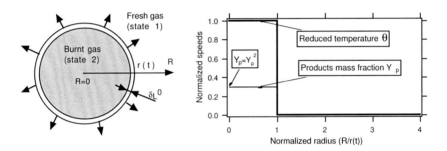

Figure 2.29: Spherical flame.

Measuring flame speeds is more complex because both the flow and the flame move. Assumptions are required to deduce flow and flame speeds from $r(t)$. These assumptions are all based on the flame thickness and can be dangerous.

Flame speeds expressions for zero flame thickness A first level of precision, implicitly accepted by most authors, corresponds to neglecting the flame thickness δ_L^0. Under this assumption, both flame and flow speeds can be derived. First, a relationship between the consumption speed s_c and the sphere radius $r(t)$ is obtained by writing the conservation equation for the products mass fraction of the reaction Y_p:

$$\frac{\partial \rho Y_P}{\partial t} + \frac{\partial}{\partial x_i}(\rho(u_i + V_{k,i})Y_P) = \dot{\omega}_P \tag{2.115}$$

Integrating this equation between $r = 0$ and $r = \infty$ in spherical coordinates yields an equation for the total mass of products M_p:

$$\frac{dM_2}{dt} = \frac{d}{dt}\left(\int_0^\infty \rho Y_P dV\right) = \int_0^\infty \dot{\omega}_P dV \tag{2.116}$$

because diffusive and convective fluxes of products are zero at $r = 0$ and $r = \infty$. The reaction rate term on the RHS of Eq. (2.116) is directly linked to the consumption flame speed if the flame is supposed to be thin and perfectly spherical:

$$\int_0^\infty \dot{\omega}_P dV = 4\pi r(t)^2 \int_0^\infty \dot{\omega}_P dr = 4\pi r(t)^2 \rho_1 s_c Y_P^2 \tag{2.117}$$

using Eq. (2.27) where Y_P^2 is the products mass fraction in the fully burnt gases (Fig. 2.29). On the other hand, the total mass of products M_p in Eq. (2.116) is:

$$M = \int_0^\infty \rho Y_P dV = \rho_2 Y_P^2 \frac{4\pi}{3} r(t)^3 \tag{2.118}$$

so that replacing Eq. (2.118) and Eq. (2.117) into Eq. (2.116) gives s_c as a function of $r(t)$:

$$\boxed{s_c = \frac{\rho_2}{\rho_1} \frac{d}{dt} r(t)} \tag{2.119}$$

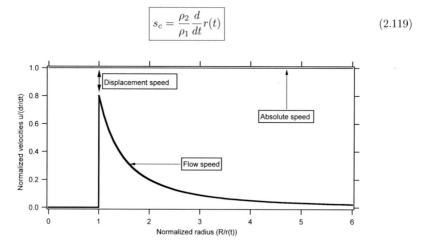

Figure 2.30: Flow and flame speeds in a spherical flame assuming zero flame thickness.

If one assumes zero flame thickness, the displacement speed can be also obtained from the measurement of dr/dt. First, the flow speed $u(r)$ is obtained as follows: within the bubble of burnt gases, for $R < r(t)$, $u(r)$ is zero, the burnt gases are stagnant. For $R > r(t)$, $u(r)$ can be evaluated by writing the continuity equation between $r = 0$ and a given position R. The variation of the total mass within the sphere of radius R is equal to the mass flux of fresh gases pushed outside the sphere:

$$\frac{d}{dt}\left(\frac{4}{3}\pi\rho_2 r(t)^3 + \frac{4}{3}\pi\rho_1\left(R^3 - r(t)^3\right)\right) = -4\pi R^2 \rho_1 u(R) \tag{2.120}$$

$$\text{or} \quad \boxed{u(R) = \left(\frac{r(t)}{R}\right)^2 \left(1 - \frac{\rho_2}{\rho_1}\right)\frac{d}{dt}r(t)} \tag{2.121}$$

The flow velocity $u(R)$ decreases with $1/R^2$ for large R values (Fig. 2.30). At the flame front $(R = r(t))$, $u(R)$ is discontinuous. Its maximum value is $(1 - \rho_2/\rho_1)dr/dt$. If this value is retained to evaluate the displacement speed $s_d = s_a - u$:

$$\boxed{s_d = \frac{\rho_2}{\rho_1}\frac{d}{dt}r(t) = s_c} \tag{2.122}$$

which provides the same estimation of the flame speed as Eq. (2.119).

Flame speeds expressions for non-zero flame thickness: Eq. (2.119) or Eq. (2.122) are the standard approximations used by most experimentalists to obtain a flame speed from the measurement of $r(t)$. For finite flame thickness, however, it is not possible to demonstrate any of these equations and all corrections which are introduced for finite flame thickness have a direct impact on the flame speeds and a drastic effect on the Markstein lengths. In addition to this issue, Eq. (2.119) or Eq. (2.122) raise multiple problems in practice:

- Spherical flames are always stretched: to obtain the unstretched flame speed s_L^0, a model linking flame speeds and stretch is mandatory. This model has often been the linear relation given by Eq. 2.106: the usual method is to fit both s_L^0 and the Markstein length L_a on a curve giving the flame speed versus stretch. The results obtained with this method depend on the model chosen to link flame speed to stretch. Many recent papers show that Eq. 2.106 is not adequate for this exercice and that methods based on non-linear relations are more precise. These relations do not provide displacement flame speeds relative to the fresh gas but displacement flame speeds relative to the burnt gases (called s_b here). Therefore they also provide Markstein lengths relative to the burnt gases (called L_b) (Ronney and Sivashinsky [567], Halter et al. [267]). A simplified expression for this class of non-linear relations is (Chen [124], Halter et al. [267]):[xviii]

$$\frac{s_b}{s_b^0}\ln\left(\frac{s_b}{s_b^0}\right) = -2\frac{L_b}{r(t)} \quad \text{or} \quad \left(\frac{s_b}{s_b^0}\right)^2 \ln\left(\frac{s_b}{s_b^0}\right)^2 = -2\frac{L_b\kappa}{s_b^0} \tag{2.123}$$

since the flame stretch κ is $\frac{2}{r}\frac{dr}{dt} = \frac{2}{r}s_b$. Using speeds relative to the burnt gases makes sense for this flame because burnt gases are stagnant: s_b is equal to dr/dt. Eq. 2.123 is a good model to obtain s_b^0 and L_b. Finding s_L^0 and L_a from s_b^0 and L_b is much more difficult however. In most cases, authors simply assume that $s_L^0 = s_b^0\frac{\rho_2}{\rho_1}$. There is no simple relation between L_b and L_a. As a consequence, measuring L_a in spherical flames (to use it for example in G equation models for turbulent premixed flames: see § 5.4) is difficult.

[xviii]This expression degenerates to the linear expression: $s_b = s_b^0 - \frac{L_b}{s_b^0}\kappa$ for small values of the stretch κ.

- Independently of the relation (linear or not) between flame speed and flame stretch used to obtain flame speeds from measurements of $r(t)$, Eq. (2.119), (2.122) or   2.123 all require the knowledge of the density ratio $\frac{\rho_2}{\rho_1}$ between fresh and burnt gases which is usually estimated from an equilibrium computation to obtain the burnt gas temperature: any level of radiative loss could change the burnt gas temperature and modify this ratio (Ronney and Sivashinsky [567]).

- The ignition phase used to start the flame may also lead to non homogeneities in the profiles of T and ρ in the burnt gases and to values of $\frac{\rho_2}{\rho_1}$ differing from equilibrium values and difficult to determine precisely: Kelley and Law [335] show that the first phases of spherical flame experiments should not be used to measure flame speeds.

- In most spherical flame experiments, the flame is placed within a bomb so the last instants of the propagation can not be used either: pressure goes up and wall effects modify the flame.

- Finally, at high pressure and for rich flames, thermodiffusive instabilities appear (§2.8) leading to cellular flames and impossible measurements of flame speeds (Wu et al. [714]).

	Consumption speed s_c	Absolute speed $s_a(\Theta)$	Displacement speed $s_d(\Theta)$
Expression:	$\frac{\rho_2}{\rho_1}\frac{d}{dt}r(t)$	$\frac{d}{dt}r(t)$	$\approx \frac{\rho_2}{\rho_1}\frac{d}{dt}r(t)$
Experiments:	Yes	Yes	Difficult
Computations:	Yes	Yes	Difficult

Table 2.14: Flame speed expressions for spherical flames if the flame thickness is zero. The "experiments" and "computations" lines indicate whether corresponding speeds can be obtained from measurements and/or from computations.

As a result, spherical flame speed measurements remain difficult exercices despite their apparent simplicity. The evaluations of flame speeds using a zero flame thickness assumption are summarized in Table 2.14. Even though these expressions are sometimes used, they do not offer sufficient precision especially if estimates of Markstein lengths (the derivatives of flame speeds versus stretch) are sought. More precise estimates for flame speeds can be derived for non-zero flame thickness. Starting from Eq. (2.116), this can be done by providing better estimates for M_p: the burnt mass M_p must include not only the fully burnt gases (between $r = 0$ and $r = r(t)$) but also the burnt gases within the flame front itself (between $r = r(t)$ and $r = r(t) + \delta_L^0$). This second contribution is small but must be retained. It is also difficult to evaluate because it requires a model for $Y_P(r)$ which is not known. Its magnitude, however can be evaluated by assuming a mean value for the product ρY_P within the flame zone as follows:

$$\int_{r(t)}^{r(t)+\delta_L^0} \rho Y_P dV = \frac{1}{2}\delta_L^0 4\pi r(t)^2 \rho_2 Y_P^2 \qquad (2.124)$$

Using this expression to write that the time derivative of M_p (Fig. 2.29) is given by Eq. (2.117) leads to an expression of s_c including the effects of finite flame thickness:

$$s_c = \left[1 + \frac{\delta_L^0}{r(t)}\right]\frac{\rho_2}{\rho_1}\frac{d}{dt}r(t) \qquad (2.125)$$

For large spherical flames, r/δ_l is large and the usual zeroth-order relation (2.119) used by Aung et al. [21] is recovered. Retaining the more general expression (2.125) shows why Markstein lengths measurements from spherical flames are difficult (Poinsot [517]): the small correction to the flame speed on the RHS of Eq. (2.125) does not change the value of s_c considerably but it changes the slope of s_c versus stretch considerably. The difference ΔL_a between Markstein lengths L_a^1 computed using Eq. (2.122) (at zero flame thickness) or L_a^2 using Eq. (2.125) (at non zero flame thickness) is simple to evaluate :

$$\Delta L_a = L_a^2 - L_a^1 = 0.5\delta_L^0 \rho_2/\rho_1 \qquad (2.126)$$

which is of the order of the flame thickness δ_L^0. Since the Markstein lengths are of the same order, the error introduced by using Eq. (2.122) to evaluate Markstein lengths can be large (Dowdy et al. [183], Poinsot [517]).

2.8 Instabilities of laminar flame fronts

Throughout this chapter, laminar premixed fronts have been assumed to have a stable structure and to propagate along the flame normal while conserving a planar one-dimensional shape. This is not always the case and various instability modes can appear along premixed flame fronts (Joulin and Mitani [317], Sivashinsky [616], Williams [710], Clavin [137]). For example, laminar premixed flames exhibit intrinsic instabilities (called thermodiffusive) which are controlled by the relative importance of reactant molecular and heat diffusion (i.e. by the Lewis number L_e of the most deficient reactant) as illustrated in Fig. 2.31:

- If $L_e < 1$, when the flame front is convex towards the fresh gases, reactants diffuse towards burnt gases faster than heat diffuse towards cold fresh gases. These reactants are heated and then burn faster, increasing the local flame speed s_L which is higher than the speed s_L^0 of a planar flame front. On the other hand, for fronts convex towards the burnt gases, reactants diffuse in a large zone and the flame velocity is decreased compared to s_L^0. This situation is unstable: the flame front wrinkling (as well as the flame surface) increases.

- When the species molecular diffusivity is lower than the heat diffusivity ($L_e > 1$), a similar analysis shows that the flame is stable: the flame surface decreases.

The transition from stable ($L_e > 1$) to unstable ($L_e < 1$) flames can be triggered by using light fuels (usually hydrogen) and going from rich (where the deficient reactant is O_2 for which $L_e \simeq 1.1$)) to lean flames (where the deficient reactant is hydrogen with $L_e \simeq 0.3$). Thermodiffusive instabilities are observed for example in lean laminar hydrogen-air flames where they lead to the formation of cellular flames. Fig. 2.32 shows an example of cell formation on a hydrogen - propane / air flame at 5 bars (Law et al. [372]): the flame is smooth for rich mixtures but cellular for lean mixtures. Cell formation increases with pressure.

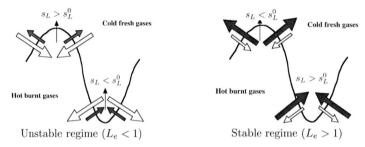

Figure 2.31: Sketch of thermodiffusive instabilities. For $L_e < 1$, molecular diffusion (empty arrows) is larger than heat diffusion (filled arrows) and the wrinkling of the flame front is enhanced by differential flame speeds (left figure). For $L_e > 1$ (right figure), a stable planar flame is obtained.

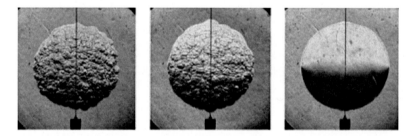

Figure 2.32: Cell formation in spherical hydrogen / propane laminar flames (Law et al. [372]) at 5 bars. Left: $\phi = 0.6$, center: $\phi = 1.$, right $\phi = 1.4$.

Thermodiffusive instabilities are not the only instability mechanism in laminar flames: a complete discussion of laminar flame front instabilities is out of the scope of this book and interested readers are referred to Williams [710] and Clavin [137]. In most cases and especially in turbulent flames, these instabilities are often neglected (Chapters 4 to 6). However, recent research suggests that thermodiffusive mechanisms could be the source of additional flame wrinkling in turbulent flames (§ 5.5.3).

Chapter 3

Laminar diffusion flames

3.1   Diffusion flame configurations

In many combustion systems, the perfectly premixed combustion mode discussed in Chapter 2 can not be used because it is either too dangerous or too complicated to premix reactants before they enter the combustor. For those systems, non-premixed regimes (also called diffusion regimes) have to be used. Diffusion flames[i] constitute a specific class of combustion problems where fuel and oxidizer are not mixed before they enter the combustion chamber: for these flames, mixing must bring reactants into the reaction zone fast enough for combustion to proceed. In premixed flames, mixing of fuel and oxidizer is performed before combustion and does not require any attention: it becomes one of the main issues (if not the first) in diffusion flames and its modeling also becomes one essential question for simulations. The literature on diffusion flames is as abundant as on premixed flames (Linan and Crespo [398], Bilger [49, 51], Peters [498], Barlow [29]) and this chapter concentrates on the basic notions required for numerical studies of such flames.

Fig. 3.1 presents a simple diffusion flame configuration. Instead of one state (the premixed reactants) for the premixed flame, two boundary states must now be considered: fuel (which may be diluted in other gases) on the left and oxidizer (diluted or not) on the right side. Fuel and oxidizer diffuse towards the reaction zone where they burn and generate heat. Temperature is maximum in this zone and diffuses away from the flame front towards the fuel and oxidizer streams. In Fig. 3.1, there is no fuel on the oxidizer side and no oxygen on the fuel side. This is a usual situation for diffusion flames in practical systems but not a systematic one: in certain flames, for example in many flames of the TNF (Turbulent Non-premixed Flame) workshop (*www.sandia.gov/TNF*), the fuel stream can contain fuel but also oxygen. This case is not considered in this chapter for simplicity reasons.

Fig. 3.1 illustrates a number of important considerations:

---

[i]This section is available as a video at *elearning.cerfacs.fr/combustion*: see Diffusion Flames (part 1) and Diffusion Flames (part 2) .

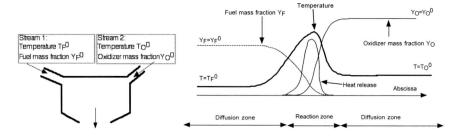

Figure 3.1: Basic non-premixed flame configuration (left) and structure (right).

- Far away on each side of the flame, the gas is either too rich or too lean to burn. Chemical reactions can proceed only in a limited region, where fuel and oxidizer are mixed adequately. The most favorable mixing is obtained where fuel and oxidizer are in stoichiometric proportions: a diffusion flame usually lies along the points where mixing produces a stoichiometric mixture.

- The flame structure plotted on Fig. 3.1 is steady only when strain is applied to the flame, i.e. when fuel and oxidizer streams are pushed against each other at given speeds (Fig. 3.2b). In a pure one-dimensional unstrained case, the flame spreads with time t (Fig. 3.2a), gets choked in its combustion products and the reaction rate slowly decreases as $1/\sqrt{t}$, as described in Section 3.4.1.

- A diffusion flame does not exhibit a reference "speed" as premixed flames (§ 2.7.1): the flame is unable to propagate towards fuel because of the lack of oxidizer and it cannot propagate towards oxidizer stream because of the lack of fuel. Accordingly, the reaction zone does not move significantly relatively to the flow field. Being unable to propagate "against" the flow, diffusion flames are more sensitive to velocity perturbations, and especially to turbulence, than premixed flames.

- A diffusion flame does not have a reference "thickness": the unstretched flame of Fig. 3.2a grows up indefinitely with time while the thickness of stretched flames of Fig. 3.2b depends essentially on stretch and can take a very wide range of values. Again, this is very different from premixed flames where a thickness may be introduced and depends on the fluid properties and the flame speed (§ 2.5).

- In terms of industrial applications, mixing is also the key characteristic of diffusion flames. These flames are simpler to design and to build: no premixing, with a given equivalence ratio, is required. They are also safer to operate because they do not propagate. However, their burning efficiency is reduced compared to premixed flames because mixing reduces the speed at which chemical reactions may proceed.

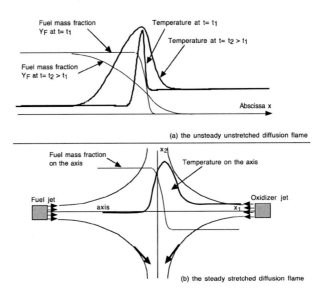

Figure 3.2: Unsteady unstretched (a) and steady stretched (b) laminar diffusion flames.

Many fundamental concepts related to diffusion flames are necessary to understand how such flows are solved for in combustion codes. Section 3.2 presents these notions (mixture fraction, flame structure, mixing problem) and shows how solving for a diffusion flame is usually decoupled into two problems: the first is related to the mixing processes between fuel and oxidizer; the second addresses the combustion process (the flame structure) once mixing is achieved. Section 3.3 presents a few classical results on flame structure in the simplest case where chemistry is infinitely fast while Section 3.4 presents complete solutions, including resolution of the mixing problem, for the same situation. Extensions to more realistic chemistry models and to real flames are discussed in Section 3.5 and 3.6.

3.2 Theoretical tools for diffusion flames

Many studies of diffusion flames assume idealized situations using the passive scalar (or mixture fraction) notion that is the starting point of the analysis. To describe this concept, assumptions are introduced to allow simple derivations. Very few of these assumptions are satisfied in a real flame and Section 3.6 shows that real flames differ from the ideal situation studied in this section. Qualitatively, however, the present results are the common basis of all diffusion flame studies.

Considering a single-step chemical reaction ($M = 1$) with N species:

$$\sum_{k=1}^{N} \nu'_k \mathcal{M}_k \rightleftharpoons \sum_{k=1}^{N} \nu''_k \mathcal{M}_k \qquad (3.1)$$

the assumptions made to analyze idealized diffusion flames are the following:

- H1 - thermodynamic pressure is constant and Mach numbers are small.

- H2 - all the diffusion coefficients D_k of chemical species are equal to $\mathcal{D}$. Fick's law, without velocity correction, is used for diffusion velocities.

- H3 - the heat capacities C_{pk} of chemical species are equal and independent of temperature: $C_{pk} = C_p$.

3.2.1   Passive scalars and mixture fraction

Consider first the case where reaction (3.1) involves only fuel (F), oxidizer (O) and products (P):

$$\nu_F F + \nu_O O \rightleftharpoons \nu_P P \qquad (3.2)$$

The mass fraction Y_k of each species (F, O, and P) follows a balance equation given by:

$$\frac{\partial \rho Y_k}{\partial t} + \frac{\partial}{\partial x_i}(\rho u_i Y_k) = \frac{\partial}{\partial x_i}\left(\rho \mathcal{D} \frac{\partial Y_k}{\partial x_i}\right) + \dot{\omega}_k \qquad (3.3)$$

Species reaction rates $\dot{\omega}_k$ are all related to the single-step reaction rate $\mathcal{Q}$ (Eq. 1.22):

$$\boxed{\dot{\omega}_k = W_k \nu_k \mathcal{Q}} \qquad (3.4)$$

so the oxidizer reaction rate is linked to the fuel reaction rate:

$$\boxed{\dot{\omega}_O = s \dot{\omega}_F} \quad \text{with} \quad s = \frac{\nu_O W_O}{\nu_F W_F} \qquad (3.5)$$

where s is the mass stoichiometric ratio defined in Eq. (1.28). The reaction rate for temperature is also obviously linked to the fuel reaction rate through Eq. (2.17):

$$\boxed{\dot{\omega}_T = -Q \dot{\omega}_F} \qquad (3.6)$$

Using these relations, the conservation equations for fuel, oxidizer and temperature become:

$$\frac{\partial \rho Y_F}{\partial t} + \frac{\partial}{\partial x_i}(\rho u_i Y_F) = \frac{\partial}{\partial x_i}\left(\rho \mathcal{D} \frac{\partial Y_F}{\partial x_i}\right) + \dot{\omega}_F \qquad (3.7)$$

$$\frac{\partial \rho Y_O}{\partial t} + \frac{\partial}{\partial x_i}(\rho u_i Y_O) = \frac{\partial}{\partial x_i}\left(\rho \mathcal{D} \frac{\partial Y_O}{\partial x_i}\right) + s \dot{\omega}_F \qquad (3.8)$$

$$\frac{\partial \rho T}{\partial t} + \frac{\partial}{\partial x_i}(\rho u_i T) = \frac{\partial}{\partial x_i}\left(\frac{\lambda}{C_p} \frac{\partial T}{\partial x_i}\right) - \frac{Q}{C_p} \dot{\omega}_F \qquad (3.9)$$

Combining Eq. (3.7) to (3.9) two by two, assuming unity Lewis numbers ($Le = \lambda/\rho C_p \mathcal{D} = 1$) shows that the three quantities:

$$Z_1 = sY_F - Y_O \quad ; \quad Z_2 = \frac{C_p T}{Q} + Y_F \quad ; \quad Z_3 = s\frac{C_p T}{Q} + Y_O \tag{3.10}$$

follow the same balance equation, without source terms:

$$\boxed{\frac{\partial \rho Z}{\partial t} + \frac{\partial}{\partial x_i}(\rho u_i Z) = \frac{\partial}{\partial x_i}\left(\rho \mathcal{D} \frac{\partial Z}{\partial x_i}\right)} \tag{3.11}$$

Z is a passive (or conserved) scalar and changes because of diffusion and convection but not reaction.[ii] The variable Z_2 is directly linked to the quantity $Y + \Theta$ introduced in premixed flames (§ 2.4.3): $Z_2 = (Y + \Theta)Y_F^1 + C_p T_1/Q$. In perfectly premixed flames, $Y + \Theta$ is constant and equal to unity everywhere (see Eq. 2.35). For diffusion flames Z_2 is not constant because fuel and oxidizer are not mixed before combustion. However, Z_2 is a passive scalar indicating that mixing can still be studied independently from combustion.

The three variables Z_1, Z_2 and Z_3, defined in Eq. (3.10) follow the same balance equation but have different boundary conditions summarized in Table 3.1 (notations are defined on Fig. 3.1).

Passive scalar Z	Fuel value Z_i^F	Oxidizer value Z_i^O
Z_1	sY_F^0	$-Y_O^0$
Z_2	$\frac{C_p T_F^0}{Q} + Y_F^0$	$\frac{C_p T_O^0}{Q}$
Z_3	$s\frac{C_p T_F^0}{Q}$	$s\frac{C_p T_O^0}{Q} + Y_O^0$

Table 3.1: Boundary conditions for the passive scalars defined in Eq. (3.10). Y_F^0 and Y_O^0 are fuel and oxidizer mass fractions in pure fuel and oxidizer streams respectively (reactants may be diluted). T_F^0 and T_O^0 denote the corresponding temperatures.

Normalized z_j variables are defined by:

$$z_j = \frac{Z_j - Z_j^O}{Z_j^F - Z_j^O} \quad \text{for } j = 1, 2, 3 \tag{3.12}$$

All reduced variables z_j follow the same convection/diffusion balance equation:

$$\frac{\partial \rho z_j}{\partial t} + \frac{\partial}{\partial x_i}(\rho u_i z_j) = \frac{\partial}{\partial x_i}\left(\rho \mathcal{D} \frac{\partial z_j}{\partial x_i}\right) \tag{3.13}$$

[ii]Reaction still plays an indirect role in Z controlling temperature and, therefore, density and velocity fields.

and have the same boundary conditions: $z_j = 1$ in the fuel stream and $z_j = 0$ in the oxidizer stream (Table 3.2). All these variables are therefore equal:[iii]

$$z_1 = z_2 = z_3 = z \tag{3.14}$$

where z is called the mixture fraction and measures the local fuel/oxidizer ratio. Expressing z using the boundary conditions given in Table 3.1 (corresponding to the simplified but general case where there is no fuel in the oxidizer stream and no oxygen in the fuel stream) leads to:

$$z = \frac{sY_F - Y_O + Y_O^0}{sY_F^0 + Y_O^0} = \frac{\frac{C_p}{Q}(T - T_O^0) + Y_F}{\frac{C_p}{Q}(T_F^0 - T_O^0) + Y_F} = \frac{\frac{sC_p}{Q}(T - T_O^0) + Y_O - Y_O^0}{\frac{sC_p}{Q}(T_F^0 - T_O^0) - Y_O^0} \tag{3.15}$$

The first part of Eq. (3.15) may be recast as:

$$z = \frac{1}{\phi + 1}\left(\phi\frac{Y_F}{Y_F^0} - \frac{Y_O}{Y_O^0} + 1\right) \tag{3.16}$$

where the equivalence ratio ϕ is introduced:

$$\phi = sY_F^0/Y_O^0 \tag{3.17}$$

This equivalence ratio corresponds to the equivalence ratio which would be obtained when premixing the *same* mass of fuel and oxidizer streams. It does not correspond to the overall (or global) equivalence ratio ϕ_g inside a burner, depending both on ϕ and on fuel and oxidizer flow rates (see § 3.3.4).

The previous derivations are valid in multi-dimensional flows and for any combustion regime: they could also be used in premixed flames. But, in perfectly premixed flows, this concept is not useful as z is constant everywhere.

3.2.2   Flame structure in mixture fraction space

The introduction of the mixture fraction z allows to reduce the number of variables. Eq. (3.15) shows that all species, for example, are function of the mixture fraction z and temperature T:

$$Y_k = f_k(z, T) \quad \text{for} \quad k = 1, N \tag{3.18}$$

Even though this is a useful simplification of the initial problem, one more step needs to be taken using the following assumption:

- H4 - the structure of the diffusion flame depends on the mixture fraction z and on time t only. Temperature and species mass fractions can be written:

$$T = T(z, t) \quad \text{and} \quad Y_k = Y_k(z, t) \tag{3.19}$$

Variable	Fuel value	Oxidizer value
Fuel mass fraction	Y_F^0	0
Oxidizer mass fraction	0	Y_O^0
Temperature	T_F^0	T_O^0
Mixture fraction z	1	0

Table 3.2: Boundary conditions for species mass fractions, temperature and the mixture fraction z defined by Eq. (3.12).

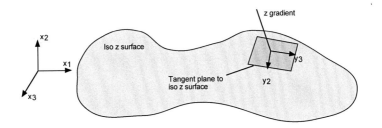

Figure 3.3: Variable change for diffusion flame sheets (Williams [710], Peters [502]).

The functions $T(z,t)$, $Y_k(z,t)$ of Eq. (3.19) define the *flame structure*. The assumption H4 can be introduced and justified in multiple ways. Formally, it is a variable change in the species equations (3.3) from (x_1, x_2, x_3, t) to (z, y_2, y_3, t) where y_2 and y_3 are spatial variables in planes parallel to iso-z surfaces (Fig. 3.3). In the resulting equation, terms corresponding to gradients along the flame front (gradients along y_2 and y_3) are neglected in comparison to the terms normal to the flame (gradients along z) (see Williams [710], Peters [502] for details and alternative derivations). Physically, all these derivations imply that the flame structure is locally one-dimensional and depends only on time and on the coordinate normal to the flame front (or on z). In a multi-dimensional flow, this assumption requires that the flame be thin compared to other flow and wrinkling scales. Each element of the flame front can then be viewed as a small laminar flame also called *flamelet*: this flamelet view is the basis of many models for turbulent combustion (Chapt. 4 to 6). Under this hypothesis, the species mass fraction balance equations (3.3) may be rewritten:

$$\rho \frac{\partial Y_k}{\partial t} + Y_k \left[\frac{\partial \rho}{\partial t} + \frac{\partial}{\partial x_i}(\rho u_i) \right] + \frac{\partial Y_k}{\partial z} \left[\rho \frac{\partial z}{\partial t} + \rho u_i \frac{\partial z}{\partial x_i} - \frac{\partial}{\partial x_i} \left(\rho \mathcal{D} \frac{\partial z}{\partial x_i} \right) \right]$$

[iii]This property holds at any time if it is verified at the initial time. If not (for example, when a diffusion flame is ignited by a hot spot at $t = 0$), it becomes true after a few typical diffusion times.

$$- \ \rho \mathcal{D} \left(\frac{\partial z}{\partial x_i} \frac{\partial z}{\partial x_i} \right) \frac{\partial^2 Y_k}{\partial z^2} = \dot{\omega}_k \tag{3.20}$$

The two terms within brackets in the LHS of Eq. (3.20) vanish because of continuity and mixture fraction (Eq. 3.13) balance equations:

$$\boxed{\rho \frac{\partial Y_k}{\partial t} = \dot{\omega}_k + \rho \mathcal{D} \left(\frac{\partial z}{\partial x_i} \frac{\partial z}{\partial x_i} \right) \frac{\partial^2 Y_k}{\partial z^2} = \dot{\omega}_k + \frac{1}{2} \rho \chi \frac{\partial^2 Y_k}{\partial z^2}} \tag{3.21}$$

where the scalar dissipation rate χ has been introduced:[iv]

$$\boxed{\chi = 2\mathcal{D} \left(\frac{\partial z}{\partial x_i} \frac{\partial z}{\partial x_i} \right)} \tag{3.22}$$

The temperature equation can also be recast in the same way:

$$\boxed{\rho \frac{\partial T}{\partial t} = \dot{\omega}_T + \frac{1}{2} \rho \chi \frac{\partial^2 T}{\partial z^2}} \tag{3.23}$$

Eq. (3.21) and (3.23) are called the flamelet equations.[v] They are key elements in many diffusion flame theories: in these equations, the only term depending on spatial variables (x_i) is the scalar dissipation rate χ which controls mixing (because it controls the gradients of z). Once χ is specified, the flamelet equations can be entirely solved in z space to provide the flame structure, i.e. the temperatures and species as functions of mixture fraction z and time t, as supposed in Assumption H4:

$$T = T(z,t) \quad \text{and} \quad Y_k = Y_k(z,t) \tag{3.24}$$

Although this is not explicit in the present notation, the T and Y_k functions are parametrized by the scalar dissipation rate χ: different scalar dissipation levels lead to different flame structures.

The scalar dissipation rate χ has the dimension of an inverse time (like strain). It measures the z-gradients and the molecular fluxes of species towards the flame. It is directly influenced by strain: when the flame strain rate increases, χ increases (§ 3.4.2). An estimate of the mixing layer thickness is $\sqrt{\mathcal{D}/\chi}$.

3.2.3   The steady flamelet assumption

The flamelet structure obtained from Eq. (3.21) and (3.23) depends both on time t and on mixture fraction z. It can be used in two ways:

[iv]Various definitions of the scalar dissipation rate may be found in the literature, including, or not, the density ρ and the factor 2.

[v]Extended flamelet equations including effects of non-unity Lewis number, variable molecular weights or radiative heat losses can also be derived: see Pitsch and Peters [513, 514] or Peters [502].

- Unsteady laminar flamelets. The dependence of the T and Y_k functions versus time can be conserved, leading to a class of approach called "unsteady flamelets".

- Steady laminar flamelets. The structure of the flamelet can be assumed to be steady, even though the flow itself (and especially the z field) depends on time. In this case:

$$\boxed{T = T(z)} \quad \text{and} \quad \boxed{Y_k = Y_k(z)} \tag{3.25}$$

To simplify the presentation, this steady flamelet approximation will be used in the following, except when mentioned explicitly. Note that the T and Y_k functions are still parametrized by the scalar dissipation rate level.

Using Eq. (3.25), Eq. (3.21) and (3.23) reduce to:

$$\boxed{\dot{\omega}_k = -\frac{1}{2} \underbrace{\rho\chi}_{\text{mixing}} \underbrace{\frac{\partial^2 Y_k}{\partial z^2}}_{\text{reaction}}} \quad \text{and} \quad \boxed{\dot{\omega}_T = -\frac{1}{2} \underbrace{\rho\chi}_{\text{mixing}} \underbrace{\frac{\partial^2 T}{\partial z^2}}_{\text{reaction}}} \tag{3.26}$$

Eq. (3.26) shows that reaction rates for species or temperature depend on z and χ only. Flow information is entirely contained in the scalar dissipation rate χ whereas chemical effects are incorporated through the flame structure in z-space. This important simplification is emphasized in the following section.

3.2.4 Decomposition into mixing and flame structure problems

Mixture fraction appears as the basic variable for most theories of laminar flames and essentially decouples diffusion flame computations (finding $T(x_i, t)$ and $Y_k(x_i, t)$) into two problems:

- A mixing problem (problem 1) where Eq. (3.13) must be solved to obtain the mixture fraction field $z(x_i, t)$ as a function of spatial coordinates x_i and time t.

- A flame structure problem (problem 2) where the links between flame variables (mass fractions $Y_k(z)$, solutions of Eq. (3.21) and temperature $T(z)$, solution of Eq. (3.23)) and z are used to construct all flame variables.

Both problems must be solved to determine the flame variables: knowing z only would provide the entire field of variable combinations such as $Z_1 = sY_F - Y_O$, $Z_2 = C_pT/Q + Y_F$ or $Z_3 = sC_pT/Q + Y_O$ but not the variables T, Y_F or Y_O themselves. To obtain these variables, additional assumptions on the flame structure must be used to link flame variables to the mixture fraction and obtain $T(z)$, $Y_F(z)$ or $Y_O(z)$. Section 3.2.5 discusses these assumptions.

Figure 3.4 summarizes how the problem of computing diffusion flame is usually split into two sub-problems: flame structure and mixing. A steady flamelet approximation is used as discussed in Section 3.2.3 but the same concept applies for unsteady flamelets. All aspects related to the flow (geometry, boundary conditions) must be treated in the mixing problem. On the other hand, all chemistry information is gathered in the flame structure part.

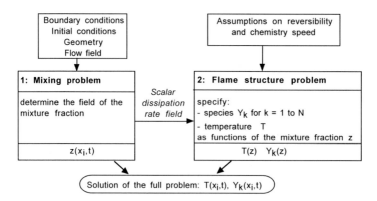

Figure 3.4: Decomposition into two problems: flame structure (right) and mixing (left). The $T(z)$ and $Y_k(z)$ functions may depend on additional parameters (like time or scalar dissipation rate).

3.2.5   Models for diffusion flame structures

The introduction of mixture fraction allows analytical solutions for diffusion flames using additional assumptions discussed here:

- Equilibrium (or fast chemistry): assuming that chemistry is infinitely fast, i.e. that chemical time scales are shorter than all other flow characteristic times (chemical reaction is faster than diffusion and flow time scales) is called the "equilibrium" (or "fast chemistry") assumption. It allows simplification of the problem enough to provide, in some cases, analytical solutions for flame structures (§ 3.3). This assumption implies that chemical reactions proceed locally so fast that equilibrium is instantaneously reached.

- Irreversibility: assuming that reaction (3.2) proceeds only from left to right (the reverse constant of Eq. (3.2) is zero) allows additional simplifications.

Combining assumptions of infinitely fast chemistry (equilibrium) and irreversibility leads to Table 3.3.

1. For infinitely fast and irreversible chemistry, fuel and oxidizer cannot exist at the same time. This important simplification is analyzed in Section 3.3. This simplest "equilibrium" assumption is called "irreversible fast chemistry". Here, the $T(z)$ and $Y_k(z)$ functions of Fig. 3.4 do not depend on the scalar dissipation rate.

2. Under infinitely fast, but reversible chemistry, fuel, oxidizer and products mass fractions are linked by the equilibrium relation:

$$\frac{Y_F^{\nu_F} Y_O^{\nu_O}}{Y_P^{\nu_P}} = K(T) \qquad\qquad (3.27)$$

where $K(T)$ is the reaction equilibrium constant at temperature T. This relation links local mass fractions and temperature. In this situation, fuel and oxidizer may be found simultaneously at the same location at the same time. The $T(z)$ and $Y_k(z)$ functions of Fig. 3.4 do not depend on the scalar dissipation rate.

3. For an irreversible but not infinitely fast chemical reaction, fuel and oxidizer may also exist simultaneously. The overlap between fuel and oxidizer profiles depends now on flow time scales and especially on the scalar dissipation rate: the $T(z)$ and $Y_k(z)$ functions of Fig. 3.4 must be parametrized by the scalar dissipation rate.

4. In the general case (finite rate chemistry and reversible reaction), no specific guess can be made on the flame structure and the $T(z)$ and $Y_k(z)$ functions depend on the scalar dissipation rate.

5. A specific case of interest is mentioned in the last line of Table 3.3: chemistry can also be "frozen": no reaction takes place and pure mixing between fuel and oxidizer proceeds. The $T(z)$ and $Y_k(z)$ functions do not depend on the scalar dissipation rate.

	Fast chemistry (equilibrium): $\dot{\omega}_k = 0$	Finite rate chemistry (non equilibrium) $\dot{\omega}_k \neq 0$
Irreversible chemistry	F and O cannot coexist (independently of χ) Section 3.3	F and O may overlap in reaction zone (depending on χ) Section 3.5.2
Reversible chemistry	F, O and P are in equilibrium ($\chi = 0$) Section 3.5.1	No simple model for this case
Frozen (pure mixing)	F and O mix but do not burn	Not applicable

Table 3.3: Equilibrium (fast chemistry) and reversibility assumptions.

Each entry in Table 3.3 corresponds to different models described in the following sections. The first column of Table 3.3 deserves some attention. For all "equilibrium" cases, the reaction rate $\dot{\omega}_k$ is zero. According to Eq. (3.26), this can be obtained in different ways:

$$\dot{\omega}_k = 0 \implies \begin{cases} \dfrac{\partial^2 Y_k}{\partial z^2} = 0 \\ \quad \text{or} \\ \chi = 0 \end{cases} \tag{3.28}$$

The first condition, $\partial^2 Y_k / \partial z^2 = 0$, is fulfilled when species mass fractions depend linearly on z: $Y_k = \alpha_k z + \beta_k$, where α_k and β_k are constants. As a consequence, Eq. (3.28) is satisfied in three cases:

- **Irreversible infinitely fast chemistry.** The first solution is to have $\partial^2 Y_k / \partial z^2 = 0$ and corresponds to a infinitely thin flame separating fresh and burnt gases. On both sides of the flame, temperature and species profiles are linear versus z (§ 3.3) but their slopes are discontinuous at the flame front. The reaction rate is zero everywhere except at the flame front where it is infinite.

- **Reversible fast chemistry.** The reaction rate is also zero in Eq. (3.28) if $\chi = 0$: all molecular fluxes are negligible compared to reaction rates. Chemical reactions take place without mixing and reach a local equilibrium defined by Eq. (3.27).

- **Frozen chemistry (pure mixing).** If combustion does not proceed at all ("frozen" chemistry), pure mixing takes place. The solution to such a mixing problem satisfies $\partial^2 Y_k / \partial z^2 = 0$. The "pure mixing" solution is:

$$\boxed{Y_F = Y_F^0 z} \quad \text{and} \quad \boxed{Y_O = Y_O^0 \, (1 - z)} \tag{3.29}$$

The temperature on the mixing line is a mass average (weighted by z) of the fuel and oxidizer temperatures:

$$\boxed{T(z) = z T_F^0 + (1 - z) T_O^0} \tag{3.30}$$

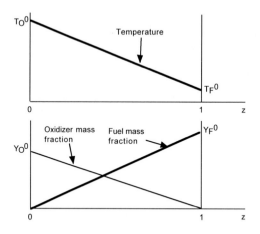

Figure 3.5: Pure mixing with frozen chemistry between fuel and oxidizer.

This solution corresponds to pure mixing, without chemical reaction, between fuel (F) and oxidizer (O) streams. Fig. 3.5 presents the structure in the z-diagram for such a flow: temperature and mass fractions at any point in the flow are plotted versus mixture fraction z at the same point. This structure is one of the (trivial) solutions to the diffusion flame problem. It has one useful application: in a given flow (even within the burnt gases if the flow is reacting), if the local mixture fraction z is known, Eq. (3.29) can be used to obtain the local equivalence ratio Φ:

$$\Phi = \frac{sY_F^m}{Y_O^m} = \frac{sY_F^0}{Y_O^0}\frac{z}{1-z} \qquad (3.31)$$

where Y_F^m and Y_O^m are the mass fractions of the fuel and oxidizer if they would have mixed without burning and therefore correspond to the mixing line of Eq. (3.29).

The next section presents results for reacting situations, first for equilibrium and finally for non-equilibrium cases.

3.3 Flame structure for irreversible infinitely fast chemistry

The first approach to solve Problem 2 (the flame structure) mentioned in Section 3.2.4 with combustion is to assume infinitely fast chemistry (first line in Table 3.3): fuel and oxidizer cannot be found together at the same location because their combustion rate is infinitely fast compared to all other time scales in the flame. This is the derivation used initially by Burke and Schumann [98]. For simplicity, it is assumed here that there is no fuel in the oxidizer stream and no oxygen in the fuel stream.

3.3.1 The Burke-Schumann flame structure

In this case, flame variables and mixture fraction are simply related by setting either $Y_O = 0$ (on the fuel side) or $Y_F = 0$ (on the oxidizer side) in Eq. (3.16):

- **On the fuel side** $(z > z_{st})$

$$
\begin{aligned}
Y_F(z) &= zY_F^0 + (z-1)\frac{Y_O^0}{s} = Y_F^0\frac{z-z_{st}}{1-z_{st}} \\
Y_O(z) &= 0. \\
T(z) &= zT_F^0 + (1-z)T_O^0 + \frac{QY_F^0}{C_p}z_{st}\frac{1-z}{1-z_{st}}
\end{aligned} \qquad (3.32)
$$

- **On the oxidizer side** $(z < z_{st})$:

$$
\begin{aligned}
Y_F(z) &= 0. \\
Y_O(z) &= Y_O^0(1 - \frac{z}{z_{st}}) \\
T(z) &= zT_F^0 + (1-z)T_O^0 + \frac{QY_F^0}{C_p}z
\end{aligned} \qquad (3.33)
$$

where the flame position in the z-space, z_{st}, is determined by expressing that the flame is located where both Y_F and Y_O are zero. At this location, z is equal to its stoichiometric value z_{st} given by Eq. (3.15) :

$$z_{st} = \frac{1}{1 + \dfrac{sY_F^0}{Y_O^0}} = \frac{1}{1 + \dfrac{\nu_O W_O Y_F^0}{\nu_F W_F Y_O^0}} = \frac{1}{1 + \phi} \qquad (3.34)$$

where $\phi = sY_F^0/Y_O^0$ is the equivalence ratio.[vi]

Typical values of ϕ and z_{st} are listed in Table 3.4 for usual fuels. The value of z_{st} has a direct physical consequence: for low z_{st}, the flame lies close to the oxidizer side while it is located close to the fuel side for large values of z_{st}. For hydrocarbon jet flames (pure fuel injected into air), z_{st} is small (of the order of 0.05): the flame front is located close to the air stream.

Fuel / oxidizer		Y_F^0	Y_O^0	ν_F	ν_O	s	ϕ	z_{st}
Pure H_2 /	Pure O_2	1	1	1	0.5	8	8.00	0.111
Pure H_2 /	Air	1	0.23	1	0.5	8	34.8	0.028
Pure CH_4 /	Pure O_2	1	1	1	2	4	4.00	0.200
Pure CH_4 /	Air	1	0.23	1	2	4	17.4	0.054
Diluted CH_4 /	Pure O_2	0.05	1	1	2	4	0.20	0.833
Diluted CH_4 /	Air	0.05	0.23	1	2	4	0.87	0.535
Pure C_3H_8 /	Pure O_2	1	1	1	5	3.64	3.64	0.216
Pure C_3H_8 /	Air	1	0.23	1	5	3.64	15.8	0.059

Table 3.4: Examples of values of mass stoichiometric ratio s (Eq. 3.5), equivalence ratio ϕ (Eq. 3.17) and stoichiometric mixture fraction z_{st} (Eq. 3.34). Diluted methane is arbitrary defined here as a mixture of methane (mass 5 %) and nitrogen (95 %).

The flame structure for infinitely fast irreversible chemistry (i.e. the so called Burke and Schumann solution [98]) is displayed in Fig. 3.6. On this figure, the "mixing" lines are also displayed. These lines correspond to states where fuel and oxidizer would mix without reaction (Eq. 3.29). These mixing lines are important in ignition or quenching problems and more generally for all flames which do not burn vigorously. They determine one extreme state of the flow where mixing takes place without reaction: for such cases, the diffusion flame is only a diffusive layer in which fuel and oxidizer mix like in a non-reacting flow. In a given laminar or turbulent diffusion flame, measuring and plotting T, Y_F and Y_O in a z diagram gives a useful picture of the flame. All points must be located between the mixing and the equilibrium lines

---

[vi]Note that this solution verifies Eq. (3.28) analyzed in Section 3.2.5 but does not require the assumptions (i.e. one-dimensional steady diffusion flame) introduced to derive Eq. (3.26).

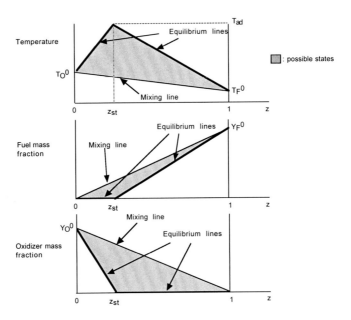

Figure 3.6: Diffusion flame structure in the mixture fraction z diagram for irreversible infinitely fast chemistry (Burke and Schumann solution [98]) and pure mixing without chemical reaction.

(no other state is possible). When most points are located close to the mixing line, the flame is almost extinguished or not ignited yet. On the other hand, z diagrams where points are located close to the combustion line indicate vigorous flames. How close these points can be to the ideal combustion lines is determined by chemistry as discussed in the following sections.

3.3.2 Maximum local flame temperature in a diffusion flame

Without heat losses, the maximum flame temperature (i.e. the adiabatic flame temperature for a diffusion flame) is reached for $z = z_{st}$ (Eq. 3.32 or Eq. 3.33):[vii]

$$T_{ad} = z_{st}T_F^0 + (1 - z_{st})T_O^0 + \frac{QY_F^0}{C_p}z_{st} = \frac{1}{1+\phi}\left(T_F^0 + T_O^0\phi + \frac{QY_F^0}{C_p}\right) \qquad (3.35)$$

[vii]This expression only holds for a single irreversible reaction, equal Lewis numbers and a constant heat capacity C_p.

Eq. (3.35) may be recovered following a more intuitive approach directly linked to the equilibrium assumption: suppose that z_{st} mass units of fuel are extracted from the fuel stream and mixed with $(1 - z_{st})$ mass units of oxidizer extracted from the oxidizer stream (Fig. 3.7). The temperature of this fresh mixture is $z_{st}T_F^0 + (1 - z_{st})T_O^0$. According to Eq. (3.29), the fuel mass fraction in the mixture is $Y_F^0 z_{st}$. Burning this mixture to equilibrium at constant pressure increases its temperature by $QY_F^0 z_{st}/C_p$. The final temperature is $z_{st}T_F^0 + (1 - z_{st})T_O^0 + QY_F^0 z_{st}/C_p$ recovering Eq. (3.35). The same approach may be used to reconstruct the complete temperature field $T(z)$. It can also be extended to multiple reactions as long as they all reach equilibrium. Note, however, that this formalism only holds when all Lewis numbers are unity and a unique mixture fraction z may be defined.

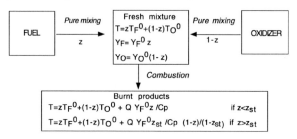

Figure 3.7: Equilibrium assumption to determine the temperature of a diffusion flame for unity Lewis number as a function of mixture fraction z.

3.3.3   Maximum flame temperature in diffusion and premixed flames

It is interesting to compare the maximum temperature reached in a diffusion flame with the adiabatic flame temperature obtained in a premixed flame given by Eq. (2.28). If the fuel and the oxidizer have equal initial temperatures ($T_F^0 = T_O^0 = T_0$), the maximum temperature for the diffusion flame is given by Eq. (3.35):

$$T_{ad}^{diff} = T_0 + \frac{QY_F^0}{C_p}z_{st} \tag{3.36}$$

Consider now the fuel stream and mix it in stoichiometric proportions with oxidizer. Eq. (3.29) shows that the fuel mass fraction in this mixture will be $Y_F^0 z_{st}$. Using Eq. (2.28) shows that the temperature of this stoichiometric premixed flame is:

$$T_{ad}^{prem} = T_0 + \frac{QY_F^0 z_{st}}{C_p} \tag{3.37}$$

which is exactly the temperature obtained for the diffusion flame in Eq. (3.36): the maximum temperature reached in a diffusion flame is the temperature of the stoichiometric premixed flame which can be formed by mixing the fuel stream with oxidizer.

3.3.4 Maximum and mean temperatures in diffusion burners

Consider a burner fed by fuel (stream 1, mass flow rate $\dot{m}_1$, mass fraction Y_F^0) and oxidizer (stream 2, mass flow rate $\dot{m}_2$, mass fraction Y_O^0) as displayed on Fig 3.8. The global equivalence ratio ϕ_g (i.e. the equivalence ratio obtained if all fuel and oxidizer flow rates would mix perfectly) is (see Eq. 1.33 and 1.34):

$$\phi_g = \phi \frac{\dot{m}_1}{\dot{m}_2} \tag{3.38}$$

Inside the burner, the flame is located at the stoichiometric zone $z = z_{st}$ and its maximum temperature is given by Eq. (3.35):

$$\boxed{T_{ad} = z_{st} T_F^0 + (1 - z_{st}) T_O^0 + \frac{Q Y_F^0 z_{st}}{C_p} = \frac{T_F^0 + \phi T_O^0}{1 + \phi} + \frac{Q Y_F^0}{C_p (1 + \phi)}} \tag{3.39}$$

This maximum temperature T_{ad} reached inside the burner does not depend on mass flow rates or on the global equivalence ratio ϕ_g. T_{ad} is only a function of free stream temperatures, T_F^0 and T_O^0, equivalence ratio ϕ and inlet fuel mass fraction Y_F^0.

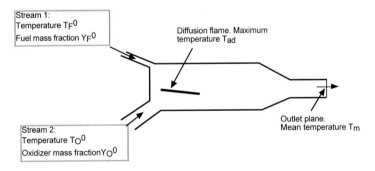

Figure 3.8: Maximum and mean outlet temperatures in a diffusion burner.

The mean temperature T_m reached at the outlet of the combustion chamber after complete combustion corresponds to the temperature obtained once a fuel mass flow rate $\dot{m}_1$ has completely mixed and burnt with an oxidizer flow rate $\dot{m}_2$. The mixture temperature before combustion is:

$$T_m^0 = \frac{\dot{m}_1}{\dot{m}_1 + \dot{m}_2} T_F^0 + \frac{\dot{m}_2}{\dot{m}_1 + \dot{m}_2} T_O^0 = \frac{T_F^0}{1 + \phi/\phi_g} + \frac{T_O^0}{1 + \phi_g/\phi} \tag{3.40}$$

Fuel and oxidizer mass fractions in such a mixture are given by:

$$Y_F = \frac{\dot{m}_1 Y_F^0}{\dot{m}_1 + \dot{m}_2} = \frac{Y_F^0}{1 + \phi/\phi_g} \quad \text{and} \quad Y_O = \frac{\dot{m}_2 Y_O^0}{\dot{m}_1 + \dot{m}_2} = \frac{Y_O^0}{1 + \phi_g/\phi} \tag{3.41}$$

The equivalence ratio of this virtual premixing is $sY_F/Y_O = \phi_g$.

Then, the temperature after complete combustion, T_m, at the burner outlet is:

$$T_m = \frac{T_F^0}{1 + \phi/\phi_g} + \frac{T_O^0}{1 + \phi_g/\phi} + \frac{Q}{C_p} \min\left(\frac{Y_F^0}{1 + \phi/\phi_g}, \frac{Y_O^0}{s(1 + \phi_g/\phi)}\right) \qquad (3.42)$$

$$\text{or} \quad \boxed{T_m = \frac{T_F^0}{1 + \phi/\phi_g} + \frac{T_O^0}{1 + \phi_g/\phi} + \frac{QY_F^0}{C_p\,(\phi + \phi_g)} \min\left(\phi_g, 1\right)} \qquad (3.43)$$

Fig. 3.9 shows the variations of T_{ad} and T_m versus global equivalence ratio ϕ_g for a methane/air diffusion flame. As already pointed out, the maximum temperature T_{ad} does not depend on ϕ_g but the mean temperature T_m varies strongly with ϕ_g. Both temperatures are equal only for for $\phi_g = 1$.[viii] Note that even though the results of Fig. 3.9 provide useful insights into the temperatures reached in diffusion flames, they are not expected to be quantitatively accurate because of the assumptions on chemistry (single-step chemistry) and thermodynamic data (constant C_p).

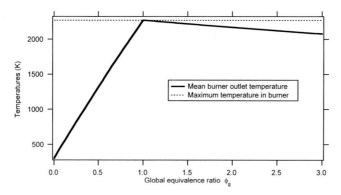

Figure 3.9: Maximum and mean outlet temperatures in a methane/air diffusion burner versus global equivalence ratio ϕ_g. $Y_F^0 = 1$, $Y_O^0 = 0.23$, $T_F^0 = T_O^0 = 300K$. The mass stoichiometric coefficient is $s = 4$, the equivalence ratio $\phi = 17.4$. The heat capacity is $C_p = 1400$ $J/kg/K$ and $Q = 50100$ kJ/kg (ideal single-step reaction).

[viii]This finding has important consequences for pollutant formation. For example, nitric oxide (NO_x) formation is mainly controlled by temperature. Since the maximum temperature of a diffusion burner does not depend on ϕ_g, pollution levels cannot be adjusted easily using $\dot{m}_1$, $\dot{m}_2$ or ϕ_g: independently of these parameters, the diffusion flame always reaches the same maximum temperature T_{ad} and generates high NO_x levels in stoichiometric regions (i.e. in the vicinity of $z = z_{st}$).

3.4   Full solutions for irreversible fast chemistry flames

As soon as an assumption is made for the flame structure, the functions linking the temperature T and species mass fractions Y_k to the mixture fraction z are known: the problem of solving for T and Y_k reduces to computing the mixture fraction field as a function of space and time (problem 1 in Section 3.2.4 and Fig. 3.4). The z balance equation is (Eq. 3.13):

$$\frac{\partial \rho z}{\partial t} + \frac{\partial}{\partial x_i}(\rho u_i z) = \frac{\partial}{\partial x_i}\left(\rho \mathcal{D}\frac{\partial z}{\partial x_i}\right) \tag{3.44}$$

which is a simple diffusion/convection equation but is still coupled to the flame structure in the general case through density (i.e. temperature) and velocity fields. Solving this equation has been the topic of multiple theoretical studies in the past (Linan [397], Linan and Crespo [398], Peters [502]) and this text presents only the simplest cases, generally assuming a constant density, to illustrate the main results.

3.4.1   Unsteady unstrained one-dimensional diffusion flame with infinitely fast chemistry and constant density

A one-dimensional unstrained diffusion flame is now considered (Fig. 3.10). x denotes the direction normal to the flame front. As previously described, flame structure relations (3.32) to (3.33) provide the expected links between species mass fractions, temperature and mixture fraction $z(x)$ (x is the spatial coordinate). Once again, $z(x)$ is still unknown. Moreover, while the flame structure is generic, the diffusion problem depends on the geometrical configuration: initial and boundary conditions determine $z(x,t)$. In a constant pressure flame, density ρ and

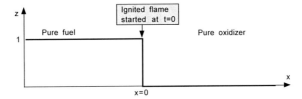

Figure 3.10: Initialization of an unstrained time-dependent diffusion flame.

temperature T are related by $\rho(z) = \rho_1 T_1/T(z)$ where index 1 corresponds to a reference state (usually the fuel stream). Eq. (3.13) is then written:

$$\frac{\partial \rho(z) z}{\partial t} + \frac{\partial}{\partial x}\left(\rho(z) u z\right) = \frac{\partial}{\partial x}\left(\rho(z)\mathcal{D}\frac{\partial z}{\partial x}\right) \tag{3.45}$$

showing that the mixture fraction z field cannot be determined without assumptions on the flame structure $\rho(z)$. In fact, problems 1 (mixing) and 2 (flame structure) are strongly coupled and cannot be solved independently.

Many diffusion flame studies overcome this difficulty assuming constant density flows.[ix] In this situation, mixing and flame structure problems are decoupled and Eq. (3.13) becomes:

$$\frac{\partial z}{\partial t} + \frac{\partial}{\partial x}(uz) = \frac{\partial}{\partial x}\left(\mathcal{D}\frac{\partial z}{\partial x}\right)$$

(3.46)

A diffusion flame in a constant density zero velocity flow is first considered. At time $t = 0$, profiles corresponding to pure fuel for negative x and pure oxidizer for positive x are set (Fig. 3.10). Accordingly, the initial z-field is:

$$z(x, t = 0) = 1 - H(x)$$

(3.47)

where H is the Heaviside function. Boundary conditions are:

$$z(-\infty, t) = 1 \quad ; \quad z(+\infty, t) = 0$$

(3.48)

If the flow is not moving before ignition, it will not at later times because density is constant: velocity can be set to zero. Assuming a constant diffusion coefficient $\mathcal{D}$, the z-balance equation reduces to:[x]

$$\frac{\partial z}{\partial t} = \mathcal{D}\frac{\partial^2 z}{\partial x^2}$$

(3.49)

corresponding to the usual heat diffusion equation. Replacing variables (x, t) by $\eta = x/2\sqrt{\mathcal{D}t}$ leads to:

$$\frac{\partial^2 z}{\partial \eta^2} + 2\eta\frac{\partial z}{\partial \eta} = 0$$

(3.50)

which has the simple solution verifying initial (3.47) and boundary (3.48) conditions:

$$z = \frac{1}{2}\left[1 - \mathrm{erf}(\eta)\right] \quad \text{with} \quad \eta = \frac{x}{2\sqrt{\mathcal{D}t}}$$

(3.51)

The exponential error function is defined as:

$$\mathrm{erf}(\eta) = \frac{2}{\sqrt{\pi}}\int_0^\eta e^{-x^2}\, dx$$

(3.52)

It verifies $\mathrm{erf}(-\infty) = -1$ and $\mathrm{erf}(+\infty) = 1$ and is tabulated in mathematical handbooks or available in scientific computational libraries.

The mixture fraction $z(x, t)$ follows a similarity solution $z(x, t) = z(\eta)$. Like in any diffusion problem in an infinite medium, no natural length scale is associated to this solution. A penetration length may be defined as $\Delta = 2\sqrt{\mathcal{D}t}$: z depends only on x/Δ. The thickness of the unstrained diffusion region increases with time as $\sqrt{\mathcal{D}t}$.

[ix]This assumption is, a priori, very crude. In fact, using the Howarth-Dorodnitzyn transformation, balance equations are formally the same for constant and non constant density flows as shown in Section 3.4.5.

[x]In most combustion studies, $\rho\mathcal{D}$ is assumed to be constant. Combining this assumption with constant density leads to a constant diffusion coefficient $\mathcal{D}$.

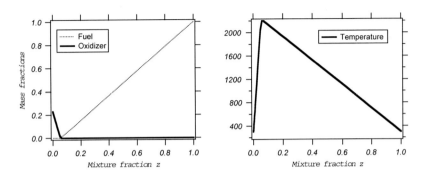

Figure 3.11: Flame structure in the z diagram for a CH_4/air ideal diffusion flame. The inlet air and fuel temperatures are equal to 300 K. The z stoichiometric value is $z_{st} = 0.054$ (Table 3.4).

As an example, Fig. 3.11 displays the flame structure $(T(z), Y_F(z)$ and $Y_O(z))$ for a one-dimensional flame of pure methane and air. For this case, Table 3.4 indicates that $z_{st} = 0.054$. The maximum flame temperature obtained here is 2200 K using a heat of reaction $Q = 50100$ kJ/kg (Table 2.1) and $C_p = 1400$ J/kg/K. Eq. (3.51) provides the evolution of z versus $\eta = x/\Delta$: Fig. 3.12 shows the z profile obtained at a given instant. Since temperature and species mass fractions are directly linked to z through the relations shown in Fig. 3.11, they can also be obtained and are displayed in Fig. 3.12.

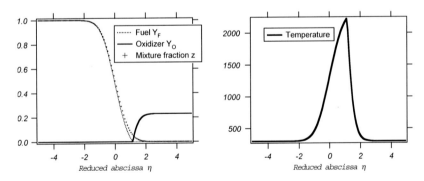

Figure 3.12: Flame structure in the physical space for a CH_4/air ideal diffusion flame. Air is preheated at 600 K, fuel temperature is 300 K. The reduced abscissa is $\eta = x/2\sqrt{\mathcal{D}t}$.

The flame position x_f is given at each instant:

$$\eta_f = \frac{x_f}{2\sqrt{\mathcal{D}t}} = \mathrm{erf}^{-1}(1 - 2z_{st}) = \mathrm{erf}^{-1}\left(\frac{\phi - 1}{\phi + 1}\right) \tag{3.53}$$

For this flame, $\eta_f = 1.14$ and the flame position in physical space is given by $x_f = 2.28\sqrt{\mathcal{D}t}$. Even though the flame is slightly moving, the corresponding velocity dx_f/dt is always small compared to a premixed flame speed.[xi]

The fuel reaction rate per unit flame area, $\dot{\Omega}_F$, may be expressed integrating Eq. (3.7) between x_f^- and x_f^+ where x_f^- and x_f^+ are two points located on both sides of the flame front, infinitely close to it (see Fig. 3.13):[xii]

$$\dot{\Omega}_F = \int_{x_f^-}^{x_f^+} \dot{\omega}_F dx = -\left[\rho D \frac{\partial Y_F}{\partial x}\right]_{x_f^-}^{x_f^+} = \left[\rho D \frac{\partial Y_F}{\partial x}\right]_{x=x_f^-} = \left[\rho D \frac{\partial Y_F}{\partial z}\right]_{x=x_f^-}\left[\frac{\partial z}{\partial x}\right]_{x=x_f^-} \tag{3.54}$$

$$\text{or} \quad \boxed{\dot{\Omega}_F = \rho D \frac{Y_F^0}{1 - z_{st}}\left[\frac{\partial z}{\partial x}\right]_{x=x_f^-} = -\rho \frac{Y_F^0}{2(1 - z_{st})}\sqrt{\frac{D}{\pi t}}e^{-\eta_f^2}} \tag{3.55}$$

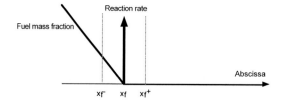

Figure 3.13: Estimation of the reaction rate for a diffusion flame with infinitely fast chemistry.

This reaction rate goes to zero like $1/\sqrt{t}$: the diffusion of reactants towards the reaction zone (and the combustion rate) is slowed down because of the accumulation of products near the flame front. As time goes by, an unstrained diffusion flame gets choked in its own products. The only solution to keep a diffusion flame burning and also to build a steady canonical problem for combustion studies is to strain the flame as done in the next section, by pushing the reactants against each other.

[xi]More generally, the flame is moving towards the deficient reactant: fuel for $\phi < 1$ and oxidizer for $\phi > 1$. It stays at $x_f = 0$ for stoichiometric conditions ($\phi = 1$).

[xii]The integrated reaction rate is finite even though chemistry is infinitely fast. In this situation, the combustion rate is not limited by chemical processes in the flame zone but by molecular diffusion rates of the fuel and oxidizer towards the reaction zone, according to:

$$\dot{\Omega}_F = \left[\rho D \frac{\partial Y_F}{\partial x}\right]_{x=x_f^-} = -s\left[\rho D \frac{\partial Y_O}{\partial x}\right]_{x=x_f^+}$$

3.4.2 Steady strained one-dimensional diffusion flame with infinitely fast chemistry and constant density

The steady strained diffusion flame is the main prototype flame for diffusion regimes (Fig. 3.14). It can be created in an experiment by sending a stream containing fuel against a stream containing oxidizer (Fig. 3.14). For such a flame, all previous results providing the flame structure in the z diagram remain valid but the mixing problem is different. The flame is steady because the flow is strained: the mixture fraction z depends on x only (no time dependance). Assuming constant density, the imposed velocity field corresponds to:

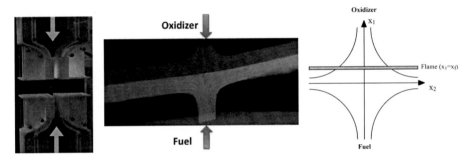

Figure 3.14: Steady strained one-dimensional diffusion flame. Left: laboratory set-up. Middle: flow visualization. Right: axis and 1D model. Figures of EM2C laboratory (ECP).

$$u_1 = -ax_1 \quad \text{and} \quad u_2 = ax_2 \tag{3.56}$$

which satisfies the continuity equation. The $x_1 = 0$ plane is a stagnation plane and a is the strain rate (s^{-1}), assumed to be constant.[xiii]

The z balance equation in such a flame is:

$$\frac{\partial \rho z}{\partial t} + \frac{\partial}{\partial x_1}(\rho u_1 z) + \frac{\partial}{\partial x_2}(\rho u_2 z) = \frac{\partial}{\partial x_1}\left(\rho D \frac{\partial z}{\partial x_1}\right) + \frac{\partial}{\partial x_2}\left(\rho D \frac{\partial z}{\partial x_2}\right) \tag{3.57}$$

Even though the z-field is one-dimensional, the term $\partial(\rho u_2 z)/\partial x_2$ must be retained because u_2 depends on x_2. Using the continuity equation, the z equation may be rewritten under a non-conservative form:

$$\rho \frac{\partial z}{\partial t} + \rho u_1 \frac{\partial z}{\partial x_1} + \rho u_2 \frac{\partial z}{\partial x_2} = \frac{\partial}{\partial x_1}\left(\rho D \frac{\partial z}{\partial x_1}\right) + \frac{\partial}{\partial x_2}\left(\rho D \frac{\partial z}{\partial x_2}\right) \tag{3.58}$$

[xiii]In a real burner, the stagnation point flow configuration is achieved by placing fuel and oxidizer jets face to face. The strain rate at the flame is not known a priori in such cases because the velocity field needs to be measured and strain is not constant along the flame normal, leading to some difficulties in the definition of strain. However, the order of magnitude of the flame strain is easy to estimate from the velocities of the jets U_1 and U_2 and the distance between the jets H: $a = (|U_1| + |U_2|)/H$.

On the axis normal to a steady strained flame, assuming constant density and diffusion coefficient, this z equation then reduces to:

$$- ax_1 \frac{\partial z}{\partial x_1} = D \frac{\partial^2 z}{\partial x_1^2} \tag{3.59}$$

Replacing x_1 by $\zeta = x_1 \sqrt{a/2D}$ gives:

$$\frac{\partial^2 z}{\partial \zeta^2} + 2\zeta \frac{\partial z}{\partial \zeta} = 0 \tag{3.60}$$

which is Eq. (3.50), with identical boundary conditions (Eq. 3.48): $z(+\infty) = 0$ and $z(-\infty) = 1$. The solution is then:

$$\boxed{z = \frac{1}{2}\left[1 - \mathrm{erf}(\zeta)\right] \qquad \text{with} \qquad \zeta = x_1 \sqrt{\frac{a}{2D}}} \tag{3.61}$$

Comparing expressions for ζ (steady strained flame) and η (unsteady unstrained flame):

$$\zeta = x_1 \sqrt{\frac{a}{2D}} \quad \text{and} \quad \eta = \frac{x_1}{2\sqrt{Dt}} \tag{3.62}$$

shows that the strain rate a and the inverse of time $1/2t$ play similar roles. An unsteady unstrained flame at time t has exactly the same spatial structure as a steady strained flame with a strain $a = 1/2t$. All solutions derived for the unsteady unstrained flame can be simply extended to the steady strained flame by replacing t by $1/2a$ in the previous expressions. For example, the integrated fuel reaction rate along the flame normal $\dot{\Omega}_F$ is:

$$\dot{\Omega}_F = \int_{x_{1f}^-}^{x_{1f}^+} \dot{\omega}_F \, dx_1 = -\left[\rho D \frac{\partial Y_F}{\partial x_1}\right]_{x_{1f}^-}^{x_{1f}^+} = \rho D \left[\frac{\partial Y_F}{\partial x_1}\right]_{x_1 = x_{1f}^-} \tag{3.63}$$

$$\text{or} \qquad \boxed{\dot{\Omega}_F = -\rho \frac{Y_F^0}{1 - z_{st}} \sqrt{\frac{aD}{2\pi}} e^{-\zeta_f^2}} \tag{3.64}$$

where ζ_f corresponds to the flame location and is given by:

$$\zeta_f = x_{1f} \sqrt{\frac{a}{2D}} = \mathrm{erf}^{-1}(1 - 2z_f) = \mathrm{erf}^{-1}\left(\frac{\phi - 1}{\phi + 1}\right) \tag{3.65}$$

For $\phi < 1$, or $z_{st} > 0.5$ the flame is located on the fuel side ($x_{1f} < 0$) of the stagnation plane $x_1 = 0$. For $\phi > 1$ ($z_{st} < 0.5$), $x_{1f} > 0$ and the flame is located on the oxidizer side of the stagnation plane. The flame front is always located on the deficient reactant side and lies on the stagnation plane only when $\phi = 1$ ($z_{st} = 0.5$), i.e. when reactants are in stoichiometric proportions.

As shown in Section 3.2.2, the scalar dissipation rate of the mixture fraction, χ, is a key quantity in diffusion flame descriptions. For a one-dimensional strained flame with constant density,[xiv] the scalar dissipation rate χ is given, from Eq. (3.61), by:

$$\chi = 2\mathcal{D} \left(\frac{\partial z}{\partial x_1} \right)^2 = \frac{a}{\pi} \exp \left(-\frac{a}{\mathcal{D}} x_1^2 \right) \tag{3.66}$$

depends on the location x_1 and is maximum on the stagnation plane ($x_1 = 0$). Combining Eq. (3.61) and (3.66) leads to:

$$\chi = \frac{a}{\pi} \exp \left(-2 \left[\mathrm{erf}^{-1} (1 - 2z) \right]^2 \right) = \chi_0 \exp \left(-2 \left[\mathrm{erf}^{-1} (1 - 2z) \right]^2 \right) = \chi_0 F(z) \tag{3.67}$$

where χ_0 is the maximum value of the scalar dissipation rate in the steady strained flame, corresponding to the stagnation plane ($x_1 = 0$). For infinitely fast irreversible chemical reaction, its value on the flame front is:

$$\chi_f = \frac{a}{\pi} \exp \left[-2 \left(\mathrm{erf}^{-1} \left(\frac{\phi - 1}{\phi + 1} \right) \right)^2 \right] \tag{3.68}$$

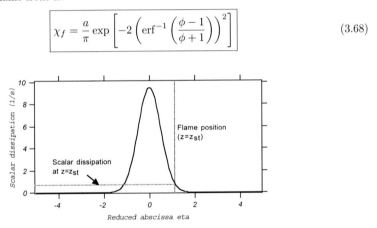

Figure 3.15: Scalar dissipation rate versus reduced abscissa η in a constant density methane/air flame (strain rate $a = 30\,s^{-1}$).

For example, Fig. 3.15 shows the profile of scalar dissipation rate χ corresponding to the constant density flame example displayed on Fig. 3.12. Assuming a typical value $\mathcal{D} = 1.5 \, 10^{-5} \, m^2/s$ and an equivalent strain rate of $30 \, s^{-1}$, maximum values of the scalar dissipation rate are of the order of $10 \, s^{-1}$. The stoichiometric value of scalar dissipation rate is obtained using Eq. (3.68) and is much lower: $\chi_{st} = 0.9 \, s^{-1}$.

[xiv]This expression for the scalar dissipation rate χ does not require an infinitely fast chemistry assumption and comes from Eq. (3.60) and boundary conditions $z(+\infty) = 0$ and $z(-\infty) = 1$.

Relations (3.66) and (3.68) show that scalar dissipation rate and strain rate are closely related. In a steady one-dimensional strained flame, the strain rate a is constant whereas the scalar dissipation rate χ depends on the spatial location x. On the other hand, strain rates are only linked to flow field characteristics (local velocity gradients) whereas scalar dissipation rates measure mixing properties (in fact, mixture fraction gradients), incorporate mass fraction values through z and are able to handle partially premixed situations (the equivalence ratio ϕ is found in Eq. 3.68).

3.4.3   Unsteady strained one-dimensional diffusion flame with infinitely fast chemistry and constant density

In the previous section, the structure of a steady stained one-dimensional flame with infinitely fast chemistry, assuming constant density, has been described. The extension of this study to transient phenomena is interesting. Starting from a steady strained one-dimensional diffusion flame (strain rate a_0), the strain rate is supposed to be instantaneously set to a new value a at time $t = 0$. The z-balance equation (3.59) is replaced by:

$$\frac{\partial z}{\partial t} - a x_1 \frac{\partial z}{\partial x_1} = \mathcal{D} \frac{\partial^2 z}{\partial x_1^2} \tag{3.69}$$

with the same boundary conditions: $z(-\infty, t) = 1$ (pure fuel) and $z(+\infty, t) = 0$ (pure oxidizer). As a steady solution is expected for negative times (strain rate a_0) and for infinite positive times (strain rate a), the unsteady solution is searched as:

$$\boxed{z = \frac{1}{2} \left[1 - \operatorname{erf} \left(\sqrt{\frac{a}{2\mathcal{D}}} f(t) x_1 \right) \right]} \tag{3.70}$$

with:

$$f(t \leq 0) = \sqrt{\frac{a_0}{a}} \quad ; \quad f(t = +\infty) = 1 \tag{3.71}$$

Substituting Eq. (3.70) into Eq. (3.69) leads to:

$$\frac{\partial f}{\partial t} - a f + a f^3 = 0 \tag{3.72}$$

which has an explicit solution:

$$f(t) = \sqrt{\frac{a_0 e^{2at}}{a + a_0 \left(e^{2at} - 1 \right)}} \tag{3.73}$$

Accordingly, the flame response time to a strain rate change is of the order of $1/a$ and may be non negligible, despite of the infinitely fast chemistry assumption (this time corresponds to a diffusion time, controlling the flame response). For example, for typical strain rates between 10 s^{-1} and 1000 s^{-1}, this response time lies between 1 and 100 ms, corresponding to a downstream distance of 0.01 to 1 m in a 10 m/s flow. These unsteady effects are easy to identify using Eq. (3.70): the unsteady flame submitted to a strain $a(t)$ has the same structure at time t as a steady flame submitted to a strain $a^{eq} = a(t)f(t)^2$. Knowing a^{eq} completely determines the flame structure. This "equivalent" strain rate a^{eq} is, using Eq. (3.73):

$$a^{eq} = af^2(t) = a\frac{a_0 e^{2at}}{a + a_0\left(e^{2at} - 1\right)} \tag{3.74}$$

As an example, Fig. 3.16 shows the equivalent strain rate controlling a diffusion flame submitted to a step function of strain from a_0 to $10a_0$.

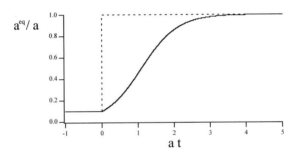

Figure 3.16: Response of a one-dimensional laminar diffusion flame to an instantaneous change of the strain rate. At time $t = 0$, the strain rate induced by the flow (----) field suddenly increases from a_0 to a (here $a/a_0 = 10$.). The equivalent strain rate a^{eq} (Eq. 3.74) is plotted as a function of the reduced time $a\,t$ (———).

This flame response time to strain rate changes has various consequences:

- A laminar diffusion flame is able to sustain high strain rates (higher than the extinction strain rate determined in steady flames, see § 3.5.2) if it is not submitted to these during too long times (typically of the order of $1/a$).

- A diffusion flame acts as a low pass filter and cannot react to high frequencies (typically higher than a) perturbations (Darabiha [163]).

- The equivalent strain rate notion is interesting because an unsteady strained flame may be described as a steady strained one. This is a way to introduce unsteady effects in flamelet models (see Chapt. 6) for turbulent combustion (Haworth et al. [278]).

The previous results are summarized in Table 3.5. A second unsteady strained flame solution (Cuenot and Poinsot [159]) has been added where a step function for z is used at initial time $t = 0$ (i.e. $z(x, t = 0) = 1 - H(x)$ where H is the Heaviside function). This situation is the limiting case $a_0 = +\infty$ of the previous unsteady case.

Physical parameters

Stoichiometric ratio s	$s = (\nu_O W_O)/(\nu_F W_F)$
Equivalence ratio ϕ	$\phi = s Y_F^0/Y_O^0$
Stoichiometric mixture fraction z_{st}	$z_{st} = \dfrac{1}{1 + s Y_F^0/Y_O^0} = \dfrac{1}{\phi + 1}$
Adiabatic flame temperature T_{ad}	$T_{ad} = z_{st} T_F^0 + (1 - z_{st}) T_O^0 + Q Y_F^0 z_{st}/C_p$

Solution of mixing problem $z(x)$

Mixture fraction $z(x)$	$\dfrac{1}{2}\left[1 - \text{erf}\left(x\sqrt{\kappa/(2D)}\right)\right]$
Scalar dissipation rate χ	$\kappa/\pi \exp\left(-\kappa x^2/D\right)$
Integrated reaction rate $\dot\Omega_F$	$\dfrac{\rho Y_F^0}{1 - z_{st}}\sqrt{\dfrac{D\kappa}{2\pi}}\, e^{-\left(\text{erf}^{-1}\left(\frac{\phi-1}{\phi+1}\right)\right)^2}$

Description of flame structure (z diagram)

	Fuel side	Oxidizer side
$Y_F(z)$	$Y_F^0(z - z_{st})/(1 - z_{st})$	0.
$Y_O(z)$	0.	$Y_O^0(1 - z/z_{st})$
$T(z)$	$z T_F^0 + (1 - z)T_O^0 + \dfrac{Q Y_F^0}{C_p}\dfrac{(1 - z)z_{st}}{1 - z_{st}}$	$z T_F^0 + (1 - z)T_O^0 + \dfrac{Q Y_F^0 z}{C_p}$

Equivalent strain rate κ

Unsteady unstrained flame (§ 3.4.1)	$1/2t$
Steady strained flame (§ 3.4.2)	a
Unsteady strained flame (1) (§ 3.4.3)	$a/(1 - e^{-2at})$
Unsteady strained flame (2) (§ 3.4.3)	$\dfrac{a_0 e^{2at}}{a + a_0(e^{2at} - 1)}$

Table 3.5: Summary of main analytical results for one-dimensional diffusion flames with constant density (Cuenot and Poinsot [159]). The unsteady unstrained flame and the unsteady strained flame (1) start at time $t = 0$ with an Heaviside function ($z(x, t = 0) = 1 - H(x)$). The initial solution for the unsteady strained flame (2) corresponds to a steady strained flame (strain rate a_0). At time $t = 0$, the strain rate is suddenly set to a. Solutions are expressed in terms of an equivalent strain rate κ.

3.4.4 Jet flame in an uniform flow field

Another simple example of diffusion flame is the steady two-dimensional jet flame (Fig. 3.17).

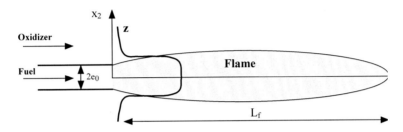

Figure 3.17: Jet diffusion flame. A plane fuel jet (height $2e_0$) is injected with an oxidizer coflow.

A plane fuel jet (fuel mass fraction Y_F^0, density ρ_F^0 and inlet velocity u_F^0) is injected into an oxidizer coflow (oxidizer mass fraction Y_O^0, density ρ_O^0 and inlet velocity u_O^0). The flow is assumed to be uniform and one-dimensional to lead to a simple analytical solution:

- constant inlet mass flow rate: $\rho_F^0 u_F^0 = \rho_O^0 u_O^0 = constant$.

- one-dimensional flow: $u_2 = u_3 = 0$.[xv]

- $\rho \mathcal{D}$ is assumed to be constant ($\rho \mathcal{D} = \rho_F^0 \mathcal{D}_{\mathcal{F}} = \rho_O^0 \mathcal{D}_O$).

Under these assumptions, the continuity equation (1.36) reduces to:

$$\frac{\partial (\rho u_1)}{\partial x_1} = 0 \Longrightarrow \rho u_1 = \rho_F^0 u_F^0 = \rho_O^0 u_O^0 = constant \qquad (3.75)$$

The z-balance equation (3.44) becomes similar to the usual heat diffusion balance equation:

$$\rho_F^0 u_F^0 \frac{\partial z}{\partial x_1} = \rho_F^0 \mathcal{D}_{\mathcal{F}} \frac{\partial^2 z}{\partial x_2^2} \qquad (3.76)$$

with the boundary conditions:

- $x_1 = 0$
  - For $x_2 < -e_0$ or $x_2 > e_0$, $z = 0$.
  - For $-e_0 < x_2 < e_0$, $z = 1$.
- $\lim_{x_2 \to +\infty}(z) = \lim_{x_2 \to -\infty}(z) = 0$.

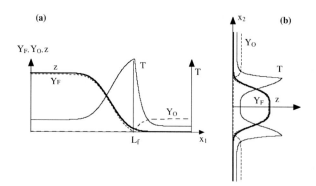

Figure 3.18: Mixture fraction (z), fuel (Y_F) and oxidizer (Y_O) mass fractions and temperature (T) in a planar jet diffusion flame (Fig. 3.17). Chemical parameters (Y_F^0, Y_O^0, ϕ, z_{st},...) correspond to a pure methane/air flame (Table 3.4).

The solution of Eq. (3.76) leads to a mixture fraction field given by:[xvi]

$$z\left(x_1, x_2\right) = \frac{1}{2\sqrt{\pi \alpha x_1}} \int_{-e_0}^{+e_0} \exp\left(-\frac{(x_2 - y')^2}{4\alpha x_1}\right) dy' \qquad (3.77)$$

where $\alpha = \mathcal{D}_F/u_F^0$. For large values of the downstream location x_1 compared to the initial jet diameter $2e_0$, Eq. (3.77) reduces to:

$$z\left(x_1, x_2\right) \approx \frac{e_0}{\sqrt{\pi \alpha x_1}} \exp\left(-\frac{x_2^2}{4\alpha x_1}\right) \qquad (3.78)$$

Having $z(x_1, x_2)$, the flame structure is fully determined as fuel and oxidizer mass fractions and temperature are functions of the mixture fraction z (Eq. 3.32 to 3.33). Profiles along the jet axis x_1 are displayed on Fig. 3.18a. Transverse profiles along x_2 are given on Fig. 3.18b. The flame length L_f may be defined as $z(x_1 = L_f, x_2 = 0) = z_{st}$. From Eq. (3.78):

$$L_f = \frac{e_0^2 u_F^0}{\pi \mathcal{D}_F} (\phi + 1)^2 = \frac{e_0}{\pi} R_e (\phi + 1)^2 \qquad (3.79)$$

where $R_e = e_0 u_F^0 / \mathcal{D}_F$ is the fuel jet Reynolds number. The flame length increases linearly with the fuel jet velocity u_F^0 and the fuel jet Reynolds number R_e.[xvii]

[xv]This assumption, initially introduced by Burke and Schumann [98], is not true. A boundary layer assumption ($u_2 \ll u_1$, keeping only transverse gradient of the axial velocity $\partial u_1/\partial x_2$), would be more adapted. Nevertheless, results do not strongly differ and the proposed assumption leads to a simple analytical solution.

[xvi]Considering round coaxial jets instead of planar jets leads to Bessel functions.

[xvii]This result is true as long as the flow remains laminar (see Chapt. 4): for large values of the Reynolds

3.4.5 Extensions to variable density

The previous results have been derived assuming constant density. This assumption is not as crucial in diffusion flames as in premixed flames but may be relaxed using the Howarth-Dorodnitzyn transformation (see Linan and Crespo [398], Williams [710] or Cuenot and Poinsot [159] for mathematical details). In this transformation, the spatial variable x is replaced by a "mass-weighted coordinate" X defined as:

$$X = \frac{1}{\rho_0} \int_{x_0}^{x} \rho(x', t)\, dx' \tag{3.80}$$

where x_0, corresponding to density ρ_0, is a reference location and could be the stagnation plane ($x_0 = 0$) or the flame front ($x_0 = x_f$). The Howarth-Dorodnitzyn approximation may be used with unsteady balance equations under classical boundary layer approximation Williams [710] but is simply illustrated here, as an example, for steady one-dimensional strain flame. The velocity field is now given by the balance continuity equation:

$$\frac{\partial \rho u}{\partial x} = -\frac{\partial \rho v}{\partial y} = -\rho a \tag{3.81}$$

The mixture fraction balance equation reduces to:

$$\rho u \frac{\partial z}{\partial x} = \frac{\partial}{\partial x}\left(\rho \mathcal{D} \frac{\partial z}{\partial x}\right) \tag{3.82}$$

Replacing x by X (Eq. 3.80) leads to:

$$\frac{\partial}{\partial x} = \frac{\partial X}{\partial x}\frac{\partial}{\partial X} = \frac{\rho}{\rho_0}\frac{\partial}{\partial X} \tag{3.83}$$

The continuity equation (3.81) becomes:

$$\frac{\partial \rho u}{\partial X} = -\rho_0 a \quad \Longrightarrow \quad \rho u = -\rho_0 a X \tag{3.84}$$

assuming that $X = 0$ ($x_0 = 0$) corresponds to the stagnation plane. The mixture fraction balance equation (3.82) is then rewritten:

$$-\rho_0 a X \frac{\rho}{\rho_0}\frac{\partial z}{\partial X} = \frac{\rho}{\rho_0}\frac{\partial}{\partial X}\left(\frac{\rho}{\rho_0}\rho \mathcal{D} \frac{\partial z}{\partial X}\right) \tag{3.85}$$

leading to, if $\rho^2 \mathcal{D} = \rho_0^2 \mathcal{D}_0$ is supposed to be constant:[xviii]

$$-a X \frac{\partial z}{\partial X} = \mathcal{D}_0 \frac{\partial^2 z}{\partial X^2} \tag{3.86}$$

---

number, a transition towards turbulent flows is expected.

[xviii]This assumption $\rho^2 \mathcal{D} = constant$ is usual in analytical derivations for diffusion flames.

which is exactly Eq. (3.59) with the same boundary conditions $z(-\infty) = 1$ and $z(+\infty) = 0$. The solution can be obtained from Table 3.5, replacing x by X and defining η by (see, for example, Cuenot and Poinsot [159]):

$$\eta = \sqrt{\frac{\kappa}{\mathcal{D}_0}} X \qquad (3.87)$$

The Howarth-Dorodnitzyn transformation is a useful tool for analytical derivations and allows flame numerical simulations using a constant density code. Unfortunately, to come back to physical space, replacing the "mass-weighted coordinate" X by the actual spatial coordinate x involves inverting Eq. (3.80) and is generally not obvious without additional assumptions.

3.5   Extensions of theory to other flame structures

The irreversible infinitely fast chemistry assumption allows derivations of diffusion flame basic properties but has to be relaxed to address more realistic cases.

3.5.1   Reversible equilibrium chemistry

When chemical reactions controlling a diffusion flame are not irreversible, fuel, oxidizer and products may coexist at the same location, leading to a more complex flame structure. Even though chemistry may proceed infinitely fast, the flame structure differs from the one observed for irreversible infinitely fast chemistry: at each point in the z diagram, fuel, oxidizer and products mass fractions must satisfy the equilibrium condition (3.27). An example of corresponding flame structure is displayed on Fig. 3.19. This structure does not depend on any flow characteristic time since chemistry is assumed to be infinitely fast and scalar dissipation χ is zero.

3.5.2   Finite rate chemistry

All results presented in Sections 3.3 and 3.4 assume an infinitely fast chemistry, compared to all other time scales. When this assumption is no longer valid, the flame structure becomes more complex and is expected to depend on flow times. Flow effects on diffusion flame structure are generally quantified using the Damköhler number:

$$\boxed{D_a^{fl} = \frac{\tau_f}{\tau_c}} \qquad (3.88)$$

where τ_f and τ_c are respectively flow and chemical time scales. Defining this flow time scale τ_f is a first difficulty. For an unsteady unstrained flame (Fig. 3.2a), there is no flow-imposed reference time and the proper time τ_f is the age of the flame so that the Damköhler number increases with time. For a strained flame (Fig. 3.2b), a possible time scale is the inverse of

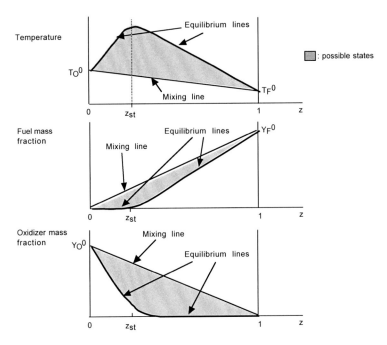

Figure 3.19: Diffusion flame structure in z diagram for reversible infinitely fast chemistry (equilibrium).

flame strain $1/a$ so that the Damköhler number is constant as long as strain is constant. For the moment, only steady strained flames are considered.

For infinitely fast chemistry, the chemical time τ_c is small compared to the flow time scale τ_f and the Damköhler number is infinite. When D_a^{fl} takes finite values, finite rate chemistry becomes important and must be taken into account. In practice, chemistry effects are only important in the zone where reaction takes place and, like for premixed flames, this zone usually remains small (see Fig. 3.1). Outside this region, combustion is zero and all concepts developed for infinitely fast chemistry apply. For example, the z-diagram is only affected in the vicinity of the flame front i.e. for z of the order of z_{st}. Fig. 3.20 shows the evolution of z diagrams when chemistry gets slower. Fuel and oxidizer now exist together in the reaction zone. The maximum temperature is lower than the temperature found for infinitely fast chemistry. But outside the reaction zone, the flame structure is identical.

Describing the details of the analyses required to construct solutions for strained diffusion flames with finite rate chemistry is beyond the scope of this text. Multiple results of these anal-

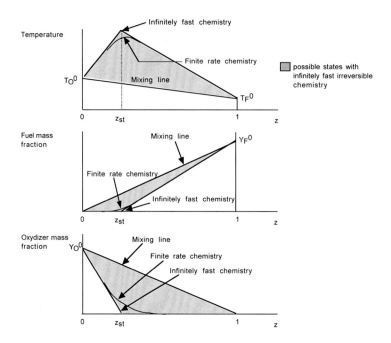

Figure 3.20: Evolution of z diagrams when chemistry changes from infinitely fast to finite rate chemistry (irreversible reaction).

yses, however, are required to understand these flames and perform numerical computations of their structure. These results are now briefly summarized.

As evidenced by Eq. (3.21) and (3.26), and also confirmed by asymptotic analysis, the scalar dissipation rate χ is a key quantity in diffusion flame studies. The scalar dissipation rate measures mixture fraction gradients, is directly related to the strain rate (see Eq. 3.66)[xix] and appears as a relevant quantity to define a flow time scale τ_f entering the Damköhler number definition: this mixing time scale may be estimated as the inverse of the scalar dissipation at the stoichiometric point: $\tau_f \approx 1/\chi_{st}$.

Various definitions may be found in the literature for the Damköhler number D_a^{fl}: asymptotic analysis (Linan [397], Cuenot and Poinsot [159], Vervisch and Poinsot [670]) provides its

---

[xix]Eq. (3.66) holds for steady one-dimensional constant density strained diffusion flames and does not require an infinitely fast chemistry assumption.

most relevant form. When the fuel reaction rate is written (see Eq. (1.24) and (1.25)):

$$\dot{\omega}_F = \nu_F W_F A \left(Y_F \frac{\rho}{W_F} \right)^{\nu_F} \left(Y_O \frac{\rho}{W_O} \right)^{\nu_O} e^{-\frac{T_a}{T}} \tag{3.89}$$

the Damköhler number should be:

$$
\begin{aligned}
D_a^{fl} = \quad & 32 \frac{\nu_F A}{\chi_{st}} \rho_f^{\nu_O + \nu_F - 1} \phi^{\nu_O} (1 - z_{st})^2 \left(\frac{Y_F^0}{W_F} \right)^{\nu_F - 1} \left(\frac{Y_O^0}{W_O} \right)^{\nu_O} \cdot \\
& \left(\frac{T_{ad}^2 / T_a}{Q Y_F^0 / C_p} \right)^{\nu_O + \nu_F + 1} e^{-\frac{T_a}{T_{ad}}}
\end{aligned}
\tag{3.90}
$$

where Y_F^0 and Y_O^0 are the fuel and oxidizer mass fractions in the fuel and oxidizer streams respectively, ρ_f is the density at the stoichiometric point, ϕ the equivalence ratio and χ_{st} the scalar dissipation at the stoichiometric point: $\chi_{st} = 2(\lambda_f / \rho_f C_p) |\nabla z|_f^2$ (this result is obtained assuming that $\rho\lambda = \rho_f \lambda_f$ is constant). T_{ad} is the adiabatic flame temperature given by Eq. (3.35).

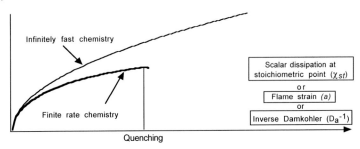

Figure 3.21: Integrated reaction rate $\dot{\Omega}_F$ as a function of strain rate a, stoichiometric scalar dissipation rate χ_{st} or inverse of the Damköhler number D_a^{fl} for infinitely fast and finite rate chemistry.

The evolution of stagnation point flames with Damköhler number changes has been studied in terms of maximum temperature and integrated reaction rate $\dot{\Omega}_F$ using asymptotic methods (Linan [397], Clavin and Li nán [140], Williams [710]). Fig. 3.21 shows how the integrated reaction rate depends on scalar dissipation (or on strain or on the inverse of the Damköhler number): increasing strain rate on diffusion flames first promotes combustion because the straining velocity field brings more fuel and oxidizer to the reaction zone. This evolution is also predicted for infinitely fast chemistry (see Table 3.5 or Eq. 3.64), showing that the magnitude of $\dot{\Omega}_F$ increases like the square root of the strain rate. But, for sufficiently large strain rates, chemistry becomes a limiting factor: chemical reactions have more difficulty keeping up with the rate at which fuel and oxidizer enter the reaction zone. Eventually, chemistry becomes too slow to burn the incoming reactants and quenching occurs for a value of the Damköhler number (provided by asymptotic theory) $D_a^{fl,q}$. For unity Lewis number and if one of the two streams is preheated, the quenching Damköhler is (Cuenot and Poinsot [159]):

$$D_a^{fl,q} = (1.359m)\frac{2}{\nu_O!}\left[1 - \frac{m}{2}(1 + \nu_O)\right] \tag{3.91}$$

where

$$m = 2(1 - z_{st})\left(1 - \frac{T_O^0 - T_F^0}{QY_F^0/C_p}\right) - 2 \tag{3.92}$$

A more general scaling is proposed by Peters [502] for the quenching scalar dissipation χ_{st}^q:

$$\chi_{st}^q = \frac{z_{st}^2(1 - z_{st})^2}{\tau_c^p} \tag{3.93}$$

where τ_c^p is simply the flame time corresponding to a premixed stoichiometric flame: $\tau_c^p = \delta/s_L^0 = \mathcal{D}/(s_L^0)^2$. This scaling illustrates the link between premixed and diffusion flame parameters: if the stoichiometric speed of the premixed flame is large, the quenching scalar dissipation of the diffusion flame is also large.

3.5.3   Summary of flame structures

Table 3.6 summarizes flame structures as a function of assumptions used for reversibility and equilibrium. On the left side, infinitely fast chemistry (equilibrium) assumptions lead to structures independent on the strain rate applied to the flame. On the right side, finite rate chemistry effects (non equilibrium) increase with strain rate (i.e. when the Damköhler number decreases). For very low strain rates values, the infinitely fast structure is recovered. Note that a reversible equilibrium flame produces a structure similar to finite rate chemistry flames at fixed strain.

3.5.4   Extensions to variable Lewis numbers

The previous analysis assumed that all Lewis numbers were equal to unity to introduce mixture fraction concepts. This assumption may also be relaxed. For every species having a non-unity Lewis number, a new passive scalar must be introduced but the mathematics can be worked out. Examples of such studies are given in Seshadri and Peters [610], Seshadri et al. [611], Cuenot and Poinsot [159], Seshadri [609] or Pitsch and Peters [513].

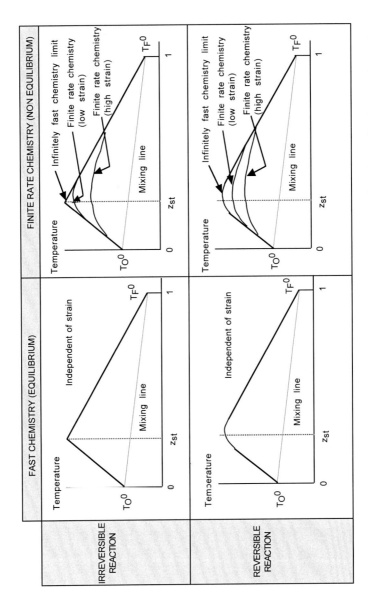

Table 3.6: Summary of diffusion flame structures plotted for temperature versus the mixture fraction z, using various assumptions on reversibility and chemistry speed.

3.6 Real laminar diffusion flames

3.6.1 One-dimensional codes for laminar diffusion flames

Even though the analysis derived in the previous section is useful to understand diffusion flame, the corresponding derivations are usually not exact for real flames for various reasons:

- Multiple chemical species, including radicals and multiple reactions have to be taken into account. Fuel does not react with oxygen simply through a single reaction $F + O \rightarrow P$. Some of these reactions may be reversible.

- Species molecular diffusion coefficients are generally not equal. Species like H_2 or H diffuse much faster than heavy molecules.

- Heat $(\lambda/(\rho C_p))$ and species (D_k) diffusivities differ so that the analogy needed between heat and species in the ideal flame theory is never satisfied.

These phenomena make analytical solutions difficult to derive. However, numerical solutions which do not require simplifications can still be performed and full computations of one-dimensional diffusion flames are performed easily today (Darabiha and Candel [164], Barlow and Chen [30], Pitsch and Peters [513]), as done for premixed flames in Section 2.3.: solvers for one-dimensional diffusion flames are available in CHEMKIN *www.reactiondesign.com*, COSILAB *www.rotexo.com/cms*) or CANTERA *code.google.com/p/cantera*. For example, Fig. 3.22 displays temperature and species mass fraction profiles in a H_2 - O_2 diffusion flame computed with CHEMKIN at atmospheric pressure (Vermorel [668]). The hydrogen stream temperature is 300 K and the oxygen is heated to 750 K. The strain rate is 300 s^{-1}.

3.6.2 Mixture fractions in real flames

Two mechanisms limit the usefulness of a mixture fraction defined by Eq. (3.10): (1) fuel and oxidizer do not react through a single reaction and multiple dissociations take place and (2) all species as well as temperature in real flames have different diffusivities, leading to differential diffusion effects. As a consequence, the Z_i's defined from fuel and oxidizer mass fractions and temperature in Eq. (3.10) are not passive scalars. The question is then : can a true mixture fraction be defined in a real flame ? This section tries to address this question by discussing the effects of Mechanism I (dissociations) and Mechanism 2 (differential diffusion) in real flames.

The effects of dissociations (Mechanism 1) can be avoided by constructing a mixture fraction from atomic elements (and not from species) as described below. Consider the generic case of N species reacting through M chemical reactions where the jth reaction is written:

$$\sum_{k=1}^{N} \nu'_{kj} \mathcal{M}_k \rightleftharpoons \sum_{k=1}^{N} \nu''_{kj} \mathcal{M}_k \quad \text{for} \quad j = 1, M \tag{3.94}$$

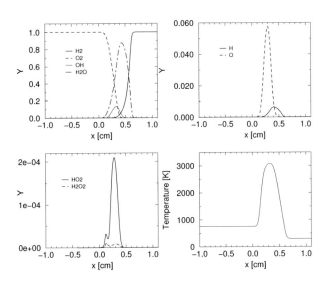

Figure 3.22: Structure of a H_2-O_2 diffusion flame at atmospheric pressure computed with full chemistry and transport. Strain rate: $300\ s^{-1}$. From Vermorel [668]. Chemical scheme from Table 1.5.

Each species contains 1 to P elementary elements. For most hydrocarbon flames $P = 4$: C, O, H, N. The mass fraction of the p-element ($p = 1$ to P) is defined as:

$$Z_p = \sum_{k=1}^{N} a_{kp} \frac{W_p}{W_k} Y_k = W_p \sum_{k=1}^{N} a_{kp} \frac{Y_k}{W_k} \tag{3.95}$$

where a_{kp} is the number of elements of type p in species k: for example, if the species k is propane (C_3H_8) and if carbon (C) is the element p: $a_{kp} = 3$. The a_{kp} values do not depend on chemical reactions taking place between species.

Now, species may be consumed or produced during chemical reactions but elements are always conserved so that, for reaction j:

$$\sum_{k=1}^{N} a_{kp}(\nu'_{kj} - \nu''_{kj}) = \sum_{k=1}^{N} a_{kp}\nu_{kj} = 0. \tag{3.96}$$

Multiplying each species conservation equations (1.37) by $a_{kp}W_p/W_k$ and summing them from $k = 1$ to N yields a balance equation for Z_p:

$$\frac{\partial \rho Z_p}{\partial t} + \frac{\partial}{\partial x_i}(\rho u_i Z_p) = \frac{\partial}{\partial x_i}\left(\rho \mathcal{D} \frac{\partial Z_p}{\partial x_i}\right) + S_p \tag{3.97}$$

If Mechanism 2 has a limited influence, i.e. if all molecular diffusion coefficients are assumed to be equal ($D_k = \mathcal{D}$), expressing $\dot{w}_k$ from Eq. (1.22) and using the conservation relation (3.96), the source term S_p for Z_p is:

$$S_p = \sum_{j=1}^{M} \sum_{k=1}^{N} \frac{W_p}{W_k} a_{kp} \dot{w}_{kj} = \sum_{j=1}^{M} \sum_{k=1}^{N} W_p a_{kp} (\nu'_{kj} - \nu''_{kj}) \mathcal{Q}_j = W_p \sum_{j=1}^{M} \mathcal{Q}_j \sum_{k=1}^{N} a_{kp} \nu_{kj} = 0 \quad (3.98)$$

Therefore, a convection/diffusion balance equation without source term is derived for Z_p:

$$\boxed{\frac{\partial \rho Z_p}{\partial t} + \frac{\partial}{\partial x_i}(\rho u_i Z_p) = \frac{\partial}{\partial x_i}\left(\rho \mathcal{D} \frac{\partial Z_p}{\partial x_i}\right)} \quad (3.99)$$

showing that all Z_p's can be used to evaluate mixture fractions z_p's by writing

$$z_p = \frac{Z_p - Z_P^1}{Z_p^2 - Z_p^1} \quad (3.100)$$

where 1 and 2 designate the oxidizer and fuel stream respectively. In practice if the molecular diffusion coefficients are not equal, Z_p does not have to be a true mixture fraction. Diffusion flames experts propose to combine Z_p's to construct a 'better' mixture fraction. For example, the mixture fraction definition (Barlow and Franck [31]) proposed by Bilger et al. [53] and used by the TNF workshop (*www.sandia.gov/TNF*) mixes Z_C and Z_H: this combination limits the effects of differential diffusion and offers the best approximation to a true mixture fraction.

To illustrate the differences between mixture fraction definitions, consider the H_2-O_2 flame displayed on Fig. 3.22 ($z_{st} = 0.111$). The species used in the computation were: H_2, H, O_2, O, H_2O, OH, H_2O_2, HO_2 and N_2 ($N = 9$). Three elements are considered H, O and N ($P = 3$). The stoichiometric ratio s is 8. The scalar z_1 defined by Eq. (3.15) and constructed using mass fractions of fuel and oxidizer is given for this flame by:

$$z_1 = \frac{s Y_{H_2} - Y_{O_2} + Y_{O_2}^0}{s Y_{H_2}^0 + Y_{O_2}^0} = \frac{s Y_{H_2} - Y_{O_2} + 1}{9} \quad (3.101)$$

A passive scalar Z_H defined for the H element for example is:

$$Z_H = W_H \left(\frac{2Y_{H_2}}{W_{H_2}} + \frac{Y_H}{W_H} + \frac{2Y_{H_2O}}{W_{H_2O}} + \frac{Y_{OH}}{W_{OH}} + \frac{Y_{HO_2}}{W_{HO_2}} + \frac{2Y_{H_2O_2}}{W_{H_2O_2}} \right) \quad (3.102)$$

and the corresponding mixture fraction definition is, according to Eq. (3.12):

$$z_H = \frac{Z_H - 0}{2Y_{H_2}^0 W_H / W_{H_2} - 0} \quad (3.103)$$

For the O element, a passive scalar is:

$$Z_O = W_O \left(\frac{2Y_{O_2}}{W_{O_2}} + \frac{Y_O}{W_O} + \frac{Y_{H_2O}}{W_{H_2O}} + \frac{Y_{OH}}{W_{OH}} + \frac{2Y_{HO_2}}{W_{HO_2}} + \frac{2Y_{H_2O_2}}{W_{H_2O_2}} \right) \quad (3.104)$$

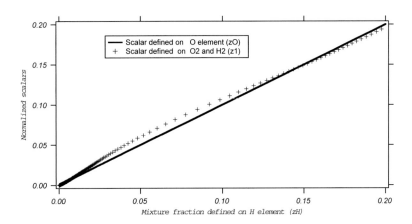

Figure 3.23: Variations of a scalar z_1 (Eq. 3.101) based on fuel and oxidizer mass fractions and of a scalar z_O (Eq. 3.105) based on the oxygen element versus mixture fraction z_H (Eq. 3.103) in the H_2 - O_2 diffusion flame displayed on Fig. 3.22.

The corresponding mixture fraction is then:

$$z_O = \frac{Z_O - 2Y_{O_2}^0 W_O/W_{O_2}}{0 - 2Y_{O_2}^0 W_O/W_{O_2}} \tag{3.105}$$

The two mixture fractions z_O and z_H defined from elements are equal (Fig. 3.23), showing that Mechanism 2 (differential diffusion) has a limited effect on mixture fractions defined on elements in this flame. However, the scalar z_1 defined by Eq. (3.15) is not equal to z_H showing that z_1 is not a mixture fraction anymore. This is mainly due to the existence of additional radicals and reactions in the mixture (Mechanism 1).

Fig. 3.24 displays the flame structure versus valid mixture fractions (such as z_O or z_H): hydrogen and oxygen fuel mass fractions roughly follow the ideal flame structure but overlap in the flame region, because of finite rate chemistry and reversibility effects. Moreover, the oxygen mass fraction deviates from the ideal line even outside the reaction zone (this is due to non-equal Lewis numbers effects). Finally, Fig. 3.25 shows temperature profiles plotted versus z_H. Three computations are presented:

- the full one-dimensional computation (thick line) of the diffusion flame obtained with complete chemistry (Fig. 3.22) and an exact model for molecular transport (Lewis numbers are not supposed to be unity)

- an equilibrium computation (see § 3.3.2) for a single irreversible reaction (thin line). To use this technique, all Lewis numbers must be supposed equal to unity. For such a flame

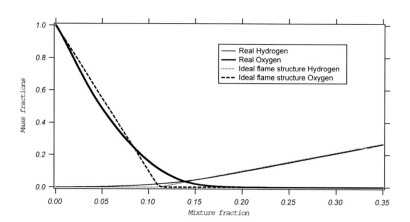

Figure 3.24: Fuel and oxygen mass fractions versus mixture fraction z_H (or z_O) in the H_2 - O_2 diffusion flame displayed on Fig. 3.22 compared with the ideal flame structure described in Section 3.2 (dotted lines).

the variations of the heat capacity C_p (going from pure hydrogen to pure oxygen) are so large that the ideal flame temperature solution (Eq. (3.35)) makes no sense. But a local variable C_p value given by $C_p = z_H C_{p,H2} + (1 - z_H)C_{p,O2}$ can be used to account for the variations of $C_{p,H2}$ and $C_{p,O2}$ with temperature. Although the shape of the result is correct, the predicted temperature levels are wrong because dissociations at high temperature are not captured using a single reaction,

- an equilibrium computation with unity Lewis numbers (square symbols) using the full chemical scheme.

The assumptions used for each method are summarized in Table 3.7. The flame computation (numbered 1) corresponds to the exact solution (if the chemical scheme is correct); the second technique (numbered 2) assumes that the equilibrium technique can be used (all Lewis numbers are unity) and that a single-step reaction is sufficient to obtain the final flame state (no dissociation) and the third one (numbered 3 in Table 3.7 and in Fig. 3.25) uses an equilibrium assumption but computes this equilibrium using the full chemical scheme so that dissociations are accounted for. Obviously, method 2 fails to capture the temperature profile: dissociations at high temperature are very important for such high-temperature flames and cannot be neglected. On the other hand, method 3 captures the temperature profile because dissociations are accounted for. However, the slight shift observed between methods 1 and 3 indicates that the equilibrium assumption is not fully satisfied here: this is mainly due to the high diffusivity of H_2 and H atoms which make the assumption of equal unity Lewis numbers approximate in such flames. For hydrocarbon/air flames at lower temperatures, the three

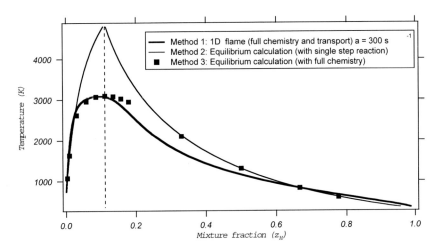

Figure 3.25: Variations of temperature versus mixture fraction z_H in the H_2 - O_2 diffusion flame displayed on Fig. 3.22. Methods are summarized in Table 3.7.

techniques would give much closer results.

	Method	Description	Limitations
1	1D flame computation	Full transport for all species and full chemistry	None (exact solution)
2	equilibrium assumption	Lewis = 1 for all species and single step chemistry	No dissociation and approximate transport
3	equilibrium assumption	Lewis = 1 for all species and complex chemistry	Approximate transport

Table 3.7: Comparison of three methods to compute temperature in a H_2-O_2 diffusion flame (strain rate = 300 s^{-1}): (1) one-dimensional flame computation with full chemistry (2) equilibrium with single step chemistry and (3) equilibrium with full chemistry .

Chapter 4

Introduction to turbulent combustion

4.1 Interaction between flames and turbulence

When flows entering a flame front are turbulent, the laminar flame mode studied in previous chapters is replaced by a regime where turbulence and combustion interact. Turbulent combustion is encountered in most practical combustion systems such as rockets, internal combustion or aircraft engines, industrial burners and furnaces... while laminar combustion applications are almost limited to candles, lighters and some domestic furnaces. Studying and modeling turbulent combustion processes is therefore an important issue to develop and improve practical systems (i.e. to increase efficiency and reduce fuel consumption and pollutant formation). As combustion processes are difficult to handle using analytical techniques, numerical combustion for turbulent flames is a fast growing area. But numerical simulations of turbulent reacting flows remain complex:

- Combustion, even without turbulence, is an intrinsically complex process involving a large range of chemical time and length scales. Some of the chemical phenomena controlling flames take place in short times over thin layers[i] and are associated with very large mass fractions, temperature and density gradients. The full description of chemical mechanisms in laminar flames may require hundreds of species and thousands of reactions leading to considerable numerical difficulties (Chapt. 2).

- Turbulence itself is probably the most complex phenomenon in non-reacting fluid mechanics. Various time and length scales are involved and the structure and the description of turbulence remain open questions. The literature on this topic is enormous and

---

[i]Chemical time scales depend on considered reactions. In most practical combustion devices, fuel oxidation times are short. On the other hand, carbon monoxide (CO) oxidation to carbon dioxide (CO_2) is slower and formation times of thermal nitrogen oxides (NO_x) are even longer.

probably proportional to the difficulty of the task.

- Turbulent combustion results from the two-way interaction of chemistry and turbulence. When a flame interacts with a turbulent flow, turbulence is modified by combustion because of the strong flow accelerations through the flame front induced by heat release, and because of the large changes in kinematic viscosity associated with temperature changes. This mechanism may generate turbulence, called "flame-generated turbulence" or damp it (relaminarization due to combustion). On the other hand, turbulence alters the flame structure, which may enhance the chemical reaction but also, in extreme cases, completely inhibit it, leading to flame quenching.

The objective of this chapter is to introduce basic notions about turbulent combustion which apply to all regimes (premixed, non-premixed, partially premixed). First, elementary concepts about turbulence are briefly recalled (§ 4.2). Qualitative experimental results, evidencing the influence of turbulent motions on combustion are then described (§ 4.3). The three main numerical approaches used in turbulence combustion modeling are presented (§ 4.4). Reynolds averaged Navier Stokes (RANS) equations describe mean flow fields and are adapted to practical industrial simulations (§ 4.5). In direct numerical simulations (DNS), all characteristic length and time scales are resolved but this approach is limited to academic situations (§ 4.6). In large eddy simulations (LES), larger scales are explicitly computed whereas the effects of smaller ones are modeled (§ 4.7). In this chapter, balance equations are presented and advantages and limitations of each approach are discussed. More refined descriptions and models are developed in Chapter 5 for turbulent premixed flames (reactants are perfectly mixed before entering the combustion chamber) and in Chapter 6 for non-premixed situations (reactants are separately introduced into the chamber). This chapter ends with a brief summary about the practical incorporation of complex chemistry features in turbulent combustion descriptions (§ 4.8).

4.2   Elementary descriptions of turbulence

This section describes some basic concepts of turbulence relevant to understand turbulent combustion approaches. Most results are given without any proof but the reader will find more information in textbooks such as Hinze [293], Lesieur [380], Piquet [511], Pope [535].

Turbulence may be characterized by fluctuations of all local properties and occurs for sufficiently large Reynolds numbers, depending on the system geometry. Any property f is usually split into mean $(\overline{f})$ and fluctuating (f') contributions:[ii]

$$f = \overline{f} + f' \tag{4.1}$$

The turbulence strength is generally characterized by the turbulence intensity I which is the ratio between the root mean square of the fluctuations f' and the mean value $\overline{f}$:

$$I = \sqrt{\overline{f'^2}}/\overline{f} \tag{4.2}$$

In some situations, the local value $\overline{f}$ may be replaced by a relevant reference mean value $\overline{f}_0$. For example, in boundary layers, the turbulence intensity is usually determined as the ratio of velocity fluctuations divided by the mean free stream velocity. Typical values of the turbulence intensity I go from 0 (in a laminar flow) to tens of percent in typical wall-bounded flows: the local velocity in a turbulent flow may deviate from its mean value by tens of percent.

Nevertheless, turbulence intensity is not a sufficient parameter to describe turbulent combustion. An important issue is how the turbulence energy is distributed over the different length scales present in the flow field and which length scales carry enough energy to interact with the flame front. Turbulent fluctuations are associated with different scales ranging from the largest, the integral length scale l_t, to the smallest one, the Kolmogorov length scale η_k. The integral scale is usually close to the characteristic size of the flow. For example, in a ducted flow, the integral scale is of the order of the duct size. A Reynolds number $Re(r)$ is introduced for each turbulent scale as:

$$Re(r) = \frac{u'(r)r}{\nu} \tag{4.3}$$

where $u'(r)$ is the characteristic velocity of the motion of size r and ν is the flow kinematic viscosity.[iii] When r corresponds to the integral scale l_t, the corresponding Reynolds number is the integral Reynolds number:

$$Re_t = Re(l_t) = u'l_t/\nu \tag{4.4}$$

which is usually high (100 to 2000 in most combustion devices). Since the Reynolds number represents the ratio of inertia to viscous forces, the largest scales in a turbulent flow are mainly controlled by inertia and are not affected by viscous dissipation.

[ii]This averaging process is usually defined as an ensemble average (i.e. average of a large number of realizations at the same instant of the same flow field). For steady mean flow fields, this average is replaced by time averages over a sufficiently long period t, according to:

$$\overline{f} = \frac{1}{t}\int_0^t f(t')\,dt'$$

This last situation is implicitly assumed here.

[iii]This relation, usual for homogeneous and isotropic turbulence, assumes that the velocity $u'(r)$ associated to a motion of size r is only function of r. More refined formulations, based on fractal theories are available (Meneveau and Sreenivasan [434]).

For homogeneous isotropic turbulence (Hinze [293]), the energy of the large scales flows to the smaller scales through the Kolmogorov cascade (Kolmogorov [354]). The energy flux from one scale to another (due to non-linear terms $u_i u_j$) is constant along scales and is given by the dissipation ε of the kinetic energy k. This dissipation ε is estimated as the ratio of the kinetic energy, $u'^2(r)$ divided by the time scale $r/u'(r)$:

$$\varepsilon = \frac{u'^2(r)}{r/u'(r)} = \frac{u'(r)^3}{r} \tag{4.5}$$

Along the cascade, the Reynolds number $Re(r)$ goes down from Re_t to values close to unity, where inertia and viscous forces balance. This limit determines the smallest scale found in the turbulent flow, the Kolmogorov scale η_k, controlled by viscosity and by the dissipation rate ε of the turbulent kinetic energy k (Kolmogorov [354]):

$$\eta_k = \left(\nu^3/\varepsilon\right)^{1/4} \tag{4.6}$$

corresponding to a unity Reynolds number:

$$Re_k = Re(\eta_k) = \frac{u'_k \eta_k}{\nu} = \frac{\varepsilon^{1/3} \eta_k^{4/3}}{\nu} = 1 \tag{4.7}$$

The ratio of the integral length scale, l_t, to the Kolmogorov length scale, η_k, comparing the largest and smallest turbulence eddies, is then expressed from (4.4), (4.5) and (4.6):

$$\frac{l_t}{\eta_k} = \frac{u'^3/\varepsilon}{\left(\nu^3/\varepsilon\right)^{1/4}} = Re_t^{3/4} \tag{4.8}$$

As with laminar flames (§ 2.6), flame strain is an important quantity for turbulent combustion. It measures the fractional rate of increase of the flame front area. Eq. (2.89) shows that strain is directly linked to velocity gradients: to first order, the strain $\kappa(r)$ induced on a flame front by an eddy of size r may be assumed to scale with $u'(r)/r$ which is the simplest estimate for the velocity gradients created by this eddy. Then:

$$\kappa(r) = u'(r)/r = \left(\varepsilon/r^2\right)^{1/3} \tag{4.9}$$

In the same way, the characteristic time scale of an eddy of size r is:

$$\tau_m(r) = r/u'(r) = \left(r^2/\varepsilon\right)^{1/3} = 1/\kappa(r) \tag{4.10}$$

The Kolmogorov (η_k) and integral (l_t) length scales induce strain values given by:

$$\kappa\left(\eta_k\right) = \sqrt{\frac{\varepsilon}{\nu}} \quad ; \quad \kappa\left(l_t\right) = \frac{\varepsilon}{u'^2} \approx \frac{\varepsilon}{k} \tag{4.11}$$

where u'^2 measures the turbulent kinetic energy k. Although the scales close to the Kolmogorov length have the smallest sizes and velocities, they generate the highest stretch[iv] and:

$$\frac{\kappa(\eta_k)}{\kappa(l_t)} = \sqrt{\frac{l_t u'}{\nu}} = \sqrt{Re_t} \qquad (4.12)$$

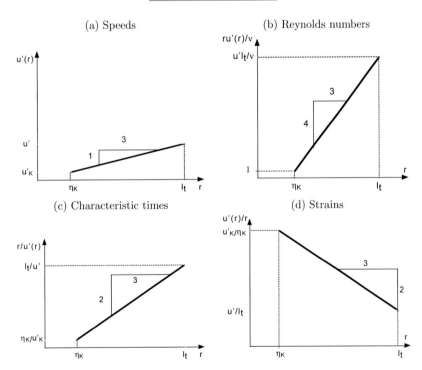

Figure 4.1: Eddy speeds (a), Reynolds numbers (b), characteristic time scales (c) and strains (d) as a function of size r in a log-log diagram.

Figure 4.1 displays the velocity $u'(r)$, the Reynolds number $Re(r)$, the characteristic time $r/u'(r)$ and strain $\kappa(r) = u'(r)/r$ as a function of the scale r in a log-log diagram.

In the previous description, turbulence is supposed to behave like isotropic homogenous turbulence at each point of the reacting flow: obviously, this assumption is not true in real systems but corresponds to the best available universal description.

[iv]Kolmogorov eddies also have the shortest life times $r/u'(r)$ which leads to some controversies about their actual effect on a flame front (see § 5.2.3).

4.3   Influence of turbulence on combustion

The main effect of turbulence on combustion is to increase the combustion rate, as shown in this section recalling two well-known experimental results, first for a premixed flame (§ 4.3.1) and second for a jet diffusion flame (§ 4.3.2).

4.3.1   One-dimensional turbulent premixed flame

Consider a statistically one-dimensional premixed flame propagating in a turbulent flow (Fig. 4.2).

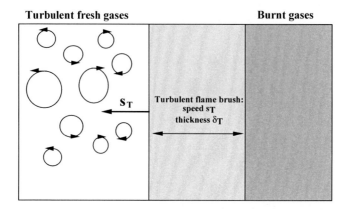

Figure 4.2: Statistically one-dimensional premixed flame propagating in a turbulent flow field. An animation of one of the first simulations of this flow, at Stanford Center for Turbulence Research in 1989, is available at *elearning.cerfacs.fr/combustion/illustrations/DNS-1989*.

In this situation, the "mean" flame brush is a planar flame, moving relatively to the flow field with a turbulent displacement speed s_T.[v] Experimentalists have known for a long time that changing the turbulence level before starting combustion in a vessel may change the time needed for total combustion and, accordingly the turbulent flame speed. In his book, Laffitte [362] presents combustion times measured in a stirred vessel in 1918 (Wheeler [706, 707]) showing that the combustion rate is maximum (the combustion time is minimum) when the reactants are mixed in stoichiometric proportions and increases when the flow becomes turbulent (Fig. 4.3). At that time, Laffitte [362] noted that *"the turbulent flame speed was always larger than two times the laminar flame speed."* The factor of two observed by Wheeler is obviously not generic of all turbulent flames and more precise measurements lead to empirical

---

[v]The turbulent flame speed s_T is qualitatively introduced here as a measure of the overall reaction rate and is precisely defined in Chapter 5.

relations such as Abdel-Gayed et al. [3] and Gulder [258]:

$$\frac{s_T}{s_L} \approx 1 + \frac{u'}{s_L} \qquad (4.13)$$

where u' is the rms (root mean square) of the velocity fluctuations (or the square root of the turbulent kinetic energy k). This approximate expression shows that premixed combustion is enhanced by turbulent motions. For large values of the velocity fluctuations, the turbulent flame speed s_T becomes roughly independent of the laminar flame speed s_L ($s_T \approx u'$). Experiments also show that the mean turbulent flame brush thickness δ_T is always larger than the laminar flame thickness δ_L^0.

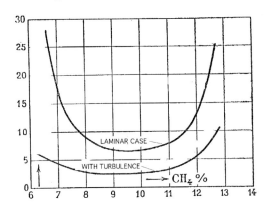

Figure 4.3: Combustion time (time needed to reach the maximum pressure in a closed vessel) for a methane/air flame with and without turbulence, plotted as a function of the proportion of CH_4 in the reactant mixture, corresponding to the equivalence ratio ϕ (stoichiometric proportions correspond to about 10 % of methane). Time units correspond to 10^{-2} s (Wheeler [706], Laffitte [362]).

4.3.2 Turbulent jet diffusion flame

In this configuration (Fig. 4.4), a jet of fuel (usually pure) is injected into ambient air. The flame length L_f can be measured (Fig. 4.5) as a function of the Reynolds number $Re = Ud/\nu$ where U, d and ν are respectively the initial velocity, the diameter and the kinematic viscosity of the fuel jet stream (Hottel and Hawthorne [297]).

The flame length L_f is found to first linearly increase with the fuel flow rate or the Reynolds number R_e. For a sufficiently high Reynolds number, the flow becomes turbulent and the flame length L_f decreases before reaching a constant value independent on the Reynolds number R_e. The transition point between laminar and turbulent region of the flame moves closer to

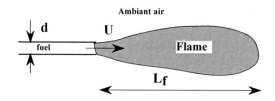

Figure 4.4: Jet flame configuration.

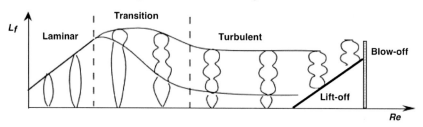

Figure 4.5: Length L_f of a jet flame (Fig. 4.4) as a function of the jet Reynolds number $R_e = (Ud/\nu)$. Figure adapted from Hottel and Hawthorne [297].

the injector lip. For sufficiently high injection velocities, the flame is lifted from the burner ("lifted flame")[vi] and then may be extinguished by "blow-off."

Since the flame length L_f remains constant when the Reynolds number (or the injection velocity, corresponding to the fuel mass flow rate) increases, the reaction rate per unit volume must be enhanced by turbulence: combustion becomes more efficient when turbulence increases, at least up to the occurrence of lift-off and blow-off phenomena.

4.4   Computational approaches for turbulent combustion

The description of turbulent combustion processes using Computational Fluid Dynamics (CFD) may be achieved using three levels of computations:

- Reynolds Averaged Navier Stokes (or RANS) computations have historically been the first possible approach because the computation of the instantaneous flow field in a turbulent flame was impossible. Therefore, RANS techniques were developed to solve

---

[vi]Examples of DNS of lifted turbulent diffusion flames (§ 4.4) for ethylene/air (Yoo et al. [724]) and hydrogen/air (Yoo et al. [723]) can be found at *elearning.cerfacs.fr/combustion/illustrations/SANDIAethylene* and *elearning.cerfacs.fr/combustion/illustrations/SANDIAhydrogen* (prepared by Hongfeng Yu, SANDIA).

for the mean values of all quantities. The balance equations for Reynolds or Favre (i.e. mass-weighted) averaged quantities are obtained by averaging the instantaneous balance equations. The averaged equations require closure rules: a turbulence model to deal with the flow dynamics in combination with a turbulent combustion model to describe chemical species conversion and heat release. Solving these equations provide averaged quantities corresponding to averages over time for stationary mean flows or averages over different realizations (or cycles) for periodic flows like those found in piston engines (i.e. phase averaging). For a stabilized flame, the temperature predicted with RANS at a given point is a constant corresponding to the mean temperature at this point, whatever the temperature history is (Fig. 4.6).[vii] RANS models are still the standard approach in all commercial codes for combustion today.

- The second level corresponds to large eddy simulations (LES). The turbulent large scales are explicitly calculated whereas the effects of smaller ones are modeled using subgrid closure rules. The balance equations for large eddy simulations are obtained by filtering the instantaneous balance equations (§ 4.7.1). LES determine the instantaneous position of a "large scale" resolved flame front but a subgrid model is still required to take into account the effects of small turbulent scales on combustion. LES would capture the low-frequency variations of temperature (Fig. 4.6). LES models have become the standard research tools in most of the community and are slowly transferred to industry today (Gourdain et al. [250, 251], Vermorel et al. [669]) where they are used for cases where RANS models are known to be imprecise (unsteady flows, ignition, quenching, swirling flows, cycle-to-cycle variations in internal combustion engines, combustion instabilities).

- The third level of combustion simulations is direct numerical simulations (DNS) where the full instantaneous Navier-Stokes equations are solved without any model for turbulent motions: all turbulence scales are explicitly determined and their effects on combustion are captured. DNS would predict all time variations of temperature (Fig. 4.6) exactly like a high-resolution sensor would measure them in an experiment. Developed in the last twenty years thanks to the development of high performance computers, DNS have changed the analysis of turbulent combustion but are still limited to simple academic flows (typically, combustion in a small cubic box) even though recent breakthroughs in the field of High Performance Computing show that DNS might be applicable to realistic combustors very soon (Chen et al. [120], Moureau et al. [458]).

RANS, LES and DNS properties are summarized in terms of energy spectrum in Fig. 4.7. All spatial frequencies in the spectrum are resolved in direct numerical simulations, whereas only the largest ones (up to a cut-off wave number k_c) are computed in LES (the effects of motions smaller that the cut-off length scale, having a wave number k larger than k_c, are modeled). By construction, LES is expected to tend toward DNS when the cut-off length

---

[vii]In the limit case of infinitely thin premixed flame fronts, the mean temperature directly measures the probability to be in burnt gases while the instantaneous temperature alternates between its fresh and fully burnt gas values (see Section 5.1.3 and Eq. 5.8). See also § 4.5.6.

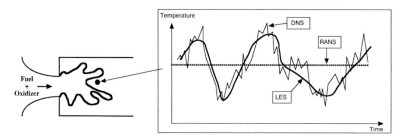

Figure 4.6: Time evolutions of local temperature computed with DNS, RANS or LES in a turbulent flame brush.

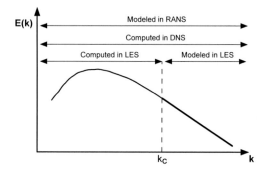

Figure 4.7: Turbulence energy spectrum plotted as a function of wave numbers. RANS, LES and DNS are summarized in terms of spatial frequency range. k_c is the cut-off wave number used in LES (log-log diagram).

scale (i.e. the LES filter size) goes to zero. In RANS, only mean flow fields are resolved: no turbulent motion is explicitly captured.

In terms of computational requirements, CFD for non-reacting and reacting flows follow similar trends: DNS is the most demanding method and is limited to fairly low Reynolds numbers and simplified geometries. LES works with coarser grids (only larger scales have to be resolved) and may be used to deal with higher Reynolds numbers but require subgrid scale models. The computation quality and the results accuracy are directly linked to these physical subgrid models. In current engineering practice, RANS is extensively used because it is less demanding in terms of resources but its validity is limited by the closure models describing turbulence and combustion.

DNS methods are limited in terms of parameter range and geometry to academic situations. For example, a DNS simulation of a three-dimensional turbulent flame at atmospheric pressure

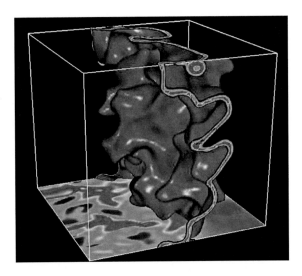

Figure 4.8: DNS of a premixed flame interacting with three-dimensional isotropic turbulence (Boger et al. [65]). An isosurface of temperature is visualized. The reaction rate is presented in two planes which are normal to the mean flame front. The vorticity field, corresponding to turbulent motions, is also displayed in the bottom plane.

typically requires 1 to 2 million grid points and the computational box corresponds to a physical size of $5 \times 5 \times 5$ mm^3. Fig. 4.8 shows an example of DNS result corresponding to an instantaneous realization of a premixed flame front interacting with isotropic turbulence (Trouvé and Poinsot [652], Boger et al. [65], Boughanem and Trouvé [77]).

The advantage of RANS is its applicability to any configuration and operating conditions: a standard RANS mesh can contain 10^5 points and the domain of calculation may be as large as needed. For example Fig. 4.9a shows an isosurface of mean high temperature (1100 K) in a turbulent premixed flame stabilized by swirl (see § 6.2.3) obtained with RANS. The configuration corresponds to a 1:1 burner of a large-scale industrial gas turbine (Selle et al. [601]). On the isosurface, the average temperature is 1100 K but RANS does not explicitly solve for possible turbulent fluctuations around this mean value.

Why do similar problems treated with DNS and RANS require so different grid sizes ($\Delta x \simeq$ 10 to 50 microns for DNS and 1 to 5 mm for RANS)? DNS has to describe the smallest scales contained in the flow field and to resolve the inner instantaneous structure of the flame front (Fig. 4.8). In many cases this last condition determines the grid size as shown in § 2.4.4. For hydrocarbon/air flames at atmospheric pressure, fronts have a thickness of the order of 0.1 mm so that mesh sizes of the order of microns are required. In contrast, RANS considers an average flame front which extends over a broader region: only mean turbulence characteristics

(a) RANS result	(b) LES result
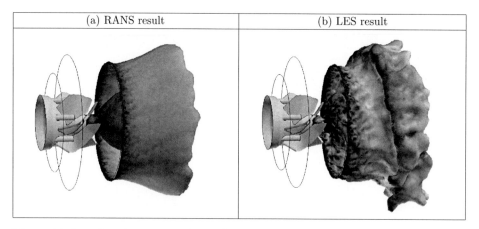	

Figure 4.9: Isosurface of temperature (1100 K) during turbulent combustion in a swirled combustor (see geometry in § 10.3, Selle [600]). (a): RANS (mean field), (b): LES (instantaneous field).

and average statistical position of the front are solved for, as shown in Fig. 4.10a. As a consequence the stiffness associated with the chemistry of the flame front is avoided. Typical mean flame brushes in burners (Abdal-Masseh et al. [1]), aircraft or piston engine (Boudier et al. [75], Cant and Bray [111]) have a thickness of 1 to 2 cm and may be easily resolved with a 2 mm mesh. Engineering codes using RANS techniques (the majority of current computational tools) never resolve the inner structure of the flame and provide average flowfields featuring scales which are much larger than the instantaneous flame thickness.

Large-eddy simulations are an intermediate tool between DNS and RANS. LES methods have been used extensively in many non reacting flows and have provided reliable predictions in a variety of applications (see for example, Herring et al. [283], Moin and Kim [450] or Akselvoll and Moin [5]). The treatment of reacting flows with similar concepts is less well established. While some advances have been made (Veynante and Poinsot [677], Angelberger et al. [13], Boger et al. [65], Pierce and Moin [508], Selle et al. [601], Janicka and Sadiki [307], Pitsch [512], Duwig [195], Schmitt et al. [594], Bini and P. [54], Fiorina et al. [216], Lecocq et al. [374]) research is still required on this topic. It is in particular necessary to construct methods for the calculation of the "large scale" flame front and to develop subgrid scale models. Fig. 4.9b gives an example of instantaneous LES field (Selle [600]) in the same geometry as the RANS result (Fig. 4.9a). Obviously, the instantaneous flame surface obtained with LES contains much more turbulent scales than the averaged field given by the RANS code.

The velocity fields obtained by RANS or LES also illustrate the basic differences between the two approaches (Fig. 4.10). While the field of axial velocity obtained with RANS is very smooth (Fig. 4.10a), the LES field exhibits much more unsteady structures: in terms of physics, the LES captures more turbulent activity; in terms of numerical resolution, the grid required

(a) RANS result	(b) LES result

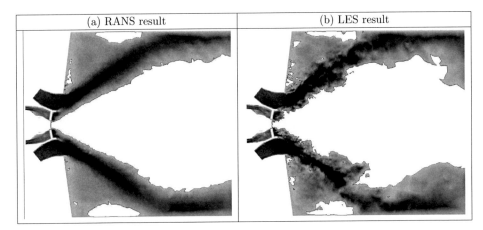

Figure 4.10: Axial velocity fields during turbulent combustion in a swirled combustor (see geometry in § 10.3). (a): RANS (mean field), (b): LES (instantaneous field). The zones within the black line are backflow regions (A. Giauque, private communication).

for RANS can be very coarse because gradients are small. On the other hand, for LES, the grid must be fine and the numerical method non dissipative in order to capture the small motions evidenced in Fig. 4.10b. Considering also that RANS codes compute only one state (the converged flow) while LES codes must resolve the flow in time, the cost of a typical LES computation is often 100 to 1000 times higher than a RANS computation. However, despite its cost, LES is well adapted for many combustion studies (see examples in Chapter 10):

- Large structures in turbulent flows depend on the system geometry whereas small structures are generally assumed to have more universal features. Accordingly, models are probably more suited to describe these small structures.

- Most reacting flows exhibit large scale coherent structures (Coats [143]). Such structures are also observed when combustion instabilities occur. These instabilities are due to a coupling between heat release, hydrodynamic flow field and acoustic waves (see Chapt. 8). They have to be avoided because they induce noise, variations of the system characteristics, large heat transfers and may lead to the system destruction. LES is a powerful tool to predict the occurrence of such instabilities and to numerically test passive or active control systems.

- The knowledge of large-scale turbulent motions may be used to infer the effects of the unresolved smaller ones: for example, during the Kolmogorov cascade, the energy flows from large (resolved) structures to (unresolved) smaller scales. In fact, subgrid scale models are generally based on similarity assumptions between large and small scales while dynamic procedures automatically adjust subgrid scale model constants from the known resolved field.

- Large eddy simulations also allow a better description of the turbulence/combustion interactions.[viii] As large structures are explicitly computed in LES, instantaneous fresh and burnt gases zones, where turbulence characteristics are quite different (see § 5.1.3 and Fig. 5.11), are clearly identified, at least at the resolved level (see, for example, Fig. 4.10b). This is a significant advantage of LES compared to RANS in which models have to take into account (at a given spatial location) the probability of being in fresh or in burnt gases. This identification of the instantaneous distribution of cold fresh and hot burnt gas zones in LES also facilitates the description of phenomena mainly linked to burnt gases such as pollutant formation or radiative heat transfer (Goncalves dos Santos et al. [246], Coelho [145], Roger et al. [564]).

Comparisons between RANS, LES and DNS are summarized in Table 4.1. In terms of numerics, the difference between the three approaches lies in the effective diffusion used in the simulation: in RANS, the turbulent viscosity is large. Moreover, the artificial viscosity introduced by the numerical method itself is also large to minimize the CPU time (by using time implicit codes) and to increase the code robustness (by using upwinded low-order spatial schemes). As a result, the effective Reynolds number of the simulation is low: the computed flow is not even turbulent and it behaves like a steady laminar flow (with a complex local viscosity in which turbulent and artificial viscosities dominate). On the other hand, in DNS, high-order numerical methods are used and no turbulent viscosity is introduced: the computed flow is turbulent and displays unsteady motions naturally. LES appears once again as an intermediate tool: turbulent diffusion coefficients are smaller than in RANS but larger than in DNS. Numerical methods for LES must be less dissipative (centered schemes in space and explicit formulations in time) than in RANS and closer to DNS precision. Therefore, a good LES must be turbulent in the sense that it must naturally produce unsteady flow motions.

A way to reduce the high computational costs linked to LES of a full system is to combine RANS and LES solvers for different parts of the flow domain. The basic idea is to use RANS where it is sufficient, and apply LES where this approach provides better results (typically, flow separation or combustion zones). For example, Schluter et al. [593] applied this technique to the simulation of an aeronautic gas turbine: RANS is used for compressor and turbine while the combustion chamber is described by LES. Inlet and outlet boundary conditions must be adapted: mean flow characteristics should be extracted from LES when entering a RANS domain while the transition from RANS to LES requires the generation of an unsteady flow with given mean properties (Schluter et al. [592]).

The previous analysis may also be illustrated from experimental data. This point is of importance as such data are required to validate numerical simulations. In Fig. 4.11a, a

---

[viii]Note that in practice the description of turbulence / combustion interactions is generally limited in RANS. Turbulence characteristics enter RANS combustion models only through a single turbulent time scale and, sometimes, a length scale, more often related to the integral turbulence time and length scales, respectively, while there is no direct influence of combustion on the turbulence model, except through the mean density, modified by the heat release.

Approach	Advantages	Drawbacks
RANS	- "coarse" numerical grid - geometrical simplification (2D flows, symmetry,...) - "reduced" numerical costs	- only mean flow field - models required
LES	- unsteady features - reduced modeling impact (compared to RANS)	- models required - 3D simulations required - needs precise codes - numerical costs
DNS	- no models needed for turbulence/combustion interaction - tool to study models	- prohibitive numerical costs (fine grids, precise codes) - limited to academic problems

Table 4.1: Comparison between RANS, LES and DNS approaches for numerical simulations of turbulent combustion.

planar laser induced fluorescence (PLIF) imaging of the OH radical is displayed in a turbulent premixed propane/air flame stabilized behind a wedge. This radical is an intermediate species appearing during propane combustion and its gradient is generally assumed to correspond to the flame front location. Accordingly, the instantaneous flame front is visualized and, for similar spatial resolutions, this experimental image would correspond to a DNS result. Assuming a sufficiently thin flame front (i.e. "flamelet," see Chapt. 5), the instantaneous flame front may be extracted from Fig. 4.11a (Fig. 4.11b). Note that such a geometry is probably too large to be simulated using DNS.

Such instantaneous flame images may be either ensemble-averaged or filtered to extract RANS and LES fields. For example, Fig. 4.12 displays the result of a LES filter acting on Fig. 4.11b to extract the LES resolved reaction rate (in fact, the subgrid scale flame surface density, see § 5.4.5). At locations 2, 4 and 11 cm, some flame front motions are not resolved in the LES but correspond to filtered reaction rates that have to be described through subgrid scale models.

Ensemble averaging of instantaneous flame front images provides RANS fields. Fig. 4.13 presents a mean temperature field, averaged over 200 instantaneous images. In this situation, the "average" flame brush is broad, except in the vicinity of the flame holder, where the flame is almost laminar (accordingly, an ad-hoc flame stabilization model is probably required for practical simulations). The thickness of this flame brush (a few cm) is not related to any laminar flame thickness. It only measures the width of the zone where the flame has a non-zero

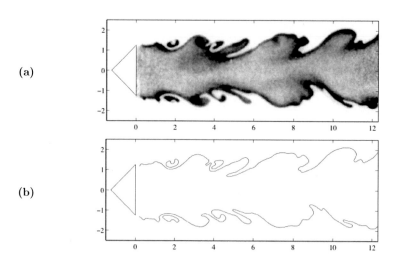

Figure 4.11: Flame front visualization in a turbulent premixed propane / air flame stabilized behind a triangular-shape flame holder. (a): laser induced fluorescence of the OH radical (grey regions denote burnt gases). (b): instantaneous flame front extracted from (a). Spatial coordinates are displayed in cm (R. Knikker, private communication, 2000).

probability of passage. All information on instantaneous flame structures, clearly apparent in Fig. 4.11 and still visible at the resolved scale level in Fig. 4.12, is lost. These effects must be incorporated in simulations through turbulence combustion models.

The mean field of Fig. 4.13 was obtained by averaging instantaneous images. It could also have been created using single point measurements. For validation purposes, the level of experimental techniques must match the characteristics of numerical tools:

- Averaged fields (velocities, temperature, species mass fractions), corresponding to RANS simulations, may be obtained using single point measuring technique (Laser Doppler velocimetry, thermocouple, single point Raman scattering), at least for statistical steady state regimes or for periodic flow fields (phase averaging).

- DNS and LES-like data require instantaneous resolved three-dimensional flow fields (in fact, in the previous figures, a two-dimensional instantaneous flow field is assumed). DNS fields correspond to raw data whereas LES fields are obtained by spatial filtering (see § 4.7). Specific experimental measurements for DNS and LES development and validation are not common yet because they require time- and space- resolved diagnostics.

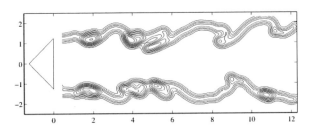

Figure 4.12: Instantaneous LES filtered reaction rate in a turbulent premixed propane/air flame stabilized behind a triangular-shape flame holder, extracted from Fig. 4.11b.

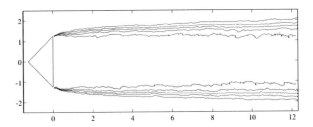

Figure 4.13: Averaged temperature field, corresponding to RANS simulations and obtained averaging over 200 instantaneous images as Fig. 4.11. A binary instantaneous temperature (fresh and burnt gases temperatures separated by the instantaneous flame front) is assumed.

4.5 RANS simulations for turbulent combustion

Balance equations for the mean quantities in RANS simulations are obtained by averaging the instantaneous balance equations. This averaging procedure introduces unclosed quantities that have to be modeled, using turbulent combustion models.

4.5.1 Averaging the balance equations

The natural starting point for averaging is the instantaneous balance equations for mass, species, momentum and enthalpy, obtained from § 1.1:

$$\frac{\partial \rho}{\partial t} + \frac{\partial}{\partial x_i}(\rho u_i) = 0 \tag{4.14}$$

$$\frac{\partial \rho u_j}{\partial t} + \frac{\partial}{\partial x_i}(\rho u_i u_j) + \frac{\partial p}{\partial x_j} = \frac{\partial \tau_{ij}}{\partial x_i} \tag{4.15}$$

$$\frac{\partial(\rho Y_k)}{\partial t} + \frac{\partial}{\partial x_i}(\rho u_i Y_k) = -\frac{\partial}{\partial x_i}(V_{k,i} Y_k) + \dot{\omega}_k \quad \text{for} \quad k = 1, N \tag{4.16}$$

$$\frac{\partial \rho h_s}{\partial t} + \frac{\partial}{\partial x_i}(\rho u_i h_s) = \dot{\omega}_T + \frac{Dp}{Dt} + \frac{\partial}{\partial x_i}\left(\lambda \frac{\partial T}{\partial x_i}\right) - \frac{\partial}{\partial x_i}\left(\rho \sum_{k=1}^{N} V_{k,i} Y_k h_{s,k}\right) + \tau_{ij}\frac{\partial u_i}{\partial x_j} \tag{4.17}$$

In constant density flows, Reynolds averaging consists in splitting any quantity f into a mean, $\overline{f}$, and a fluctuating, f' component ($f = \overline{f} + f'$). Using this procedure with the mass conservation equation (4.14) leads to (averaging and derivating operators may be exchanged):

$$\frac{\partial \overline{\rho}}{\partial t} + \frac{\partial}{\partial x_i}(\overline{\rho u_i}) = \frac{\partial \overline{\rho}}{\partial t} + \frac{\partial}{\partial x_i}\left(\overline{\rho}\,\overline{u}_i + \overline{\rho' u_i'}\right) = 0 \quad \text{or} \quad \frac{\partial \overline{\rho}}{\partial t} + \frac{\partial}{\partial x_i}\left(\overline{\rho}\,\overline{u}_i\right) = -\frac{\partial}{\partial x_i}\left(\overline{\rho' u_i'}\right) \tag{4.18}$$

where an unclosed quantity $\overline{\rho' u_i'}$ corresponding to the correlation between density and velocity fluctuations appears and requires modeling. This term also acts as a mass source term for the mean flow field ($\overline{\rho}, \overline{u}_i$) which is awkward to handle in CFD codes: for example, the average mass flow rates using Reynolds averaging may not be a conserved quantity in a steady flow. Reynolds averaging for variable density flows introduces many other unclosed correlations between any quantity f and density fluctuations $\overline{\rho' f'}$. To avoid this difficulty, mass-weighted averages (called Favre averages) are usually preferred (Favre [206], Williams [710], Kuo [361]):

$$\boxed{\widetilde{f} = \frac{\overline{\rho f}}{\overline{\rho}}} \tag{4.19}$$

Any quantity f may be split into mean and fluctuating components as:

$$f = \widetilde{f} + f'' \quad \text{with} \quad \widetilde{f''} = 0 \tag{4.20}$$

Using this formalism, the averaged balance equations become:

• **Mass**

$$\frac{\partial \overline{\rho}}{\partial t} + \frac{\partial}{\partial x_i}(\overline{\rho}\widetilde{u}_i) = 0 \tag{4.21}$$

• **Momentum**

$$\frac{\partial \overline{\rho}\widetilde{u}_i}{\partial t} + \frac{\partial}{\partial x_i}(\overline{\rho}\widetilde{u}_i\widetilde{u}_j) + \frac{\partial \overline{p}}{\partial x_j} = \frac{\partial}{\partial x_i}\left(\overline{\tau}_{ij} - \overline{\rho u_i'' u_j''}\right) \tag{4.22}$$

• **Chemical species**

$$\frac{\partial(\overline{\rho}\widetilde{Y}_k)}{\partial t} + \frac{\partial}{\partial x_i}(\overline{\rho}\widetilde{u}_i\widetilde{Y}_k) = -\frac{\partial}{\partial x_i}\left(\overline{V_{k,i} Y_k} + \overline{\rho u_i'' Y_k''}\right) + \overline{\dot{\omega}}_k \quad \text{for} \quad k = 1, N \tag{4.23}$$

- **Enthalpy**

$$\frac{\partial \overline{\rho}\widetilde{h}_s}{\partial t} + \frac{\partial}{\partial x_i}(\overline{\rho}\widetilde{u}_i\widetilde{h}_s) = \overline{\dot{\omega}}_T + \overline{\frac{Dp}{Dt}} + \frac{\partial}{\partial x_i}\left(\overline{\lambda\frac{\partial T}{\partial x_i}} - \overline{\rho u_i''h_s''}\right) + \overline{\tau_{ij}\frac{\partial u_i}{\partial x_j}} - \frac{\partial}{\partial x_i}\left(\overline{\rho\sum_{k=1}^{N}V_{k,i}Y_k h_{s,k}}\right)$$

$$(4.24)$$

where

$$\overline{\frac{Dp}{Dt}} = \overline{\frac{\partial p}{\partial t}} + \overline{u_i\frac{\partial p}{\partial x_i}} = \frac{\partial \overline{p}}{\partial t} + \widetilde{u}_i\frac{\partial \overline{p}}{\partial x_i} + \overline{u_i''\frac{\partial p}{\partial x_i}} \qquad (4.25)$$

These equations are now formally identical to the classical Reynolds averaged equations for constant density flows. Even though Favre averaging seems to offer a simple and efficient route for reacting flows, it must be kept in mind that:

- There is no simple relation between Favre $(\widetilde{f})$ and Reynolds $(\overline{f})$ averages. A relation between these two quantities requires the knowledge, or the modeling, of density fluctuation correlations, $\overline{\rho'f'}$ which remain hidden in Favre average quantities:

$$\overline{\rho}\widetilde{f} = \overline{\rho}\,\overline{f} + \overline{\rho'f'} \qquad (4.26)$$

- Reynolds and Favre averages may strongly differ, as shown in the case of infinitely thin flame fronts in premixed combustion in §5.1.3 (Fig. 5.8).

- Comparisons between numerical simulations, providing Favre averages, $\widetilde{f}$, with experimental data are not obvious. Most experimental techniques provide Reynolds averages $\overline{f}$ (for example when averaging thermocouple data) but differences between $\overline{f}$ and $\widetilde{f}$ may be significant, as shown in § 5.1.3.

4.5.2 Unclosed terms in Favre averaged balance equations

The objective of turbulent combustion modeling is to propose closures for the unknown quantities found in Eq. (4.21) to (4.24):

Reynolds stresses $(\widetilde{u_i''u_j''})$

These terms are closed by a turbulence model. The closure may be done directly or by deriving balance equations for the Reynolds stresses. Most combustion works are based on the classical turbulence models developed for non-reacting flows, such as the $k - \varepsilon$ model, simply rewritten in terms of Favre averaging. Heat release effects on the Reynolds stresses are generally not explicitly taken into account.

Species $(\widetilde{u_i''Y_k''})$ and enthalpy $(\widetilde{u_i''h_s''})$ turbulent fluxes.

These fluxes are generally closed using a classical gradient assumption:

$$\boxed{\overline{\rho}\widetilde{u_i''Y_k''} = -\frac{\mu_t}{Sc_{kt}}\frac{\partial \widetilde{Y}_k}{\partial x_i}} \tag{4.27}$$

where μ_t is the turbulent viscosity, estimated from the turbulence model, and Sc_{kt} a turbulent Schmidt number for species k. Nevertheless, theory and experiments (Libby and Bray [386], Shepherd et al. [614]) have shown that this gradient assumption is wrong in some turbulent premixed flames: counter-gradient turbulent transport (i.e. in an opposite direction compared to the one predicted from Eq. 4.27) can be observed in weak turbulence flames (§ 5.1.3 and 5.3.8).

Laminar diffusive fluxes for species or enthalpy

These molecular terms are generally neglected against turbulent transport, assuming a sufficiently large turbulence level (large Reynolds numbers limit). They may also be retained by adding a laminar diffusivity to the turbulent viscosity μ_t in Eq. (4.27). For example, species laminar diffusion fluxes are generally modeled as:

$$\boxed{\overline{V_{k,i}Y_k} = -\overline{\rho D_k \frac{\partial Y_k}{\partial x_i}} \approx -\overline{\rho}\overline{D}_k\frac{\partial \widetilde{Y}_k}{\partial x_i}} \tag{4.28}$$

where $\overline{D}_k$ is a "mean" species molecular diffusion coefficient. Note also that the laminar heat diffusion flux in the enthalpy equation (4.24) is generally rewritten as:

$$\overline{\lambda \frac{\partial T}{\partial x_i}} = \overline{\lambda}\frac{\partial \widetilde{T}}{\partial x_i} \tag{4.29}$$

where $\overline{\lambda}$ denotes a mean thermal diffusivity.

Species chemical reaction rates $\overline{\dot{\omega}}_k$.

Modeling these mean reaction rates is the objective of most studies on turbulent flames: these issues are discussed in Chapters 5 and 6.

Pressure-velocity correlation $\overline{u_i''\partial p/\partial x_i}$.

This term, found in Eq. (4.25), is simply neglected in most RANS codes.

Of course, these equations, coupled to ad-hoc models, allow only the determination of mean quantities that may be quite different from instantaneous quantities (Fig. 4.6).

4.5.3 Classical turbulence models for the Reynolds stresses

Following the turbulence viscosity assumption proposed by Boussinesq (Hinze [293], Tennekes and Lumley [644], Pope [535]), the turbulent Reynolds stresses $\overline{\rho u_i'' u_j''}$ are generally described using the viscous tensor τ_{ij} expression retained for newtonian fluids (Eq. (1.15)):[ix]

$$\overline{\rho u_i'' u_j''} = \overline{\rho} \widetilde{u_i'' u_j''} = -\mu_t \left(\frac{\partial \tilde{u}_i}{\partial x_j} + \frac{\partial \tilde{u}_j}{\partial x_i} - \frac{2}{3} \delta_{ij} \frac{\partial \tilde{u}_k}{\partial x_k} \right) + \frac{2}{3} \overline{\rho} k \tag{4.30}$$

where μ_t is a turbulent dynamic viscosity ($\mu_t = \overline{\rho} \nu_t$, where ν_t is the turbulent kinematic viscosity) and δ_{ij} is the Kronecker symbol. The last term in Eq. (4.30) has been added to recover the right expression for the turbulent kinetic energy k as:

$$k = \frac{1}{2} \sum_{k=1}^{3} \widetilde{u_k'' u_k''} \tag{4.31}$$

The question is now to evaluate the turbulent viscosity μ_t. Three main approaches have been proposed: algebraic expressions which do not require any additional balance equation, one-equation closure, and two-equations closure.

Zero-equation model: Prandtl mixing length model

Prandtl [541] has proposed to link turbulent viscosity to the velocity gradient via an algebraic expression as:[x]

$$\mu_t = \overline{\rho} l_m^2 \left| \widetilde{S} \right| \tag{4.32}$$

where $\widetilde{S}$ is the mean stress tensor, defined as:

$$\widetilde{S}_{ij} = \frac{1}{2} \left(\frac{\partial \tilde{u}_i}{\partial x_j} + \frac{\partial \tilde{u}_j}{\partial x_i} \right) \tag{4.33}$$

and l_m is a mixing length to be given. Various empirical relations have been proposed to model l_m but depend strongly on the flow geometry.

[ix]Note that the last term between parenthesis in the right hand side of Eq. (4.30) is equal to zero for constant density flows according to the mass conservation equation (4.21) and then does not appear in usual turbulence textbooks.

[x]These turbulence models have been developed for non reacting, constant density flows and are written in terms of classical unweighted Reynolds averages. Their extension to reacting flows remains an open question (see Chapt. 5) but is generally conducted by simply replacing Reynolds by Favre averages in model expressions as done here.

One-equation model: Prandtl-Kolmogorov

A more general formulation incorporates a closure of the balance equation for the turbulent kinetic energy k. The turbulent viscosity is then modeled as:

$$\mu_t = \bar{\rho} C_\mu l_{pk} \sqrt{k} \qquad (4.34)$$

where C_μ is a model constant (generally chosen as $C_\mu = 0.09$) and l_{pk} is a characteristic length to be given. Once again, empirical relations are required for l_{pk}.

Two-equations model: $k - \varepsilon$

In this approach (Jones and Launder [315]), the turbulent viscosity is estimated as:

$$\mu_t = \bar{\rho} C_\mu \frac{k^2}{\varepsilon} \qquad (4.35)$$

where the turbulent kinetic energy k and its dissipation rate ε are described by closure of two balance equations:

$$\frac{\partial}{\partial t}(\bar{\rho} k) + \frac{\partial}{\partial x_i}(\bar{\rho} \tilde{u}_i k) = \frac{\partial}{\partial x_i}\left[\left(\mu + \frac{\mu_t}{\sigma_k}\right)\frac{\partial k}{\partial x_i}\right] + P_k - \bar{\rho}\varepsilon \qquad (4.36)$$

$$\frac{\partial}{\partial t}(\bar{\rho}\varepsilon) + \frac{\partial}{\partial x_i}(\bar{\rho}\tilde{u}_i\varepsilon) = \frac{\partial}{\partial x_i}\left[\left(\mu + \frac{\mu_t}{\sigma_\varepsilon}\right)\frac{\partial \varepsilon}{\partial x_i}\right] + C_{\varepsilon1}\frac{\varepsilon}{k}P_k - C_{\varepsilon2}\bar{\rho}\frac{\varepsilon^2}{k} \qquad (4.37)$$

The source term P_k is given by:

$$P_k = -\bar{\rho}\widetilde{u_i'' u_j''}\frac{\partial \tilde{u}_i}{\partial x_j} \qquad (4.38)$$

where the Reynolds stresses $\bar{\rho}\widetilde{u_i'' u_j''}$ are determined using Boussinesq expression (4.30). The model constants are usually:

$$C_\mu = 0.09 \quad ; \quad \sigma_k = 1.0 \quad ; \quad \sigma_\varepsilon = 1.3 \quad ; \quad C_{\varepsilon1} = 1.44 \quad ; \quad C_{\varepsilon2} = 1.92 \qquad (4.39)$$

This model is very popular because of its simplicity and cost effectiveness. It also provides turbulent time scale estimates, respectively k/ε and $\sqrt{\varepsilon/\nu}$ for integral and Kolmogorov length scales which are used in turbulent combustion models. Nevertheless, this model has some well-known drawbacks:

- Exact balance equations for k and ε may be derived but are very difficult to close without strong assumptions. For example, Eq. (4.36) and (4.37) implicitly assume high Reynolds number, homogeneous and isotropic turbulence and have to be adapted for low Reynolds number flows.

- Algebraic laws for Reynolds stresses and/or for certain source terms in Eqs. (4.36) and (4.37) are generally required to predict flow fields in the vicinity of walls (Chapt. 7).

- Velocity fluctuations due to low frequency motions associated to intermittency and flapping are underestimated.

- The $k - \varepsilon$ model has also to be modified for compressible flows. These effects are generally taken into account through the model constant C_μ, becoming a function of convective Mach numbers, and splitting the turbulent kinetic energy dissipation rate ε into solenoidal (ε_s) and dilatational (ε_h) contributions (Sarkar et al. [588], Zeman [730]).

- To provide a better description of energy exchanges between turbulent scales, multi-scale $k - \varepsilon$ models have been proposed. The basic idea is to split the turbulence spectrum in several zones having their own turbulent kinetic energy k_i and dissipation rate ε_i (Kim [346]).

Extensions

Usual turbulence models such as $k - \varepsilon$ assume isotropic turbulence, but practical flows are often anisotropic. Such phenomena can be incorporated through more sophisticated modeling. The simplest approaches are known as Algebraic Stress Models (ASM). In these models, the Boussinesq formulation (4.30) is no longer retained and algebraic expressions are derived for the Reynolds stresses, $\overline{\rho u_i'' u_j''}$ which depends on turbulent kinetic energy k, dissipation rates ε, mean strain tensor $\widetilde{S}$ or mean rotational tensor. The second way is to derive and close balance equations for the Reynolds stresses, $\overline{\rho u_i'' u_j''}$. This approach corresponds to second-order modeling and leads to Reynolds Stresses Models (RSM). More details may be found in review papers (Hallback et al. [265], Launder [366]) or textbooks (Pope [535]).

4.5.4 A first attempt to close mean reaction rates

A direct approach to evaluate mean reaction rates is first discussed in this section. This simple formalism, based on series expansion, illustrates the difficulties arising from the non-linear character of chemical sources.

Consider a simple irreversible reaction between fuel (F) and oxidizer (O):

$$F + s O \rightarrow (1 + s)P$$

where the fuel mass reaction rate $\dot{\omega}_F$ is expressed from the Arrhenius law as:

$$\dot{\omega}_F = -A_1 \rho^2 T^{\beta_1} Y_F Y_O \exp\left(-\frac{T_A}{T}\right) \qquad (4.40)$$

where A is the pre-exponential constant and T_A the activation temperature. Assuming a constant pressure p, this reaction rate is rewritten, using the perfect gas law ($\rho = (pW)/(RT)$, Eq. 1.4):

$$\dot{\omega}_F = -A_1 \frac{pW}{R} \rho T^{\beta_1 - 1} Y_F Y_O \exp\left(-\frac{T_A}{T}\right) \qquad (4.41)$$

As the reaction rate is highly non-linear, the averaged reaction rate $\overline{\dot{\omega}}_F$ cannot be easily expressed as a function of the mean mass fractions $\widetilde{Y}_F$ and $\widetilde{Y}_O$, the mean density $\overline{\rho}$ and the mean temperature $\widetilde{T}$. The first simple idea is to expand the mean reaction rate $\overline{\dot{\omega}}_F$ as a Taylor series of the temperature fluctuation T'', using:

$$\exp\left(-\frac{T_A}{T}\right) = \exp\left(-\frac{T_A}{\widetilde{T}}\right)\left(1 + \sum_{n=1}^{+\infty} P_n \frac{T''^n}{\widetilde{T}^n}\right) \quad ; \quad T^{b-1} = \widetilde{T}^{b-1}\left(1 + \sum_{n=1}^{+\infty} Q_n \frac{T''^n}{\widetilde{T}^n}\right) \tag{4.42}$$

where P_n and Q_n are given by:

$$P_n = \sum_{k=1}^{n} (-1)^{n-k} \frac{(n-1)!}{(n-k)!\left[(k-1)!\right]^2 k} \left(\frac{T_A}{\widetilde{T}}\right)^k \quad ; \quad Q_n = \frac{(b-1)(b-2)...(b-n)}{n!} \tag{4.43}$$

The mean reaction rate $\overline{\dot{\omega}}_F$ becomes, using $pW/R = \overline{\rho}\widetilde{T}$ (Borghi [70]):

$$\overline{\dot{\omega}}_F = -A_1\overline{\rho}^2\widetilde{T}^{\beta_1}\widetilde{Y}_F\widetilde{Y}_O \exp\left(-\frac{T_A}{\widetilde{T}}\right)\left[1 + \frac{\widetilde{Y_F''Y_O''}}{\widetilde{Y}_F\widetilde{Y}_O} + (P_1 + Q_1)\left(\frac{\widetilde{Y_F''T''}}{\widetilde{Y}_F\widetilde{T}} + \frac{\widetilde{Y_O''T''}}{\widetilde{Y}_O\widetilde{T}}\right)\right.$$
$$\left. + (P_2 + Q_2 + P_1Q_1)\left(\frac{\widetilde{T''^2}}{\widetilde{T}^2} + \frac{\widetilde{Y_F''T''^2}}{\widetilde{Y}_F\widetilde{T}^2} + \frac{\widetilde{Y_O''T''^2}}{\widetilde{Y}_O\widetilde{T}^2}\right) + ...\right] \tag{4.44}$$

Equation (4.44) leads to various difficulties. First, new quantities such as $\widetilde{Y_F''Y_O''}$, $\widetilde{T''^n}$ and $\widetilde{Y_k''T''^n}$ have to be closed, using algebraic expressions or transport equations. Because of non linearities, large truncation errors are also introduced when only few terms of the series expansion are taken into account. Expression (4.44) is complicated but is only valid for a simple irreversible reaction: it cannot be extended to realistic chemical schemes. For these reasons, reaction rate closures in turbulent combustion are not based on Eq. (4.44) but are derived from physical analysis, briefly summarized in Section 4.5.5 and described in Chapters 5 and 6.

Nevertheless, this approach is used in some practical simulations where chemical times are not negligible compared to flow times, for example in supersonic reacting flow fields (Villasenor et al. [689]) or to describe chemical reactions in atmospheric boundary layer where the temperature T may be roughly assumed to be constant (Nieuwstadt and Meeder [472]). In these situations, only the first two terms in the series expansion are kept. A segregation factor $\alpha_s = \widetilde{Y_F''Y_O''}/\widetilde{Y}_F\widetilde{Y}_O$ is introduced to write the mean reaction rate as:

$$\overline{\dot{\omega}}_F = -A_1\overline{\rho}^2\widetilde{T}^{\beta_1}\widetilde{Y}_F\widetilde{Y}_O \exp\left(-T_A/\widetilde{T}\right)(1 + \alpha_s) \tag{4.45}$$

The segregation factor α_s measures the mixing between fuel and oxidizer ($\alpha_s = 0$ for perfectly mixed reactants and $\alpha_s = -1$ for perfectly separated ones). This factor is modeled or provided by a balance equation.

4.5.5 Physical approaches to model turbulent combustion

As shown in Section 4.5.4, a proper turbulent combustion description cannot be based on a simple mathematical expansion around mean values. Therefore, reaction rate closures are generally developed from physical analysis, comparing chemical and turbulent time scales (see Chapters 5 and 6). According to Veynante and Vervisch [678], most combustion models are derived from one of the three following approaches illustrated in Fig. 4.14.

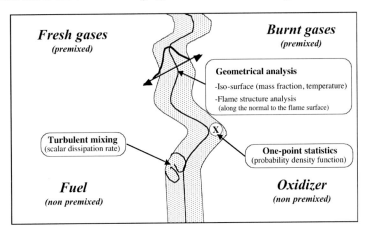

Figure 4.14: Modeling approaches for turbulent combustion: geometrical analysis (the flame front is identified to a surface), mixing description (the reaction rate is assumed to be controled by the mixing rate, i.e. the scalar dissipation rate) or pure statistical approach (probability density function formalism), following the analysis proposed by Veynante and Vervisch [678].

Geometrical analysis

The flame front is identified as a geometrical surface evolving in the turbulent flow field. This surface may be related to the global flame brush as done in the level set G-equation framework (section 5.3.4) but is generally linked to the instantaneous iso-surface of a mass or mixture fraction. This formalism is usually combined with flamelet assumptions (each flame element is assumed to behave as a laminar flame). In this situation, mean reaction rates are estimated as the product of the available flame area per unit volume (the so-called flame surface density) multiplied by the mean reaction rate per unit of flame area (see Sections 5.3.6 and 6.4.6).

Turbulent mixing

Under the assumption that chemical time scales are shorter than turbulent time scales (large Damköhler numbers, Sections 5.2 and 6.3), reaction rates are controled by turbulent mixing rates. The challenge is then to model these turbulent mixing rates, generally expressed in terms of scalar dissipation rates (Section 6.4.3 and Eq. 6.34). Note that simple popular models such as Eddy-Break-Up (Section 5.3.3) and Eddy-Dissipation Concept (Section 6.4.4) are derived from this analysis.

One-point statistics

In principle, this last approach does not require assumptions on the flame structure such as a flamelet hypothesis or that of mixing-controlled combustion:[xi] mean reaction rates are expressed combining instantaneous reaction rates given from Arrhenius law (Eq. 1.24), $\dot{\omega}_k(\Psi_1, \ldots \Psi_N)$ with the joint probability density function $p(\Psi_1, \Psi_2 \ldots, \Psi_N)$ to have given values of the thermochemical variables (i.e. species mass fractions, temperature...)$\Psi_1, \Psi_2, \ldots \Psi_N$:

$$\overline{\dot{\omega}}_k = \int_{\Psi_1, \ldots \Psi_N} \dot{\omega}_k\left(\Psi_1, \ldots, \Psi_N\right) p(\Psi_1, \Psi_2 \ldots, \Psi_N)\, d\Psi_1\, \Psi_2 \ldots d\Psi_N \qquad (4.46)$$

This formalism is detailed in Section 5.3.7 for turbulent premixed flames and in Section 6.4.6 for turbulent non-premixed flames.

Comments

Even though the previous approaches are based on different physical concepts, they are closely related as evidenced by Veynante and Vervisch [678]. To derive the mathematical relations between modeling tools is beyond the scope of this book and the reader is referred to the corresponding paper. These relations are useful to understand the exact implications of the physical hypothesis underlying the model developments. According to these findings, no approach displays a decisive advantage over others and results will mainly depend on the ability to close unknown quantities. Note also that the unknown quantities, flame surface density, scalar dissipation rate or probability density functions respectively, may be determined either by an algebraic expression from known quantities or through a balance equation as evidenced in the two following chapters.

4.5.6   A modeling challenge: flame flapping and intermittency

Before deriving any model, as described in Chapter 5 and 6, challenges in reaction rate $\overline{\dot{\omega}}_k$ modeling should be emphasized. First, from a mathematical point of view, the strong non linearity of the Arrhenius law with temperature makes averaging a difficult issue, as shown

---

[xi]Of course, additional assumptions are required in practice to determine unknown quantities. Note also that this statistical description may be combined with flamelet assumptions to derive simple models for primitive variables in turbulent non-premixed combustion (Sections 6.4.2 and 6.4.5).

above (§ 4.5.4), because the average of a strongly non-linear function cannot be estimated using the value of the function for mean values (first term in Eq. (4.44)).

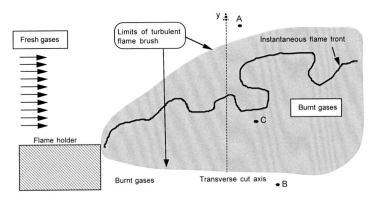

Figure 4.15: Turbulent flame brush.

A more physical insight on this statement may be given, for example, considering a turbulent premixed flame brush (Fig. 4.15) in which the mean temperature transverse profiles at a given axial location are displayed in Fig. 4.16. This flame corresponds to the usual situation of a "stabilized" flame where burnt gases recirculating behind the flame holder ignite the incoming fresh gases. This flame is unsteady because of turbulence, but RANS models try to predict mean values only so that the result of a RANS code is independent of time.

As shown in Fig. 4.15, the flame is wrinkled and displaced by the incoming turbulence. The extreme positions reached by the instantaneous flame during its movement determine the width of the averaged turbulent flame brush at a given location. Simply looking at a turbulent flame (after averaging by eyes, a procedure similar to Reynolds or Favre averaging) reveals flame brushes of a few cm. Laminar flame thicknesses range from a few micrometers to a fraction of a millimeter (Chapt. 2). Obviously, characteristics of instantaneous and averaged flames are very different: mean temperature profiles are much broader than instantaneous temperature profiles as displayed in Fig. 4.16. Since the mean reaction is non zero at every location reached by the flame during its flapping movements, mean reaction rate profiles are also broader than instantaneous reaction rate profiles. A convenient method to consider fuel reaction rates is to plot them versus reduced temperature Θ. Fig. 4.17 shows a typical laminar rate profile ($\dot{\omega}_F$ vs Θ) and a typical turbulent rate profile ($\overline{\dot{\omega}}_F$ vs $\widetilde{\Theta}$). As in physical space, mean reaction rate profiles in Θ space are much broader than laminar ones. This finding has strong implications for numerical resolution: while a code solving laminar flame equations must resolve fronts of 0.1 mm thickness, RANS turbulent combustion solvers have to resolve fronts which are much thicker and less demanding in terms of grid resolution.

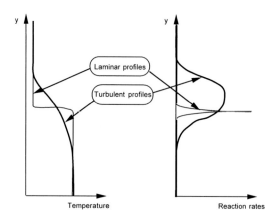

Figure 4.16: Comparison of laminar and turbulent profiles for temperature and reaction rates along a transverse axis of Fig. 4.15.

Flapping motions may also be analyzed in terms of intermittency. Fig. 4.15 shows that a given location in the turbulent flame brush may contain either pure fresh gases (point A), fully burnt products (point B) or a succession of fresh and burnt gases (point C). Assuming a sufficiently thin flame front, compared to turbulent motions (which is discussed in subsequent chapters), temperature measurements at a given location produce a telegraphic signal as a function of time (Fig. 4.18). An intermittency between fresh (temperature T_1) and burnt (temperature T_2) is observed. This has various consequences for RANS modeling:

- Averaged temperatures $\widetilde{T}$ are not representative of instantaneous temperatures: $\widetilde{T}$ mainly measures the probability of finding fresh or burnt gases at a given location.

- RANS closures have to take into account intermittency phenomena between fresh and burnt gases in turbulent premixed flames or between fuel and oxidizer streams in non-premixed situations: properties may be quite different on each side of the flame. For example, in premixed flames, turbulence is generally higher in the fresh gases (viscous effects are enhanced by high temperatures). Nevertheless, Reynolds stresses, $\widetilde{\rho u_i'' u_j''}$, are supposed to incorporate turbulence in fresh and in burnt gases, weighted by the probability of finding fresh or burnt gases.[xii] Classical turbulence models, developed for non-reacting constant density flows (§ 4.5.3) are not designed for this difficult task.

[xii] This point is analyzed more precisely in § 5.1.3.

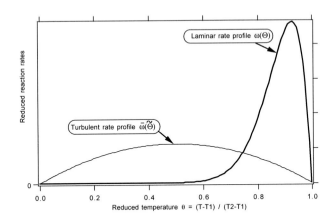

Figure 4.17: Reaction rate profiles versus temperature in a turbulent flame brush.

- For CFD code users, knowing that the mean temperature at a given point is low does not mean that very high levels of temperature cannot be reached for short durations at this point; but only that the probability of finding hot burnt gases at this point is low. Accordingly, for example, RANS results may be misleading to design wall cooling devices (Chapt. 7).

The main conceptual difference between RANS and LES modeling lies in intermittency phenomena. As LES are instantaneous simulations, intermittency does not have to be modeled because at a given time, the flame position is known at the resolved scale level. LES models are only introduced to describe unresolved flame structure and reaction rate at subgrid scale levels. On the other hand, as described above, intermittency must be incorporated in RANS models, because, as only averaged flow fields are computed, they have to take into account, implicitly or explicitly, the probability to find the flame at a given location.

4.6 Direct numerical simulations (DNS)

Initiated in the eighties, Direct Numerical Simulations (DNS) have changed turbulent combustion studies and modeling. Solving the flow equations (4.14) to (4.17), without any turbulence model, DNS have offered a new way to investigate flame/turbulence interactions and significant progress has been achieved both for models and for fundamentals of turbulent combustion (Givi [243, 244], Poinsot et al. [526], Vervisch and Poinsot [670], Hilbert et al. [289]). A complete numerical simulation of the three–dimensional balance equations describing a chemically reacting flow and including multispecies transport, realistic thermodynamics and complex chemistry was out of reach in 2000 but the introduction of massively parallel systems and the

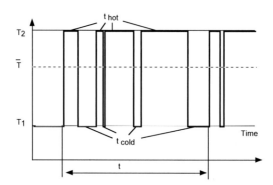

Figure 4.18: Passage of flame structures for infinitely fast chemistry.

adaptation of DNS codes to these machines have allowed to reach grids of the order of a few billion points with realistic chemistry, bringing DNS to levels of precision never reached before (Mizobuchi et al. [445], Lignell et al. [396], Bisetti et al. [57], Chen et al. [120], Chen [121]).

4.6.1   The role of DNS in turbulent combustion studies

Even though highly precise DNS are available today, they are not always needed or may be too expensive so that various levels of simplification been introduced. In fact, such simplifications are also often required to understand the basic mechanisms controlling a specific phenomenon. Assumptions may be used to isolate an elementary ingredient of turbulence/combustion inter-actions, in a manner inaccessible to experiments. For example, heat release may be suppressed to study the influence of turbulence on chemical reaction without the simultaneous feedback effects of chemistry on the flow field through density and fluid properties variations. On the other hand, caution has to be taken with results obtained using a given set of assumptions and idealizations. DNS provides the best results only when conducted in conjunction with theoretical analysis and experiments.

This section describes DNS as a numerical tool for turbulent combustion analysis and presents its practical limitations. Important results achieved using DNS are detailed in Chapter 5 for turbulent premixed flames and in Chapter 6 for non-premixed ones.

4.6.2   Numerical methods for DNS

DNS of reacting flows differs in many ways from DNS of non-reacting situations where the fundamental limitation is determined by the turbulence Reynolds number. The maximum Reynolds number which can be reached without combustion is determined by the number of grid points as described below. The simulation of reacting flows requires a set of balance equations and the selection of chemical kinetics and species transport properties. The initial flow configuration has to be set-up with great care. The Reynolds number upper limit is also controlled by the number of grid points, but another condition is imposed by the proper resolution of the flame inner structure. The main issues and trade-offs encountered in the field of DNS are listed below. The following aspects are successively considered: formulation, description of chemistry, initial and boundary conditions, dimensions, description of heat losses, algorithm selection.

Formulation: incompressible, low Mach number and compressible

Since multiple formulations may be derived for reacting flows equations (Chapt. 1), the first issue is to choose a form for the conservation equations. Most DNS of non-reacting flows have been performed for incompressible (constant-density) flows. For reacting flows, many options may be retained depending on the acceptable simplifications for a certain application. DNS of reacting flows may rely on the constant density ("thermodiffusive") approximation, low-Mach number formulations (variable density formulations where acoustic waves are filtered out) or fully compressible flow descriptions (variable density, variable pressure).

While constant density formulations yield interesting information on some mechanisms governing turbulent flames, they are limited by the absence of flame-induced flow modifications due to heat release. In thermodiffusive formulations, temperature variations can be taken into account in the evaluation of reaction rates (see Clavin [136] for applications of this approximation in laminar flame theory and Rutland and Ferziger [578] for a typical direct simulation) if a modified state equation decouples the temperature from density and pressure field. Under this approximation, the essential stiffness of Arrhenius kinetics is retained but the conversion of chemical species and the corresponding heat release do not influence the density.

A less restrictive formulation relies on the low-Mach number approximation where density may change due to temperature variations but remains independent of pressure. In this formulation, acoustic waves are eliminated so that the numerical time step is no longer limited by the classical Courant-Friedrichs-Lewy (CFL) condition.[xiii] This formulation is well-suited for low-speed flows, typically encountered in subsonic combustion. Nevertheless, it cannot be retained in studying combustion instabilities where flow field, acoustic field and chemical reaction interact (Chapt. 8). It remains also questionable when pressure gradients are involved in scalar turbulent transport (terms (VI) and (VII) in Eq. (5.119)).

Despite the higher cost, fully compressible formulations have some advantages which explain why they have been used in many DNS of reacting flows: flame/acoustics interaction effects are captured, combustion in high-speed flows may be studied, and an easier treatment

---

[xiii]The Courant-Friedrichs-Lewy condition prescribes that an acoustic wave cannot move over more than one computational grid size Δx during one computational time step Δt. Accordingly, the possible time step is limited as $\Delta t \leq \Delta x / c$ where c is the sound speed. The CFL number is defined as $CFL = c\Delta t / \Delta x$ and should remain lower than unity in explicit compressible codes. Implicit compressible codes are generally able to work with higher CFL numbers but require the resolution of an implicit equation for pressure.

of boundary conditions is offered (Chapt. 9). With an explicit time advancement scheme the CFL criterion limits the time step and the computational cost becomes important, especially in low-speed flows. Nevertheless, in practical simulations, this time step is often limited by the chemical reaction rate, and not by acoustic wave propagation, so that the fully compressible formulation does not induce additional cost.

Chemical system selection

In addition to the form retained for the flow field equations (incompressible, low Mach Number or compressible flows), a DNS of reacting flows requires a description of chemistry. Specialists in chemistry argue that a realistic computation of hydrocarbon/air flames requires, at least, twenty chemical species while simulation experts point out that numerical constraints of unsteady computations in three dimensions make such a computation practically impossible. The choice of the chemical scheme essentially depends on the question being investigated. Studies of the folding of premixed flames in low-intensity turbulence may be carried out with the simplest chemistry or even with no kinetics at all by simply tracking the flame as a propagating front. On the other hand, investigation of pollutant formation in a turbulent flame requires a reasonably complete chemical scheme. The latter computation is much more realistic (and expensive) but the former may also be quite informative. Valuable results on the development of turbulent flames and their modeling have been deduced from simulations based on front tracking (Yeung et al. [721]) showing that physical intuition is often more important than the largest possible computer resources.

Initial and boundary conditions

The choice of initial configuration and boundary conditions introduces additional difficulties. Most cold flow simulations are carried out in periodic domains. Reacting flows preclude using periodic conditions at least in one direction (a planar premixed flame separates fresh and burnt gases and a diffusion flame take place between fuel and oxidizer streams) and more refined boundary conditions have to be specified, describing for example inlet and outlet flows (see Chapt. 9). The precision of these conditions should match that of the numerical solver. Parasitic phenomena may couple inlet and outlet boundaries when the numerical scheme has a very low numerical viscosity. Under these circumstances, numerical waves, traveling on the grid and propagating from outlet to inlet, have been observed (Buell and Huerre [97], Poinsot and Lele [519], Baum [38]). For incompressible or low Mach number formulations (Orlanski [484], Rutland and Ferziger [578], Zhang and Rutland [731]), the specification of boundary conditions preventing such phenomena requires a fine tuning with the pressure solver used inside the domain. Another solution is to sacrifice a certain part of the computational domain near the outlet, used as a buffer zone where perturbations are damped by a high artificial viscosity before reaching the outlet. For compressible flows, Poinsot and Lele [519] present a method based on characteristic analysis (Thompson [648]) for direct numerical simulation of compressible reacting flows that has been validated in many different situations (see Chapt. 9). This method was later extended to multi-species flows with complex chemistry (Baum et al.

[40], Moureau et al. [456]) and real gas (Okong'o and Bellan [480]). Higher-order formulations of the same techniques for non-reacting flows may also be found in Giles [235], Colonius et al. [148] and multiple improvements have been proposed for example to inject turbulence in DNS and LES (Yoo and Im [725], Prosser [545], Guezennec and Poinsot [256]).

Initial conditions may also be difficult to set and limit the possible configurations to be studied. For example, DNS of turbulence/combustion interactions require the initial specification of a given turbulent flow field, compatible with the mass and momentum conservation equations and having a prescribed spectrum. At the initial time, this turbulent field is superimposed to a laminar flame, generally planar. This situation is clearly non physical and an adaptation time is required. To be relevant, the initial flame has to be issued from a previous one-dimensional laminar DNS. In the absence of forcing, turbulence decays with time whereas the flame front is wrinkled by flow motions. Then, no steady state situation may be reached limiting the possible conclusions of the simulations, generally analyzed after several eddy turnover times. Injection of a well-defined turbulent flow field in the numerical domain is possible but difficult and expensive: see van Kalmthout and Veynante [664] for supersonic incoming flows, and, for subsonic incoming flows Rutland and Cant [576] (low-Mach number formulation), Guichard [257], Vervisch et al. [673], Prosser [545], Guezennec and Poinsot [256] (fully compressible formulation).

Two-dimensional versus three-dimensional DNS

Because computer resources are limited, it is often necessary to perform reacting flow simulations in two dimensions, thereby missing all three-dimensional effects of real turbulence. This approximation is generally not suitable for non-reacting flows because turbulent fluctuations are intrinsically three-dimensional. For premixed combustion, however, direct simulations (Cant et al. [113]) show that the probability of finding locally cylindrical (2D) flame sheets is higher than the probability of finding 3D spheroidal flame surfaces (§ 5.5.5). Two-dimensional flames appear more probable even though the flow field ahead of these flames is fully three-dimensional. Considering the prohibitive cost of three-dimensional reacting flow computations, two-dimensional simulations remain quite valuable. This is especially true when dealing with "flame/vortex" interactions where the dynamics of a flame front interacting with isolated vortex structures is examined (§ 5.2.3). Flame/vortex studies yield useful information on turbulent combustion (see Laverdant and Candel [367], Poinsot et al. [528] or Ashurst [16]) This simple problem is also well-suited for comparisons with experimental investigation (Jarosinski et al. [309], Roberts and Driscoll [560], Roberts et al. [561], Lee et al. [375], Roberts et al. [562], Driscoll et al. [187], Mantel et al. [418], Thevenin et al. [647]). The comparison of two and three-dimensional simulations shows that, in terms of turbulent transport, no clear difference appears and that the criterion proposed to delineate between gradient and counter-gradient regimes is in very good agreement with both DNS (Veynante et al. [683]). But, on the other hand, for the numerical cost of a single three-dimensional DNS, thirty two-dimensional DNS can be performed allowing the exploration of a large range of physical parameters.

Description of heat losses

Direct numerical simulations of reacting flows should include a description of heat transfer by radiation and convection. Heat losses from the reactive region govern flame quenching processes (Patnaik and Kailasanath [493]) and thus determine the combustion regime (Poinsot et al. [523]) or the flame evolution near a wall. Detailed models of radiation require complicated descriptions of the spectral characteristics of the main chemical species and the solution of the radiative transfer equations. Simplified assumptions (Williams [710]) have been used up to now to avoid the added complexity of the general formulation (see however Soufiani and Djavdan [622], Daguse et al. [162], Wu et al. [715], Coelho [144], Amaya et al. [9] for realistic radiative models coupled to combustion codes).

Numerical schemes

The DNS of flows (with or without reaction) requires extremely precise numerical methods: these schemes must be able to propagate vortices over long distances without changing their velocity (dispersion effects) or their amplitude (dissipation effects). This is a very difficult task and building such schemes is beyond the objective of this book[xiv]

Multiple numerical algorithms have been used for DNS of reacting flows. To simulate constant density flames, classical incompressible DNS codes developed for cold flows and generally based on spectral methods may be used. These schemes are accurate but limited to periodic boundary conditions. For this reason, recent simulations have relied on alternative higher-order finite difference schemes (Lele [378], Sengupta [606], Sengupta et al. [607]) or mixed schemes which use spectral methods in two directions and a finite difference method along the non-periodic direction (Nomura and Elgobashi [477], Nomura [476]). Spatial derivatives in the non-periodic direction are estimated by higher-order upwind schemes or by compact Pade approximates (Lele [378]).

Fig. 4.19 summarizes the wide range of formulations used for DNS of turbulent flames (diffusion or premixed). For example, three-dimensional constant density codes applied to DNS of cold flows may be used without modification to study the wrinkling of material surfaces by turbulence (Yeung et al. [721], Ashurst and Barr [17], Cattolica et al. [115]). The propagation of premixed flames with a specified flame speed in a turbulent flowfield may be studied introducing a transport equation for a field variable G (Osher and Sethian [485], Ashurst et al. [19], Ashurst [14], Barr [33]). While the computed flow differs from real flames (no chemistry and in most cases no heat release effects), this formulation provides valuable information on premixed flames for a reasonable computational cost. In the middle of Fig. 4.19, three-dimensional computations (Ashurst et al. [20], Trouvé and Poinsot [652], Rutland and

---

[xiv]Readers interested in a simple tutorial in dispersion and dissipation effects in CFD will find a simple example and a simulation tool at *elearning.cerfacs.fr/numerical/schemes/1Dscheme/index.php*. They can also learn about basic methods for CFD (mesh and discretization) at *elearning.cerfacs.fr/numerical/schemes/mesh/index.php*. An example of recent CFD solvers applied to the case of a vortex convection is available at *elearning.cerfacs.fr/numerical/benchmarks/vortex2d/*. This simple test case allows to visualize how a vortex (the typical flow prototype which DNS must propagate without modification) is convected over long distances by some of the most well-known DNS codes.

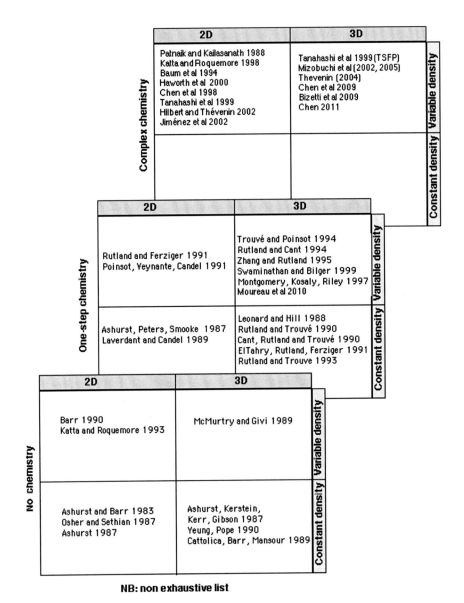

NB: non exhaustive list

Figure 4.19: Examples of direct numerical simulations (DNS) of turbulent flames.

Trouvé [579], Zhang and Rutland [731], Swaminathan and Bilger [634], Montgomery et al. [452], Leonard and Hill [379], Rutland and Ferziger [578], Laverdant and Candel [367], Rutland and Trouvé [580], Cant et al. [113], Tahry et al. [636], Poinsot et al. [523]) performed for premixed flames with simple chemistry (Arrhenius law, variable density, variable viscosity) or for diffusion flames with infinitely fast chemistry require about 100 times more CPU hours for each run. At the top of the diagram (Fig. 4.19), complex chemistry computations in 2D or 3D require the largest computer resources: calculations are limited to small box sizes and cannot be repeated systematically. A few direct numerical simulations of H_2-O_2 or CH_4-air flames in two or three dimensions with complex chemistry, variable density, and multispecies transport models have been reported in recent years (Jiménez et al. [311], Patnaik et al. [494], Tanahashi et al. [639], Haworth et al. [275], Baum et al. [39], Tanahashi et al. [638], Hilbert and Thévenin [287], Katta and Roquemore [325], Patnaik et al. [494], Echekki and Chen [196], Chen et al. [122], Tanahashi et al. [638], Katta and Roquemore [324], Mizobuchi et al. [445, 444], Thevenin [645]). The revolution of parallel computing after 2005 has produced DNS with meshes of the order of billions of points (Chen et al. [120], Bisetti et al. [57], Gourdain et al. [250], Chen [121], Moureau et al. [458]) which can now be compared directly to real experiments.

Most direct simulations of turbulent combustion have been based on regular non-adaptive meshes because turbulent flames move rapidly in the whole domain, exhibit considerable wrinkling and cannot be easily treated with self-adaptive gridding. While adaptive meshes work well in simple geometry (Darabiha et al. [165], Giovangigli and Smooke [238], Dervieux et al. [173]), there are few examples of DNS applications. Lagrangian methods and especially random-vortex methods (RVM), which are grid free, are not emphasized here because our attention is focused on techniques which solve the Navier-Stokes equations.

4.6.3   Spatial resolution and physical scales

Direct numerical simulation grids must ensure that:

- the calculation is performed in the largest possible domain to resolve the large scales,

- the mesh is fine enough to resolve the smallest scales (usually Kolmogorov scales),

- the mesh is fine enough to resolve the inner structure of the flame.

Resolution of turbulence scales

Turbulent scales are correctly resolved when the largest and smallest eddies are captured by the grid mesh. This leads to a standard condition derived as follows. Consider a computational domain with a typical size L. The mesh comprises N points in each dimension leading to a typical cell size $\Delta x = L/N$. The turbulent flow may be characterized by the large-scale velocity fluctuations u' and integral length scale l_t. The size of the domain should be at least of the order of one integral scale l_t ($L = N\Delta x \geq l_t$). The smallest scale of turbulent eddies η_k is estimated from the Kolmogorov cascade arguments: $\eta_k \simeq l_t/(Re_t)^{3/4}$, according to Eq. (4.8). This scale is resolved by the computation if it is larger than the mesh size: $\eta_k > \Delta x$. Combining the previous expressions leads to:

$$\frac{l_t}{\eta_k} < N \quad \text{or} \quad N > Re_t^{3/4} \quad \text{or equivalently} \quad \boxed{Re_t < N^{4/3}} \tag{4.47}$$

These inequalities determine the number of grid points N required in each direction for a given Reynolds number Re_t or the limiting value of the Reynolds number for a selected number of grid points in each direction.

Resolution of chemical scales

The inner flame structure has also to be resolved on the computational mesh. In the following, this constraint is discussed for premixed flames because non-premixed flames have no characteristic thicknesses and require a different treatment (Chapt. 3 and 6).

The proper resolution of chemical scales depends strongly on the type of chemical scheme used in the DNS. When simple descriptions for chemistry are used (one-step irreversible reaction), calculations show that the resolution of the inner structure of the flame requires at least ten to twenty grid points ($Q \simeq 20$). In other words, the flame thickness δ_L^0 should extend over $Q \simeq 20$ elementary cells. In terms of flame thicknesses, the size of the computational domain is then given by $L \simeq (N/Q)\delta_L^0$. For standard hydrocarbon flames at room temperature $\delta_L^0 \simeq 0.5$ mm so that a 1024^3 grid would yield a box size of about $L \simeq 25$ mm. This condition also leads to an upper limit for the turbulence integral length scale l_t which must be smaller than L to provide converged statistics:

$$\frac{l_t}{\delta_L^0} < \frac{L}{\delta_L^0} < \frac{N}{Q} \tag{4.48}$$

Another expression may be obtained by replacing δ_L^0 with the diffusive flame thickness $\delta \simeq \nu/s_L^0$ (see § 2.5 for definition of thicknesses: δ is approximate but sufficient for this discussion). The Damköhler number, $Da = \tau_m/\tau_c$, compares a mechanical time scale τ_m and a chemical time scale τ_c. These two times may be estimated as $\tau_m(l_t) = \tau_t = l_t/u'$ and $\tau_c = \delta/s_L^0.$[xv] Then, the product of the Reynolds number by the Damköhler number is:

$$Re_t\, Da = \frac{l_t^2 s_L^0}{\nu\delta} = \left(\frac{l_t}{\delta}\right)^2 \tag{4.49}$$

leading to the computational grid condition (since δ and δ_L^0 are of the same order):

$$Re_t\, Da < (N/Q)^2 \tag{4.50}$$

[xv]The turbulent time scale is chosen here as the characteristic time scale of the largest turbulence structure, l_t. The chemical time corresponds to the time required by the flame front to propagate over a distance δ. Using $\delta \simeq \nu/s_L^0$, $\tau_c = \nu/s_L^{0\,2}$ may also be viewed as a characteristic diffusion time.

For a given Reynolds number satisfying condition (4.47), the Damköhler number is bounded by expression (4.50). This condition is relatively strong as shown by the following example. Assuming that $N = 1000$ and $Q = 20$, then $Re_t < 10^4$ according to (4.47) and $Re_t\, Da < 2500$ according to (4.50). For a turbulence Reynolds number $Re_l = 1000$, the Damköhler number cannot exceed 2.5, a value far from the large Damköhler numbers assumption used in most turbulent combustion models.

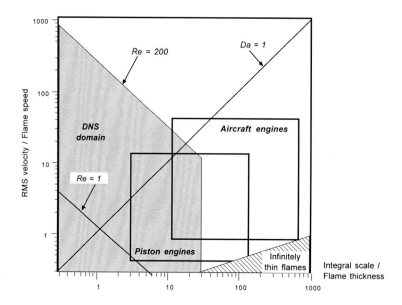

Figure 4.20: Resolution requirements of direct numerical simulation (DNS) methods: the shaded domain may be accessed with DNS. This diagram is displayed for a grid comprising $N = 600$ points in each direction with $Q = 20$ grid points inside the flame front. The maximum turbulence Reynolds number is $Re_t = 200$ (maximum Damköhler number $Da = 4.5$). The resolution of turbulence and flame structures impose $l_t/\delta < N/Q$. The infinitely thin flame zone is defined here as $\delta < \eta_k/10$.

Requirements for resolution of chemical scales impose a severe limitation on the parameter range that may be explored using DNS. These conditions are illustrated in Fig. 4.20, where operating constraints are plotted in terms of l_t/δ and u'/s_L^0. Assuming that the grid comprises 600 points in each direction and $Q = 20$, the Reynolds number is theoretically limited to $Re_t = 5000$ but should not exceed $Re_t = 200$ to reach reasonably high Damköhler numbers. For $Re_t = 200$, the maximum value of the Damköhler number, given by Eq. (4.50), is $Da = 4.5$. The domain which may be explored with DNS is shown as a grey region in Fig. 4.20.

This region is bounded above by the constraint on the turbulence Reynolds number (line $Re_t = (u'/s_L^0)(l_t/\delta) = 200$) and on the right by the condition $l_t/\delta = N/Q < 30$.

The diagram also shows that for small values of the integral scale l_t compared to the flame thickness δ, the resolution limit is defined by the first condition (4.47) on the Reynolds number. The largest integral scale l_t is usually set by the limit (4.50) induced by flame resolution.

Note that for fixed costs, the number of grid points N in one direction may be larger for two-dimensional calculations compared to three-dimensional simulations. As a consequence, the range of parameters explored in two dimensional computation may be wider.

The regions of the diagram of Fig. 4.20 corresponding to practical applications (for example IC engines) are overlapping with the domain of application of DNS. One may therefore claim that DNS may be used to address problems of practical importance. Another interesting result is that methods assuming an infinitely thin flame front (fast chemistry approximation in Table 4.19) are not suited to most practical problems because the separation between turbulent and chemical scales is generally not large enough to justify such an assumption.[xvi]

Fig. 4.20 corresponds to simple chemistry simulations. When complex chemical schemes are used, the domain where DNS is possible is much smaller because stiffer concentration gradients have to be resolved.

4.7 Large eddy simulations (LES)

The objective of large eddy simulations is to explicitly compute the largest structures of the flow field (typically structures larger than the computational mesh size) whereas the effects of the smallest ones are modeled (see Fig. 4.7). This technique is widely used for non-reacting flows, as evidenced in review papers (Piomelli and Chasnov [510], Ferziger [209], Lesieur [381], Lesieur and Metais [382], Piomelli [509], Sagaut [581], Meneveau and Katz [431], Geurts [230]) and is developing rapidly for combustion modeling.

4.7.1 LES filters

In LES, variables are filtered in spectral space (components greater than a given cut-off frequency are suppressed) or in physical space (weighted average over a given volume). The filtered quantity f is defined as:[xvii]

$$\overline{f}(\mathbf{x}) = \int f(\mathbf{x}')F(\mathbf{x} - \mathbf{x}')\,d\mathbf{x}' \qquad (4.51)$$

where F is the LES filter. The usual LES filters are shown in Fig. 4.21:

[xvi]The infinitely thin flame limit is defined here for a flame thickness δ ten times lower than the smallest turbulent length scale, i.e. the Kolmogorov scale ($\delta < \eta_k/10$). This limit is more constraining than the flamelet regime defined in Chapter 5.

[xvii]To simplify, similar notations $\overline{f}$ and $\widetilde{f}$ are used here in RANS and LES. In RANS context, these quantities denote ensemble averages whereas they correspond to filter quantities in large eddy simulations.

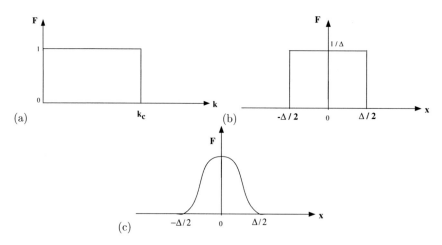

Figure 4.21: Common spatial filters used in large eddy simulations. (a) cut-off filter in spectral space; (b) box filter in physical space; (c) gaussian filter in physical space.

- **A cut-off filter in spectral space** (Fig. 4.21a):

$$F(k) = \begin{cases} 1 & \text{if } k \leq k_c = \pi/\Delta \\ 0 & \text{otherwise} \end{cases} \qquad (4.52)$$

where k is the spatial wave number. This filter keeps length scales larger than the cut-off length scale 2Δ, where Δ is the filter size.

- **A box filter in physical space** (Fig. 4.21b):

$$F(\mathbf{x}) = F(x_1, x_2, x_3) = \begin{cases} 1/\Delta^3 & \text{if} \quad |x_i| \leq \Delta/2, \ i = 1, 2, 3 \\ 0 & \text{otherwise} \end{cases} \qquad (4.53)$$

where (x_1, x_2, x_3) are the spatial coordinates of the location $\mathbf{x}$. This filter corresponds to an averaging over a cubic box of size Δ.

- **A Gaussian filter in physical space** (Fig. 4.21c):

$$F(\mathbf{x}) = F(x_1, x_2, x_3) = \left(\frac{6}{\pi\Delta^2}\right)^{3/2} \exp\left[-\frac{6}{\Delta^2}\left(x_1^2 + x_2^2 + x_3^2\right)\right] \qquad (4.54)$$

All these filters are normalized:

$$\int_{-\infty}^{+\infty} \int_{-\infty}^{+\infty} \int_{-\infty}^{+\infty} F(x_1, x_2, x_3) \, dx_1 dx_2 dx_3 = 1 \qquad (4.55)$$

For variable density ρ, a mass-weighted Favre filtering is introduced according to:

$$\overline{\rho}\,\widetilde{f}(\mathbf{x}) = \int \rho\, f(\mathbf{x}')\, F(\mathbf{x} - \mathbf{x}')\, d\mathbf{x}' \tag{4.56}$$

The filtered quantity $\overline{f}$ is resolved in the numerical simulation whereas $f' = f - \overline{f}$ corresponds to the unresolved part (i.e. the subgrid scale part, due to the unresolved flow motions). Balance equations for large eddy simulations are obtained by filtering the instantaneous balance equations (4.14) to (4.17). This operation should be carefully conducted:

- Contrary to RANS averaging, the filtered value of a LES perturbation is not zero: $\overline{f'} \neq 0$. Filtered and double filtered values are not equal in general:[xviii] $\overline{\overline{f}} \neq \overline{f}$. This is also true for Favre filtering: $f = \widetilde{f} + f''$, $\widetilde{f''} \neq 0$ and $\widetilde{\widetilde{f}} \neq \widetilde{f}$.

- The derivation of balance equations for the filtered quantities $\overline{f}$ or $\widetilde{f}$ requires the exchange of filter and derivative operators. This exchange is valid only under restrictive assumptions and is wrong, for example, when the filter size, corresponding to the mesh size, varies with spatial location. Ghosal and Moin [231] have investigated this point in detail but, in general, the uncertainties due to this operator exchange are neglected and their effects are assumed to be incorporated in the subgrid scale models. When the filter size varies with time, for example in piston engines, time commutation errors must also be accounted for (Moureau et al. [459]).

4.7.2 Filtered balance equations

Filtering the instantaneous balance equations leads to the following equations, formally similar to the Reynolds averaged balance equations derived in § 4.5.1:

- **Mass**

$$\frac{\partial \overline{\rho}}{\partial t} + \frac{\partial}{\partial x_i}(\overline{\rho}\,\widetilde{u}_i) = 0 \tag{4.57}$$

- **Momentum**

$$\frac{\partial \overline{\rho}\,\widetilde{u}_i}{\partial t} + \frac{\partial}{\partial x_i}(\overline{\rho}\,\widetilde{u}_i\widetilde{u}_j) + \frac{\partial \overline{p}}{\partial x_j} = \frac{\partial}{\partial x_i}\left[\overline{\tau}_{ij} - \overline{\rho}\left(\widetilde{u_iu_j} - \widetilde{u}_i\widetilde{u}_j\right)\right] \tag{4.58}$$

- **Chemical species**

$$\frac{\partial(\overline{\rho}\,\widetilde{Y}_k)}{\partial t} + \frac{\partial}{\partial x_i}(\overline{\rho}\,\widetilde{u}_i\widetilde{Y}_k) = \frac{\partial}{\partial x_i}\left[\overline{V_{k,i}Y_k} - \overline{\rho}\left(\widetilde{u_iY_k} - \widetilde{u}_i\widetilde{Y}_k\right)\right] + \overline{\dot{\omega}}_k \quad k = 1, N \tag{4.59}$$

[xviii]Filtered and double filtered values are equal when a cut-off filter in the spectral space is used: wave numbers larger than k_c are suppressed.

- **Enthalpy**

$$\frac{\partial \overline{\rho} \widetilde{h}_s}{\partial t} + \frac{\partial}{\partial x_i}(\overline{\rho} \widetilde{u}_i \widetilde{h}_s) = \overline{\frac{Dp}{Dt}} \quad + \quad \frac{\partial}{\partial x_i}\left[\overline{\lambda \frac{\partial T}{\partial x_i}} - \overline{\rho}\left(\widetilde{u_i h_s} - \widetilde{u}_i \widetilde{h}_s\right)\right] + \overline{\tau_{ij}\frac{\partial u_i}{\partial x_j}}$$

$$- \frac{\partial}{\partial x_i}\left(\overline{\rho \sum_{k=1}^{N} V_{k,i}Y_k h_{s,k}}\right) + \overline{\dot{\omega}}_T \qquad (4.60)$$

where

$$\overline{\frac{Dp}{Dt}} = \frac{\partial \overline{p}}{\partial t} + \overline{u_i \frac{\partial p}{\partial x_i}} \qquad (4.61)$$

In this set of equations, the following unclosed quantities must be modeled:

- **Unresolved Reynolds stresses** $(\widetilde{u_i u_j} - \widetilde{u}_i \widetilde{u}_j)$, requiring a subgrid scale turbulence model.

- **Unresolved species fluxes** $\left(\widetilde{u_i Y_k} - \widetilde{u}_i \widetilde{Y}_k\right)$ and **enthalpy fluxes** $\left(\widetilde{u_i h_s} - \widetilde{u}_i \widetilde{h}_s\right)$.

- **Filtered laminar diffusion fluxes** for species and enthalpy. As in RANS, these molecular fluxes may be either neglected or modeled through a simple gradient assumption such as:

$$\overline{V_{k,i}Y_k} = -\overline{\rho} D_k \frac{\partial \widetilde{Y}_k}{\partial x_i} \quad \text{and} \quad \overline{\lambda \frac{\partial T}{\partial x_i}} = \overline{\lambda} \frac{\partial \widetilde{T}}{\partial x_i} \qquad (4.62)$$

- **Filtered chemical reaction rate** $\overline{\dot{\omega}}_k$.

- **The pressure velocity term** $\overline{u_i(\partial p/\partial x_i)}$ is usually approximated by $\widetilde{u}_i(\partial \overline{p}/\partial x_i)$.

These filtered balance equations, coupled to ad-hoc subgrid scale models may be numerically solved to determine instantaneous filtered fields. Compared to direct numerical simulations, the description of the unresolved small scales is lost. Compared to Reynolds ensemble averaging, large eddy simulations provide instantaneous resolved fields.

Finding models for the unknown terms in balance equations for LES (Eq. (4.57) to (4.60)) may follow concepts developed in RANS approaches, for example by using global quantities such as the subgrid scale turbulent kinetic energy and its dissipation rate. Nevertheless, in large eddy simulations, an additional information is available because large scale turbulent motions are numerically resolved. Closure models may be based on similarity assumptions, using the known largest structures to estimate the effects of the smaller ones.

4.7.3 Unresolved fluxes modeling

The objective of this section is to summarize the main approaches developed in non reacting flows to model unresolved transport terms: Reynolds stresses $\mathcal{T}_{ij} = (\widetilde{u_i u_j} - \widetilde{u}_i \widetilde{u}_j)$, scalar fluxes $(\widetilde{u_i Y_k} - \widetilde{u}_i \widetilde{Y}_k)$ and enthalpy fluxes $(\widetilde{u_i h_s} - \widetilde{u}_i \widetilde{h}_s)$. Detailed discussions about subgrid modeling may be found, for example, in Lesieur and Metais [382], Piomelli and Chasnov [510], Ferziger [209], Lesieur [381], Piomelli [509], Sagaut [581], Meneveau and Katz [431], Pope [535] or Geurts [230]. These models have been derived assuming constant density flows and are presented here in this situation.

Smagorinsky model

The Smagorinsky [617] subgrid-scale model is popular because of its simple formulation. Unresolved momentum fluxes are expressed according to the Boussinesq assumption (Eq. 4.30):[xix]

$$\boxed{\mathcal{T}_{ij} - \frac{\delta_{ij}}{3}\mathcal{T}_{kk} = -\nu_t \left(\frac{\partial \overline{u}_i}{\partial x_j} + \frac{\partial \overline{u}_j}{\partial x_i}\right) = -2\nu_t \overline{S}_{ij}} \tag{4.63}$$

where ν_t is a subgrid scale viscosity, modeled from dimensional arguments as:

$$\nu_t = C_S^2 \, \Delta^{4/3} \, l_t^{2/3} \, |\overline{S}| = C_S^2 \, \Delta^{4/3} \, l_t^{2/3} \, \left(2\overline{S}_{ij}\overline{S}_{ij}\right)^{1/2} \tag{4.64}$$

where l_t is the turbulence integral length scale, C_S a model constant, and $\overline{S}$ the resolved shear stress (components $\overline{S}_{ij}$, defined in Eq. 4.63). Eq. (4.64) is simplified assuming that the integral scale l_t is of the order of the grid size $l_t \approx \Delta$:

$$\boxed{\nu_t = (C_S\Delta)^2 \, |\overline{S}| = (C_S\Delta)^2 \, \left(2\overline{S}_{ij}\overline{S}_{ij}\right)^{1/2}} \tag{4.65}$$

The isotropic contribution $\mathcal{T}_{kk}$ in Eq. (4.63), corresponding to twice the subgrid scale turbulent kinetic energy, is unknown and is usually absorbed into the filtered pressure $\overline{p}$.[xx] In the

---

[xix]Summing the three isotropic contributions $\mathcal{T}_{ii}$ shows that Eq. (4.63) is consistent only when $\partial \overline{u}_k / \partial x_k = 0$, i.e. for constant density flows. For variable density flows, Eq. (4.63) must be adapted using Favre filtered quantities and incorporating the trace of the strain rate tensor to the Reynolds stresses:

$$\mathcal{T}_{ij} - \frac{\delta_{ij}}{3}\mathcal{T}_{kk} = -\nu_t \left(\frac{\partial \widetilde{u}_i}{\partial x_j} + \frac{\partial \widetilde{u}_j}{\partial x_i} - \frac{2}{3}\delta_{ij}\frac{\partial \widetilde{u}_k}{\partial x_k}\right) = -2\nu_t \left(\widetilde{S}_{ij} - \frac{\delta_{ij}}{3}\widetilde{S}_{kk}\right)$$

[xx]For compressible flows, $\mathcal{T}_{kk}$ is generally modelled using the Yoshizawa's expression Yoshizawa [726]:

$$\mathcal{T}_{kk} = 2C_I\overline{\rho}\Delta^2 \left|\widetilde{S}\right|^2$$

where C_I is a model constant and $|\widetilde{S}| = (2\widetilde{S}_{ij}\widetilde{S}_{ij})^{1/2}$ with:

$$\widetilde{S}_{ij} = \frac{1}{2}\left(\frac{\partial \widetilde{u}_i}{\partial x_j} + \frac{\partial \widetilde{u}_j}{\partial x_i}\right)$$

case of homogeneous isotropic turbulence, the model constant is estimated as $C_S \approx 0.2$. Unfortunately, C_S depends on the flow configuration. Moreover the Smagorinsky model is known as being too dissipative, especially near walls.

Scale similarity model

This subgrid-model proposed by Bardina et al. [27, 28] assumes that unresolved stresses are mainly controlled by the largest unresolved structures, similarly to the lowest resolved ones. This analysis leads to the following expression:

$$\boxed{\mathcal{T}_{ij} = \overline{\overline{u}_i \overline{u}_j} - \overline{u}_i \, \overline{u}_j}$$ (4.66)

The principle of the scale similarity model is summarized on Fig. 4.22.

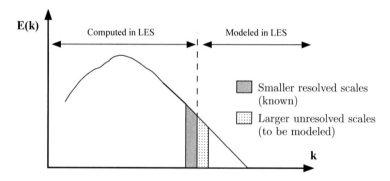

Figure 4.22: Scale similarity modeling.

In Eq. (4.66) all quantities can be obtained by filtering the resolved field $\overline{u}_i$. This closure was found to be insufficiently dissipative, and it is generally coupled to the Smagorinsky model to derive mixed models (Bardina et al. [28], Piomelli [509]). The value, and the variability, of the Smagorinsky model constant, C_S is then decreased.

Germano dynamic model

The objective of the Germano et al. [228] dynamic model is to estimate small scale dissipation from the knowledge of the resolved eddies (Fig. 4.23). The Smagorinsky approach is improved through an automatic determination of the model constant $C_S(\underline{x}, t)$ depending on time and space. A test filter, $\widehat{Q}$, having a size $\widehat{\overline{\Delta}}$ larger than the LES filter (size $\overline{\Delta}$) is introduced. The unresolved subgrid momentum fluxes are:

$$\mathcal{T}_{ij} = \overline{u_i u_j} - \overline{u}_i \overline{u}_j$$ (4.67)

The unresolved fluxes at the test level are:

$$T_{ij} = \widehat{\overline{u_i u_j}} - \widehat{\overline{u}}_i \, \widehat{\overline{u}}_j \tag{4.68}$$

The two previous relations are combined to give the Germano identity:

$$\boxed{\underbrace{\widehat{\overline{u}_i \, \overline{u}_j} - \widehat{\overline{u}}_i \, \widehat{\overline{u}}_j}_{\mathcal{L}_{ij}} = T_{ij} - \widehat{\mathcal{T}_{ij}}} \tag{4.69}$$

where the left hand side term, $\mathcal{L}_{ij}$, is determined by filtering the resolved LES velocity field, $\overline{u}_i$ at the test level $\widehat{\Delta}$. Estimating the Reynolds stresses $\mathcal{T}_{ij}$ et T_{ij} from the Smagorinsky model leads to:

$$\mathcal{T}_{ij} - \frac{\delta_{ij}}{3} \, \mathcal{T}_{kk} = -2\,C\,\overline{\Delta}^2 \, |\overline{S}| \, \overline{S}_{ij} = -2\,C\,\alpha_{ij} \tag{4.70}$$

$$T_{ij} - \frac{\delta_{ij}}{3} \, T_{kk} = -2\,C\,\widehat{\Delta}^2 \, |\widehat{\overline{S}}| \, \widehat{\overline{S}}_{ij} = -2\,C\,\beta_{ij} \tag{4.71}$$

where C is the parameter to determine and α_{ij} and β_{ij} are introduced to simplify notations.

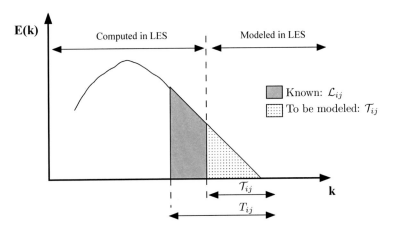

Figure 4.23: Graphical representation of the Germano identity (4.69) in the energy spectrum. The unknown unresolved Reynolds stresses at the filter level ($\mathcal{T}_{ij}$) and at the test filter level (T_{ij}) are related through $\mathcal{L}_{ij}$ which is the LES resolved part of the unresolved Reynolds stresses T_{ij}.

Then, the *Germano identity* is rewritten as:

$$\boxed{\mathcal{L}_{ij} - \frac{\delta_{ij}}{3} \, \mathcal{L}_{kk} = 2\,C \, (\widehat{\alpha_{ij}} - \beta_{ij})} \tag{4.72}$$

providing five independent equations[xxi] for the unknown "model constant" C so that C may be determined using optimization procedures. This model seems to be very efficient in a large number of applications and was extended to compressible turbulence (Moin et al. [451]). In practical applications, to avoid negative values leading to numerical difficulties, C is not determined locally but averaged in homogeneous directions or along streamlines following a Lagrangian procedure (Meneveau et al. [435]). These various procedures are compared by Sarghini et al. [587].

The dynamic procedure is presented here in its original version based on the Smagorinsky model but may be applied to others, starting from the Germano identity (4.69). For example, Zang et al. [729] and Vreman et al. [694] develop a dynamic formulation of the Bardina et al. [28] mixed model while Vreman et al. [695] compare Smagorinsky, mixed and Clark et al. [135] gradient models as well as their dynamic versions for the simulation of a temporal turbulent mixing layer. You and Moin [727, 728] investigate a dynamic formalism for the Vreman [693] turbulence model.[xxii]

Structure function models

Developed by Lesieur and coworkers [381, 382], these models are based on a theoretical analysis of turbulence in spectral space (Eddy Damped Quasi Normal Markovian, or EDQNM, approximation, (Lesieur [380]) and on the subgrid scale viscosity concept. The subgrid scale dynamic viscosity is determined as:

$$\nu_t\left(\mathbf{x}, \Delta\right) = 0.105\, C_K^{-3/2}\, \Delta \sqrt{F_2\left(\mathbf{x}, \Delta\right)} \qquad (4.73)$$

where $C_K = 1.4$ is the Kolmogorov constant and F_2 the structure function defined as:

$$F_2\left(\mathbf{x}, \Delta\right) = \left[\overline{\mathbf{u}}\left(\mathbf{x} + \mathbf{r}\right) - \overline{\mathbf{u}}\left(\mathbf{x}\right)\right]^2 \quad \text{with} \quad \sqrt{\mathbf{r}^2} = \Delta \qquad (4.74)$$

In practice, F_2 is estimated from the grid points found in the vicinity of the location $\mathbf{x}$.

A filtered structure function model was proposed by Ducros et al. [192] (see also Lesieur and Metais [382], Lesieur [381]) to avoid the high dissipation level of the large eddies observed with Eq. (4.73). The resolved velocity field is first high-pass filtered to eliminate the largest turbulent structures before estimating the structure function F_2. The subgrid viscosity is then:

$$\nu_t\left(\mathbf{x}, \Delta\right) = 0.0014\, C_K^{-3/2}\, \Delta \sqrt{\overline{F}_2\left(\mathbf{x}, \Delta\right)} \qquad (4.75)$$

where $\overline{F}_2$ is the filtered structure function.

[xxi]For constant density flows, as assumed in model derivation, $\mathcal{L}_{11}$, $\mathcal{L}_{22}$ and $\mathcal{L}_{33}$ are not independent because $\sum_{k=1}^{3} \overline{S}_{kk} = \sum_{k=1}^{3} \widehat{\overline{S}}_{kk} = 0$ (mass conservation).

[xxii]Note that You and Moin [727, 728] look for a global value of the model parameter (i.e. a unique value over the entire flow at a given time), a procedure that appears more suitable for complex flows where no homogenous direction is available to average the model parameter and avoid numerical instabilities. However, this approach is possible with the Vreman [693] model which can predict vanishing subgrid scale momentum transport in regions where the flow is fully resolved, whatever the value of the model parameter is, but would not be relevant with the usual Smagorinsky [617] model which requires a zero model parameter in such regions.

Unresolved scalar transport

As in RANS, LES unresolved scalar fluxes are often described using a gradient assumption:

$$\boxed{\widetilde{u_iY_k} - \tilde{u}_i\,\tilde{Y}_k = -\frac{\nu_t}{Sc_k}\frac{\partial\tilde{Y}_k}{\partial x_i}} \tag{4.76}$$

where Sc_k is a subgrid scale Schmidt number. The subgrid scale viscosity ν_t is estimated from the unresolved Reynolds stresses models (Smagorinsky, Germano, structure function models).

4.7.4 Simple filtered reaction rate closures

The objective of this section is to describe simple models for the LES filtered reaction rate $\bar{\dot{\omega}}_k$ which are supposed to apply both to premixed and diffusion flames. The first one (§ 4.7.4) is the extension of RANS models using series development (§ 4.5.4) whereas the second one (§ 4.7.4) extends similarity concepts to model the subgrid filtered reaction rate. None of these general techniques are efficient to handle all possible situations and specific models are required for each regime. These models are described in Chapter 5 for premixed flames and in Chapter 6 for non-premixed flames. Of course, they are generally based on the same physical approaches briefly summarized in Section 4.5.5 for RANS.

Arrhenius law based on filtered quantities

The simplest model is to assume perfect mixing at the subgrid scale level, neglecting subgrid scale fluctuations. The filtered reaction rate is then:

$$\bar{\dot{\omega}}_F = A_1\bar{\rho}^2\tilde{Y}_F\tilde{Y}_O\tilde{T}^{\beta_1}\exp\left(-T_A/\tilde{T}\right) \tag{4.77}$$

This expression implicitly assumes that the turbulent subgrid time scale τ_t is shorter than all chemical time scales τ_c ($\tau_t \ll \tau_c$). It may be used with reasonable accuracy for reacting flows in the atmospheric boundary layer (Nieuwstadt and Meeder [472]) but not in most combustion applications.

A more refined approach is to keep the second term in the series development (see Eq. (4.44) in RANS context):

$$\bar{\dot{\omega}}_F = A_1\bar{\rho}^2\tilde{Y}_F\tilde{Y}_O\tilde{T}^{\beta_1}\exp\left(-\frac{T_A}{\tilde{T}}\right)\left[1 + \frac{\widetilde{Y_FY_O} - \tilde{Y}_F\tilde{Y}_O}{\tilde{Y}_F\tilde{Y}_O}\right] \tag{4.78}$$

where the subgrid scale segregation factor $\alpha_{sgs} = (\widetilde{Y_FY_O} - \tilde{Y}_F\tilde{Y}_O)/\tilde{Y}_F\tilde{Y}_O = 0$ when the fuel and oxidizer are perfectly mixed at the subgrid level and $\alpha_{sgs} = -1$ for an infinitely fast reaction. The α_{sgs} factor may either be presumed or found solving a balance equation for $(\widetilde{Y_FY_O} - \tilde{Y}_F\tilde{Y}_O)$ (Meeder and Nieuwstadt [429]). Such a formulation is justified when temperature fluctuations are negligible (for example in the case of the dispersion of pollutants in the atmospheric boundary layer) but not for turbulent flames.

Scale similarity assumptions

Germano et al. [229] have proposed to extend scale similarity assumptions, widely used for Reynolds stresses, to the reaction rate modeling. For a constant density flow without heat release, the filtered reaction rate $\overline{\dot{\omega}}_k$ is proportional to $\overline{Y_F Y_O}$.[xxiii] Assuming similarity between two filtering levels (respectively noted $\overline{f}$ and $\widehat{f}$), the unresolved reaction rate is expressed as:

$$\overline{Y_F Y_O} - \overline{Y}_F \overline{Y}_O = k_{fg} \left(\widehat{\overline{Y_F}\overline{Y}_O} - \widehat{\overline{Y}}_F \widehat{\overline{Y}}_O \right) \tag{4.79}$$

This analysis is attractive because of its simplicity and its similarity with the Germano dynamic model for unresolved Reynolds stresses. Unfortunately, a priori tests against DNS data have revealed a disappointing result: the similarity constant k_{fg} is found to strongly depend on the mesh size and on the Damköhler number.

An increase of the Damköhler number corresponds to a thinner reaction zone and the test filter $\widehat{Q}$ underestimates the unresolved production term (a large fraction of the chemical production occurs at the subgrid level), requiring a higher similarity constant. On the other hand, as the mesh size decreases, the reaction rate estimated from the similarity filter $\widehat{Q}$ increases (an increasing part of the reaction rate occurs between subgrid, $\overline{Q}$, and similarity, $\widehat{Q}$, filter levels) and, the similarity constant decreases. Eq. (4.79) is not appropriate for flames where length scale effects have to be incorporated (comparison between flame thickness, flame wrinkling and mesh size).

Scale similarity models (DesJardin and Frankel [175]) have been developed for the filtered reaction rate $\overline{\dot{\omega}}_k$ of species k. After a priori (against DNS data) and a posteriori tests (i.e. actual large eddy simulations), they recommend the Scale Similarity Filtered Reaction Rate Model (SSFRRM). The filtered reaction rate is decomposed in a resolved and a subgrid part contribution

$$\overline{\dot{\omega}}_k = \dot{\omega}_k \left(\overline{\rho}, \widetilde{T}, \widetilde{Y}_1, \widetilde{Y}_2, ..., \widetilde{Y}_n \right) + \underbrace{\overline{\dot{\omega}_k \left(\rho, T, Y_1, Y_2, ...Y_n \right)} - \dot{\omega}_k \left(\overline{\rho}, \widetilde{T}, \widetilde{Y}_1, \widetilde{Y}_2, ..., \widetilde{Y}_n \right)}_{\dot{\omega}_{SGS}} \tag{4.80}$$

The filtered reaction rate has been decomposed into filtered large-scale and subgrid scale contributions. Filtering again Eq. (4.80) and using the same decomposition strategy leads to:

$$\overline{\overline{\dot{\omega}}}_k = \dot{\omega}_k \left(\overline{\overline{\rho}}, \widetilde{\widetilde{T}}, \widetilde{\widetilde{Y}}_1, ..., \widetilde{\widetilde{Y}}_n \right) + \underbrace{\overline{\dot{\omega}_k \left(\overline{\rho}, \widetilde{T}, \widetilde{Y}_1, ..., \widetilde{Y}_n \right)} - \dot{\omega}_k \left(\overline{\overline{\rho}}, \widetilde{\widetilde{T}}, \widetilde{\widetilde{Y}}_1, ..., \widetilde{\widetilde{Y}}_n \right)}_{\mathcal{L}_\omega} + \overline{\dot{\omega}}_{SGS} \tag{4.81}$$

This expression is closed invoking scale similarity, according to:

$$\dot{\omega}_{SGS} = K \mathcal{L}_\omega \tag{4.82}$$

[xxiii] As density is assumed to be constant, classical Reynolds ($\overline{f}$, Eq. 4.51) and mass-weighted Favre filters ($\widetilde{f}$, Eq. 4.56) are equivalent.

where K is a model constant to be specified. Since Arrhenius laws are still used to provide $\dot{\omega}_k (\rho, T, Y_1, Y_2, ..., Y_n)$, this formulation includes finite chemistry effects and stabilization processes. Nevertheless, as already discussed, length scale effects should be incorporated in the modeling constant K.

4.7.5 Dynamic modeling in turbulent combustion

Dynamic models, where model parameters are automatically adjusted taking advantage of the knowledge of resolved scales (see Germano dynamic model in section 4.7.3), have been found to be effective in describing unresolved stresses in LES. Extending dynamic procedures to combustion models appears to be a promising approach. However, aerodynamics and combustion are very different: most of the aerodynamic flow energy is transported by large scale resolved flow motions[xxiv] whereas combustion is mainly a subgrid scale phenomenon (the flame thickness is generally lower than the LES grid mesh (§ 5.4)). Simple models for the filtered fuel reaction rate may be expressed as:

$$\overline{\dot{\omega}}_F = \dot{\omega}_F \left(\widetilde{Q}, \overline{\Delta} \right) \left[1 + \alpha f \left(u'_{\overline{\Delta}}, \dots \right) \right] \tag{4.83}$$

where $\dot{\omega}_F(\widetilde{Q}, \overline{\Delta})$ is the resolved reaction rate depending only on known quantities $\widetilde{Q}$ such as filtered temperature and species mass fractions and on the filter size $\overline{\Delta}$. $f(u'_{\overline{\Delta}}, \dots)$ is a function of subgrid scale parameters such as the subgrid scale turbulence intensity $u'_{\overline{\Delta}}$ and α a model parameter. $\alpha f(u'_{\overline{\Delta}}, \dots) \dot{\omega}_F(\widetilde{Q}, \overline{\Delta})$ models the unresolved fuel reaction rate.

A dynamic procedure expresses that the filtered reaction rate at a test scale $\widehat{\Delta}$ larger than the filter scale may be given either by filtering Eq. (4.83) at scale $\widehat{\Delta}$ or directly using the model at this scale (Germano-like identity, Eq. 4.69):[xxv]

$$\widehat{\dot{\omega}_F \left(\widetilde{Q}, \overline{\Delta} \right) \left[1 + \alpha f \left(u'_{\overline{\Delta}}, \dots \right) \right]} = \dot{\omega}_F \left(\widehat{\widetilde{Q}}, \widehat{\Delta} \right) \left[1 + \alpha f \left(u'_{\widehat{\Delta}}, \dots \right) \right] \tag{4.84}$$

When combustion is mainly due to subgrid scale contribution (i.e. $\alpha f(u'_{\overline{\Delta}}, \dots) \gg 1$ in Eq. 4.83), Eq. (4.84) reduces to:

$$\alpha \widehat{\dot{\omega}_F \left(\widetilde{Q}, \overline{\Delta} \right) f \left(u'_{\overline{\Delta}}, \dots \right)} \approx \alpha \dot{\omega}_F \left(\widehat{\widetilde{Q}}, \widehat{\Delta} \right) f \left(u'_{\widehat{\Delta}}, \dots \right) \tag{4.85}$$

[xxiv]The ratio of the resolved turbulent kinetic energy over the total turbulent kinetic energy is a criterion to check the quality of an LES (Pope [536]). This ratio is typically expected to be of the order of 80 %.

[xxv]In practice, this local identity is not used as it stands here for clarity. The comparison of the reaction rate estimated at the filter and test size levels is meaningful only by averaging the reaction rate over a small volume. Then, Eq. (4.84) is recast as:

$$\left\langle \widehat{\dot{\omega}_F \left(\widetilde{Q}, \overline{\Delta} \right) \left[1 + \alpha f \left(u'_{\overline{\Delta}}, \dots \right) \right]} \right\rangle = \left\langle \dot{\omega}_F \left(\widehat{\widetilde{Q}}, \widehat{\Delta} \right) \left[1 + \alpha f \left(u'_{\widehat{\Delta}}, \dots \right) \right] \right\rangle$$

where $\langle \rangle$ denotes averaging over a small volume. See Charlette et al. [117] for details.

where α vanishes leading to an ill-posed problem (Charlette et al. [117]).[xxvi] This difficulty may be overcome by looking for an exponential dependance for $\overline{\dot{\omega}}_F$ and recasting Eq. (4.83) as:

$$\overline{\dot{\omega}}_F = \dot{\omega}_F\left(\widetilde{Q},\overline{\Delta}\right)\left[1 + f\left(u'_{\underline{\Delta}},\dots\right)\right]^\alpha \tag{4.86}$$

In principle, the exponent α may depend on various parameters such as turbulence level, Reynolds number, location in the flow field (for example proximity to walls) and time. Note that if α is constant and verifies $0 < \alpha < 1$, the fractal model (Gouldin [249], Gouldin et al. [247], Gulder [260]) is recovered and the fractal dimension D of the flame surface is related to α as $\alpha = D - 2$.

The Germano-like identity (4.84) becomes:

$$\widehat{\dot{\omega}_F\left(\widetilde{Q},\overline{\Delta}\right)\left[1 + f\left(u'_{\underline{\Delta}},\dots\right)\right]^\alpha} = \dot{\omega}_F\left(\widehat{\widetilde{Q}},\widehat{\Delta}\right)\left[1 + f\left(u'_{\underline{\widehat{\Delta}}},\dots\right)\right]^\alpha \tag{4.87}$$

The dynamic determination of the α parameter is then given by:

$$\alpha = \frac{\log\left[\widehat{\dot{\omega}_F\left(\widetilde{Q},\overline{\Delta}\right)}\Big/\dot{\omega}_F\left(\widehat{\widetilde{Q}},\widehat{\Delta}\right)\right]}{\log\left[\left(1+f\left(u'_{\underline{\Delta}},\dots\right)\right)\Big/\left(1+f\left(u'_{\underline{\widehat{\Delta}}},\dots\right)\right)\right]} \tag{4.88}$$

assuming that the subgrid scale parameters such as $u'_{\underline{\Delta}}$ are constant over the test filter size volume. The problem is now well-posed and this dynamic approach has been successfully used by Charlette et al. [117], Knikker et al. [353] and Wang et al. [697].

4.7.6 Resolution constraints in LES

LEs of a reacting flow must resolve the flow scales and the flame scales. For the flow structures, it is possible to provide simple resolution constraints for LES (as done for DNS in Section 4.6.3). First, the integral length scale has to be contained in the computational domain, i.e. $l_t < N\Delta x$, where Δx denotes the LES mesh size. Most models derived to describe unresolved fluxes are based on similarity assumptions requiring the cut-off scale, $l_{cut-off}$, between resolved and unresolved structures to be in the inertial range of the turbulence spectrum, i.e: $l_t > l_{cut-off} > \eta_k$. Assuming that $l_{cut-off} = q\eta_k$ with $1 < q < Re_t^{3/4}$, the resolution of scale $l_{cut-off}$ requires $l_{cut-off} > \Delta x$, leading to:

$$qN > Re_t^{3/4} \quad \text{with} \quad q > 1 \tag{4.89}$$

Compared to DNS, condition (4.47) has been replaced by the less restrictive one (4.89). In the diagram of Fig. 4.20, the upper limit, given by the constraint on the Reynolds number, moves upward.

[xxvi]However, with the fine numerical grids available today (mesh sizes of the order of laminar flame thickness), resolved and subgrid scale contributions become of the same order of magnitude. Then, one might expect to look for a linear dependence, according to Eq. (4.83).

For the flame scales, requirements for LES depend directly on the model used for the description of chemistry and there is no simple rule to determine mesh sizes required for reacting LES. In practical LES computations, the internal structure of the flame fronts is not resolved on the mesh and the right limit in the diagram (Fig. 4.20) does not hold any more so that the chemical limits depend on the subgrid scale model retained for combustion.

Compared to RANS simulations, LES are, of course, expensive. Usual simplifications used in RANS to decrease their cost (symmetry conditions, two-dimensional mean flows) cannot be retained in LES: a proper description of unsteady turbulent motions requires three-dimensional simulations. Averaged and global quantities (mean, rms, correlation functions, energy spectra,...) may also be extracted from LES but require large computational times and databases.

4.7.7 Numerical methods for LES

Using LES or DNS described in § 4.6.2 and § 4.6.3 leads to similar procedures: the objective is to compute unsteady large turbulence motions and the method must handle unsteady flow fields (at the resolved scale) with adequate boundary and initial conditions. The numerical precision of the algorithm becomes a key point: subgrid scale models should not be offset by numerical diffusion. A useful numerical test is to compare simulations with and without subgrid models to check that the LES model has a significant effect compared to numerical dissipation.

The properties required for a numerical scheme to be used in LES are an open issue in the combustion community. The methodologies used in present LES codes come from two sources: (1) the DNS community has adapted its methods to incorporate LES subgrid models (an easy task) and to be able to handle complex geometries and hybrid meshes (a much more difficult task because it required moving from structured solvers to methods working on hybrid meshes); (2) on the other side, the RANS community has been able to handle complex geometry configurations for a long time and it has changed its turbulent viscosity models from k-ε approaches to LES subgrid models. Both types of LES solvers codes can be found in the literature. The main difference between these solvers is accuracy. The DNS community has always insisted on using high-order high-fidelity numerical techniques (centered finite-difference schemes or spectral methods, see Section 4.6.2) while numerical methods used in most RANS solvers focus on robustness (reasonable levels of upwinding for spatial differentiation) and efficiency (implicit schemes in time).[xxvii]

There is no doubt that using high fidelity schemes preserves the quality of the solutions. The question is that it is also much more expensive and that LES might actually not need

---

[xxvii]Readers interested in learning more on dispersion and dissipation effects in CFD will find a simple example and a simulation tool at *elearning.cerfacs.fr/numerical/schemes/1Dscheme/index.php.* They can also learn about basic methods for CFD (mesh and discretization) at *elearning.cerfacs.fr/numerical/schemes/mesh/index.php.* An example of recent CFD solvers applied to the case of a vortex convection (the CO-VO test of CERFACS) is available at *elearning.cerfacs.fr/numerical/benchmarks/vortex2d/* . This simple test case allows to visualize how a vortex is convected over long distances by some well-known DNS/LES codes.

such an accuracy: high-order schemes have a maximum (positive) effect on small vortices, scales which are in any case not fully resolved in LES. Therefore, many practitioneers of LES have argued that using second-order spatial schemes was sufficient for LES. In many cases, the artificial viscosity introduced by an approximate spatial or temporal differentiation scheme is even blended with the subgrid scale turbulent viscosity (Oran and Boris [482]). Moreover, since low-order implicit schemes (coming from the RANS world) run faster than centered explicit schemes (coming from the DNS community), they can also use finer grids and run over longer physical times. As a consequence, today, this issue is not settled. When commercial CFD solvers will really try to address the LES market (which is a large one, much larger than for DNS which remains a specificity of academic laboratories), this question will probably become even more controversial. Right now, only a few LES solvers for combustion have been tested extensively and their development continues at a high pace.

Finally, two issues related to computer science problems control the efficiency of LES solvers for reacting flows (Gourdain et al. [251]):

- Efficiency on highly parallel systems. The computational task associated to LES performed in realistic configurations is such that they must be performed on thousands of processors.Writing a solver able to use efficiently 10 to 100 000 processors has become a mandatory starting point for these codes. This can be a difficult task especially when intense post processing is needed: post processing is most often a non parallel task, requiring multiple communications between processors. For example, finding the maximum temperature or the average pressure when the domain is decomposed into 50 000 sub domains can be more expensive than the computation itself if it is not done correctly. The infrastucture needed to write such codes has become large and this explains why the effort today in this field has focused on a limited number of solvers, some of them distributed as open source codes (Open Foam, *www.openfoam.com*) or others open to a large academic community (AVBP, *www.cerfacs.fr/4-26334-The-AVBP-code.php*, Gourdain et al. [250]) or YALES2 (*www.coria-cfd.fr/index.php/YALES2*).

- Quality of the mesh. All LES practitioners recognize that the most important parameter controlling the results of an LES is the quality of the mesh. DNS solvers use only Cartesian (parallelepipedic) grids where the mesh size changes very slowly while RANS solvers can work with very distorted irregular unstructured meshes. For LES, especially in complex geometries, RANS meshes can not be used directly: most good LES codes diverge immediately on such grids because of their limited artificial viscosity. Even if the code does not diverge, the mesh density has a direct effect on the solution and mesh refinement exercices are required to verify that the mean fields converge correctly when the mesh becomes smaller (Wolf et al. [713], Boudier et al. [74]). The mesh density, however, is not the only parameter controlling the quality of the LES: rapid variations in element shapes and sizes directly decrease the quality of the solution. As a consequence, constructing unstructured meshes which are adapted for LES of reacting flows is a very important aspect of LES. Today, this task must also be thought as a parallel task: LES solvers today (like YALES2 for example *www.coria-cfd.fr/index.php/YALES2*) can handle meshes containing 20 billion cells but have to generate the mesh themselves because mesh generators cannot create meshes of this size on a single processor. Moreover domain decomposition tools have the same problem: they can not partition very large domains on single processor machines and parallel decomposition tools are required (see for example PARMETIS *glaros.dtc.umn.edu/gkhome/metis/parmetis/overview*). Finally, adapting the LES mesh to the solution during the computation is also a promising path for efficiency and precision.

4.7.8 Comparing large eddy simulations and experimental data

Multiple studies present comparisons of LES data with experimental results. Even though the idea of comparing quantities (velocities, temperatures,species) obtained by LES with quantities measured in experiments is a reasonable one, it is actually a complex exercice because LES and experiments provide quantities which are averaged differently and can not be compared directly:

- LES provide unsteady and spatially-filtered quantities. These instantaneous quantities cannot be directly compared to experimental flow fields. Only statistical quantities extracted from LES and experiments are expected to match as subgrid scale models are devised using statistical arguments (Pope [535, 536]).

- To extract LES filtered quantities from experiments would require to measure three-dimensional instantaneous flow fields. Even though such experiments have already been reported (van der Bos et al. [661], Tao et al. [641] who performed 3D PIV, or Upton et al. [659] who display 3D instantaneous flame front in a turbulent Bunsen burner), three-dimensional instantaneous data are generally not available. Note also that such processing would require to specify the LES filter used in the simulation which is generally not explicitly determined in practical computations.

- LES simulations provide Favre (mass weighted) filtered quantities whereas most diagnostic techniques are expected to provide unweighted filtered quantities.

The following discussion compares statistical quantities such as means and variances in experiments and large eddy simulations (see Veynante and Knikker [674] for details). For clarity, the discussion is first conducted for constant density flows. Spatially filtered quantities are noted $\overline{f}$ (respectively $\widetilde{f}$ when mass-weighted) and $\langle f \rangle$ denote usual time or ensemble averages (respectively $\{f\}$ for Favre averages).

Constant density flows

The time-averaged spatially filtered quantity $\langle \overline{f} \rangle$ of any variable f is given by:

$$\langle \overline{f} \rangle (\mathbf{x}) = \frac{1}{T} \int_0^T \overline{f}(\mathbf{x}, t) \, dt = \frac{1}{T} \int_0^T \left[\int f(\mathbf{x}', t) \, F(\mathbf{x}' - \mathbf{x}) \, d\mathbf{x}' \right] dt$$

$$= \int \left[\frac{1}{T} \int_0^T f\left(\mathbf{x}', t\right) dt \right] F\left(\mathbf{x}' - \mathbf{x}\right) d\mathbf{x}' \qquad (4.90)$$

Then

$$\boxed{\langle \overline{f} \rangle = \overline{\langle f \rangle}} \qquad (4.91)$$

The time (or ensemble) average of a filtered quantity f is equal to the filtered local averaged quantity because spatial filter and time-average operators may be exchanged. Assuming that the filter size Δ remains small compared to the spatial evolution of $\langle f \rangle$ also allows to estimate $\langle \overline{f} \rangle$ as $\langle \overline{f} \rangle \approx \langle f \rangle$.

The variance of the quantity f may be expressed as:

$$\langle f^2 \rangle - \langle f \rangle^2 = \left[\langle \overline{f}^2 \rangle - \langle \overline{f} \rangle^2 \right] + \left[\langle f^2 \rangle - \langle \overline{f}^2 \rangle \right] + \left[\langle \overline{f} \rangle^2 - \langle f \rangle^2 \right] \qquad (4.92)$$

Assuming that the filter size Δ remains small compared to the spatial evolution of $\langle f \rangle$ and $\langle f^2 \rangle$ gives $\langle \overline{f} \rangle \approx \langle f \rangle$ and $\langle f^2 \rangle \approx \langle \overline{f^2} \rangle$. Eq. (4.92) becomes:

$$\boxed{\langle f^2 \rangle - \langle f \rangle^2 \approx \underbrace{\left[\langle \overline{f}^2 \rangle - \langle \overline{f} \rangle^2 \right]}_{\text{Variance of } \overline{f}} + \underbrace{\left[\langle \overline{f^2} - \overline{f}^2 \rangle \right]}_{\text{Subgrid scale variance}}} \qquad (4.93)$$

The variance of the quantity f is the sum of the variance of the filtered quantity $\overline{f}$, provided by LES, and the time (or ensemble) average of the subgrid scale variance $\overline{f^2} - \overline{f}^2$. To compare RMS quantities obtained in experiments and numerical simulations, this last contribution must be expressed:

• When $f = u_i$ is a velocity component, Eq. (4.93) becomes:

$$\langle u_i{}^2 \rangle - \langle u_i \rangle^2 \approx \left[\langle \overline{u}_i{}^2 \rangle - \langle \overline{u}_i \rangle^2 \right] + \left[\overline{\langle u_i u_i} - \overline{u}_i \overline{u}_i \rangle \right] \qquad (4.94)$$

where the subgrid scale variance, $\overline{u_i u_i} - \overline{u}_i \overline{u}_i$, corresponding to the unresolved momentum transport, is modeled by the subgrid scale model and may be averaged over time. This relation is easily extended to subgrid scale Reynolds stresses:

$$\langle u_i u_j \rangle - \langle u_i \rangle \langle u_j \rangle \approx \left[\langle \overline{u}_i \overline{u}_j \rangle - \langle \overline{u}_i \rangle \langle \overline{u}_j \rangle \right] + \langle \overline{u_i u_j} - \overline{u}_i \overline{u}_j \rangle \qquad (4.95)$$

where the first RHS term corresponds to the resolved momentum transport known in the simulation. The second term is the time-average of the subgrid scale Reynolds stresses, explicitly modeled in LES.

- When f is a scalar such as temperature, mixture or mass fraction, the subgrid scale variance in the last term of Eq. (4.93) is generally not explicitly modeled in simulation, even though some models are proposed in the framework of subgrid scale probability density functions. For example, Cook and Riley [151] propose a scale similarity assumption to model the subgrid scale variance of the mixture fraction Z (see § 6.5.1):

$$\overline{Z^2} - \overline{Z}^2 = C_Z \left(\widehat{\overline{Z}^2} - \widehat{\overline{Z}}^2 \right) \tag{4.96}$$

where C_Z is a model parameter and $\widehat{Q}$ denotes a test filter larger than the LES filter.

Variable density flows

For variable density flows, Eq. (4.91) is rewritten for ρf, leading to:

$$\boxed{\langle \overline{\rho \widetilde{f}} \rangle = \overline{\langle \rho f \rangle} = \overline{\langle \rho \rangle} \{f\}} \tag{4.97}$$

where $\widetilde{f}$ and $\{f\}$ denote Favre (mass-weighted) spatial filter and averaging operators respectively. Comparison requires to extract from experiment the time (or ensemble) average $\langle \rho f \rangle$ of the quantity ρf, which is generally not available. Nevertheless, under the assumption that the filter size remains small against the spatial evolution of mean quantities, $\langle \overline{\rho} \rangle \{f\} \approx \langle \rho \rangle \{f\}$ and $\langle \overline{\rho} \rangle \approx \langle \rho \rangle$ lead to:

$$\boxed{\{f\} = \frac{\langle \rho f \rangle}{\langle \rho \rangle} \approx \frac{\langle \overline{\rho \widetilde{f}} \rangle}{\langle \overline{\rho} \rangle}} \tag{4.98}$$

Accordingly, the Favre average $\{f\}$ may be estimated by averaging the LES field $\widetilde{f}$ weighted by the resolved density $\overline{\rho}$. On the other hand, to simply average the LES field versus time will not provide the actual Favre average $\{f\}$. Indeed, the time average value of $\widetilde{f}$ is:

$$\langle \widetilde{f} \rangle (\mathbf{x}) = \frac{1}{T} \int_0^T \frac{\overline{\rho \widetilde{f}}}{\overline{\rho}} \, dt = \frac{1}{T} \int_0^T \left[\frac{\int \rho \left(\mathbf{x}', t\right) f \left(\mathbf{x}', t\right) F \left(\mathbf{x} - \mathbf{x}\right) d\mathbf{x}'}{\int \rho \left(\mathbf{x}', t\right) F \left(\mathbf{x} - \mathbf{x}\right) d\mathbf{x}'} \right] dt \tag{4.99}$$

which is not equal to $\langle \overline{\rho \widetilde{f}} \rangle / \langle \overline{\rho} \rangle$ because filtering and averaging operator cannot be exchanged.

The variance of the quantity f may be expressed as:

$$\langle \rho \rangle \left(\{f^2\} - \{f\}^2 \right) = \langle \rho f^2 \rangle - \frac{\langle \rho f \rangle^2}{\langle \rho \rangle} \tag{4.100}$$

$$= \left(\langle \overline{\rho} \left(\widetilde{f} \right)^2 \rangle - \frac{\langle \overline{\rho \widetilde{f}} \rangle^2}{\langle \overline{\rho} \rangle} \right) + \left(\langle \rho f^2 \rangle - \langle \overline{\rho} \left(\widetilde{f} \right)^2 \rangle \right) + \left(\frac{\langle \overline{\rho \widetilde{f}} \rangle^2}{\langle \overline{\rho} \rangle} - \frac{\langle \rho f \rangle^2}{\langle \rho \rangle} \right)$$

Assuming that the spatial length scale of averaged quantities are small compared to the LES filter:

$$\langle \overline{\rho} \rangle \approx \langle \rho \rangle \quad ; \quad \langle \overline{\rho}\widetilde{f} \rangle = \langle \overline{\rho f} \rangle \approx \langle \rho f \rangle \quad ; \quad \langle \overline{\rho}\widetilde{f^2} \rangle = \langle \overline{\rho f^2} \rangle \approx \langle \rho f^2 \rangle \tag{4.101}$$

Eq. (4.101) becomes:

$$\{f^2\} - \{f\}^2 \approx \underbrace{\frac{1}{\langle \overline{\rho} \rangle} \left(\langle \overline{\rho} \left(\widetilde{f} \right)^2 \rangle - \frac{\langle \overline{\rho}\widetilde{f} \rangle^2}{\langle \overline{\rho} \rangle} \right)}_{\text{Resolved}} + \underbrace{\frac{1}{\langle \overline{\rho} \rangle} \langle \overline{\rho} \left(\widetilde{f^2} - \left(\widetilde{f} \right)^2 \right) \rangle}_{\text{Subgrid-scale}} \tag{4.102}$$

The RHS terms of this equation are the variance of the resolved field, which can be measured using the LES field, and the time-average of the subgrid scale variance, which must be modeled. Previous comments in section 4.7.8 still hold:

- When $f = u_i$ is a velocity component, the subgrid scale variance $\widetilde{u_i u_i} - \widetilde{u}_i \widetilde{u}_i$ found in Eq. (4.102) is described by the subgrid scale model. The previous result may be extended to Reynolds stresses:

$$\langle \rho \rangle \left(\{u_i u_j\} - \{u_i\}\{u_j\} \right) \approx \left(\langle \overline{\rho}\widetilde{u}_i \widetilde{u}_j \rangle - \frac{\langle \overline{\rho}\widetilde{u}_i \rangle \langle \overline{\rho}\widetilde{u}_j \rangle}{\langle \overline{\rho} \rangle} \right) + \langle \overline{\rho} \left(\widetilde{u_i u_j} - \widetilde{u}_i \widetilde{u}_j \right) \rangle \tag{4.103}$$

  where the subgrid scale variance in the last RHS term is modeled in simulations.

- When f denotes a scalar field such as temperature, mixture fraction or species mass fractions, the subgrid variance $\overline{\rho}(\widetilde{f^2} - \widetilde{f}^2)$ is generally not explicitly modeled.

These findings show that the comparison of LES statistics with experimental data requires cautions, especially when Favre (mass-weighted) operators are involved (Veynante and Knikker [674]). To estimate local variances from LES results requires consideration of subgrid scale variances (Eq. 4.93 and 4.102). An other technique would be to extract from experiments the filtered quantities computed in LES, but this approach is a challenge for experimentalists as it requires three-dimensional measurements (van der Bos et al. [661], Tao et al. [641], Upton et al. [659]) and the precise definition of the effective filter used in the simulations. Comparisons between experiments and LES should be clarified in the near future. First preliminary investigations, still to be confirmed, show that Eqs. (4.98) and (4.99) give similar results in practical simulations (private communications by S. Roux and H. Pitsch).

4.8 Chemistry for turbulent combustion

4.8.1 Introduction

The full description of chemical reactions in flames may involve hundreds of species and thousands of reactions. Handling such complex chemical schemes in turbulent combustion is still impossible for three main reasons:

- One additional balance equation is required for each species.

- Chemical reaction rates and transport coefficients are complex functions of species mass fractions and temperature. Increasing the number of chemical reactions dramatically increases the computational time.

- A major theoretical difficulty lies in the coupling between turbulence and combustion. As chemical reactions involve a large range of chemical time scales, this coupling cannot be handled through a single turbulent time such as the integral l_t/u' or the Kolmogorov η_k/u'_k time scales (§ 4.2), as done in usual turbulent combustion models.

This section addresses only the two first questions. The third one is discussed in § 4.5 and Chapters 5 and 6. Various approaches have been proposed to reduce chemical schemes and are briefly summarized in the following. They are all based on the common idea that fastest chemical time scales can be neglected.[xxviii]

4.8.2 Global schemes

The development of global schemes from complex chemical schemes can be done "by hand" and relies on two main assumptions:

- Quasi-steady state approximation: some intermediate species or radicals are assumed to have reached an equilibrium state. These species do not evolve any more, their mass fractions are constant and their overall reaction rates are negligible (the production rate equals the consumption rate).

- Partial equilibrium: some elementary reactions of the chemical scheme are assumed to have reached equilibrium.

For example, starting from an detailed mechanism by Smooke [621], Peters [499] (see also Peters [502]) proposes a four-step global chemical scheme for methane, including seven species:

$$
\begin{array}{rlrcl}
\text{(I)} & CH_4 + 2H + H_2O & = & CO + 4H_2 \\
\text{(II)} & CO + H_2O & = & CO_2 + H_2 \\
\text{(III)} & H + H + M & = & H_2 + M \\
\text{(IV)} & O_2 + 3H_2 & = & 2H + 2H_2O
\end{array}
\qquad (4.104)
$$

[xxviii] Reducing chemical schemes is, of course, also interesting to compute laminar flames or perform direct numerical simulations but, as this book is not devoted to chemistry, these procedures are only described here as a way to incorporate complex chemistry features in turbulent flow simulations.

where the four reaction rates are determined from limiting steps of the chemistry, using quasi-steady state and partial equilibrium approximations, leading to:

$$
\begin{aligned}
\dot{\omega}_I &= k_{11}\,[CH_4]\,[H] \\
\dot{\omega}_{II} &= \frac{k_{9f}}{K_3}\frac{[H]}{[H_2]}\left([CO]\,[H_2O]-\frac{1}{K_{II}}\,[CO_2]\,[H_2]\right) \\
\dot{\omega}_{III} &= k_5\,[H]\,[O_2]\,[M] \\
\dot{\omega}_{IV} &= k_{1f}\frac{[H]}{[H_2]^3}\left([O_2]\,[H_2]^3-\frac{1}{K_{IV}}\,[H]^2\,[H_2O]^2\right)
\end{aligned}
\tag{4.105}
$$

The reaction rates are written in terms of the species molar concentrations $[X_k]=\rho Y_k/W_k$. k_{1f}, k_5, k_{9f} and k_{11} are respectively the constant rates of the elementary reactions:

$$
\begin{aligned}
(1f) && H+O_2 &\longrightarrow OH+O \\
(5) && H+O_2+M &\longrightarrow HO_2+M \\
(9f) && CO+OH &\longrightarrow CO_2+H \\
(11) && CH_4+H &\longrightarrow CH_3+H_2
\end{aligned}
\tag{4.106}
$$

K_3 is the equilibrium constant of the elementary reaction:

$$
OH+H_2 = H+H_2O
\tag{4.107}
$$

and K_{II} and K_{IV} are the equilibrium constants of the global reactions (II) and (IV).

A similar analysis was performed by Jones and Lindstedt [316] for hydrocarbons C_nH_{2n+2} up to butane ($n=4$) leading to the four-step global chemical scheme:

$$
\begin{aligned}
(I) && C_nH_{2n+2}+\frac{n}{2}O_2 &\rightarrow nCO+(n+1)H_2 \\
(II) && C_nH_{2n+2}+nH_2O &\rightarrow nCO+(2n+1)H_2 \\
(III) && H_2+\frac{1}{2}O_2 &\rightleftharpoons H_2O \\
(IV) && CO+H_2O &\rightleftharpoons CO_2+H_2
\end{aligned}
\tag{4.108}
$$

Corresponding rates are given in Table 4.2. Note that the global reaction rate of the third reaction involves a negative water concentration exponent, which may lead to practical difficulties in numerical simulations. The authors propose an alternative formulation, referred as III* in Table 4.2, avoiding this dependence but providing a reduced accuracy in fuel lean regions.

   This derivation of global chemical schemes is attractive but leads to various difficulties. First, the identification of limiting steps, quasi-steady state and equilibrated reactions in a complex chemical scheme is a difficult task requiring an expert knowledge of chemistry. In addition, the reduction of the computational work is lower than expected: the number of chemical species and chemical reactions is decreased but reaction rates have more complicated

Reaction	Reaction Rate	Reaction rate constant			
		n	A	b	E
I	$k_I(T) [C_n H_{2n+2}]^{1/2} [O_2]^{5/4}$	1	0.44 x 10^{12}	0	30,000
		2	0.42 x 10^{12}	0	30,000
		3	0.40 x 10^{12}	0	30,000
		4	0.38 x 10^{12}	0	30,000
II	$k_{II}(T) [C_n H_{2n+2}] [H_2O]$	1 − 4	0.30 x 10^{09}	0	30,000
III	$k_{III}(T) [H_2]^{1/2} [O_2]^{9/4} [H_2O]^{-1}$	1	0.25 x 10^{17}	−1	40,000
		2	0.35 x 10^{17}	−1	40,000
		3	0.30 x 10^{17}	−1	40,000
		4	0.28 x 10^{17}	−1	40,000
IV	$k_{IV}(T) [CO] [H_2O]$	1 − 4	0.275 x 10^{10}	0	20,000
III*	$k_{III}^*(T) [H_2]^{1/4} [O_2]^{3/2}$	1	0.68 x 10^{16}	−1	40,000
		2	0.90 x 10^{16}	−1	40,000
		3	0.85 x 10^{16}	−1	40,000
		4	0.75 x 10^{16}	−1	40,000

Table 4.2: Reaction rates proposed by Jones and Lindstedt [316] for the global chemical scheme (4.108) for hydrocarbons $C_n H_{2n+2}$ up to butane ($n = 4$). Reaction rate constants are expressed as $k_i = AT^b \exp(-E/RT)$. Despite a reduced accuracy, reaction rates $(III)^*$ may replace reaction rates (III) to avoid numerical difficulty because of the negative exponent of water concentration in (III). Units: kg, m, s, kmol, K.

expressions (see, for example, the system 4.105) and often stiffer mathematical formulations. These reaction rates can also contain molar concentrations with negative exponents (see $[H_2]$ in reaction rates $\dot\omega_{II}$ and $\dot\omega_{IV}$ in the previous Peters' scheme) leading to practical difficulties, especially to initiate the simulation. These difficulties have pushed research in two directions: automatic chemistry reduction methods and tabulated chemistries (§ 4.8.3).

4.8.3   Automatic reduction - Tabulated chemistries

Intrinsic Low Dimensional Manifold (ILDM)

As with other procedures to reduce chemical schemes, the Intrinsic Low Dimensional Manifold (ILDM) approach proposed by Maas and Pope [411, 412] takes advantage of the large range of chemical time scales. Starting from different initial compositions leading to the same equilibrium condition, the temporal evolution of a chemical system depends on initial conditions (Fig. 4.24). But, after a certain time t_M, which is generally small, the chemical system may be described by a reduced set of variables in the composition (i.e. mass fractions) space. In Fig. 4.24, between point M and the equilibrium composition (point E), the mass fraction Y_B

(for example, the water mass fraction Y_{H_2O} for hydrocarbon combustion) may be expressed as a function of the species A mass fraction Y_A (for example the carbon dioxide mass fraction, Y_{CO_2}). The attracting curve ME (in general, an hyper-surface in the composition space) is the so-called low-dimensional manifold.

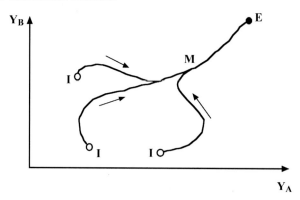

Figure 4.24: Temporal evolution, indicated by arrows, of a reacting mixture in the mass fraction space (Y_A, Y_B) starting from different initial compositions denoted I. After a certain time t_M, the composition is described by a low dimensional manifold (curve ME) where the mass fractions Y_B is directly linked to the phase coordinate Y_A before reaching equilibrium (E) after time t_E.

The mathematical formalism to automatically identify and describe the attracting surface from a complex chemical scheme is beyond the scope of this book. The basic idea, however, is to determine the eigenvalues (which are, in fact, the inverse of the characteristic chemical time scales) of the chemical scheme and to take into account only the largest time scales. Then, species mass fractions and reaction rates may be determined as functions of a reduced set of variables (in Fig. 4.24, the mass fraction Y_B is a function of Y_A after time t_M). This reduced set may contain a "progress variable" measuring the evolution of the reaction (for example the CO_2 mass fraction Y_{CO_2} or the sum of carbon monoxide and dioxide mass fractions $Y_{CO_2}+Y_{CO}$ for hydrocarbon combustion) and a description of the mixing through a "mixture fraction" (for example, the nitrogen mass fraction Y_{N_2}). A look-up table is then built with entries corresponding to the variables of the reduced set and searched using multilinear interpolations.

Flame prolongation of ILDM - Flamelet generated manifold

The ILDM formalism is based on a strong mathematical foundation and provides very good results for high temperatures close to equilibrium values. Unfortunately, low temperature regions are not well described. In fact, these regions are not covered by ILDM and are usually determined only by linear interpolations. This drawback has no importance for steady flames where reaction rates are mainly controlled by the highest temperatures but may lead to difficulties, for example, to describe ignition, transient and diffusion phenomena. To overcome this limit, Gicquel et al. [234], Fiorina et al. [214], van Oijen et al. [666], de Goey et al. [169] have independently proposed similar approaches called "Flame prolongation of ILDM" (FPI) and "Flamelet generated manifold" (FGM) respectively. The basic idea is to generate look-up tables from simulations of one-dimensional laminar premixed flames using complex chemical schemes.[xxix] Reaction rates and species mass fractions are then tabulated as functions of a limited set of coordinates (progress variable, mixture fraction,...).[xxx] As shown by Gicquel et al. [234] this approach recovers the ILDM results for high temperatures and provides better results in low temperature regions. It can be viewed as a prolongation of the ILDM. But, as pointed out by de Goey et al. [169], the mathematical background of FPI or FGM is weaker when compared to ILDM.

Chemical tables become very large when they include the effects of several parameters (progress variable, mixture fraction, enthalpy, dilution by burnt gases,...), leading to practical difficulties on massively parallel machines: their size may be incompatible with duplication in the local memory of each processor while a shared memory implementation would be prohibitive in terms of communications. A solution is to take advantage of the self-similarity behaviour of premixed flames, as suggested by Ribert et al. [555] or Wang et al. [698] for laminar flame elements and Veynante et al. [684] or Fiorina et al. [215] for turbulent flames. The initial table is then split into a set of much smaller sub tables.

4.8.4 In situ adaptive tabulation (ISAT)

The exploration of chemical look-up tables which take into account more than two or three coordinates may become prohibitive in terms of computational costs (memory access, multilinear interpolations). On the other hand, only a very small part of the table is generally used during the simulation because only a small part of the composition space is accessed. To overcome these difficulties, Pope [534] and Yang and Pope [719] propose to build the chemical table as needed on the fly during the computation (*in situ*). The principle of this approach is briefly summarized here and the reader is referred to the above papers for details.

The thermochemical composition $\Phi = (\phi_1, \phi_2, ..., \phi_i, ...)$ of a mixture evolves with time in the composition space according to:

$$d\Phi/dt = \mathbf{S}\left[\Phi(t)\right] \tag{4.109}$$

where $\mathbf{S}[\Phi(t)]$ denotes the chemical source term and ϕ_i represents the composition space components (species mass fractions, temperature or enthalpy,...). Starting from a chemical composition Φ^0 at time t_0, the composition at time $t_0 + \Delta t$ is given by $\Phi(t_0 + \Delta t) = \mathbf{R}(\Phi^0)$

[xxix] Using laminar premixed flames for chemistry tabulation has already been proposed by Bradley et al. [78, 79].
[xxx] Note that other coordinates may be added. For example, Fiorina et al. [213] have included the enthalpy as a third coordinate together with a progress variable and a mixture fraction, to describe non-adiabatic partially premixed flames.

where $\mathbf{R}(\Phi^0)$ is the reaction mapping obtained by integrating Eq. (4.109) between times t_0 and $t_0 + \Delta t$.

Each table entry contains the thermochemical composition Φ^0, the reaction mapping $\mathbf{R}(\Phi^0)$ and the mapping gradient $\mathbf{A}(\Phi^0) = (\partial R_i(\Phi)/\partial \phi_j)$ measuring the sensitivity of the reaction mapping to changes in composition and provides the coefficients required for linear interpolations. The entry is complemented with the size of the region of accuracy where a reaction mapping may be estimated from this entry by a linear interpolation with an error below a tolerance ε_{tol} prescribed by the user. When the reaction mapping $\mathbf{R}(\Phi^q)$ is required for a query composition Φ^q, the closest composition Φ^0 in the table is first determined through a binary tree. Three actions are then possible:

- If Φ^q lies in the region of accuracy of the existing table entry Φ^0, a simple linear interpolation is performed (*retrieve*):

$$\mathbf{R}(\Phi^q) = \mathbf{R}(\Phi^0) + \mathbf{A}(\Phi^0)\left(\Phi^q - \Phi^0\right) \tag{4.110}$$

- If Φ^q is outside the region of accuracy of the table entry Φ^0, $\mathbf{R}(\Phi^q)$ is determined by integration of Eq. (4.109) and is compared to the linear interpolation (4.110) providing the corresponding error ε. Two cases are then considered:

  - If the error ε is lower than the tolerance ε_{tol} prescribed by the user, the size of the region of accuracy of the table entry Φ^0 is increased (*growth*).
  - If the error ε is larger than ε_{tol}, a new table entry is generated (*addition*).

As the table is empty when the computation starts, most queries lead initially to a generation of new table entries. Then, when the low dimensional manifold becomes populated, additional entries are only rarely required. The practical implementation of the ISAT procedure to determine whether a table entry is available or not is not obvious. Nevertheless, this approach, developed for detailed chemical schemes in the transported probability density function framework (sections 5.3.7 and 6.4.5), has been found to be very efficient compared to a direct integration (speed-ups larger than 1000 have been reported in some problems).[xxxi] ISAT, which is now available in some commercial codes, has been used for laminar flame calculations (Singer and Pope [615]) or in large eddy simulations (Pope [536]).

[xxxi]ISAT is a very efficient method to reduce numerical costs linked to chemistry computation but since all species involved in the chemical scheme must be solved for to enter the database, the computational task remains significant compared to reduced schemes.

Chapter 5

Turbulent premixed flames

5.1 Phenomenological description

Laminar premixed combustion corresponds to the propagation of a flame front in a mixture of fresh premixed reactants. For usual hydrocarbon/air flames at atmospheric pressure, the front moves at a speed s_L^0 (of the order of 20 to 100 cm/s for most hydrocarbon fuels at atmospheric pressure) and has a thickness δ_L^0 of the order of 0.1 mm (Chapt. 2). In a turbulent premixed flame, this front interacts with turbulent eddies (often designated as vortices although they are not necessarily vortex-like structures) which may have speeds of the order of tens of m/s and sizes ranging from a few millimeters to a few meters. This interaction may lead to a strong increase of the mass consumption rate and of the overall flame thickness, as described in Section 4.3.1. This section provides observations regarding turbulent premixed flames and a number of classical theoretical analyses required to understand the models implemented in most codes for turbulent premixed flames.

5.1.1 The effect of turbulence on flame fronts: wrinkling

The first description of turbulent combustion is due to Damköhler (1940) and introduces wrinkling as the main mechanism controlling turbulent flames. A turbulent flame speed s_T is defined as the velocity needed at the inlet of a control volume V (see notation in Fig. 5.1) to keep a turbulent flame stationary in the mean inside this volume. For a one-dimensional turbulent flame propagating along x_1, writing the mean fuel mass fraction balance equation (4.23) in the reference frame of the flame and using continuity ($\overline{\rho}\tilde{u}_1 = \rho_1 s_T$) leads to:

$$\rho_1 s_T \frac{\partial \widetilde{Y_F}}{\partial x_i} = -\frac{\partial}{\partial x_i}\left(\overline{V_{F,i}Y_F} + \overline{\rho}\widetilde{u_i''Y_F''}\right) + \bar{\dot{\omega}}_F \qquad (5.1)$$

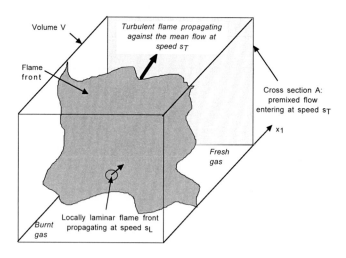

Figure 5.1: Flame wrinkling by turbulence.

Integrating this equation from $x_1 = -\infty$ to $x_1 = +\infty$ and canceling the diffusion terms far away from the flame front gives:

$$A\rho_1 Y_F^1 s_T = -\int_V \dot{\omega}_F \, dV \qquad (5.2)$$

where $\dot{\omega}_F$ is the local fuel reaction rate (the rate at which the reactants are consumed by the chemical reaction) and ρ_1 and Y_F^1 are respectively the density and the fuel mass fraction in the fresh gases. A is the area of the box cross section. Eq. (5.2) is established for a box where the turbulent flame is statistically stationary (Fig. 5.1) and expresses that the fuel mass flow rate entering the control box is totally consumed by combustion (this is true for lean mixtures). The flame is also assumed to remain in the box for an indefinitely long time, although it certainly moves inside this box. This definition is an extension of Eq. (2.24) derived for laminar flames.

Correlations between the fresh gases RMS velocity u' and the turbulent flame speed s_T, such as the simplest one proposed in Eq. (4.13), are numerous (Hakberg and Gosman [264], Abdel-Gayed et al. [3], Yakhot et al. [716], Duclos et al. [189], Peters [501]) and they basically all show the same trend, displayed in Fig. 5.2: s_T first increases, roughly linearly, with u', then levels off ("bending effect") before total quenching occurs for too intense turbulence. Damköhler (1940) explains the initial increase of s_T by a simple phenomenological model assuming that each point of the flame surface moves locally at the laminar flame speed s_L:

the local burning rate per unit area is then given by $\rho_1 Y_F^1 s_L^0$. If A_T measures the total flame area, the total reaction rate in the volume V is:

$$- \int_V \dot{\omega}_F dV = A_T \rho_1 Y_F^1 s_L^0 \qquad (5.3)$$

Using Eq. (5.2) to eliminate the integrated reaction rate $\int_V \dot{\omega}_F dV$ in Eq. (5.3) leads to:

$$\boxed{\frac{s_T}{s_L^0} = \frac{A_T}{A}} \qquad (5.4)$$

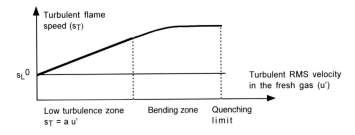

Figure 5.2: Variations of the turbulent flame speed with RMS turbulent speed

Eq. (5.4) shows that the increase of the turbulent flame speed s_T compared to the laminar flame speed s_L^0 is due to the increase of the total flame surface A_T, allowing a higher consumption rate for the same cross section A. The ratio $\Xi = A_T/A$ is a flame wrinkling factor and corresponds to the ratio of the available flame surface area divided by its projection in the propagating direction. As the ratio A_T/A increases with increasing Reynolds number Re, the turbulent flame speed increases with Re (Kuo [361], Duclos et al. [189], Peters [501]). Any model predicting that A_T/A goes up with u' gives a physical reasonable result. However, the prediction of the bending of the s_T curve is more difficult and predicting the quenching limits almost impossible (see § 4.6 for computations of quenching limits). Many semi-phenomenological models for s_T may be found in the literature (see Kuo [361] for a simple review) but both experimental and theoretical results show considerable scattering. This discrepancy may be due to measurement errors and poor modeling. However, a more likely explanation is that the concept of a unique turbulent flame speed depending only on u' is only an academic notion (Gouldin [248]): in practice, s_T is conditioned by experimental boundary conditions, turbulence spectrum or initial conditions (Cheng and Shepherd [126]). Accordingly, the quest for a universal expression for s_T vs u' has probably no practical interest and displaying correlations between s_T and u' is not a proof of the quality of models.

5.1.2   The effect of flame fronts on turbulence

Most studies of turbulent combustion are concerned with the effects of turbulence on the flame front. However, the flame also modifies the turbulent flow field.

First, when temperature changes from one side of the flame front to the other, kinematic viscosity and therefore local Reynolds numbers change accordingly. The kinematic viscosity ν increases roughly as $T^{1.7}$ for air. For a flame with a temperature ratio $T_2/T_1 = 8$, the Reynolds number is about 40 times smaller in burnt than in fresh gases. This effect may lead to relaminarization (a turbulent flow might become laminar after ignition).

A second important effect of the flame is flow acceleration through the flame front. For subsonic combustion, Eq. (2.104) shows that the flow accelerates through the flame front from u_1 to $u_1 + s_L^0(\rho_1/\rho_2 - 1) = u_1 + s_L^0(T_2/T_1 - 1)$. This velocity increase may be significant: for typical hydrocarbon flames, the speed difference through the flame front due to combustion is of the order of 4 m/s (for $T_2/T_1 = 8$ and $s_L^0 = 0.5$ m/s). This acceleration, occurring through very thin regions (typical flame thicknesses are of the order of 0.1 mm), modifies the turbulent flow field. The vorticity field is also affected by velocity and density changes leading to the so-called "flame-generated turbulence." The instantaneous balance equation for the vorticity vector $\vec{\Omega} = (\nabla \times \vec{u})/2$ is (assuming a constant kinematic viscosity ν):

$$\boxed{\frac{\partial \vec{\Omega}}{\partial t} + \vec{u} \cdot \nabla \vec{\Omega} = \underbrace{\left(\vec{\Omega} \cdot \nabla\right) \vec{u}}_{I} + \underbrace{\nu \nabla^2 \vec{\Omega}}_{II} - \underbrace{\vec{\Omega}\left(\nabla \cdot \vec{u}\right)}_{III} - \underbrace{\nabla \frac{1}{\rho} \times \nabla p}_{IV}} \qquad (5.5)$$

where RHS terms represent respectively the change in vorticity due to vortex stretching (I), viscous dissipation (II), density changes[i] (III) and the baroclinic torque (IV), corresponding to vorticity generation because of pressure and density gradients. The two last terms are induced by combustion. The effects of flames on turbulence depend on situations. Some flows becomes laminar ("relaminarization") when burning (Lewis and Von Elbe [383]) while some studies suggest that turbulence is increased in the burnt gas.

Mueller et al. [460] have experimentally investigated vorticity generation through a premixed flame. A toroidal vortex is convected through a planar laminar premixed flame. For low vortex strengths, corresponding to low turbulence intensities, a counter-rotating flame-generated vorticity was observed (Fig. 5.3). On the other hand, when vortex strengths are large (high turbulence intensities), the vortex crosses the flame front and remains almost unaffected. These results are summarized in Fig. 5.4.

More generally, the definition of turbulence in flames, related to an actual physical meaning, is questionable in premixed combustion. Such flows may be viewed as two-phase flows: a "fresh gases" phase and a "burnt gases" phase with different characteristics. Because of thermal expansion due to heat release, fresh gases are heavy and cold whereas burnt gases are hot and light. The dilatation through the flame induces different mean velocities on both sides of the flame front ($\overline{u}^u$ in the fresh gas and $\overline{u}^b$ in the burnt gas), as illustrated in Fig. 5.5. For the

---

[i]For a constant density flow, the mass balance equation reduces to $\nabla \cdot \mathbf{u} = 0$.

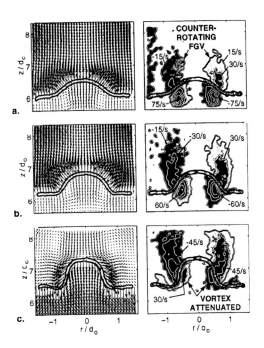

Figure 5.3: Velocity (left) and vorticity fields (right) measured during the interaction of a weak toroidal vortex with a planar laminar flame, at three successive times, a, b and c. A counter-rotating flame-generated vorticity (FGV) is observed when the vortex crosses the flame front (Reprinted by permission of Elsevier Science from Mueller et al. [460] © the Combustion Institute).

point referenced A, located in the fresh gases and never "seeing" any burnt gas, the definition of the RMS turbulent velocity u'_u is clear. In the same way, turbulence is well defined in the burnt gases for a point like B. However, at a point C located in the mean reaction zone, the velocity signal oscillates between two states: one state observed when C is surrounded by fresh gases and the other when it is surrounded by burnt gases. Simply computing an RMS velocity u' from the velocity signal at point C leads to very large values biased by the velocity jump $\overline{u}^b - \overline{u}^u$ through the flame front, as quantified by a simple analysis in the following section. Using this "turbulent" velocity in any model produces non physical results. This effect is due to intermittency and is not often included in models. The only method to alleviate this problem is to use conditional quantities to compute the turbulent velocity conditioned in the fresh or in the burnt gases (see § 5.1.3). The RMS velocity is the velocity used naturally by experimentalists and theoreticians to characterize turbulence: the u' quantity found in all text

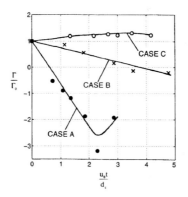

Figure 5.4: Total circulation Γ (normalized by the initial vortex circulation Γ_0) as a function of time during the interaction of a toroidal vortex with a planar laminar flame. In Case A (weak vortex), the incident circulation is eliminated and the flame produces a counter-rotating circulation (i.e. $\Gamma \leq 0$) that is twice the magnitude of the incident circulation. In Case B (intermediate vortex strength), the incident circulation is nearly eliminated by the flame front. For intense vortices, the initial circulation is not affected by the flame crossing (Case C). Reprinted by permission of Elsevier Science from Mueller et al. [460] © the Combustion Institute.

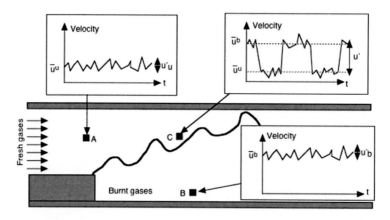

Figure 5.5: Definition of turbulence in a turbulent premixed flame.

books on turbulent combustion is tacitly the turbulence level in the fresh gases u'_u. In RANS codes, however, conditional models are most often too complex to be used (Duclos et al. [191]) and the interpretation of the u' values computed with RANS inside a flame front remains an open question.[ii] This question is critical because turbulence quantities (and especially the turbulence time ε/k) are directly controlling the mean reaction rate in RANS codes (see § 5.3). Non physical behaviors of RANS codes are often observed because "turbulence" in the flame brush, computed with classical turbulence models, is meaningless. This question is discussed in Sections 5.1.3 and 5.3 to model turbulent reaction and transport terms.

Another important point coming from this two phase flow structure of turbulent flames lies in buoyancy effects. Fresh gases are heavy and cold while burnt gases are light and hot. Accordingly, external forces (gravity) or pressure gradients act in different ways on fresh and burnt gases as simply shown in Fig. 5.6. Gravity forces are generally negligible in practical applications but may become predominant in large fires where flow motions are mainly controlled by natural convection (pool fires or forest fires among others). But most practical flames are ducted and accordingly submitted to large pressure gradients. These buoyancy effects may lead to unexpected phenomena such as counter-gradient turbulent transport where turbulent scalar fluxes have a direction opposed to the one predicted by Eq. (4.27). This point is discussed later (§ 5.3.8). These buoyancy effects are illustrated in Fig. 5.7, which compares the instantaneous structure of a turbulent premixed flame without (a) and with (b) externally imposed favorable pressure gradient (i.e. a pressure decreasing from fresh to burnt gases sides of the flame). In the case of an imposed favorable pressure gradient, the flame surface, and accordingly the turbulent flame speed, is decreased.

5.1.3 The infinitely thin flame front limit

An interesting tool to analyze turbulent premixed flames corresponds to an infinitely thin flame front (this assumption is discussed in next sections). This analysis was first proposed by Bray and Moss [87] in the derivation of the so-called BML (i.e. Bray-Moss-Libby) model.

Bray-Moss-Libby (BML) analysis

Only the basic analysis of the BML model is described here: modeling closures are discussed in Section 5.3.5. For an infinitely thin flame, the reduced temperature Θ may only have two values: $\Theta = 0$ in fresh gases and $\Theta = 1$ in fully burnt ones. The probability density function $p(\Theta)$ of the reduced temperature Θ has two peaks and may be written:

$$\boxed{p(\Theta) = \alpha\, \delta(\Theta) + \beta\, \delta(1 - \Theta)} \tag{5.6}$$

[ii]Experimental and direct numerical simulation (DNS) results, on the other hand, may be post-processed using conditioned quantities (Shepherd et al. [614]).

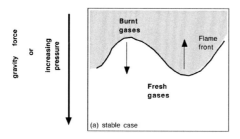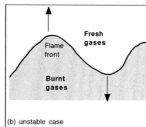

Figure 5.6: Relative motions of fresh (heavy and cold) and burnt (light and hot) gases submitted to a pressure gradient or a gravity force. Stable case(a): the pressure gradient tends to reduce the flame front wrinkling, decreases the overall reaction rate and induces a counter-gradient turbulent transport. Unstable case (b): the flame front wrinkling is promoted by the pressure gradient, increasing the overall reaction rate and a gradient turbulent transport is enhanced.

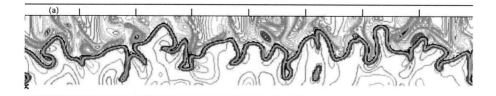

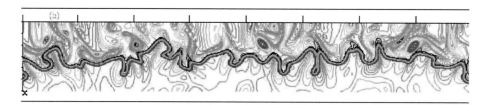

Figure 5.7: Superimposed instantaneous temperature and vorticity fields, extracted from DNS of turbulent premixed flames (Veynante and Poinsot [675], Reprinted with permission by Cambridge University Press): (a) free flame, no externally imposed pressure gradient; (b) imposed favorable pressure gradient (decreasing pressure from fresh (top) to burnt (bottom) gases).

where δ is the Dirac-δ function and α and β are respectively the probability to have fresh and fully burnt gases. Accordingly, $\alpha + \beta = 1$. The mean value $\overline{f}$ of any quantity f is given by:

$$\overline{f} = \int_0^1 f(\Theta)p(\Theta)\, d\Theta = \alpha\, \overline{f}^u + \beta\, \overline{f}^b \tag{5.7}$$

where $\overline{f}^u$ and $\overline{f}^b$ are respectively the conditional averages of f in fresh and burnt gases. Then:

$$\overline{\Theta} = \int_0^1 \Theta p(\Theta)\, d\Theta = \alpha(\Theta = 0) + \beta(\Theta = 1) = \beta \tag{5.8}$$

showing that the Reynolds average reduced temperature $\overline{\Theta}$ is the probability to be in burnt gases. The Favre average temperature is given by:

$$\overline{\rho\Theta} = \overline{\rho}\widetilde{\Theta} = \rho_b\beta = \rho_b\overline{\Theta} \tag{5.9}$$

where ρ_b is the density of the burnt gases. The mean density is given by:

$$\overline{\rho} = \alpha\rho_u + \beta\rho_b = (1 - \beta)\,\rho_u + \beta\rho_b \tag{5.10}$$

where ρ_u is the density of fresh gases. This relation may be recast as:

$$\overline{\rho}\left(1 + \tau\widetilde{\Theta}\right) = \rho_u = \rho_b\left(1 + \tau\right) \tag{5.11}$$

where τ is the heat release factor, defined as:

$$\boxed{\tau = \frac{\rho_u}{\rho_b} - 1 = \frac{T_b}{T_u} - 1} \tag{5.12}$$

where T_u and T_b are respectively the fresh and burnt gases temperatures, assuming a constant pressure combustion. Combining Eq. (5.9) and (5.11) leads to the determination of α and β:

$$\boxed{\alpha = \frac{1 - \widetilde{\Theta}}{1 + \tau\widetilde{\Theta}} \quad ; \quad \beta = \frac{(1 + \tau)\widetilde{\Theta}}{1 + \tau\widetilde{\Theta}}} \tag{5.13}$$

Another interesting relation is:

$$\boxed{\widetilde{Q} = \alpha\frac{\rho_u}{\overline{\rho}}\overline{Q}^u + \beta\frac{\rho_b}{\overline{\rho}}\overline{Q}^b = \left(1 - \widetilde{\Theta}\right)\overline{Q}^u + \widetilde{\Theta}\,\overline{Q}^b} \tag{5.14}$$

showing that the Favre average value of any quantity Q is a weighted average of mean values in fresh and burnt gases, where the weighting coefficient is the mean reduced temperature $\widetilde{\Theta}$. This simple analysis has various consequences discussed in the following sections.

Relations between Favre and Reynolds averaging

Under the assumption of a thin flame front, Eqs. (5.8) and (5.13) lead to a simple relation between Reynolds $(\overline{\Theta})$ and Favre $(\widetilde{\Theta})$ averages:

$$\boxed{\overline{\Theta} = \frac{(1+\tau)\widetilde{\Theta}}{1+\tau\widetilde{\Theta}}} \tag{5.15}$$

This relation corresponds, as already shown in Eq. (4.26) of Section 4.5.1, to an implicit model for the cross correlation of the density and the reduced temperature fluctuations:

$$\boxed{\overline{\rho'\Theta'} = \overline{\rho}\left(\widetilde{\Theta} - \overline{\Theta}\right) = -\overline{\rho}\frac{\tau\widetilde{\Theta}\left(1-\widetilde{\Theta}\right)}{1+\tau\widetilde{\Theta}}} \tag{5.16}$$

Relations (5.15) and (5.16) are displayed on Fig. 5.8 and 5.9 for various values of the heat release factor τ. The difference between $\overline{\Theta}$ and $\widetilde{\Theta}$ is large for usual values of τ (typically from 5 to 7).

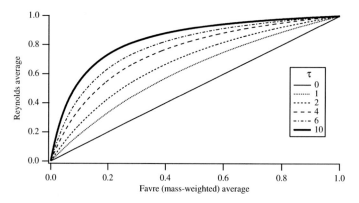

Figure 5.8: Reynolds average temperature $\overline{\Theta}$ as a function of the Favre average temperature $\widetilde{\Theta}$ for various values of the heat release factor τ, assuming a bimodal distribution ($\Theta = 0$ or $\Theta = 1$) of the reduced temperature Θ (Eq. 5.15).

Turbulent fluxes and countergradient turbulent transport

Under the BML assumption, the turbulent fluxes of Θ are also easily expressed as:

$$\boxed{\overline{\rho\mathbf{u}''\Theta''} = \overline{\rho}\left(\widetilde{\mathbf{u}\Theta} - \widetilde{\mathbf{u}}\widetilde{\Theta}\right) = \overline{\rho}\widetilde{\Theta}(1 - \widetilde{\Theta})\left(\overline{\mathbf{u}}^{b} - \overline{\mathbf{u}}^{u}\right)} \tag{5.17}$$

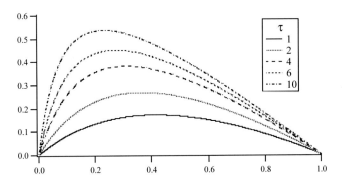

Figure 5.9: Correlation $-\overline{\rho'\Theta'}/\bar{\rho}$ as a function of the Favre averaged progress variable $\widetilde{\Theta}$ for various values of the heat release factor τ, assuming a bimodal distribution ($\Theta = 0$ or $\Theta = 1$) of the reduced temperature Θ (Eq. 5.16).

where $\overline{u}^u$ and $\overline{u}^b$ are the conditional mean velocity in fresh and burnt gases respectively.

This expression can been used to analyze counter-gradient phenomena: consider a statistically one-dimensional turbulent premixed flame propagating in the fresh gases along the x-axis oriented towards burnt gases. Because of thermal expansion, $\overline{u}^b$ is expected to be larger than $\overline{u}^u$, leading to a positive turbulent flux as suggested by Eq. (5.17). On the other hand, a classical gradient assumption:

$$\overline{\rho u''\Theta''} = -\frac{\mu_t}{Sc_t}\frac{\partial \widetilde{\Theta}}{\partial x}$$

(5.18)

predicts a negative flux. This counter-gradient turbulent transport (i.e. in the opposite direction than the one predicted using a gradient assumption) is generally explained by differential buoyancy effects induced by pressure gradients acting on heavy fresh gases and on light burnt gases (see Fig. 5.6). This phenomenon is observed both experimentally (Libby and Bray [386], Shepherd et al. [614]) and in direct numerical simulations (Veynante et al. [683]) but expression (5.17) should be used with care because conditional velocities are not simply related to mean velocities as discussed in Veynante et al. [683] (§ 5.3.8).

A simple physical insight into counter-gradient turbulent transport (Veynante et al. [682]) can be obtained by observing a premixed propane/air flame stabilized behind an obstacle (Fig. 5.10). The first part of the chamber (referred to as region A) is controlled by the vortices shed behind the flame holder. These eddies turn clockwise (counterclockwise) in the upper (lower) flame sheet, as in classical Von Kármán vortex streets but they are symmetric because of thermal expansion. When the centerline velocity increases in region B (because of expansion induced by the heat release), the upper (lower) coherent structures start to turn counterclockwise (clockwise). A simple geometrical analysis, based on Eq. (5.17), leads to the results presented in Table 5.1. For example, in region A, for $x_2 > 0$, a higher axial velocity ($u_1'' > 0$) is due to a fresh gases fluid particle ($\Theta'' < 0$), leading to $\widetilde{u_1''\Theta''} < 0$, denoting a gradient turbulent transport as $\partial\widetilde{\Theta}/\partial x_1 > 0$. A higher transverse velocity ($u_2'' > 0$) is due to a fluid particle moving upstream and coming from burnt gases ($\Theta'' > 0$). Then, $\widetilde{u_2''\Theta''}$ is positive, corresponding to a gradient turbulent transport $\partial\widetilde{\Theta}/\partial x_2 < 0$. According to Table 5.1, the transverse turbulent flux $\widetilde{u_2''\Theta''}$ is always of gradient type. But the change in structures rotation corresponds to a transition between gradient and counter-gradient transport for the downstream turbulent flux $\widetilde{u_1''\Theta''}$. Note that the turbulent fluxes are of gradient type close to the flame holder as expected to allow flame stabilization.

Turbulent stresses and turbulent kinetic energy

Under the BML assumption and combining Eq. (5.14) with relations:

$$\widetilde{u_i''u_j''} = \widetilde{u_iu_j} - \widetilde{u}_i\widetilde{u}_j \quad ; \quad \overline{u_i'u_j'}^u = \overline{u_iu_j}^u - \overline{u}_i^u\overline{u}_j^u \quad ; \quad \overline{u_i'u_j'}^b = \overline{u_iu_j}^b - \overline{u}_i^b\overline{u}_j^b \qquad (5.19)$$

Reynolds stresses $\widetilde{u_i''u_j''}$ are also expressed as:

$$\boxed{\widetilde{u_i''u_j''} = \underbrace{(1 - \widetilde{\Theta})\overline{u_i'u_j'}^u}_{\text{fresh gases}} + \underbrace{\widetilde{\Theta}\overline{u_i'u_j'}^b}_{\text{burnt gases}} + \underbrace{\widetilde{\Theta}(1 - \widetilde{\Theta})\left(\overline{u}_i^b - \overline{u}_i^u\right)\left(\overline{u}_j^b - \overline{u}_j^u\right)}_{\text{intermittency}}} \qquad (5.20)$$

and appear as a weighted average of fresh and burnt gases Reynolds stresses, corresponding to real turbulence and to an additional term corresponding to intermittency between fresh and burnt gases (see point C in Fig. 5.5). This last term is not related to turbulent motions. Eq. (5.20) may be rewritten in terms of an "apparent" turbulent kinetic energy, $\widetilde{k}$:

$$\widetilde{k} = \frac{1}{2}\sum_i \widetilde{u_i''^2} = \underbrace{(1 - \widetilde{\Theta})\,\overline{k}^u}_{\text{fresh gases}} + \underbrace{\widetilde{\Theta}\,\overline{k}^b}_{\text{burnt gases}} + \underbrace{\frac{1}{2}\widetilde{\Theta}(1 - \widetilde{\Theta})\left[\sum_i \left(\overline{u}_i^b - \overline{u}_i^u\right)^2\right]}_{\text{intermittency}} \qquad (5.21)$$

where $\overline{k}^u$ and $\overline{k}^b$ are the actual turbulent kinetic energy in fresh and in burnt gases respectively. Once again, an additional term, corresponding to intermittency between fresh and burnt gases and not to actual turbulent motions, occurs. Because of the intermittency term, $\widetilde{k}$ measures velocity fluctuations which do not correspond to the real turbulence levels either in the fresh or in the burnt gases.[iii]

[iii] The intermittency terms in Eqs (5.20) and (5.21) appear because the actual turbulence in fresh and burnt gases should be defined relatively to the conditional mean velocities $\overline{\mathbf{u}}^u$ and $\overline{\mathbf{u}}^b$, respectively, while velocity fluctuations $\mathbf{u}''$ entering mean Reynolds stresses, $\widetilde{u_i''u_j''}$, and turbulent kinetic energy, $\widetilde{k}$, are defined relatively to the Favre average velocity $\widetilde{\mathbf{u}}$ which has no physical meaning in terms of turbulence.

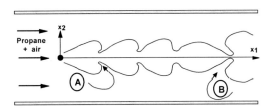

Figure 5.10: Coherent structure dynamics in a turbulent premixed propane/air flame stabilized behind a flame holder (Veynante et al. [682]).

Region	$\overline{u}_1^b - \overline{u}_1^u$	$\dfrac{\partial \widetilde{\Theta}}{\partial x_1}$	$\widetilde{u_1''\Theta''}$	$\overline{u}_2^b - \overline{u}_2^u$ (for $x_2 > 0$)	$\dfrac{\partial \widetilde{\Theta}}{\partial x_2}$ (for $x_2 > 0$)	$\widetilde{u_2''\Theta''}$
A	< 0	> 0	G	> 0	< 0	G
B	> 0	> 0	CG	> 0	< 0	G

Table 5.1: Simple geometrical analysis, based on Eq. (5.17), of the flame structure dynamics displayed in Fig. 5.10. G and CG denote respectively gradient and counter-gradient turbulent transport.

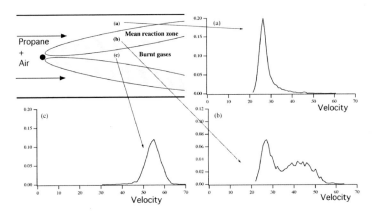

Figure 5.11: Velocity measurements in a V-shape turbulent premixed flame stabilized behind a small rod (top). Velocity probabilities are displayed in fresh gases (location a), in the mean reaction zone (b) and in burnt gases (c) (Veynante et al. [682]).

This point can be demonstrated experimentally by conditional velocity measurements (Cheng and Shepherd [125], Cho et al. [130]) illustrated in Fig. 5.11. Laser Doppler velocity measurements have been performed in a V-shape turbulent premixed flame stabilized behind a small rod (Veynante et al. [682], see Fig. 5.10). In the fresh gases region (location a), a Gaussian-type probability density function (pdf) is observed as in a classical turbulent flow field. The RMS velocity is directly related to the turbulence level. In burnt gases (location c), the same shape is found. But, in the mean reaction zone (location b) a two peak histogram is found corresponding to intermittency between fresh and burnt gases. The apparent turbulence level (i.e. the RMS velocity) is due to turbulence in fresh gases (first term in Eq. (5.21)), in burnt gases (second term in Eq. (5.21)) and to intermittency. As the conditional averaged axial velocity is higher in the burnt gases, the turbulent transport is counter-gradient (region B in Fig. 5.10 and Table 5.1).

5.2   Premixed turbulent combustion regimes

As described in Section 4.5.4, a direct approach to model the mean reaction rate based on the series expansion of the Arrhenius law cannot be retained because of the large number of unclosed quantities (correlations between species concentrations and temperature fluctuations) and of the large truncation errors due to high non linearities. Therefore, the derivation of models must be based on physical analysis and comparisons of the various time and length scale involved in combustion phenomena. These analyses lead to the so-called "turbulent combustion diagrams" where various regimes are identified and delineated introducing non-dimensional characteristic numbers. Diagrams defining combustion regimes in terms of length and velocity scales ratios have been proposed by Barrère [34], Bray [83], Borghi [71], Borghi and Destriau [73], Peters [500, 501], Williams [710], Abdel-Gayed and Bradley [2]. Knowing the turbulence characteristics (integral length scale, turbulent kinetic energy and its dissipation rate among other characteristics), these diagrams indicate whether the flow contains flamelets (thin reaction zones), pockets or distributed reaction zones. This information is essential to build a turbulent combustion model. A continuous flame front, without holes, cannot be modeled in the same way than a flame which is broken into many small pockets and where combustion does not take place along a sheet but in a more distributed manner.

These diagrams are mainly based on intuitive arguments and introduce order of magnitude arguments rather than precise demonstrations. The derivation is also based on strong assumptions on turbulence which are discussed in Section 5.2.1 and used to build classical combustion diagrams in Section 5.2.2. Results obtained from direct numerical simulations (DNS) as well as from experimental data are then presented to derive more refined diagrams in Section 5.2.3.

5.2.1   A first difficulty: defining u'

Most heuristic derivations of turbulent combustion models use various assumptions and approximations:

- Turbulence is supposed to behave everywhere like isotropic homogeneous turbulence.

- Turbulence is characterized through its RMS velocity u' and its integral scale l_t.

Although the first assumption is commonly used in all RANS approaches, the second one is more dangerous. Using the RMS velocity u' (or the kinetic turbulent energy $\tilde{k}$) to quantify the velocity fluctuations in a flame has no theoretical basis in a premixed flame. Eq. (5.21) shows that $\tilde{k}$ is not well defined except far from the flame front. In experiments, k is the RMS velocity in the fresh gases and this is the implicit assumption used by most experimentalists when correlations between combustion speeds and RMS velocities are presented. In a multi-dimensional code, however, $\tilde{k}$ is a local quantity. Its value at the flame front is biased by intermittency.[iv] Using this value to obtain a turbulent time for a combustion model is not a soundly based method even though this approach is used in most existing codes.

5.2.2 Classical turbulent premixed combustion diagrams

In a first approach, turbulent premixed combustion may be described as the interaction between a flame front (thickness δ and speed s_L^0)[v] and an ensemble of "eddies" (representing turbulence) with sizes ranging from the Kolmogorov (called η_k) to the integral (called l_t) scales and characteristic speeds ranging from the Kolmogorov (called u'_k) to the integral RMS (u') velocities. If turbulence is supposed to be homogeneous and isotropic, the speed $u'(r)$ and the size r of any eddy participating to the turbulence cascade are linked by Eq. (4.5):

$$\frac{u'(r)^3}{r} = \varepsilon \qquad (5.22)$$

where ε is the local dissipation rate of turbulent kinetic energy (Fig. 4.1). This assumption is useful to imagine how a turbulent flow may interact with a premixed front because it provides estimates of speeds and times variations with r. For example (Eq. (4.10) and Fig. 4.1), a typical turbulent time of an eddy of size r is:

$$\tau_m(r) = \frac{r}{u'(r)} = \frac{r^{2/3}}{\varepsilon^{1/3}} \qquad (5.23)$$

Comparing this characteristic time to a typical flame time scale τ_c (defined by $\tau_c = \delta/s_L^0$)[vi] to build a reduced number $D_a(r) = \tau_m(r)/\tau_c$ suggests scenarios for flame/vortex interaction: for large $D_a(r)$, chemical times are small compared to the eddy time and turbulence is not able

---

[iv]The turbulence levels are probably poorly evaluated anyway because usual turbulence models do not take into account variable density effects induced by flame fronts.

[v]As indicated in Section 4.6.3, the flame thickness is usually estimated as $\delta = \nu/s_L^0$ instead of using the actual thickness δ_L^0 defined in Section 2.5 to simplify the analysis (unity "flame Reynolds number" $\delta s_L^0/\nu = 1$).

[vi]This time scale is the time needed for the flame to move on a distance corresponding to its own thickness δ. It may also be viewed as a characteristic diffusion time scale because $\tau_c = \delta/s_L^0 = \delta^2/\nu$.

to affect the flame inner structure in a significant way. On the other hand, low values of $D_a(r)$ imply long chemical time scales and a flame strongly modified by the turbulent eddies.[vii]

The Damköhler number $D_a(r)$ changes when r goes from the Kolmogorov size η_k to the integral scale l_t. Which values of r (which turbulent eddies) are the most relevant in controlling the flame structure? This question is still unsolved in general and controls many assumptions introduced later for models. Classical approaches introduce two reduced numbers corresponding to the limiting values of r:

- The Damköhler number D_a is defined for the largest eddies and corresponds to the ratio of the integral time scale τ_t to the chemical time scale (see § 4.6.3):

$$D_a = D_a(l_t) = \frac{\tau_t}{\tau_c} = \frac{\tau_m\,(l_t)}{\tau_c} = \frac{l_t/u'(l_t)}{\delta/s_L^0} \tag{5.24}$$

- The Karlovitz number K_a corresponds to the smallest eddies (Kolmogorov) and is the ratio of the chemical time scale to the Kolmogorov time:

$$K_a = \frac{1}{D_a(\eta_k)} = \frac{\tau_c}{\tau_k} = \frac{\tau_c}{\tau_m\,(\eta_k)} = \frac{u'(\eta_k)/\eta_k}{s_L^0/\delta} \tag{5.25}$$

Using Eq. (4.5), (4.6) and (2.74), this number may also be recast in various forms:

$$K_a = \left(\frac{l_t}{\delta}\right)^{-1/2} \left(\frac{u'}{s_L^0}\right)^{3/2} = \left(\frac{\delta}{\eta_k}\right)^2 = \frac{\sqrt{\varepsilon/\nu}}{s_L^0/\delta} \tag{5.26}$$

The turbulence Reynolds number Re_t, based on integral length scale characteristics, may also be expressed as:

$$Re_t = \frac{u'l_t}{\nu} = \left(\frac{u'}{s_L^0}\right)\left(\frac{l_t}{\delta}\right) \tag{5.27}$$

leading to the relation:

$$Re_t = D_a^2\,K_a^2 \tag{5.28}$$

For large values of the Damköhler number ($D_a \gg 1$), chemical times are shorter than the integral turbulence time. Accordingly, turbulence is not able to affect the inner flame structure

---

[vii] All these analyses are implicitly based on a single-step irreversible reaction. In real flames, a large number of chemical species and reactions have to be included (several hundred species and several thousand reactions for propane burning in air). These reactions may correspond to a large range of chemical time scales. For example, propane oxidation may be assumed to be fast compared to turbulent time scales. On the other hand, the CO_2 formation from carbon monoxide (CO) and OH radical in the burnt gases is quite slower with chemical times of the same order as turbulent times. Nitric oxide formation is also generally very slow.

which remains close to a laminar flame, wrinkled by turbulence motions ("flamelet" limit). In this case, the mean burning rate may be estimated from the burning rate of a laminar flame multiplied by the overall flame surface. On the other hand, when the Damköhler number is low ($D_a \ll 1$), the chemical time is larger than turbulent times. The overall reaction rate is therefore controlled by chemistry whereas reactants and products are mixed by turbulence motions. This regime is the so-called "perfectly stirred reactor." This limiting case is quite easy to model: in this situation, reactants and products are continuously mixed in a time shorter than the chemical time. The mean reaction rate may then be estimated as the reaction rate computed using mean values (i.e. keeping only the first term in the series expansion 4.44).

$K_a < 1$ $(D_a > 1)$	$K_a > 1$ and $D_a > 1$	$D_a \ll 1$
Flamelets	Thickened flames	Well stirred reactor
Flame is thinner	Small turbulent scales	All turbulent time scales are
than all turbulent scales	may enter the flame front	smaller than the chemical time scale

Table 5.2: Classical regimes of turbulent premixed combustion.

Using Damköhler and Karlovitz numbers, various combustion regimes may be identified in terms of length (l_t/δ) and velocity (u'/s_L^0) ratios (Table 5.2):

- When $K_a < 1$, the chemical time scale is shorter than any turbulent time scales and the flame thickness is smaller than the smallest turbulent scale, the Kolmogorov scale. In this regime, the flame front is thin, has an inner structure close to a laminar flame and is wrinkled by turbulence motions. This "thin flame regime" or "flamelet regime" may be divided into two regions, depending on the velocity ratio u'/s_L^0:

  - $u' < s_L^0$: the speed of turbulent motions is too low to wrinkle the flame front up to flame interactions. This regime is identified as a "wrinkled flamelet regime."

  - $u' > s_L^0$: as the turbulent motion velocities become larger than the flame speed, turbulent motions become able to wrinkle the flame front up to flame front interactions leading to the formations of pockets of fresh and burnt gases. This regime is identified as a "thin flame regime with pockets" or "corrugated flamelet regime."

- For $\tau_k < \tau_c < \tau_t$ ($K_a > 1$ and $D_a > 1$) the turbulent integral time scale is still larger than the chemical time scale but the Kolmogorov scales are smaller than the flame thickness and are able to modify the inner flame structure. The flame can no longer be identified as a laminar flame front but is still a wrinkled flame. This regime is known as "thickened flame regime" or "distributed reaction zones." According to Eq. (5.26), the stretch induced by Kolmogorov scales becomes larger than the critical "flame stretch" s_L^0/δ possibly leading to flame quenching as discussed below.

- For $D_a < 1$, turbulent motions have shorter characteristic times than the chemical reaction time τ_c: mixing is fast and the overall reaction rate is mainly limited by chemistry. This regime tends toward the "well-stirred reactor" limit ($D_a \ll 1$).

The line separating corrugated flamelets and distributed reaction regimes corresponds to the condition $K_a = 1$ and is known as the Klimov-Williams criterion.

These regimes may be plotted on a combustion diagram as a function of lengths (l_t/δ) and velocities (u'/s_L^0) ratios as in Fig. 5.12, using a log-log scale.

Peters [501] has also proposed to identify combustion regimes using two characteristic thicknesses: the flame thickness δ, and the reaction zone thickness, δ_r ($\delta_r \ll \delta$):

- When $\delta_r < \delta < \eta_k$, a "thin flame regime" is identified as previously. As an example, Fig. 5.14a presents a DNS computation for such a regime.

- When $\delta > \eta_k$, Kolmogorov scales are able to enter and to thicken the flame preheat zone. The question is now: are Kolmogorov scales able to enter the reaction zone? This situation occurs when the reaction thickness, δ_r becomes larger than the Kolmogorov size, η_k, i.e. when the Karlovitz number reaches a transition value $K_{a,r}$, corresponding to $\delta_r = \eta_k$:

$$\boxed{K_{a,r} = \left(\frac{\delta}{\eta_k}\right)^2 = \left(\frac{\delta}{\delta_r}\right)^2 \left(\frac{\delta_r}{\eta_k}\right)^2 = \left(\frac{\delta}{\delta_r}\right)^2} \tag{5.29}$$

For most premixed flames, $\delta/\delta_r \approx 10$, corresponding to a transition for $K_{a,r} \approx 100$. Then, two regimes are identified:

- When $1 < K_a < K_{a,r}$ (i.e. $\delta_r < \eta_k < \delta$), turbulent motions are able to enter and modify the flame preheat zone but not the reaction zone, which remains close to a wrinkled laminar reaction zone. This regime is the "thickened-wrinkled flame regime:" a DNS example of such flames is displayed in Fig. 5.14b.

- For $K_a > K_{a,r}$ (i.e. $\eta_k < \delta_r < \delta$), both diffusion and reaction zone are affected by turbulent motions. No laminar structure could be longer identified. This regime is called "thickened flame regime."

These regimes are identified in the diagram in Fig. 5.13 and a scheme of the three regimes, proposed by Borghi and Destriau [73] is plotted in Fig. 5.15.

5.2.3 Modified combustion diagrams

The classical analysis developed in the previous section to define turbulent premixed combustion regimes is useful to provide a first view of combustion regimes but is also well known to fail in many situations because of different deficiencies:

- All the analysis is derived assuming an homogeneous and isotropic frozen (i.e. unaffected by heat release) turbulence.

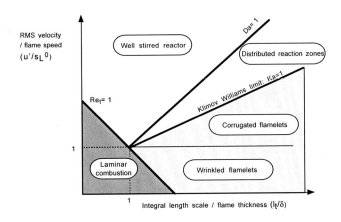

Figure 5.12: Classical turbulent combustion diagram: combustion regimes are identified in terms of length (l_t/δ) and velocity (u'/s_L^0) ratios using a log-log scale (Peters [500]).

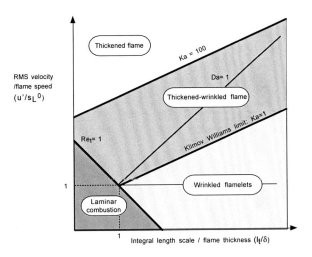

Figure 5.13: Modified turbulent combustion diagram proposed by Peters [501]: combustion regimes are identified in terms of length (l_t/δ) and velocity (u'/s_L^0) ratios (log-log scale).

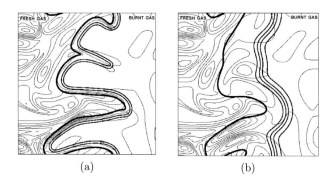

Figure 5.14: DNS of (a) a wrinkled flamelet regime and (b) a thickened-wrinkled flame regime. Vorticity field (thin lines) and reaction rate (bold lines). Very thick line denotes the fresh gases boundary of the preheat zone. Same initial turbulent field for both simulations. The flame thickness is 5 times larger in case (b) than in (a). In case (a) the whole flame structure remains laminar-like. In case (b) the preheat zone is modified by small turbulent scales.

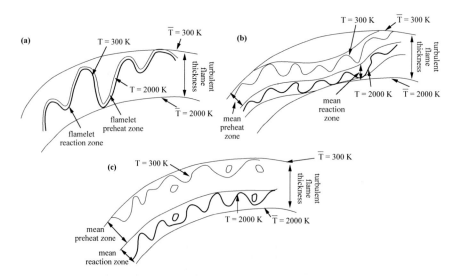

Figure 5.15: Turbulent premixed combustion regimes proposed by Borghi and Destriau [73] illustrated in a case where the fresh and burnt gas temperatures are 300 and 2000 K respectively: (a) wrinkled flamelet (thin wrinkled flame), (b) thickened-wrinkled flame, (c) thickened flame.

- Criterions and regime limits are only based on order of magnitude estimations and not on precise derivations. For example, the Klimov-Williams criterion defining the ability of a Kolmogorov vortice to enter the flame structure could correspond to a Karlovitz number $K_a = 0.1$ or $K_a = 10.$, instead of $K_a = 1$.

- The Kolmogorov scale η_k may be too small, or have too small velocities u'_k (compared to the flame front thickness and speed) to affect the flame efficiently. For this reason, Peters [502] suggests to retain the Gibson scale, l_g, defined as the size of the eddy turning at the laminar flame speed $(u'(l_g) = s^0_L; \; l_g = (s^0_l)^3/\varepsilon > \eta_k)$, as the minimum turbulent scale able to wrinkle the flame front in the thin flame regime ($K_a < 1$).

- As the Kolmogorov scales (η_k and u'_k) and the flame scales (δ and s^0_L) are linked by the same relations to diffusion coefficients ($\eta_k u'_k/\nu \simeq \delta s^0_L/\nu \simeq 1$ (Eq. 4.7) where ν is the kinematic viscosity), viscous dissipation is important for all structures having a scale close to the flame thickness. Kolmogorov vortices are the most efficient in terms of induced strain rate but, because of viscous dissipation, have a short lifetime and therefore only limited effects on combustion. For example, these structures are probably unable to effectively quench the flame.

- Scales smaller than the flame front thickness induce high local curvature and associated thermo-diffusive effects which may counteract the influence of strain.

- The previous arguments show that the interaction between a given vortex and a flame front is essentially unsteady. The flame response depends on how long it is submitted to the vortex stretch and how fast the vortex is dissipated by viscous effects.

Following the previous comments, a more refined diagram should be derived analyzing the ability of vortices to quench a premixed flame front and the importance of unsteady phenomena.

Quenching in turbulent premixed combustion

Flame quenching occurs when a flame front is submitted to external perturbations such as heat losses or sufficiently strong aerodynamic stretch to decrease the reaction rate to a negligible value, and, in some cases, to completely suppress the combustion process. For example, asymptotic studies of laminar stagnation point flame established by the counterflow of reactants and products (Bush and Fendell [99], Libby and Williams [387], Libby et al. [391]) reveal that stretch may decrease the flame speed by a considerable amount. Libby et al. [391] show that quenching by stretch may occur in non-adiabatic flows or when the Lewis number (defined as the ratio of the thermal diffusivity to the reactant diffusivity: $Le = \lambda/(\rho C_p \mathcal{D})$) is greater than unity. These results have been confirmed by numerical methods (Darabiha et al. [165], Giovangigli and Smooke [238, 239]) and experimental studies (Ishizuka and Law [304], Sato [589], Law et al. [371]). These have already been presented in Section 2.7.3 and Fig. 2.24 to 2.26 give a brief summary of the effects of stretch on a laminar flame front with and without heat losses. All these studies have been performed for laminar flames but, assuming a thin flame front in the wrinkled flame regime, they should also be valid in turbulent flames.

When no quenching occurs in a turbulent premixed flame, the flame zone is "active" everywhere and may be analyzed as an interface separating fresh unburnt cold reactants from hot burnt products. This regime is called a *flamelet regime* here and defined as (Fig. 5.16):[viii] *A turbulent premixed reacting flow is in a flamelet regime when a line connecting any point A in fresh gases to another point B in burnt products crosses (at least) one active flame front.*

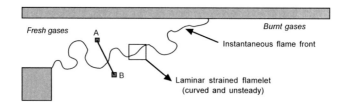

Figure 5.16: Flamelet assumption: definition of flamelet regimes.

When the local stretch induced by turbulent motions on the flame front becomes sufficiently large to quench the flame at a given location, combustion stops in the vicinity of this point and fresh reactants diffuse into the products without burning. In this situation, the description of the reacting flow becomes much more complex and standard flamelet approaches are no longer valid.

Therefore, quenching in a turbulent premixed flame determines the limit between two fundamentally different behaviors (i.e. flamelets or no flamelets) and appears as an important mechanism in the description and modeling of turbulent combustion. Flame elements are usually assumed to quench in turbulent flows for conditions similar to laminar stagnation point flames (Bray [83]). The parameter controlling the similarity between turbulent flamelets and laminar stagnation point flames is flame stretch (see § 2.6). This assumption is justified, once again, from asymptotic theories (Clavin and Williams [141], Clavin and Joulin [139]) which show that, under certain assumptions (mainly low levels of stretch), the whole flame structure and many important flame parameters, such as displacement and consumption speeds, depend only on stretch. For example, the displacement speed s_d defined by Eq. (2.99) is given by:

$$\frac{s_d}{s_L^0} = 1 - \frac{\mathcal{M}}{s_L^0}\,\kappa, \tag{5.30}$$

where $\mathcal{M}$ is the Markstein length, a characteristic length scale depending on thermal and mass

---

[viii]This definition is not as restrictive as the usual one. In various other works, the flamelet regime corresponds to a thin flame front having the internal structure of a one-dimensional laminar flame. In the present definition, the flamelet regime corresponds only to a continuous flame front without quenching. The inner flame structure can differ from laminar flame cases.

diffusive properties of the reactant mixture.[ix]

The flame stretch κ appearing in (5.30) is defined as for laminar flames, in terms of flame and flow kinematic and geometrical properties (Eq. (2.78)):

$$\kappa = \frac{1}{A} \frac{dA}{dt} \tag{5.31}$$

When $\kappa > 0$, the flame front is positively stretched (generally simply called "stretched"). The simplest example of a positively stretched flame is the planar stagnation point flame studied in Section 2.6. Many stretched flamelets are also found in the leading edges of turbulent flames where flame surface is produced. Flame quenching is expected when κ becomes of the order of the inverse of the flame time $\tau_c = \delta/s_L^0$, i.e. when the Karlovitz number $K_a = \kappa\delta/s_L^0 = \kappa\tau_c$ is of order unity. When $\kappa < 0$, the flame front is negatively stretched (or "compressed"). A typical example of a compressed flame is a flame front curved towards the fresh gases or the tip of a Bunsen burner flame (Fig. 2.27). Expression (5.30) indicates that, in the limit of small stretch values, the flamelet response to flow perturbations may be described using only the stretch κ. Curvature and strain play similar roles in flame stretch, suggesting an important simplification: the flamelet behavior may be studied only considering planar strained flames, which are simpler to set and investigate than curved flames. In other words, according to asymptotic analysis, a curved flame and a planar flame feature the same dynamics if they have the same total stretch. Therefore, one may conclude that studies of planar strained flames are sufficient to understand flame/flow interaction and this explains why plane strain effects have been extensively studied while curvature effects have been relatively neglected.[x]

Unfortunately, various difficulties are associated to this simple description:

- First, the asymptotic relation (5.30) is developed assuming low flame stretch values. Its extension to high stretch values (and strong curvature) has no rigorous basis.

- The instantaneous structure of a turbulent flame (Fig. 5.17) evidences a second difficulty: a flame front embedded in a turbulent shear layer is positively stretched at certain locations (typically in vortex braids) and strongly curved (and therefore negatively stretched or compressed) where the flame is wrapped around the vortices. This sketch reveals that planar positively stretched flamelets cannot describe the regions where the front is strongly curved towards the fresh gases. Since most turbulent flames involve large stretch values and highly curved flame fronts, these questions have to be addressed to develop a satisfactory local flamelet model.

- Geometrical considerations suggest that vortices should be larger than the length scales corresponding to the flame front (typically the thermal thickness δ_L^0) to be able to actually stretch the flame. Accordingly, small scales should not be included in a description which only relies on stretch.

[ix]This relation is used in studies of turbulent premixed flame propagation to express the flame front displacement speed (Ashurst et al. [19], Peters [501]).

[x]Counterflow strained planar flames are also the prototype of simple steady-state flames, very well suited for detailed experimental investigations.

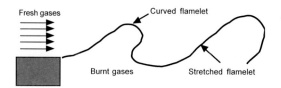

Figure 5.17: Stretched and curved flamelets in a turbulent flame.

- In laminar stagnation point flames, the flame front is planar and submitted to constant stretch. In a turbulent flame, the flame front is stretched by turbulent eddies. Therefore, induced stretches vary because eddies move with respect to the flame. Thus, the flame is also curved when stretched. Curvature effects may be very important (Mikolaitis [441]) and should be accounted for.

- Finally, viscous effects may modify the vortex structure and decrease the stretch induced on the flame front before quenching occurs.

Time and scale-dependent effects

Flame/vortex interactions in a turbulent flow are intrinsically time-dependent: information extracted from laminar stagnation point flames submitted to steady stretch might not be relevant for turbulent premixed flames. More importantly, a turbulent flow is not restricted to one type of eddy but features a complex combination of vortices including scales ranging from the Kolmogorov scale η_k to the integral scale l_t. As described in Section 4.2, each scale may be characterized by a length scale r, a velocity perturbation $u'(r)$ and induces a stretch $u'(r)/r$ (Fig. 4.1). Using only the smallest or the largest scale to describe flame/turbulence interaction is not sufficient: an analysis of the effects of all scales is required and may be performed using the "spectral diagram" introduced in Fig. 5.18.

Using the description of eddies in turbulence (§ 4.2), a turbulent flow field is represented in the spectral diagram by a straight line denoted as "turbulence line" and bounded by the Kolmogorov and integral scales. Each scale present on the turbulence line has a different effect on the flame front. Some vortices may lead to quenching, some may induce formations of fresh gases pockets, while others may be dissipated by viscous effects before any interaction with the flame structure. In the same turbulent reacting flow, all three types of vortices may be found at the same time: a description based on one scale cannot take all mechanisms into account.

The interaction between a flame and a vortex can be characterized by three non-dimensionalized numbers (Fig. 5.18) depending on the length scale r considered:

- $V_r(r) = u'(r)/s_L^0$ compares the turbulent velocity fluctuation $u'(r)$ associated to the length scale r and the laminar flame speed. A necessary condition for strong interactions is that the speed induced by the vortex be greater than the flame speed, i.e. $V_r(r) > 1$.

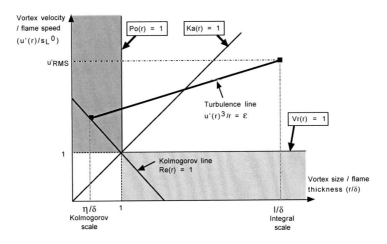

Figure 5.18: Principle of spectral diagram for premixed flame vortex interaction (log-log scale).

- The Karlovitz number for the scale r is:

$$K_a(r) = \frac{u'(r)/r}{\delta/s_L^0} \simeq \frac{1}{Re(r)^{1/2}} \left(\frac{\delta}{\eta_k} \right)^2 \qquad (5.32)$$

where $Re(r)$ is the Reynolds number associated to the scale r. $K_a(r)$ coincides with the Karlovitz number of Eq. (5.26) when r is the Kolmogorov length scale $r = \eta_k$. A necessary condition for flame quenching due to stretch corresponds to $K_a(r) > 1$.

- The vortex power is measured by the ratio of the vortex lifetime r^2/ν to the chemical time δ/s_L^0:

$$P_o(r) = \frac{r^2 s_L^0}{\nu \delta} \simeq \left(\frac{r}{\delta} \right)^2 \qquad (5.33)$$

This number may be viewed as the ratio of the penetration length of the vortex into the flame front (before its eventual dissipation by viscous effects) to the flame front thickness. Vortices with a power lower than unity ($P_o(r) < 1$) are dissipated by viscous effects before they affect the flame front. $P_o(r)$ is also a good measure of curvature effects arising from the interaction of a vortex of size r with a flame front of thickness δ.

The Klimov-Williams criterion may be reconsidered from this analysis: according to this criterion, the Kolmogorov scales may quench the flame front. In the spectral diagram (Fig. 5.18), the Kolmogorov scales belong to the line $Re(\eta_k) = u'(\eta_k)\eta_k/\nu \simeq u'(\eta_k)\eta_k/s_L^0\delta = 1$.

When the Kolmogorov length scale is larger than the flame thickness ($\eta_k > \delta$), the corresponding flow conditions fall below the line $V_r(r) = 1$. The vortex speed is lower than the flame speed leading to a "weak" interaction. On the other hand, if $\eta_k < \delta$, the power $P_o(\eta_k)$ of the vortex is small (although its velocity may be high) and the fluctuation is dissipated by viscous effects before any interaction with the flame. In both cases, Kolmogorov scales are unable to quench a flame front. Clearly, the interaction between a single vortex and a flame front involves more than a single non-dimensional number (for example, the Karlovitz number) and must be studied in more detail as described in the next section.

DNS of flame/vortex interactions

The interaction of isolated deterministic vortices with flame fronts is a pre-requisite to understanding the interaction of a turbulent flow field, viewed as a collection of vortices, with flames. Flame/vortex interactions have received much attention using numerical techniques (Karagozian and Marble [322], Laverdant and Candel [368], Ashurst and McMurtry [18], Rutland and Ferziger [577], Poinsot et al. [523], Mantel et al. [418], Samaniego and Mantel [584]) or experiments (Jarosinski et al. [309], Roberts and Driscoll [560], Roberts et al. [562], Mueller et al. [460], Samaniego and Mantel [584]). Since the size and velocity of the vortical structure may be controlled independently, the aerodynamic perturbation of the flame front is precisely defined. A typical flame/vortex configuration is displayed in Fig. 5.19. At the initial time, two counter-rotating vortices are generated upstream of a laminar flame front. The flow is symmetrical with respect to the $y = 0$ axis and subsequently, only the upper half part of the domain is calculated and displayed. The vortex-pair configuration generates large flame stretch values and interacts efficiently with the flame front because of its self-induced velocity.

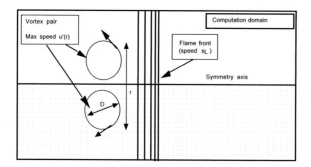

Figure 5.19: Typical initial geometry for DNS of flame/vortex interaction.

An important aspect linked to the choice of the equations used for the DNS deals with the introduction of heat loss models into the computation. These losses are mainly due to radiation. Laminar flame results show that they are essential control parameters for flame quenching (see § 2.7.3). If a DNS is performed without modeling heat losses (something which is possible for DNS but not for an actual flame), flames might be too resistant to strain: Patnaik and Kailasanath [493] show that the level of heat losses used in flame/vortex interaction DNS controls the occurrence of quenching. On the other hand, modeling heat losses in real flames is a challenge in itself and corresponding models cannot yet be included in a DNS. An intermediate solution is to follow asymptotic methods and use a simplified approach for radiative heat losses where the flux lost ($\dot{Q}$ in Eq. (1.54)) is simply proportional to T^4- T_0^4: $\dot{Q} = \varepsilon_R \sigma (T^4 - T_0^4)$ where ε_R denotes the local emissivity of the gas and T_0 is a reference "cold" temperature at infinity (Poinsot et al. [523]). In this case, the difficulty is to choose a level of emissivity for the gas. More sophisticated models may be found in recent DNS (Patnaik and Kailasanath [493]) but the uncertainties on the level of radiation losses remain high.

Simulations of Poinsot et al. [523] are performed for an arbitrary value of ε_R inducing quenching for realistic values of stretch. Simulations also include heat release, variable density and viscosity. The temperature ratio between fresh and burnt gases is 4 and the Lewis number is 1.2. The length scale r used to characterize the size of the perturbation is the sum of the vortex diameter D and of the distance between vortex centers (Fig. 5.19). The velocity scale $u'(r)$ is defined as the maximum velocity induced by the vortex pair. Calculations are carried out for a broad range of parameters $0.81 < r/\delta_L < 11$ and $1 < u'(r)/s_L^0 < 100$.

An example of results is plotted in Figs. 5.20 and 5.21 for a case where the vortex pair size and speed are high enough to induce quenching of the flame front ($r/\delta = 4.8$ and $u'(r)/s_L^0 = 28$). Figures 5.20 and 5.21 respectively display the temperature (Θ) and reaction rate ($\dot{\omega}$) fields at four instants. The reduced variable $t^+ = t/\tau_c$ measures the time with respect to the flame characteristic time $\tau_c = \delta/s_L^0$.

At $t^+ = 0.8$, the vortex pair has stretched and curved the flame but the inner flame structure is preserved and no quenching is observed. The largest Karlovitz number $K_a = \kappa \delta/s_L^0$ is found on the axis and reaches about three. While quenching might be expected for $K_a = 1$, burning proceeds even when Karlovitz numbers reach larger values. At $t^+ = 1.6$, quenching appears on the downstream side of the pocket of fresh gases previously formed by the vortex pair. These gases are pushed rapidly into regions where the burnt gases have been cooled due to heat losses (Fig. 5.20). This effect, combined with the high stretch generated by the vortices, causes almost complete extinction of the pocket after it has been separated from the bulk of the fresh gases. At times $t^+ = 2.0$ and $t^+ = 2.4$, the pocket of fresh gases is convected through the burnt gases without burning except near its tail. In this case, the flame front is locally quenched by the vortex pair and, in addition, unburnt mixture has crossed the flame.

Spectral combustion diagrams

A spectral diagram based on calculations of flame/vortex interactions (and not only on dimensional analysis) may be constructed (Poinsot et al. [523]). Fig. 5.22 presents an example of a spectral diagram obtained for a Lewis number of 1.2 and including strong heat losses.

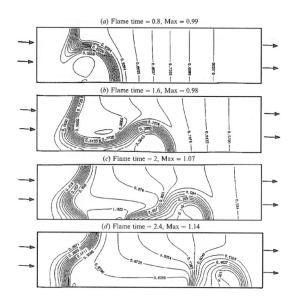

Figure 5.20: Reduced temperature fields at different instants during flame vortex interaction (Poinsot et al. [523], Reprinted with permission by Cambridge University Press).

The outcome of a flame/vortex interaction depends on the scale r and on the vortex velocity $u'(r)$. Four typical regimes are identified:

1. a local quenching of the front,

2. the formation of a pocket of fresh gases in the burnt gases without quenching,

3. a wrinkled flame front,

4. a negligible global effect without noticeable flame wrinkling or thickening.

Two curves are plotted in Fig. 5.22:

- The quenching curve distinguishes vortices locally quenching the flame front.

- The cut-off limit (Gulder and Smallwood [259]) corresponds to vortices inducing an increase of the total reaction rate of about 5 %. A best fit for this inner cut-off length scale l_{inner} is derived from DNS:

$$\boxed{l_{inner}/\delta_L^0 = 0.2 + 5.5 \left(\varepsilon \delta_L^0/s_L^{0\ 3}\right)^{-1/6}}$$

$$(5.34)$$

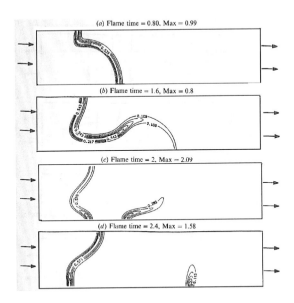

(a) Flame time = 0.80, Max = 0.99

(b) Flame time = 1.6, Max = 0.8

(c) Flame time = 2, Max = 2.09

(d) Flame time = 2.4, Max = 1.58

Figure 5.21: Reaction rate fields at different instants during flame-vortex interaction (Poinsot et al. [523], Reprinted with permission by Cambridge University Press).

where $\varepsilon \delta_L^0 / {s_L^0}^3$ is a reduced turbulence dissipation rate. This cut-off limit is the inner limit which should be used in a fractal description of premixed flame surfaces.

Spectral diagrams may also be constructed experimentally (Roberts et al. [562]). Large differences should be expected between experiments and simple chemistry computations such as the DNS of Poinsot et al. [523]. Qualitatively, however, the trends of the experimental results are well reproduced by DNS as shown on Fig. 5.23.

Modified combustion diagram

A turbulent premixed combustion diagram may be deduced from the spectral diagram displayed in Fig. 5.22 under the following assumptions:

1. A single vortex structure interacts at a given time with the flame front.

2. Any turbulent structure located in the quenching zone of the spectral diagram locally quenches the flame front and induce a distributed reaction regime.

These assumptions are rather crude. For example, turbulent scales in the quenching zone do not quench the flame front if the corresponding energy density is too low. Therefore,

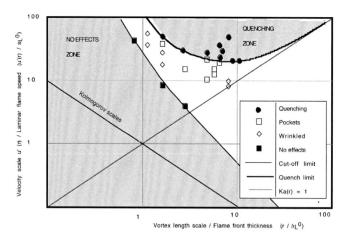

Figure 5.22: Spectral diagram obtained from Direct Numerical Simulations of flame vortex interaction (Poinsot et al. [523]).

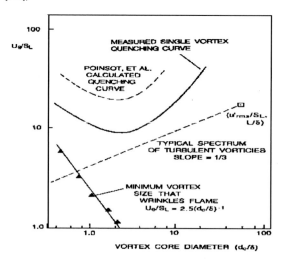

Figure 5.23: Spectral diagram obtained from experiments: d_c and U_θ are respectively the size and the rotating velocity of the vortex whereas δ and S_L correspond to thickness and speed of the laminar flame (Reprinted by permission of Elsevier Science from Roberts et al. [562], © the Combustion Institute).

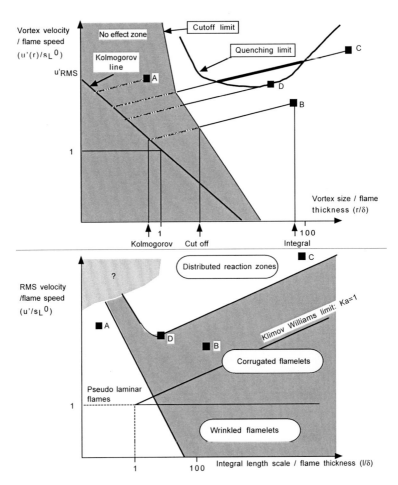

Figure 5.24: Spectral diagram and corresponding turbulent combustion diagram based on DNS of flame/vortex interactions.

assumption (2) is probably too strong and not satisfied. However, these hypothesis lead to a
"worse case" quenching interaction diagram. Nevertheless, the following construction, based
on DNS, is probably more precise than analysis based on simple dimensional arguments.

Under the previous assumptions, the construction of a new turbulent combustion diagram
based on the spectral diagram of Fig. 5.22 is straightforward. A turbulent field of type B
(Fig. 5.24) contains inefficient scales (dashed line) and scales able to corrugate the flame front
but unable to quench it (solid line). Point B therefore corresponds to a flamelet regime. In the
case of field A, even the integral scale is not sufficiently energetic to interact with the flame
and the latter remains pseudo-laminar. Turbulent field C contains scales that may locally
quench the flame (double-width solid line). These scales are larger and faster by orders of
magnitude than the Kolmogorov scale. Type C turbulence creates a turbulent flame which
cannot satisfy flamelet assumptions.

Comparing this diagram (Fig. 5.24) with the classical diagram (Fig. 5.12) reveals that
the domain where distributed reaction zones are expected has been displaced upwards by at
least an order of magnitude towards more intense turbulence levels. Taking into account the
important value of heat losses used for this computation, the flamelet domain is expected to
be even larger in most practical cases. Peters [502] has also pointed out that the quenching
limit in Fig. 5.24 roughly corresponds to line $K_a = 100$, separating thickened-wrinkled and
thickened flame regimes in his own diagram (Fig. 5.13).

5.3 RANS of turbulent premixed flames

Phenomenological descriptions and turbulent combustion diagrams are useful to understand
turbulent combustion but do not provide a mathematical framework for numerical simulations.
The derivation of Reynolds average Navier-Stokes (RANS) equations has been previously
described (see § 4.5). For premixed flames, equations (4.21) to (4.24) are generally first
simplified for practical simulations.

5.3.1 Premixed turbulent combustion with single one-step chemistry

A usual assumption in turbulent premixed combustion modeling is to consider a single one-
step, irreversible chemical reaction, as in Section 2.4:

$$R \text{ (reactants)} \quad \rightarrow \quad P \text{ (products)} \tag{5.35}$$

The fuel reaction rate $\dot{\omega}_F$ is expressed (Eq. 2.37) as:

$$\dot{\omega}_F = B\rho Y_F \exp\left(-T_a/T\right) \tag{5.36}$$

where the temperature exponent β_1 in the preexponential constant is 0. The preexponential
constant B is negative. T_1, T_2 and T_a are respectively the fresh gases, the adiabatic flame
and the activation temperatures. The reactant mass fraction Y_F is non-dimensionalized using

the initial reactant mass fraction in fresh gases Y_F^1: $Y = Y_F/Y_F^1$. Y varies from 1 in the fresh gases to 0 in the burnt gases.

Most turbulent combustion models assume constant pressure (see § 1.2.1), unity Lewis numbers (see § 2.4.3) and adiabatic conditions. Under these three assumptions, the relation linking the reduced temperature $\Theta = C_p(T - T_1)/QY_F^1$ to the reduced reactant mass fraction Y derived in Eq. (2.35) is still valid in turbulent flows:[xi]

$$\Theta + Y = 1 \tag{5.37}$$

Therefore, only the Θ (or the Y) equation needs to be retained. Θ, increasing from $\Theta = 0$ in fresh gases to $\Theta = 1$ in fully burnt gases, is called the *progress variable*. The system to solve for a turbulent low-speed premixed flame then reduces to:

$$\frac{\partial \bar{\rho}}{\partial t} + \frac{\partial}{\partial x_i}(\bar{\rho}\tilde{u}_i) = 0 \tag{5.38}$$

$$\frac{\partial \bar{\rho}\tilde{u}_j}{\partial t} + \frac{\partial}{\partial x_i}(\bar{\rho}\tilde{u}_i\tilde{u}_j) + \frac{\partial \bar{p}}{\partial x_j} = \frac{\partial}{\partial x_i}\left(\bar{\tau}_{ij} - \overline{\rho u_i'' u_j''}\right) \tag{5.39}$$

$$\frac{\partial(\bar{\rho}\tilde{\Theta})}{\partial t} + \frac{\partial}{\partial x_i}(\bar{\rho}\tilde{\Theta}\tilde{u}_i) = \frac{\partial}{\partial x_i}\left(\overline{\rho D}\frac{\partial \tilde{\Theta}}{\partial x_i} - \overline{\rho u_i''\Theta''}\right) + \bar{\dot{\omega}}_\Theta \tag{5.40}$$

where $\dot{\omega}_\Theta = -\dot{\omega}_F/Y_F^1$ is the reaction rate for the reduced temperature Θ. In Eq. (5.40), the averaged thermal diffusion term in Eq. (4.24) has been simply modeled as:

$$\overline{\rho D\frac{\partial \Theta}{\partial x_i}} = \overline{\rho D}\frac{\partial \tilde{\Theta}}{\partial x_i} \tag{5.41}$$

The initial set of averaged equations is simplified since only $\bar{\rho}$, $\tilde{u}_i$ and $\tilde{\Theta}$ must be solved for. But, as previously described (§ 4.5.2), the corresponding equations contain three unclosed terms requiring modeling:

- the turbulent stress tensor $\overline{\rho u_i'' u_j''}$,

- the mean reaction rate $\bar{\dot{\omega}}_\Theta$,

- the turbulent scalar transport term $\overline{\rho u_i''\Theta''}$

How these terms influence mean values is a key issue in turbulent combustion modeling. Such terms require closure assumptions and models to express them as functions of the solved mean quantities (namely $\bar{\rho}$, $\tilde{u}_i$ and $\tilde{\Theta}$) or as solutions of additional conservation equations:

[xi]In Section 2.4.3, the relation $Y + \Theta = 1$ has been proved in a steady flame. The same demonstration holds in an unsteady turbulent flame when initial conditions also satisfy the same property. When initial conditions do not satisfy $Y + \Theta = 1$, the flame relaxes towards this state after initial conditions are forgotten.

- models for Reynolds stresses in the momentum equation, $\overline{\rho u_i'' \widetilde{u_j''}}$ have been discussed in Section 4.5.3. These turbulent stresses are usually viewed as additional stresses and modeled through a turbulent viscosity ν_t (Boussinesq assumption).

- Two unknown terms are then really specific of the introduction of combustion in Navier-Stokes equations: the mean reaction rate $\overline{\dot{\omega}}_\Theta$ and the scalar turbulent transport $\overline{\rho u_i'' \Theta''}$. A large portion of the literature in turbulent combustion focuses on the modeling of the mean reaction rate $\overline{\dot{\omega}}_\Theta$. These models are discussed in Section 5.3.2 to 5.3.7. Models for scalar turbulent fluxes are generally closed using a gradient assumption (see Eq. (4.27)) and are presented in Section 5.3.8.

5.3.2   The "no-model" or Arrhenius approach

The simplest approach is to neglect the effects of turbulence on turbulent combustion and to retain only the first term in the Taylor series (4.44) in Section 4.5.4. The reaction rate is then expressed as:

$$\overline{\dot{\omega}}_\Theta = \dot{\omega}_\Theta(\widetilde{\Theta}) = -B\overline{\rho}(1 - \widetilde{\Theta}) \exp\left(-\frac{T_a}{T_1 + (T_2 - T_1)\widetilde{\Theta}} \right) \tag{5.42}$$

This is equivalent to supposing that the mean reaction rate corresponds to the reaction rate obtained using mean local values $\overline{\rho}$ and $\widetilde{\Theta}$. This model is relevant only when chemical time scales are larger than turbulent time scales ($\tau_c \gg \tau_t$, low Damköhler number limit), corresponding to the "well stirred reactor" regime (Fig. 5.12) where reactants mix rapidly and burn slowly. This approach may be useful for simple analysis and is encountered for some specific applications such as supersonic combustion and chemical reactions in atmospheric boundary layers (see § 4.5.4). In most situations, this model is completely inadequate: Fig. 4.17 shows that $\dot{\omega}_\Theta(\widetilde{\Theta})$ is never a good estimate of $\overline{\dot{\omega}}_\Theta(\Theta)$. Estimating the mean reaction rate by the reaction rate based on mean quantities leads to unacceptable errors (usually orders of magnitude).

5.3.3   The Eddy Break Up (EBU) model

Proposed by Spalding [623, 624] (see also Kuo [361]), the Eddy Break Up (EBU) model is based on a phenomenological analysis of turbulent combustion assuming high Reynolds ($Re \gg 1$) and Damköhler ($Da \gg 1$) numbers. A simple idea (opposite to the Arrhenius model of § 5.3.2), is to consider that chemistry does not play any explicit role while turbulent motions control the reaction rate: the reaction zone is viewed as a collection of fresh and burnt gaseous pockets transported by turbulent eddies. Then, the mean reaction rate is mainly controlled by a characteristic turbulent mixing time τ_t and the temperature fluctuations $\widetilde{\Theta''^2}$ and is expressed as:

$$\overline{\dot{\omega}}_\Theta = C_{EBU}\, \overline{\rho}\, \frac{\sqrt{\widetilde{\Theta''^2}}}{\tau_{EBU}} \tag{5.43}$$

C_{EBU} is a model constant of the order of unity. The turbulence time τ_t is estimated from the turbulence kinetic energy k and its dissipation rate ε according to:

$$\tau_{EBU} = k/\varepsilon \tag{5.44}$$

which is an estimate of the characteristic time of the integral length scales of the turbulent flow field (§ 4.2 in Chapt. 4). To first order, the largest vortices, close to the integral length scale, are assumed to produce the strongest flapping motions. Since k and ε are required in Eq. (5.44), the Eddy Break Up closure is generally used together with the k-ε turbulence model (see § 4.5.3).

Eq. (5.43) requires an estimate for the fluctuations $\widetilde{\Theta''^2}$. A first analysis assuming that the flame is infinitely thin leads to the simple result:

$$\overline{\rho\widetilde{\Theta''^2}} = \overline{\rho\left(\Theta - \widetilde{\Theta}\right)^2} = \overline{\rho}\left(\widetilde{\Theta^2} - \widetilde{\Theta}^2\right) = \overline{\rho}\widetilde{\Theta}\left(1 - \widetilde{\Theta}\right) \tag{5.45}$$

because temperature can only take two values, $\Theta = 0$ (in the fresh gases) or $\Theta = 1$ (in the fully burnt gases) so that $\Theta^2 = \Theta$. The final EBU model for the mean reaction rate is:[xii]

$$\boxed{\overline{\dot{\omega}}_\Theta = C_{EBU}\,\overline{\rho}\,\frac{\varepsilon}{k}\widetilde{\Theta}\left(1 - \widetilde{\Theta}\right)} \tag{5.46}$$

This model is attractive because the reaction rate is written as a simple function of known mean quantities without additional transport equations. The Eddy-Break-Up model is found in most commercial codes. Despite its success, its basic form (5.46) has an obvious limitation: it does not include any effects of chemical kinetics. The preexponential constant B or the activation temperature T_a do not appear in Eq. (5.46). However, the EBU model generally gives better results than the simple Arrhenius model. Fig. 5.25 compares variations of mean reaction rates predicted by the EBU and by the Arrhenius models: the EBU formula predicts a non-zero reaction rate at all points where the averaged temperature $\widetilde{\Theta}$ is not 0 or 1 as revealed by experiments (see Fig. 4.17). The Arrhenius model would predict a mean reaction rate located around $\widetilde{\Theta} = 0.9$ and zero everywhere else, as displayed in Fig. 5.25.

Some adjustments of the model constant C_{EBU} have been proposed to incorporate chemical features (Said and Borghi [582]). In commercial codes, the EBU model is sometimes coupled to the Arrhenius law (§ 5.3.2) to limit the mean reaction rate using chemistry information. The Eddy-Break-Up model also tends to overestimate the reaction rate, especially in highly strained regions, where the ratio ε/k is large (flame-holder wakes, walls and so on). Note

---

[xii] A comparison shows that Eqs. (5.43) and (5.46) are not compatible. According to Eq. (5.45), a square root is missing in Eq. (5.46) compared to Eq. (5.43). This square root was initially introduced for "dimensional" arguments but leads to various physical and mathematical problems which can be illustrated using the KPP analysis presented in Section 5.3.10: this analysis shows that a proper model should have a finite derivative $d\overline{\dot{\omega}}_\Theta/d\widetilde{\Theta}$ for $\widetilde{\Theta} = 0$ and $\widetilde{\Theta} = 1$. This is not the case when the mean reaction rate is written $[\widetilde{\Theta}(1 - \widetilde{\Theta})]^{1/2}$ so the expression $\widetilde{\Theta}(1 - \widetilde{\Theta})$ was retained (Borghi, private communication, 1999).

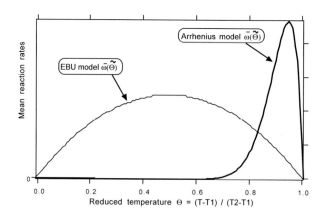

Figure 5.25: Comparing the Arrhenius and the EBU models in a turbulent flame brush.

however that the estimate of the characteristic time τ_{EBU} is quite arbitrary,[xiii] as discussed in Section 5.3.9, and could be modeled using other assumptions, leading to other results. For example, the ITNFS model, devised by Meneveau and Poinsot [432] improves the predictive capacities of the EBU model at low numerical costs (Bailly et al. [25]).

5.3.4 Models based on turbulent flame speed correlations

Turbulent premixed flames may be described in terms of a global turbulent flame speed s_T, as mentioned in Section 4.3.1. From experimental data (Abdel-Gayed and Bradley [2], Abdel-Gayed et al. [3], Gulder [258]) or theoretical analysis (Renormalization Group Theory, Yakhot et al. [716]), the turbulent flame speed s_T may be modeled by:

$$\frac{s_T}{s_L} = 1 + \alpha \left(\frac{u'}{s_L} \right)^n \tag{5.47}$$

where α and n are two model constants close to unity. u' is the turbulent velocity (i.e the RMS velocity). The flame front propagation is then described in term of a "G-equation" (Kerstein

---

[xiii]In preliminary versions of the EBU model, developed to simulate a turbulent premixed flame stabilized behind a flame-holder (Spalding [623, 624]), the characteristic time τ_{EBU} was simply estimated from the transverse gradient of the mean axial velocity, $|\partial \widetilde{u}/\partial y|^{-1}$, corresponding to the strain rate induced by large scale coherent motions.

et al. [342], Karpov et al. [323]):

$$\boxed{\bar{\rho}\frac{\partial G}{\partial t} + \bar{\rho}\widetilde{u}_i\frac{\partial G}{\partial x_i} = \rho_0 s_T \left|\nabla G\right|} \tag{5.48}$$

where ρ_0 is the fresh gas density and the turbulent flame brush is associated to a given level G^* of a G field.[xiv] Far from the front when G is not close to G^*, the G-field has no particular physical meaning.

Unfortunately, the turbulent flame speed s_T is not a well defined quantity (Gouldin [248]). Experimental data exhibit a large scatter and depend on various parameters (chemistry characteristics, turbulence scales, flow geometry among others). Eq. (5.48) also leads to various numerical difficulties. This equation tends to induce "flame cusps", generally avoided adding a diffusive term (G second spatial derivative) in the right hand side of the equation. But this term slightly modifies the propagation speed of the flame front.[xv] The coupling between the G-equation with mass-fraction or energy balance equations is also not obvious: G-equation requires the turbulent displacement speed of the flame front whereas conservation equations need the consumption speed of the flame brush. As for laminar flames (see § 2.7.1), these quantities may be quite different.

While this formulation is not particularly well suited to close Favre averaged transport equations, it may be of interest in the context of large eddy simulations (see § 5.4). Such a description may also be useful for very large scale combustion system simulations. The G-equation formalism does not require to resolve the turbulent flame brush thickness in the computation but only the G-field which may be quite larger, with smoother gradients (Smiljanovski et al. [618]).

A more refined formalism based on G-equation has been developed by Peters [501, 502], briefly described page 242 in Section 5.3.6.

5.3.5 The Bray Moss Libby (BML) model

Known under the initials of its authors, Bray, Moss and Libby, this model, first proposed in 1977, has been the subject of many improvements (see papers by Bray, Moss and Libby, and then by Bray, Champion and Libby). Combining a statistical approach using probability density functions and a physical analysis, the BML model has evidenced some special features of turbulent premixed combustion such as counter-gradient turbulent transport and flame turbulence generation, already described in Section 5.1.3.

A one-step, irreversible chemical reaction between fresh gases (R) and combustion products (P) is considered. Usual assumptions are introduced to simplify the model formulation: perfect gases, incompressible flow, constant heat capacities and unity Lewis numbers. The probability

---

[xiv]In practice, G is often chosen as the signed distance to the flame front (i.e. to the G^* surface).

[xv]Some authors (Karpov et al. [323], Lipatnikov and Chomiak [401]) introduce a turbulent diffusive term (i.e. $\nu_t\partial^2 G/\partial x_i^2$) predicting a continuously increasing flame brush thickness propagating at the mean turbulent flame speed s_T.

density function of the progress variable Θ at a given location $\mathbf{x}$ is expressed as a sum of fresh, fully burnt and burning gases contributions (Fig. 5.26):

$$p(\Theta, \mathbf{x}) = \underbrace{\alpha(\mathbf{x})\delta(\Theta)}_{\text{fresh gases}} + \underbrace{\beta(\mathbf{x})\delta(1 - \Theta)}_{\text{burnt gases}} + \underbrace{\gamma(\mathbf{x})\, f(\Theta, \mathbf{x})}_{\text{burning gases}} \qquad (5.49)$$

where α, β and γ respectively denotes the probability to have, at location $\mathbf{x}$, fresh gases, burnt gases and reacting mixture. $\delta(\Theta)$ and $\delta(1 - \Theta)$ are respectively the Dirac delta functions corresponding to fresh gases ($\Theta = 0$) and fully burnt ones ($\Theta = 1$).

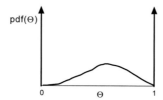

Figure 5.26: Probability density function in turbulent premixed combustion.

The normalization of the probability density function ($\int_0^1 p(\Theta, \mathbf{x})\, d\Theta = 1$) leads to the following conditions:

$$\alpha + \beta + \gamma = 1 \quad \text{and} \quad \int_0^1 f(\Theta, x)\, d\Theta = 1 \qquad (5.50)$$

with $f(0) = f(1) = 0$.

The BML model is developed assuming large Reynolds and Damköhler numbers. Since the flame front is thin, the probability to be in burning gases is low ($\gamma \ll 1$). An intermittency between fresh gases ($\Theta = 0$) and burnt gases ($\Theta = 1$) is observed and Eq. (5.49) reduces to:

$$p(\Theta, \mathbf{x}) = \alpha(\mathbf{x})\delta(\Theta) + \beta(\mathbf{x})\delta(1 - \Theta) \qquad (5.51)$$

At a given location $\mathbf{x}$ inside the mean reaction zone, the Θ signal has a telegraphic shape, displayed in Fig. 5.27. According to Section 5.1.3, this assumption determines the values of probability α and β and leads to interesting relations between Reynolds and Favre averages and expressions for turbulent fluxes evidencing intermittency effects between fresh and burnt gases. Unfortunately, this analysis does not provide the mean reaction rate $\bar{\dot{\omega}}_\Theta$ because:

$$\bar{\dot{\omega}}_\Theta(\mathbf{x}) = \int_0^1 \dot{\omega}(\Theta)p(\Theta, \mathbf{x})\, d\Theta = \gamma(\mathbf{x}) \int_0^1 \dot{\omega}(\Theta)f(\Theta, \mathbf{x})\, d\Theta \approx 0 \qquad (5.52)$$

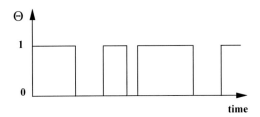

Figure 5.27: Intermittency between fresh and fully burnt gases at a location **x** in the reaction zone. This signal corresponds to a bimodal ($\Theta = 0$ and $\Theta = 1$) probability density function.

As the probability γ to be in burning gases has been neglected, the mean reaction rate cannot be estimated from this expression. Since the origin of the BML model, three main approaches have been successively proposed to close the mean reaction rate $\bar{\dot{\omega}}_\Theta$. The first two formulations, based on scalar dissipation rate and on flame crossing frequency, are discussed here. The later one, derived in terms of flame surface densities, is described in Section 5.3.6.

Scalar dissipation rate formulation

Starting from the instantaneous balance equation for Θ:

$$\frac{\partial \rho \Theta}{\partial t} + \frac{\partial}{\partial x_i}\left(\rho u_i \Theta\right) = \frac{\partial}{\partial x_i}\left(\rho D \frac{\partial \Theta}{\partial x_i}\right) + \dot{\omega}_\Theta \tag{5.53}$$

Bray and Moss [87] derived a balance equation for $\Theta(1 - \Theta) = \Theta - \Theta^2$:

$$\frac{\partial}{\partial t}\left[\rho \Theta(1-\Theta)\right] + \frac{\partial}{\partial x_i}\left[\rho u_i \Theta(1-\Theta)\right] = \frac{\partial}{\partial x_i}\left(\rho D \frac{\partial}{\partial x_i}\left[\Theta(1-\Theta)\right]\right) + 2\rho D \frac{\partial \Theta}{\partial x_i}\frac{\partial \Theta}{\partial x_i} - 2\Theta \dot{\omega}_\Theta + \dot{\omega}_\Theta \tag{5.54}$$

Under the BML model assumptions, the reduced temperature Θ is equal to zero or to unity. Then, $\Theta(1 - \Theta) = 0$ and the balance equation (5.54) reduces to:

$$2\rho D \frac{\partial \Theta}{\partial x_i}\frac{\partial \Theta}{\partial x_i} = 2\Theta \dot{\omega}_\Theta - \dot{\omega}_\Theta \tag{5.55}$$

leading to, after averaging:

$$\boxed{\bar{\dot{\omega}}_\Theta = \frac{1}{2\Theta_m - 1}\left(\overline{2\rho D \frac{\partial \Theta}{\partial x_i}\frac{\partial \Theta}{\partial x_i}}\right) = \frac{\bar{\rho}\tilde{\chi}_\Theta}{2\Theta_m - 1}} \tag{5.56}$$

where Θ_m is defined as:

$$\Theta_m = \frac{\overline{\Theta \dot{\omega}_\Theta}}{\bar{\dot{\omega}}_\Theta} = \frac{\int_0^1 \Theta \dot{\omega}_\Theta f(\Theta) d\Theta}{\int_0^1 \dot{\omega}_\Theta f(\Theta) d\Theta} \tag{5.57}$$

and $\overline{\rho \chi_\Theta} = \overline{\rho} \widetilde{\chi_\Theta}$ is the scalar dissipation rate of the reduced temperature Θ.

The mean reaction rate $\overline{\dot{\omega}}_\Theta$ is related to the dissipation rate $\widetilde{\chi}_\Theta$, describing turbulent mixing, and to Θ_m, characterizing chemical reaction. A balance equation may be derived, and solved, for the scalar dissipation rate, as done, for example, by Mantel and Borghi [417]. A simpler solution is to postulate a linear relaxation of the fluctuations as:

$$\overline{\rho \chi_\Theta} = \overline{\rho} \widetilde{\Theta''^2} / \tau_t \qquad (5.58)$$

where a turbulent mixing time scale, τ_t is introduced. A balance equation may be derived and closed for the progress variable variance $\widetilde{\Theta''^2}$ as shown in Section 5.3.7 but, assuming an intermittency between fresh and burnt gases ($\Theta = 0$ or $\Theta = 1$), $\Theta^2 = \Theta$. Then, according to Eq. (5.45):

$$\overline{\dot{\omega}}_\Theta = \frac{1}{2\Theta_m - 1} \overline{\rho} \frac{\varepsilon}{k} \widetilde{\Theta} \left(1 - \widetilde{\Theta}\right) \qquad (5.59)$$

where τ_t has been estimated from the turbulent kinetic energy k and its dissipation rate ε as $\tau_t = k/\varepsilon$ (Eq. 5.44). The expression (5.46) proposed by Spalding in the Eddy-Break-Up model is recovered. The BML model may then be viewed as a theoretical derivation of the Eddy-Break-Up (EBU) model, initially based on a phenomenological approach. Compared to EBU, the BML model incorporates chemistry features through Θ_m.

Flame crossing frequencies

This analysis (Bray et al. [89], Bray and Libby [86]) recognizes that the mean reaction rate at a given location depends more on the passage (or crossing) frequency of the flame front at this point than on the local mean temperature or species mass fractions. Fig. 5.28 shows temperature signals in a turbulent flame. Points like A (on the cold side of the flame brush) or B (on the hot side) both exhibit very few passages of flame fronts and have a low mean reaction rate. Point B has not a mean reaction rate significantly higher than point A. This is very different from a laminar case (see Fig. 2.8) where reaction rates based on Arrhenius expressions peak at high temperature values. In the center of the flame brush, many flame crossings are found at point C and the mean reaction rate is high. This simple observation suggests that the mean reaction can be expressed as the product of the flame crossing frequency f_c by the reaction rate per flame crossing $\dot{\omega}_c$:

$$\overline{\dot{\omega}}_\Theta = \dot{\omega}_c f_c \qquad (5.60)$$

The flame crossing frequency is then estimated from a statistical analysis of the telegraphic equation (temperature signals are viewed as a telegraphic signal, Fig. 5.27), leading to:

$$f_c = 2 \frac{\overline{\Theta} \left(1 - \overline{\Theta}\right)}{\widehat{T}} \qquad (5.61)$$

where $\widehat{T}$ is a mean period of the telegraphic signal, related to turbulent motions. This expression leads to the following comments:

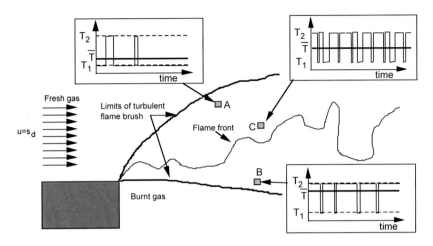

Figure 5.28: The temperature signal at different points in a turbulent flame.

- The factor 2 comes from the fact that two crossing flame are found from a signal period (one from fresh to burnt gases, the other from burnt to unburnt gases).

- The crossing frequency is expressed in terms of Reynolds averaged reduced temperature $\overline{\Theta}$ which can be replaced by the Favre-averaged temperature using Eq. (5.15), leading to:

$$f_c = 2 \frac{1+\tau}{(1+\tau\widetilde{\Theta})^2} \frac{\widetilde{\Theta}(1-\widetilde{\Theta})}{\widehat{T}} \qquad (5.62)$$

- The crossing frequency f_c is easy to measure in experiments and requires to record the temperature signal as a function of time at a given location, for example using thermocouples, Mie or Rayleigh scattering.

Eq. (5.61) is generally closed by estimating $\widehat{T}$ from a characteristic turbulent time τ_t. The reaction rate per crossing flame $\dot{\omega}_c$ needed in Eq. (5.60) is usually modeled as:

$$\dot{\omega}_c = \frac{\rho_0 s_L^0}{\delta_L^0 / t_t} \qquad (5.63)$$

where ρ_0 is the unburnt gases density, s_L^0 and δ_L^0 are respectively the speed and the thickness of the laminar flame. The flame transit time t_t measures the time required to cross a flame front and corresponds to the time for transition between the $\Theta = 0$ and $\Theta = 1$ levels of the reduced temperature, as shown in Fig. 5.29.

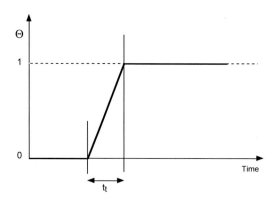

Figure 5.29: Definition of the flame transit time t_t in the flame crossing frequency BML model.

The mean reaction rate is then given by:

$$\overline{\dot{\omega}}_\Theta = 2\frac{\rho_0 s_L^0}{\delta_L^0/t_t}\frac{\varepsilon}{k}\overline{\Theta}\left(1 - \overline{\Theta}\right) \qquad (5.64)$$

using $\widehat{T} = \tau_t = k/\varepsilon$. An EBU-like expression is recovered when the transit time t_t is estimated from the laminar flame thickness δ_L^0 and speed s_L^0 as $t_t = \delta_L^0/s_L^0$.

Estimating this reaction rate per crossing flame is difficult in practice so that expression (5.60) has been later recast in terms of flame surface densities, as described below (§ 5.3.6). Note that BML formulations propose algebraic expressions for the reaction rate $\overline{\dot{\omega}}_\Theta$ but focus on a turbulent transport description, taking into account the possible occurrence of counter-gradient features and flame-generated turbulence, as evidenced in Section 5.1.3, through balance equations for scalar turbulent fluxes $\widetilde{u_i''\Theta''}$ and Reynolds stresses $\widetilde{u_i''u_j''}$.

5.3.6   Flame surface density models

In the previous section, the turbulent mean reaction rate was quantified in terms of flame front crossing frequency. Another approach, also valid under flamelet assumptions, is to describe the mean reaction rate in term of flame surface area, as the product of the flame surface density Σ (i.e. the available flame surface area per unit volume) by the local consumption rate per unit of flame area, $\rho_0\langle s_c\rangle_s$ (Marble and Broadwell [419], Candel et al. [110], Pope [530], Bray et al. [90]):

$$\boxed{\overline{\dot{\omega}}_\Theta = \rho_0\langle s_c\rangle_s\Sigma} \qquad (5.65)$$

where ρ_0 is the fresh gases density and $\langle s_c\rangle_s$ is the average flame consumption speed along the surface. The flame surface density Σ (unity: m^2/m^3) measures the flame front convolutions. A high flame surface density at a given location in the flow corresponds to a high turbulent reaction rate. The main advantage of this approach is to separate complex chemistry features, incorporated into the average flame speed $\langle s_c \rangle_s$, from turbulent/combustion interactions modeled by the flame surface density Σ.

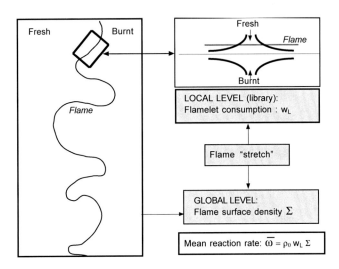

Figure 5.30: Flame surface density concepts for turbulent premixed flames.

Fig. 5.30 gives a simple picture of flame surface density models. The turbulent flame is viewed as an ensemble of small laminar flame elements (*flamelets*) supposed here to have a structure similar to a laminar stagnation point flame. The consumption rate per unit flame surface s_c of these flamelets may be computed (including complex chemistry) using a simple model of a laminar planar stagnation point flame (Giovangigli and Smooke [239]). The corresponding results are stored in a flamelet library where the laminar consumption rate per unit flame surface, $s_c(\kappa)$, is tabulated for a range of stretch values κ, fresh gases equivalence ratio, temperature among other possible parameters. The mean flamelet consumption speed $\langle s_c \rangle_s$ is then given by (Vervisch and Veynante [671], Veynante and Vervisch [678]):

$$\langle s_c \rangle_s = \int_0^{+\infty} s_c(\kappa) \, p(\kappa) \, d\kappa \tag{5.66}$$

where $p(\kappa)$ is the probability to have the stretch rate κ on the flame surface. Bray [84] introduces a "stretch factor" I_0 to link the mean flamelet consumption speed $\langle s_c \rangle_s$ to the unstretched laminar flame speed s_L^0 and to take into account possible flame quenching:

$$\langle s_c \rangle_s = I_0 s_L^0 \tag{5.67}$$

According to Eq. (5.66), I_0 is defined as:

$$I_0 = \frac{1}{s_L^0} \int_0^{+\infty} s_c(\kappa) \, p(\kappa) \, d\kappa \tag{5.68}$$

In most practical implementations, $p(\kappa)$ is assumed to be a Dirac function: $p(\kappa) = \delta(\kappa - \overline{\kappa})$, where $\overline{\kappa}$ denotes the mean local stretch rate, generally identified as the inverse of turbulent time scale $(\overline{\kappa} \approx \varepsilon / k)$.[xvi] Then:

$$\langle s_c \rangle_s \approx s_c(\overline{\kappa}) \qquad \text{and} \qquad I_0 \approx s_c(\overline{\kappa}) / s_L^0 \tag{5.71}$$

DNS (Haworth and Poinsot [277]) generally show that I_0 remains of the order of unity. So, to first order, strain effects are neglected in some models which simply set $I_0 = 1$ and $\langle s_c \rangle_s = s_L^0$.

The challenge is now to provide a model for the flame surface density Σ. This may be done using a simple algebraic expression or solving a balance equation.

Algebraic expressions for the flame surface density

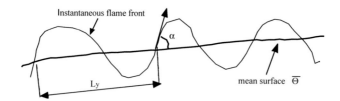

Figure 5.31: BML flame surface modeling quantities. L_y is the mean flame length scale. The orientation factor $\sigma_y = \overline{\cos \alpha}$ is the mean cosine angle of the instantaneous flame front with the $\overline{\Theta}$ iso-surface. The number of flame crossings per unit length along the $\overline{\Theta}$ surface is of the order of $2/L_y$.

[xvi]To avoid the use of flamelet libraries, Bray [84] proposes, from the experimental data obtained by Abdel-Gayed et al. [4], the following expression for I_0:

$$I_0 = 0.117 K_a^{-0.784} / (1 + \tau) \tag{5.69}$$

where τ is the heat release factor and K_a a Karlovitz number estimated as:

$$K_a = 0.157 \left(\frac{u'}{s_L^0} \right)^2 \left(\frac{u' l_t}{\nu} \right)^{-1/2} = 0.157 \left(\frac{u'}{s_L^0} \right)^2 Re_t^{-1/2} \tag{5.70}$$

Bray et al. [90] have recast Eq. (5.60) in terms of flame surface density, leading to:

$$\Sigma = n_y / \sigma_y \tag{5.72}$$

where n_y measures the number of flamelet crossings per unit length (spatial frequency) along a constant $\overline{\Theta}$ direction. The flamelet orientation factor σ_y is the mean cosine angle of the instantaneous flame front with the $\overline{\Theta}$ iso-surface (Fig. 5.31) and is assumed to be an universal model constant ($\sigma_y \approx 0.5$). Eq. (5.61) is then rewritten:[xvii]

$$\Sigma = \frac{g}{\sigma_y} \frac{\overline{\Theta}\left(1 - \overline{\Theta}\right)}{L_y} = \frac{g}{\sigma_y} \frac{1 + \tau}{(1 + \tau\widetilde{\Theta})^2} \frac{\widetilde{\Theta}(1 - \widetilde{\Theta})}{L_y} \tag{5.73}$$

where g is a model constant of order unity and L_y the wrinkling length scale of the flame front, generally modeled as proportional to the integral length scale l_t:

$$L_y = C_l l_t \left(\frac{s_L^0}{u'}\right)^n \tag{5.74}$$

where the constants C_l and n are of order unity. Modeling $\langle s_c \rangle_s$ as $\langle s_c \rangle_s = s_L^0$ and assuming $n = 1$ leads to:

$$\overline{\dot{\omega}}_\Theta = \rho_0 \frac{g}{C_l \sigma_y} \frac{u'}{l_t} \overline{\Theta}\left(1 - \overline{\Theta}\right) \tag{5.75}$$

As l_t / u' corresponds to a characteristic time of integral length scale and may be modeled as $\tau_t = k/\varepsilon$, an expression similar to Eqs. (5.46), (5.59) and (5.64) is recovered. As already pointed out, the turbulent time l_t / u' in expression (5.75) may be replaced using the ITNFS formulation of Meneveau and Poinsot [432], as done by Bailly et al. [25]. Flame surface densities Σ are more difficult to measure than flame front crossing frequencies f_c because flame front visualizations are required to estimate Σ (Veynante et al. [681, 682]). But, on the other hand, $\langle s_c \rangle_s$ may be easily estimated from laminar flame theories or computations.

The flame surface density may also be derived from fractal theories, leading to Gouldin et al. [247]:

$$\Sigma = \frac{1}{L_{outer}} \left(\frac{L_{outer}}{L_{inner}}\right)^{D-2} \tag{5.76}$$

where L_{inner} and L_{outer} are respectively the inner and outer cut-off length scales (the flame surface is assumed to be fractal between these two scales). D is the fractal dimension of the flame surface. The cut-off scales are generally estimated as the turbulence Kolmogorov η_k and the integral l_t length scales. Cut-off scales obtained from DNS such as expression (5.34) could also be used.

[xvii]The BML model is first based on a bimodal probability density function assumption (statistical analysis, Eq. 5.51). Its derivation leads to a reaction rate proportional to the scalar dissipation rate (mixing description, Eq. 5.56). Finally, the model is recast in terms of flame surface density (geometrical description, Eq. 5.73). This derivation evidences the links between the various physical approaches available for turbulent combustion modeling described in Section 4.5.5. These links are rigourously derived in Veynante and Vervisch [678].

Balance equation for the flame surface density

Various forms of conservation equations for the flame surface density Σ may be found in the literature. These equations may be derived from heuristic arguments (Marble and Broadwell [419], Darabiha et al. [166]) or constructed from more rigorous considerations (Pope [530], Candel and Poinsot [109], Trouvé and Poinsot [652], Vervisch et al. [672]). According to Pope [530], the surface density of the iso-temperature Θ^* surface is given by:

$$\boxed{\Sigma = \overline{|\nabla\Theta|\,\delta(\Theta-\Theta^*)} = \left(\overline{|\nabla\Theta|\,|\Theta=\Theta^*}\right)p(\Theta^*)} \qquad (5.77)$$

where $\delta(\Theta)$ is the Dirac δ function, $(\overline{|\nabla\Theta|\,|\Theta=\Theta^*})$ is the conditional average of $|\nabla\Theta|$ for $\Theta=\Theta^*$ and $p(\Theta^*)$ is the probability to find $\Theta=\Theta^*$ at the given location. As qualitatively described in Section 4.5.6, the mean flame surface density Σ contains local informations on the instantaneous flame front through $(\overline{|\nabla\Theta|\,|\Theta=\Theta^*})$, but also the probability $p(\Theta^*)$ to find the flame front at the given location (i.e. intermittency).

An exact balance equation for the flame surface density (identified as the $\Theta=\Theta^*$ iso-surface) may be derived from this definition and the balance equation for the reduced temperature Θ (Trouvé and Poinsot [652], Vervisch et al. [672]). This equation may be written:

$$\frac{\partial\Sigma}{\partial t}+\frac{\partial}{\partial x_i}\left(\langle u_i\rangle_s\Sigma\right)+\frac{\partial}{\partial x_i}\left[\langle s_d n_i\rangle_s\Sigma\right]=\underbrace{\left\langle(\delta_{ij}-n_i n_j)\frac{\partial u_i}{\partial x_j}\right\rangle_s\Sigma+\left\langle s_d\frac{\partial n_i}{\partial x_i}\right\rangle_s\Sigma}_{\langle\kappa\rangle_s\Sigma} \qquad (5.78)$$

where s_d is the displacement speed of the flame relatively to fresh gases, n_i are the component of the unit vector $\vec{n}$ normal to the flame front and pointing towards the fresh gases ($\vec{n}=-\nabla\Theta/|\nabla\Theta|$). The flame front curvature is given by $\nabla\cdot\vec{n}=\partial n_i/\partial x_i$. The surface averaged operator (i.e. average along the flame surface) $\langle\,\rangle_s$ is defined as:

$$\langle Q\rangle_s = \frac{\overline{Q\,|\nabla\Theta|\,\delta(\Theta-\Theta^*)}}{\overline{|\nabla\Theta|\,\delta(\Theta-\Theta^*)}} \qquad (5.79)$$

The three terms in the LHS of the Σ balance equation (5.78) correspond respectively to unsteady effects, to the flame surface convection by the flow field and to the normal propagation of the flame.[xviii] The first term in the RHS expresses the action of the tangential strain rate

---

[xviii]This last term is generally neglected in practice, assuming that the propagation velocity in the normal direction, $\langle s_d n_i\rangle_s$, of the order of the laminar flame speed s_L^0, is negligible compared to the convection velocity $\langle u_i\rangle_s$. This assumption is not always true as shown by Veynante et al. [682] from experimental data who propose, for an infinitely thin flame front and assuming that $s_d=s_L^0$, to retain the exact relation:

$$\frac{\partial}{\partial x_i}\left[\langle s_d n_i\rangle_s\Sigma\right]=-s_L^0\frac{\partial}{\partial x_i}\left(\frac{\partial\overline{\Theta}}{\partial x_i}\right)=-s_L^0\Delta\overline{\Theta}$$

on the flame surface and the last term corresponds to combined propagation/curvature effects. The sum of these two effects corresponds to the stretch rate $\langle \kappa \rangle_s$ acting on the flame surface. This stretch rate is the surface averaged stretch rate κ acting on the premixed flame element (see Eq. (2.84) in Chapt. 2). This exact balance equation leads to the following comments:

- Many effects are implicitly incorporated in the flame front propagation speed, s_d, which may differ significantly from the laminar flame speed s_L^0 (Poinsot et al. [524]). As discussed for laminar premixed flames (Chapter 2), displacement speeds are more difficult to predict than consumption speeds s_c for which the approximation $s_c \approx s_L^0$ is usually correct to first order.

- This derivation assumes that a single iso-Θ^* surface corresponds to the flame front. This is true when the flame is infinitely thin. But, in some situations, for example direct numerical simulation data where the flame is not infinitely thin, the flame front, identified as the location of the maximum reaction rate, may differ from the Θ^* iso-surface. In other words, this Θ^* surface may be not representative of the flame front features. Choosing a value for Θ^* then becomes a difficult issue. To overcome this difficulty, a "generalized flame surface density" extending definition (5.77) can be defined as, following Veynante and Vervisch [678]:

$$\overline{\Sigma} = \int_0^1 \Sigma \, d\Theta^* = \int_0^1 \overline{|\nabla\Theta| \delta(\Theta - \Theta^*)} \, d\Theta^* = \overline{|\nabla\Theta|} \qquad (5.80)$$

The balance equation for $\overline{\Sigma}$ is formally similar to Eq. (5.78) using the "generalized" surface averaged operator as:

$$\langle Q \rangle_s = \overline{Q\,|\nabla\Theta|}/\overline{|\nabla\Theta|} \qquad (5.81)$$

- The flame surface density balance equation is unclosed and requires modeling for the turbulent flux of flame surface, the propagation speed s_d, strain rate and curvature effects. Using the Favre decomposition $(u_i = \widetilde{u}_i + u_i'')$, convection and strain rate terms may be split into mean flow and turbulent contributions:

$$\langle u_i \rangle_s \Sigma = \widetilde{u}_i \Sigma + \langle u_i'' \rangle_s \Sigma \qquad (5.82)$$

and

$$\left\langle (\delta_{ij} - n_i n_j) \frac{\partial u_i}{\partial x_j} \right\rangle_s = \underbrace{(\delta_{ij} - \langle n_i n_j \rangle_s) \frac{\partial \widetilde{u}_i}{\partial x_j}}_{\kappa_m} + \underbrace{\left\langle (\delta_{ij} - n_i n_j) \frac{\partial u_i''}{\partial x_j} \right\rangle_s}_{\kappa_t} \qquad (5.83)$$

where κ_m and κ_t correspond to the strain rate acting of the flame surface and induced by the mean flow field and the turbulent motions, respectively.

Using Eq. (5.82) and (5.83), the flame surface density equation (5.78) becomes:

$$\frac{\partial \Sigma}{\partial t} + \frac{\partial \tilde{u}_i \Sigma}{\partial x_i} = -\frac{\partial}{\partial x_i}(\langle u_i'' \rangle_s \Sigma) + \kappa_m \Sigma + \kappa_t \Sigma + \left\langle s_d \frac{\partial n_i}{\partial x_i} \right\rangle_s \Sigma \qquad (5.84)$$

Various closures may be found in the literature for Eq. (5.84) and are briefly summarized in Table 5.3. The closed Σ equation is generally written as:[xix]

$$\boxed{\frac{\partial \Sigma}{\partial t} + \frac{\partial \tilde{u}_i \Sigma}{\partial x_i} = \frac{\partial}{\partial x_i}\left(\frac{\nu_t}{\sigma_c} \frac{\partial \Sigma}{\partial x_i}\right) + \kappa_m \Sigma + \kappa_t \Sigma - D} \qquad (5.85)$$

where D a consumption term. In this expression, the turbulent flux of flame surface density is expressed using a classical gradient assumption, ν_t is the turbulent viscosity and σ_Σ a flame surface turbulent Schmidt number. The D term must be introduced because surface strain rate contributions κ_m and κ_t are generally positive as shown in Section 5.5.3. Without a destruction term, the flame surface density balance equation would predict an infinite growth of flame area (a property which holds for non reacting material surfaces but not for flames which annihilate when they interact). Whether this destruction term is only due to curvature effects (last RHS term in Eq. 5.84) or should incorporate additional features (flame front interactions, for example) is still an open question. Additional physical phenomena can be incorporated in Eq. (5.85). For example, Paul and Bray [496] propose a term to describe the increase of flame surface area due to thermodiffusive (or Darrieus-Landau) instabilities (non-unity Lewis numbers, see Section 2.8 in Chapt. 2).

A simple phenomenological closure may be derived as follows (Marble and Broadwell [419], Darabiha et al. [166]). First, the flame stretch generated by the turbulent flow may be estimated as $\kappa = \varepsilon/k$, using the integral time scale as a flame time. The flame surface consumption term is assumed to be proportional to the mean reaction rate, $\langle s_c \rangle_s \Sigma$, and inversely proportional to the available reactants per unit of flame area measured by $(1 - \tilde{\Theta})/\Sigma$. Then, a simple closed balance equation for Σ is:[xx]

$$\frac{\partial \Sigma}{\partial t} + \frac{\partial \tilde{u}_i \Sigma}{\partial x_i} = \frac{\partial}{\partial x_i}\left(\frac{\nu_t}{\sigma_c} \frac{\partial \Sigma}{\partial x_i}\right) + \alpha_0 \frac{\varepsilon}{k} \Sigma - \beta_0 \langle s_c \rangle_s \frac{\Sigma^2}{1 - \tilde{\Theta}} \qquad (5.86)$$

where α_0 and β_0 are two model constants. The $\langle s_c \rangle_s$ term is the consumption speed computed using complex chemistry and is the only chemical parameter appearing in balance equations (5.65) and (5.85). It can be computed using one-dimensional laminar flame codes discussed in Section 2.3. Eq. (5.86) is now closed and can be implemented in solvers. Assuming equilibrium between source and sink terms in this equation leads to:

$$\overline{\dot{\omega}}_\Theta = \rho_0 \frac{\alpha_0}{\beta_0} \frac{\varepsilon}{k} \left(1 - \tilde{\Theta}\right) \qquad (5.87)$$

[xix]The flame surface density Σ measures the flame area per unit volume (m^2/m^3). The flame surface density per unit mass $S = \Sigma/\bar{\rho}$ (m^2/kg) is sometimes introduced to solve a balance equation for $\bar{\rho}S$ that may be easier to implement in numerical solvers.

[xx]This expression is the CFM1 model in Table 5.3, neglecting the κ_m contribution and with $C = 0$.

MODEL	$\kappa_m \Sigma$	$\kappa_t \Sigma$	D
CPB [112]	$A_{ik}\dfrac{\partial \widetilde{u}_k}{\partial x_i}\Sigma$	$\alpha_0 C_A \sqrt{\dfrac{\varepsilon}{\nu}}\Sigma$	$\beta_0 \langle s_c \rangle_s \dfrac{2 + e^{-aR}}{3(1 - \widetilde{\Theta})}\Sigma^2$ $R = \dfrac{(1 - \widetilde{\Theta})\varepsilon}{\Sigma \langle s_c \rangle_s k}$
CFM1 [189]	$A_{ik}\dfrac{\partial \widetilde{u}_k}{\partial x_i}\Sigma$	$\alpha_0 \dfrac{\varepsilon}{k}\Sigma$	$\beta_0 \dfrac{\langle s_c \rangle_s + C\sqrt{k}}{1 - \widetilde{\Theta}}\Sigma^2$
CFM2-a [189]	$A_{ik}\dfrac{\partial \widetilde{u}_k}{\partial x_i}\Sigma$	$\alpha_0 \Gamma_K \dfrac{\varepsilon}{k}\Sigma$	$\beta_0 \dfrac{\langle s_c \rangle_s + C\sqrt{k}}{1 - \widetilde{\Theta}}\Sigma^2$
CFM2-b [189]	$A_{ik}\dfrac{\partial \widetilde{u}_k}{\partial x_i}\Sigma$	$\alpha_0 \Gamma_K \dfrac{\varepsilon}{k}\Sigma$	$\beta_0 \dfrac{\langle s_c \rangle_s + C\sqrt{k}}{\widetilde{\Theta}\left(1 - \widetilde{\Theta}\right)}\Sigma^2$
CFM3 [682]	$A_{ik}\dfrac{\partial \widetilde{u}_k}{\partial x_i}\Sigma$	$\alpha_0 \Gamma_K \dfrac{\varepsilon}{k}\Sigma$	$\beta_0 \langle s_c \rangle_s \dfrac{\Theta^* - \widetilde{\Theta}}{\widetilde{\Theta}\left(1 - \widetilde{\Theta}\right)}\Sigma^2$
MB [417]	$E\dfrac{\widetilde{u_i'' u_k''}}{k}\dfrac{\partial \widetilde{u}_k}{\partial x_i}\Sigma$	$\alpha_0 \sqrt{Re_t}\dfrac{\varepsilon}{k}\Sigma$ $+\dfrac{F}{\langle s_c \rangle_s}\dfrac{\varepsilon}{k}\widetilde{u_i''\Theta''}\dfrac{\partial \widetilde{\Theta}}{\partial x_i}$	$\dfrac{\beta_0 \langle s_c \rangle_s \sqrt{Re_t}\Sigma^2}{\widetilde{\Theta}\left(1 - \widetilde{\Theta}\right)\left(1 + c\dfrac{\langle s_c \rangle_s}{\sqrt{k}}\right)^{2\gamma}}$
CD [128]		$\alpha_0 \lambda \dfrac{\varepsilon}{k}\Sigma$ if $\kappa_t \leq \alpha_0 K\dfrac{\langle s_c \rangle_s}{\delta_L}$	$\beta_0 \dfrac{\langle s_c \rangle_s}{1 - \widetilde{\Theta}}\Sigma^2$
CH1 [131]		$\alpha_0 \sqrt{\dfrac{\varepsilon}{15\nu}}\Sigma$	$\beta_0 \dfrac{\langle s_c \rangle_s}{\widetilde{\Theta}\left(1 - \widetilde{\Theta}\right)}\Sigma^2$
CH2 [131]		$\alpha_0 \dfrac{u'}{l_{tc}}\Sigma$	$\beta_0 \dfrac{\langle s_c \rangle_s}{\widetilde{\Theta}\left(1 - \widetilde{\Theta}\right)}\Sigma^2$

Table 5.3: Source and consumption terms in the Σ-balance equation (5.85). Re_t is the turbulent Reynolds number. α_0, β_0, γ, λ, Θ^* ($0 < \Theta^* < 1$), C_A, a, c, C, E and K are model parameters. A_{ik} correspond to the orientation factors $\left(\delta_{ij} - \langle n_i n_j \rangle_s\right)$ found in Eq. (5.83) for κ_m. These may be modeled according to Cant et al. [112] or Veynante et al. [682] but κ_m is often neglected against κ_t. Γ_K is the efficiency function in the ITNFS model (Eq. 5.125). In the CH model, $u' \approx \sqrt{k}$ is the RMS turbulent velocity and l_{tc} is an arbitrary length scale introduced for dimensional consistency and combined to α_0 as a single constant. An additional term, not directly linked to the flame surface density Σ, is found in κ_t in the MB model. This term may be viewed as an anisotropic contribution to κ_t. As evidenced in Eq. (5.83), the theoretical expression of κ_t contains flame orientation factors n_i: this term is generally modeled using isotropic expressions such as ε/k. The consumption speed $\langle s_c \rangle_s$ is assumed to be equal to the laminar flame speed s_L^0, also identified as the flame displacement speed found in Eq. (5.78).

recovering an Eddy-Break-Up type model.[xxi] This shows that the EBU model can be viewed as a simplified flame surface density model.[xxii]

Equations (5.65) and (5.85) are enough to close the system of equations (5.38) to (5.40) and solve for mean values. Chemistry and turbulence have been treated independently.

Flame surface density models have been applied to turbulent premixed flames stabilized behind bluff bodies (Maistret et al. [415]) but also to combustion in piston engines (Cheng and Diringer [128], Boudier et al. [75], Duclos et al. [190], Choi and Huh [131]). They provide a fairly good prediction of chemistry effects (for example, the influence of the equivalence ratio) on turbulent combustion. Note, however, that, as flame source terms are proportional to the flame surface density Σ, these models are not able to handle flame ignition without ad-hoc submodels (Boudier et al. [75], Veynante et al. [682], Duclos and Colin [188]). Flame surface density models are also equivalent to a number of other flamelet models such as the Mantel and Borghi [417] model derived from a balance equation for the scalar dissipation rate (Eq. 5.56) and recast under the flame surface density formulation (Table 5.3). Comparisons of various flame surface density models may be found in Duclos et al. [189] or in Choi and Huh [131]. For most models using Eq. (5.85) , the turbulent flame speed may be deduced analytically for one-dimensional flames propagating in frozen turbulence (see § 5.3.10).

A related approach: the level set formalism

Peters proposes a formalism based on a level-set approach, or a G-equation, for local, instantaneous flame element (Peters [501, 502]):

$$\rho \frac{\partial G}{\partial t} + \rho u_i \frac{\partial G}{\partial x_i} = \rho_0 s_d |\nabla G| \tag{5.88}$$

where the flame front is identified as the surface $G = G_0$. s_d is the displacement speed of the flame element relatively to the fresh gases (density ρ_0) and may be expressed in terms of laminar flame speed s_L^0, strain rate, curvature and Markstein numbers, among others. Peters [502] proposes s_d expressions suited to flamelet and to corrugated flame regimes.

Instantaneous Eq. (5.88) is then averaged and closure schemes are proposed both for $\widetilde{G}$ and $\widetilde{G''^2}$. A balance equation is also proposed for $\sigma = \overline{|\nabla G|}$, directly linked to the flame surface density (Eq. 5.80, see also Vervisch and Veynante [671] or Veynante and Vervisch [678]). In fact, the same derivation could be conducted identifying the G-field to the progress variable or the reduced temperature Θ.[xxiii] This approach is mathematically similar to a flame surface

---

[xxi]In fact, the preliminary version of EBU is recovered (Spalding [623]). Limiting the combustion in the flame region defined by $\widetilde{\Theta}(1 - \widetilde{\Theta})$ allows to express the consumption term as $\beta_0 \langle s_c \rangle_s \Sigma^2/\widetilde{\Theta}(1 - \widetilde{\Theta})$ (CFM2b type closure in Table 5.3) and leads to EBU expression (5.46).

[xxii]Note that EBU has been derived assuming a mixing controlled combustion. Once again, this shows the links between the various physical concepts involved in turbulent combustion models (see § 4.5.5).

[xxiii]But Θ may be not resolved in the numerical simulation while G is. This level-set formalism is also developed for corrugated flame regimes and, a priori, does not require a flamelet assumption. The inner structure of the flame, corresponding to the Θ-field, is not described. The flame is only viewed as a propagating front and the challenge is to model the flame front displacement speed s_d.

density description but differs in the assumptions introduced and in the closure developments. Details are out of the scope of this book and the reader is referred to the book by Peters [502], devoting a large part to this level set description.

5.3.7 Probability density function (pdf) models

The probability density function $p(\Theta^*)$ measures the probability that the reduced temperature Θ takes values between Θ^* and $\Theta^* + d\Theta^*$:

$$p(\Theta^*)\,d\Theta^* = Probability\,(\Theta^* \leq \Theta < \Theta^* + d\Theta^*) \tag{5.89}$$

From this definition, pdf are normalized so that:

$$\int_0^1 p(\Theta^*)\,d\Theta^* = 1 \tag{5.90}$$

The information contained in a pdf is essential for combustion phenomena. For example, the mean temperature and its variance can be directly extracted from the pdf:

$$\overline{\Theta} = \int_0^1 \Theta^* p(\Theta^*)\,d\Theta^* \quad \text{and} \quad \overline{\Theta'^2} = \int_0^1 \left(\Theta^* - \overline{\Theta}\right)^2 p(\Theta^*)\,d\Theta^* \tag{5.91}$$

For an adiabatic, single reaction, with unity Lewis numbers, the mean reaction rate is:

$$\boxed{\overline{\dot{\omega}}_\Theta = \int_0^1 \dot{\omega}_\Theta(\Theta^*) p(\Theta^*)\,d\Theta^*} \tag{5.92}$$

A mass-weighted probability density function $\widetilde{p}$ is also introduced as $\overline{\rho}\widetilde{p}(\Theta) = \rho p(\Theta)$. Any Favre-averaged quantity $\widetilde{f}$ may then be determined as:

$$\boxed{\overline{\rho}\widetilde{f} = \overline{\rho f} = \int_0^1 \rho(\Theta^*) f(\Theta^*) p(\Theta^*)\,d\Theta^* = \overline{\rho}\int_0^1 f(\Theta^*)\widetilde{p}(\Theta^*)\,d\Theta^*} \tag{5.93}$$

These expressions are easily extended when several species mass fractions Y_i have to be taken into account in addition to temperature, for example when Lewis numbers are not unity or to incorporate complex chemistry features by considering the joint probability $p(\Psi_1, \Psi_2 \ldots, \Psi_N)$:

$$\text{Prob}\,(\Psi_1 \leq Y_1 < \Psi_1 + d\Psi_1, .., \Psi_N \leq Y_N < \Psi_N + d\Psi_N) = p(\Psi_1, .., \Psi_N)\,d\Psi_1 \ldots d\Psi_N \tag{5.94}$$

for a given location, with the normalization relation:

$$\int_{\Psi_1, \Psi_2, \ldots \Psi_N} p(\Psi_1, \Psi_2 \ldots, \Psi_N)\,d\Psi_1\,d\Psi_2 \ldots d\Psi_N = 1 \tag{5.95}$$

where Ψ_1, Ψ_2,..., Ψ_N are the thermochemical variables such as mass fractions and tempera-ture.[xxiv] Any averaged quantity $\overline{f}$ is then determined as:

$$\overline{f} = \int_{\Psi_1, \Psi_2, \ldots \Psi_N} f(\Psi_1, \ldots, \Psi_N)\, p(\Psi_1, \Psi_2 \ldots, \Psi_N)\, d\Psi_1\, d\Psi_2 \ldots d\Psi_N \qquad (5.96)$$

or, in terms of Favre averaged:

$$\widetilde{f} = \int_{\Psi_1, \Psi_2, \ldots \Psi_N} f(\Psi_1, \ldots, \Psi_N)\, \widetilde{p}(\Psi_1, \Psi_2 \ldots, \Psi_N)\, d\Psi_1\, d\Psi_2 \ldots d\Psi_N \qquad (5.97)$$

where $\overline{\rho}\, \widetilde{p}(\Psi_1, \ldots, \Psi_N) = \rho(\Psi_1, \ldots, \Psi_N)p(\Psi_1, \ldots, \Psi_N)$.

This stochastic description has many theoretical advantages. Probability density functions may be defined in any turbulent reacting flow field. They contain all the required information to describe unsteady reacting flow fields. These functions may also be extracted from experimental data or direct numerical simulations (statistical analysis of one-point measurements).

Eq. (5.92) and (5.96) are exact. Quantities such as $\dot{\omega}_\Theta(\Theta^*)$ or $f(\Psi_1, \ldots, \Psi_N)$ are provided from chemistry and laminar flame studies. The difficulty is to determine the pdf (which changes at every point in the flow field). Two main paths have been proposed (Pope [532, 533], Dopazo [182]): to presume the pdf shape or to solve a balance equation for the pdf.

Presumed pdf approach

In general, a pdf function can take any shape and exhibit multiple extrema. It contains information not only on the mean value of the variable but also on its variance (first moment) and on all higher moments. For many combustion applications, however, pdf functions often present common features, suggesting that these functions can be described using a limited number of parameters. A possible approach (Williams [710]) is then to suppose that the pdf has a fixed shape, parametrized using, for example, only one or two parameters. The logical parameters to use are the moments of the variable: mean quantities and/or first moment (variance). The BML model described above (§ 5.3.5) is a presumed pdf model: the pdf of the progress variable Θ is assumed to be bimodal and only two flow states is considered: fresh gases ($\Theta = 0$) and burnt gases ($\Theta = 1$).

More sophisticated pdf shapes may be used to construct other models and the literature provides multiple examples of presumed pdf shapes (Borghi [72], Bray et al. [90], Ribert et al. [554], Robin et al. [563]). The most popular pdf shape is the so-called β-function:

$$\widetilde{p}(\Theta) = \frac{1}{B(a,b)}\Theta^{a-1}(1-\Theta)^{b-1} = \frac{\Gamma(a+b)}{\Gamma(a)\Gamma(b)}\Theta^{a-1}(1-\Theta)^{b-1} \qquad (5.98)$$

[xxiv]Flow field variables such as velocity components may also be introduced in the joint probability (Pope [532, 533], Dopazo [182]). In this situation, turbulence models are no longer required (turbulence motions are directly described through the joint pdf) but this approach is very expensive.

where $B(a, b)$ is a normalization factor:

$$B(a, b) = \int_0^1 \Theta^{a-1}(1-\Theta)^{b-1} d\Theta \tag{5.99}$$

and the Γ function, defined as:

$$\Gamma(x) = \int_0^{+\infty} e^{-t} t^{x-1} dt \tag{5.100}$$

is usually tabulated or found in scientific libraries.

The pdf parameters a and b are determined plugging Eq. (5.98) into the definitions of the two first moments of the reduced temperature, $\widetilde{\Theta}$ and $\widetilde{\Theta''^2}$:

$$\widetilde{\Theta} = \int_0^1 \Theta^* \widetilde{p}(\Theta^*) d\Theta^* \quad \text{and} \quad \widetilde{\Theta''^2} = \int_0^1 \left(\Theta^* - \widetilde{\Theta}\right)^2 \widetilde{p}(\Theta^*) d\Theta^* \tag{5.101}$$

leading to:

$$a = \widetilde{\Theta}\left[\frac{\widetilde{\Theta}(1-\widetilde{\Theta})}{\widetilde{\Theta''^2}} - 1\right] \quad ; \quad b = \frac{a}{\widetilde{\Theta}} - a \tag{5.102}$$

Inversely, knowing a and b, the mean temperature $\widetilde{\Theta}$ and its variance $\widetilde{\Theta''^2}$ are given by:

$$\widetilde{\Theta} = \frac{a}{a+b} \quad ; \quad \widetilde{\Theta''^2} = \frac{ab}{(a+b)^2(a+b+1)} \tag{5.103}$$

The β-functions are generally retained to presume pdf because they are able to change continuously from pdf shapes with one or two peaks to Gaussian shapes (Fig. 5.32). Unfortunately, they cannot describe distributions combining a peak for $\Theta = 0$ (pure fresh gases) or $\Theta = 1$ (fully burnt gases) with an intermediate maximum within the range $0 < \Theta < 1$ (burning mixture). This simplified approach is used in some industrial simulations.[xxv] Of course, an additional balance equation for the progress variable variance $\widetilde{\Theta''^2}$ has to be closed and solved.

[xxv] Presumed pdf approaches may also be coupled to other models. Fuel oxidation is fast and may be modeled using flamelet assumptions and flame surface density models. On the other hand, nitric oxide (NO_x) formation is slower and occur in burnt gases, mainly controlled by gases temperature. This NO_x formation may then be modeled using a presumed β-pdf based on temperature. Note also that, as NO_x and most pollutants involve very small quantities (ppm), they are negligible against main species and have no influence on global balances (heat release rate, main species mass fractions, temperature). Accordingly, they may be estimated by postprocessing simulation results.

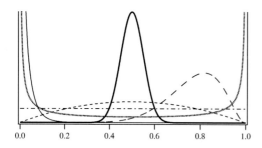

Line	a	b	$\widetilde{\Theta}$	$\widetilde{\Theta''^2}$
— · —	1.0	1.0	0.50	0.08333
- - - -	2.0	2.0	0.50	0.05000
——	50.	50.	0.50	0.00247
········	0.2	0.2	0.50	0.17857
— ·· —	10.	3.0	0.77	0.01267
——	0.2	20.	0.01	0.00046

Figure 5.32: Examples of temperature β-pdf shapes for various values of parameters (a, b) and corresponding $\widetilde{\Theta}$ and $\widetilde{\Theta''^2}$ values. The a and b parameters are linked to the mean reduced temperature $\widetilde{\Theta}$ and its variance $\widetilde{\Theta''^2}$ by Eq. (5.102).

In RANS, a balance equation is derived, closed and solved for the temperature variance $\widetilde{\Theta''^2}$. Multiplying by Θ the instantaneous balance equations for Θ in conservative form (Eq. 5.53):

$$\frac{\partial \rho \Theta}{\partial t} + \frac{\partial}{\partial x_i}\left(\rho u_i \Theta\right) = \frac{\partial}{\partial x_i}\left(\rho D \frac{\partial \Theta}{\partial x_i}\right) + \dot\omega_\Theta \tag{5.104}$$

and in non conservative form:

$$\rho \frac{\partial \Theta}{\partial t} + \rho u_i \frac{\partial \Theta}{\partial x_i} = \frac{\partial}{\partial x_i}\left(\rho D \frac{\partial \Theta}{\partial x_i}\right) + \dot\omega_\Theta \tag{5.105}$$

and summing them provides a balance equation for Θ^2:

$$\frac{\partial \rho \Theta^2}{\partial t} + \frac{\partial}{\partial x_i}\left(\rho u_i \Theta^2\right) = \frac{\partial}{\partial x_i}\left(\rho D \frac{\partial \Theta^2}{\partial x_i}\right) - 2\rho D \frac{\partial \Theta}{\partial x_i}\frac{\partial \Theta}{\partial x_i} + 2\Theta \dot\omega_\Theta \tag{5.106}$$

Similarly, a balance equation is derived for the square of the mean temperature $\widetilde{\Theta}^2$, multiplying Eq. (5.40) by $\widetilde{\Theta}$:

$$\frac{\partial \rho \widetilde{\Theta}^2}{\partial t} + \frac{\partial}{\partial x_i}\left(\rho \widetilde{u_i} \widetilde{\Theta}^2\right) = 2\widetilde{\Theta}\frac{\partial}{\partial x_i}\left(\rho D \frac{\partial \widetilde{\Theta}}{\partial x_i} - \overline{\rho u_i'' \Theta''}\right) + 2\widetilde{\Theta}\overline{\dot\omega}_\Theta \tag{5.107}$$

Subtracting Eq. (5.107) from the averaged Eq. (5.106) provides a balance equation for the reduced temperature variance $\widetilde{\Theta''^2} = \widetilde{\Theta^2} - \widetilde{\Theta}^2$:

$$
\frac{\partial \bar{\rho} \widetilde{\Theta''^2}}{\partial t} + \frac{\partial}{\partial x_i}\left(\bar{\rho} \tilde{u}_i \widetilde{\Theta''^2}\right) = \underbrace{\frac{\partial}{\partial x_i}\left(\overline{\rho D \frac{\partial \Theta''^2}{\partial x_i}}\right) + 2\overline{\Theta'' \frac{\partial}{\partial x_i}\left(\rho D \frac{\partial \widetilde{\Theta}}{\partial x_i}\right)}}_{\text{molecular diffusion}}
$$

$$
\underbrace{- \frac{\partial}{\partial x_i}\left(\overline{\rho u_i'' \Theta''^2}\right)}_{\text{turbulent transport}} \underbrace{- 2\overline{\rho u_i'' \Theta''}\frac{\partial \widetilde{\Theta}}{\partial x_i}}_{\text{production}} \underbrace{- 2\overline{\rho D \frac{\partial \Theta''}{\partial x_i}\frac{\partial \Theta''}{\partial x_i}}}_{\text{dissipation}} \underbrace{+ 2\overline{\Theta'' \dot{\omega}_\Theta}}_{\text{reaction}}
$$

(5.108)

This equation is discussed in more details for non-premixed flames in Section 6.4.3. Usual closures are only briefly presented here:

- Molecular diffusion terms are generally neglected against turbulent transport in RANS, assuming large Reynolds numbers.

- Turbulent transport and production term are closed using gradient assumptions:

$$
\overline{\rho u_i'' \Theta''^2} = -\bar{\rho}\frac{\nu_t}{S_{ct_1}}\frac{\partial \widetilde{\Theta''^2}}{\partial x_i} \tag{5.109}
$$

$$
\overline{\rho u_i'' \Theta''}\frac{\partial \widetilde{\Theta}}{\partial x_i} = -\bar{\rho}\frac{\nu_t}{S_{ct_2}}\frac{\partial \widetilde{\Theta}}{\partial x_i}\frac{\partial \widetilde{\Theta}}{\partial x_i} \tag{5.110}
$$

where S_{ct_1} and S_{ct_2} are two turbulent Schmidt numbers.

- The scalar dissipation rate of the Θ fluctuations is linked to a turbulent mixing time τ_t using a linear relaxation assumption:[xxvi]

$$
\overline{\rho D \frac{\partial \Theta''}{\partial x_i}\frac{\partial \Theta''}{\partial x_i}} = \bar{\rho} C_\Theta \frac{\widetilde{\Theta''^2}}{\tau_t} = \bar{\rho} C_\Theta \frac{\varepsilon}{k}\widetilde{\Theta''^2} \tag{5.111}
$$

where C_Θ is a model constant of order unity.

- The reaction term measures correlations between reduced temperature fluctuations and reaction rate and is directly provided by the probability density function:

$$
\overline{\Theta'' \dot{\omega}_\Theta} = \overline{\left(\Theta - \widetilde{\Theta}\right)\dot{\omega}_\Theta} = \int_0^1 \left(\Theta^* - \widetilde{\Theta}\right)\dot{\omega}_\Theta\left(\Theta^*\right)p\left(\Theta^*\right)d\Theta^* \tag{5.112}
$$

using relations (5.57) and (5.59).

[xxvi]Note that the scalar dissipation rate entering Eqs (5.108) and (5.111) is defined from the local gradient of the reduced temperature fluctuation $\partial \Theta''/\partial x_i$ while the gradient of the instantaneous reduced temperature $\partial \Theta/\partial x_i$ is retained in Eq. (5.56). They differ by the gradient of the mean reduced temperature $\partial \widetilde{\Theta}/\partial x_i$ which is generally negligible in RANS. This point is discussed in more details in Section 6.4.3 (Chapt. 6).

These simple closure schemes neglect some phenomena: for example, counter-gradient turbulent transport is not taken into account by gradient assumptions in Eqs. (5.109) and (5.110). They also involve some rough assumptions: as discussed in Section 6.4.3, the linear relaxation assumption (5.111) has been devised for mixing in homogeneous flows, without $\widetilde{\Theta}$-gradients.

This presumed pdf approach provides good results when only one parameter, such as a reduced temperature or progress variable Θ is required to describe chemical reaction. When more than one variable is needed for chemistry (for example, two or more species in addition to temperature), constructing a multi-dimensional pdf becomes more difficult (Lockwood and Naguib [402], Pope [532], Gutheil [263]). Nevertheless, a strong, and wrong, assumption is sometimes introduced: chemical variables are supposed to be statistically independent to split the joint probability density function as a product of single variable probability density functions:

$$p(\Psi_1, \Psi_2, \dots, \Psi_N) \approx p(\Psi_1)p(\Psi_1)\dots p(\Psi_N) \qquad (5.113)$$

expressing each single variable pdf using β-functions. But this assumption does not hold in practical situations because species mass fractions and temperature are closely related in flames and, accordingly, are not statistically independent.

Balance equation for the probability density function

An exact balance equation may be derived for a multi-species, mass-weighted probability density function $\widetilde{p}(\Psi_1, \Psi_2 \dots, \Psi_N)$ starting from the definition:

$$\overline{\rho}\, \widetilde{p}\,(\Psi_1, \Psi_2, \dots, \Psi_N) = \overline{\rho\,(\Psi_1, \Psi_2, \dots, \Psi_N)\, \delta\,(Y_1 - \Psi_1)\, \delta\,(Y_2 - \Psi_2)\dots\delta\,(Y_N - \Psi_N)} \quad (5.114)$$

where $\delta()$ is the Dirac function. This derivation is out of the scope of this book (see, for example Pope [532], Dopazo [182], Vervisch et al. [672], Veynante and Vervisch [678]) but its result is interesting to comment. This equation reads:

$$
\overline{\rho}\frac{\partial \widetilde{p}}{\partial t} + \overline{\rho}\widetilde{u}_k \frac{\partial \widetilde{p}}{\partial x_k} = \quad - \underbrace{\frac{\partial}{\partial x_k}\left[\overline{\rho}\,\overline{(u_k''|\underline{Y} = \underline{\Psi})}\,\widetilde{p}\right]}_{\text{Turbulent convection}}
$$

$$
- \underbrace{\overline{\rho}\sum_{i=1}^{N}\frac{\partial}{\partial \Psi_i}\left[\left(\frac{1}{\rho}\frac{\partial}{\partial x_k}\left(\rho D \frac{\partial Y_i}{\partial x_k}\right)|\underline{Y} = \underline{\Psi}\right)\widetilde{p}\right]}_{\text{Molecular diffusion}}
$$

$$
- \underbrace{\overline{\rho}\sum_{i=1}^{N}\frac{\partial}{\partial \Psi_i}\left(\frac{1}{\rho}\dot{\omega}_i\,(\Psi_1, \Psi_2, \dots, \Psi_N)\,\widetilde{p}\right)}_{\text{Chemical reaction}}
$$

$$(5.115)$$

where $\overline{(Q|\underline{Y} = \underline{\Psi})}$ correspond to a conditional averaging of Q for the sampling values Ψ_i.

The first three terms in equation (5.115) correspond respectively to unsteady evolution, convection by the mean flow field and convection due to turbulent motions.[xxvii] These convection terms describe the pdf evolution in the physical (i.e. flow field) space. The last two terms corresponds respectively to molecular diffusion and chemical reaction and describe a pdf evolution in the composition space (Ψ_i), because of mixing and combustion.

The main interest of the balance pdf equation is that the chemical reaction term in Eq. (5.115) depends only on chemical variables and does not require any modeling. Accordingly, the pdf balance equation approach is able to handle any complex chemical scheme. Unfortunately, the molecular diffusion term, often referred as the "micromixing term", is unclosed and is difficult to model. This finding is not surprising: as the one-point pdf describes the chemical composition at any location, one-point quantities such as the chemical reaction rate, which depend only on the local composition, are naturally closed. But spatial gradient terms involved in molecular diffusion processes require additional length scale informations which are not incorporated in the one-point pdf formalism.

Pdf balance equations are not solved directly: generally Monte-Carlo methods are used where stochastic "fluid particles" are introduced to describe the chemical composition (see books or review papers by Pope [532, 533], Dopazo [182], Fox [219], Haworth [279]). Although this method is general and powerful, at least when ad hoc models are provided for molecular mixing terms, its practical application to industrial cases remains difficult and time consuming. However, this approach is now available in some commercial codes.

5.3.8 Modeling of turbulent scalar transport terms

When the mean reaction term $\overline{\dot{\omega}}$ is modeled using one of the formulations described in previous sections, the closure of turbulent scalar fluxes, $\overline{\rho u_i'' \Theta''}$ remains controversial. Classical gradient transport assumptions (Eq. 4.27) are generally used in turbulent combustion models (Darabiha et al. [166], Maistret et al. [415], Candel et al. [105], Cant et al. [112]):

$$\boxed{\overline{\rho u_i'' \widetilde{\Theta''}} = \overline{\rho u_i'' \Theta''} = -\overline{\rho} \frac{\nu_t}{Sc_\Theta} \frac{\partial \widetilde{\Theta}}{\partial x_i}} \tag{5.116}$$

where ν_t is the turbulent kinetic viscosity, provided by the turbulent model and Sc_Θ a turbulent Schmidt number, assumed to be constant. This choice is guided by practical reasons:

- Expression (5.116) is directly inspired from turbulent scalar transport models in non-reacting, constant density flows. For such flows, Eq. (5.116) may be derived using an equilibrium assumption and simple closure schemes in the $\overline{\rho u_i'' \widetilde{\Theta''}}$ balance equation.

- Few studies are available on turbulent scalar transport in combustion. Non-constant density reacting flows are difficult to describe and most turbulence studies are limited to

---

[xxvii]This statistical formalism may also be extended to joint velocity/composition pdf $p(u_1, u_2, u_3, \Psi_1, \ldots, \Psi_N)$. In this situation, turbulence model are no longer required but additional terms are found in the pdf balance equation (Pope [532]).

constant density situations, without chemical reactions. On the other hand, combustion experts have mainly focused their attention on the closure of the reaction rate term, $\bar{\dot{\omega}}_\Theta$.

- From a numerical point of view, Eq. (5.116) leads to simple implementations and increases the stability of CFD codes because the modeled term is a diffusive contribution simply added to the laminar diffusion term:

$$\frac{\partial(\bar{\rho}\widetilde{\Theta})}{\partial t} + \frac{\partial}{\partial x_i}(\bar{\rho}\widetilde{u}_i\widetilde{\Theta}) = \frac{\partial}{\partial x_i}\left(\bar{\rho}\left(\overline{D} + \frac{\nu_t}{Sc_\Theta}\right)\frac{\partial\widetilde{\Theta}}{\partial x_i}\right) + \bar{\dot{\omega}}_\Theta \qquad (5.117)$$

Eq. (5.117) also explains why the model used for molecular transport has a limited impact in turbulent combustion codes: D is usually much smaller than the turbulent diffusivity ν_t/Sc_Θ in RANS codes and can simply be neglected.

However both experimental data (Libby and Bray [386], Shepherd et al. [614]) and theoretical analysis (Libby and Bray [386], Bray et al. [90], Bray [84]) have pointed out the existence of counter-gradient scalar turbulent transport in certain flames where even the sign in Eq. (5.116) would be wrong. This is consistent with Eq. (5.17) in Section 5.1.3 and is due to differential buoyancy effects on cold, heavy fresh gases and on hot, light burnt gases (Fig. 5.6). Despite these evidences, the practical importance of counter-gradient turbulent transport remains controversial.

DNS studies (Veynante et al. [683], Veynante and Poinsot [675], Rutland and Cant [576]) reveal that different flames feature different turbulent transport properties. For instance, in Fig. 5.33, the scalar fluxes from two DNS of planar turbulent flames are plotted versus $\widetilde{\Theta}$ and are found to have opposite signs. Mean and conditional average velocities across the turbulent flame brush are displayed in Fig. 5.34 for the two DNS simulations:

- One of the DNS (the Rutland database) corresponds to low turbulence levels ($u'/s_L^0 = 1$): the burnt gases conditional velocity, $\bar{u}^b$, is higher than the fresh gases conditional velocity, $\bar{u}^u$, leading to counter-gradient turbulent transport in agreement with Eq. (5.17).

- On the other hand, the second DNS database (CTR) used higher turbulence levels (homogeneous isotropic decaying turbulence from an initial level $u'/s_L^0 = 10$): the fresh gases conditional velocity is higher than the burnt gases conditional velocity. Although this result is surprising ($\bar{u}^b$ is expected to be larger than $\bar{u}^u$ because of thermal expansion due to the heat release), it is consistent with expression (5.17) and a gradient turbulent transport.

In both cases, the Bray-Moss-Libby (BML) model is able to predict, through Eq. (5.17), the turbulent flux type (gradient or counter-gradient). In fact, conditional averages are not intuitive quantities and should be handled with care. As shown in Fig. 5.34, conditional burnt gas velocities cannot be expected to be always higher than conditional fresh gas velocities.

Counter-gradient diffusion ($\overline{\rho u_i''\Theta''}/(\partial\widetilde{\Theta}/\partial x_i) > 0$) occurs when the flow field near the flame is dominated by thermal dilatation due to chemical reaction, whereas gradient diffusion

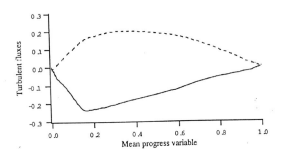

Figure 5.33: Variations of the turbulent $\widetilde{\Theta}$-flux $\overline{\rho u''\Theta''}$ across the turbulent flame brush versus mean progress variable $\widetilde{\Theta}$. Two DNS databases corresponding to statistically one-dimensional premixed flames propagating in a three-dimensional isotropic turbulence (variable density, single-step Arrhenius kinetics chemistry) are compared. Results from the Center for Turbulence Research database (CTR), exhibiting a gradient turbulent transport (solid line), are compared with results from DNS performed by C.J. Rutland (dashed line) where counter-gradient turbulent transport is found (Veynante et al. [683], Reprinted with permission by Cambridge University Press).

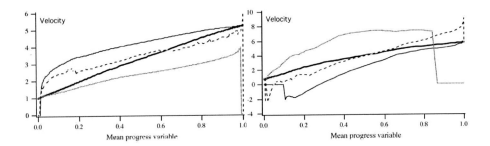

Figure 5.34: Conditional velocities across the turbulent flame brush versus mean progress variable $\widetilde{\Theta}$ in the Rutland (top) and the CTR (bottom) databases. Favre averaged velocity $\widetilde{u}$ (——), fresh gases conditional velocity, $\overline{u}^u$ (········), burnt gases conditional velocity, $\overline{u}^b$ (——) and flame front conditional velocity, $\langle u \rangle_s$ (– – – –). Velocities are normalized by the laminar flame speed s_L^0 (Veynante et al. [683], Reprinted with permission by Cambridge University Press).

$(\overline{\rho u_i'' \Theta''}/(\partial \widetilde{\Theta}/\partial x_i) < 0)$ occurs when the flow field near the flame is dominated by the turbulent motions (Veynante et al. [683]). For high turbulence levels, the flame is not able to impose its own dynamic to the flow field and turbulence transport is expected to be of gradient type as for any passive scalar. On the other hand, for low turbulence level cases, the flame is able to impose its own acceleration (through thermal expansion due to heat release) to the flow field and the turbulent transport may become counter-gradient (conditional velocities are higher in fresh gases than in burnt ones). Consistent with the Bray-Moss-Libby theory, DNS[xxviii] suggests that the occurrence of gradient or counter-gradient turbulent diffusion is determined by the ratio of turbulence intensity divided by the laminar flame speed, u'/s_L^0, and by the heat release factor, τ (Eq. 5.12). Veynante et al. [683] introduce a "Bray number" defined as:

$$N_B = \frac{\tau s_L^0}{2\alpha u'}$$

(5.118)

where α is a function of order unity to take into account the limited ability of small vortices to wrinkle the flame front. When the length scale ratio l_t/δ_L^0 decreases, α decreases. Gradient (counter-gradient) turbulent transport is promoted by high (low) values of u'/s_L^0 and low (high) values of τ, corresponding to $N_B \leq 1$ ($N_B \geq 1$). This criterion matches experimental data (Kalt [321]).

For typical premixed flames, the heat release factor τ is about 5 to 7. According to the simple criterion (5.118), counter-gradient transport should be expected when $u'/s_L^0 \leq 3$. Note also that buoyancy effects are enhanced in ducted flames, because of pressure gradients (Veynante and Poinsot [675]). Counter-gradient (gradient) turbulent transport are promoted under favorable (adverse) pressure gradients, i.e. pressure decreasing (increasing) from fresh to burnt gases. Counter-gradient transport also tends to decrease the turbulent flame speed (i.e. the overall reaction rate), the flame surface wrinkling and the overall flame brush thickness (see Fig. 5.7).

The existence of counter-gradient turbulent scalar transport in turbulent premixed combustion implies that simple algebraic closures based on gradient assumption and eddy viscosity concepts should be replaced by higher-order models. In the Bray-Moss-Libby model, second-order closures are proposed for the exact balance equation for the turbulent scalar fluxes $\overline{\rho u_i'' \Theta''}$. This balance equation, derived from momentum and progress variable balance

---

[xxviii] Veynante et al. [683] have analyzed turbulent scalar transport using both two- and three-dimensional DNS of a statistically one-dimensional turbulent premixed flame propagating in an homogeneous turbulence. Results obtained with both types of simulations are similar but, because of computational costs, only two 3D DNS are available whereas a large range of parameters is explored using two-dimensional simulations.

equations, is:

$$
\begin{array}{c}
\underbrace{\dfrac{\partial \overline{\rho u_i'' \Theta''}}{\partial t}}_{(I)} + \underbrace{\dfrac{\partial \widetilde{u}_j \overline{\rho u_i'' \Theta''}}{\partial x_j}}_{(II)} = \underbrace{- \dfrac{\partial \overline{\rho u_j'' u_i'' \Theta''}}{\partial x_j}}_{(III)} - \underbrace{\overline{\rho u_j'' u_i''} \dfrac{\partial \widetilde{\Theta}}{\partial x_j}}_{(IV)} \\[3em]
\underbrace{- \overline{\rho u_j'' \Theta''} \dfrac{\partial \widetilde{u}_i}{\partial x_j}}_{(V)} - \underbrace{\overline{\Theta''} \dfrac{\partial \overline{p}}{\partial x_i}}_{(VI)} - \underbrace{\overline{\Theta'' \dfrac{\partial p'}{\partial x_i}}}_{(VII)} \\[3em]
\underbrace{- \overline{u_i'' \dfrac{\partial \mathcal{J}_k}{\partial x_k}}}_{(VIII)} + \underbrace{\overline{\Theta'' \dfrac{\partial \tau_{ik}}{\partial x_k}}}_{(IX)} + \underbrace{\overline{u_i'' \dot{\omega}_\Theta}}_{(X)}
\end{array}
\tag{5.119}
$$

where $\mathcal{J}_k$ is the molecular diffusion flux of Θ and τ_{ik} is the viscous stress tensor. In Eq. (5.119), (I) accounts for unsteady effects, (II) represents transport by the mean flow field, (III) transport by the turbulent flow field, (IV) and (V) are source terms due to mean progress variable and mean velocity gradients, (VI) represents the effect of mean pressure gradients and (VII) is the fluctuating pressure term, (VIII) and (IX) are dissipation terms, and (X) is the velocity-reaction rate correlation.

The closure of Eq. (5.119) is made difficult by the large number of terms appearing in the right hand side as well as by their intrinsic complexity. Direct numerical simulations can be used to analyze these different terms and thereby evaluate the general feasibility of the second-order closure approach. A typical DNS evaluation of all terms appearing in Eq. (5.119) is presented in Fig. 5.35. The analysis reveals the dominant terms in Eq. (5.119) as well as the nature of their contribution. For instance, Fig. 5.35 shows that while the dissipation terms (VIII) and (IX) are of the same order and act to promote gradient diffusion $(\overline{\rho u'' \Theta''}/(\partial \widetilde{\Theta}/\partial x) < 0)$, the pressure terms (VI) and (VII), and the velocity-reaction rate correlation (X), strongly promote counter-gradient diffusion $(\overline{\rho u'' \Theta''}/(\partial \widetilde{\Theta}/\partial x) > 0)$.

Figure 5.35 also displays the imbalance term (the algebraic sum of all terms of Eq. (5.119) which should be zero) found when numerically closing the $\widetilde{\Theta}$-flux budget in (5.119). This imbalance is due to inherent numerical errors involved in the simulations as well as in the post-processing of the data. Its magnitude remains small, which suggests that DNS can indeed be used to analyze the variations of second-order moments as Domingo and Bray [180] did to derive closures for the pressure fluctuation term. Such high-order models are almost never found in CFD codes (see an example in Bailly et al. [25]) because of their costs.[xxix] In fact, their complexity and the models uncertainties are too high to justify their implementation.

[xxix] Second order closures for the turbulent scalar fluxes $\overline{\rho u_i'' \Theta''}$ (three additional balance equations) are used together with second order closures for Reynolds stresses $\overline{\rho u_i'' u_j''}$ (six additional balance equations). Note that $\overline{\rho u_i'' u_j''}$ appear in term (IV) in the $\overline{\rho u_i'' \Theta''}$ balance equation (5.119).

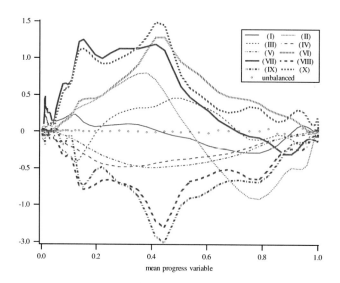

Figure 5.35: Variations of the different terms appearing in the $\widetilde{\Theta}$-flux budget across the turbulent flame brush. Results obtained in DNS of three-dimensional isotropic turbulence with variable density, single-step Arrhenius kinetics chemistry. In this case, counter-gradient turbulent transport is observed (Veynante et al. [683]).

However, the limitations imposed by gradient formulations for the turbulent transport terms remain strong and high-order formulations should be developed in the future to significantly improve RANS simulations. However, large eddy simulation (LES) appears as a very powerful alternative to describe scalar turbulent transport: as shown in Section 5.4.6 and Fig. 5.49, counter-gradient transport may be directly predicted at the resolved scale level without ad-hoc modeling.

5.3.9   Modeling of the characteristic turbulent flame time

All RANS models require information on turbulent flame characteristic time scales. This information may be expressed either as a characteristic turbulent time τ_t, a flame crossing frequency, f_c, a scalar dissipation rate or a flame stretch, κ (which has the dimension of a frequency, i.e. inverse of a time). The issue is often critical in practical simulations. Some models like EBU, BML, CFM or MB (Table 5.3) assume that integral scales control the flame wrinkling so that the integral time scale is a proper turbulent flame time:

$$\kappa = \frac{1}{\tau_t} = f_c \approx \kappa(l_t) = \frac{\varepsilon}{k} \tag{5.120}$$

Other models (CPB and CH1 in Table 5.3) assume that small scales (i.e. Kolmogorov scales) control flame wrinkling so that Kolmogorov scaling is used for the flame time (§ 4.2):

$$\kappa = \frac{1}{\tau_{\eta_k}} = f_c \approx \kappa(\eta_K) = \sqrt{\frac{\varepsilon}{\nu}} \qquad (5.121)$$

These expressions lead to very different flame times. Eq. (4.12) shows that they differ by a ratio $\sqrt{Re_t}$:

$$\frac{\kappa(\eta_k)}{\kappa(l_t)} = \sqrt{\frac{l_t u'}{\nu}} = \sqrt{Re_t} \qquad (5.122)$$

Both expressions are equally arbitrary and usually constitute the weakest link in many turbulent combustion models:

- There is no reason to assume that only one turbulent scale (large or small) controls the flame time and the turbulent flame structure. A wide range of scales, from Kolmogorov to integral scales, is likely to be involved.

- Flame characteristic scales should also appear in any expression for characteristic times describing turbulence/combustion interaction. A very thick flame is not wrinkled by turbulence motions like a very thin flame and this should be taken into account.

A more precise approach is to derive a balance equation for characteristic times τ_t of the turbulence/combustion interaction, as proposed, for example by Mantel and Borghi [417] starting from a scalar dissipation rate balance equation.[xxx]

A simpler technique (ITNFS: Intermittent Turbulent Net Flame Stretch) has been proposed by Meneveau and Poinsot [432], using DNS of flame/vortex interaction by Poinsot et al. [523] (see § 5.2.3) together with multifractal theories (Meneveau and Sreenivasan [433, 434]). The basic idea is to estimate the strain rate induced by a given pair of counter-rotating vortices (size r and velocity u'). This strain rate is then integrated over all possible turbulent scales, from Kolmogorov to integral length scales, assuming that each scale acts independently. The total turbulent strain rate is then written:

$$\kappa = \alpha_0 \Gamma_K \left(\frac{u'}{s_L^0}, \frac{l_t}{\delta_L^0} \right) \frac{\varepsilon}{k} \qquad (5.124)$$

[xxx]Mantel and Borghi [417] have derived a balance equation for the scalar dissipation rate:

$$\overline{\chi} = D \overline{\frac{\partial \Theta}{\partial x_i} \frac{\partial \Theta}{\partial x_i}} \qquad (5.123)$$

assuming constant density flows. This scalar dissipation corresponds to the inverse of a characteristic turbulent mixing time and may be related to the stretch rate κ. As shown in Section 5.3.5, this scalar dissipation rate $\overline{\chi}$ is directly related to the mean reaction rate through Eq. (5.56) and contains time information (Eq. (5.58)). This balance equation can also be recast in terms of flame surface density equation (MB model in Table 5.3).

where u' is the turbulent RMS velocity in fresh gases, s_L^0 is the unstrained laminar flame speed, l_t is the integral length scale, δ_L^0 the thermal flame thickness and α_0 a model constant. The efficiency function Γ_K is fitted from DNS data:

$$\log_{10}(\Gamma_K) = -\frac{1}{(s+0.4)}\exp\left(-(s+0.4)\right) + (1 - \exp\left(-(s+0.4)\right))\left(\sigma_1\left(\frac{u'}{s_L^0}\right)s - 0.11\right)$$
(5.125)

where

$$s = \log_{10}\left(\frac{l_t}{\delta_L^0}\right) \quad \text{and} \quad \sigma_1\left(\frac{u'}{s_L^0}\right) = \frac{2}{3}\left(1 - \frac{1}{2}\exp\left[-\left(\frac{u'}{s_L^0}\right)^{1/3}\right]\right)$$
(5.126)

This efficiency function takes into account the reduced ability of small vortices to wrinkle the flame front. When the length scale ratio l_t/δ_L^0 tends towards zero, Γ_K also decreases, reducing the effective flame strain rate, as displayed on Fig. 5.36. Γ_k only slightly depends on the velocity ratio u'/s_L^0. Note also that the efficiency function does not reach a constant level when l_t/δ_L^0 increases because increasing l_t/δ_L^0 keeping u'/s_L^0 constant corresponds to an implicit increase of the turbulent Reynolds number Re_t.

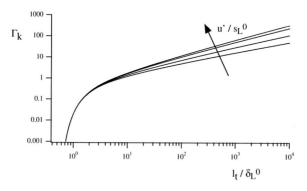

Figure 5.36: ITNFS efficiency function Γ_k given by Eq. (5.125) as a function of the length scale ratio l_t/δ_L^0 for several values of the velocity ratio u'/s_L^0 (0.1; 1.0; 10; 100).

This model provides significant improvements when used in EBU, BML or in flame surface density models (see CFM2-a and CFM2-b models in Table 5.3 and Duclos et al. [189]). For example, an ITNFS-EBU formulation can be written as:

$$\overline{\dot{\omega}}_\Theta = C_{EBU}\overline{\rho}\Gamma_K\left(\frac{u'}{s_L^0}, \frac{l}{\delta_L^0}\right)\frac{\varepsilon}{k}\widetilde{\Theta}(1 - \widetilde{\Theta})$$
(5.127)

This approach introduces in the EBU model a sensitivity to chemistry and also tends to decrease the mean reaction rate in highly strained regions when turbulent scales are small (in these regions the EBU model generally overestimates reaction rates). Expression (5.127) has been successfully used by Bailly et al. [25] and Lahjaily et al. [363].

5.3.10   Kolmogorov-Petrovski-Piskunov (KPP) analysis

This section presents a simple theoretical tool to analyze turbulent combustion models. This analysis is conducted under some restrictive assumptions such as frozen turbulence (turbulent flow field is not affected by combustion) and can only be derived for some combustion models. It is, however, an efficient way to study basic model trends.

The Kolmogorov-Petrovski-Piskunov (KPP) analysis is illustrated here using an example. More details may be found in Hakberg and Gosman [264], Fichot et al. [211] or Duclos et al. [189]. Assuming an EBU-like (see § 5.3.3) combustion model:

$$\overline{\dot{\omega}}_\Theta = C\overline{\rho}\frac{1}{\tau_m}\widetilde{\Theta}\left(1 - \widetilde{\Theta}\right) \qquad (5.128)$$

where τ_m is a turbulent mechanical time and C a model constant, the balance equation for a statistically one-dimensional steady propagating turbulent flame is:

$$\rho_0 s_T \frac{\partial \widetilde{\Theta}}{\partial x} = \overline{\rho}\frac{\nu_t}{\sigma_\Theta}\frac{\partial^2 \widetilde{\Theta}}{\partial x^2} + C\overline{\rho}\frac{1}{\tau_m}\widetilde{\Theta}\left(1 - \widetilde{\Theta}\right) \qquad (5.129)$$

where ρ_0 is the fresh gases density and σ_Θ a turbulent Schmidt number. A gradient description of turbulent fluxes is assumed. Turbulence is frozen so that the turbulent time τ_m and the dynamic viscosity $\overline{\rho}\nu_t$ are constant in space and in time.

The basic idea of the KPP analysis is to look for an exponential solution of Eq. (5.129) at the flame leading edge (i.e. when $\widetilde{\Theta}$ tends towards $\widetilde{\Theta} = 0$). Keeping first order $\widetilde{\Theta}$ terms, Eq. (5.129) reduces to:

$$\rho_0 s_T \frac{\partial \widetilde{\Theta}}{\partial x} = \rho_0 \frac{\nu_t}{\sigma_\Theta}\frac{\partial^2 \widetilde{\Theta}}{\partial x^2} + C\rho_0 \frac{1}{\tau_m}\widetilde{\Theta} \qquad (5.130)$$

which has a solution when the discriminant Δ is positive or equal to zero:

$$\Delta = s_T^2 - 4\frac{C}{\sigma_\Theta}\frac{\nu_t}{\tau_m} \geq 0 \qquad (5.131)$$

leading to a continuum of solutions for the turbulent flame speed s_T:

$$s_T \geq 2\sqrt{\frac{C}{\sigma_\Theta}\frac{\nu_t}{\tau_m}} \qquad (5.132)$$

The KPP theorem shows that the actual solution of Eq. (5.129) corresponds to the lowest turbulent flame speed:

$$\boxed{s_T = 2\sqrt{\frac{C}{\sigma_\Theta}\frac{\nu_t}{\tau_m}}} \qquad (5.133)$$

This expression displays the influence of the turbulent time modeling on the turbulent flame speed. For example, Table 5.4 gives turbulent flame speeds when the turbulent viscosity is modeled using the $k - \varepsilon$ model ($\nu_t = C_\mu k^2/\varepsilon$, see § 4.5.3), for three expressions for the turbulent time τ_t (integral time scale, Kolmogorov time scale and ITNFS time scale, see § 5.3.9). Relations derived in Section 4.2 have been used.[xxxi]

Turbulent flame time	τ_m	Turbulent flame speed s_T	s_T/s_L^0
Kolmogorov	$\sqrt{\dfrac{\nu}{\varepsilon}}$	$2\sqrt{\dfrac{CC_\mu}{\sigma_\Theta}}\,Re_t^{1/4}u'$	$2\sqrt{\dfrac{CC_\mu}{\sigma_\Theta}}\left(\dfrac{l_t}{\delta_L^0}\right)^{1/4}\left(\dfrac{u'}{s_L^0}\right)^{5/4}$
Integral	$\dfrac{k}{\varepsilon}$	$2\sqrt{\dfrac{CC_\mu}{\sigma_\Theta}}\,u'$	$2\sqrt{\dfrac{CC_\mu}{\sigma_\Theta}}\,\dfrac{u'}{s_L^0}$
ITNFS	$\dfrac{1}{\Gamma_k\left(\frac{u'}{s_L^0},\frac{l_t}{\delta_L^0}\right)}\dfrac{k}{\varepsilon}$	$2\sqrt{\dfrac{CC_\mu}{\sigma_\Theta}}\Gamma_k\left(\dfrac{u'}{s_L^0},\dfrac{l_t}{\delta_L^0}\right)u'$	$2\sqrt{\dfrac{CC_\mu}{\sigma_\Theta}}\Gamma_k\left(\dfrac{u'}{s_L^0},\dfrac{l_t}{\delta_L^0}\right)\dfrac{u'}{s_L^0}$

Table 5.4: Turbulent flame speed s_T for various values of the turbulent time scale τ_t used to model the mean reaction rate $\bar{\dot{\omega}}_\Theta$ estimated from the KPP theory (Eq. 5.133). The turbulent viscosity is modeled from the $k - \varepsilon$ model as $\nu_t = C_\mu k^2/\varepsilon$. The rms velocity, u' is given by $u' = \sqrt{k}$. Laminar flame speed s_L^0 and thickness δ_L^0 are assumed linked through the relation $\delta_L^0 s_L^0/\nu \approx 1$.

This analysis shows that the turbulent flame speed predicted by the three models increases with u'. Using the Kolmogorov time scale as the turbulent flame time leads to a turbulent flame speed which is higher than with the integral time scale. On the other hand, ITNFS expression predicts a lower turbulence flame speed when the length scale ratio l_t/δ_L^0 is low because the turbulence efficiency on the flame front wrinkling is reduced (Fig. 5.37).[xxxii]

Of course, this kind of analysis is possible only under restrictive assumptions (frozen turbulence, flame propagation controlled by the turbulent flame leading edge) and can be conducted only with some models. The turbulent flame speed itself is not a very useful quantity as experimental results display a large scatter. Nevertheless, the KPP analysis provides a simple way to predict model trends. It can be extended to two equations models, as done by Duclos et al. [189] for flame surface density descriptions.

[xxxi]Note that the laminar flame speed s_L^0 is not recovered when the turbulence level decreases (i.e. for $u' = 0$): most simple turbulent combustion models are designed for large turbulent Reynolds numbers Re_t for which s_L^0 should be negligible compared to s_T.

[xxxii]More refined ITNFS formulations, including the possible occurrence of flame quenching, are able to reproduce turbulent flame speed bending and flame quenching at high turbulence level (Duclos et al. [189]).

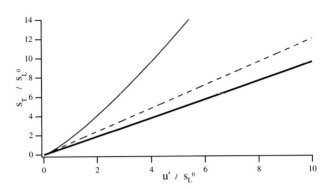

Figure 5.37: Turbulent flame speed s_T/s_L^0 versus turbulent velocity u'/s_L^0, predicted by the KPP analysis for an EBU-like model using Kolmogorov (——), integral (----) and ITNFS (——) turbulent characteristic times. Frozen turbulence. $C_{EBU} = 4.$, $C_\mu = 0.09$ and $l_t/\delta_L^0 = 4$.

5.3.11   Flame stabilization

Statistically steady turbulent flames require flame stabilization mechanisms. The objective of this section is to briefly describe these mechanisms and to evidence the corresponding difficulties for turbulent flame numerical simulations. Additional discussion on the effects of walls on turbulent flames is given in Chapter 7.

Two main mechanisms are generally proposed to stabilize a turbulent premixed flame:

- **Low speed zone.** Creating a low speed region in the flow speed allows the flame stabilization (Beer and Chigier [43]). In this situation, the turbulent flame speed is able to sustain the incoming flow velocity leading to flame stabilization. This objective is generally achieved using a so-called flame-holder (see Fig. 5.38) or a swirling flow (Gupta et al. [261], Syred [635], Huang and Yang [300], Galley et al. [225]), both inducing a large recirculation zone.

- **Continuous ignition.** In this case, the incoming reactants are continuously ignited through a heat source such as a pilot flame (small secondary flame), hot wire, hot gas stream or an electrically sustained plasma, as displayed in Fig. 5.39. Note that this mechanism may also be involved when using a recirculation zone, viewed as a hot gases "tank."

None of these mechanisms is explicitly modeled in most turbulent premixed combustion models. These models are generally designed to predict a turbulent flame speed s_T (see, for example, § 5.3.10) and are based on fast chemistry assumptions (i.e. the flame exists and has reached an equilibrium state). However, RANS models, through s_T, generally predict flame stabilization in low speed regions such as recirculation zones. But the exact flame stabilization

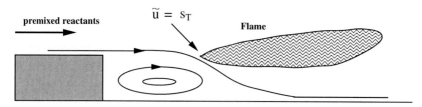

Figure 5.38: Turbulent premixed flame stabilization using a low speed zone (recirculation zone). The flame is stabilized in a location where the turbulent flame speed s_T is able to sustain the flow velocity $\widetilde{u}$.

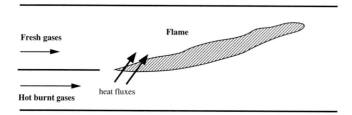

Figure 5.39: Turbulent premixed flame stabilization using a hot gases stream providing the required heat fluxes. Longitudinal velocities are larger than the turbulent flame speed. Experiment by Moreau [453].

location is not correctly predicted because these models do not account for actual ignition mechanisms which involve complex chemistry features and control initial regions of flames in Fig. 5.38 and 5.39.

An experimental evidence of modeling difficulties is displayed in Fig. 5.40 where experimental data achieved in a turbulent V-shape premixed propane/air flame stabilized behind a small cylindrical rod (Veynante et al. [682]) are compared. Flame surface surface density fields are obtained from laser tomography and mean reaction rates are estimated from CH radical emission. Close to the stabilization rod, the flame surface density Σ is high whereas the mean reaction rate remains quite low. In this region, fresh and burnt gases are separated by an interface (the probability to find this interface is high so that flame surface densities are large) where combustion is started but not yet fully established. Accordingly, in the flame surface density modeling approach, some submodel should account for ignition processes (i.e. non-equilibrium combustion features) in the local reaction rate per unit flame surface, $\rho_0 \langle s_c \rangle_s$ (Eq. 5.65), which is not the case in classical flamelet approaches assuming that flame elements have reached an equilibrium state. Simple models such as algebraic Eddy-Break-Up or BML models ignore transient ignition effects clearly apparent on Fig. 5.40 and predict that the turbulent flame is anchored to the stabilization rod.

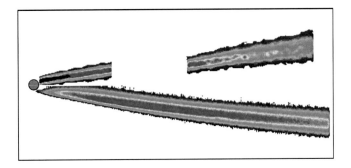

Figure 5.40: Flame surface density (half top) extracted from laser tomography imaging and mean reaction rate (half bottom) estimated from CH radical emission measured in a V-shape turbulent premixed propane/air flame stabilized downstream a small cylindrical rod. Flame surface density data (half top), extracted from two different data sets, are not available from 30 to 70 mm downstream the rod (Veynante et al. [682]).

Simple flame surface density models based on a balance equation for Σ are also unable to directly describe a flame stabilized using a hot gases stream (pilot flame) in high speed flows (Fig. 5.39).[xxxiii] Such models, as others, predict a stabilization through a turbulent flame speed s_T and then are only able to stabilize a flame when low speed zones are encountered. Moreover, Σ-balance equations and most closure schemes are derived implicitly assuming that the flame is established. All source terms in these equations are proportional to Σ or Σ^2 (see Table 5.3, page 241) and the equations cannot generate flame surface densities where there is no initial flame surface. Most models have the same drawbacks. On the other hand, simple algebraic models, such as Eddy-Break-Up model (see § 5.3.3 or § 5.3.10), predict a flame stabilization when fresh and burnt gases mix (i.e. when $\widetilde{\Theta}(1-\widetilde{\Theta})$ is non-zero), and, accordingly, are able to stabilize a turbulent flame with a hot gases stream (Fig. 5.39), strongly anchored to the injector lip. Nevertheless, they completely miss the flame stabilization mechanism and transient chemical effects.

The description of flame stabilization mechanisms remains a difficult challenge for turbulent combustion modeling. Three main points must be enhanced:

- Flame ignition and stabilization involve complex chemistry features and generally cannot be handled using simple chemical schemes.

[xxxiii]A rough submodel to overcome this difficulty and describe such a flame stabilization is to continuously impose in the numerical simulation an initial flame surface density Σ_0 at an ad-hoc location.

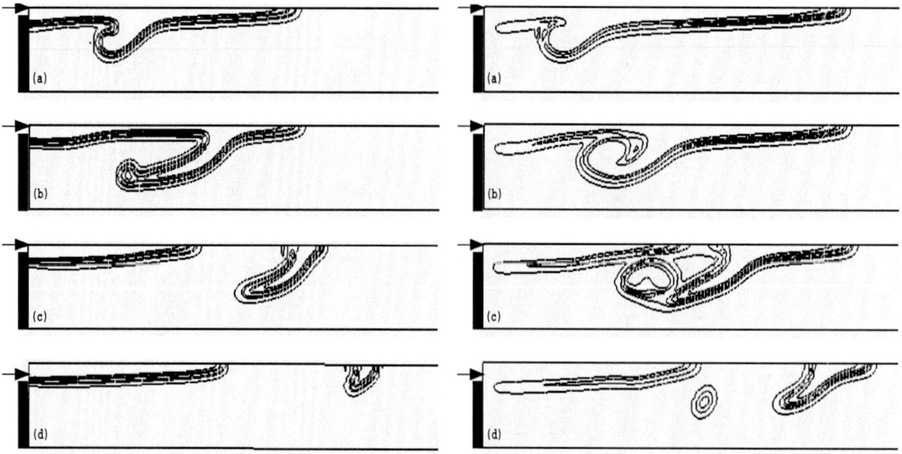

Figure 5.41: Time evolution of reaction rate fields in a premixed flame stabilized behind a downstream facing step and submitted to a velocity jump. Left: adiabatic step wall. Right: cold wall, the wall temperature is set equal to the fresh gases temperature (DNS by Veynante and Poinsot [676]).

- Ignition often occurs in low turbulence or laminar flow regions such as boundary or mixing layers in the vicinity of injector lips. For example, in spark-ignited engines, the initial flame is laminar, grows and later becomes turbulent. Boudier et al. [75] have proposed a submodel to describe this mechanism in a flame surface density modeling context. Taking into account ignition time, spark energy and flow conditions, this submodel determines when the flame becomes turbulent and the initial flame surface density to be imposed in the turbulent code. This model has been refined by Duclos and Colin [188].

- Ignition and flame stabilization take generally place in the vicinity of walls (injector lips, backward facing step inducing recirculation zones,...). Wall effects such as heat transfer and catalytic effects have to be taken into account and may strongly affect the stabilization and the evolution of the flame (see Chapt. 7). This point is illustrated on Fig. 5.41 where the time evolution of a premixed laminar flame stabilized behind a backward facing step is plotted for two limiting cases: adiabatic (left) and cold (right) flame holder (Direct numerical simulations by Veynante and Poinsot [676]). The flame response to an inlet velocity jump is directly controlled by the flame holder thermal condition: the small lift-off distance induced by the cold wall (right) leads to a very different flame surface evolution compared to the adiabatic wall (left).

5.4 LES of turbulent premixed flames

RANS modeling of turbulent premixed combustion has been discussed in the previous section. Models for large eddy simulations (LES) are now briefly reviewed.

5.4.1 Introduction

Development of RANS combustion models started about 40 years ago with the pioneering work of Spalding [623] followed some years later by the Eddy Break Up model (Spalding [624]). On the other hand, large eddy simulations started during the eighties for non-reacting, constant density flow fields and only by the end of the 20th century for combustion. Accordingly, LES is still at a relatively early stage for reacting flows and only the basic principles of the main proposed approaches are summarized here.

A difficult problem is encountered in large eddy simulations of premixed flames: the thickness δ_L^0 of a premixed flame is about 0.1 to 1 mm and is generally much smaller than the LES mesh size Δ as plotted in Fig. 5.42. The progress variable, Θ (i.e. non dimensionalized fuel mass fraction or temperature) is a very stiff variable of space and the flame front cannot be resolved in the computation, leading to numerical problems. In fact, the most important contribution to the reaction rate probably occurs at the subgrid scale level suggesting that LES could be impossible for reacting flows (Pope [533]).

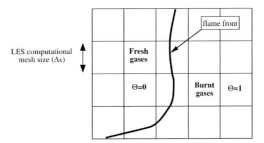

Figure 5.42: Comparison between premixed flame thickness δ_L^0 and LES mesh size Δ_x. The flame front separates fresh gases (progress variable $\Theta = 0$) from burnt gases ($\Theta = 1$).

To overcome this difficulty, three main approaches have been proposed: simulation of an artificially thickened flame, use of a flame front tracking technique (G-equation), or filtering with a Gaussian filter larger than the mesh size. In certain LES approaches, this theoretical problem is sometimes avoided by developing subgrid scale models for filtered reaction rates and unresolved scalar transport which increase the flame thickness, either through turbulent diffusion or through numerical diffusion.[xxxiv] Probability density function formulations

---

[xxxiv]This point may be of importance when data are extracted from DNS or experiments for model validations.

(§ 5.3.7) could also be extended to LES but, as this approach has been mainly developed for non premixed combustion, it is described in Chapter 6.

5.4.2   Extension of RANS models: the LES-EBU model

A first idea is to extend classical RANS closures to large eddy simulations. For example, the Eddy-Break-Up model (see § 5.3.3) may be recast as:

$$\boxed{\overline{\dot{\omega}}_\Theta = C_{EBU}\overline{\rho}\frac{1}{\tau_t^{SGS}}\widetilde{\Theta}\left(1-\widetilde{\Theta}\right)}$$
(5.134)

where τ_t^{SGS} is a subgrid turbulent time scale, estimated as:[xxxv]

$$\tau_t^{SGS} \approx \frac{l_\Delta}{u'_{SGS}} \approx \frac{\Delta}{\sqrt{k^{SGS}}}$$
(5.135)

where l_Δ is the subgrid turbulent length scale, identified as the filter size Δ and u'_{SGS} a subgrid scale turbulent velocity. The subgrid turbulent kinetic energy k^{SGS} may be given from an algebraic expression or a balance equation. In this formalism, the flame thickness problem is not taken into account: this LES-EBU model is used together with a gradient model for scalar subgrid scale transport to ensure a resolved $\widetilde{\Theta}$ field in numerical simulations.

This simple formulation has not been extensively tested (Fureby and Løfstrøm [223], Fureby and Møller [224]) but two shortcomings may be anticipated: the Eddy Break up model has known deficiencies in RANS context (reaction rate independent of chemical reaction, overestimation of the reaction rate in zones of strong shears among others). In an LES context, the model constant C_{EBU} seems to be strongly dependent on various parameters (flow conditions, mesh size). As discussed in Section 4.7.4, length scale ratios (LES filter size, flame thickness, and subgrid scale flame front wrinkling) should probably be incorporated.

5.4.3   Artificially thickened flames

An attractive solution to propagate a premixed flame on a coarse grid was proposed by Butler and O'Rourke [100]. Following simple theories of laminar premixed flame (Williams [710], Kuo [361]), the flame speed s_L and the flame thickness δ_L^0 may be expressed as (see Tables 2.5 and

---

[xxxv]More refined expressions, taking into account the reduced ability of small vortices to wrinkle the flame front, could be developed, extending ITNFS formalism (see § 5.3.9) to LES (Angelberger et al. [13], Colin et al. [147], Charlette et al. [118]).

2.8):[xxxvi]

$$s_L^0 \propto \sqrt{D_{th}B} \quad . \quad ; \quad \delta_L^0 \propto \frac{D_{th}}{s_L^0} = \sqrt{\frac{D_{th}}{B}}$$

(5.136)

where D_{th} is the thermal diffusivity and B the preexponential constant. If the thermal diffusivity is increased by a factor F while the preexponential constant is decreased by F, the flame thickness δ_L^0 is multiplied by F while the flame speed is maintained. For sufficiently large F values, the thickened flame front is resolved on the LES computational mesh (see Fig. 5.43).

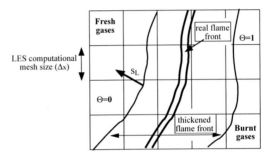

Figure 5.43: Thickened flame approach. The laminar flame is artificially thickened but its flame speed is conserved.

Since the reaction rate is still expressed using Arrhenius law, various phenomena can be accounted for without requiring ad-hoc submodels (for example, ignition, flame stabilization or flame/wall interactions). This route has been found very powerful, at least when the flow scales are much larger than the laminar flame thickness, as in combustion instabilities (see Chapt. 8 and 10).

When the flame is thickened from δ_L^0 to $F\delta_L^0$, the interaction between turbulence and chemistry is modified because the Damköhler number, D_a, comparing turbulent (τ_t) and chemical (τ_c) time scales (see § 5.2.2):

$$D_a = \frac{\tau_t}{\tau_c} = \frac{l_t}{u'}\frac{s_l}{\delta_L^0}$$

(5.137)

[xxxvi]The following derivation is performed for a single step reaction with a preexponential constant B but can be extended to multi-step chemistry. This result is a property of convection/diffusion/reaction balance equations and may be proved by replacing the spatial coordinate x by x/F in the balance equation for a 1D steady propagating flame:

$$\rho_0 s_L^0 \frac{\partial \Theta}{\partial x} = \frac{\partial}{\partial x}\left(\rho D_{th}\frac{\partial \Theta}{\partial x}\right) + \dot{\omega}_\Theta$$

is decreased by a factor F and becomes D_a/F.

As already discussed in Section 5.3.9, when the ratio between the turbulent length scale and the laminar flame thickness, l_t/δ_L^0, is decreased, the flame becomes less sensitive to turbulence motions. This ratio is decreased by a factor F when the flame is thickened. This point has been investigated using DNS by Angelberger et al. [13] and Colin et al. [147] (Fig. 5.44).[xxxvii] An efficiency function E, corresponding to a subgrid scale wrinkling factor, has been derived to account for this effect. This efficiency function extends the ITNFS concept (Eq. 5.125) to LES and depends on velocity (u'/s_L) and length scale $(\Delta/F\delta_L^0)$ ratios. In practice, the thickened flame approach is implemented by changing the diffusivity and the reaction rate according to

$$
\begin{array}{lcccc}
\text{Diffusivity:} & D_{th} & \longrightarrow & F\,D_{th} & \longrightarrow & E\,F\,D_{th} \\
\text{Preexponential constant:} & B & \longrightarrow & B/F & \longrightarrow & E\,B/F \\
& & \text{thickening} & & \text{wrinkling}
\end{array}
$$

According to Eq. (5.136), the flame speed s_L^0 and the flame thickness δ_L^0 become respectively:

$$ s_T^0 = E s_L^0 \qquad \text{and} \qquad \delta_T = F\delta_L^0 \tag{5.138} $$

where s_T^0 is the subgrid scale turbulent flame speed.

(a) 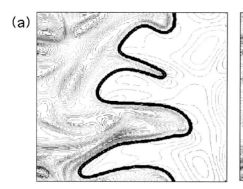 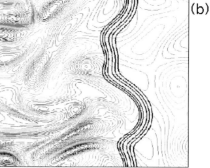 (b)

Figure 5.44: DNS of flame turbulence interactions. Reaction rate and vorticity fields are superimposed. (a) reference flame; (b) flame artificially thickened by a factor $F = 5$. Because of the change in the length scale ratio l_t/δ_L^0, combustion/turbulence interaction is changed and the thickened flame is less wrinkled by turbulence motions. This effect can be parametrized using a subgrid scale model.

[xxxvii]Starting from the DNS by Colin et al. [147], Charlette et al. [118] have proposed a refined expression for the efficiency E, correcting its behaviour in limiting cases. Dynamic formalisms for the automatic adjustment of the efficiency function parameter may be found in Charlette et al. [117] and Wang et al. [697].

In practice, implementing the TFLES model in a code is achieved by modifying the equation (1.47) for species k into:

$$\frac{\partial}{\partial t}\rho Y_k + \frac{\partial}{\partial x_i}\rho(u_i + V_i^c)Y_k = \frac{\partial}{\partial x_i}\left(\rho EFD_k\frac{W_k}{W}\frac{\partial X_k}{\partial x_i}\right) + \frac{E\dot{\omega}_k}{F} \tag{5.139}$$

where F is the thickening factor and E the efficiency function. The same modification is operated on the energy equation. The initial TFLES model has been extended to work on other flame regimes (partially premixed flames for example) by using a thickening factor which varies with local position to thicken only reaction zones and not mixing regions (Légier [376], Kuenne et al. [360]). This extended TFLES model is discussed in § 6.5.3.

5.4.4 The G - equation

The G-equation formalism adopts a view which is opposite to the thickened flame approach: the flame thickness is set to zero and the flame front is described as a propagating surface tracked using a field variable $\widetilde{G}$ (Fig. 5.45). In LES, the resolved flame brush is associated to the iso-level $\widetilde{G} = G^*$. The resolved $\widetilde{G}$ field does not need to follow the progress variable Θ gradients and can be smoothed out to be resolved on the LES mesh.

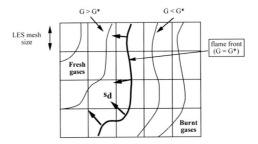

Figure 5.45: Flame front and G-field. The flame front is identified as a given surface $G = G^*$ of a G field, generally related to the distance to the flame front.

The G-equation is written as (Kerstein et al. [342]):

$$\frac{\partial \bar{\rho}\widetilde{G}}{\partial t} + \frac{\partial \bar{\rho}\tilde{u}_i\widetilde{G}}{\partial x_i} = \rho_0 \bar{s}_T \left|\nabla\widetilde{G}\right| \tag{5.140}$$

A model for the subgrid scale "turbulent" flame speed $\bar{s}_T$ is needed. This closure is generally based on Eq. (5.47):

$$\frac{\bar{s}_T}{s_L} = 1 + \alpha \left(\frac{\overline{u'}}{s_L}\right)^n \tag{5.141}$$

where $\overline{u'}$ is the subgrid scale turbulence level which may be estimated as:

$$\overline{u'} \approx \Delta \left|\widetilde{S}\right| = \Delta\sqrt{\left|2\widetilde{S}_{ij}\widetilde{S}_{ij}\right|} \tag{5.142}$$

where $\widetilde{S}_{ij}$ are the components of the resolved shear stresses. The constants α and n have to be specified. Im et al. [303] has proposed a dynamic determination for α when $n = 1$. In many cases, $\overline{u'}$ - $\overline{s}_T$ correlations obtained in experiments or used in RANS models are directly used in LES without further justification, replacing the turbulent rms velocity by the subgrid scale turbulent velocity.

Equation (5.140) is a formulation corresponding to a simple physical analysis (displacement of the resolved flame front with the displacement speed $\overline{s}_T$). Nevertheless, as already pointed out (§ 5.3.4), the turbulent flame speed is not a well-defined quantity and no universal model is available. Eq. (5.140) also induces numerical and theoretical difficulties: flame cusps avoided adding artificial diffusivity, coupling between displacement and consumption speeds (Piana et al. [505], Janicka and Sadiki [307]). Despite these drawbacks, the G-equation is a popular technique for large eddy simulations of turbulent premixed combustion (Pitsch [512]).

5.4.5   Flame surface density LES formulations

Another approach is to filter the Θ (or mass fractions or temperature) balance equation:

$$\frac{\partial \rho\Theta}{\partial t} + \frac{\partial \rho u_i \Theta}{\partial x_i} = \frac{\partial}{\partial x_i}\left(\rho D \frac{\partial \Theta}{\partial x_i}\right) + \dot{\omega}_\Theta = \rho s_d |\nabla\Theta| \tag{5.143}$$

where s_d is the local displacement speed (Eq. 2.99) of the iso-surface Θ, leading to:[xxxviii]

$$\frac{\partial \overline{\rho}\widetilde{\Theta}}{\partial t} + \frac{\partial \overline{\rho}\widetilde{u}_i\widetilde{\Theta}}{\partial x_i} + \frac{\partial}{\partial x_i}\left(\widetilde{\overline{\rho u_i \Theta}} - \overline{\rho}\widetilde{u}_i\widetilde{\Theta}\right) = \frac{\partial}{\partial x_i}\left(\overline{\rho D \frac{\partial \Theta}{\partial x_i}}\right) + \overline{\dot{\omega}}_\Theta = \overline{\rho s_d |\nabla\Theta|} \tag{5.144}$$

As already pointed out, the flame front (and the gradient of the progress variable Θ) is generally too thin to be resolved on the LES computational mesh. Nevertheless, following Boger et al. [65], the filtered progress variable $\overline{\Theta}$ may be resolved using a physical space Gaussian filter F expressed by Eq. (4.54) with a filter size Δ larger than the computational mesh size Δ_m as displayed on Fig. 5.46. Accordingly, the filtered flame front is numerically resolved with about $2\Delta/\Delta_m$ grid points.[xxxix] Compared to an arbitrary G-field (G-equation), the progress variable Θ has a main advantage: Θ and related quantities, such as flame surface densities, are physically defined and may be extracted from DNS or experimental measurements.

[xxxviii]Note that using the displacement speed s_d, Eq. (5.143) is similar to a G-equation (5.140) where the $\widetilde{G}$ field is identified as the Θ field.

[xxxix]The form of the LES filter does not explicitly appear in Eq. (5.144) and is generally not used to close and solve it. It would appear only when LES results are validated against experimental or DNS data to filter measurements results.

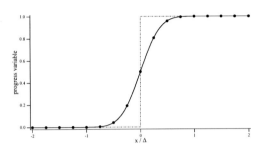

Figure 5.46: Effect of a spatial Gaussian filter (Eq. 4.54) having a size Δ larger than the mesh size Δ_m (here $\Delta = 4\,\Delta_m$). Unfiltered Θ (— · —) and filtered progress variable $\overline{\Theta}$ (——) versus x/Δ where x is the spatial coordinate. The progress variable Θ is not resolved on the computational mesh denoted by ($\bullet$) whereas the filtered progress variable $\overline{\Theta}$ is resolved with about $2\,\Delta/\Delta_m = 8$ grid points in the filtered flame front (Boger et al. [65]).

The RHS term in Eq. (5.144), $\overline{\rho s_d |\nabla\Theta|}$ may be modeled as (Boger et al. [65]):

$$\boxed{\overline{\rho s_d |\nabla\Theta|} \approx \rho_u s_L \Sigma = \rho_u s_L \Xi \left|\nabla\overline{\Theta}\right|} \qquad (5.145)$$

where ρ_u and s_L are respectively the fresh gases density and the laminar flame speed. Σ is the subgrid scale flame surface density (i.e. the flame surface density per unit volume at the subgrid scale level) and Ξ the subgrid scale flame wrinkling factor (i.e. the ratio between the subgrid scale flame surface and its projection in the propagating direction). Models are then required for Σ and Ξ. Proposed approaches are formally identical to the ones developed in RANS context. Algebraic expressions (Boger et al. [65], Boger and Veynante [64]), similarity models (Knikker et al. [352, 353]) or balance equations (Boger et al. [65], Weller et al. [701], Hawkes and Cant [272], Richard et al. [556]) may be proposed either for Σ or Ξ. As shown in Fig. 4.12, this flame surface density may be extracted from experimental data.

Duwig [195] proposes to extract the contribution $\rho_u s_L |\nabla\overline{\Theta}|$ in Eq. (5.145) from filtered one-dimensional laminar flame elements (i.e. flamelets) and to tabulate it as a function of the filtered progress variable $\widetilde{\Theta}$. The F-TACLES model (Filtered TAbulated Chemistry for LES) follows a similar idea: one-dimensional laminar premixed flames computed taking into account complex chemistry features are filtered and corresponding reaction rate, molecular diffusion and unresolved transport (Eq. 5.148) terms are tabulated as functions of the filtered progress variable $\widetilde{\Theta}$, the filter size Δ and other useful parameters such as filtered mixture fraction (Fiorina et al. [216], Auzillon et al. [23, 24]). The turbulence / combustion interaction is then modelled through the wrinkling factor Ξ, estimated from algebraic expression such as the ones proposed by Colin et al. [147] or Charlette et al. [118]. Colin and Truffin [146] have developed a spark-ignition submodel in the flame surface density balance equation formalism.

5.4.6   Scalar fluxes modeling in LES

Unresolved scalar fluxes are generally described from a simple gradient assumption (Eq. 4.76):

$$\boxed{\widetilde{u_i \Theta} - \widetilde{u}_i\, \widetilde{\Theta} = -\frac{\nu_t}{Sc_k}\frac{\partial\widetilde{\Theta}}{\partial x_i}}$$
(5.146)

However, the analysis of the Boughanem and Trouvé [77] DNS database (Fig. 4.8) by Boger et al. [65] has shown that gradient or counter-gradient unresolved fluxes may be observed in LES like in RANS (see § 5.3.8), depending on the turbulence level and heat release rate (Fig. 5.47). Pfadler et al. [503] confirm that the gradient model (5.146) is unsuitable for the premixed turbulent flames they investigate experimentally. Nevertheless, unresolved LES fluxes are lower than in RANS so that model uncertainties have less dramatic consequences in LES than in RANS.

Since counter-gradient transport may be explained by differential buoyancy effects between cold fresh and hot burnt gases, all characteristic length scales are involved. Accordingly, the unresolved scalar flux increases almost linearly with the filter size Δ (Fig. 5.48) but its type (gradient or counter-gradient) does not change. Thereafter, a portion of the counter-gradient phenomena is expected to be directly described in large eddy simulations through resolved motions, even when a subgrid scale gradient-type closure is used. This point is evidenced in Fig. 5.49: Boger and Veynante [64] have performed large eddy simulations of a V-shape turbulent premixed propane/air flame stabilized behind a triangular flame-holder (an instantaneous progress variable $\widetilde{\Theta}$ field is displayed in Fig. 5.49a). Fields are averaged over time to obtain a mean flow field (Fig. 5.49b) similar to RANS predictions.

The contribution of the turbulent transport due to resolved motions is explicitly computed in LES and may be extracted from simulations by evaluating $\overline{\rho u''\Theta''}$ using the LES fields. It would have to be modeled in RANS computations. Three transverse profiles of the LES resolved contribution to the downstream turbulent transport are displayed on Fig. 5.50. Close to the flame-holder, this turbulent transport is of gradient type but becomes counter-gradient further downstream, according to the analysis conducted in Fig. 5.10. This shows that countergradient turbulent transport, at least at the resolved level, is easily recovered in LES even using a simple gradient subgrid scale model. Such a prediction would be very difficult in RANS simulations, requiring a second-order modeling (Bailly et al. [25]).

Another important point has to be considered when analyzing unresolved scalar fluxes in reacting, and more generally variable density flows. For a one-dimensional laminar steady propagating premixed flame (see § 2.4.5), the mass continuity equation in the flame reference frame leads to:

$$\rho u = \rho_u s_L = constant$$
(5.147)

where ρ_u is the density in the fresh gases and s_L the laminar flame speed. Then, the unresolved scalar transport becomes:

$$\boxed{\overline{\rho}\left(\widetilde{u\Theta} - \widetilde{u}\widetilde{\Theta}\right) = \overline{\rho u\Theta} - \overline{\rho u}\widetilde{\Theta} = \rho_u s_L\left(\overline{\Theta} - \widetilde{\Theta}\right)}$$
(5.148)

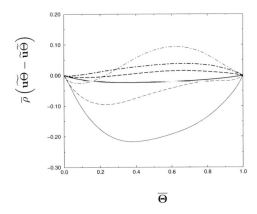

Figure 5.47: Unresolved $\widetilde{\Theta}$-flux, $\overline{\rho}(\widetilde{u\Theta} - \widetilde{u}\widetilde{\Theta})$ versus filtered progress variable $\overline{\Theta}$ for various cases, depending on the heat release factor τ. $\tau = 0.5$ (——); $\tau = 2$ (— — —) and $\tau = 6$ (—·—). Thin lines correspond to RANS turbulent transport. Fluxes are normalized by $\rho_0 s_L$. DNS of Boughanem and Trouvé [77] (Fig. 4.8). Data analysis from Boger et al. [65].

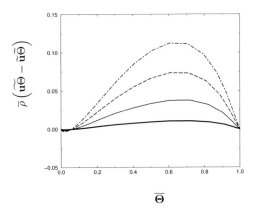

Figure 5.48: Unresolved $\widetilde{\Theta}$-flux, $\overline{\rho}(\widetilde{u\Theta} - \widetilde{u}\widetilde{\Theta})$ versus filtered progress variable $\overline{\Theta}$ (bold lines), for different values of the filter size Δ in a case exhibiting counter-gradient unresolved transport (case $\tau = 6$. in Fig. 5.47). LES filter size are Δ_0 (——); $2\Delta_0$ (——); $3\Delta_0$ (— — —) and $4\Delta_0$ (—·—). Fluxes are made non-dimensional using $\rho_0 s_L$. Initial DNS database from Boughanem and Trouvé [77] (see an example of DNS field in Fig. 4.8). Data analysis from Boger et al. [65].

(a): instantaneous field of the resolved progress variable $\widetilde{\Theta}$

(b): time-averaged $\widetilde{\Theta}$ field

Figure 5.49: Large eddy simulations of a turbulent premixed propane/air flame stabilized behind a triangular shape flame-holder (experiment conducted at ENSMA Poitiers). Inlet velocity: $U_{in} = 5.75\,m/s$; equivalence ratio: $\phi = 0.65$; blockage ratio: 50 % (Boger and Veynante [64]).

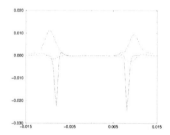

Figure 5.50: Transverse profiles of the resolved turbulent fluxes $\overline{\rho u''\widetilde{\Theta}''}$ in the configuration of Fig. 5.49 for three locations: 2 cm (——), 6 cm (- - - -) and 10 cm (—·—) behind the flame holder. $\overline{\rho u''\widetilde{\Theta}''} > 0$ indicates counter-gradient transport (Boger and Veynante [64]).

For an adiabatic constant pressure laminar flame with unity Lewis number, reduced temperature Θ and density ρ are directly related:

$$\rho = \frac{\rho_u}{1 + \tau\Theta} \tag{5.149}$$

where τ is the heat release factor, linking fresh (T_u) and burnt (T_b) gases temperatures ($\tau = T_b/T_u - 1$). Then:

$$\boxed{\overline{\rho}\left(\widetilde{u\Theta} - \widetilde{u}\widetilde{\Theta}\right) = \rho_u s_L \frac{\rho_u}{\overline{\rho}}\left[\overline{\left(\frac{1}{1+\tau\Theta}\right)\Theta} - \overline{\left(\frac{\Theta}{1+\tau\Theta}\right)}\right] \geq 0} \tag{5.150}$$

where positive x values correspond to burnt gases ($\Theta = 1$). Eq. (5.150) shows that the filtering operation induces unresolved counter-gradient scalar fluxes even in a laminar flame. Such a contribution is not taken into account in model expression (5.146) but should be incorporated in models to ensure a correct prediction of a subgrid planar laminar flame.

A similar result is achieved for unresolved Reynolds stresses, leading to:

$$\boxed{\overline{\rho}\left(\widetilde{uu} - \widetilde{u}\widetilde{u}\right) = \overline{\rho u u} - \overline{\rho u}\widetilde{u} = \rho_u s_L \left(\overline{u} - \widetilde{u}\right)} \tag{5.151}$$

so that a laminar contribution should also be incorporated in unresolved Reynolds stresses modeling.[xl] This has also a reverse implication. Because of thermal expansion due to heat release, resolved velocity gradients and resolved shear stresses contain both information on turbulence and on thermal expansion and are non-zero for laminar flames. Accordingly, these quantities are not well suited to extract actual turbulence information to model, for example, the subgrid scale flame front wrinkling due to turbulence motions. Dilatation-free quantities, such as vorticity, have to be introduced to estimate turbulence characteristics (see Colin et al. [147]).

5.5 DNS of turbulent premixed flames

The previous sections suggest that understanding and modeling turbulent premixed flames are often difficult because the knowledge of basic mechanisms controlling these flames is not sufficient. Direct numerical simulations (DNS) are powerful tools to analyze these mechanisms.

5.5.1 The role of DNS in turbulent combustion studies

Numerical techniques for DNS and specific limitations induced by reacting flows have been discussed in Section 4.6.2. This section is mainly devoted to an analysis of turbulent flame structures, in connection with RANS description. Explicit references to flamelet models, discussed in Section 5.3.6, will be made.

Flamelet models assume that turbulent reacting flows may be treated as collections of laminar flames convected, strained and curved by turbulence. Then, the following three questions may be specifically addressed using DNS:

1. When are flamelet assumptions valid? This question has been already discussed when DNS data was used to derive new turbulent combustion diagrams (§ 5.2.3).

2. Assuming the reacting flow field may be described in terms of flamelets, how is the local flame structure influenced by turbulence (§ 5.5.3)?

3. What is the amount of flame surface density (defined as the flame surface per unit volume) available for combustion (§ 5.5.5)?

[xl]A similar analysis should also be conducted in RANS to ensure a correct prediction of a laminar flame by turbulent combustion models. But, in practical simulations, Reynolds numbers are assumed to be very high and usual models are unable to describe a laminar flame when the turbulence level becomes zero. In LES, this point is much more important as the flame may become laminar and unwrinkled at the subgrid scale level, especially when the filter size Δ decreases.

In discussions of simulations and their implications for modeling, it is important to recognize that comparisons between turbulent combustion models (RANS or LES) and DNS may be carried out at two different levels:

- Some low-level modeling assumptions may be checked using DNS without performing any RANS or LES simulations (*a priori* testing). For example, flamelet assumptions, strain rate distributions, curvature probability density functions, occurrence of local quenching, or occurrence of counter-gradient transport may be evaluated using DNS results only.

- On the other hand, global comparisons between DNS and models may be carried out after simulations (*a posteriori* testing) by computing the same flame with DNS and with RANS (or LES). For example, the total reaction rate (or equivalently the turbulent flame speed) obtained from DNS may be compared to model predictions for the same flow conditions.

5.5.2   DNS database analysis

Different levels of DNS analysis

RANS and LES models are based on a number of assumptions related to the structure of flames embedded in turbulence which are difficult to check experimentally. DNS has been commonly used in the last twenty years to investigate these questions. This section presents some DNS results to illustrate the potential and the limits of these approaches.

The first issue is to define the relevant quantities to be extracted from DNS. A flame front, and correspondingly a direction of strong inhomogeneity (along the normal to the flame front) may be identified in most turbulent premixed flames. In this situation, four levels of analysis may be developed (Fig. 5.51):

- Level 0: each quantity $f(\mathbf{x})$ is analyzed instantaneously and individually, for example to build probability density functions. This most obvious data processing equally suits DNS data and experimental measurements based on laser point measurements. In the following, the data processing is oriented towards flamelet analysis and this single point analysis is no longer retained.

- Level 1: if a thin flame front is identified, each flame element may be analyzed along its normal direction. Variables are a function of the position along the local flame normal direction.

- Level 2: ensemble-averaged quantities are extracted from DNS taking mean values over flame elements located at similar positions along the mean flame normal direction: averaged variables are then functions of the coordinate normal to the mean flame front position or of a characteristic variable which changes monotonically from one side of the flame to the other like the mean reduced temperature $\widetilde{\Theta}$.

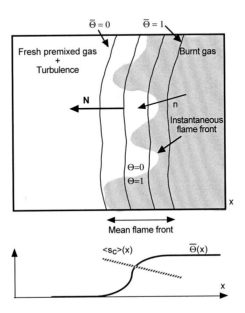

Figure 5.51: Post processing of DNS of turbulent premixed flames. n denotes the normal vector to the local instantaneous flame front ($0 < \Theta < 1$) whereas N is the normal vector to the mean flame front (defined by $\overline{\Theta}$) and gives the mean propagation direction.

- Level 3: space-average variables are determined at this level by integration over a volume larger than the flame brush thickness so that the result integrates all flamelets present in the flame brush.

Consider for example the fuel consumption speed defined by Eq. (2.102):

$$s_c = -\frac{1}{\rho_1 Y_F^1} \int_{-\infty}^{+\infty} \dot{\omega}_F \, d\mathbf{n} \qquad (5.152)$$

The consumption speed s_c is a physical property of the local instantaneous flame front and characterizes the inner structure of the reaction zone. Now s_c may be averaged in planes parallel to the mean flame front: in a DNS where the mean flame propagation is the x -axis, averaging s_c for all flame elements found in a $y - z$ plane provides a mean speed $< s_c >$ which is a function of x only. Finally $< s_c >$ may be averaged along x (or equivalently s_c may be averaged along the whole flame surface or over the all DNS volume) to yield a space-averaged quantity $<\widehat{s_c}>$:

$$\boxed{<\widehat{s_c}> = \frac{1}{A_T}\int_{A_T} s_c dA}$$

(5.153)

where A_T is the total flame surface area in the volume of interest V and dA designates a flame surface element. These three flame speeds s_c, $< s_c >$ and $<\widehat{s_c}>$ describe different aspects of the flame/turbulence interaction (Table 5.5).

LEVEL	Quantity	
LOCAL	s_c	function of position along the flame surface
ENSEMBLE AVERAGED (RANS) or SPATIAL FILTERING (LES)	$< s_c >$	function of location along direction normal to the mean flame front
SPACE AVERAGED	$<\widehat{s_c}>$	independent of space coordinates

Table 5.5: Levels of analysis used to interpret DNS results.

One common assumption of current flamelet models is that each flame element behaves like a steady laminar stagnation point flame submitted to a turbulent strain rate κ acting in its tangent plane. It is not always clear whether this is assumed at the local level or at some (ensemble or space) averaged level. In fact, the degree of attention that one should pay to the local flame features depends on the modeling objectives. For example, the mean reaction rate $\langle\widehat{\omega}_F\rangle$ within a given volume V is determined by the product of the space-averaged consumption speed times the flame surface area A_T per unit volume:

$$\langle\widehat{\omega}_F\rangle = \rho_1 Y_1 <\widehat{s_c}> \frac{A_T}{V}$$

(5.154)

Note that A_T in Eq. (5.154) is a global space-averaged statistical mean as well. In this expression, a detailed description of the local flame speed s_c is not required because only the space-averaged speed $<\widehat{s_c}>$ is used. However, when properties like flame quenching or pollutant formation are studied, a more accurate description of the local flame structure becomes necessary and mean values like $<\widehat{s_c}>$ are no longer sufficient.

DNS studies of the links between the local values of s_c are first described (§ 5.5.3) because they do not rest on a specific model. The other levels are considered next together with their implications for turbulent combustion modeling.

Analyzing flamelet models using DNS

Most turbulent combustion models are based on a flamelet assumption, where the flame remains sufficiently thin, compared to turbulence length scales, and the inner flame structure is close to a laminar flame. Model derivations are often conducted for infinitely thin flame fronts (see, for example, BML analysis in § 5.1.3). Unfortunately, flame fronts are not thin in DNS because the inner flame structure has to be numerically resolved, using, at least, about eight to ten grid points in simple chemistry (see § 4.6.3). Accordingly, DNS data analysis in developing flamelet models should be conducted with care. This point, illustrated in Fig. 5.52, is important and may lead to misunderstandings.

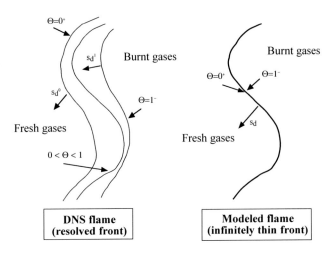

Figure 5.52: DNS data analysis. The flame resolved in DNS is not infinitely thin while most models assume a zero thickness front.

When assuming an infinitely thin flame front, the first step is to identify the relevant iso-Θ surface for analysis. Generally, a given value of $\Theta = \Theta^*$, corresponding to the maximum value of the reaction rate in planar laminar flames is retained ($\Theta^* \approx 0.8$), as done in most processed results presented below. Nevertheless, this iso-surface may not be representative of the overall flame properties. For example, Θ^* may not correspond to the maximum reaction rate when the flame front is wrinkled.

An important flame property is the front displacement speed, s_d (see § 2.7.1), denoting the speed of the flame front relatively to unburnt gases ($\Theta = 0$). This quantity is difficult to extract from DNS: the local displacement speed s_d^* (i.e. the displacement speed of the iso-surface Θ^*, relative to the local flow speed) may be computed using Eq. (2.101). The speed required for modeling is not this displacement speed but the global speed of the flame (supposed to have zero thickness) relative to the fresh gases s_d. In a laminar flame, these speeds are linked by $\rho_0 s_d = \rho^* s_d^*$, where ρ_0 and ρ^* are respectively the density for $\Theta = 0$ (fresh gases) and for $\Theta = \Theta^*$. Using the same law in a turbulent flame gives an estimate for s_d

which measures (approximately because the density correction is based on a one-dimensional analysis) the displacement speed of the iso-surface Θ^* relatively to fresh gases. Nevertheless, this displacement speed does not characterize the global flame displacement speed relatively to fresh gases but only the chosen Θ^*-level. If the flame thickness is locally changing, isolevels of Θ^* may have different displacement speed values: Fig. 5.53 shows probability density distributions of s_d^* versus Θ^* extracted from two-dimensional flame/turbulence interactions DNS (Hilka [290]). For $\Theta^* = 0.2$, the distribution is shifted towards negative values denoting that the corresponding iso-surface is mainly moving towards the burnt gases. On the other hand, for $\Theta^* = 0.9$, most values are positive (iso-surface moving towards fresh gases). In this situation, the flame front thickness is mainly decreasing at the observed time. More generally, the fact that the displacement speed pdf are not Dirac functions simply shows that this pdf contains information on the "global" front speed but also on its thickness evolution with time. It also demonstrate how much care must be taken when Θ^* value is chosen to post-process DNS data: negative displacement speeds obviously have no meaning in the initial framework of thin flamelets and many authors can get confused by the analysis of their DNS.

To overcome this difficulty, it is possible to introduce an integrated displacement speed (Hilka [290]), measuring the overall flame displacement:

$$\widehat{s}_d = \int_0^l s_d \, d\mathbf{n} \tag{5.155}$$

where the integration is performed along the local normal to the flame front. This "global" analysis always provides positive flame front displacement speeds, with a mean value around the laminar flame speed s_L, as shown in Fig. 5.53. This analysis is obviously closely related to the "generalized" flame surface density proposed by Veynante and Vervisch [678] and briefly described in § 5.3.6.

5.5.3   Studies of local flame structures using DNS

Effects of strain, curvature and stretch on flamelet structure

Flamelet models assume that the local reactive layer is similar to a steady laminar flame submitted to the same local strain rate (§ 5.3). DNS results show that the local reactive layer structure is more complex and that curvature and unsteady effects, in addition to strain, also control the local physical structure of the reaction zone, at least in certain regimes (Haworth and Poinsot [276], Rutland and Trouvé [579], Poinsot et al. [523]). The typical configuration used for such studies is displayed in Fig. 5.51: an initially planar flame is placed at $t = 0$ in a flow in which a "synthetic" turbulence has been generated.

DNS showing the importance of flame curvature were first obtained by Ashurst et al. [20]. Computations of constant density two-dimensional flames submitted to random vortex excitations indicated that the Lewis number was a controlling parameter (the Lewis number is the ratio of thermal to species diffusivity). For $Le = 0.5$, the flame developed an instability similar to those found in laminar flames studies (Clavin [136], Buckmaster and Ludford [95]).

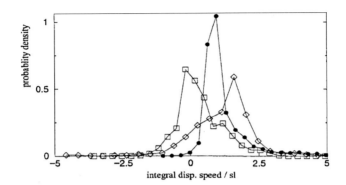

Figure 5.53: Probability density distributions of displacement speed s_d, relative to the fresh gases. Rectangles: $\Theta^* = 0.2$; Diamonds $\Theta^* = 0.9$; Dots: integrated displacement speed across the flame front, $\widehat{s}_d$, according to Eq. (5.155) (Hilka [290]).

Flame elements which are convex towards the unburnt mixture receive proportionally more fresh reactants than they lose heat, their flame speed increases and they propagate even faster towards the fresh gases. This leads to a strong growth of the flame surface and to an unstable development of perturbations.

The local physical structure of premixed flames embedded in homogeneous turbulent flow fields was investigated with a two-dimensional variable density code (Haworth and Poinsot [277]), a three-dimensional constant density code (Rutland and Trouvé [579, 580]) and various three-dimensional variable density codes (Trouvé and Poinsot [652], Rutland and Cant [576], Boughanem and Trouvé [77]). Interestingly enough, all these codes provided similar correlations between flame speeds, curvature and strain. Fig. 5.54 shows the strong relation found between the local flame speed s_c and the flame front curvature $1/R$ especially for Lewis numbers differing from unity (Rutland and Trouvé [579]). Consistent with laminar flame theory, the correlation between the local curvature $1/R$ and the local flame speed s_c depends on the Lewis number: no correlation is found for a unity Lewis number, and opposite effects are observed for Lewis numbers greater or smaller than unity.

While curvature effects are generally neglected, compression effects may be also ignored arguing that the flame front tends to align locally with the most extensive strain rate direction (Ashurst et al. [19], Rutland and Trouvé [579]) so that the average tangential strain rate along the flame surface is positive ($\langle \widehat{\kappa} \rangle > 0$). Therefore positively stretched flame elements are more probable than compressed elements. DNS results also indicate that negatively stretched (compressed) elements exist along the flame sheet (Yeung et al. [721], Cant et al. [113]) and should be considered in the modeling.

As argued in the RANS framework (§ 5.2.3), stretch (defined in § 2.6) is the natural parameter to use in a flamelet approach for turbulent combustion: since it incorporates both

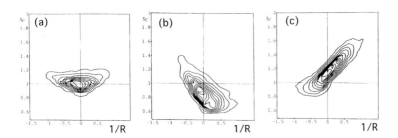

Figure 5.54: Correlation between local curvature $1/R$ and local consumption speed s_c for three values of the Lewis number: (a) Lewis=1, (b) Lewis=1.2 and (c) Lewis = 0.8 (Rutland and Trouvé [579]).

curvature and strain effects, it should offer a proper interface between flamelet libraries and turbulent flame elements. However, attempts to obtain such correlations from DNS data with simple chemistry models have failed for the moment. For example correlations of s_c with local flame stretch do not reveal a clear trend (Haworth and Poinsot [276]). More generally, the estimation of stretch is quite difficult because it involves calculations of velocity derivatives in one plane and also because it requires an evaluation of the displacement velocity s_d.

Unsteadiness also determines in many ways the local flamelet structure (Trouve [651]). The response time of a premixed flame is of the order of the flame transit time and is not always negligible. High strain rates generated by turbulence usually last for a time which is inverse to this strain rate, i.e. a short time. This time may be not sufficient for the flame to react to the straining field: the flame structure then does not match the prediction of a steady flamelet library (Meneveau and Poinsot [432]). To refine the treatment of this problem (i.e. to take into account the flamelet response time), one needs a better understanding of the persistence of strain in turbulent flows, a property that is at present not well quantified. The challenge is to follow a flame element and compare time histories of strain rate and flame dynamics (Yeung et al. [721]).

Practical implications for flame speeds used in flamelet models

Averaged flame speeds such as $< s_c >$ or $< s_d >$ may be extracted from DNS (Fig. 5.51) and plotted in terms of the progress variable $\overline{\Theta}$ instead of N (by definition, the mean progress variable $\overline{\Theta}$ is a monotonic function of N).

Variations of $< s_c >$ (Fig. 5.55) and $< s_d >$ (Fig. 5.56) with $\overline{\Theta}$ show that the flamelets do not burn or move at the same speeds when they are at the leading edge of the flame brush ($\overline{\Theta} = 0$) or at the trailing edge ($\overline{\Theta} = 1$) and that this behavior is Lewis number dependent (Trouvé and Poinsot [652]). A first transition is observed for the consumption speed at $Le = 1$. Below this value (see $Le = 0.8$ in Fig. 5.55), the flame elements at the leading edge of the flame brush burn faster than at the trailing edge indicating a possible instability. However,

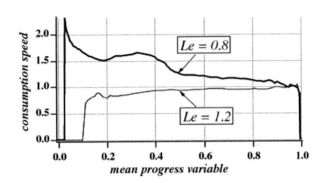

Figure 5.55: Evolution of the consumption speed $< s_c >$ (normalized by s_L^0) versus progress variable $\overline{\Theta}$ for the 3D DNS of Trouvé and Poinsot [652] (Reprinted with permission by Cambridge University Press) for two different Lewis numbers.

these flame elements still move more slowly than at the trailing edge of the flame as shown in Fig. 5.56 so that the flame brush thickness does not grow rapidly.

If the Lewis number is decreased further (see $Le = 0.3$ in Fig. 5.56), the displacement speed of the leading edge takes large values, an effect which is characteristic of the formation of fingers of burnt gases growing into the fresh gases. This dramatically increases the total flame surface and the reaction rate as shown in Fig. 5.57 (Trouvé and Poinsot [652]).

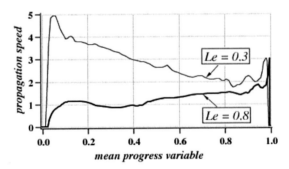

Figure 5.56: Evolution of the displacement speed $< s_d >$ (normalized by s_L^0) versus progress variable $\overline{\Theta}$ for the 3D DNS of Trouvé and Poinsot [652] (Reprinted with permission by Cambridge University Press) for two different Lewis numbers.

Flamelet models do not use velocities depending on $\overline{\Theta}$ such as $< s_c >$ or $< s_d >$ because they need space-averaged quantities such as $< \widehat{s_c} >$. The main issue is then to estimate

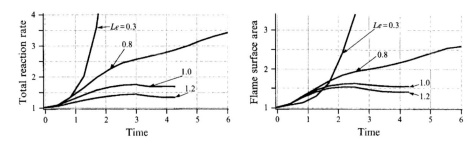

Figure 5.57: Total reaction rate (left) and total flame surface area (right) plotted as a function of time, made non-dimensional using the initial turbulent eddy turnover time, for various Lewis number Le in the 3D DNS of Trouvé and Poinsot [652] (Reprinted with permission by Cambridge University Press).

$< \widehat{s_c} >$ from quantities given by Reynolds or Favre average transport equations. For example, assumptions like those given in Table 5.5 are typically used to relate $< \widehat{s_c} >$ and the strain rate $\langle \widehat{\kappa} \rangle$ (see Table 5.6). The function f is obtained either from simple relations derived from asymptotics and experiments (Law et al. [371], Law [369], Searby and Quinard [599], Clavin and Williams [141]) or from numerical computations of laminar steady stagnation point flames, including complex chemistry which are stored in so called flamelet libraries (Giovangigli and Smooke [238], Rogg [566]). The h function is usually supposed to be equal to f without other justification than a fast chemistry assumption.

LEVEL	Stretch	Flame speed	Relation	
LOCAL	κ	s_c	s_c	$= \quad f(\kappa)$
ENSEMBLE AVERAGED	$\langle \kappa \rangle$	$< s_c >$	$< s_c >$	$= \quad g(\langle \kappa \rangle)$
SPACE AVERAGED	$\langle \widehat{\kappa} \rangle$	$< \widehat{s_c} >$	$< \widehat{s_c} >$	$= \quad h(\langle \widehat{\kappa} \rangle)$

Table 5.6: Flamelet models for the consumption speeds at the different levels of analysis.

As indicated in the case of simple chemistry calculations (§ 5.5.4), curvature is locally more important than strain rate so that local stretch and local flame speed do not correlate ($s_c \neq f(\kappa)$). These findings tend to invalidate flamelet models which consider elementary strained plane laminar flames as the prototype configuration for turbulent combustion and to make the search for a proper h function an impossible task. However, local quantities are not critical in flamelet models. For example, Eq. (5.154) shows that the reaction rate at a given point of the computational mesh only requires quantities that are space-averaged over the computational volume, like the flamelet speed $< \widehat{s_c} >$: although the space-averaged model for $< \widehat{s_c} >$ may bear only a loose relation to the local physical structure of the flame front, this model is valuable if it provides good estimates for average quantities. For example, as shown by Rutland and Trouvé [579], Trouvé and Poinsot [652] or Haworth and Poinsot [277] in the case of two- or three-dimensional premixed flames in homogeneous turbulence, the pdfs of flame curvature are nearly symmetric with near-zero mean value. Since the correlation of s_c with curvature is roughly linear, curvature effects cancel out in the mean and the flamelet speed $< \widehat{s_c} >$ does not exhibit any significant dependence on curvature, as predicted by Bray [84] or Becker et al. [41]. While the local and instantaneous physical structure of the reaction zone does not correlate with the instantaneous strain rate acting on the flame, strain effects are still present as may be seen in Fig. 5.54 by slicing the joint pdfs along a line corresponding to zero curvature. When curvature is zero, only strain effects remain: depending on the value of the Lewis number, the local flame speeds s_c are shifted from the one-dimensional unstretched laminar value (increased for a Lewis number smaller than one, decreased otherwise). These trends are consistent with laminar flame theory (Libby et al. [391], Williams [710]) and have been observed in three-dimensional simulations with variable or constant density (Rutland and Trouvé [579], Trouvé and Poinsot [652]) as well as in two dimensional simulations with variable density and larger Reynolds numbers (Haworth and Poinsot [277]). Contrary to curvature effects, modifications of the flame structure due to turbulent straining do not cancel out when averaged along the flame surface and the flamelet speed $< \widehat{s_c} >$ is indeed affected by the mean strain. Hence, while curvature determines the local physical characteristics of the reaction zone, global features like the flamelet speed do not depend on curvature and they may be described in terms of the response of stagnation point flames to strain.

Recommendations for flame speeds in flamelet models

As far as models are concerned, an important question is to know whether information obtained from flamelet libraries can be applied to turbulent flames to obtain, for example, flame properties like $< \widehat{s_c} >$ and correlate these with the turbulent flow properties. As already seen, in the mean, curvature effects may be neglected and the problem is reduced to the determination of the function h relating the flamelet speed $< \widehat{s_c} >$ to the mean strain rate $\langle \widehat{\kappa} \rangle$. As a first approximation, this function h is assumed to have a laminar-like behavior (i.e. h coincides with the function f obtained from flamelet libraries) but this question remains open.[xli] Possible functional forms for h based on recent direct simulation results have been proposed (Bray and Cant [85], Haworth and Poinsot [277]), but this issue cannot be addressed before a proper model for the mean strain rate (averaged over a computational cell of the RANS code) is derived.

However, the problem may not be of great importance because variations of $< \widehat{s_c} >$ remain

---

[xli] A more refined option is to introduce a probability density function $p(\kappa)$ to describe the stretch distribution:

$$< \widehat{s_c} > = \int_0^{+\infty} s_c(\kappa) \, p(\kappa) \, d\kappa = \int_0^{+\infty} f(\kappa) \, p(\kappa) \, d\kappa$$

A log normal distribution is generally retained for $p(\kappa)$ (see § 6.4.5, Effelsberg and Peters [198]).

small when compared to the variation of other quantities which determine the total reaction rate: results of simulations (Ashurst et al. [20], Rutland and Trouvé [579], Haworth and Poinsot [276]) indicate that the flamelet speed $< \widehat{s_c} >$ only differs by 10 to 30 percent from the one-dimensional unstrained laminar value s_L^0 even for high turbulence levels. These results may serve as the basis to further simplifications in the models. In contrast, the flame surface density $\Sigma_T = A_T/V$ is a very strong function of the turbulent flow field and may change by an order of magnitude because of the stirring process associated with the turbulent motions. Hence, as far as modeling the time-averaged reaction rate is concerned, the evolution of the flame surface density (Cant et al. [112], Maistret et al. [415], Pope and Cheng [531], Duclos et al. [189]) appears to be the key problem (see § 5.5.5).

5.5.4 Complex chemistry simulations

The first DNS of turbulent premixed flames were derived assuming one-step irreversible chemistry (Table 4.19). After 1990, new DNS codes have been developed to incorporate complex chemistry. Results obtained for H_2-O_2 flames (Baum et al. [39]), for methane/air flames (Hilka et al. [291, 292], Echekki and Chen [196], Chen et al. [122], Tanahashi et al. [638]) or for propane/air flames (Haworth et al. [275], Jiménez et al. [311]) have rapidly shown that there are indeed differences between simple and complex chemistry computations. Furthermore these simulations open new possibilities for DNS as quantitative chemical information may now be extracted from them.

DNS with complex chemistry requires considerable computer resources. Instead of six balance equations (five to describe the flow field and one for the deficient species) in simple chemistry, $5 + M$ conservation equations have now to be solved, where M is the number of species, of the order to 10 to 100. Thermodynamic functions, transport coefficients (viscosity, conductivity, and binary diffusion coefficients) and reaction rates have also to be evaluated in terms of the local temperature and species mass fractions.

Numerical and physical models required for this type of computations are described for example in a series of papers on laminar cellular flames (Patnaik et al. [494], Patnaik and Kailasanath [491, 492]) or turbulent flames (Baum et al. [39], Echekki and Chen [196], Chen et al. [122, 120], Chen [121]). Implementations of such calculations even on supercomputers raise specific problems of memory and CPU times (Stoessel et al. [627], Chen et al. [120], Chen [121]). An additional difficulty is related to the treatment of boundary conditions when compressible solvers are used. Since the sound speed changes with the species mass fractions, identification of waves near boundaries, a basic ingredient of the specification of boundary conditions (Hirsch [294], Poinsot and Lele [519], Baum et al. [40], Moureau et al. [456]), becomes more complex (Chapt. 9).

Local flame structures obtained from complex chemistry DNS

Figure 5.58 shows an example of DNS results obtained for a very lean H_2/O_2 flame. The grid is two-dimensional and the Miller et al. [442] 9-species/19 reactions chemical scheme (Table 1.5) is used. Initial conditions correspond to a planar laminar flame interacting with

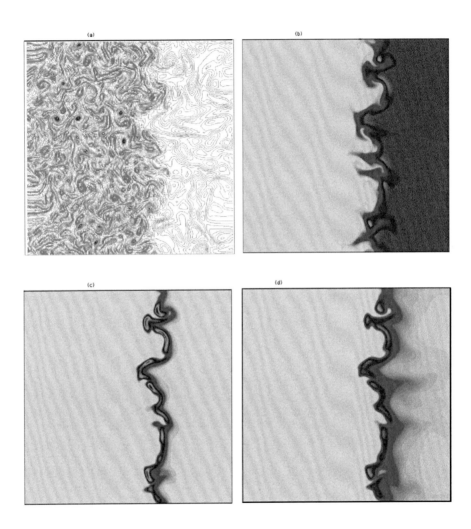

Figure 5.58: DNS of a turbulent H_2/O_2 flame with the 9-species/19-reactions Miller scheme (Baum et al. [39]. Reprinted with permission by Cambridge University Press): vorticity (a), temperature (b), heat release (c) and OH mass fraction (d) fields.

decaying turbulence, imposed at $t = 0$ according to a Von Kármán-Pao spectrum (Baum et al. [39]). The initial turbulent Reynolds number in the fresh gases $(u'l_t/\nu)$ is 289, the velocity (u'/s_L^0) and the length scale (l_t/δ_L^0) ratio are respectively 30 and 1.4. The equivalence ratio is 0.35. The fresh gases temperature is 300 K. The flame speed s_L^0 is 11 cm/s. The total box size is 2.5 cm in each direction. The figure is taken after one turnover time of the large scale perturbations at the initial time. Conclusions of Baum et al. [39] can be summarized as follows:

- Flames simulated with complex chemistry remain flamelet-like for most investigated cases. No quenching is observed along the flame front.

- Flames simulated with complex chemistry align preferentially along extensive strain rates like simple chemistry flames. The curvature pdfs remain symmetric with near-zero mean value.

- A striking difference with simple chemistry results is that complex chemistry flames are more sensitive to strain than simple chemistry flames. Their thickness changes strongly with strain and the local consumption speed s_c correlates rather well with strain, a result which is opposite to the one obtained with simple chemistry computations. However, like simple chemistry flames, the space-averaged flame speed $< \widehat{s_c} >$ remains of the order of the laminar flame speed s_L^0, except for unstable flames.

- Comparison of predictions of a flamelet library (based on planar steady strained flames with the same chemical and transport models as for the DNS) and DNS results was also given by (Baum et al. [39]). This result gives more credit to the flamelet library concept than simple chemistry computations did.

Direct numerical simulations and experimental imaging techniques

Valuable information for experiments may also be extracted from complex chemistry DNS. For example, the correlation between OH or CH radical levels in turbulent flames and the local reaction rate is often assumed to be strong enough so that OH or CH emission images (obtained for example using spontaneous or induced emission techniques, Khose-Hoinghaus and Jeffries [343]) may be interpreted qualitatively and sometimes quantitatively in terms of local reaction rate (Becker et al. [41], Samaniego [583], Samaniego and Mantel [584]).

For H_2/O_2 flames, the correlation between the maximum reaction rate along the flame front and the corresponding OH concentration [39] shows that OH may be used as an indicator of reaction rate in a turbulent flame only for very lean cases (equivalence ratio smaller than 0.5) and for cool reactants ($T < 400\,K$). For methane/air flames, the correlation between OH concentrations and reaction rate is much higher (simulation performed with 17 species and 45 reactions (Hilka et al. [292]). The correlation is even better when other radicals such as CH_2O are used as shown in Fig. 5.59. It is worth remembering that local concentrations obtained from DNS cannot be directly identified with the level of light emission from these species or to the fluorescence signal detected in laser induced fluorescence experiments. Emission is not

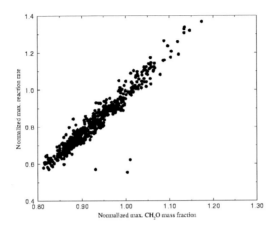

Figure 5.59: Correlation between CH_2O concentration and maximum reaction rate along the flame front for a turbulent methane/air flame (equivalence ratio = 1.0; T_u = 298 K) [291].

always linearly related to the local concentration of radicals. However, it is possible to infer the light emission level in some simple cases and to compare DNS results with experiments. This is done for example by Hilka et al. [292] or Mantel et al. [418] who use DNS results to interpret measurements of Samaniego and Mantel [584] for a methane-air flame interacting with a vortex pair.

5.5.5 Studying the global structure of turbulent flames with DNS

Flame surface geometry

DNS has been extensively used to study the statistics of the velocity derivatives in various turbulent non-reacting flows. These studies characterize the properties of the vorticity field and the structure of the strain rate tensor. For instance, DNS shows that the most probable structure for the strain rate tensor corresponds to two extensive and one compressive eigendirections and that the corresponding eigenvalues are well approximated by the ratios (3:1:-4) (Ashurst et al. [19], Yeung et al. [721]). Another result is that the vorticity vector tends to align with the intermediate strain rate eigendirection (Ashurst et al. [19]). DNS was also used to probe the simulated flows for the possible presence of coherent motions. For instance, one important result is that the intense vorticity tends to be organized in elongated, tube-like, coherent structures called "worms" (Kerr [336], She et al. [612], Ruetsch and Maxey [573], Vincent and Meneguzzi [690], Jiménez et al. [312]). The worms have a high probability for an extensional strain rate in the direction of the vorticity vector, i.e. along the axis of the vortex tube.

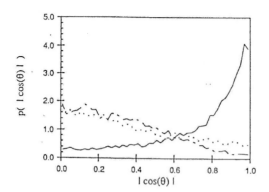

Figure 5.60: Probability density function of $|cos(\theta)|$, θ is the angle between the flame normal and the principle strain rate eigenvectors: compressive strain (solid line); intermediate strain (dashed line); extensive strain (long-dashed line). DNS of three-dimensional isotropic turbulence with constant density, single-step, Arrhenius kinetics chemistry (Reprinted by permission of Elsevier Science from Rutland and Trouvé [580] © the Combustion Institute).

Different objectives are adopted in studies of turbulent combustion where the vorticity field and the strain rate tensor are analyzed in the reaction zone, in a reference frame attached to the flame. One of the early objectives of three-dimensional DNS of turbulent flames was to determine the most probable local flame-flow configuration and in particular the orientation of the flame normal with respect to the local vorticity vector and strain rate eigenvectors. As shown in Fig. 5.60, the flame normal is found to align preferentially with the most compressive strain direction. This result is consistent with the flamelet picture of flame elements that are positively strained in their plane. Also, since vorticity tends to align with the intermediate strain direction (Ashurst et al. [19]), the vorticity vector is found to lie preferentially in the plane of the flame (Rutland and Trouvé [580]).

An important issue to quantify flame wrinkling is the local flame surface geometry. The local geometry of a three-dimensional flame surface is conveniently described using the curvature shape factor, H_k. Here, H_k is defined as the smallest principal curvature divided by the largest curvature and is constrained to lie between -1 and 1. When $H_k = -1$, the surface is a spherical saddle point ; when $H_k = 0$, the surface is cylindrically curved ; when $H_k = 1$, the surface is spherically curved. A typical DNS result is displayed in Fig. 5.61 where the most probable values for the shape factor are close to zero: the most probable shape for the flame surface is that of a cylinder (Pope et al. [537], Ashurst [15], Cant et al. [113], Rutland and Trouvé [580]). This result supports studies of two-dimensional, steady stretched cylindrical flames or studies of two-dimensional, unsteady flame/vortex interactions as relevant simplifications of three-dimensional problems.

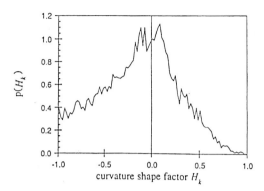

Figure 5.61: Probability density function of the flame curvature shape factor H_k. DNS of three-dimensional isotropic turbulence with constant density, single-step, Arrhenius chemistry (Reprinted by permission of Elsevier Science from Rutland and Trouvé [580] © the Combustion Institute).

Production and dissipation of flame surface area

In the flamelet regime, the flame is viewed as an infinitesimally thin, propagating surface progressing at variable speed into the turbulent premixed flow. To first order, the principal effect of turbulence in flamelet combustion is to wrinkle the flame surface through velocity fluctuations and greatly increase its total area. In the flamelet theory, this effect is described by the flame surface area per unit volume Σ, also called the flame surface density. The flamelet theory has produced an exact (but unclosed) evolution equation for the flame surface density, called the Σ-equation (Pope [530], Candel and Poinsot [109], Trouvé and Poinsot [652], Vervisch et al. [672], Veynante and Vervisch [678]) already described in § 5.3.6 (see Eq. (5.78)):

$$\frac{\partial \Sigma}{\partial t} + \frac{\partial \widetilde{u_i} \Sigma}{\partial x_i} + \frac{\partial \langle u_i'' \rangle_s \Sigma}{\partial x_i} + \frac{\partial \langle s_d n_i \rangle_s \Sigma}{\partial x_i} = \langle \kappa \rangle_s \Sigma, \qquad (5.156)$$

where the intervening quantities have been defined in Section 5.3.6.

Eq. (5.156) has the form of a standard turbulent transport equation where basic physical mechanisms like transport by the mean flow field, transport by the turbulent flow field, transport by flame propagation, production or destruction by flame stretch, are described explicitly. The Σ-equation provides a proper description of the flame surface dynamics and many current models for the mean reaction rate are based on modeled formulations of Eq. (5.156) (Duclos et al. [189]). Closure models are required in this equation, in particular for the turbulent diffusion velocity, $\langle u_i'' \rangle_s$, and for the turbulent flame stretch, $\langle \kappa \rangle_s$. DNS is well-suited to provide basic information on those quantities (Trouvé et al. [654]).

As seen in Eq. (5.156), the mean flame stretch, $\langle \kappa \rangle_s$, gives the local rate of change of mean flame surface area. If $\langle \kappa \rangle_s$ is positive, the mean flame surface grows locally; if negative, the mean flame surface contracts. The expression of flame stretch as a function of flow and flame quantities is given by Eq. (2.89):

$$\kappa = \nabla_t \cdot \vec{u} - s_d / \mathcal{R} \qquad (5.157)$$

where $\nabla_t \cdot \vec{u}$ is the strain rate acting in the flame tangent plane and $1/\mathcal{R}$ is the flame surface curvature, as given by the divergence of the flame normal vector: $1/\mathcal{R} = -\nabla.\vec{n}$. In the laminar flames of Fig. 2.20, either one of the two terms contributing to stretch was zero: stretched planar stagnation point flames have zero curvature while spherical flames have zero strain in the flame tangent plane. In a turbulent flame, both terms are expected to be important and DNS provides useful results on their respective orders of magnitude and on stretch. The mean flame stretch then features two components:

$$\langle \kappa \rangle_s = \langle \nabla_t \cdot \vec{u} \rangle_s - \langle s_d / \mathcal{R} \rangle_s \qquad (5.158)$$

Among these two components, the aerodynamic stretch $\langle \nabla_t \cdot \vec{u} \rangle_s$ has received the most attention since aerodynamic straining occurs in many turbulent flow problems and applies to propagating surfaces as well as to material surfaces. The statistical distribution of tangential strain rate, $\nabla_t \cdot \vec{u}$, has been described using DNS in a series of related studies: material surfaces evolving in stationary, isotropic turbulent flow (Yeung et al. [721]); passive propagating surfaces with infinitely fast chemistry and constant propagation speed s_d, evolving in stationary, isotropic turbulent flow (Girimaji and Pope [241]); passive flame surfaces with constant density, finite-rate chemistry, evolving in decaying, isotropic turbulent flow (Cant et al. [113], Rutland and Trouvé [580]); flame surfaces with variable density, finite-rate chemistry, evolving in decaying, isotropic turbulent flow (Trouvé and Poinsot [652]).

For material surfaces, the statistical properties of $\nabla_t \cdot \vec{u}$ are found to be related to the Kolmogorov scales. The surface-averaged value of $\nabla_t \cdot \vec{u}$ is then well approximated by:

$$\langle \nabla_t \cdot \vec{u} \rangle_s \approx 0.28 / \tau_k \qquad (5.159)$$

where $\tau_k = \sqrt{\varepsilon/\nu}$ is the Kolmogorov time scale (Yeung et al. [721]). Fig. 5.62 presents a typical probability density distribution of $\nabla_t \cdot \vec{u}$ and shows that while the mean stain rate is positive along a material surface, the probability for compressive straining is 20 %. Similar results are found in studies of propagating surfaces with infinitely fast or finite-rate chemistry, and low to moderate propagation speeds (Cant et al. [113], Girimaji and Pope [241], Rutland and Trouvé [580]). At high propagation speeds, propagating surfaces behave like randomly-oriented surfaces (Fig. 5.62) and the average strain rate decreases to zero (Girimaji and Pope [241]). These results provide valuable limiting cases of more general expressions used to predict the mean stretch experienced by a turbulent flame (Meneveau and Poinsot [432]).

Comparisons between model predictions and DNS results can also be used to test experimental methodologies. For instance, the flame surface density is a quantity that requires access to three-dimensional spatial information and that cannot be measured directly using current experimental techniques. In the Bray-Moss-Libby model (Eq. 5.72), the flame surface density is written as a flamelet crossing frequency, n_y, divided by a flamelet orientation factor, σ_y (Bray et al. [90], Bray [84]). The three-dimensional information is conveyed by the

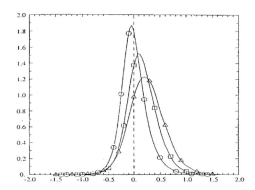

Figure 5.62: Probability density function of Kolmogorov-scaled stain rate, $\nabla_t \cdot \mathbf{u}/\sqrt{\varepsilon/\nu}$, acting on material and randomly-oriented surfaces: material surface with area-weighted statistics (triangles); material surface with unweighted statistics (squares); randomly-oriented surface (circles). Results obtained from three-dimensional, stationary, isotropic turbulence DNS (Reprinted by permission of Elsevier Science from Yeung et al. [721] © the Combustion Institute).

flamelet orientation factor, σ_y, assumed to be constant. This assumption is of great practical significance since it puts Σ at the level of n_y, *i.e.* at an experimentally accessible level. The crossing frequency n_y can be measured via, for example, thermocouple signals, Mie or Rayleigh scattering or laser tomography techniques. The assumption, $\sigma_y = constant$, is tested in Fig. 5.63 where σ_y is plotted across the turbulent flame brush, at two different instants in the simulations. The DNS test shows that the flamelet orientation factor is approximately constant in the simulations, $\sigma_y \approx 0.7$. This result is in agreement with the Bray-Moss-Libby formulation and supports experimental estimates of the flame surface density based on direct measurements of the flamelet crossing frequency.

DNS also allow refined comparisons between model predictions and experimental data. Scalar dissipation rates as well as flame surface densities entering combustion models are directly linked to the norm of the instantaneous three-dimensional gradient of the progress variable, $|\nabla\Theta|$ through Eqs (5.56) and (5.77), respectively. Unfortunately, most refined experiments are limited to two-dimensional measurements (planar imaging, Khose-Hoinghaus and Jeffries [343]).[xlii] The question is then: to what extent two-dimensional measurements of the instantaneous progress variable gradient, $|\nabla\Theta|$ may be used to infer their three-dimensional characteristics? This point is investigated by Hawkes et al. [273] for scalar dissipation rates and Halter et al. [266], Veynante et al. [685] and Hawkes et al. [274] for flame surface densities. Of course, additional assumptions are required to link two- and three-dimensional information:

[xlii]Note that some recent attempts to determine the instantaneous three-dimensional shape of turbulent flames may be found in literature (see, for example, Upton et al. [659]), but are still limited to simple configurations (Bunsen burner), require an important diagnostic set-up and cannot be routinely used.

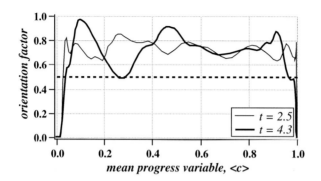

Figure 5.63: DNS of three-dimensional, variable density flames: variations of the flamelet orientation factor σ_y across the turbulent flame brush. The two solid curves correspond to two different instants in the simulations. The dashed line is the Bray-Moss-Libby prediction (Trouvé and Poinsot [652] Reprinted with permission by Cambridge University Press).

- For isotropic scalar field distributions, two- (Σ^{2D}) and three- (Σ^{3D}) flame surface densities are linked by (Veynante et al. [685], Hawkes et al. [274]):

$$\Sigma^{3D} = \frac{4}{\pi}\Sigma^{2D} \qquad (5.160)$$

so that 2D measurements underestimate the flame surface density by about 30%. Eq. (5.160) is well verified for high turbulence levels (Hawkes et al. [274]). Note that Hawkes et al. [274] also analyse the terms of the flame surface density balance equation under this isotropic assumption.

- Veynante et al. [685] propose a refined expression when the measuring plane contains the downstream direction, x, and is a plane of symmetry of the mean flow field, either by translation (slot burner) or by rotation (axisymmetric Bunsen burner):

$$\Sigma^{3D} = \left(\sqrt{1 + \langle n_y^{2D} n_y^{2D} \rangle_s^{2D} - \langle n_y^{2D} \rangle_s^{2D} \langle n_y^{2D} \rangle_s^{2D}} \right) \Sigma^{2D} \qquad (5.161)$$

where n_y^{2D} is the component of the unit vector normal to the instantaneous flame front in the transverse direction y, while $\langle \cdot \rangle_s^{2D}$ denotes average along the flame surface, both measured in the 2D plane. Equation (5.161) assumes that fluctuations in the transverse directions are similar in (y-direction) and out of (z-direction) the measuring plane. This expression gives excellent results even for isotropy (Veynante et al. [685], Hawkes et al. [274]) but requires the extraction of vectors normal to the flame front.

Figure 5.64 compares 2D measurements and estimations given by Eqs (5.160) and (5.161) to DNS results in the case of a turbulent axisymmetric Bunsen burner (Veynante et al. [685]). In this case, Eq. (5.161) provides excellent results while assuming isotropy tends to overestimate the flame surface density.

Turbulent V-shape flame

Most DNS are conducted in time decaying turbulence: an isotropic and homogeneous turbulence is set as initial conditions but is not sustained and decays with time. As no steady state is reached, statistical analysis should be conducted with care.[xliii] Being able to study the propagation of a turbulent flame into a non-decaying turbulent field is the topic of multiple DNS present studies. This can be achieved by adding a well-defined homogeneous isotropic turbulence to an inlet mean flow field. Because of the high numerical precision of DNS codes, this injection requires a careful treatment of acoustic waves in compressible codes that will not be detailed here (see Chapter 9 and Guichard [257], Vervisch et al. [673]. The situation is rather simple when the mean flow is supersonic because acoustic waves cannot travel upstream toward the domain inlet (see § 6.6.3). An alternative solution is to use low-Mach number codes (Alshaalan and Rutland [6]) if acoustic effects can be neglected.

The injection of turbulence through the numerical domain inlet gives access to mean steady state flow characteristics and to the extraction of relevant statistics. But another question arises: which type of flame should be studied? Two possibilities exist:

- (1) use a freely propagating flame (as done for most DNS of flames propagating in decaying turbulence) or

- (2) use a stabilized flame (for example a flame anchored on a rod).

Solution (1), the stabilization of a statistically one-dimensional freely propagating premixed flame in a turbulent flow field, is very difficult to obtain: it cannot be achieved experimentally and it is expected to be as difficult to create numerically because of the following reasons:

- The injected turbulence is stable over time but is spatially decaying as usual grid turbulence: when the premixed flame moves upstream, it encounters higher turbulence levels, is more wrinkled by turbulence motions, and propagates upstream faster. On the other hand, a premixed flame moving downstream finds lower turbulence levels and its wrinkling and its turbulent propagation speed decrease. The overall result is that the flame is intrinsically unstable.

- To achieve a statistically steady state would require either a very large inlet section or a continuous inlet flow speed adaptation and a large numerical domain to avoid flame elements at the leading or trailing edge of the flame from touching the boundaries of the computational domain.

[xliii]Statistics are generally extracted when an equilibrium is reached between flame wrinkling and decaying turbulence and time-averages can be identified as spatial averages because of the homogeneous flow field.

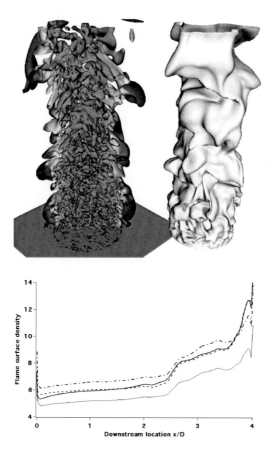

Figure 5.64: Top: DNS of a round turbulent jet flame: Q-criterion (left), visualizing vortices (Hussain and Jeong [301]), and flame surface (right). Bottom: downstream evolution of the total transverse flame surface density defined as $\Sigma^{tot} = \int_{-\infty}^{+\infty} \int_{-\infty}^{+\infty} \Sigma \, dy \, dz$, where y and z denote transverse directions. Bold line: true flame surface density as extracted from DNS; thin line: 2D measurements; bold dashed line: 3D flame surface reconstructed using Eq. (5.161); bold dotted-dashed line: 3D flame surface reconstructed assuming isotropy (Eq. 5.160). Flame surface densities are non-dimensionalised using the jet diameter D. From Veynante et al. [685].

- To avoid negative inlet speeds, low turbulence levels must be used (typically u' must be less than the mean inlet flow speed) for which the flame / turbulence interaction is weak and not of great interest.

Therefore solution (2) constitutes a better choice even though the stabilization must be mimicked by a ad hoc device. It also allows to use large inlet flow velocities and large turbulence intensities. An example of Solution (2) is given by Vervisch et al. [673] who investigate a V-shape flame evolving in a spatially decaying homogeneous isotropic turbulence (Fig. 5.65). The flame is stabilized by a local energy release mimicking a hot wire found in some experiments. Two separate Navier-Stokes solvers evolve simultaneously in time: a DNS spectral solver generates a forced synthetic grid-turbulence which is fed into a combustion DNS code for the flame zone.

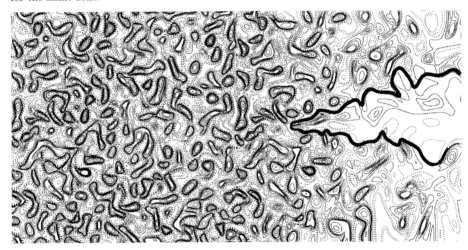

Figure 5.65: Instantaneous snapshot of a premixed methane/air V-shape flame stabilized in a spatially decaying turbulence. The vorticity field (continuous lines: positive values; dashed lines: negative vorticity values) is superimposed to the reaction rate (bold lines). The turbulent flow in the left part of the domain is generated by the spectral code. The flame develops in the turbulence in the right part. The velocity ratio comparing the inlet turbulent velocity u' to the laminar flame speed s_L^0 is $u'/s_L^0 = 1.25$. (L. Vervisch, 2004, private communication; see also Vervisch et al. [673]). An animation of this computation is available at *elearning.cerfacs.fr/combustion/illustrations/V-Flame-Vervisch/*.

When a statistically steady state is reached, various statistics can be extracted from the mean flow field. For example, Fig. 5.66 displays the mean progress variable $\widetilde{\Theta}$ obtained when averaging instantaneous fields of Fig. 5.65, corresponding to a V-shape flame, as expected. The profiles of the progress variable turbulent fluxes $\widetilde{u''\Theta}$ are displayed for three downstream locations and two initial turbulence levels in Fig. 5.67: in agreement with the analysis proposed in Section 5.1.3 (Fig. 5.10 and Table 5.1) and the large eddy simulations in Section 5.4.6 (Figs. 5.49 and 5.50), these turbulent fluxes are of gradient type in the vicinity of the flame stabilization point and become counter-gradient further downstream. Note also that the BML expression (Eq. 5.17) provides satisfactory estimates of the turbulent fluxes, even though the flame is not strictly infinitely thin in the DNS.

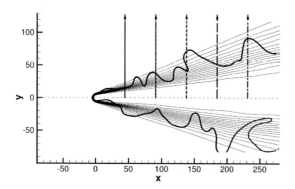

Figure 5.66: Favre averaged progress variable $\widetilde{\Theta}$ field obtained from instantaneous fields similar to Fig. 5.65. Fourteen levels between $\widetilde{\Theta} = 0.1$ and $\widetilde{\Theta} = 0.98$ are displayed (thin lines). An instantaneous field of the burning rate is superimposed (bold lines). Locations where profiles are extracted are evidenced by vertical lines (L. Vervisch, 2004, private communication; see also Vervisch et al. [673]).

These DNS have also been used to test an improved model for the scalar dissipation rate $\widetilde{\chi}_\Theta$ of the progress variable. This scalar dissipation rate is linked to the mean reaction rate in the Bray-Moss-Libby model framework (Eq. 5.56) and is found in the balance equation for the variance $\widetilde{\Theta''^2}$ (Eq. 5.108). It is usually modelled assuming a linear relaxation as $\widetilde{\chi}_\Theta = \widetilde{\Theta''^2}/\tau_t$ (Eq. 5.58) where τ_t is a turbulent time that may be estimated from the turbulent kinetic energy k and its dissipation rate ε as $\tau_t = k/\varepsilon$. Taking advantage of the relations between modeling tools derived by Veynante and Vervisch [678], Vervisch et al. [673] propose to rely on the scalar dissipation rate $\widetilde{\chi}_\Theta$ to the flame surface density Σ as:

$$\overline{\rho}\widetilde{\chi}_\Theta = \overline{2\rho D \left|\nabla\Theta\right|^2} \approx (2\Theta_m - 1)\, \rho_0 s_L^0 \Sigma \tag{5.162}$$

where ρ_0 is the fresh gas density and Θ_m has been introduced in Eq. (5.57). The derivation is beyond the scope of this book and the reader is referred to the above paper for details.[xliv] As evidenced in Fig. 5.68, this model provides good results.

[xliv]Eq. (5.162) is actually a model for the scalar dissipation rate $2\rho D |\nabla\Theta|^2$ when Eq. (5.108) requires a model for $2\rho D |\nabla\Theta''|^2$. These two quantites are linked by:

$$\overline{2\rho D|\nabla\Theta|^2} = \overline{2\rho D|\nabla\widetilde{\Theta}|^2} + \overline{4\rho D|\nabla\Theta''||\nabla\widetilde{\Theta}|} + \overline{2\rho D|\nabla\Theta''|^2}$$

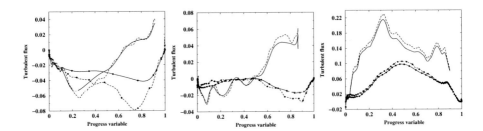

Figure 5.67: Axial turbulent fluxes $\widetilde{u''\Theta}$ extracted at three locations corresponding, from left to right, to the first, third and fifth lines in Fig. 5.66. Two initial turbulence levels $u'/s_L^0 = 1.25$ (lines with symbols) and $u'/s_L^0 = 2.5$ (lines) are plotted. Dashed lines correspond to the BML expression (Eq. 5.17). From L. Vervisch (2004, private communication), see also Vervisch et al. [673].

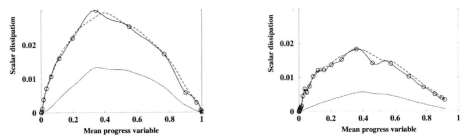

Figure 5.68: Transverse profiles of scalar dissipation rate $\widetilde{\chi}_\Theta$ extracted from DNS (lines with circles), modelled by a linear relaxation assumption $\widetilde{\chi}_\Theta = (\varepsilon/k)\widetilde{\Theta''^2}$ (lines) and model of Eq. 5.162) (dashed lines). Profiles extracted along left vertical line in Fig. 5.66 for two turbulence levels: $u'/s_L^0 = 1.25$ (left) and $u'/s_L^0 = 2.5$ (right). Private communication by L. Vervisch (see also Vervisch et al. [673]).

5.5.6 DNS analysis for large eddy simulations

DNS databases can also be used to investigate subgrid scale models for large eddy simulations (LES). Compared to the analysis performed for RANS models in the previous sections, the only major difference is the averaging procedure (Table 5.5) where ensemble averaging (or

---

where the two first terms of the RHS are usually neglected assuming a large Reynolds number (see § 6.4.3). Obviously, $\overline{2\rho D|\nabla\Theta''|^2}$ should vanish when $\widetilde{\Theta''^2}$ goes to zero while $\overline{2\rho D|\nabla\Theta|^2}$ is expected to go to $\overline{2\rho D|\nabla\widetilde{\Theta}|^2}$. This difficulty is addressed in Vervisch et al. [673] who propose the simple correction:

$$\overline{2\rho D|\nabla\Theta''|^2} \approx \frac{\widetilde{\Theta''^2}}{\widetilde{\Theta}\left(1 - \widetilde{\Theta}\right)} (2\Theta_m - 1) \rho_0 s_L^0 \Sigma$$

which has been successfully used in Eq. (5.108) by Fiorina et al. [214].

time averaging) procedures must be replaced by spatial filtering (see § 4.7.1).

For example, starting from a DNS of a premixed flame front interacting with three-dimensional decaying isotropic homogenous turbulence (Fig. 4.8), terms in the filtered progress variable balance equation (5.144) may be extracted for model analysis (Fig. 5.69). In this situation, filtered laminar diffusion fluxes are not negligible (as generally assumed in RANS) and of the same order as the unresolved convective fluxes.

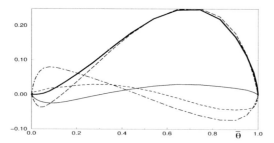

Figure 5.69: Terms of the $\widetilde{\Theta}$-balance equation (5.144). Resolved $\nabla.(\overline{\rho}\widetilde{u}\widetilde{\Theta})$ ($-\,-\,-$) and unresolved convective fluxes $\nabla.[\overline{\rho}(\widetilde{u\Theta} - \widetilde{u}\widetilde{\Theta})]$ ($-\!\!-\!\!-$), molecular diffusion $\overline{\nabla.(\rho D\nabla\Theta)}$ ($-\,-\,-\,-$) and reaction rate $\overline{\dot{\omega}}_\Theta$ ($-\!\!\!-\!\!\!-$) vs filtered progress variable $\overline{\Theta}$. The unsteady term $\partial\overline{\rho}\widetilde{\Theta}/\partial t$ ($-\cdot-$) is estimated from the sum of the other terms of Eq. (5.144). All terms normalized by $\rho_u s_L/\delta_L$ (Boger et al. [65]).

Subgrid scale flame surface densities (Eq. (5.145)) may also be extracted (Fig. 5.70), validating a BML-like subgrid scale flame surface density model (Eq. (5.73)).

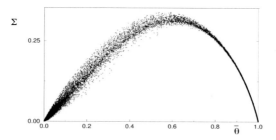

Figure 5.70: Subgrid scale flame surface density (Eq. 5.145) versus filtered progress variable $\overline{\Theta}$. Flame surface densities are normalized by $1/\delta_L^0$ (Boger et al. [65]).

5.5.7   DNS of realistic premixed combustors

Until 2006, most DNS were performed with solvers using structured single-block meshes and finite difference (or spectral) algorithms. An advantage of these techniques is that high-order numerical methods can be used and that their CPU efficiency is very high. An obvious drawback is that they are limited to simple geometries and can not be used in real combustors. This explains why most DNS were performed in cubic boxes or in situations where the geometry could be described with very simple meshes. Recently, progresses in CFD methods and increase of CPU powers have brought two essential new capacities (Gourdain et al. [250], Chen et al. [120], Moureau et al. [457, 458], Chen [121]): (1) the number of points has increased from typically 1 million to 1 billion points and (2) high-order efficient schemes can now be used on unstructured meshes. As a consequence, DNS can now be performed in real systems (Bell et al. [44], Sankaran et al. [586], Moureau et al. [458]). Even if this is true only for small, low pressure combustors using simplified chemistry descriptions, this is a major breakthrough which will allow to study flame structures in real cases and not only in cubic boxes: swirled flames for example are difficult to study with classical DNS tools but can be tackled with these new DNS codes on unstructured meshes.

One example of recent DNS is given here using the results of Moureau et al. [458] who performed a low-Mach number DNS of the PRECCINSTA burner (described in Section 10.2 where it is computed with compressible LES techniques on grids of the order of 1 to 10 million cells). Using new numerical methods for reacting flows on unstructured grids, Moureau et al repeated this computation on a 2.6 billion cell grid on which no LES subgrid model is necessary for the flame or the flow.

Fig. 5.71 shows an instantaneous view (for the non-reacting flow) of the so-called "Q" criterion (Hussain and Jeong [301]) which visualizes vortices and shows the very wide range of scales captured by DNS in such a complex geometry. With combustion, Fig. 5.72 displays a field of instantaneous reaction rate showing all wrinkling scales which are fully resolved on the grid. In such a DNS, all scales present in the swirled region are resolved and the flame front itself is meshed. As a result, the turbulent flow can be completely analyzed. Moreover, the DNS results can be used to check RANS or LES subgrid models in a realistic case (Moureau et al. [458]). Note that even at this level of mesh refinement, such computations are not yet true DNS near walls where boundary layers would require finer meshes. For the shear regions and for the flame itself where most of the important phenomena take place, this is not a major issue but it will become one when such computations will be used to analyze the structure of the flow created in the swirlers for example where walls have important effects.

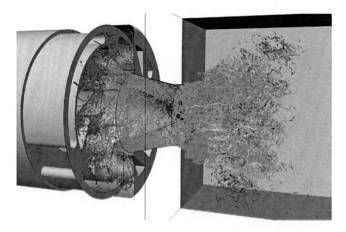

Figure 5.71: Instantaneous snapshot of Q criterion in a swirled premixed methane/air combustor (see description in Section 10.2). An animation of this computation is available at *elearning.cerfacs.fr/combustion/illustrations/moureau-short/*.

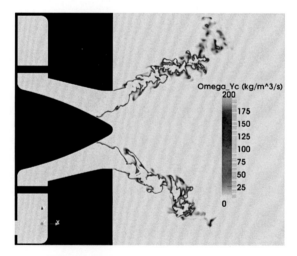

Figure 5.72: Instantaneous snapshot of reaction rate in a swirled premixed methane/air combustor (see description in Section 10.2). An animation of this computation is available at *elearning.cerfacs.fr/combustion/illustrations/Moureau-hot/*.

Chapter 6

Turbulent non premixed flames

6.1 Introduction

Turbulent non-premixed flames are encountered in a large number of industrial systems for two main reasons. First, compared to premixed flames, non-premixed burners are simpler to design and to build because a perfect reactant mixing, in given proportions, is not required. Non-premixed flames are also safer to operate as they do not exhibit propagation speeds and cannot flashback or autoginite in undesired locations.[i] Accordingly, turbulent non-premixed flame modeling is a usual challenge assigned to combustion codes in industrial applications.

Most mechanisms described for turbulent premixed flames (Chapt. 5) are also found in non-premixed flames: flame-generated vorticity, viscous effects, stretching. But specific processes make non-premixed flames probably more difficult to understand and to describe than turbulent premixed flames. First, reacting species have to reach, by molecular diffusion, the flame front before reaction. Hence, non-premixed flames are also called diffusion flames. During this travel, they are exposed to turbulence and their diffusion speeds may be strongly modified by turbulent motions. The overall reaction rate is often limited by the species molecular diffusion towards the flame front. Then, in many models, the chemical reaction is assumed to be fast, or infinitely fast, compared to transport processes.

Section 6.2 presents the physics of diffusion flames and their specificities in terms of flame structure and stabilization mechanisms. The different combustion regimes for turbulent non-premixed flames are discussed in Section 6.3. RANS models for non-premixed flames are described in Section 6.4 while Section 6.5 presents LES techniques. Finally, a few recent DNS results are given in Section 6.6.

---

[i]However, as burning in premixed regimes is the only way to control maximum flame temperatures (see § 3.3.3), and then nitric oxide emissions, there is now a clear tendency to promote reactant premixing in practical applications.

6.2   Phenomenological description

6.2.1   Typical flame structure: jet flame

A typical example of turbulent non-premixed flame is displayed in Fig. 6.1, providing the large eddy simulation (LES) instantaneous resolved temperature field of the so-called methane/air jet "Sandia D-flame."[ii] This long flame exhibits the usual features of diffusion flames: an initial zone near the injection orifice where the flame is thin and a downstream region where the burnt gases occupy a large portion of the domain. Small premixed flames (pilot flames) are used to stabilize the flame near the jet exit. Fig. 6.1 corresponds to an instantaneous flame view. Direct observation provides an average view displayed in Fig. 6.2. Examples of RANS computation for this flame are also displayed in Fig. 6.2. Understanding and modeling such flames are the objectives of the numerical tools described in this chapter.

6.2.2   Specific features of turbulent non-premixed flames

Compared to premixed flames, turbulent non-premixed flames exhibit some specific features that have to be taken into account, and may lead to additional difficulties, in combustion modeling. This section briefly discusses and summarizes some of these features.

First, non-premixed flames do not propagate: they are located where fuel and oxidizer meet. This property is useful for safety purposes but it also has consequences on the chemistry/interaction turbulence: without propagation speed, a non-premixed flame is unable to impose its own dynamics on the flow field and is more sensitive to turbulence. Diffusion flames are also more sensitive to stretch than turbulent premixed flames: critical stretch values for extinction of diffusion flames are one order of magnitude smaller than for premixed flames. A diffusion flame is more likely to be quenched by turbulent fluctuations and flamelet assumptions are not justified as often as for turbulent premixed combustion.

Important points are in buoyancy, natural convection and entrainment effects. Buoyancy effects have already been evidenced in turbulent premixed flames (see § 5.1.2) but may be enhanced in non-premixed flames: pressure gradients or gravity forces induce differential effects on fuel, oxidizer and combustion products streams (and not only on fresh and burnt gases as in premixed flames). For example, pure hydrogen/air flames use reactants having quite different densities. Molecular diffusion may also be strongly affected (differential diffusivity effects). The simplest diffusion flame is a fuel jet discharging in ambient air. In this situation, oxidizer is provided to the flame zone through air entrainment and natural convection (Fig. 6.3). Such situations are simple from a technological point of view but correspond to difficult numerical

---

[ii]The Combustion Research Facility (CRF) of the Sandia National Laboratories (Livermore, California, U.S.A.) collects and makes available a large number of experimental data sets about turbulent non-premixed combustion in several flow configurations (http://www.ca.sandia.gov/tdf) providing well defined test cases for turbulent combustion modeling. Proceedings and summaries of the International Workshops on Measurement and Computation of Turbulent non-premixed Flames that aim to share experimental data and to compare model predictions are also available on the Sandia web site (http://www.ca.sandia.gov/tdf/Workshop.html).

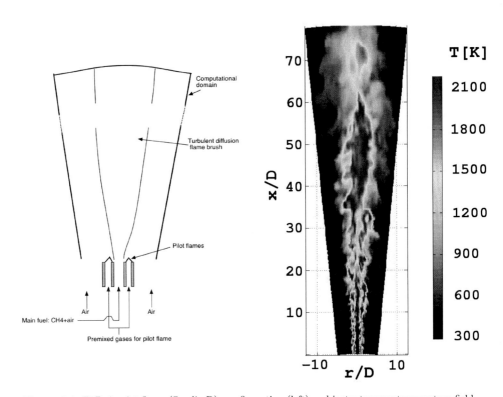

Figure 6.1: Diffusion jet flame (Sandia D): configuration (left) and instantaneous temperature field obtained by Large Eddy Simulation (right). (H. Steiner, private communication, 1999).

simulations.[iii]

Non-premixed flame stabilization is also a challenging problem, both for experimentalists and for numerical simulations. This point is discussed in the next section.

6.2.3 Turbulent non-premixed flame stabilization

Flames in practical combustors and furnaces must first be ignited, for example with a spark. After this first ignition, the incoming reactants must be continuously mixed and ignited by

---

[iii]The problem comes from boundary conditions. Ambient air is difficult to describe: to specify a constant pressure requires large computational domain whereas smaller domains need to provide velocity and turbulence characteristic profiles for the entrained air.

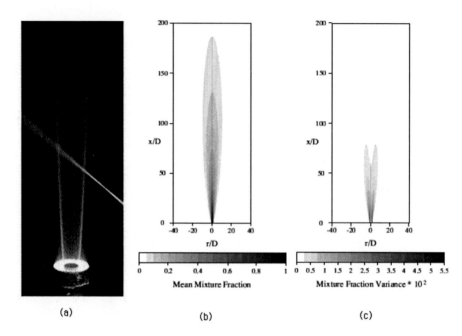

Figure 6.2: Sandia D flame. Direct view (a) and RANS computation: fields of mean mixture fraction z (b) and of variance of z (c) (E. Riesmeier and H. Pitsch, private communication, 1999).

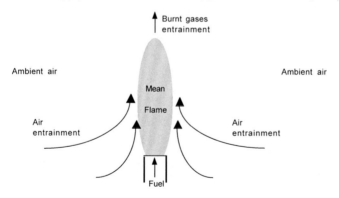

Figure 6.3: Turbulent non-premixed flame. A fuel jet decharges in ambient air. Reaction zone is fed by oxidizer because of air-entrainment.

the hot gases present in the chamber, for combustion to continue. This process, called flame stabilization, is a central design criterion for combustion chambers, especially at high powers: insufficient stabilization can result in a combustor which cannot be operated safely or which oscillates dangerously (see Chapt. 8). Predicting flame stabilization is also an unsolved challenge for numerical combustion codes. Most models actually ignore the problem completely by assuming that the flame front is ignited everywhere.[iv] For example, assuming infinitely fast chemistry or assuming any type of ignited flame structure (like in flamelet models, see § 6.4) directly implies that combustion is active for any layer where fuel and oxidizer meet. This assumption may be acceptable for certain flows but it is often used in cases where it is not true leading to erroneous results. The most obvious drawback of such models is that they predict stabilization and combustion for any flow rates (even very large), something which is obviously wrong: most combustion chambers quench when the flow rates of fuel and oxidizer are increased beyond certain limits. This section presents the usual stabilization methods employed in burners. The choice of these methods is a function of the inlet speeds of the reactants (or equivalently of the power of the combustor). Table 6.1 summarizes these strategies which are then discussed in more details in the second part of this section. Models are presented in the following sections: very few of them can actually predict flame stabilization.

Inlet speeds	Stabilization method	Stabilization mechanism
Very low ($< s_L^0$)	None needed	Rim stabilized flames
Low ($< 5s_L^0$)	None needed	Triple flames
Large ($> 10s_L^0$)	Add another "pilot" flame	Flame stabilized on hot gases
	Heat up one of the reactants	Auto ignition
	Create a recirculation zone using a dump or swirl	Flame stabilized on its own burnt gases

Table 6.1: Stabilization methods and mechanisms as a function of the inlet speeds (or of the power). s_L^0 is the stoichiometric laminar premixed flame speed.

Rim-stabilized flames

When the inlet reactant speeds are small (typically less than the laminar flame speed of a stoichiometric premixed flame), the diffusion flame can stabilize directly at the splitter plate separating the fuel and oxidizer streams (Fernandez et al. [207]). This regime (Fig. 6.4) is seldom observed in real burners because the splitter plate can suffer from excessive heat transfer and because it corresponds to very small powers and usually laminar flows. The

---

[iv]From a chemical point of view, chemical species and reaction paths involved in ignition and auto-ignition mechanisms are generally not the same than in propagating flames.

transition from such a regime to a lifted flame depends on the flow velocities but also on the velocity gradients at the walls (Fernandez et al. [207]).

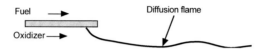

Figure 6.4: Diffusion flame stabilization on the rim of the splitter plate.

Triple flames

First observed experimentally by Phillips [504], triple flames are often involved in the stabilization of lifted laminar diffusion flames. In this situation, mixing between fuel and oxidizer occurs upstream of the flame ignition point. Two premixed flames and a diffusion flame are observed (Fig. 6.5). These triple flames have been widely studied both experimentally (Kioni et al. [348, 349], Plessing et al. [516]), theoretically (Dold [179]) and numerically (Ruetsch et al. [574], Domingo and Vervisch [181], Ghosal and Vervisch [232]).

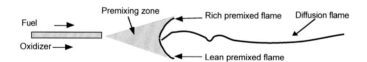

Figure 6.5: Diffusion flame stabilization with a triple flame.

Fig. 6.6 shows a direct view of a triple flame in a laminar flow (Kioni et al. [348, 349]) and confirms that these structures are indeed observed for laminar flames. One important result is the ability of triple flames to propagate (and accordingly to sustain incoming reactant streams) with velocities slightly higher than the corresponding laminar flame speed because triple flames are able to modify the upstream flow field.

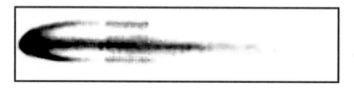

Figure 6.6: Triple flame visualization in a laminar flow (Kioni et al. [348]).

Whether triple flames also play a role in stabilization mechanisms of turbulent non-premixed combustion is still a controversial issue but DNS (Domingo and Vervisch [181]) and experimental results (Schefer and Goix [590], Upatnieks et al. [658]) show that triple flame-like structures are found in the stabilization regions of turbulent lifted flames. Instantaneous velocity measurements in a lifted jet diffusion flame (Muniz and Mungal [463]) show that, despite a mean flow velocity larger than the flame speed, a triple-flame is able to sustain, the flame front is always located in a region where the instantaneous flow velocity is of the order of magnitude of the laminar flame speed and continuously moves to satisfy this condition. However, total flame blow-off is observed when the instantaneous velocity of the flow is everywhere and constantly larger than the flame speed. Muller et al. [462] (see also Chen et al. [123]) have developed a turbulent combustion model devoted to the stabilization of lifted non-premixed flames, based on the G-equation formalism (§ 5.3.4).

Pilot flames

Like many diffusion flames where the fuel speed is high, the Sandia "D-flame" displayed in Fig. 6.2 cannot be stabilized without pilot flames: small premixed flames are used in the vicinity of the jet exit to ensure flame ignition and stabilization (see a rough sketch in Fig. 6.7). This technique is efficient but requires the use of a secondary premixed flame and all related components (secondary supply, control). From a numerical point of view, this pilot flame may be described as a heat source or an injection of hot burnt gases.

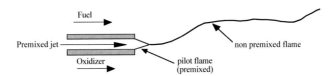

Figure 6.7: Turbulent non-premixed flame stabilization using a pilot flame. A secondary premixed flame is used to ensure the flame ignition and stabilization.

Auto-ignition

When one of the fuel or oxidizer streams is sufficiently hot, the flame stabilization may be ensured by auto-ignition processes inside the mixing layer (Fig. 6.8), independently of the inlet speeds. This situation is found in supersonic combustion (scramjets: supersonic ramjets) where the air stream is sufficiently hot because of compression effects to ensure the flame ignition. The technical challenge lies in the ignition distance δ_i which must be as short as possible. Auto-ignition is also encountered in Diesel engines where air is heated by compression before fuel injection and in staged gas turbines where pure fuel is injected into the hot gases produced by a first burner. From a numerical point of view, these situations are difficult to handle because ignition mechanisms, generally linked to complex chemistry features, have to be incorporated in models.

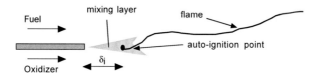

Figure 6.8: Turbulent non-premixed flame stabilization by auto-ignition processes. One of the reactant streams is sufficiently hot to ensure an ignition inside the mixing layer.

Dump geometries

Triple flames can stabilize only in flows where the velocity is of the order of the flame speed. In practical burners, flow speeds are much larger and other stabilization mechanisms must be found. One solution is to create a recirculation zone which acts as a hot burnt gases tank providing the energy to ignite incoming reactants. This recirculation zone can be created in two different ways:

- sudden expansion (dump geometries) in which the recirculation zone is created by the burner geometry: the usual configuration corresponds to the backward facing step (Keller et al. [333]) which is well known for turbulence studies in non-reacting flows but many more configurations can be found in real burners.

- swirl (see next section).

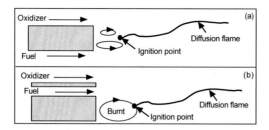

Figure 6.9: Turbulent non-premixed flame stabilization in recirculation zones.

Different configurations are encountered in practice for dump combustors, as summarized in Fig. 6.9. In the so-called "bluff-body" case (Fig. 6.9a), fuel and oxidizer are separated by a large step which generate recirculation zones and mixing between fuel and oxidizer. Recirculation zone characteristics strongly depend on relative fuel and oxidizer injection velocities. In other cases, fuel and oxidizer are injected on the same side of the bluff body where a large recirculation of burnt products stabilizes combustion. (Fig. 6.9b).

These two situations are not yet well predicted using numerical simulations.[v] In fact, bluff-body experimental data show that, because of recirculation zones, fuel is transported towards the oxidizer stream and oxidizer towards the fuel stream, a phenomenon which is not correctly accounted for by classical turbulent transport models. For the configuration (b) in Fig. 6.9, oxidizer has to be transported across the fuel stream towards the burnt gases recirculation zone. Once again, usual turbulence and scalar transport models are generally not sufficient to reproduce this mechanism. A key point lies in the correct description of turbulent boundary layers and wall boundary conditions, especially at the injector lips.

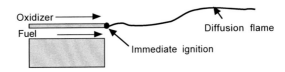

Figure 6.10: Turbulent non-premixed flame stabilization in a dump combustor (see Fig. 6.9b) assuming equilibrium chemistry. The flame is anchored at the burner lip separating fuel and oxidizer.

Note also that assuming equilibrium chemistry, as done in most classical turbulent non-premixed flame models, predicts that diffusion flames are always anchored at the burner lip separating fuel and oxidizer (Fig. 6.10).

Swirl-stabilized flames

For large powers and inlet flow speeds, creating a recirculation zone behind a sudden expansion may not be sufficient to ensure flame stabilization while minimizing pressure losses. For such cases, swirl offers another stabilization mechanism used in multiple industrial turbulent non-premixed flames (Beer and Chigier [43], Gupta et al. [261]).

Swirl corresponds to a rotating movement of the incoming reactants and is produced upstream of the combustion chamber by vanes or lateral injection. Swirling the flow creates a low-speed region on the combustion chamber axis (Fig. 6.11). Without combustion, the size and the strength of this low-speed zone depend on the swirl level:

- for low swirl levels, the axial velocity is decreased on the axis. After ignition, this can promote flame stabilization not only on the lateral recirculation zones produced by the dump but also on the axis,

---

[v]See, for example, proceedings of the International Workshops on Measurement and Computation of Turbulent non-premixed Flames (http://www.ca.sandia.gov/tdf/Workshop.html).

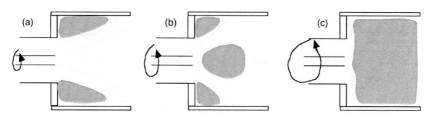

Figure 6.11: Non-reacting swirled flows in combustion chamber. Shaded zones correspond to recirculating flow. Swirl intensities increase from Cases (a) to (c).

- for higher swirl levels, this low speed zone becomes a recirculation zone (negative axial velocities) and is used as a stabilization point for incoming gases in the reacting case. Compared to dump geometries, this configuration has the advantage to stabilize the flame far from the walls,

- for very large swirls, the lateral recirculation zones disappear and the whole chamber is almost filled by a large axial recirculation zone. The fresh gases flow along the walls of the chamber (wall jet flow). Increasing swirl also has drawbacks: when the recirculation zone is too large, the flame can flashback into the injection systems and burn them.

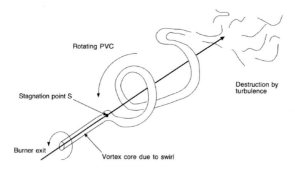

Figure 6.12: Topology of a precessing vortex core (PVC).

Such processes are used in most gas turbines: various geometries may be encountered, using one rotating or several co- or contra-rotating flows. Note that swirl is also used to break liquid fuel jets. The prediction of such swirl-stabilized flames requires a proper description of the flow field (usual turbulence models such as $k - \varepsilon$ are not very well suited to rotating flows) and to take into account finite chemistry effects. Examples of LES of swirled stabilized flames are given in Chapter 10.

Swirling flows can exhibit a very large range of topologies, mainly depending on the swirl number (see the review on vortex breakdown in Lucca-Negro and O'Doherty [407]). For high values of the swirl number, the central recirculation zone may oscillate. This phenomenon is often referred to as precessing vortex core (PVC). Fig. 6.12 shows the topology of a precessing vortex core. The vortex aligned with the axis of the chamber (due to the swirl) breaks down at the stagnation point S in a spiral form. In most flames, the flow inside the spiral is recirculated. The entire structure rotates around the axis of the chamber, causing large perturbations which can be the source of instabilities.

6.2.4 An example of turbulent non-premixed flame stabilization

As an example of the complexity of diffusion flame stabilization, Fig. 6.13 displays the geometrical configuration of a two-dimensional turbulent non-premixed burner where two propane jets are injected in air coflows. Two backward facing steps are used to stabilize the turbulent flame. Depending on conditions (air and propane flow rates), various flame structures are observed as summarized in Fig. 6.14.

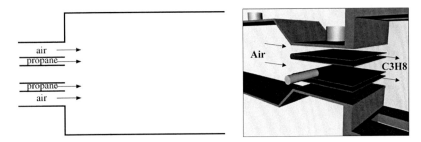

Figure 6.13: Two-dimensional turbulent non-premixed flame burner. Two propane jets are injected in coflowing air streams (B. Varoquié, private communication, 2000; see also Varoquié et al. [667] or Légier et al. [377]).

For low values of the reactants flow rates, the flame is stabilized in the vicinity of the fuel lips. An instantaneous PLIF visualization of the OH radical (Fig. 6.15) shows that flames start along the fuel jet axis and are slightly lifted from the lips (the flame is not anchored on the burner lips): for such a flow, four stoichiometric lines begin at the fuel injectors so that four triple flames would be expected. The structure revealed by the PLIF method is more complex and intrinsically unsteady: the eddies shed behind the injectors distort the flame structures and merges them. A more global view of the flow is given in Fig. 6.16a which shows an image of mean CH radical emission for an "anchored" flame. Since the mean flow is two-dimensional, this picture is obtained simply by collecting the light emitted by CH and integrates transverse variations. It is also averaged over time.

For larger propane mass flow rates, the flame is lifted from the injector and is stabilized

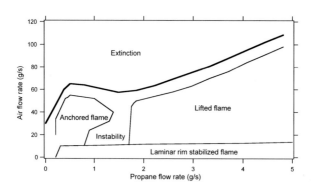

Figure 6.14: Flame regimes observed in the turbulent non-premixed combustion burner of Fig. 6.13 as a function of air and propane mass flow rates (B. Varoquié, private communication, 2000; see also Varoquié et al. [667] or Légier et al. [377]).

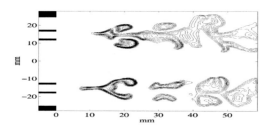

Figure 6.15: Instantaneous laser induced fluorescence imaging of OH for the "anchored flame" regime in Fig. 6.14 (Varoquié et al. [667], Légier et al. [377]).

by recirculation zones induced by the backward facing steps (Fig. 6.16b). Large air mass flow rates lead to the flame blow-out (extinction). These regimes are separated by transition zones, referred here as "instability" where the flame structure is found to oscillate between two regimes.

Comparing Fig. 6.16 (a) and (b) shows two very different stabilization regimes: the first one ("anchored flame") involves triple flame structures close to the flame holder (Fig. 6.15) made possible by the low injection speeds while the second ("lifted flame") corresponds to high speeds and a stabilization ensured by the recirculating gases.

Relevant numerical simulations of turbulent non-premixed flames should be able to recover these various combustion regimes. Flame stabilization and location are of importance for practical industrial applications. Unfortunately, simple but widely used models cannot reproduce these experimental findings. For example, Fig. 6.17 displays the mean temperature

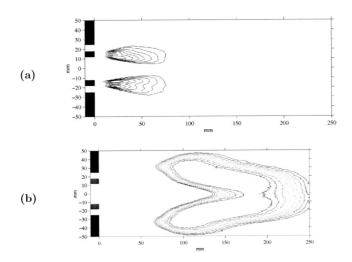

Figure 6.16: Mean CH radical emission in the burner of Fig. 6.13 for the two regimes of Fig. 6.14. (a): "anchored flame" regime. (b): "lifted flame" regime. (Varoquié et al. [667], Légier et al. [377]).

and reaction rate fields obtained using the Magnussen EDC model based on an infinitely fast chemistry assumption (see § 6.4.4). This model assumes that fuel and oxidizer burn as soon as they meet. Accordingly, the flame is directly anchored on the injector lips separating fuel and oxidizer. This result is clearly not in agreement with experimental results because the infinitely fast assumption is too crude. More refined modeling is required.

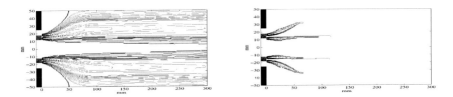

Figure 6.17: Mean temperature (left) and reaction rate (right) fields as obtained using RANS and the Eddy Dissipation Concept (§ 6.4.4) (Varoquié et al. [667], Légier et al. [377]).

6.3   Turbulent non-premixed combustion regimes

As for turbulent premixed flames (see § 5.2), combustion regimes have to be identified to support model developments because simple mathematical approaches based on Arrhenius law series expansions are not relevant (§ 4.5.4). But, compared to premixed flames, regimes description is more difficult in turbulent non-premixed combustion. First, reactants have to mix before reaction and chemical reactions are generally limited by mixing. On the other hand, fast mixing, compared to chemistry, may lead to premixed combustion. The second difficulty arises from the fact that non-premixed flames do not exhibit well-defined characteristic scales: a diffusion flame does not feature a propagation speed and the local flame thickness depends on flow conditions (see Chapt. 3). Before deriving a diagram for turbulent non-premixed combustion regimes, a first step is to analyze flame/vortex interactions using DNS.

6.3.1   Flame/vortex interactions in DNS

Similarly to premixed combustion (see § 5.2.3), the ability of turbulent vortices to affect, modify and eventually quench a laminar diffusion flames is an important ingredient of turbulent combustion models and has been studied using direct numerical simulations (Cuenot and Poinsot [158], Thevenin et al. [646], Renard et al. [549]). The objective of these studies is to understand flame/turbulence interactions and to derive a diagram for turbulent non-premixed combustion regimes.

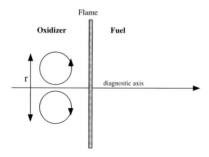

Figure 6.18: Laminar diffusion flame interacting with a pair of counter-rotating vortices.

As pointed out in Section 3.4, diffusion flames exhibit no well-defined flow-independent length and time scales. The thickness of an unstrained diffusion flame increases with time and such flames have no propagation speed. On the other hand, the thickness of strained flames depends on flow motions and is not an intrinsic flame characteristic. However, in flame/vortex interactions, flame scales can be defined unambiguously.

As an example, the flame/vortex interaction study of Cuenot and Poinsot [158] is now described. To analyze their DNS (Fig. 6.18), Cuenot and Poinsot [158] introduce scales as follows:

- **Flame scales** are defined using initial conditions of the simulation. The initial flame thickness δ_i is estimated as:

$$\delta_i = \left(\frac{1}{|\nabla z|}\right)_{z=z_{st}} = \sqrt{\frac{2\mathcal{D}_{st}}{\chi_{st}}} \tag{6.1}$$

where χ_{st} is the scalar dissipation rate at the stoichiometric point $z = z_{st}$ at time $t = 0$. $\mathcal{D}_{st}$ is the stoichiometric value of the molecular diffusion coefficient. A chemical time scale τ_c is defined from asymptotic theories (Linan [397], Cuenot and Poinsot [159], Vervisch and Poinsot [670]) as:

$$\tau_c = \frac{1}{\chi_{st}D_a^{fl}} \tag{6.2}$$

where D_a^{fl} is the flame Damköhler number[vi] given by Eq. (3.90). A "flame velocity" is then defined as $u_f = \delta_i/\tau_c$.

- **Flow scales** correspond to the vortex characteristics (size r, as defined on Fig. 6.18, and speed u') at the beginning of the simulation.

According to these definitions, two non-dimensional numbers are evidenced (Table 6.2):

- A length scale ratio: r/δ_i.

- A velocity ratio: u'/u_f.

	Length scale	Velocity scale
Flame	$\delta_i = (1/|\nabla z|)_{z=z_{st}} = \sqrt{2\mathcal{D}_{st}/\chi_{st}}$	δ_i/τ_c
Vortex	r	u'
Ratio	r/δ_i	$u'\tau_c/\delta_i$

Table 6.2: Characteristic length and velocity scales introduced to analyze DNS flame/vortex interactions. The chemical time, τ_c is estimated from asymptotic theories according to Eq. (6.2).

Flame/vortex interaction regimes may then be identified in a log-log diagram based on velocity $(u'\tau_c/\delta_i)$ and length (r/δ_i) scale ratios, as already done for premixed flames (see § 5.2.3). Two characteristic lines appear:

[vi]This Damköhler number compares molecular diffusion and chemical time scales and is only a function of the local flame structure. It does not take into account a vortex time scale.

- A constant Damköhler number D_a, comparing vortex and chemical times:

$$D_a = \frac{r/u'}{\tau_c} = \frac{r}{\delta_i} \left(\frac{u'}{\delta_i/\tau_c} \right)^{-1} \tag{6.3}$$

corresponds to a line of slope $+1$ in a $(u'\tau_c/\delta_i, r/\delta_i)$ log-log diagram. Higher Damköhler numbers correspond to lower lines in the diagram.

- A vortex Reynolds number is defined as:

$$Re_{vortex} = \frac{u'r}{\nu} = \frac{\tau_d}{\tau_c} \left(\frac{u'}{\delta_i/\tau_c} \right) \left(\frac{r}{\delta_i} \right) \tag{6.4}$$

where τ_d/τ_c compares diffusion ($\tau_d = \delta_i^2/\nu$) and chemical (τ_c) times. For a given initial flame thickness δ_i and a given chemical time τ_c, constant vortex Reynolds numbers correspond to lines of slope -1 in such a diagram.

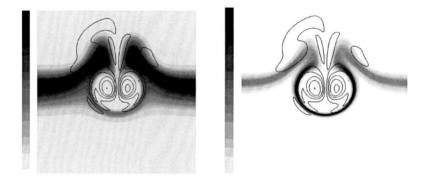

Figure 6.19: DNS of the interaction of a pair of counter-rotating vortices with a laminar diffusion flame (case A in Fig. 6.20 and 6.21). Left: temperature field superimposed to vorticity (lines) field. Right: reaction rate and vorticity (lines) fields (Cuenot and Poinsot [158]).

Cuenot and Poinsot [158] performed two-dimensional direct numerical simulations of a pair of counter-rotating vortex interacting with a laminar diffusion flame, using one-step, irreversible, finite rate chemistry following an Arrhenius law. A typical snapshot is displayed in Fig. 6.19. Various regimes summarized on Fig. 6.20 are identified and analyzed comparing maximum flame temperature and total reaction rate to asymptotic theory results (Fig. 6.21).

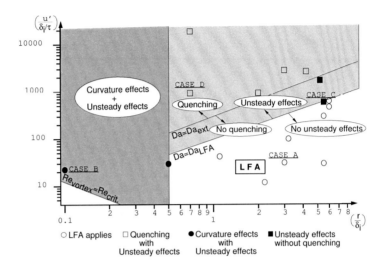

Figure 6.20: Laminar diffusion flame/vortex interaction spectral log-log diagram. Regime plotted versus velocity and length scale ratios defined in Table 6.2 (Cuenot and Poinsot [158]).

The reference Damköhler number corresponding to the extinction of a steady laminar stagnation point flame is D_a^{SE}. Four typical situations and two transition Damköhler numbers, D_a^{LFA} and D_a^{ext}, were identified from DNS results and compared to D_a^{SE}:

(1) For sufficiently large Damköhler numbers ($D_a > D_a^{LFA}$), the steady laminar flamelet assumption (LFA) applies. The flame front behaves like a laminar flame element having the same scalar dissipation rate and flamelet modeling is relevant. In this situation, chemistry is sufficiently fast to follow flow changes induced by the vortices. Both maximum temperature and reaction rate are in very good agreement with laminar flame theory, as shown on Fig. 6.21A. The limit of this regime corresponds to $D_a^{LFA} = 2D_a^{SE}$

(2) In case B (small length scale ratio), a strong curvature of the flame front is observed and molecular and heat diffusion along tangential direction to the flame front become non negligible: large discrepancies are observed for maximum temperature and total reaction rate compared to asymptotic theories (Fig. 6.21B).

(3) For case C ($D_a^{ext} < D_a < D_a^{LFA}$), compared to case A, the Damköhler number decreases (or the vortex speed u' increases). The chemical time becomes non negligible compared to the vortex characteristic time and the chemistry is not sufficiently fast to instantaneously "follow" the flow changes as in LFA regime. In this situation, unsteady effects become important and are clearly evidenced in Fig. 6.21C. The temporal evolution of the flame lags the temporal evolution of the flow and, accordingly, also lags results from asymptotic theories.

(4) When the strain rate induced by the vortex on the flame front becomes too strong

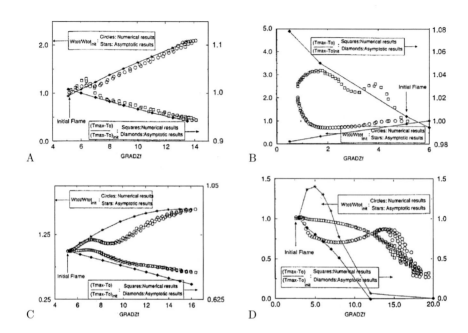

Figure 6.21: Maximum reduced temperatures and total reaction rates from DNS and asymptotic theories, plotted in terms of a reduced $|\nabla z|$, extracted along the axis line (Fig. 6.18). Conditions are displayed in Fig. 6.20. Case A: laminar flamelet assumption (LFA) is valid. B, strong curvature effects are observed. C: strong unsteady effects. D: flame quenching (Cuenot and Poinsot [158]).

$(D_a < D_a^{ext})$, quenching occurs (case D). But, as evidenced on Fig. 6.21D, strong unsteady effects are observed and the quenching is found for lower Damköhler values than expected from flamelet libraries and asymptotic theories: the quenching Damköhler number was measured from DNS: $D_a^{ext} = 0.4 D_a^{SE}$.

Such a classification has been investigated both numerically and experimentally by Thevenin et al. [647]. These authors find similar results but identify some additional regimes. The complete description of these regimes is out of the scope of this book.

These flame/vortex analysis show that the laminar flamelet assumption (LFA), identifying the turbulent flame as a collection of steady strained laminar flame elements, is probably valid over a larger domain than expected from asymptotic theories. This finding is due to unsteady effects. In fact, a diffusion flame is able to sustain larger strain rates than expected from steady state flame analysis, when it is not submitted to these strain rates during too long a time (see § 3.4.3 and Darabiha [163]).

Unfortunately, this spectral diagram (i.e. defining the flame response as a function of vortex size and speed) cannot be easily used to determine turbulent non-premixed combustion regimes as was done for premixed combustion in Section 5.2.3 and Fig. 5.24. As already pointed out, the difficulty lies in the fact that diffusion flames have no well-defined length, time and velocity scales. Accordingly, the precise classification of turbulent flame regimes is still an open question. In the following, a simple classification is proposed based on transition Damköhler numbers D_a^{LFA} and D_a^{ext}, introducing an explicit link between turbulent time scales and molecular diffusion characteristic time $1/\chi_{st}$.

6.3.2   Scales in turbulent non-premixed combustion

Like in turbulent premixed flames studies, turbulence may be parametrized using integral, l_t, and Kolmogorov, η_k, length scales (see § 4.2). For the flame front, however, various length scales may be introduced in non-premixed regimes (Fig. 6.22). Two main length scales are related to diffusion flames:

- The diffusion layer thickness, l_d. This thickness may be defined as the thickness of the zone where the mixture fraction changes, indicating reactants mixing ($0 < z < 1$). In this region, fuel and oxidizer may coexist for non infinitely fast chemistry and are diluted with reaction products. In mixture fraction space, this thickness is defined as $\Delta z = 1$.

- The reaction zone thickness, l_r, corresponding to the region where the reaction rate is non zero. In mixture fraction space, this layer has a thickness $(\Delta z)_r$ and lies around the stoichiometric $z = z_{st}$ iso-surface.

These two length scales cannot be compared to thermal and reaction thicknesses of laminar premixed flames: they depend on time and on flow conditions and may vary independently. For example, for infinitely fast chemistry, $l_r = 0$ (and corresponds to $z = z_{st}$) whereas l_d is finite (see, for example, Fig. 3.18 in § 3.4.4).

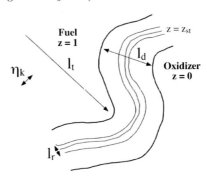

Figure 6.22: Characteristical length scales in turbulent non-premixed combustion.

The problem is now to estimate flame thicknesses as functions of relevant parameters. As shown in Chapter 3 (§ 3.5.2), laminar diffusion flames may be characterized by a Damköhler number comparing local flow time τ_f and chemical time τ_c (Eq. 3.88):

$$D_a^{fl} = \frac{\tau_f}{\tau_c} \approx \frac{1}{\chi_{st}\tau_c}$$

(6.5)

where χ_{st} is the mixture fraction scalar dissipation rate for the stoichiometric value $z = z_{st}$. χ_{st} also measures the mixture fraction gradient (Eq. 3.22) and can be used to estimate the local laminar diffusive layer thickness l_d^{lam} according to:[vii]

$$l_d^{lam} \approx \sqrt{\mathcal{D}_{st}/\chi_{st}}$$

(6.6)

where $\mathcal{D}_{st}$ is the value of the molecular diffusivity on the stoichiometric surface.

This analysis is extended to turbulent non-premixed flames to link the mean diffusive layer thickness l_d to the mean scalar dissipation rate of the mixture fraction conditioned on the stoichiometric surface $z = z_{st}$, $\widetilde{\chi}_{st}$:

$$l_d \approx \sqrt{\mathcal{D}_{st}/\widetilde{\chi}_{st}}$$

(6.7)

where $\widetilde{\chi}_{st}$ is defined as:

$$\overline{\rho}\widetilde{\chi}_{st} = 2\left(\overline{\rho\mathcal{D}\left|\nabla z\right|^2 |z_{st}}\right)$$

(6.8)

$(\overline{Q|z_{st}})$ denotes a conditional average of Q on the stoichiometric surface $z = z_{st}$. $\widetilde{\chi}_{st}$ is generally unknown and cannot be easily estimated from known quantities without additional assumptions. Assuming that the flame structure is controlled by the strain rate due to turbulent motions, the local diffusion layer may be viewed as a steady constant density strained diffusion layer and Eq. (3.67) gives:

$$\chi = \chi_0 \exp\left(-2\left[\text{erf}^{-1}\left(2z-1\right)\right]^2\right) = \chi_0 F(z) = \chi_{st}F(z)/F(z_{st})$$

(6.9)

Then:

$$\widetilde{\chi} = \frac{1}{\overline{\rho}}\int_0^1 \left(\overline{\rho\chi|z}\right)p(z)\,dz = \widetilde{\chi}_{st}\int_0^1 \frac{F(z)}{F(z_{st})}\widetilde{p}(z)\,dz = \widetilde{\chi}_{st}\mathcal{F}\left(\widetilde{z},\widetilde{z''^2}\right)$$

(6.10)

relating $\widetilde{\chi}_{st}$ to $\widetilde{\chi}$. The notation $\mathcal{F}(\widetilde{z},\widetilde{z''^2})$ implicitly assumes that the mass weighted probability density function $\widetilde{p}(z)$ depends on $\widetilde{z}$ and $\widetilde{z''^2}$, as in a β-function (see § 6.4.2). Note that $\widetilde{\chi}_{st}$ measures the mean local diffusive thickness l_d whereas $\widetilde{\chi}$ incorporates additional features. For example, in the infinitely thin diffusive layer limit, $\widetilde{\chi}_{st} \to +\infty$ but $\widetilde{\chi}$ is mainly governed by

---

[vii]Compared to Table 6.2, a factor $\sqrt{2}$ is missing for consistency reasons. Defining diffusive layer thickness l_d as $l_d = \sqrt{\mathcal{D}_{st}/\chi_{st}}$ and diffusion time as $\tau_f = 1/\chi_{st}$ is consistent with the classical diffusion time relation $\tau_f = l_d^2/\mathcal{D}_{st}$ and is sufficient for the present analysis which is limited to orders of magnitude.

pure oxidizer $(z = 0)$ and pure fuel $(z = 1)$ regions leading to $\widetilde{\chi} \to 0$ (In fact, as $F(z = 0) = F(z = 1) = 0$, $\mathcal{F}(\widetilde{z}, \widetilde{z''^2}) \to 0$).[viii]

The stoichiometric value of the scalar dissipation rate, $\widetilde{\chi}_{st}$, may also be used to estimate a diffusion time scale τ_f according to:

$$\tau_f \approx \left(\widetilde{\chi}_{st}\right)^{-1} \tag{6.11}$$

The local flame Damköhler number is then:

$$D_a^{fl} = \tau_f/\tau_c \approx \left(\widetilde{\chi}_{st}\tau_c\right)^{-1} \tag{6.12}$$

A "flame velocity" U_d is sometimes introduced from the diffusive thickness l_d and the chemical time scale τ_c: $U_d = l_d/\tau_c$.[ix]

For a single chemical reaction between fuel (F) and oxidizer (O):

$$\nu_F F + \nu_O O \longrightarrow P \tag{6.13}$$

Asymptotic theories (Linan [397]) show that reaction and diffusion layer thicknesses in laminar flames may be related through the Damköhler number D_a^{fl} as:

$$l_r/l_d \approx \left(D_a^{fl}\right)^{-1/a} \tag{6.14}$$

where $a = \nu_F + \nu_O + 1$. As expected, higher is the Damköhler number D_a^{fl}, thinner is the reaction zone.

These scales are summarized in Table 6.3. But, once again, all the intervening quantities cannot be easily a priori determined and strongly depend on local flow conditions.

6.3.3 Combustion regimes

The objective is now to identify turbulent non-premixed combustion regimes by comparing characteristic flame scales to characteristic turbulent scales. But, unfortunately, non-premixed flames have no intrinsic length scales and strongly depend on flow conditions. Accordingly, further analysis requires additional assumptions (in fact, a model to relate flame scales to flow scales).

[viii]Relation (6.10) links the mean scalar dissipation rate $\widetilde{\chi}$ to its conditionally averaged stoichiometric value $\widetilde{\chi}_{st}$, but $\widetilde{\chi}$ estimations are very difficult. This quantity is generally described from a turbulent time τ_t and the mixture fraction variance $\widetilde{z''^2}$ (already found in $\mathcal{F}(\widetilde{z}, \widetilde{z''^2})$) as detailed in Section 6.4.3:

$$\widetilde{\chi} \approx \widetilde{z''^2}/\tau_t \approx \widetilde{z''^2}\varepsilon/k$$

This linear relaxation model supposes a homogenous and isotropic mixing, without mean mixture fraction gradients, an assumption which is clearly wrong in flames where a diffusive layer separates fuel $(z = 1)$ and oxidizer $(z = 0)$ streams.

[ix]Note that U_d compares a thickness and a time and has the dimension of a velocity but does not correspond to a flame propagation speed. Such a quantity is only introduced to conveniently describe some results, for example by Cuenot and Poinsot [158] (see § 6.3.1).

	Thickness	Time	"velocity"
Diffusive layer	$l_d \approx \sqrt{\mathcal{D}_{st}/\widetilde{\chi}_{st}}$	$\tau_f \approx 1/\widetilde{\chi}_{st} = l_d^2/\mathcal{D}_{st}$	l_d/τ_f
Reactive layer	$l_r = l_d \left(D_a^{fl}\right)^{-1/a}$	$\tau_c = 1/\left(D_a^{fl}\widetilde{\chi}_{st}\right)$	l_r/τ_c

Table 6.3: Characteristic flame scales in turbulent non-premixed flames. D_a^{fl} is the Damköhler number $(D_a^{fl} = (\tau_c\widetilde{\chi}_{st})^{-1})$.

The flame front is wrinkled and affected by turbulent motions. Regimes classification is first based on comparison between chemical time τ_c and a turbulent time to be identified. In the following analysis, the shortest turbulent time, corresponding to the worst case, is retained (chemical times are usually shorter than turbulence time). Assuming homogeneous and isotropic turbulence, maximum strain rates and shortest turbulent times are due to Kolmogorov scales (see § 4.2 and Fig. 4.1). Then, to first order, diffusive thickness (l_d) and time ($1/\widetilde{\chi}_{st}$) are assumed to be controlled by Kolmogorov motions (size η_k, time τ_k):[x]

$$l_d \approx \eta_k \qquad \text{and} \qquad \tau_f = \left(\widetilde{\chi}_{st}\right)^{-1} \approx \tau_k \qquad (6.15)$$

Note that these definitions ensure a unity Reynolds number for Kolmogorov structures:

$$\frac{\eta_k u_k}{\mathcal{D}_{st}} = \frac{\eta_k^2}{\mathcal{D}_{st}\tau_k} = \frac{l_d^2}{\mathcal{D}_{st}\tau_f} = 1 \qquad (6.16)$$

The integral length scale, l_t, is of the order of the mean mixing zone thickness, l_z, estimated from the mean mixture fraction gradient:

$$l_t \approx l_z \approx \left(|\nabla\widetilde{z}|\right)^{-1} \qquad (6.17)$$

The flame structure and the combustion regime depend on the chemical characteristic time τ_c. For fast chemistry (low τ_c values and large Damköhler numbers), the flame is very thin ($l_r \ll l_d \approx \eta_k$) and may be identified to a laminar flame element ("flamelet"). For larger values of the chemical time τ_c, l_r becomes of the same order as η_k. Then, according to Section 3.5.2, departures from laminar flame structures and unsteady effects are expected. For low Damköhler numbers, or large chemical times, extinctions occur.

This qualitative and intuitive analysis is difficult to summarize on a single combustion diagram as done for turbulent premixed combustion because the local flame scales depend on the local flow conditions. In the following, a simple (and rough) description based on two characteristic ratios is presented:

- a time ratio τ_t/τ_c comparing the turbulence integral characteristic time τ_t and the chemical time τ_c. This ratio corresponds to the Damköhler number D_a introduced for turbulent premixed combustion but is not the Damköhler number relevant for the local non-premixed flame structure ($D_a^{fl} = 1/\tau_c\chi_{st}$).

---

[x]This assumption is quite crude and assumes that the flame is strained by Kolmogorov motions, neglecting possible negative strain regions (compression) or viscous dissipation of Kolmogorov structures.

- a length scale ratio l_t/l_d comparing integral length scale l_t and diffusive thickness l_d. As $l_d \approx \eta_k$, $l_t/l_d \approx Re_t^{3/4}$ (Eq. 4.8), where Re_t is the turbulence Reynolds number.

The time ratio (or the Damköhler number) is recast as:

$$Da = \frac{\tau_t}{\tau_c} = \frac{\tau_t}{\tau_k}\frac{\tau_k}{\tau_c} \approx \frac{\tau_t}{\tau_k}\frac{2}{\widetilde{\chi}_{st}\tau_c} \approx 2\sqrt{Re_t}D_a^{fl} \qquad (6.18)$$

Constant Damköhler numbers D_a^{fl} correspond to lines of slope $1/2$ in a log-log (D_a, Re_t) diagram. For sufficiently fast chemistry, the flame is expected to have a laminar flame (LF) structure. According to Cuenot and Poinsot [158] (§ 6.3.1), this condition may be written as $D_a^{fl} \geq D_a^{LFA}$. Extinction occurs for large chemical times, i.e. when $D_a^{fl} \leq D_a^{ext}$. Results may then be summarized on a combustion diagram (Fig. 6.23).

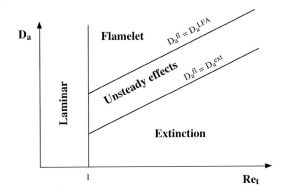

Figure 6.23: Regimes for turbulent non-premixed combustion as a function of the Damköhler number $Da = \tau_t/\tau_c$ (based on the turbulence integral time scale τ_t and the chemical time τ_c) and the turbulent Reynolds number Re_t.

Such a turbulent combustion diagram should be used with great care. The local flame thickness and speed depend on the local flow conditions such as local strain rates and may be affected by unsteady effects (see, for example, the flame response time analyzed in § 3.4.3). In a given burner, the flame structure may strongly depend on the spatial location. For example, a flamelet structure may be encountered close to the injectors while a partial extinction followed by a re-ignition may be found downstream. Some strong assumptions have been introduced in this derivation. For example, the local diffusion thickness l_d and time τ_f are supposed to be controlled by the Kolmogorov length scales. This assumption needs to be validated: Kolmogorov length scales induce the highest strain rate but have a short lifetime because of viscous dissipation (see Chapt. 4). Negative strains (flame compression) have also been neglected. In fact, classification of turbulent non-premixed combustion regimes is a controversial subject and different diagrams, introducing various parameters such as scalar dissipation rate, mixture fraction variance $\widetilde{z''^2}$,... may be found in the literature (Borghi [72], Bray and Peters [88], Libby and Williams [389], Peters [502]).

6.4   RANS of turbulent non-premixed flames

The general mathematical framework for RANS modeling of turbulent non-premixed flames has been already described in Chapter 4 (§ 4.5). Compared to turbulent premixed flames, the main difference lies in boundary conditions and in the use of the mixture fraction variable z, introduced in Section 3.2.1 (Eq. 3.16). Classical assumptions used to average the conservation equations are discussed in Section 6.4.1. Models using infinitely fast chemistry assumptions are then presented in Section 6.4.2.: these models require specific efforts to express scalar dissipation which are discussed in Section 6.4.3. Sections 6.4.4 to 6.4.6 describe models able to incorporate finite rate chemistry effects into turbulent combustion models.

6.4.1   Assumptions and averaged equations

Classical models for turbulent non-premixed flames are usually derived under the following assumptions:[xi]

- H1 - The thermodynamic pressure is constant and Mach numbers are small (see § 1.2.1).

- H2 - Species heat capacities are equal and constant ($C_{pk} = C_p$).

- H3 - Molecular diffusion follows Fick's law and molecular diffusivities D_k are equal for all species ($D_k = \mathcal{D}$).

- H4 - Lewis numbers are equal to unity ($Le = \lambda/\rho C_p \mathcal{D} = 1$).

- H5 - Fuel and oxidizer streams are separately introduced into the combustion chamber with reference state (T_F^0, Y_F^0) for fuel and (T_O^0, Y_O^0) for oxidizer.

Under these assumptions, for a single one-step chemistry in adiabatic flows (no heat losses), fuel (Y_F) and oxidizer (Y_O) mass fractions and temperature (T) are linked through the mixture fraction z (Eq. 3.15):

$$z = \frac{sY_F - Y_O + Y_O^0}{sY_F^0 + Y_O^0} = \frac{\frac{C_p}{Q}(T-T_O^0) + Y_F}{\frac{C_p}{Q}(T_F^0-T_O^0) + Y_F^0} = \frac{\frac{sC_p}{Q}(T-T_O^0) + Y_O - Y_O^0}{\frac{sC_p}{Q}(T_F^0-T_O^0) - Y_O^0} \qquad (6.19)$$

For flames where assumptions H2 to H4 are not satisfied (multi-step chemistry, heat losses), mixture fraction variables are based on atomic elements (see § 3.6.2) and link species mass fractions.

[xi]Among these assumptions, equal and constant heat capacities and unity Lewis numbers may be clearly wrong in actual flames. They can be relaxed using more complex formulations (see Linan et al. [400], Pitsch and Peters [513, 514], Barlow et al. [32]).

The simplified equation set is (see Eq. 4.21 to 4.24):

$$\frac{\partial \bar{\rho}}{\partial t} + \frac{\partial}{\partial x_i}(\bar{\rho}\tilde{u}_i) = 0 \tag{6.20}$$

$$\frac{\partial \bar{\rho}\tilde{u}_i}{\partial t} + \frac{\partial}{\partial x_j}(\bar{\rho}\tilde{u}_i\tilde{u}_j) + \frac{\partial \bar{p}}{\partial x_j} = \frac{\partial}{\partial x_i}\left(\overline{\tau_{ij}} - \overline{\rho u_i'' u_j''}\right) \tag{6.21}$$

$$\frac{\partial(\bar{\rho}\tilde{Y}_k)}{\partial t} + \frac{\partial}{\partial x_i}(\bar{\rho}\tilde{u}_i\tilde{Y}_k) = \frac{\partial}{\partial x_i}\left(\overline{\rho D_k \frac{\partial Y_k}{\partial x_i}} - \overline{\rho u_i'' Y_k''}\right) + \bar{\omega}_k \quad \text{for} \quad k = 1, N \tag{6.22}$$

$$\frac{\partial \bar{\rho}\tilde{z}}{\partial t} + \frac{\partial}{\partial x_i}(\bar{\rho}\tilde{u}_i\tilde{z}) = \frac{\partial}{\partial x_i}\left(\overline{\rho D \frac{\partial z}{\partial x_i}} - \overline{\rho u_i'' z''}\right) \tag{6.23}$$

For a single step (irreversible or reversible) chemistry between fuel and oxidizer in adiabatic flows, fuel and oxidizer mass fractions, temperature and the mixture fraction z are related through Eq. (6.19). Therefore, for example, only balance equations for the fuel mass fraction $\tilde{Y}_F$ and the mixture fraction $\tilde{z}$ are needed. Mean oxidizer mass fraction $\tilde{Y}_O$ and temperature $\tilde{T}$ are then directly determined from $\tilde{Y}_F$ and $\tilde{z}$.

This set of equations contains unclosed terms: turbulent fluxes such as $\widetilde{u_i'' u_j''}$, $\widetilde{u_i'' Y_k''}$ or $\widetilde{u_i'' z''}$ and reaction terms $\bar{\omega}_k$. Reynolds stresses $(\widetilde{u_i'' u_j''})$ are closed using classical turbulence models (see § 4.5.3). Turbulent scalar transport $(\widetilde{u_i'' Y_k''}$ and $\widetilde{u_i'' z''})$ is usually modeled using a gradient assumption (Eq. 4.27). Some experiments (Hardalupas et al. [269]) and DNS (Luo and Bray [409], Luo [408]) show counter-gradient transport in turbulent non-premixed flames but, compared to premixed flames (§ 5.3.8), this point remains an open topic. Modeling the reaction rate term $\bar{\omega}_k$ is the key difficulty in turbulent non-premixed combustion simulations.

According to Section 3.2.4, laminar diffusion flame computations may be split into two problems:

- a mixing problem providing the mixture fraction field $z(x_i, t)$,

- a flame structure problem where species mass fractions, Y_k, temperature T, and reaction rates $\dot{\omega}_k$ are expressed as functions of the mixture fraction z.

This remains true for turbulent flames and most of the theoretical arguments derived in Section 3.2 can be repeated for the structure of the flamelets found in a turbulent diffusion flame. In such a flame, the two problems to solve are:

- a mixing problem providing the average mixture fraction field $\tilde{z}(x_i, t)$, and some of its higher moments (for example $\widetilde{z''^2}$),

- a flame structure problem where species mass fractions, Y_k, temperature T and reaction rates $\dot{\omega}_k$ are expressed as functions of the mixture fraction z. These functions are formulated as conditional expressions $(Y_k|z^*, T|z^*)$ since Y_k or T may depend on multiple parameters in a turbulent flow.

The complexity added by turbulence, compared to laminar diffusion flames, comes from the averaging procedures. To determine average values, the mean value of z is not sufficient: higher z moments are needed and, if possible, a full pdf of z. When the pdf of z, $p(z)$ is known, averaged species mass fraction $(\widetilde{Y}_k)$, averaged temperature $(\widetilde{T})$ or averaged reaction rate $(\overline{\dot{\omega}}_k)$ are given by:

$$\overline{\rho}\widetilde{Y}_k = \int_0^1 \left(\overline{\rho Y_k | z^*} \right) p(z^*) \, dz^* \quad ; \quad \overline{\rho}\widetilde{T} = \int_0^1 \left(\overline{\rho T | z^*} \right) p(z^*) \, dz^* \tag{6.24}$$

$$\overline{\dot{\omega}}_k = \int_0^1 \left(\overline{\dot{\omega}_k | z^*} \right) p(z^*) \, dz^* \tag{6.25}$$

where $(\overline{Q|z^*})$ denotes the conditional average of quantity Q for a given value of the mixture fraction $z = z^*$, depending on z^* and various quantities such as the scalar dissipation rate. $p(z^*)$ is the z-probability density function (pdf).

Eq. (6.24) and (6.25) suggest that two different levels are available to model turbulent non-premixed flames:

- The **primitive variable method** is based on Eq. (6.24). Assumptions are made on the flame structure to provide conditional quantities $(\overline{\rho Y_k | z^*})$ and $(\overline{\rho T | z^*})$, for example from flamelet (or laminar flame) libraries or through balance equations (CMC modeling, see § 6.4.5). Species mass fractions (Eq. 6.22) and temperature balance equations are no longer required and mean reaction rates $\dot{\omega}_k$ are not modeled: RANS codes solve only for flow variables $(\overline{\rho}, \widetilde{u}_i,...)$ and mixture fraction variables $(\widetilde{z}, \widetilde{z''^2},...)$ to estimate, directly or indirectly, the probability density function $p(z^*)$. This approach is described in Section 6.4.2 and 6.4.5.

- In the **reaction rate approach**, balance equations for species mass fractions (Eq. 6.22) and, eventually, for temperature, are solved. Accordingly, reaction rates $\overline{\dot{\omega}}_k$ have to be modeled as for turbulent premixed combustion. These models may be based on Eq. (6.25) and also use laminar flame libraries for $(\overline{\dot{\omega}_k | z^*})$. This method is presented assuming infinitely fast chemistry[xii] in Section 6.4.4 and for finite reaction rate chemistry in Section 6.4.6.

The primitive variable method is clearly less time-consuming than the reaction rate approach because species mass fractions and temperature balance equations are no longer required, but it is valid only under restrictive assumptions. On the other hand, the reaction

---

[xii]As for laminar diffusion flames, assuming infinitely fast chemistry does not mean infinite reaction rates. In this situation, reaction rates are controlled by molecular diffusion and take finite values.

rate method is able to take into account various additional effects such as compressibility, heat losses or secondary reactants injections, at least when $(\overline{\dot{\omega}_k|z^*})$ can be modeled. Nevertheless, one has to be aware that, even under the same assumptions, the two approaches are not a priori equivalent and may lead to quite different results. In the primitive variable method, mean species mass fractions $\widetilde{Y}_k$ are directly computed from $(\overline{\rho Y_k|z^*})$ and $p(z^*)$ using Eq. (6.24). In the reaction rate approach, mean reaction rates $\overline{\dot{\omega}}_k$ are first determined from $(\overline{\dot{\omega}_k|z^*})$ and $p(z^*)$ with Eq. (6.25) and mean species mass fractions $\widetilde{Y}_k$ are solutions of Eq. (6.22). In this last case, turbulent fluxes $\widetilde{u_i'' Y_k''}$ are modeled and taken into account while they are not incorporated in the primitive variable method. Accordingly, assuming a classical gradient turbulent transport, computations using the reaction rate approach lead to larger turbulent flame brushes than with the primitive variable method (Vervisch, 2000, private communication).

Table 6.4 summarizes the presentation chosen for these models.

	Infinitely fast chemistry	Finite rate chemistry
Primitive variables: solve for $\widetilde{z}$ and deduce $\widetilde{T}$ and $\widetilde{Y}_k$ from library	Section 6.4.2	Section 6.4.5
Reaction rates: solve for $\overline{\dot{\omega}}_k$ taking $(\overline{\dot{\omega}_k|z^*})$ from libraries and advance $\widetilde{T}$ and $\widetilde{Y}_k$ from balance equations	Section 6.4.4	Section 6.4.6

Table 6.4: Classification of RANS models for turbulent non-premixed flames.

6.4.2 Models for primitive variables with infinitely fast chemistry

As shown in Chapter 3 (§ 3.3), for infinitely fast irreversible chemistry with unity Lewis number and adiabatic combustion (no heat losses), instantaneous mass fractions Y_k and temperature T are directly linked to the mixture fraction z through relations $Y_k(z)$ and $T(z)$ given in Eq. (3.32) to (3.33). For reversible infinitely fast chemistry, the flame structure is determined from the equilibrium relation (3.27) and depends only on the mixture fraction z (see Fig. 3.6). In fact, for infinitely fast chemistry, reversible or not, conditional averages $(\overline{\rho Y_k|z^*})$ and $(\overline{\rho T|z^*})$ in Eq. (6.24) reduce to:

$$\left(\overline{\rho Y_k|z^*}\right) = \rho\left(z^*\right) Y_k\left(z^*\right) \quad ; \quad \left(\overline{\rho T|z^*}\right) = \rho\left(z^*\right) T\left(z^*\right) \tag{6.26}$$

Mean species mass fractions and temperature are then obtained from

$$\overline{\rho}\widetilde{Y}_k = \int_0^1 \rho(z^*) Y_k(z^*) p(z^*)\, dz^* \quad ; \quad \overline{\rho}\widetilde{T} = \int_0^1 \rho(z^*) T(z^*) p(z^*)\, dz^* \tag{6.27}$$

or, in terms of mass-weighted probability density function, $\widetilde{p}(z^*) = \rho(z^*)p(z^*)/\overline{\rho}$:

$$\widetilde{Y_k} = \int_0^1 Y_k(z^*)\widetilde{p}(z^*)\,dz^* \quad ; \quad \widetilde{T} = \int_0^1 T(z^*)\widetilde{p}(z^*)\,dz^* \qquad (6.28)$$

Therefore, the determination of $\widetilde{Y_k}$ and $\widetilde{T}$ reduces to the determination of the probability density function $\widetilde{p}(z)$ of the mixture fraction z. The determination of the pdf of mixture fraction in turbulent flows is still an open field of research (O'Brien [478], Pope [532], Chen et al. [119], Fox et al. [218], Dopazo [182], Fox [219], Haworth [279]). Like for turbulent premixed combustion (§ 5.3.7), this probability density function may be either presumed or solution of a balance equation.

For engineering computations, a widely used, but approximate, solution is to presume the shape of the pdf using simple analytical functions. The β function, already introduced for turbulent premixed flames (§ 5.3.7) is the most popular presumed pdf function and depends only on two parameters, the mean mixture fraction $\widetilde{z}$ and its variance $\widetilde{z''^2}$:

$$\widetilde{p}(z) = \frac{1}{B(a,b)}z^{a-1}(1-z)^{b-1} = \frac{\Gamma(a+b)}{\Gamma(a)\Gamma(b)}z^{a-1}(1-z)^{b-1} \qquad (6.29)$$

where the normalization factor $B(a,b)$ and the Γ function are defined by Eq. (5.99) and (5.100).

The pdf parameters a and b are determined from $\widetilde{z}$ and its variance $\widetilde{z''^2}$ as:

$$a = \widetilde{z}\left[\frac{\widetilde{z}(1-\widetilde{z})}{\widetilde{z''^2}} - 1\right] \quad ; \quad b = \frac{a}{\widetilde{z}} - a \qquad (6.30)$$

to ensure:

$$\widetilde{z} = \int_0^1 z^*\widetilde{p}(z^*)\,dz^* \quad \text{and} \quad \widetilde{z''^2} = \int_0^1 (z^* - \widetilde{z})^2\,\widetilde{p}(z^*)\,dz^* \qquad (6.31)$$

In practice, to save computational resources, the β-function parameters a and b (Eq. 6.30), as well as the mean quantities $\widetilde{Y_k}$ and $\widetilde{T}$ (Eq. 6.28) are never computed on the fly during the simulation. Mean quantities entering the computation, such as the mean temperature $\widetilde{T}$ (see Fig. 6.24 below) are directly pre-tabulated as functions of the mean and the variance of the mixture fraction, $\widetilde{T}(\widetilde{z}, \widetilde{z''^2})$.

Typical shapes of β-pdf are displayed on Fig. 5.32 in Chapter 5. β-functions are found to mimic quite correctly real mixture fraction pdfs in a variety of cases. Nevertheless, despite their flexibility, β functions are unable to describe distributions with a singularity for $z = 0$ or $z = 1$ and an additional intermediate maximum in the range $0 < z < 1$ (Peters [502]). It must be emphasized that using a presumed pdf depending only on two parameters (a and b) is a very important assumption since this pdf should contain most of the information about the interaction between turbulence and combustion.

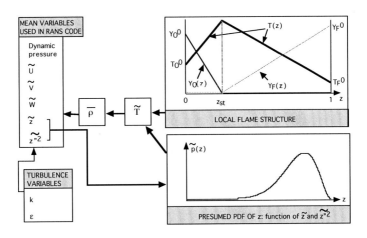

Figure 6.24: Presumed pdf method for infinitely fast irreversible chemistry.

All building blocks to construct a typical presumed pdf method for turbulent non-premixed flames with infinitely irreversible fast chemistry are displayed in Fig. 6.24, when the $k - \varepsilon$ turbulence model is used to describe Reynolds stresses and turbulent fluxes.[xiii]

On the left of Fig. 6.24, the RANS code is solving the Favre-averaged balance equations. This includes an equation for dynamic pressure (usually a Poisson solver in low Mach number codes), the three momentum equations to find the average velocities $\widetilde{u}_i$, the mixture fraction equation for $\widetilde{z}$ and an additional equation for the variance $\widetilde{z''^2}$. The only input to these equations coming from the flame is the mean density field $\overline{\rho}$ obtained from the flame structure and the mixture fraction pdf. The pdf input parameters are the mean mixture fraction $\widetilde{z}$ and its variance $\widetilde{z''^2}$. These quantities must be solved for by the RANS code (a balance equation for $\widetilde{z''^2}$ is derived and closed, as discussed in the next section). These equations are closed using a turbulent viscosity ν_t (for the momentum equations), a turbulent diffusivity D_t (for the mixture fraction equation), determined with the $k - \varepsilon$ turbulence model (two additional balance equations, see § 4.5.3) and expressed as functions of the turbulent kinetic energy k and its turbulent dissipation rate ε.[xiv] This algorithm may be applied to steady mean flow fields or to unsteady mean flows. In this last case, the algorithm is repeated for each time

---

[xiii]In practice, expressions (6.28) are pre-processed before the simulations and mean mass fractions and mean temperature are directly stored as functions of $\widetilde{z}$ and $\widetilde{z''^2}$.

[xiv]Because of the assumptions used here, there is no need to solve mass fraction equations: mass fractions may be obtained by post-processing results (Eq. 6.28) but are not required for the resolution. In such an approach, models are not needed for mean reaction rates which never appear in the balance equations.

step.

Of course, as for turbulent premixed flames, an alternative route to the presumed pdf method is to solve a balance equation for $p(z)$ (Pope [532], Dopazo [182], Fox [219], Haworth [279]). This equation is similar to Eq. (5.115), without source terms.

6.4.3   Mixture fraction variance and scalar dissipation rate

An estimate of the mixture fraction variance, $\widetilde{z''^2}$, is still required to determine β-functions (Eq. 6.30). In RANS, $\widetilde{z''^2}$ is generally given as a solution of a balance equation.[xv] The balance equation for $\widetilde{z''^2}$ is derived as, and corresponds to, the balance equation for $\widetilde{\Theta''^2}$ in premixed combustion (5.108), without reaction rate term (z is a passive scalar):

$$\frac{\partial \bar{\rho}\widetilde{z''^2}}{\partial t} + \frac{\partial}{\partial x_i}\left(\widetilde{\bar{\rho}u_i z''^2}\right) = \quad - \quad \underbrace{\frac{\partial}{\partial x_i}\left(\overline{\rho u_i'' z''^2}\right)}_{\text{turbulent transport}} + \underbrace{\frac{\partial}{\partial x_i}\left(\overline{\rho D\frac{\partial z''^2}{\partial x_i}}\right) + 2\overline{z''\frac{\partial}{\partial x_i}\left(\rho D\frac{\partial \widetilde{z}}{\partial x_i}\right)}}_{\text{molecular diffusion}}$$

$$- \underbrace{2\overline{\rho u_i'' z''}\frac{\partial \widetilde{z}}{\partial x_i}}_{\text{production}} - \underbrace{2\overline{\rho D\frac{\partial z''}{\partial x_i}\frac{\partial z''}{\partial x_i}}}_{\text{dissipation}} \tag{6.32}$$

where:

$$\bar{\rho}\widetilde{\chi_p} = \overline{2\rho D\left(\frac{\partial z''}{\partial x_i}\right)^2} \tag{6.33}$$

is the scalar dissipation rate of the fluctuations of the mixture fraction field z. This scalar dissipation rate measures the decay of $\widetilde{z''^2}$ as evidenced in the simplest case of homogeneous flows (no mean mixture fraction $\widetilde{z}$ gradients). In this situation, Eq. (6.32) reduces to:

$$\frac{d\bar{\rho}\widetilde{z''^2}}{dt} = -2\overline{\rho D\frac{\partial z''}{\partial x_i}\frac{\partial z''}{\partial x_i}} = -\bar{\rho}\widetilde{\chi_p} \tag{6.34}$$

In the literature, multiple expressions have been associated with the terminology *scalar dissipation rate*. First, depending on authors, the scalar dissipation rate may or may not include the density and the factor 2. But its definition may also be based on the mixture fraction field z, as for laminar diffusion flame structure (see Eq. 3.22 in § 3.2.2), or on the mixture fraction fluctuations z''. The total scalar dissipation rate $\widetilde{\chi}$ may be written:

$$\bar{\rho}\widetilde{\chi} = \overline{2\rho D\frac{\partial z}{\partial x_i}\frac{\partial z}{\partial x_i}} = \underbrace{2\overline{\rho D}\frac{\partial \widetilde{z}}{\partial x_i}\frac{\partial \widetilde{z}}{\partial x_i}}_{\bar{\rho}\widetilde{\chi_m}} + 4\overline{\rho D\frac{\partial z''}{\partial x_i}\frac{\partial \widetilde{z}}{\partial x_i}} + \underbrace{2\overline{\rho D\frac{\partial z''}{\partial x_i}\frac{\partial z''}{\partial x_i}}}_{\bar{\rho}\widetilde{\chi_p}} \tag{6.35}$$

[xv] In LES, similarity assumptions are generally introduced (see § 6.5) to avoid such a balance equation.

For constant density flows, the second term in the RHS vanishes and Eq. (6.35) reduces to:

$$\widetilde{\chi} = \widetilde{\chi}_m + \widetilde{\chi}_p \tag{6.36}$$

where $\widetilde{\chi}_m$ measures the scalar dissipation rate due to the mean $\widetilde{z}$ field while $\widetilde{\chi}_p$ measures the scalar dissipation rate due to the turbulent fluctuations of z (z'' field). Neglecting mean gradients against fluctuations gradients, as usually done in RANS, Eq. (6.35) leads to:

$$\overline{\rho}\widetilde{\chi} = \overline{2\rho\mathcal{D}\frac{\partial z}{\partial x_i}\frac{\partial z}{\partial x_i}} \approx \overline{2\rho\mathcal{D}\frac{\partial z''}{\partial x_i}\frac{\partial z''}{\partial x_i}} = \overline{\rho}\widetilde{\chi}_p \tag{6.37}$$

These definitions of the scalar dissipation rate are summarized in Table 6.5.

Name	Definition	Use
Total	$\overline{\rho}\widetilde{\chi} = \overline{2\rho\mathcal{D}\dfrac{\partial z}{\partial x_i}\dfrac{\partial z}{\partial x_i}}$	Laminar flame structure (Eq. 3.22)[xvi]
Perturbations	$\overline{\rho}\widetilde{\chi}_p = \overline{2\rho\mathcal{D}\dfrac{\partial z''}{\partial x_i}\dfrac{\partial z''}{\partial x_i}}$	Dissipation of scalar variance $\widetilde{z''^2}$ (Eq. 6.32)
Mean	$\overline{\rho}\widetilde{\chi}_m = \overline{2\rho\mathcal{D}}\dfrac{\partial \widetilde{z}}{\partial x_i}\dfrac{\partial \widetilde{z}}{\partial x_i}$	Usually neglected in RANS (then $\widetilde{\chi} \approx \widetilde{\chi}_p$)

Table 6.5: Definitions and use of the mixture fraction scalar dissipation rates.

Closure schemes now have to be proposed for the variance $\widetilde{z''^2}$ balance equation (6.32):

- The first RHS term of Eq. (6.32) corresponds to transport by turbulent motions and is modeled using a classical gradient assumption:

$$\overline{\rho u_i'' z''^2} = -\overline{\rho}\frac{\nu_t}{S_{ct_1}}\frac{\partial \widetilde{z''^2}}{\partial x_i} \tag{6.38}$$

where ν_t is the turbulent viscosity, provided by the turbulence model (see § 4.5.3) and S_{ct_1} a turbulent Schmidt number, generally of the order of unity.

- Molecular diffusion terms in Eq. (6.32) are usually neglected against turbulent transport, assuming sufficiently large Reynolds numbers or modeled using an expression similar to Eq. (6.38), replacing the turbulent viscosity ν_t by the flow viscosity ν.

[xvi]According to Eq. (3.21), the laminar flame structure depends on the local instantaneous scalar dissipation rate $\chi = 2\mathcal{D}\dfrac{\partial z}{\partial x_i}\dfrac{\partial z}{\partial x_i}$ which is simply averaged here.

- The unknown contribution $\overline{\rho u_i'' z''}$ in the production term is also modeled using a gradient transport assumption:

$$\overline{\rho u_i'' z''}\frac{\partial \tilde{z}}{\partial x_i} = -\overline{\rho}\frac{\nu_t}{S_{ct_2}}\frac{\partial \tilde{z}}{\partial x_i}\frac{\partial \tilde{z}}{\partial x_i} \qquad (6.39)$$

where S_{ct_2} is a turbulent Schmidt number.

- As evidenced in Eq. (6.34), the scalar dissipation rate $\tilde{\chi}_p$ measures the decay of the mixture fraction fluctuations estimated by the variance $\widetilde{z''^2}$. In fact, this scalar dissipation rate $\tilde{\chi}_p$ plays for the mixture fraction z the same role as the dissipation rate of the kinetic energy, ε, with the velocity field. This analogy is often used to model $\tilde{\chi}_p$ with the turbulent mixing time $\tau_t = k/\varepsilon$:

$$\tilde{\chi}_p = c\frac{\widetilde{z''^2}}{\tau_t} = c\frac{\varepsilon}{k}\widetilde{z''^2} \qquad (6.40)$$

where c is a model constant of order unity. This relation simply expresses that scalar dissipation time and turbulence dissipation time are proportional:

$$\frac{\widetilde{z''^2}}{\tilde{\chi}_p} = \frac{1}{c}\frac{k}{\varepsilon} \qquad (6.41)$$

The closed equation for $\widetilde{z''^2}$ used in most RANS codes is therefore:

$$\boxed{\frac{\partial \overline{\rho}\widetilde{z''^2}}{\partial t} + \frac{\partial}{\partial x_i}\left(\overline{\rho}\tilde{u}_i\widetilde{z''^2}\right) = \frac{\partial}{\partial x_i}\left(\overline{\rho}\frac{\nu_t}{S_{ct_1}}\frac{\partial \widetilde{z''^2}}{\partial x_i}\right) + 2\overline{\rho}\frac{\nu_t}{S_{ct_2}}\frac{\partial \tilde{z}}{\partial x_i}\frac{\partial \tilde{z}}{\partial x_i} - c\overline{\rho}\frac{\varepsilon}{k}\widetilde{z''^2}} \qquad (6.42)$$

This equation can be solved together with Eq. (6.20), (6.21) and (6.23).

An interesting extension of infinitely fast chemistry approaches is to also assume constant density. In this situation, as shown on Fig. 6.24, there is no feedback from the flame structure onto the flow (this feedback is due to thermal expansion and is expressed in terms of density $\overline{\rho}$). Accordingly, the flow field may be computed independently of the flame structure (see Fig. 6.25) and the flame may be reconstructed a posteriori from $\tilde{z}$ and $\widetilde{z''^2}$. This property allows to interpret any non-reacting computation carrying a scalar $\tilde{z}$ and its variance $\widetilde{z''^2}$ as a "diffusion flame" (Jiménez et al. [313]). The same property is also true in experiments: any scalar z field in a non-reacting flow may be interpreted as a flame when a local flame structure is chosen and constant density is assumed (Bilger [50]).

6.4.4   Models for mean reaction rate with infinitely fast chemistry

The previous analysis does not need any closure for the reaction rate. In fact, the mean reaction rate $\overline{\dot{\omega}}_k$ is never even computed because the primitive variables (temperature and

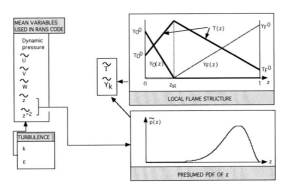

Figure 6.25: Principle of a presumed pdf method for infinitely fast chemistry and constant density: all flame information can be extracted a posteriori from the non-reacting flow field.

species mass fractions) are all linked directly to the mixture fraction. However, this approach is not always possible: when pressure waves propagate into the domain (compressible code) or when other source or sink terms have to be taken into account (for example, heat losses), pressure or temperature may be decoupled from the mixture fraction and it becomes more convenient to explicitly work with reaction rates (see 6.4.1).

Two main approaches have been proposed to model reaction rates in a turbulent non-premixed flame assuming infinitely fast chemistry. The first one extends the Eddy-Break-Up concept (§ 5.3.3), the second analyzes the flame structure in the mixture fraction space.

Eddy Dissipation Concept (EDC)

The Eddy Dissipation Concept, devised by Magnussen and Mjertager [413], directly extends the Eddy-Break-Up model (EBU, see § 5.3.3) to non-premixed combustion. The fuel mean burning rate, $\overline{\dot{\omega}}_F$, is estimated from fuel ($\widetilde{Y}_F$), oxidizer ($\widetilde{Y}_O$) and products ($\widetilde{Y}_P$) mean mass fractions and depends on a turbulent mixing time, estimated from integral length scales as $\tau_t \approx k/\varepsilon$:

$$\overline{\rho \dot{\omega}}_F = C_{mag}\overline{\rho}\,\frac{1}{\tau_t}\,\min\left(\widetilde{Y}_F, \frac{\widetilde{Y}_O}{s}, \beta\frac{\widetilde{Y}_P}{(1+s)}\right) \approx C_{mag}\overline{\rho}\,\frac{\varepsilon}{k}\,\min\left(\widetilde{Y}_F, \frac{\widetilde{Y}_O}{s}, \beta\frac{\widetilde{Y}_P}{(1+s)}\right) \quad (6.43)$$

where C_{mag} and β are two model constants. In Eq. (6.43), the reaction rate is limited by the deficient species. For finite β, this deficient species may be combustion products to take into account the existence of burnt gases, providing the energy required to ignite fresh reactants.

The comments on the EBU model (§ 5.3.3) also apply to the Magnussen model: EDC is a good model in many cases but the model constants C_{mag} and β as well as the turbulent time τ_t need to be adjusted on a case by case basis. Furthermore, EDC cannot precisely describe any ignition or stabilization mechanism since fuel and oxidizer burn as soon as they meet.[xvii]

Flame structure analysis

Mean reaction rates may also be estimated from Eq. (3.26), assuming a steady state flame structure:

$$\dot{\omega}_k = -\frac{1}{2}\rho\chi\frac{\partial^2 Y_k}{\partial z^2} \tag{6.44}$$

leading, after averaging:

$$\bar{\dot{\omega}}_k = -\frac{1}{2}\int_0^1\left[\int_0^\infty \rho\chi\frac{\partial^2 Y_k}{\partial z^2}p(\chi,z)d\chi\right]dz \tag{6.45}$$

where $p(\chi, z)$ is the joint mixture fraction/scalar dissipation rate pdf, measuring the probability that χ and z have given values at the same location at the same time. For infinitely fast chemistry, reaction rates and $\partial^2 Y_k/\partial z^2$ are Dirac-delta functions centered on the stoichiometric value $z = z_{st}$ of the mixture fraction z. In this situation, according to Table 3.5:

$$\frac{\partial Y_F}{\partial z} = \frac{Y_F^0}{1 - z_{st}}H\left(z - z_{st}\right) \quad \text{and} \quad \frac{\partial^2 Y_F}{\partial z^2} = \frac{Y_F^0}{1 - z_{st}}\delta\left(z - z_{st}\right) \tag{6.46}$$

where H and δ are respectively the Heaviside and the Dirac-delta functions. Eq. (6.45) then reduces to:

$$\boxed{\bar{\dot{\omega}}_F = -\frac{Y_F^0}{2\left(1 - z_{st}\right)}\int_0^\infty \rho\chi\, p(\chi, z_{st})\, d\chi = -\frac{Y_F^0}{2\left(1 - z_{st}\right)}\left(\overline{\rho\chi|z_{st}}\right)p(z_{st})} \tag{6.47}$$

where $\left(\overline{\rho\chi|z_{st}}\right) = \bar{\rho}\widetilde{\chi}_{st}$ is the conditional mean of $\rho\chi$ for $z = z_{st}$ and $p(z_{st})$ the probability to have $z = z_{st}$. A submodel should be provided for $\left(\overline{\rho\chi|z_{st}}\right)$. The simplest one is to assume $\left(\overline{\rho\chi|z_{st}}\right) \approx \bar{\rho}\widetilde{\chi}$. A more advanced formulation is described in the following section. Expression (6.47) may then be used to advance the system (6.20) to (6.23).

6.4.5   Models for primitive variables with finite rate chemistry

Assuming infinitely fast chemistry is clearly inadequate in many circumstances and incorporating more chemistry into turbulent combustion models is needed. As soon as finite rate

---

[xvii]In practical applications, the reaction rate in Eq. (6.43) is sometimes also limited by the Arrhenius reaction rate computed using the mean mass fractions and temperature. This is a simple, approximate way to limit the reaction rate in high strain rate zones, such as initial regions of mixing layers, and to incorporate some chemistry features for ignition or stabilization.

chemistry is introduced, the link between flow variables and mixture fraction is no longer unique and depends on the Damköhler number (see § 3.5.2 and Fig. 3.20). This point is illustrated on Fig. 6.26 which displays an ideal lifted flame with an initial mixing zone leading to ignition and an active flame followed by a local quenched zone (for example because of high turbulence).

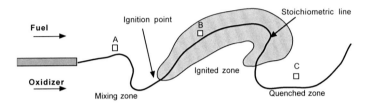

Figure 6.26: Diffusion flame structure ambiguity for finite rate chemistry: shaded zones correspond to large reaction rates.

In Fig. 6.26, knowing the mixture fraction z at a given point is not sufficient anymore to deduce local species mass fractions or temperature if chemistry is not infinitely fast: such a point could correspond to pure mixing (like point A in Fig. 6.26) or to an ignited flame (point B) or a quenched flame (point C); points A, B and C can have the same z but very different mass fractions or temperature. Additional information is required to choose which flame structure must be used. To (partially) incorporate this information in turbulent combustion models based on primitive variables (and not on reaction rates) can be achieved using flamelet concepts. This approach may then be extended through conditional momentum closures (CMC) or probability density function balance equations.

Finite rate chemistry modeling based on flamelet approaches

The basic idea of flamelet modeling is to assume that a small instantaneous flame element embedded in a turbulent flow has the structure of a laminar flame: the z-diagram structure functions described in Section 3.2 for laminar flames then hold for turbulent flame elements too. This assumption requires all reaction zones to be thin compared to turbulent flow scales, i.e. large Damköhler numbers as shown in Fig. 6.23 (Peters [498]). Fig. 6.27 shows how this concept is carried out in practice.

Some "parameters" must be conserved to represent correctly turbulent flamelets using laminar diffusion flames. The identification of these parameters is difficult. Obviously, the chemical scheme should be the same for turbulent flamelets and for laminar diffusion flames. The pressure should be the same and the conditions at infinity (mass fractions (Y_F^0, Y_O^0) and temperature (T_F^0, T_O^0)) should be conserved in a first approach (Pitsch and Peters [514], Bish and Dahm [58]). But other parameters are also needed to define a diffusion flame: strain, curvature and flamelet "age" may be important; and are retained or not in flamelet models depending on their complexity.

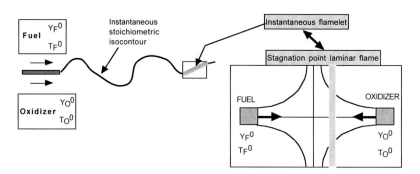

Figure 6.27: Flamelet concepts for turbulent non-premixed flames.

To simplify the presentation, the scalar dissipation rate at the flame location, χ_{st} (or equivalently the flame stretch) is the only parameter retained here but other control parameters may be added. Using only χ_{st} as an additional flame parameter also limits the capacities of the model: even though this extension allows to account for stretch effects and quenching, it cannot be used to predict flame stabilization for example. It is, however, a first step which leads to considerable complexity as shown below.

Under these assumptions, the flame structure is given by a set of functions $T(z, \chi_{st})$, $Y_k(z, \chi_{st})$, solutions of Eq. (3.21). All functions $T(z, \chi_{st})$, $Y_k(z, \chi_{st})$, may be computed for laminar stagnation point flames, independently of the turbulent code, and stored in "flamelet libraries." The mean species mass fractions are then obtained from:

$$\overline{\rho}\widetilde{Y}_k = \int_0^{+\infty} \int_0^1 \rho Y_k(z, \chi_{st})\, p\,(z, \chi_{st})\; dz\, d\chi_{st} \qquad (6.48)$$

while the mean temperature is given by:

$$\overline{\rho}\widetilde{T} = \int_0^{+\infty} \int_0^1 \rho T(z, \chi_{st})\, p\,(z, \chi_{st})\; dz\, d\chi_{st} \qquad (6.49)$$

Statistical independence or the mixture fraction z and its scalar dissipation rate χ_{st} is often assumed,[xviii] leading to:

$$p(z, \chi_{st}) = p(z)\, p(\chi_{st}) \qquad (6.50)$$

[xviii]This assumption seems, a priori, very crude. In fact, this statistical independence is quite well verified in direct numerical simulations and may be simply explained: the mixture fraction z measures the reactants mixing and is mainly related to large scale flow motions. On the other hand, χ_{st} is linked to the local flame structure (χ_{st} corresponds to a local z-gradient and measures the local diffusion zone thickness) and is governed by small scale features.

or, in terms of mass-weighted probability density function:

$$\rho p(z, \chi_{st}) = \overline{\rho} \widetilde{p}(z) \, p(\chi_{st}) \tag{6.51}$$

Probability density functions for the mixture fraction z and its scalar dissipation rate χ_{st} are usually presumed. The mixture fraction pdf $\widetilde{p}(z)$ is generally presumed using β-functions based on $\widetilde{z}$ and $\widetilde{z''^2}$ as for infinitely fast chemistry (see § 6.4.2). A presumed distribution is also required for χ_{st}. A Dirac-delta function may be retained (Pitsch and Peters [514]) if scalar dissipation is assumed to remain unchanged along the flame front:

$$p(\chi_{st}) = \delta \left(\chi_{st} - \widetilde{\chi}_{st} \right) \tag{6.52}$$

but a more physical approach is to use log normal distributions (Effelsberg and Peters [198]):

$$p(\chi_{st}) = \frac{1}{\chi_{st} \sigma \sqrt{2\pi}} \exp \left(-\frac{(\ln \chi_{st} - \mu)^2}{2\sigma^2} \right) \tag{6.53}$$

where the parameter μ is linked to the mean value of χ_{st}:

$$\widetilde{\chi}_{st} = \int_0^{+\infty} \chi_{st} p\left(\chi_{st}\right) \, d\chi_{st} = \exp \left(\mu + \frac{\sigma^2}{2} \right) \tag{6.54}$$

and σ is the variance of $\ln(\chi)$ so that:

$$\widetilde{\chi_{st}''^2} = \widetilde{\chi}_{st}^2 \left(\exp(\sigma^2) - 1 \right) \tag{6.55}$$

σ is often assumed to be constant: $\sigma = 1$ leading to $\sqrt{\widetilde{\chi_{st}''^2}}/\widetilde{\chi}_{st} = 1.31$ (Effelsberg and Peters [198]). A functional dependence of σ with turbulent Reynolds number may also be assumed such as $\sigma = 0.5 \ln(0.1 Re_t^{1/2})$ (Liew et al. [395]). But, in fact, σ has a limited practical influence on the probability density function $p(\chi_{st})$ and on final results. Fig. 6.28 shows typical lognormal distributions for two values of σ: $\sigma = 1$ gives a large variance ($\widetilde{\chi_{st}''^2}/\widetilde{\chi}_{st}^2 = 1.7$) while $\sigma = 0.25$ corresponds to a smaller variance ($\widetilde{\chi_{st}''^2}/\widetilde{\chi}_{st}^2 = 0.06$).

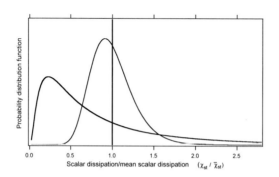

Figure 6.28: Lognormal scalar dissipation rate distribution for low ($\sigma = 0.25$, $\widetilde{\chi''^2_{st}}/\widetilde{\chi}^2_{st} = 0.06$, ——) and high ($\sigma = 1$, $\widetilde{\chi''^2_{st}}/\widetilde{\chi}^2_{st} = 1.7$, ——) values of variance (Eq. 6.53). The thick vertical line would correspond to a Dirac-delta function at $\widetilde{\chi}_{st}$ ($\widetilde{\chi''^2_{st}} = 0$).

In these formulations, $\widetilde{\chi}_{st}$ is still missing but, as already done in § 6.3.2, using results for a steady strained laminar flame with constant density (§ 3.4.2), $\widetilde{\chi}_{st}$ and $\widetilde{\chi}$ can be linked by:

$$\widetilde{\chi} = \widetilde{\chi}_{st} \int_0^1 \frac{F(z)}{F(z_{st})}\, \widetilde{p}(z)\, dz = \widetilde{\chi}_{st} \mathcal{F}\left(\widetilde{z}, \widetilde{z''^2}\right) \tag{6.56}$$

with

$$F(z) = \exp\left(-2\left[\text{erf}^{-1}\left(2z - 1\right)\right]^2\right) \tag{6.57}$$

The mean scalar dissipation rate $\widetilde{\chi}$ is usually modeled from a turbulent time (Eq. 6.40):

$$\boxed{\widetilde{\chi} = c\frac{\varepsilon}{k}\widetilde{z''^2}} \tag{6.58}$$

The organization of a pdf-flamelet model based on primitive variables is summarized in Table 6.6 and in Fig. 6.29. The resolution follows a route similar to the infinitely fast chemistry case. The RANS code solves for main flow variables as well as for $\widetilde{z}$ and $\widetilde{z''^2}$ (Fig. 6.29). Mixture fraction and scalar dissipation rate pdfs are then constructed and combined with the local flame structure (flamelet libraries) to determine all flow variables (temperature and mass fractions). Density is finally deduced from temperature and sent back to the RANS code. As for infinitely fast chemistry (§ 6.4.2), flamelet calculations are not performed on the fly and variables entering the RANS code, such as mean temperature or density are tabulated prior to computation as functions of $\widetilde{z}$, $\widetilde{z''^2}$ and $\widetilde{\chi}$.

Compared to models assuming infinitely fast chemistry (see § 6.4.2), a new element is required: finite rate chemistry effects are measured through scalar dissipation rates at the

OPERATION	RESULTS
STAGNATION POINT FLAMES:	
Store flame structure in library	$T(z, \chi_{st}) \quad Y_k(z, \chi_{st})$
IN RANS CODE:	
Solve for mixture fraction and variance	$\widetilde{z} \quad \widetilde{z''^2}$
Construct β pdf for z using $\widetilde{z}$ and $\widetilde{z''^2}$	$\widetilde{p}(z)$
Evaluate $\widetilde{\chi}$ from $\widetilde{z''^2}$, k and ε	$\widetilde{\chi} = c\widetilde{z''^2}\varepsilon/k$
Evaluate $\widetilde{\chi}_{st}$ from $\widetilde{\chi}$ and $\mathcal{F}(\widetilde{z}, \widetilde{z''^2})$	$\widetilde{\chi}_{st} = \widetilde{\chi}/\mathcal{F}(\widetilde{z}, \widetilde{z''^2})$
Construct log normal pdf for χ_{st} using $\widetilde{\chi}_{st}$	$p(\chi_{st})$
Compute mean temperature	$\widetilde{T} = \int_0^\infty \int_0^1 T(z, \chi_{st})\widetilde{p}(z)p(\chi_{st})dzd\chi_{st}$
Compute density from $\widetilde{T}$ and send back to RANS code	$\overline{\rho}$

Table 6.6: Principle of a pdf flamelet model using primitive variables.

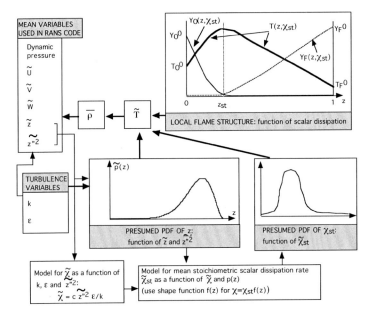

Figure 6.29: Organization of a pdf-flamelet model using primitive variables: mean species mass fractions are obtained by post-processing using Eq. (6.48) but are not required during the computation.

stoichiometric conditions. These scalar dissipation rates have to be correlated to available resolved quantities (usually mixture fraction distribution and turbulent time scales) as described
in Section 6.4.3.

The finite rate chemistry modeling is implicitly presented here using steady-state flamelet
elements. Of course, unsteady flamelets (i.e. solutions of the full Eq. 3.21) may be used and
are mandatory to incorporate unsteady features such as ignition. This has been done, for
example, in the so-called RIF (representative interactive flamelet) model developed by Barths
et al. [36] or in the models proposed by Michel et al. [440].

Conditional Momentum Closure (CMC)

In principle, the Conditional Momentum Closure (CMC) approach, independently devised by
Klimenko [350] and Bilger [52], proposes a more complex description of turbulent combustion.
The basic idea is to derive, close and solve exact balance equations for conditional species mass
fractions $\left(\overline{\rho Y_k | z^*}\right)$, corresponding to the mean value of mass fraction Y_k for a given value of
the mixture fraction $z = z^*$. The mean species mass fraction are then given by:

$$\widetilde{\rho Y_k} = \int_0^1 \left(\overline{\rho Y_k | z^*}\right) p\left(z^*\right) dz^* \tag{6.59}$$

This formalism requires (Klimenko and Bilger [351]):

- balance equations for all conditional mass fractions $\left(\overline{\rho Y_k | z^*}\right)$. An additional equation
  is needed for each z^* level. These equations also contain second order derivatives in the
  z-space and, accordingly, require a sufficiently large number of conditioning values z^* to
  be estimated with sufficient precision,

- a description of the probability density function, $p\left(z^*\right)$, generally presumed from $\widetilde{z}$ and
  $\widetilde{z''^2}$.

This approach is interesting for several reasons:

- Conditional mass fractions, $\left(\overline{\rho Y_k | z^*}\right)$ or $\left(\overline{Y_k | z^*}\right)$, are accessible to measurements.[xix]

- Some phenomena are strongly related to iso-mixture fraction surfaces. For example,
  Mastorakos et al. [422] show that auto-ignition occurs on the most reactive mixture
  fraction, z_{MR}, surface while the well-established diffusion flame corresponds to the stoichiometric mixture fraction surface.[xx]

[xix]See, for example, the database compiled in the framework of TNF workshops
www.sandia.gov/TNF/abstract.

[xx]The most reactive mixture fraction, z_{MR}, corresponds to the mixture fraction value for which the reaction
rate is maximum, taking into account that in auto-igniting systems, at least one of the reactants is preheated
(see Section 6.6.2 and Mastorakos et al. [422] for details).

- CMC could be viewed as a multi-surface model ($z = z^*$ iso-surfaces), extending and refining flame surface density formalisms.

However, $N_k \times N_z$ additional balance equations have to be closed and solved for conditional quantities $\overline{(\rho Y_k|z^*)}$, where N_k and N_z are the numbers of species and conditioning values retained, respectively, leading to very high computational costs. These costs are sometimes reduced introducing restrictive assumptions such as a slow evolution of conditional quantities $\overline{(\rho Y_k|z^*)}$ (the corresponding balance equations are then solved on coarser meshes) or homogeneity along transverse flow directions $\overline{(\rho Y_k|z^*}$ then depend only on time and downstream location). Vervisch et al. [673] propose a simplified version of this formalism where $\overline{\rho Y_k|z^*}$ are presumed from tabulated chemistry (PCM: Presumed Conditional Momentum).

Balance equations for probability density functions

There is no theoretical difficulty in deriving balance equations for probability density functions $p(z)$ in Eq. (6.28) or (6.59) and $p(z, \chi_{st})$ in Eq. (6.48). Nevertheless, this approach is generally not retained for practical simulations because it requires some assumptions on the flame structure (for example flamelet assumptions) to provide $T(z, \chi_{st})$ and $Y_k(z, \chi_{st})$. Accordingly, pdf balance equations are used in connection with mean reaction rate closures (see § 6.4.6).

6.4.6 Models for mean reaction rate with finite rate chemistry

As explained in Section 6.4.4, working with primitive variables is not always convenient and models must then be based on reaction rates $\bar{\omega}_k$ formulations. In this case, species equations are conserved and models must be developed for the average reaction rates $\bar{\omega}_k$. This derivation may be done using flamelet or statistical point approaches.

Presumed pdf flamelet models

Instead of building a flamelet library containing the relations between primitive variables (species mass fractions and temperature) and the mixture fraction z and its scalar dissipation rate χ_{st} as in Section 6.4.5, laminar reaction rates $\dot{\omega}_k(z, \chi_{st})$ may be stored in the library. The mean reaction rate $\bar{\omega}_k$ is then expressed using a pdf formulation according to:

$$\bar{\omega}_k = \int_0^1 \int_0^\infty \dot{\omega}_k(z, \chi_{st}) p(z, \chi_{st}) \, dz \, d\chi_{st} \tag{6.60}$$

The joint pdf of z and χ_{st} is also generally split into one-dimensional pdfs:

$$p(z, \chi_{st}) = p(z)p(\chi_{st}) \quad \text{or} \quad \rho p(z, \chi_{st}) = \bar{\rho}\tilde{p}(z)p(\chi_{st}) \tag{6.61}$$

β-functions are used to presume $\tilde{p}(z)$ and a log-normal distribution is generally assumed for χ_{st} (see § 6.4.5). This procedure is summarized in Fig. 6.30 and Table 6.7. The RANS solver provides $\tilde{z}$ and $\widetilde{z''^2}$. These data are then used to construct probability density functions and obtain the mean reaction rate from the flamelet library (Eq. 6.60).

OPERATION	RESULTS
LAMINAR STAGNATION POINT FLAMES:	
Store reaction rates of species k in library	$\dot{\omega}_k(z, \chi_{st})$
IN RANS CODE:	
Solve for mixture fraction and variance	$\widetilde{z} \quad \widetilde{z''^2}$
Construct β-pdf for z using $\widetilde{z}$ and $\widetilde{z''^2}$	$\widetilde{p}(z)$
Evaluate $\widetilde{\chi}$ using $\widetilde{z''^2}$, k and ε	$\widetilde{\chi} = c\widetilde{z''^2}\varepsilon/k$
Evaluate $\widetilde{\chi}_{st}$ using $\widetilde{\chi}$ and $\mathcal{F}(\widetilde{z}, \widetilde{z''^2})$	$\widetilde{\chi}_{st} = \widetilde{\chi}/\mathcal{F}(\widetilde{z}, \widetilde{z''^2})$
Construct log normal pdf for χ_{st}	$p(\chi_{st})$
Compute $\overline{\dot{\omega}}_k$ using pdfs and flamelet library	$\overline{\dot{\omega}}_k = \overline{\rho} \int_0^1 [(\dot{\omega}_k(z, \chi_{st})/\rho]\widetilde{p}(z)p(\chi_{st})dzd\chi_{st}$

Table 6.7: Principle of a pdf-flamelet model using mean reaction rates.

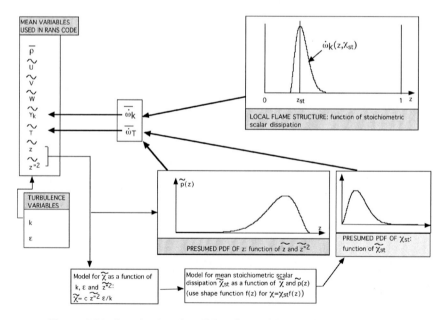

Figure 6.30: Organization of a pdf-flamelet model using mean reaction rates.

Flame surface density flamelet models

Flame surface density concepts are based on a slightly different approach. Only the reaction rate integrated along the normal direction of a strained laminar diffusion flame (stoichiometric scalar dissipation rate χ_{st}) $\dot{\Omega}_k(\chi_{st})$, is stored in the flamelet library. The mean reaction rate $\overline{\dot{\omega}}_k$ is then expressed as the product of the flame surface density Σ by the local reaction rate per unit of flame area $\dot{\Omega}_k(\chi_{st})$:

$$\overline{\dot{\omega}}_k = \overline{\dot{\Omega}_k(\chi_{st})} \, \Sigma \tag{6.62}$$

The mean surface density Σ is defined as (Pope [530], Vervisch et al. [672]):[xxi]

$$\Sigma = \left(\overline{|\nabla z| \, | z = z_{st}} \right) p(z_{st}) \tag{6.63}$$

where $\left(\overline{|\nabla z| \, | z = z_{st}} \right)$ is the conditional average of $|\nabla z|$ on the stoichiometric surface $z = z_{st}$. $\dot{\Omega}_k(\chi_{st})$ is the integrated reaction rate averaged along the flame surface. For a thin flame front, Vervisch and Veynante [671] have shown the exact relation:

$$\overline{\dot{\omega}}_k = \int_0^1 \int_0^\infty \dot{\omega}_k(z, \chi_{st}) p(z, \chi_{st}) \, dz \, d\chi_{st} = \underbrace{\left[\int_0^\infty \Omega(\chi_{st}) p(\chi_{st}) \, d\chi_{st} \right]}_{\overline{\dot{\Omega}_k(\chi_{st})}} \Sigma \tag{6.64}$$

which shows the link between pdf and flame surface density formalisms. Flame surface density models generally assume that:

$$\overline{\dot{\Omega}_k(\chi_{st})} \approx \dot{\Omega}_k \left(\widetilde{\chi}_{st} \right) \tag{6.65}$$

which is equivalent to assume a Dirac-delta function centered on $\chi = \widetilde{\chi}_{st}$ for $p(\chi_{st})$, the probability density function of the scalar dissipation rate. $\dot{\Omega}_k(\widetilde{\chi}_{st})$ is then extracted from flamelet libraries.[xxii] Another model is required to relate the average scalar dissipation rate $\widetilde{\chi}_{st}$ to turbulent quantities available in the RANS code.[xxiii]

[xxi]The flame surface is here identified to the stoichiometric mixture fraction iso-surface $z = z_{st}$ as a diffusion flame usually lies in this region (Chapter 3). But autoignition occurs on the "most reactive" mixture fraction iso-surface, z_{MR} which generally differs from z_{st} (see § 6.6.2). To overcome this difficulty and according to Veynante and Vervisch [678], Hilbert et al. [288] and Tap et al. [643], extend definition (6.63) to consider a "generalized" flame surface as:

$$\overline{\Sigma} = \int_0^1 \left(\overline{|\nabla z| \, | z = z^*} \right) p(z^*) \, dz^* = \overline{|\nabla z|}$$

This model has been successful to predict autoignition of turbulent flames (Tap and Veynante [642]).

[xxii]Flamelet libraries are generally built from one-dimensional steady laminar strained diffusion flame computations. Nevertheless, unsteady effects, incorporating the flame response time evidenced in Section 3.4.3, may be included according to Haworth et al. [278], Fichot et al. [212].

[xxiii]In fact, flame surface density models generally relate the reaction rate $\dot{\Omega}_k$ to the flame strain rate instead of the scalar dissipation rate. As these two quantities are directly linked in strained laminar diffusion flames (see Eq. 3.66), the principle remains the same.

A main issue is the derivation of a balance equation for the flame surface density Σ. Flame surface density models have been first proposed by Marble and Broadwell [419] who have derived a Σ-equation mainly from intuitive arguments. This balance equation is written, for single reaction between fuel (F) and oxidizer (O):

$$\frac{\partial \Sigma}{\partial t} + \frac{\partial \widetilde{u}_i \Sigma}{\partial x_i} = \frac{\partial}{\partial x_i}\left(\frac{\nu_t}{\sigma_c}\frac{\partial \Sigma}{\partial x_i}\right) + \alpha\kappa\Sigma - \beta\left(\frac{V_F}{\widetilde{Y}_F} + \frac{V_O}{\widetilde{Y}_O}\right)\Sigma^2 \qquad (6.66)$$

where κ is the mean strain rate acting on the flame surface and is estimated from a turbulent time scale.[xxiv] α and β are model constants. V_F and V_O are respectively the fuel and oxidizer consumption speed, estimated from one-dimensional steady laminar strain flame. According to Eq. (3.64), V_F is given by $\rho V_F = \dot{\Omega}_F$ and $V_O = sV_F$, where s is the stoichiometric mass coefficient. The source term $\kappa\Sigma$, similar to the one found in Eq. (5.85), is easily derived analyzing transport of material surfaces by turbulent flow field. The consumption term (last term in Eq. 6.66) is based on phenomenological arguments and expresses that the flame surface consumption is proportional to the reaction rate ($V_F\Sigma$ or $V_O\Sigma$) and inversely proportional to available reactants per unit of flame area (i.e. $\widetilde{Y}_F/\Sigma$ and $\widetilde{Y}_O/\Sigma$). This term is known as the "flamelet mutual annihilation term" (Marble and Broadwell [419]).

Recent analyses have formally evidenced links between flame surface density and the mixture fraction z probability density function, proving that writing an equation for Σ is actually equivalent to deriving an equation for one of the moments of the pdf of z (Pope [530], Vervisch et al. [672], Vervisch and Veynante [671]).

The principle of flame surface density models is summarized in Table 6.8 and Fig. 6.31. Balance equations for the mixture fraction or its variance are no longer required but all species and temperature equations must be conserved. These models have various advantages: working with reaction rates, they can be extended to more complex situations like compressible flows, supersonic combustion and partially premixed combustion (Veynante et al. [679], Maistret et al. [415], Candel et al. [106], Veynante et al. [680], Hélie and Trouve [281]). Since only integrated reaction rates $\dot{\Omega}_k(\chi_{st})$ are required, the corresponding libraries are smaller. However, conservation equations for all species must be solved, limiting this approach to few species.

Full statistical point models

The two approaches previously described are based on flamelet assumptions: the flame structure is assumed to correspond locally to a laminar flame element. In full statistical point models, assumptions on the flame structure are no longer required. The mean reaction rate

---

[xxiv] In the initial work of Marble and Broadwell [419] devoted to a two-dimensional mixing layer between parallel fuel and oxidizer streams, κ is estimated from the absolute value of the transverse gradient of the mean axial velocity. Other works use the integral turbulent time scale k/ε for κ but relevant time scale modeling in turbulent non-premixed combustion is still an open question.

OPERATION	RESULTS
COMPUTE LAMINAR STAGNATION POINT FLAMES:	
Store integrated reaction rates $\dot{\Omega}_k$ and $\dot{\Omega}_T$ in library	$\dot{\Omega}_k(\chi_{st}),\ \dot{\Omega}_T(\chi_{st})$
IN RANS CODE:	
Solve for flame surface density	Σ
Evaluate the mean scalar dissipation rate from k and ε	$\widetilde{\chi}_{st}$
Obtain mean species reaction rates from library	$\dot{\Omega}_k$
Compute species $(\overline{\dot{\omega}}_k)$ mean reaction rates:	$\overline{\dot{\omega}}_k = \dot{\Omega}_k(\widetilde{\chi}_{st})\,\Sigma$
Compute temperature $(\overline{\dot{\omega}}_T)$ mean reaction rate:	$\overline{\dot{\omega}}_T = \dot{\Omega}_T(\widetilde{\chi}_{st})\,\Sigma$
Advance mean species and temperature using $\overline{\dot{\omega}}_k$ and $\overline{\dot{\omega}}_T$	$\widetilde{Y}_k \quad \widetilde{T}$

Table 6.8: Principle of a flamelet model based on flame surface density concepts.

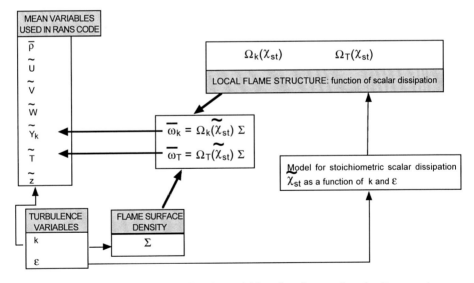

Figure 6.31: Organization of a flamelet model based on flame surface density concepts.

for species k is written:

$$\overline{\dot{\omega}_k} = \int_{Y_1=0}^1 \int_{Y_2=0}^1 \ldots \int_{Y_N=0}^1 \int_T \dot{\omega}_k(Y_1,Y_2,\ldots,Y_N,T)\, p(Y_1,Y_2,\ldots,Y_N,T)\, dY_1 dY_2 \ldots dY_N dT$$

$$(6.67)$$

where $p(Y_1,Y_2,\ldots,Y_N,T)$ is the joint probability of species and temperature. Reaction rates $\dot{\omega}_k$ are directly provided by kinetics (Arrhenius laws) such as for example, Table 1.5. The advantage of this approach is to be able to handle complex chemical schemes (reaction rates $\dot{\omega}_k$ are known) but the estimate of the joint probability density function $p(Y_1,Y_2,\ldots,Y_N,T)$ constitutes the challenge of the method. Two main routes may be followed:

Presumed pdf models.

A given shape is assumed for the probability density function, for example using β-functions or log-normal distribution, determined from available parameters such as mean mass fractions, $\widetilde{Y}_k$, and variances, $\widetilde{Y_k''^2}$. Unfortunately practical simulations show that it is very difficult to presume the shape of a joint pdf depending on more than two variables.[xxv] In practice, presumed pdf approaches are generally used together with flamelet assumptions.

Transported pdf models.

In this case, a balance equation is derived for the joint pdf. This equation is exactly the same as in premixed turbulent flames (Eq. 5.115). As already described, the reaction term is closed because it depends only on local quantities. On the other hand, the molecular mixing (or micromixing) needs closures. Various works have been conducted in this direction (see, for example, Pope [532], Dopazo [182], Fox [219] or Haworth [279]). Proposed models appear to be more efficient for turbulent non-premixed flames, governed by mixing processes, than for premixed flames controlled by a diffusion-reaction balance.

6.5   LES of turbulent non-premixed flames

Non-premixed flames appear to be mainly governed by turbulent mixing, because chemistry is generally faster than turbulent times. Accordingly, large eddy simulations for turbulent non-premixed combustion are based on mixing descriptions, through probability density functions for the mixture fraction z. A mixing approach has also been derived using a one-dimensional stochastic description of turbulent stirring ("linear eddy model").

[xxv] A simplified approach is to assume a statistical independence of pdf variables, to write:

$$p(Y_1,Y_2,\ldots,Y_N,T) = p(Y_1)p(Y_2)\ldots p(Y_N)p(T) \qquad (6.68)$$

and to presume each single variable pdf $p(Y_k)$ and $p(T)$. Nevertheless, this statistical independence does not hold because mass fractions and temperature are clearly linked in flames. For example, for infinitely fast chemistry with unity Lewis numbers, mass fractions and temperature are linear functions of the mixture fraction z (see Fig. 3.6).

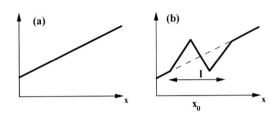

Figure 6.32: "Triplet map" used in the Linear Eddy Model (Kerstein [337]) to simulate a one-dimensional turbulent stirring process. (a) before mixing; (b) simulated mixing by a vortex of size l.

6.5.1 Linear Eddy Model

The Linear Eddy Model (LEM) approach (Kerstein [337, 338, 339, 340, 341], McMurthy et al. [427]) is based on a one-dimensional stochastic description of turbulence stirring and diffusion. In a LES framework, LEM is used to represent unresolved mixing occurring at the subgrid scale level. Subgrid scale chemical reaction and turbulent mixing are analyzed from a one-dimensional problem. Two subsequent stages are involved:

1. **Turbulent stirring mechanisms** are modeled by a rearrangement process applied to a reference one-dimensional scalar field. The initial one-dimensional scalar distribution (Fig. 6.32a) is rearranged on a given segment of size l according to Fig. 6.32b ("triplet map"). This process may be viewed as the effect of a single turbulent structure of size l located in x_0. Then, the turbulent mixing is simulated from a stochastic description where vortex locations x_0, vortex sizes l ($\eta_k \leq l \leq \Delta$, where η_k is the Kolmogorov length scale and Δ the LES filter size) and vortex frequencies λ are specified according to a given turbulence spectra.

2. **Molecular diffusion and chemical processes** are explicitly computed by solving a one-dimensional balance equations:

$$\frac{\partial \rho Y_i}{\partial t} = \frac{\partial}{\partial x}\left(\rho D_i \frac{\partial Y_i}{\partial x}\right) + \dot{\omega}_i \qquad (6.69)$$

Complex chemistry or differential diffusion effects may be easily incorporated in Eq. (6.69). LEM also provides a direct estimation of filtered mass fractions $\widetilde{Y}_i$ or temperature $\widetilde{T}$ without balance transport equations for these quantities. Nevertheless, mass fractions and temperature transports between adjacent mesh cells have to be explicitly described. Note also that a one-dimensional calculation is required in each computational cell (Eq. 6.69), leading to a heavy computational load.

LEM was successful to simulate turbulent mixing (McMurthy et al. [428]) and non-premixed combustion in some cases (McMurthy et al. [427], Menon et al. [438], Calhoon and Menon

[101], Mathey and Chollet [425]). Despite some attempts (Menon and Kerstein [436], Menon et al. [437], Smith and Menon [620]), its extension to turbulent premixed combustion raises some specific difficulties. For instance, viscous dissipation and flame front curvatures play an important role in flame/turbulence interactions (Poinsot et al. [523], Roberts et al. [562]), properties which are not accounted for in LEM formulations.

6.5.2 Probability density functions

Probability density functions, introduced above in RANS context, are easily extended to LES, both for species mass fraction or for reaction rates. Filtered species mass fractions and reaction rates are defined as (see § 4.7.1):

$$\overline{\rho}\left(\mathbf{x},t\right)\widetilde{Y}_k\left(\mathbf{x},t\right) = \int \rho\left(\mathbf{x},t\right) Y_k\left(\mathbf{x}',t\right) F\left(\mathbf{x}-\mathbf{x}'\right) d\mathbf{x}' \tag{6.70}$$

$$\overline{\dot{\omega}}_k\left(\mathbf{x},t\right) = \int \dot{\omega}_k\left(\mathbf{x},t\right) F\left(\mathbf{x}-\mathbf{x}'\right) d\mathbf{x}' \tag{6.71}$$

where F denotes the LES filter. Infinitely fast and finite rate chemistry cases are now discussed successively.

Infinitely fast chemistry

As described in Section 3.5.3, for equilibrium chemistry, mass fractions or reaction rate depend only on the mixture fraction z. Then, Eq. (6.71) may be recast as:

$$\begin{aligned} \overline{\dot{\omega}}_k &= \int \dot{\omega}_k\left(z\right) F\left(\mathbf{x}-\mathbf{x}'\right) d\mathbf{x}' \\ &= \int \int_0^1 \dot{\omega}_k\left(z^*\right) \delta\left(z\left(\mathbf{x}',t\right)-z^*\right) F\left(\mathbf{x}-\mathbf{x}'\right) dz^* d\mathbf{x}' \end{aligned} \tag{6.72}$$

where δ denotes the Dirac-delta function. Then:

$$\overline{\dot{\omega}}_k\left(\mathbf{x},t\right) = \int_0^1 \dot{\omega}_k\left(z^*\right) \underbrace{\int \delta\left(z\left(\mathbf{x}',t\right)-z^*\right) F\left(\mathbf{x}-\mathbf{x}'\right) d\mathbf{x}'}_{\text{Subgrid scale pdf } p(z^*,\mathbf{x},t)} dz^* = \int_0^1 \dot{\omega}_k\left(z^*\right) p(z^*,\mathbf{x},t) dz^*$$

where the subgrid scale probability density function, $p(z^*,\mathbf{x},t)$ has been introduced (Gao and O'Brien [226]). This probability density function may be either presumed or obtained by solving a balance equation, formally identical to the pdf-balance equation in RANS.

Cook and Riley [151] proposed to presume the z-pdf shape using a β-function (§ 6.4.2), based on the filtered mixture fraction $\widetilde{z}$ and its unresolved fluctuations $\widetilde{z''^2}$:

$$\widetilde{p}(z) = \frac{\rho\, p(z)}{\overline{\rho}} = z^{a-1}(1-z)^{b-1}\frac{\Gamma(a+b)}{\Gamma(a)\Gamma(b)} \tag{6.73}$$

where

$$a = \widetilde{z}\left(\frac{\widetilde{z}(1-\widetilde{z})}{\widetilde{z''^2}} - 1\right) \quad \text{and} \quad b = \frac{1-\widetilde{z}}{\widetilde{z}}\left(\frac{\widetilde{z}(1-\widetilde{z})}{\widetilde{z''^2}} - 1\right) \qquad (6.74)$$

An exact (but unclosed) balance equation may be derived for $\widetilde{z''^2} = \widetilde{(z - \widetilde{z})^2}$, but in LES, $\widetilde{z''^2}$ is generally estimated from resolved quantities using a scale similarity assumption:

$$\widetilde{z''^2} = \widetilde{(z - \widetilde{z})^2} = C_z\left(\widehat{\left(\widetilde{z^2}\right)} - \left(\widehat{\widetilde{z}}\right)^2\right) \qquad (6.75)$$

where $\widehat{f}$ denotes a test filter larger than the LES filter. C_z is a model parameter to be estimated. It may be constant (Cook and Riley [151]), estimated from turbulence spectrum (Cook [149], Cook and Bushe [150]) or dynamically provided through a lagrangian formulation, extending the work of Meneveau et al. [435] (Réveillon [550], Réveillon and Vervisch [551]) or using optimal estimators (Balarac et al. [26]).

Finite rate chemistry

The subgrid-scale probability density function concept can be easily extended to finite rate chemistry where species mass fractions (or reaction rates) depend on both the mixture fraction z and its scalar dissipation rate χ (Cook and Riley [152], De Bruyn Kops et al. [168]). Then:

$$\overline{\rho}\widetilde{Y}_k = \int_0^1 \int_\chi \rho Y_k\left(z^*, \chi^*\right) p\left(z^*, \chi^*\right) d\chi^* dz^* \qquad (6.76)$$

Identifying flame elements to steady one-dimensional strained diffusion flames provides a relation between the mixture fraction z and its scalar dissipation rate χ (Chapt. 3, § 3.4.2, Eq. 3.67):

$$\chi = \chi_0 F(z) = \chi_0 \exp\left(-2\left[\text{erf}^{-1}\left(2z - 1\right)\right]^2\right) \qquad (6.77)$$

where χ_0 is the scalar dissipation rate maximum value in the strained flame. Flamelet libraries data $Y_k(z^*, \chi^*)$ may then be recast in terms of flamelet maximum scalar dissipation rate χ_0:

$$\overline{\rho}\widetilde{Y}_k = \int_0^1 \int_\chi \rho Y_k\left(z^*, \chi_0^*\right) p\left(z^*, \chi_0^*\right) d\chi_0^* dz^* \qquad (6.78)$$

Assuming that the mixture fraction z and the maximum scalar dissipation rate χ_0 are statistically independent, $\widetilde{Y}_k$ is given by:

$$\overline{\rho}\widetilde{Y}_k(\mathbf{x}, t) = \int_0^1 \int_\chi \rho Y_k\left(z^*, \chi_0^*\right) p\left(z^*, \mathbf{x}, t\right) p\left(\chi_0^*, \mathbf{x}, t\right) d\chi_0^* dz^* \qquad (6.79)$$

When species mass fractions Y_k are assumed to depend weakly on the scalar dissipation rate χ_0 or when the possible range for χ_0 is not too large, Y_k may be expanded in Taylor series form, keeping only the first two terms:

$$Y_k(z, \chi_0) \approx Y_k(z, \widetilde{\chi}_0) + \left[\frac{\partial Y_k}{\partial \chi_0}\right]_{\chi_0 = \widetilde{\chi}_0} (\chi_0 - \widetilde{\chi}_0) \qquad (6.80)$$

Inserting this result into Eq. (6.79) yields:

$$\boxed{\overline{\rho}\widetilde{Y}_k(\mathbf{x}, t) = \int_0^1 \rho Y_k(z^*, \widetilde{\chi}_0)\, p(z^*, \mathbf{x}, t)\, dz^*} \qquad (6.81)$$

where $Y_k(z^*, \widetilde{\chi}_0)$ is determined from laminar flamelet solutions, using balance equations (3.26). The mean scalar dissipation rate $\widetilde{\chi}$ (supposed to be provided by existing models) and $\widetilde{\chi}_0$ are related through:

$$\widetilde{\chi}(\mathbf{x}, t) = \widetilde{\chi}_0 \int_0^1 F(z^*) p(z^*, \mathbf{x}, t)\, dz^* \qquad (6.82)$$

A β-function is chosen for $\widetilde{p}(z^*, \mathbf{x}, t) = \rho\, p(z^*, \mathbf{x}, t)/\overline{\rho}$, depending on the filtered mixture fraction $\widetilde{z}$ and its fluctuations $\widetilde{z''^2}$. A model is then required for the scalar dissipation rate $\widetilde{\chi}$ (see Girimaji and Zhou [242], Pierce and Moin [507], Cook and Bushe [150]). A simple equilibrium hypothesis gives (De Bruyn Kops et al. [168]):

$$\widetilde{\chi} = \left(\frac{\widetilde{\nu}}{P_e} + \frac{\nu_t}{Sc_t}\right)(\nabla\widetilde{z})^2 \qquad (6.83)$$

where $\widetilde{\nu}$ is the filtered laminar kinematic viscosity, P_e the Peclet number, ν_t the subgrid scale turbulent viscosity, provided by the subgrid turbulence model and Sc_t a turbulent Schmidt number.

CMC modelling

The Conditional Momentum Closure (CMC) approach, described in the RANS context in Section 6.4.5 can be extended to LES. The filtered species mass fraction are given by:

$$\boxed{\overline{\rho}\widetilde{Y}_k = \int_0^1 \left(\overline{\rho Y_k | z^*}\right) p(z^*)\, dz^*} \qquad (6.84)$$

where the conditionally filtered species mass fractions $\left(\overline{\rho Y_k | z^*}\right)$ for a given value z^* of the mixture fraction are solutions of balance equations. This approach suffers of the same drawbacks than in RANS (closure schemes, large computational costs) but has been successfully used in some situations (Navarro-Martinez and Kronenburg [464, 465], Triantafyllidis et al. [650], Garmory and Mastorakos [227]).

6.5.3   Thickened flame model

The thickened flame model (TFLES), described in Section 5.4.3, was developed initially for premixed flames. Légier et al. [377] and Schmitt et al. [594] extended it to simulate turbulent non-premixed flames, starting on the configuration discussed in § 6.2.4 and it has been used in many other non premixed flames (Sengissen et al. [605]), two-phase flames (Boileau et al. [69, 68]) or supercritical flames (Schmitt et al. [596]). For these cases, the TFLES model was modified to thicken only the zone where reactions take place by introducing a sensor to identify the reaction zone: in this zone, both diffusivity and reaction rate are modified, according to § 5.4.3, to ensure the flame thickening; outside this reaction zone, no thickening takes place. In this model called Dynamic Thickened Flame Model (DTFLES)[xxvi], the equation for species k is the same as the TFLES equation (5.139) for premixed flames:

$$\frac{\partial}{\partial t}\rho Y_k + \frac{\partial}{\partial x_i}\rho(u_i + V_i^c)Y_k = \frac{\partial}{\partial x_i}\left(\rho EFD_k\frac{W_k}{W}\frac{\partial X_k}{\partial x_i}\right) + \frac{E\dot{\omega}_k}{F} \qquad (6.85)$$

where F is the thickening factor and E the efficiency function. The only difference is that F is not constant: it is unity outside of the reaction zone and reaches its maximum value inside the reaction zone. In this zone, F depends on the ratio of the mesh size to the flame thickness and is adjusted to have typically 3 to 5 points within the reaction thickness. Eq. (6.85) has multiple advantages in complex flames. It does not depend on the combustion regime (premixed or not); in regions far from flames, $\dot{\omega}_k$ is zero, F is unity and Eq. (6.85) is the standard LES equation controlling mixing in a multispecies gas, a useful property in systems with multiple gas injections; it can handle flames with multiple feeds (for example, two different fuel inlets or two air inlets with different compositions); it degenerates to true DNS when the mesh is refined and F goes to unity everywhere; in perfectly premixed flames, it degenerates to the usual TFLES model; it captures ignition and quenching (near walls or by heat losses) because the Arrhenius chemistry is retained in $\dot{\omega}_k$ and it can be easily extended to reduced schemes by thickening all reactions.

The use of DTFLES for non-premixed flames is not well sustained theoretically: it is not obtained by a filtering operation like most LES equations; many questions remain open, such as the relevance of the efficiency function, derived from DNS of premixed flames or the differences between a flame which is thickened everywhere (TFLES) and one which is thickened only in the reaction zone (DTFLES) (Kuenne et al. [360]). However, it provides good results in practice with limited coding efforts and is often the only possible approach in complex combustors. One of the possible explanations of this success is that many practical diffusion flames actually burn in partially premixed regimes as illustrated in Fig.6.33 which displays an instantaneous TFLES field of the configuration presented in Fig. 6.13 (see § 6.2.4) in the "lifted" flame regime (the most relevant for industrial applications). The propane mass fraction Y_F field (gray scale), is superimposed to the reaction rate field and the two stoichiometric lines (bold

---

[xxvi]Note that the model is dynamic as the thickened factor is locally adjusted from the flame sensor, but not as usually thought in LES, where model parameters are automatically adjusted from the knowledge of the resolved flow field (see sections 4.7.3 and 4.7.5).

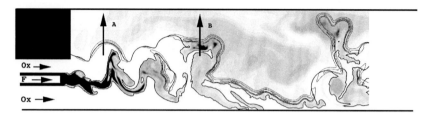

Figure 6.33: Instantaneous snapshot of the fuel mass fraction Y_F (gray scale) and reaction rate (contour lines) fields superimposed to the stoichiometric iso-surface (bold lines) extracted from an LES in the lifted flame regime of the configuration described in Section 6.2.4 (Fig. 6.13). Arrows indicate location and direction of the cuts displayed in Fig. 6.34. From Légier et al. [377].

lines). Even though fuel and oxidizer are injected separately into the burner, only few reaction zones exhibit a diffusion flame-like structure, lying around the stoichiometric iso-surface: in fact, strong mixing occurs before any combustion starts. When combustion begins, a strong rich premixed flame, leaving fuel in hot products, is observed (location B, Fig. 6.34b). This excess fuel then burns with air downstream or in the recirculation zone. In this latter case, a non-premixed flame is observed between hot fuel diluted in burnt products and fresh air (point A, Fig. 6.34a). The diffusion flame structure observed for this point differs from the usual cold fuel / oxidizer configuration retained in flamelet models because the fuel is diluted with burnt gases: on the fuel side, the maximum fuel mass fraction is $Y_F \approx 0.05$, far from the maximum value $Y_F = 1$ found in a pure propane / air diffusion flame.[xxvii] Moreover, the temperature on this fuel side also corresponds to the burnt gases temperature of rich premixed flames, a situation which is never seen in usual diffusion flames and would be difficult to tabulate.

This situation is surprising but is found in many lifted flames: in the lift-off zone, fuel (mixture fraction $z = 1$) and oxidizer ($z = 0$) mix, forming rich mixed zones because the stoichiometric mixture fraction, z_{st}, is low in usual applications (Table 3.4). These pockets then burn in rich-premixed flames, leaving unburnt fuel in combustion products. The excess fuel, diluted in hot gases, may then burn later in diffusion flames with oxidizer. This simple analysis, sustained by DNS (see Section 6.6.4), suggests that many turbulent non-premixed flames actually burn in partially premixed regimes (reactants partially before burning) which are correctly predicted by the DTFLES model but would be difficult to predict using other models because the flame structure seen here does not match any canonical situation (premixed or diffusion). More generally, the key challenge is then to handle partially premixed (or stratified) combustion regimes, i.e. where reactants are not perfectly premixed and local mixture fractions evolve continuously from zero to unity. This is generally done by combining premixed combustion models with a distribution of equivalence ratios. A complete description of partially premixed flame regimes and their modelling is out of the scope of this book.

[xxvii]For the present one-step propane / air chemistry, combustion products contain excess propane. In real systems, propane will be cracked in the reaction zone and burnt gases will contain unburnt hydrocarbons.

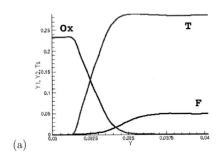
(a)

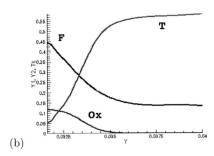
(b)

Figure 6.34: Fuel, oxidizer and temperature profiles across the flame front in locations A (left) and B (right) displayed in Fig. 6.33. From Légier et al. [377].

6.6 DNS of turbulent non-premixed flames

DNS of flame/vortex interaction have already been described to study turbulent combustion regimes (§ 6.3.1). In the following, the local flame structure is more precisely investigated (§ 6.6.1). Results on non-premixed flame autoignition are presented in Section 6.6.2. This chapter ends with some global properties of turbulent non-premixed flames (§ 6.6.3) and a description of the most recent DNS (§ 6.6.4).

6.6.1 Studies of local flame structure

A typical example of local flame structure analysis and flamelet assumption validation for turbulent non-premixed flames using DNS is given by Bédat et al. [42]. These 2D and 3D simulations use a single-step chemical scheme, tuned to match the GRI 2.11 complex scheme (Frenklach et al. [221])[xxviii] predictions for stoichiometric laminar burning velocity, adiabatic flame temperatures, main reactants concentrations and extinction strain rates both for premixed (steady) and non-premixed (steady and unsteady) strained laminar flames. As for direct numerical simulations (DNS) of turbulent premixed flames (see § 5.5), a planar laminar diffusion flame is initially superimposed to a decaying homogeneous and isotropic turbulent field. The flame front is then wrinkled and strained by turbulent motions and a typical flow field is displayed on Fig. 6.35.

DNS results are analyzed following a "flamelet" concept (Fig. 6.36): the flame surface, defined by $z = z_{st}$, is first identified. For each point of this surface, temperature (T_{st}) and scalar dissipation rate (χ_{st}) are extracted and a local Damköhler number, D_a, is determined from χ_{st} and the chemical time τ_c (see § 3.5.2 and Eq. 3.90). The flame normal is constructed and the integrated reaction rate $\int \dot{\omega}\, dn$ is computed along this normal. Since flamelet models

---

[xxviii]The GRI chemical mechanisms are available on http://euler.berkeley.edu/gri_mech/index.html.

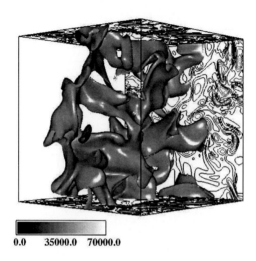

0.0   35000.0   70000.0

Figure 6.35: DNS of a turbulent non-premixed methane/air flame. The heat release rate envelope (level of 500 W cm^{-3}) and vorticity amplitude (faces of the computational domain and scale in $[s^{-1}]$) snapshots are displayed (Reprinted by permission of Elsevier Science from Bédat et al. [42] © the Combustion Institute).

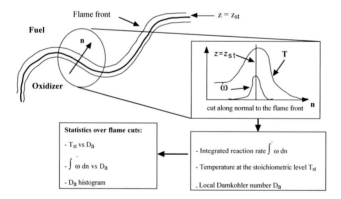

Figure 6.36: DNS analysis performed by Bédat et al. [42]. Cuts along the normal to the flame front **n** are used to extract temperature T_{st}, scalar dissipation rate χ_{st} for $z = z_{st}$ and to integrate the reaction rate along **n**. A local Damköhler number $Da = 1/(\chi_{st}\tau_c)$, where τ_c is a chemical time scale, is used as a reference quantity. The integrated reaction rate and T_{st} are plotted as a function of Da.

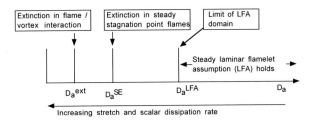

Figure 6.37: Definition of Damköhler numbers to post-process DNS results.

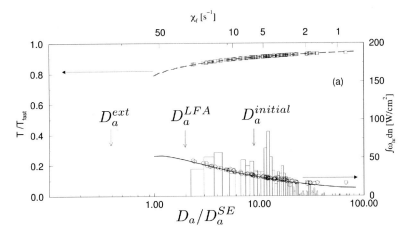

Figure 6.38: Direct numerical simulation of a turbulent methane/air diffusion flame starting using a small initial turbulence level ($u' = 1.2 \, m/s$, turbulence Reynolds number $Re_t = 18$). Results after one eddy turn-over time:
- Histograms plotted for local Damköhler numbers.
- Integrated heat release rate normal to the stoichiometric surface (○). DNS data.
- Temperature at $z = z_{st}$ (□). DNS data.
- Integrated heat release rate normal to the stoichiometric surface (———). Library data.
- Temperature at $z = z_{st}$ (– – – –). Library data.

Data are plotted as a function of a reduced local Damköhler number, D_a/D_a^{SE} where D_a^{SE} is the extinction Damköhler number for a stagnation point flame. Temperatures are normalized with the infinitely fast chemistry value (Reprinted by permission of Elsevier Science from Bédat et al. [42] © the Combustion Institute).

assume that the flame elements in the turbulent flame behave like laminar flames, $T_{st}(D_a)$ and $\int \dot{\omega}\, dn(D_a)$, extracted from DNS data, should be compared with the corresponding quantities found in laminar stagnation point flames (the so-called "flamelet libraries"). These libraries are computed separately using the same transport and chemical models as the DNS.

DNS results show that the local Damköhler number controls the flame structure. Bédat et al. [42] use three reference Damköhler numbers proposed by Cuenot and Poinsot [158] (see § 6.3.1 and Fig. 6.37) using DNS of flame / vortex interactions:

- D_a^{SE} corresponds to the local Damköhler number at extinction for a steady strained laminar diffusion flame

- D_a^{LFA} defines the limit where steady laminar flamelet approach applies,

- D_a^{ext} is the Damköhler number where extinction occurs (see § 6.3.1).

According to Cuenot and Poinsot [158] (§ 6.3.1), the two last Damköhler numbers are estimated as follows: $D_a^{LFA} = 2D_a^{SE}$ and $D_a^{ext} = 0.4D_a^{SE}$. Results are plotted on Fig. 6.38 for a low initial turbulence levels ($u' = 1.2\,m/s$, turbulence Reynolds number $Re_t = 18$) and are compared to steady strained laminar flame solutions. Fig. 6.39 displays results obtained for high turbulence level ($u' = 6.0\,m/s$, initial turbulence Reynolds number $Re_t = 92$).

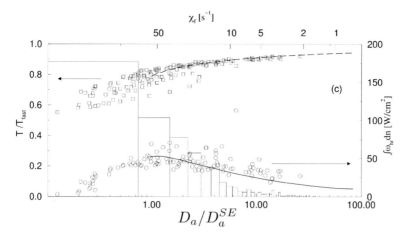

Figure 6.39: Direct numerical simulation of the local structure of a turbulent methane/air diffusion flame starting using a high initial turbulence level ($u' = 6.0\,m/s$, turbulence Reynolds number $Re_t = 92$). Lines and symbols are the same as on Fig. 6.38 (Reprinted by permission of Elsevier Science from Bédat et al. [42] © the Combustion Institute).

For the first case (Fig. 6.38), starting with a small initial turbulence level, histograms show that the local Damköhler number is larger than D_a^{LFA} for all the points on the flame surface

$z = z_{st}$ and the laminar flamelet assumption is clearly valid, as expected: both integrated heat release rate and local temperature for the stoichiometric conditions are in close agreement with flamelet library data.

As the turbulence level increases (Fig. 6.39), the turbulent characteristic time, measured as the inverse of the scalar dissipation rate for stoichiometric conditions, decreases and the Damköhler number distribution shifts towards low Damköhler values. The histogram of D_a reveals that a significant number of points on the flame surface now have a Damköhler number smaller that the extinction value D_a^{SE} found in the flamelet library. The library would predict a quenched flame for these points (zero heat release rate). This is not the case (Fig. 6.39) and even though these points burn slowly, they are not quenched yet because of unsteady effects. However, very few points are found below $D_a^{ext} = 0.4 D_a^{SE}$ which corresponds to the limit found in flame vortex interaction, confirming that this limit is more adapted to turbulent flows than D_a^{SE}. Moreover, points on Fig. 6.39 are more scattered around the laminar library data than they were for the low u' case (Fig. 6.38) even though the library remains an excellent fit for most flame elements. This scatter is due to small scale turbulent eddies entering the reaction zone and to unsteady effects.

6.6.2 Autoignition of a turbulent non-premixed flame

DNS is also a powerful tool to investigate autoignition mechanisms. Mastorakos et al. [422] studied ignition in a turbulent diffusive layer between cold fuel and hot air (Fig. 6.40). This geometry is of interest for some practical industrial situations such as ignition in Diesel internal combustion engines or supersonic combustors. In both cases, a cold fuel stream is injected into an air flow heated by compression effects. The objective of such simulations is to understand autoignition mechanisms to develop adapted models.

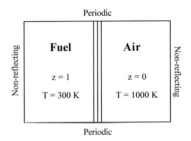

Figure 6.40: Numerical configuration used by Mastorakos et al. [422] to investigate autoignition mechanisms between cold fuel and hot air. An homogeneous and isotropic turbulence is initially superimposed to the diffusive layer.

Autoignition is studied using conditional average of the heat release rate, $(\overline{\dot{\omega}|z})$, corresponding to the mean reaction rate for a given value of the mixture fraction z. As shown in Fig. 6.41

(left), autoignition occurs for a "preferred" value of the mixture fraction, $z_{MR} = 0.12$ (the most reactive mixture fraction), corresponding to the maximum value of the reaction rate $\dot{\omega}$:

$$\dot{\omega} = A Y_F Y_O \exp\left(-T_A/T\right) \qquad (6.86)$$

whereas the stoichiometric mixture fraction value is $z_{st} = 0.055$. Before autoignition (pure mixing), $\dot{\omega}$ is proportional to $z(1-z)\exp(-T_A/T)$. For identical fuel and oxidizer temperatures, the maximum reaction rate is reached for $z_{MR} = 0.5$. When fuel and oxidizer streams have different initial temperatures, the autoignition location is shifted towards the highest temperature stream (i.e. the oxidizer stream in the simulations of Mastorakos et al. [422]). This finding, already known from asymptotic theories in laminar flames (Linan and Crespo [398]), is recovered in turbulent flow fields.

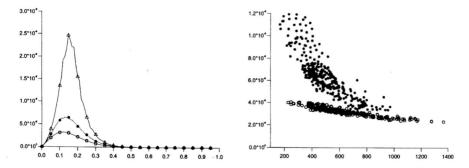

Figure 6.41: Left: conditionally averaged reaction rate $(\overline{\dot{\omega}|z})$ versus mixture fraction z for three times before autoignition. Right: scatter plots of reaction rate versus scalar dissipation rate for $0.11 < z < 0.14$ ($z_{MR} = 0.12$) for two times before autoignition. $\circ$: $t/t_{turb} = 0.52$; $\bullet$: $t/t_{turb} = 0.67$ and $\triangle$: $t/t_{turb} = 0.78$, where t_{turb} is the turbulent integral time scale. Autoignition occurs around the "most reactive" value of the mixture fraction, here $z_{MR} = 0.12$ whereas $z_{st} = 0.055$ (Reprinted by permission of Elsevier Science from Mastorakos et al. [422] © the Combustion Institute).

Reaction rates can also be plotted versus scalar dissipation rate for mixture fraction values in the vicinity of the "most reactive" mixture fraction z_{MR}. As displayed in Fig. 6.41 (right), autoignition preferentially occurs for lowest values of the scalar dissipation rate χ. To summarize, autoignition of turbulent non-premixed flames occurs on the "most reactive" mixture fraction surface ($z = z_{MR}$, depending on initial stream temperatures) in locations having the lowest scalar dissipation rates. Hilbert and Thévenin [287] achieve similar conclusions in DNS of autoignition of turbulent non-premixed H_2/air flames with complex chemistry (9 species, 37 chemical reactions). From their results, Mastorakos et al. [423] derive a model for autoignition in turbulent flow fields based on CMC (Conditional Momentum Closure, see § 6.4.5) concepts.

Fig. 6.42 compares reaction rates and maximum temperatures in a configuration similar to Fig. 6.40, with infinitely fast and finite rate chemistry, but without turbulence. With infinitely fast (or equilibrium) chemistry, the reaction rate decreases with time, according to relations derived in Section 3.4.1. The maximum temperature is constant and corresponds to the adiabatic temperature. On the other hand, with finite rate chemistry, the reaction rate is initially equal to zero, reaches a maximum value just after the autoignition time and then decreases to recover the infinitely fast chemistry solution. The maximum temperature increases with time but remains lower than its adiabatic level. This figure clearly displays the importance of the flame ignition description. In this situation, the infinitely fast chemistry approximation, assuming that the flame exists when oxidizer and fuel are in contact, is not relevant and leads to erroneous results. On the other hand, far from the autoignition location, the infinitely fast chemistry assumption holds.

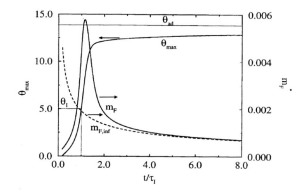

Figure 6.42: Temporal evolution of the maximum temperature θ_{max} and the total reaction rate m_F compared to the adiabatic temperature θ_{ad} and the reaction rate $m_{F,inf}$ computed using infinitely fast chemistry assumption. The flow geometry is similar to Fig. 6.40 without initial superimposed turbulence motions (van Kalmthout [662]).

The results of Mastorakos et al. [422], obtained with a temporal simulation, have also been recovered in a spatial mixing layer configuration (van Kalmthout [662]). Two parallel laminar streams of cold fuel and hot oxidizer are injected in the burner displayed on Fig. 6.43. As shown on Fig. 6.44 (left), the reaction starts for the most reaction mixture fraction z_{MR} and then moves to the vicinity of the stoichiometric value z_{st}. Downstream, the established diffusion flame lies on the z_{st} iso-surface. These findings are confirmed by the fuel mass fraction profiles plotted for various downstream locations x in the mixture fraction space (Fig. 6.44, right). Note that, far from the autoignition location, the fuel mass fraction profile evolves towards the infinitely fast chemistry solution (Fig. 3.6).

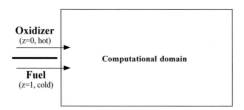

Figure 6.43: Spatial mixing layer between hot oxidizer and cold fuel streams (van Kalmthout [662]).

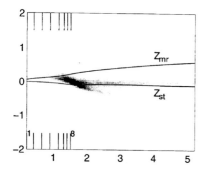
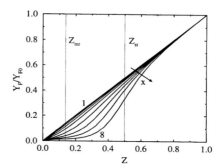

Figure 6.44: DNS reaction rate field for the spatial mixing layer between hot oxidizer and cold fuel streams (left). Transverse profiles of the fuel mass fraction Y_F plotted for various downstream locations x as a function of the mixture fraction (right) (van Kalmthout [662]).

6.6.3   Studies of global flame structure

van Kalmthout and Veynante [664] have investigated the structure of a turbulent non-premixed flame in a spatially developing two-dimensional mixing layer. A well-defined homogeneous and isotropic turbulent flow field is injected at the inlet boundary, using a virtual domain, as shown of Fig. 6.45. The flame front, identified by the stoichiometric iso-surface $z = z_{st}$ is wrinkled by turbulent motions.[xxix]

Mean (i.e. averaged along time) local reaction rates are integrated along transverse direction and plotted as a function of the downstream location for various initial turbulence Reynolds numbers in Fig. 6.46. Results are summarized in Table 6.9.

As expected, when the turbulent Reynolds number Re_t increases, the integrated reaction rate also increases. But this finding combines two phenomena (Table 6.9):

[xxix]In this simulation, the inlet turbulent flow is supersonic and acoustic waves cannot move upstream. In § 5.5.5 has been described a more recent DNS with injection of turbulence in a subsonic flow, a situation which requires special care in compressible codes because of acoustic waves travelling upstream up to the domain inlet where turbulent motions are prescribed.

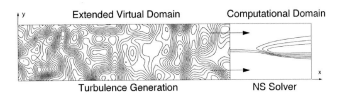

Figure 6.45: Generation of turbulence over an extended virtual domain and progressive injection into the computational domain (van Kalmthout and Veynante [664]).

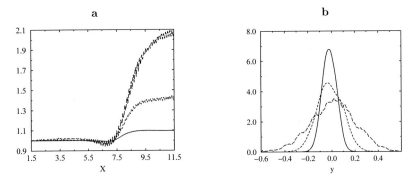

Figure 6.46: Global properties of the turbulent non-premixed flame developing in a two dimensional mixing layer: (a) mean reaction rate, $\int \bar{\dot{\omega}}_F \, dy$, (normalized by the laminar flame value and integrated along the transverse direction y) versus the downstream location x, (b) transverse profiles of the flame surface density at $x = 11$ for three turbulent Reynolds numbers: 105 (———), 201 (----) and 310 (— — —) (van Kalmthout and Veynante [663]).

- an increase of the available flame surface area due to the wrinkling of the flame front induced by turbulence motions,

- an increase of the local fuel consumption rate $\dot{\Omega}_F$ per unit of flame area explained by an increase of the local scalar dissipation rate χ_{st} at the flame front according to non-premixed laminar flame theory and confirmed by DNS results.

For example, according to Table 6.9, for $Re_t = 310$, the total reaction rate is increased by a factor of order 2 compared to the planar laminar flame. The flame surface is increased by only about 70 % when the local reaction rate per unit of flame area is also enhanced by about 25 % because of the increase of the scalar dissipation rate. Note also that the turbulent flame brush is thickened when the turbulence level increases as shown on Fig. 6.46b. The maximum flame surface density decreases, denoting a flapping flame front, but the overall available flame surface area increases.

Re_t	0	105	201	310
$\int \bar{\dot{\omega}}_F \, dy$	1.0	1.1	1.4	2.1
$\int \Sigma dy$	1.0	1.08	1.3	1.7
$\overline{(\chi \mid z = z_{st})}$	1.0	1.2	1.7	2.5

Table 6.9: Global properties of the turbulent non-premixed flame developing in a two dimensional mixing layer, normalized by planar laminar flame values ($Re_t = 0$). Results are displayed for downstream location $x = 11$ where a steady state regime is achieved (van Kalmthout and Veynante [663]).

These direct numerical simulations may also be used to check the main assumption of the flame surface density concept, i.e. to express the mean reaction rate as the product of a flame surface density and a local consumption rate (Eq. 6.62). Fig. 6.47 compares transverse profiles of the mean fuel reaction rate $\bar{\dot{\omega}}_F$, the mean flame surface density Σ and the local reaction rate estimated as $\bar{\Omega}_F = \bar{\dot{\omega}}_F / \Sigma$. This last quantity is found to be constant across the mixing layer, at least when the flame surface density (and the number of realizations used for averaging) is not too low, and depends on the conditional mean scalar dissipation rate, expected to be constant along the transverse direction because of the homogeneous and isotropic turbulence. This finding validates, in this situation, the flame surface density modeling assumptions. Van Kalmthout et al [665, 663, 664] have then carefully investigated the exact balance equation for the flame surface density Σ and its possible closure schemes. This study is beyond the scope of this book and the reader is referred to the corresponding publications.

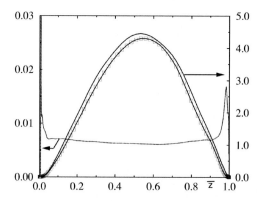

Figure 6.47: Two dimensional mixing layer: mean reaction rate $\bar{\dot{\omega}}_F$ (———), local consumption rate $\bar{\Omega}_F = \bar{\dot{\omega}}_F / \Sigma$ (·········) and flame surface density Σ (—□—) (van Kalmthout and Veynante [664]).

6.6.4 Three-dimensional DNS with complex chemistry

Recent progress in High Performance Computing have allowed impressive DNS to be performed since 2004, mainly in the USA and in Japan. At Sandia National Laboratories, 3D DNS of turbulent diffusion flames including complex chemistry have been performed and these sites (*elearning.cerfacs.fr/combustion/illustrations/SANDIAhydrogen* and *SANDIAethylene*) show examples of lifted turbulent diffusion flames for hydrogen / air (Yoo et al. [723]) and ethylene / air (Yoo et al. [724]).

Similarly, taking advantage of computers such as the "Earth Simulator" or the "Numerical Wind Tunnel" (vector parallel machine at National Aerospace Laboratory, Japan), Japanese teams have performed large 3D DNS: Yokokawa et al. [722] studied an homogeneous and isotropic turbulence (non reacting flow) using a 4096^3 numerical grid. Mizobuchi et al. [444, 445] investigated a 3D turbulent hydrogen jet flame with complex chemistry: hydrogen is injected into ambient air through a 2 mm diameter nozzle with a jet velocity of 680 m/s (Mach number: 0.54; Reynolds number based on the jet diameter: 13600). Nine species (H_2, O_2, OH, H_2O, H, O, H_2O_2, HO_2, N_2) are solved using a 17 reaction chemical model (Westbrook [704]) and Fick's law with binary diffusion coefficients. The computational domain is 4.6 cm long in the downstream direction and 6 cm wide in the two transverse directions. The rectangular grid contains about 22.8 millions grid points. The grid mesh is 2.5 times larger than the Kolmogorov length scale measured in the experiment by Cheng et al. [127] and corresponds to about 1/10 of the heat release layer width of the laminar flame.

In agreement with the experiment, a lifted flame is observed in Fig. 6.48 where an example of numerical results is displayed. This simulation clearly evidences the complexity of the flow field, far from a usual diffusion flame. Three main regions are observed:

- The flame is stabilized outside the turbulent jet and has in this region a triple flame-like structure (see Section 6.2.3).

- Most of the combustion occurs in a vigorous turbulent inner rich premixed flame.[xxx] In fact, as the stoichiometric mixture fraction is low ($z_{st} \approx 0.028$, Table 3.4), most of the hydrogen/air mixture produced between the jet nozzle and the flame is rich.

- Diffusion flame islands are observed outside of the inner rich premixed flame. These islands burn the remaining fuel or are produced by local extinction of the inner premixed flame. Their structure does not correspond to usual hydrogen/air diffusion flamelets (cold oxidizer burning with hot fuel diluted by combustion products).

These results show that the present non-premixed jet flame actually consists of partially premixed flame elements which burn most of the fuel and produce most of the heat release. In terms of models, this implies that diffusion flamelets are probably not a proper prototype for

---

[xxx]The combustion regime is identified using the flame index $F.I.$ (Yamashita et al. [718]): $F.I. = \nabla Y_{H_2} \cdot \nabla Y_{O_2}$ where Y_{H_2} and Y_{O_2} denote the hydrogen and oxygen mass fractions respectively. This index is positive (respective negative) for premixed (diffusion) flame.

the combustion zones of this jet flame: models able to handle mixing and partially premixed flames are better adapted in this case.

These DNS provide useful information as they become closer to real flames. But the difficulties of such computations do not only lie in the computational resources but also in the data storage, retrieval and processing. Assuming that 15 variables are stored (density, pressure, 3 velocity components, energy or temperature, 9 chemical species), each instantaneous flowfield contains about 342 million data elements of information representing about 2.7 Gigaoctets when stored on 64 bits words. An additional difficulty is that these DNS codes cannot handle complex geometry today.

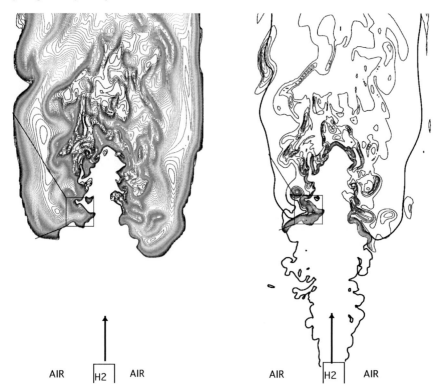

Figure 6.48: Instantaneous DNS field of a three-dimensional turbulent hydrogen lifted jet flame by Mizobuchi et al. [445]. Left: temperature; Right: heat release rate (grey scale) superimposed to the stoichiometric level of the mixture fraction (line). The flow goes from bottom to top.

Chapter 7

Flame/wall interactions

7.1 Introduction

The computation of combustion chambers requires the description of turbulent flows near walls but also of heat transfer near walls, a much more difficult question when reacting gases at high temperature flow along solid surfaces. The first property of a well-designed combustor is that its walls should survive. Since typical adiabatic flame temperatures are higher than the melting temperature of most materials used for combustor walls, this question is a critical issue in most combustors and wall cooling is a central topic for combustion experts. Combustors walls are submitted to large fluxes, typically 1 MW/m^2. High wall fluxes are observed when burnt gases are in contact with walls but the highest fluxes are found when a flame hits a wall: such flame/wall interactions are found in most practical industrial systems where they induce various effects on the overall efficiency and pollutant formation of the flame but also on the lifetime of combustion chambers. The interaction between flames and walls is a two-way process: walls are heated by the flame but the flame is quenched by the wall presence.

Most flame/wall interaction studies have been performed for premixed combustion: this chapter focuses on this combustion mode even though non-premixed devices are also submitted to similar phenomena (Delataillade et al. [172], Dabireau et al. [161]). In most combustion devices, burnt gases reach temperatures between 1500 and 2500 K while walls temperatures remain between 400 and 600 K because of cooling. The temperature decreases from burnt gas levels to wall levels in a near-wall layer which is less than 1 mm thick, leading to very large temperature gradients. Studying the interaction between flames and walls is extremely difficult from an experimental point of view because it occurs in a very thin zone near the wall: in most cases, the only measurable quantity is the unsteady wall heat flux, which is an "indirect" measurement of phenomena taking place in the gas phase. Moreover, flames approaching walls are dominated by transient effects. They do not usually touch walls and quench a few micrometers before because the low temperature of most walls inhibits chemical reactions. At the same time, the large near-wall temperature gradients lead to very high wall heat fluxes. These fluxes are maintained for short durations and their characterization is also a difficult task in experiments (Lu et al. [405], Ezekoye et al. [204]).

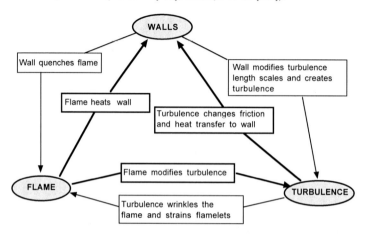

Figure 7.1: Interactions between walls, flame and turbulence.

When the flow within the chamber is turbulent, the interaction between the wall and the flame is even more complex. Fig. 7.1 shows how turbulence, walls and flames interact. In addition to the interaction between the flame and the wall, the coupling phenomena between the wall and the turbulence on one hand, and between the turbulence and the flame on the other hand, must be considered. As a result, the overall picture of flame/wall interaction in turbulent flows is quite complex and modeling still in an early stage.

Even though flame/wall interaction phenomena are not well understood, they must still be accounted for in CFD codes in some minimal way. They have recently become critical issues in CFD models for reacting flows as discussed below and in Fig. 7.2. In the following, modeling is supposed to be performed in terms of flamelet models for turbulent combustion (§ 5.3.6) and the k-ε model for the flow but is easily extended to other cases and models:

1. The first effect of the wall is to quench the flamelets which come too close to it. This effect is directly associated to an enthalpy loss from the flow to the wall so that the adiabaticity assumption used in many models (see § 5.3) fails: assumptions relating reduced temperature to fuel mass fractions (see Eq. (5.37)) in most models for turbulent premixed combustion cannot be used anymore. Another important issue is the formation of unburnt hydrocarbons left near the walls after the flame quenches. This source of pollution and reduced performance cannot be modeled without considering flame/wall interactions. Such interactions occur when flames hit planar walls or when they enter crevices. As far as turbulent combustion models are concerned, the wall also limits flame wrinkling and acts as a sink term for the flame surface density Σ.

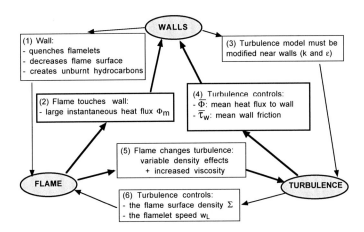

Figure 7.2: Modeling implications of turbulent combustion near walls.

2. Before quenching, flame elements induce very large heat fluxes to the wall. Most heat transfer models ignore this effect even though it controls the maximum levels of heat fluxes to be considered for cooling and structure design.

3. The presence of the wall modifies turbulence scales and near-wall effects must be included in turbulence models. This is the case even without combustion and most codes contain law-of-the-wall extensions (usually logarithmic laws for the velocity (Kays and Crawford [328]) or low Reynolds number evolutions for turbulence models). Combining wall model concepts derived for non reacting flows and turbulent combustion models involves some dangers. The most obvious limitation of combustion models near walls is that turbulent length scales decrease near walls: these scales can become smaller than the flame thickness so that flamelet models can provide non physical results. For example, the EBU model (§ 5.3) expresses the mean reaction rate as (Eq. (5.46)):

$$\overline{\dot{\omega}}_\Theta = C_{EBU}(\varepsilon/k)\widetilde{\Theta}(1 - \widetilde{\Theta}) \qquad (7.1)$$

Near walls, k-ε models predict that k goes to zero so that the EBU model predicts that $\overline{\dot{\omega}}_\Theta$ goes to infinity. In piston engine codes, for example, all EBU- based models (§ 5.3.3) predict that the flame propagates faster near the walls (almost infinitely fast) than far from the walls leading to non physical results[i].

---

[i]CFD users often suppress this difficulty by using ad-hoc modifications in the near-wall cells such as setting the mean reaction rate to zero. This should not be done and the introduction of wall effects in the turbulent combustion models (Bruneaux et al. [92, 93]) is the only path to tackle this issue.

4. Models are needed to determine the mean wall heat flux $\overline{\Phi}$ and the mean wall friction $\overline{\tau}_W$: logarithmic laws are used here for both quantities without taking into account the presence of combustion. Existing models usually neglect effects of flame/wall interaction on wall heat transfer: the wall heat flux is computed with classical thermal law-of-the-wall models (Kays and Crawford [328]) neglecting the presence of the flame. Only the presence of burnt gases near the wall is accounted for. Moreover, most law-of-the-wall models used for reacting flows were derived for constant density flows and must be modified to include effects of the large temperature gradients found in combustion.

5. The effects of flame on turbulence are similar with and without walls but are usually never accounted for in models. The effects of turbulence on flame fronts remain the same: turbulence controls flame wrinkling (the flame surface density Σ in a flamelet model) and flame strain (the flamelet consumption speed w_L).

7.2   Flame–wall interaction in laminar flows

7.2.1   Phenomenological description

The first flame/wall studies were performed for wall quenching of laminar premixed flames (Jarosinski [308], Huang et al. [299], Blint and Bechtel [61], Wichman and Bruneaux [709], Kiehne et al. [344], Lu et al. [405], Clendening et al. [142], Westbrook et al. [705]). These laminar cases may be characterized by two parameters changing with time during the inter-action: the distance y between flame and wall and the heat flux Φ through the wall. The wall distance y is usually normalized by the characteristic flame thickness $\delta = \lambda_1/(\rho_1 c_p s_L^0)$ (§ 2.5) to define a local Peclet number:

$$P = y/\delta \tag{7.2}$$

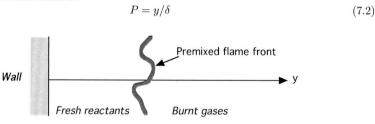

Figure 7.3: Interaction between a premixed flame and a wall.

The instantaneous wall heat flux Φ is defined by:

$$\Phi = -\lambda \, \frac{\partial T}{\partial y} \, |_W \tag{7.3}$$

where λ is the gas thermal conductivity and the index W designates wall quantities (Fig. 7.3). By convention, the y axis is normal to the wall and points from the wall into the gas so that

Φ is negative when a hot flame interacts with a cold wall. The heat flux Φ is usually scaled by the laminar reference "flame power" (the heat release per unit time and unit surface of flame $\rho_1 Y_F^1 s_L^0 Q = \rho_1 s_L^0 c_p (T_2 - T_1)$ for lean flames) to yield:

$$F = | \Phi | / (\rho_1 Y_F^1 s_L^0 Q) \tag{7.4}$$

where ρ_1 and Y_F^1 designate the fresh–gas density and fuel mass fraction, s_L^0 is the unstretched laminar flame speed, and Q is the heat of reaction (defined by $Y_F^1 Q = C_p(T_2 - T_1)$ if T_1 is the temperature of the fresh gases and T_2 is the adiabatic flame temperature). Notations shown in Table 7.1 follow Chapter 2: the subscript or superscript "1" refers to reference properties in the fresh gases and a subscript "Q" to values at quenching conditions.

	Flame/wall distance	Wall heat flux
Non reduced	y (m)	Φ (W/m^2)
Reduced	$P = y/\delta = \rho_1 c_p s_L^0 y / \lambda_1$	$F = \mid \Phi \mid / (\rho_1 Y_F^1 s_L^0 Q)$

Table 7.1: Notations for flame/wall interaction.

The flame/wall distance y and the wall heat flux Φ change with time. Consider a one-dimensional laminar flame propagating into fresh reactants towards a cold wall (Fig. 7.4). Far from the wall ($t = t_1$), the flame propagates without modification. When the flame is close enough to the wall, it starts sensing its presence ($t = t_2$). The wall extracts energy from the flame (through heat diffusion), playing a role similar to a heat loss term: the flame is weakened by this loss and slows down. A critical instant in flame/wall interaction corresponds to the flame quenching: at a wall distance y_Q, the flame stops and quenches ($t = t_3$ on Fig. 7.4). Generally, the wall heat flux Φ_Q peaks at the same instant. After quenching, the burnt gases are cooled down by the cold wall following a simple heat diffusion process.

The quenching distance y_Q is expressed by the quenching Peclet number P_Q: $P_Q = y_Q/\delta$ (Huang et al. [299], Vosen et al. [692], Lu et al. [405]). At the quenching instant, the maximum normalized heat flux F_Q and the minimum Peclet number P_Q may be correlated in laminar flows by assuming that the wall heat flux at quenching Φ_Q is due to heat conduction in the gas layer of thickness y_Q:

$$\Phi_Q \approx -\lambda(T_2 - T_w)/y_Q \tag{7.5}$$

where T_w is the wall temperature. Note that Eq. (7.5) assumes that the main wall flux is diffusion controlled and that radiation can be neglected. Radiative fluxes are often neglected in studies of flame/wall interaction because they are small compared to the maximum heat flux obtained when the flame touches the wall.

Eq. (7.5) can be used to express the scaled wall heat flux F_Q at quenching:

$$F_Q = \frac{T_2 - T_w}{T_2 - T_1} \frac{1}{P_Q} \tag{7.6}$$

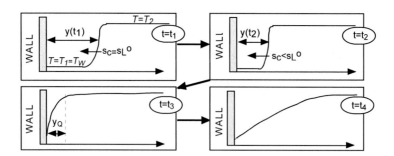

Figure 7.4: Laminar flame interacting with a cold wall. Temperature profiles at four consecutive instants t_1 to t_4. The fresh gases temperature T_1 is equal to the wall temperature T_W. Quenching occurs at $t = t_3$.

using the definition of $\delta = \lambda_1/(\rho_1 c_p s_L^0)$ and introducing the adiabatic flame temperature $T_2 = T_1 + QY_F^1/C_p$. Eq. (7.6) shows that the maximum reduced heat flux during flame/wall interaction varies like the inverse of the minimum reduced flame/wall distance.

Flame/wall interaction is observed in various configurations. Fig. 7.4 displays one possibility but others exist for premixed flames (Fig. 7.5):

- Head–on quenching (HOQ): when a flame front reaches a cold wall ($T_w = T_1$) at a normal angle, head–on quenching occurs (Fig. 7.4 and 7.5a). This case has been studied theoretically (Wichman and Bruneaux [709]), numerically (Westbrook et al. [705], Poinsot et al. [525], Popp and Baum [538]) and experimentally (Huang et al. [299], Jarosinski [308], Vosen et al. [692]). Results [ii] show that quenching occurs for Peclet numbers P_Q of the order of three. Heat flux measurements indicate values of F_Q of the order of 0.34, which are consistent with the value predicted by Eq. (7.6) with $P_Q \approx 3$: a flame stops propagating towards the wall when the heat losses to the wall are equal to about one–third of the flame power. Chemical effects (for example, equivalence ratio) also change quenching distances (Jennings [310], Kuo [361], Blint and Bechtel [61, 62]). However, the fact that F_Q is almost constant for different fuels (Huang et al. [299]) suggests that, for cold walls, the problem is thermally controlled and that a model based on a simple chemistry assumption may be used. The same conclusion was obtained by Westbrook et al. [705] by comparing computations with simple and complex chemistry.

- Side–wall quenching (SWQ): when a flame propagates parallel to a wall, only localized quenching of the flame edge near the wall occurs (Fig. 7.5b). This situation has been studied theoretically (von Kármán and Millan [691], Makhviladze and Melikov [416]),

---

[ii] An example of laminar propane-air flame interacting with a wall in a head–on quenching mode can be visualized at *www.cerfacs.fr/cfd/Gallery/movies/flame1d_v2.mov*.

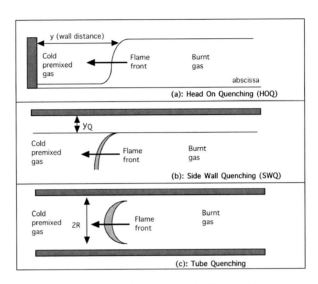

Figure 7.5: The three configurations for flame/wall interaction in laminar flows.

and experimentally (Lu et al. [405], Clendening et al. [142]) [iii]. Quenching Peclet numbers P_Q in this case are of the order of 7 suggesting values for F_Q of about 0.16 (Eq. (7.6)). Asymptotic theories of non–adiabatic flames may also be used to predict quenching distances (Williams [710]) and give the same order of magnitude for P_Q.

- Tube quenching: total flame quenching may occur in a tube if its radius R is sufficiently small (Lewis and Von Elbe [383], Jarosinski [308], Fairchild et al. [205]; Fig. 7.5c). This phenomenon was first used by Davy [167] and George Stephenson in 1818 to design mine lamps (Well [700]): these lamps are surrounded by holes with diameters smaller than the quenching distance so that a flame cannot propagate through them. A flame confined in such a box radiates light but does not allow ignition of the premixed gases outside the lamp, a useful property in mines (Fig. 7.6). Peclet numbers in this case (Aly and Hermance [8]) are based on the tube diameter $(2R)$ and are close to 50.

7.2.2 Simple chemistry flame/wall interaction

As a first example, Fig. 7.7 displays a computation of a laminar premixed flame interacting with a wall in a HOQ configuration (Poinsot et al. [525]). This simulation is performed under

---

[iii] An example of laminar hydrogen-oxygen flame interacting with a wall in a side-wall mode can be visualized at *www.cerfacs.fr/cfd/Gallery/movies/SWQ3.mov*.

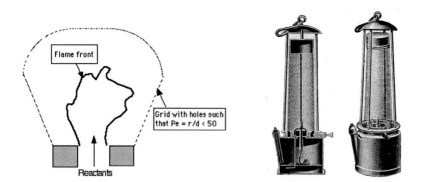

Figure 7.6: Mine lamp based on the principle of flame quenching in a small tube by walls (Davy [167]). Left: principle of the system. Right: image of Davy lamp.

the assumptions of single-step reaction, variable density and viscosity. The calculations are initialized with reactants on one side of the computational domain and products on the other; these are separated by a laminar premixed flame. The wall is located on the reactant side of the domain (Fig. 7.5a). All velocity components are zero on the wall and the wall temperature is imposed and equal to the fresh gas temperature, T_1.

Figure 7.7 presents time variations of the Peclet number $P = y/\delta$ (the normalized flame distance to the wall), of the flame power $\rho_1 s_c c_p (T_2 - T_1)$ (in this expression, only the normalized consumption flame speed s_c changes when the flame moves towards the wall) and of the normalized wall heat flux $F = |\Phi| / (\rho_1 s_L^0 c_p (T_2 - T_1))$. Time has been normalized by the flame time $t_F = \delta_L^0 / s_l^0$ (δ_L^0 is the flame thickness defined from the temperature gradient in Eq. (2.75)[iv]). The flame position corresponds to the distance between the wall and the $\Theta = 0.9$ isotherm. With this definition, the flame is still defined even after quenching has occurred. This may lead to "flames" going away from the wall as in Fig. 7.7.

The values obtained from DNS using the $\Theta = 0.9$ isotherm are $P_Q = 3.4$ and $F_Q = 0.39$. These values are in good agreement with experimental data (Lu et al. [405], Vosen et al. [692]) and with the simple model given by Eq. (7.6). The influence of chemical parameters (heat release and activation energy) on the quenching distances and maximum heat fluxes is limited (Poinsot et al. [525]). Even for large parameter changes, quenching quantities do not change by more than 25 %, confirming that the problem is essentially thermally controlled.

[iv]It is more convenient to use the real flame thickness δ_L^0 here rather than the thickness δ entering the definition of the Peclet number.

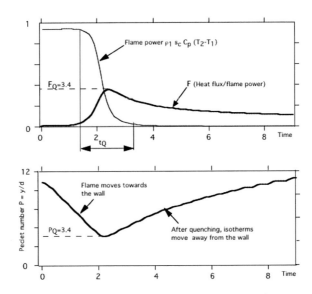

Figure 7.7: Simulation of Head on Quenching (HOQ) interaction (Poinsot et al. [525]).

7.2.3 Computing complex chemistry flame/wall interaction

Even though the effects observed in single-step chemistry studies (§ 7.2.2) are important, complex chemistry and molecular transport effects also play a role. Incorporating them in flame/wall interaction studies is difficult for the following reasons:

- The computation becomes intrinsically unsteady and none of the methods developed for steady premixed flames (§ 2.3) can be used to simplify the problem. Moreover, the resolution needed for a flame/wall interaction (especially in the near-wall zone) is usually higher than for a usual 1D propagating flame so that the computational effort is larger.

- Chemical mechanisms are developed and tested for simple flame configurations: pure ignition, propagating flame, etc. When a flame touches a wall, low-temperature kinetics become critical. Schemes which correctly predict flame speeds, flame temperatures and response to stretch may fail for flame/wall interaction. Obviously, Soret and Dufour effects (Williams [710]) have to be included.

- At the wall, catalysis may become an issue and wall reactions may have to be considered (Popp et al. [539]).

Popp and Baum [538] present a study of HOQ quenching for a stoichiometric methane/air flame interacting with a cold wall at atmospheric pressure and compare their results to experimental results (Fig. 7.8). Four chemical schemes developed for methane were tested and yielded essentially similar results. The critical part of the results validation was the prediction of maximum wall heat flux variations when the wall temperature is varied. For this test, a one-step chemistry flame/wall computation fails as it predicts a strong increase of maximum wall fluxes with wall temperature while experiments show only a limited variation of heat fluxes. Taking into account complex chemistry (Fig. 7.8) and adding surface chemistry models (Popp et al. [539]) improves the results.

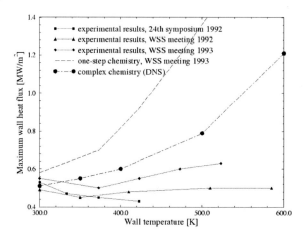

Figure 7.8: Head on Quenching (HOQ) interaction of a stoichiometric methane/air flame with a cold wall (Popp and Baum [538]). Comparison of simple chemistry simulations, complex chemistry simulations and experimental data of Lu et al. [405] and Ezekoye et al. [204].

Flame/wall interactions induce very high values of wall heat fluxes: maximum values of the heat flux of the order of 1 MW/m^2 are typical for hydrocarbon fuels at atmospheric pressure. These values go up with pressure and can reach values as large as 500 MW/m^2 for a H_2/O_2 flame interacting with a wall at high pressure. However, these fluxes are maintained for very short times, typically of the order of the flame time (a few microseconds) so that their impact on the mean wall flux is often neglected.

Table 7.2 summarizes results for maximum heat flux obtained using asymptotic analysis (Wichman and Bruneaux [709]), simple chemistry computations for a generic one-step reaction (Fuel + Oxidizer → Products, Poinsot et al. [525]), complex chemistry computation for methane/air (Popp and Baum [538]), complex chemistry computation for hydrogen/oxygen flames (Vermorel [668]) and complex chemistry computation for octane/air flames (Hasse et al. [271]). Even though assumptions and methods are very different, the order of magnitude obtained for the reduced heat flux F is still correct, suggesting that this scaling is adequate, except for hydrogen/oxygen flames.

7.3 Flame/wall interaction in turbulent flows

7.3.1 Introduction

Even though studies of laminar flame/wall interaction provide valuable information on the flame evolution during the interaction and on wall heat fluxes, the influence of turbulence on the interaction remains unknown. The interaction between a wall and a turbulent premixed flame involves all mechanisms described in Section 7.1. As an example, Fig. 7.9 shows time traces of the instantaneous local wall heat flux which would be measured with a perfect flux detector in a combustion chamber.

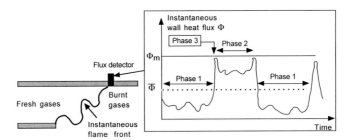

Figure 7.9: Effects of flame/wall interaction on wall heat flux.

As for temperature evolutions in a turbulent flame, heat fluxes are controlled by the intermittency between fresh and burnt gases passing along the wall: when fresh reactants are in contact with the wall (phase 1 in Fig. 7.9), heat fluxes are low. When burnt gases are found at the wall, higher levels of heat flux are observed (phase 2). Phases 1 and 2 are separated by the passage of a flame in front of the detector (phase 3): this passage corresponds to the interaction of the wall with a flame and is usually accompanied by a very intense heat flux at the wall. This complex picture of the interaction between a flame and a wall has multiple

Initial reference	Overall reaction	Approach	Chemical model	Flux Φ MW/m^2	Reduced flux F
Wichman & Bruneaux	$F + O \rightarrow P$	Theory	Simple		0.33
Poinsot et al 1993	$F + O \rightarrow P$	DNS	Simple		0.34
Popp & Baum 1997	CH_4/air - 1 bar	DNS	Complex	0.5	0.4
Vermorel 1999	H_2/O_2 - 1 bar	DNS	Complex	4.85	0.13
Hasse et al 2000	C_8H_{18}/air 10 bar	DNS	Complex	10	0.41

Table 7.2: Example of results on laminar flame/wall interaction.

consequences for modeling:

- The maximum heat flux Φ_m is due to the interaction between an active flame front and the wall. Predicting the flux level due to this interaction and its duration is a challenge in itself. This question is out of reach of RANS models. The DNS described in the next sections show that Φ_m scales with the maximum heat flux obtained at quenching for laminar flames Φ_Q, indicating that flame/wall quenching indeed controls maximum heat fluxes in turbulent combustors.

- RANS models cannot predict the maximum wall flux but should be able to predict the mean wall heat flux. DNS of quenching in laminar flows (§ 7.2.2) indicate that the duration of phase 3 is very small compared to phases 1 and 2 so that the mean flux $\overline{\Phi}$ is essentially the average of fluxes seen during phases 1 and 2. But again, intermittency makes averaging difficult: mean temperature and velocity profiles are very different during phases 1 and 2. Averaging them in a single law-of-the-wall is difficult. Moreover, during phase 2, the ratio of the gas temperature to the wall temperature T/T_W can be as large as 6 (in a piston engine, typical wall temperatures are 500 K while the burnt gases reach 2700 K) and classical logarithmic laws cannot be used anymore.

Compared to the laminar cases described in Section 7.2, the additional issues are:

- Can turbulence change the maximum wall fluxes during quenching?

- In a turbulent flame brush, flame elements close to the wall have a higher probability of quenching than elements which are far from the wall. This must be accounted for in models.

- The wall constrains the flame movement and limits the flame wrinkling, reducing the turbulent flame brush size.

- The wall affects the structure of the turbulence and leads to laminarization in the near-wall region. This induces a strong decrease of the turbulent stretch and thereby a decrease of the flame area.

- Models for mean friction and wall heat fluxes have to be revisited.

Very few experiments have tried to address these problems because of the difficulty of the task. Some DNS have been performed in two (Poinsot et al. [525]) and three dimensions (Nicolleau [467], Bruneaux et al. [92, 93], Alshaalan and Rutland [6]) and provide qualitative answers on the behavior of the flame and the impact of the interaction for models of turbulent premixed combustion.

7.3.2   DNS of turbulent flame/wall interaction

Figure 7.10 displays results of a typical DNS of flame/wall interaction in two dimensions (Poinsot et al. [525]). Heat release is taken into account as well as variable density and

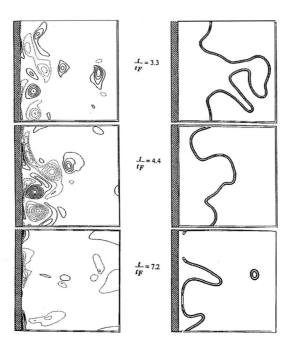

Figure 7.10: Three instants during DNS of flame/wall interaction in two dimensions. Vorticity contours and reaction rate contours (right). Time is normalized by the flame time $t_F = \delta_L^0/s_L^0$ (Reprinted by permission of Elsevier Science from Poinsot et al. [525] © the Combustion Institute).

viscosity. Vorticity fields are shown on the left hand side of the picture while heat release fields are plotted on the right-hand side. Fresh gases are trapped between the wall and the flame (as in a real piston engine) and turbulence is generated at the initial time in the whole domain. The flame is initially planar. There is no mean flow. The initial temperature of the fresh gases is equal to the wall temperature. The initial turbulence characteristics are such that $u'/s_L^0 - 6.25$ and $l_t/\delta_L^0 - 1.43$. The flame propagates towards the wall and gets eventually quenched in its vicinity (Fig. 7.10, last instant $t/t_F = 7.2$).

Post-processing DNS results allows to track the flame front characteristics, flame curvature, strain and wall heat flux distribution. Simulations reveal that turbulent flamelets behave in different ways when they reach the wall depending on their history but that the quenching distance y_Q is of the same order as in a purely laminar case: Fig. 7.11 (left) displays variations of the minimum and maximum distances between wall and flame elements. The minimum distance corresponds to a Peclet number $P_Q = 3.4$ close to the value obtained for HOQ in a

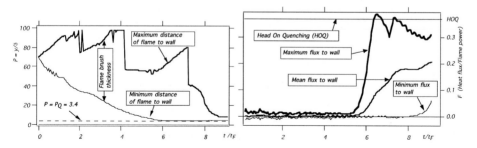

Figure 7.11: DNS of flame/wall interaction: minimum and maximum flame/wall distances versus time (left) and wall heat fluxes versus time (right) (Reprinted by permission of Elsevier Science from Poinsot et al. [525] © the Combustion Institute).

laminar flow (Fig. 7.7). The maximum wall heat flux in the turbulent case never exceeds the flux obtained in laminar head-on quenching (HOQ) situations (Fig. 7.11 right).

A drawback of such two-dimensional simulations is the fact that turbulence decays rapidly during the interaction with the flame. Qualitative information obtained from these DNS on quenching distances for example is useful but quantitative models are difficult to validate on such data. To overcome these difficulties, 3D DNS have been reported both for constant density (Bruneaux et al. [91]) or variable density (Alshaalan and Rutland [6], Gruber et al. [254]) assumptions. The configuration used in Bruneaux et al. [91] is displayed on Fig. 7.12: two flame sheets are initiated near the center plane of a periodic turbulent channel and interact with the turbulence and the wall. Since constant density is assumed, turbulence is not affected by the flame passage and its characteristics are constant and well defined (Kim et al. [345]).

These simulations show that near-wall structures (horseshoe vortices) have a strong impact on the flame when it comes close to the wall. On one hand, these structures push the flame towards the wall and lead to intense wall heat fluxes and localized flame quenching. On the other hand, these vortical structures suck fresh fluid away from the wall and carry it into the burnt gases (Fig. 7.13), creating "tongues" of fresh gases in the burnt zone (these tongues have also been identified in experiments). The tongue of fresh gases, visualized by an isosurface of temperature and located in the middle of the figure is formed by a horseshoe vortex pushing fresh gas away from the upper wall. At the same time, on the upper wall, the flame impinges on the boundary and the fuel mass fraction (visualized by gray levels on the upper walls) nearly vanishes. Maximum heat fluxes Φ_m in these simulations may reach values larger than the maximum laminar heat flux Φ_Q (by a factor of two). This significant difference between two- and three- dimensional DNS is due to structures of intense vorticity near the wall which appear in three–dimensional but not in two–dimensional computations. However, the order of magnitude remains the same than in two dimensions and suggests that maximum heat fluxes measured for laminar flames also provide reasonable estimates of maximum heat fluxes for turbulent situations.

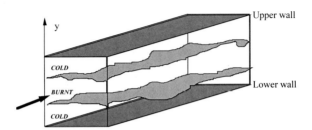

Figure 7.12: Configuration used for DNS of flame wall interaction in a periodic channel with constant density (Bruneaux et al. [93]). Two initially planar premixed flames, separated by burnt gases, move towards the walls and burn the cold fresh reactants

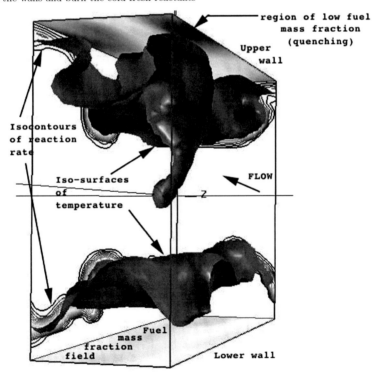

Figure 7.13: DNS of flame/wall interaction in a periodic channel (Bruneaux et al. [93]) Reprinted with permission by Cambridge University Press): flow configuration in Fig. 7.12.

7.3.3   Flame/wall interaction and turbulent combustion models

DNS show that turbulent flames are influenced by walls but incorporating this coupling into
a RANS code is still a challenge. Most models include an indirect coupling between walls
and flames: for example, walls influence turbulence time scales through the law-of-the-wall
approaches used in most codes. These modified time scales affect the mean reaction rate.
However, this coupling is usually wrong and leads to non physical results because of incom-
patibilities between near-wall models and turbulent combustion models. When code users
recognize the deficiency of such models, they often fix the problem with various ad-hoc solutions: setting reaction rates to zero in cells close to a wall is a possible solution. Obviously, it
should be avoided: there is no physical ground upon which such compromises can be justified.

A proper approach to incorporate wall effects in turbulent combustion models is to modify
models near walls using physical arguments and DNS results. One example of "law–of–the–
wall" model for reacting turbulent flows is reported in Poinsot et al. [525] in the framework of
flamelet models. In this model a global sink term D_Q for flame flame density Σ is derived
from DNS and added to the Σ balance equation in the first cell near the wall to represent the
destruction of flame surface density by wall effects (quenching and reduced wrinkling).

A more sophisticated approach is to evaluate all terms of the exact conservation equation
for the flame surface density Σ in the simulation displayed in Fig. 7.13 and use this information
to build models for additional terms induced by the wall (Bruneaux et al. [93]). The influence
of heat losses at the wall on the flame is modeled using an adiabaticity loss factor. The result
of the analysis is a modified flame surface density equation which is valid far from and close to
walls. This equation is an extension of Eq. (5.85), derived for flamelet models in the absence
of walls. This flame surface density balance equation is written:

$$\frac{\partial \Sigma}{\partial t} + \frac{\partial \tilde{u}_i \Sigma}{\partial x_i} = \frac{\partial}{\partial x_i}\left(\frac{\nu_t}{\sigma_\Sigma}\frac{\partial \Sigma}{\partial x_i}\right) \quad + \quad \alpha_0 \frac{\varepsilon}{k}\Gamma_K\left(\frac{u'}{s_L^0},\frac{l_t}{\delta_L^0}\right)\Sigma - \beta_0 \rho_0 s_{Ls}^0 Q_m \frac{\Sigma^2}{\overline{\rho Y}}$$

$$+ \quad \frac{\partial}{\partial x_i}\left[s_L^0\left(1 - \frac{1-Q_m}{\gamma_w}\right)\Sigma\right] \qquad (7.7)$$

where ρ_0 is the fresh gases density and Y the reduced reactant mass fraction ($Y = 1$ in fresh
gases and $Y = 0$ in burnt gases). The last term accounts for flame surface destruction near
the wall. γ_w is a model constant estimated from DNS as $\gamma_w = 0.3$. Q_m is a quenching factor
which is unity for flames which are far from the wall[v] and falls to zero for quenched flames.
DNS show that Q_m may be directly linked to the enthalpy loss L_H induced by the wall:[vi]

$$Q_m = e^{-2\beta L_H} \quad \text{where} \quad L_H = 1 - (\tilde{\Theta} + \tilde{Y}) \qquad (7.8)$$

This equation has been used successfully for piston engine computations (Angelberger et al.
[12], Duclos et al. [190]).

---

[v]Without wall effects ($Q_m = 1$), the CFM2-a model in Table 5.3 is recovered, neglecting the contribution
of the strain rate induced by the mean flow field.

[vi]For adiabatic flames with unity Lewis numbers, reduced mean temperature $\tilde{\Theta}$ and fuel mass fraction $\tilde{Y}$
are linked by $\tilde{\Theta} + \tilde{Y} = 1$ and $L_H = 0$ (see § 5.3.1). L_H is then a measure of heat losses ($\tilde{\Theta} + \tilde{Y} \leq 1$).

7.3.4 Flame/wall interaction and wall heat transfer models

Maximum heat fluxes discussed in the previous sections are one important aspect of flame/wall interaction because they control the maximum local load imposed on materials. But to design cooling systems, mean heat fluxes are of greater importance than maximum fluxes. RANS models cannot predict maximum fluxes but they have to predict mean heat fluxes. For these mean quantities, the interaction between active flames and wall is not the dominant factor as shown in Fig. 7.9. However, the presence of burnt gases must definitely be accounted for. This is not often the case: the traditional law-of-the-wall approach used in many codes is valid only for flows in which temperature variations remain small (typically, the ratio of gas temperature to wall temperature T/T_W must be of order unity). In combustion applications, this is rarely the case and ratios T/T_W of the order of 4 to 6 are common. This can induce very large errors on wall friction and wall heat fluxes. In this section, the principles of law-of-the-wall approaches are first described and their implementation is presented for the classical isothermal situation where T/T_W is of order unity. Then, possible extensions to cases where T/T_W is large are discussed. The basics of boundary layer theory can be found in Schlichting [591] or Kays and Crawford [328] and numerous other books on turbulent flows. Only the implementation of these laws and their limits in reacting flows are discussed.

Principle of law-of-the-wall models

In RANS codes, boundary layers are usually too thin to be resolved. The usual technique to solve this problem is to make assumptions on the structure of turbulence near the wall to avoid having to resolve it.[vii] Law-of-the-wall models provide such approximations. The flow structure between the wall and the first grid point is assumed to be similar to a boundary layer flow which would have the same velocity $\widetilde{u}_1$ at the distance y_1 from the wall (Fig. 7.14). Boundary layer flows are well known (Kays and Crawford [328]): one of their most interesting features is that they provide scaling laws for mean velocities and turbulent quantities. For example, knowing the mean[viii] velocity $\widetilde{u}_1$ at the distance y_1 from the wall in a boundary layer directly provides an estimate for the mean wall friction $\overline{\tau}_W$:

$$\boxed{\overline{\tau}_W = \mu \overline{\frac{\partial u}{\partial y}} = \rho \widetilde{u}_\tau^2} \qquad (7.9)$$

where $\widetilde{u}_\tau$ is the friction velocity. The wall heat flux $\overline{\Phi}$ is obtained in a similar way, using the mean temperature at the first grid point and the wall friction $\widetilde{u}_\tau$. If such relations hold in the flow to compute, knowing $\widetilde{u}_1$ and y_1 allows to evaluate $\overline{\tau}_W$ and $\overline{\Phi}$. Since these two quantities are sufficient to compute the flow outside the wall region, the problem is closed. When a k-ε

[vii]Low Reynolds number turbulence models (which are an alternative choice to law-of-the-wall models) are not considered here even though they are often used in aerodynamical applications. For combustion applications, law-of-the-wall models are generally used explaining why this text focuses on this approach.

[viii]Favre averaging is used in this section (see Chapt. 4).

model is used, the law-of the-wall assumption also provides an estimate for k and ε near the wall as well as boundary conditions for the turbulence model.

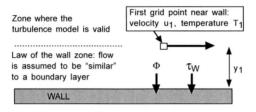

Figure 7.14: Principle of law-of-the-wall models.

Nearly-isothermal law-of-the-wall

The simplest example of law-of-the-wall relations is given below. All relations are expressed in wall units where distances are scaled by a near-wall characteristic length $y_\tau = \nu_W/\tilde{u}_\tau$ and ν_W is the kinematic viscosity at the wall. The velocity parallel to the wall is scaled by $\tilde{u}_\tau$ and the temperature by $T_\tau = \overline{\Phi}/(\rho C_p \tilde{u}_\tau)$:[ix]

$$
\boxed{y^+ = \frac{y}{y_\tau} = \frac{\tilde{u}_\tau y}{\nu_W}} \qquad \boxed{u^+ = \frac{u}{\tilde{u}_\tau}} \quad \text{and} \quad \boxed{T^+ = \frac{T_W - T}{T_\tau} = \frac{(T_W - T)\rho C_p \tilde{u}_\tau}{\overline{\Phi}}} \tag{7.10}
$$

A number of assumptions are needed to derive the law-of-the-wall relations:

- H1: negligible gradients along wall,

- H2: fully turbulent flow, stationary in the mean,

- H3: negligible pressure gradient,

- H4: low Mach number,

- H5: no chemical reactions,

- H6: perfect gases and no Soret or Dufour effects,

- H7: no radiative fluxes or external forces,

- H8: small temperature differences; T/T_W must be of order unity (nearly-isothermal assumption).

[ix]The sign convention is that, for a cold wall surrounded by hot gases, $\overline{\Phi}$ and T_τ are negative.

Some of these assumptions are not compatible with combustion. The most restrictive one is H8. Its impact can be measured by introducing an isothermicity parameter ξ:

$$\xi = -\frac{T_\tau}{T_W} = -\frac{\overline{\Phi}}{\rho_W C_p \tilde{u}_\tau T_W} \tag{7.11}$$

By convention, the isothermicity parameter is positive when the mean flux to the wall is negative, i.e. for a cold wall and vice versa (Table 7.3).

Case	Heat flux $\overline{\Phi}$	ξ
Cold wall and hot gases ($T_W < T_{gas}$)	< 0	> 0
Hot wall and cold gases ($T_W > T_{gas}$)	> 0	< 0

Table 7.3: Sign conventions for wall heat fluxes.

Using ξ, the temperature can be expressed as:

$$T = T_W \left(1 + \xi T^+\right) \tag{7.12}$$

Defining a reduced viscosity μ^+, a reduced heat coefficient λ^+ and a reduced density ρ^+:

$$\mu^+ = \mu/\mu_W, \quad \lambda^+ = \lambda/(C_p \mu_W) \quad \text{and} \quad \rho^+ = \rho/\rho_W \tag{7.13}$$

and linking the viscosity to the temperature by a polynomial law: $\mu = \mu_W (T/T_W)^b$, it is simple to show that

$$\mu^+ = (1 + \xi T^+)^b, \quad \lambda^+ = \mu^+/P_r \quad \text{and} \quad \rho^+ = 1/(1 + \xi T^+) \tag{7.14}$$

For small values of the isothermicity parameter ξ as postulated by hypothesis H8, Eq. (7.14) shows that temperature changes have no effect on the reduced viscosity, heat coefficient or density which can be considered as constant (independent of wall distance):

$$\mu^+ = 1, \quad \lambda^+ = 1/P_r \quad \text{and} \quad \rho^+ = 1 \tag{7.15}$$

showing that the flow behaves like a constant-temperature fluid in which temperature is convected like any scalar, with no feedback effect on the flow.

Under these assumptions, theoretical developments and fits on experimental results provide the relations given in Table 7.4 (Schlichting [591], Kays and Crawford [328]):

Close to the wall, in a zone called the "viscous sublayer", the reduced velocity and temperature profiles are linear with y^+. They become logarithmic further away from the wall ("log zone") as displayed in Fig. 7.15.

When a k-ε model is used, the law-of-the-wall also provides scaling for the kinetic energy k_1 and the dissipation ε_1 at the first grid point:

$$k_1 = \tilde{u}_\tau^2/(C_\mu^{1/2}) \quad \text{and} \quad \varepsilon_1 = \tilde{u}_\tau^3/(K y_1) \tag{7.16}$$

Velocity

y^+ region	Zone	Velocity
$y^+ < 10.8$	Viscous sublayer	$\widetilde{u}^+ = y^+$
$y^+ > 10.8$	Logarithmic layer	$\widetilde{u}^+ = 2.44\ln(y^+) + 5$

Temperature

y^+ region	Zone	Temperature
$y^+ < 13.2$	Viscous sublayer	$\widetilde{T}^+ = P_r y^+$
$y^+ > 13.2$	Logarithmic layer	$\widetilde{T}^+ = 2.075\ln(y^+) + 3.9$

Table 7.4: Summary of nearly-isothermal law-of-the-wall relations. P_r is the Prandtl number.

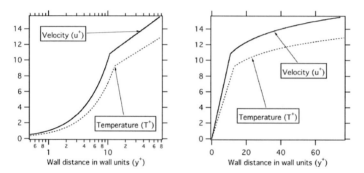

Figure 7.15: Law-of-the-wall relations for velocity and temperature in log scale (left) and linear scale (right) for a nearly isothermal flow.

where C_μ and K are model constants: $C_\mu = 0.09$ and $K = 0.41$. The first relation (giving k_1) corresponds to experimental observations showing that the ratio $k_1/\widetilde{u}_\tau^2$ was constant in most boundary layers (Bradshaw [81], Bradshaw et al. [82]). The second one (giving ε_1) is obtained by expressing the production of k (Eq. (4.38)) as a function of the wall velocity:

$$P_k = -\overline{\rho u_i'' u_j''}\frac{\partial \widetilde{u}_i}{\partial x_j} \approx \overline{\rho}\widetilde{u}_\tau^2 \frac{\widetilde{u}_\tau}{Ky} \tag{7.17}$$

and stating that P_k is equal to the dissipation $\overline{\rho}\varepsilon_1$ at the first grid point:

$$\varepsilon_1 = \widetilde{u}_\tau^3/(Ky_1) = C_\mu^{3/4}k_1^{3/2}/(Ky_1) \tag{7.18}$$

Practical implementation of nearly-isothermal law-of-the-wall models ($\xi \ll 1$)

In practice, the implementation of law-of-the-wall models depends on the discretization scheme itself: space discretization (cell-vertex or cell-centered), numerical method (finite elements, finite volumes or finite differences), time discretization (explicit or implicit) lead to different implementations and results. The link between a code and a law-of-the-wall formulation is very strong and results obtained with a given law-of-the-wall in one code may differ in another code, thereby limiting the generic character of such developments. As an example, this section shows how this coupling is usually performed in an explicit finite volume code where all variables are located on grid points (Fig. 7.14 and Table 7.5):

- Step 1. After a given time iteration, the code has computed the velocity and the temperature at all nodes close to walls: for each of these nodes, $\widetilde{u}_1$ and $\widetilde{T}_1$ are known.

- Step 2. At each node, the relations of Table 7.4 are used to construct implicit relations for the friction velocity $\widetilde{u}_\tau$ and the wall heat flux $\overline{\Phi}$. Even though their inversion is cumbersome, it is easily performed numerically. For example, for velocity, supposing that y_1^+ is larger than 10.8, the relation to invert is:

$$\widetilde{u}_1/\widetilde{u}_\tau = 2.44\ln(\widetilde{u}_\tau y_1/\nu_W) + 5 \qquad (7.19)$$

where the only unknown is $\widetilde{u}_\tau$. After resolution, it is simple to check whether y_1^+ is indeed larger than 10.8. If it is smaller, Eq. (7.19) must be replaced by the linear relation $\widetilde{u}^+ = y^+$. If y_1^+ is too large (more than 1000 in most codes), the first grid point is too far from the wall and the mesh must be refined.

- Step 3. Having $\widetilde{u}_\tau$, the wall coordinate of the first grid point is $y_1^+ = \widetilde{u}_\tau y_1/\nu_W$ and the reduced temperature of the first point is calculated from Table 7.4:

$$\widetilde{T}_1^+ = 2.075\ln(\widetilde{u}_\tau y_1/\nu_W) + 3.9 \qquad (7.20)$$

for y_1^+ larger than 13.2.

- Step 4. From $\widetilde{T}_1^+$, $\overline{\Phi}$ is obtained using Eq. (7.10):

$$\overline{\Phi} = (T_W - \widetilde{T}_1)\rho_W C_p \widetilde{u}_\tau/\widetilde{T}_1^+ \qquad (7.21)$$

- Step 5. The turbulent kinetic energy k_1 and its dissipation ε_1 at the first grid point are obtained by replacing the conservation equations of k and ε in the first wall cell by the equilibrium values of these quantities in the turbulent boundary layer:

$$k_1 = \widetilde{u}_\tau^2/(C_\mu^{1/2}) \quad \text{and} \quad \varepsilon_1 = \widetilde{u}_\tau^3/(Ky_1) \qquad (7.22)$$

- Step 6. The previous procedure has provided the mean wall friction $\overline{\tau}_W = \rho_W \widetilde{u}_\tau^2$, the mean wall flux $\overline{\Phi}$ and the values of k_1 and ε_1. This is enough in a finite volume code to integrate the flow equations above the near-wall region and obtain values for the velocities at the next time step.

Step 1	Input values: $\widetilde{u}_1$ and $\widetilde{T}_1$
Step 2	Invert Eq. (7.19): find $\widetilde{u}_\tau$
Step 3	Compute $y_1^+ = \widetilde{u}_\tau y_1/\nu_W$ and $\widetilde{T}_1^+$ using Eq. (7.20)
Step 4	Having $\widetilde{T}_1^+$, compute heat flux $\overline{\Phi} = \rho_W C_p \widetilde{u}_\tau (T_W - \widetilde{T}_1)/\widetilde{T}_1^+$
Step 5	Find turbulent values: $k_1 = \widetilde{u}_\tau^2/C_\mu^{1/2}$ and $\varepsilon_1 = \widetilde{u}_\tau^3/Ky_1$
Step 6	Advance flow equations and go to Step 1

Table 7.5: Using an equilibrium law-of-the-wall under the nearly-isothermal assumption $\xi \ll 1$.

This method works correctly in many flows but has some deficiencies. For example, near stagnation points, $\widetilde{u}_1$ goes to zero and solving Eq. (7.19) becomes inaccurate: even though $\widetilde{u}_1$ goes to zero, $\widetilde{u}_\tau$ can still take large values which cannot be predicted by Eq. (7.19). In many combustion codes, this equilibrium approach is replaced (Table 7.6) by evolutions of the model initially proposed by Chieng and Launder [129] (see also Johnson and Launder [314], Ciofalo and Collins [134] in which the law-of-the-wall assumptions are used differently):

- Step 1. The input parameters are now the mean velocity $\widetilde{u}_1$ and the mean temperature $\widetilde{T}_1$ at the first point but also the turbulent kinetic energy k_1 and its dissipation ε_1.

- Step 2. Instead of using Eq. (7.19), the friction velocity is directly obtained from the kinetic energy at the previous time step k_1 using the equilibrium relation $\widetilde{u}_\tau = k_1^{1/2} C_\mu^{1/4}$.

- Step 3. Having $\widetilde{u}_\tau$, the reduced wall distance of the first point is obtained by $y_1^+ = \widetilde{u}_\tau y_1/\nu_W$ and the reduced temperature at this point $\widetilde{T}_1^+$ is given by Eq. (7.20).

- Step 4. The wall heat flux $\overline{\Phi}$ is evaluated from $\widetilde{T}_1^+$ and $\widetilde{u}_\tau$ using Eq. (7.10): $\overline{\Phi} = (T_W - \widetilde{T}_1)\rho C_p \widetilde{u}_\tau/\widetilde{T}_1^+$.

- Step 5. The new value of k_1 is not imposed using Eq. (7.16) but is computed using the balance equation (see Eq. 4.36) in the cell near the wall. In this equation, the source term P_{k1} is evaluated using $\widetilde{u}_\tau$: $P_{k1} = \rho_W \widetilde{u}_\tau^2 \widetilde{u}_1/y_1$ and the dissipation is still evaluated by the equilibrium relation $\varepsilon_1 = \widetilde{u}_\tau^3/(Ky_1)$.

- Step 6. All flow equations (including the k equation at the first point near the wall) can be time-advanced and the cycle repeated.

Limits of the nearly-isothermal approach

The derivation of the previous law-of-the-wall models and their validation were performed for nearly isothermal flows where the isothermicity parameter of Eq. (7.11) was small and the ratio T/T_W was of order unity. In most combustion systems, these assumptions are

Step 1	Input values: $\widetilde{u}_1$, $\widetilde{T}_1$, k_1 and ε_1
Step 2	Compute $\widetilde{u}_\tau$ from k_1: $\widetilde{u}_\tau = k_1^{1/2} C_\mu^{1/4}$
Step 3	Compute $y_1^+ = \widetilde{u}_\tau y_1/\nu_W$ and $\widetilde{T}_1^+$ using Eq. (7.20)
Step 4	Having $\widetilde{T}_1^+$, compute heat flux $\overline{\Phi} = \rho_W C_p \widetilde{u}_\tau (T_W - \widetilde{T}_1)/\widetilde{T}_1^+$
Step 5	Find source terms in first cell for k equation: $P_{k1} = \rho_W \widetilde{u}_\tau^2 \widetilde{u}_1/y_1$ and $\varepsilon_1 = \widetilde{u}_\tau^3/(K y_1)$
Step 6	Advance flow equations including the k equation at first grid point and go to Step 1

Table 7.6: Using Chieng and Launder law-of-the-wall under nearly-isothermal assumption $\xi \ll 1$.

not satisfied. In a piston engine for example, fluxes of the order of 5 MW/m^2 are often encountered for pressures of 30 bars and friction velocities of the order of 1 m/s leading to ξ values larger than 0.5 (Angelberger [11]). Under these conditions, viscosity, density and heat coefficient change significantly when the wall distance increases. Temperature and velocity equations become intrinsically coupled because temperature controls density and viscosity (see Eq. 7.14). As a result, the whole basis of law-of-the-wall models must be revised. There are two situations where this problem has been identified and studied: high-speed boundary layers and reacting flows. For example, the supersonic turbulent boundary layer with or without heat transfer is well documented (Bradshaw [81], Spina et al. [625]). The case of large heat transfer and low speeds (typical of combustion) has received much less attention. Correlations providing Nusselt numbers as a function of Reynolds number and temperature ratio may be found for engineering applications but few studies have focused on deriving a law-of-the-wall which can be integrated into CFD codes (Diwakar [177], Kays and Crawford [328], Han et al. [268], Angelberger [11], Angelberger et al. [12]). One of these extensions (Han et al. [268], Angelberger et al. [12]) is described here: this approach assumes that law-of-the-wall relations can still be written for reduced mean velocity and temperature if corrected variables accounting for temperature changes are used. These variables are: the extended wall distance η^+, the extended reduced velocity ψ^+ and the extended reduced temperature Θ^+ which are linked to the wall distance y^+, the reduced density ρ^+ and the reduced temperature T^+ by:

$$d\eta^+ = (\nu_W/\nu)dy^+, \quad d\psi^+ = (\rho/\rho_W)du^+ \quad \text{and} \quad d\Theta^+ = (\rho/\rho_W)dT^+ \qquad (7.23)$$

Momentum and energy equations take the same form as in an isothermal flow if these variables are used: one can then speculate that the solution to these equations also takes the same form, simply replacing y^+ by η^+, u^+ by ψ^+ and T^+ by Θ^+ as shown in Table 7.7 (Han et al. [268], Angelberger et al. [12]). These relations relax to the nearly-isothermal case of Table 7.4 when ξ goes to zero.

Under these assumptions, a law-of-the-wall can be derived to incorporate effects of large temperature gradients. To provide a simple implementation, an additional simplification is

η^+ region	Zone	Velocity
$\eta^+ < 10.8$	Viscous sublayer	$\widetilde{\psi}^+ = \eta^+$
$\eta^+ > 10.8$	Logarithmic layer	$\widetilde{\psi}^+ = 2.44\ln(\eta^+) + 5$

Velocity

η^+ region	Zone	Temperature
$\eta^+ < 13.2$	Viscous sublayer	$\widetilde{\Theta}^+ = P_r\eta^+$
$\eta^+ > 13.2$	Logarithmic layer	$\widetilde{\Theta}^+ = 2.075\ln(\eta^+) + 3.9$

Temperature

Table 7.7: Summary of extended law-of-the-wall relations for non isothermal flows (ξ not small).

introduced to relate η^+ to y^+ and $\widetilde{\psi}^+$ to u^+ at the first grid point:

$$\eta_1^+ = \int_0^{y_1^+} \frac{\nu_W}{\nu} dy^+ \approx \frac{\nu_W}{\nu_1} y_1^+ = \frac{\widetilde{u}_\tau y_1}{\nu_1} \quad \text{and} \quad \widetilde{\psi}_1^+ = \int_0^{u_1^+} \frac{\rho}{\rho_W} du^+ \approx \frac{\rho_1}{\rho_W}\frac{\widetilde{u}_1}{\widetilde{u}_\tau} \tag{7.24}$$

showing that η_1^+ is a wall unit based on the local viscosity ν_1 while y_1^+ was based on the wall viscosity ν_W. The extended temperature Θ^+ can be expressed directly as a function of the temperature T^+ simply assuming constant pressure:

$$\Theta^+ = \int_0^{T^+} \frac{1}{1+\xi T^+} dT^+ = \frac{1}{\xi}\ln\left(1+\xi T^+\right) = \frac{1}{\xi}\ln\left(\frac{T}{T_W}\right) \tag{7.25}$$

using the definition of T^+.

The scaling for the kinetic energy k_1 remains unchanged:

$$k_1 = \widetilde{u}_\tau^2/C_\mu^{1/2} \tag{7.26}$$

Production-dissipation equilibrium is assumed in the k equation (4.36) to have dissipation:

$$P_k = -\overline{\rho u_i'' u_j''}\frac{\partial \widetilde{u}_i}{\partial x_j} \approx \overline{\rho}\widetilde{u}_\tau^2\frac{\widetilde{u}_\tau}{Ky}\frac{\rho_W}{\rho_1} = \overline{\rho}\varepsilon_1 \quad \text{so that} \quad \varepsilon_1 = \frac{\widetilde{u}_\tau^3}{Ky_1}\frac{\rho_W}{\rho_1} \tag{7.27}$$

Compared to the isothermal case (Eq. (7.18)), the dissipation at the first grid point is increased by a factor $\rho_W/\rho_1 > 1$.

The equilibrium version of the law-of-the-wall is then obtained as described in Table 7.8:

- Step 1. After a given time iteration, the velocity and the temperature $\widetilde{u}_1$ and $\widetilde{T}_1$ at all nodes close to walls are known. The kinematic viscosity ν_1 and the density ρ_1 are obtained directly from $\widetilde{T}_1$.

- Step 2. At each node, the relations of Table 7.7 are used to construct implicit relations for the friction velocity $\widetilde{u}_\tau$ and the wall heat flux $\overline{\Phi}$. For velocity, assuming η_1^+ larger than 10.8, $\widetilde{u}_\tau$ is determined by:

$$(\rho_1/\rho_W)(\widetilde{u}_1/\widetilde{u}_\tau) = 2.44\ln(\widetilde{u}_\tau y_1/\nu_1) + 5 \tag{7.28}$$

where $\widetilde{u}_\tau$ is the only unknown. After resolution, it is simple to check whether η_1^+ is indeed larger than 10.8. If it is smaller, Eq. (7.28) must be replaced by the linear relation $\widetilde{\psi}^+ = \eta^+$ and solved.

- Step 3. Having $\widetilde{u}_\tau$, the wall coordinate of the first grid point is $\eta_1^+ = \widetilde{u}_\tau y_1/\nu_1$ and the reduced temperature of the first point is calculated from Table (7.7):

$$\Theta_1^+ = 2.075 \ln\left(\eta_1^+\right) + 3.9 \qquad (7.29)$$

- Step 4. From Θ_1^+, $\overline{\Phi}$ is obtained using Eqs. (7.11) and (7.25):

$$\overline{\Phi} = -\rho_W C_p \widetilde{u}_\tau T_W / \Theta_1^+ . \ln(\widetilde{T}_1/T_W) \qquad (7.30)$$

- Step 5. The turbulent kinetic energy k_1 and its dissipation ε_1 at the first grid point are obtained by replacing the conservation equations of k and ε by the equilibrium values of these quantities in the turbulent boundary layer:

$$k_1 = \widetilde{u}_\tau^2/C_\mu^{1/2} \quad \text{and} \quad \varepsilon_1 = \widetilde{u}_\tau^3/(K y_1).\rho_W/\rho_1 \qquad (7.31)$$

- Step 6. The previous procedure has provided the mean wall friction $\overline{\tau}_W = \rho_W \widetilde{u}_\tau^2$, the mean wall flux $\overline{\Phi}$ and the values of k_1 and ε_1. Flow equations can be integrated above the near-wall region and give values for the velocities at the next time step.

Step 1	Input values: $\widetilde{u}_1$ and $\widetilde{T}_1$
Step 2	Invert Eq. (7.28): find $\widetilde{u}_\tau$.
Step 3	Compute $\eta_1^+ = \widetilde{u}_\tau y_1/\nu_1$ and Θ_1^+ using Eq. (7.29)
Step 4	Having Θ_1^+, compute heat flux $\overline{\Phi} = -\dfrac{\rho_W C_p \widetilde{u}_\tau T_W}{\Theta_1^+} \ln\left(\dfrac{\widetilde{T}_1}{T_W}\right)$
Step 5	Find turbulent values: $k_1 = \widetilde{u}_\tau^2/C_\mu^{1/2}$ and $\varepsilon_1 = \widetilde{u}_\tau^3/(K y_1)\ \rho_W/\rho_1$
Step 6	Advance flow equations and go to Step 1

Table 7.8: Tasks performed with an extended equilibrium law-of-the-wall for large ξ values.

The extension of this technique to a non-equilibrium formulation similar to the Chieng and Launder model is straightforward.

Chapter 8

Flame/acoustics interactions

8.1 Introduction

Coupling mechanisms between acoustic waves and flames control two important phenomena in the development of modern combustion systems: (1) combustion noise (because of environmental issues) and (2) combustion instabilities (because of their undesired effects on combustor performances and sometimes life time). Numerical tools are essential in those fields but a theoretical background in acoustics and especially in acoustics for reacting flows is mandatory to tackle such problems. This is the objective of this chapter.

For combustion noise, flame/acoustics coupling operate in a one-way mode: flames produce noise (Strahle [629], Putnam and Faulkner [547], Strahle [630], Candel et al. [108], Ihme et al. [302], Leyko et al. [384]) but this noise can be predicted a posteriori because it does not influence the flame itself. For combustion instabilities, coupling works both ways: flames create noise but are also influenced by noise leading to a resonant interaction and combustion instabilities in many practical systems[i]. These instabilities have been known for a long time (Rayleigh [548], Putnam [546], Williams [710], Culick and Kuentzmann [160]). A flame is not even needed to produce such coupling: as shown by Rijke [557, 558], a heated gauze placed in a tube is enough to produce a "singing" tube caused by the coupling between the acoustic modes of the duct and the unsteady heat released by the gauze (Moeck et al. [446, 447]). However, when the heat release is due to a flame, much more energy can be injected into the oscillation modes and the effects of combustion instabilities can be spectacular: in addition to inducing oscillations of all flow parameters (pressure, velocities, temperature, etc), such phenomena increase the amplitude of flame movements and the levels of heat transfer to walls; in some extreme cases, they can destroy part of the burner and induce a loss of control of the system. At the same time, burners submitted to instabilities usually have a higher efficiency: pulse combustors[ii] which are designed to oscillate have high burning rates and

---

[i]A tutorial on combustion instabilities is available: *elearning.cerfacs.fr/combustion/n7masterCourses/acoustic*.
[ii]The most famous example of pulse combustor is the V1 rocket built by Germany during World War II

wall heat fluxes which make them suitable choices for certain applications (Dec and Keller [170, 171]). The pollutant emission rates of combustors submitted to instability may also be substantially lower than those produced by stable combustion if the combustor is built to sustain such oscillations (Keller et al. [334]). However, most combustors are not designed for such regimes and combustion instabilities are usually undesired and harmful phenomena.

Many combustion instabilities are the result of a coupling between unsteady combustion processes and acoustic waves propagating in the system ducts.[iii] Even when flames are not submitted to strong combustion instabilities, acoustic waves interact with turbulent combustion in a number of situations and can modify flames at least as significantly as turbulence does: simple estimates show that velocities induced by acoustic oscillations in cavities can be of the same order as turbulent velocities (§ 8.2.2). Moreover, acoustic wavelengths in most combustion chambers are of the order of 10 cm to 3 m so that acoustic waves have a spatial coherence which can amplify their effects over the full combustion chamber (while turbulent length scales are much smaller). As a consequence, the effect of acoustics on turbulent combustion can be both significant and very different from the action of turbulence, suggesting that a proper description of certain combustion chambers must incorporate effects of acoustics. Numerically, the importance of acoustic waves also emphasizes the need for sophisticated boundary conditions: using boundary conditions which can handle correctly the transmission and the reflection of acoustic waves on boundaries becomes a critical issue (Chapt. 9).

Studies of combustion instabilities and noise are numerous (Crocco [154], Price [542], Barrère and Williams [35], Harrje and Reardon [270], Strahle [629], Mugridge [461], Yang and Culick [720], Crighton et al. [153], Candel et al. [107], Dowling [184], Martin et al. [421], Morgans and Stow [454]) and started long ago (Rayleigh [548]). Advanced simulations only begin to be utilized in this field as observed in classical books on instabilities by Lieuwen and Yang [393] and Culick and Kuentzmann [160]. This chapter focuses on generic results and theoretical tools needed to understand flame / acoustics interaction using recent simulation methods.

The presentation starts with basic notions of acoustics in non-reacting flows (§ 8.2). The objective is not to replace classical text books on acoustics (Landau and Lifchitz [364], Morse and Ingard [455], Pierce [506], Kinsler et al. [347], Crighton et al. [153]) but to provide minimum information for readers and describe the acoustic tools needed for combustion. The numerical procedures required to develop one- (§ 8.2.2 to 8.2.5 and 8.2.7) and three- dimensional (§ 8.2.6 and 8.2.10) numerical solvers for acoustic modes in cavities are described. Cases which are typical of combustors are discussed: longitudinal modes in double-duct systems (§ 8.2.8), decoupling in triple-duct systems (§ 8.2.9) and azimuthal modes in annular combustors (§ 8.2.11). A wave equation in reacting flows is then derived in Section 8.3 and the concepts of § 8.2 are generalized to reacting cases and applied in Section 8.4 to combustion instability studies. The concept of FTF (Flame Transfer Function) is introduced (§ 8.4.3) and a simplified case of a single flame placed in a constant cross-section duct is used to build a fully analytical solution and discuss flame stability (§ 8.4.4). Finally Section 8.5 shows how recent CFD tools like large eddy simulation can be used to study combustion instabilities.

(Reynst [553]) which used valves to operate in a pulsating mode.

[iii]Most unconfined flames do not exhibit strong combustion instabilities.

8.2 Acoustics for non-reacting flows

In this first section, the propagation of acoustic waves in ducts is studied in the absence of combustion. Temperature is first assumed to be constant to simplify the presentation.

8.2.1 Fundamental equations

A simple framework to introduce acoustic theory is linear acoustics in non-reacting flows. Acoustic perturbations are small amplitude changes of thermodynamic variables and velocity. These perturbations are present in all gases and appear in all codes using a compressible formulation. Equations of acoustics are derived from the main conservation equations: mass, momentum and energy. Classical elements of acoustics are first recalled in a simplified case:

- H0 - no combustion.

- H1 - zero volume forces ($f_k = 0$)

- H2 - zero volume heat sources ($\dot{Q} = 0$).

- H3 - negligible viscous forces: no viscous stresses are retained in the volume. Moreover, near walls, only the normal velocity goes to zero ("slip walls").

- H4 - linear acoustics: acoustic variables are indexed "1" and supposed to be small compared to reference quantities indexed "0": $p_1 \ll p_0$, $\rho_1 \ll \rho_0$, $u_1 \ll c_0$. Note that the reference speed is not the mean flow speed u_0 but the sound speed c_0.

- H5 - isentropic variations: under the previous assumptions (no heat release, no viscous terms), the flow remains isentropic if it is homogeneous and isentropic at the initial time $t = 0$. The energy equation may then be replaced by the isentropic relation:

$$s_0 = C_v \ln(p/\rho^\gamma) \quad \text{or} \quad p = \rho^\gamma e^{s_0/C_v} \tag{8.1}$$

where s_0 is the (constant) entropy of the flow.

- H6 - low-speed mean flow: $\vec{u}_0 = 0$.

Under these assumptions, the equations of mass, momentum and energy are:[iv]

$$\frac{\partial \rho}{\partial t} + \nabla.\rho\vec{u} = 0 \tag{8.2}$$

$$\rho\frac{\partial \vec{u}}{\partial t} + \rho\vec{u}\nabla\vec{u} = -\nabla p \tag{8.3}$$

$$p = \rho^\gamma e^{s_0/C_v} \tag{8.4}$$

[iv]Tensor notations are used in this chapter to simplify equations.

where $\vec{u}$ is the velocity vector.

An acoustic perturbation $(p_1, \vec{u}_1)$ added to the mean flow $(p_0, \vec{u}_0)$ is written:

$$\boxed{p = p_0 + p_1 \quad ; \quad \vec{u} = \vec{u}_0 + \vec{u}_1 \quad ; \quad \rho = \rho_0 + \rho_1}$$

(8.5)

Substituting p and $\vec{u}$ into Eq. (8.2) and (8.3) and conserving only first order terms gives:

$$\frac{\partial \rho_1}{\partial t} + \rho_0 \nabla . \vec{u}_1 = 0$$

(8.6)

$$\rho_0 \frac{\partial \vec{u}_1}{\partial t} + \nabla p_1 = 0$$

(8.7)

The isentropic assumption provides a direct relation between pressure and density perturbations. Linearizing Eq. (8.1):

$$p_1 = c_0^2 \rho_1 \quad \text{where} \quad c_0^2 = \left(\frac{\partial p}{\partial \rho} \right)_{s=s_0}$$

(8.8)

where c_0 is the sound speed. For a perfect gas, the sound speed is obtained using Eq. (8.4):

$$c_0 = \sqrt{\gamma \frac{p_0}{\rho_0}} = \sqrt{\gamma \frac{R}{W} T_0}$$

(8.9)

Density variations may be eliminated using Eq. (8.8), and two variables (for example p_1 and $\vec{u}_1$) are sufficient to describe acoustic waves:

$$\frac{1}{c_0^2} \frac{\partial p_1}{\partial t} + \rho_0 \nabla . \vec{u}_1 = 0$$

(8.10)

$$\rho_0 \frac{\partial \vec{u}_1}{\partial t} + \nabla p_1 = 0$$

(8.11)

These equations may be combined to obtain the well-known wave equation:

$$\boxed{\nabla^2 p_1 - \frac{1}{c_0^2} \frac{\partial^2 p_1}{\partial t^2} = 0}$$

(8.12)

Solving this wave equation often requires to retain Eq. (8.11) to impose boundary conditions.

8.2.2   Plane waves in one dimension

In one-dimensional situations (for example, acoustic waves propagating in long ducts along the z direction), the velocity field is $\vec{u}_1 = (0, 0, u_1)$ and Eq. (8.10) and (8.11) reduce to:

$$\frac{1}{c_0^2} \frac{\partial p_1}{\partial t} + \rho_0 \frac{\partial u_1}{\partial z} = 0$$

(8.13)

$$\rho_0 \frac{\partial u_1}{\partial t} + \frac{\partial p_1}{\partial z} = 0 \tag{8.14}$$

leading to the wave equation:

$$\frac{\partial^2 p_1}{\partial z^2} - \frac{1}{c_0^2} \frac{\partial^2 p_1}{\partial t^2} = 0 \tag{8.15}$$

The solution of Eq. (8.15) is the superimposition of two traveling waves (Fig. 8.1):

$$p_1 = A^+(t - z/c_0) + A^-(t + z/c_0) \tag{8.16}$$

Using Eq. (8.13) shows that:

$$u_1 = \frac{1}{\rho_0 c_0} \left(A^+(t - z/c_0) - A^-(t + z/c_0) \right) \tag{8.17}$$

Figure 8.1: One-dimensional waves in a constant cross section duct.

The pressure and velocity perturbations corresponding to the right ($z = +\infty$ direction) traveling wave A^+ are such that $p_1 = \rho_0 c_0 u_1$. For the A^- wave traveling in the $z = -\infty$ direction, pressure and velocity perturbations have opposite signs: $p_1 = -\rho_0 c_0 u_1$. This scaling between pressure and velocity perturbations involves a quantity $\rho_0 c_0$ called the *characteristic impedance* of the gas where the acoustic waves propagate. In a chamber at atmospheric pressure containing burnt gases ($\rho_0 = 0.2 \, kg/m^3$, $c_0 = 850 \, m/s$), an acoustic pressure variation of 1000 Pa, corresponding[v] to 154 dB, induces an acoustic velocity given by $1000/(\rho_0 c_0) \approx 6$ m/s, which is large compared to many turbulent speeds as mentioned earlier.

The notion of impedance is also useful to characterize wave transmission and reflection at a given section in a duct: at any z location, the acoustic effect of all parts located downstream of this section can be measured by a reduced impedance Z defined by:

$$Z = \frac{1}{\rho_0 c_0} \frac{p_1}{u_1} \tag{8.18}$$

A reflection coefficient R can be defined from the impedance as the amplitude ratio of the wave entering a given section $z = z_0$ to the wave leaving this section. The reflection coefficient is

---

[v] Decibel levels are defined from RMS pressure by $p'(dB) = 20 \log(p'/p_0')$ where the reference acoustic pressure is $p_0' = 2.10^{-5}$ Pa.

defined for a given axis orientation (to decide which wave enters or leaves the section where R is measured) and must be used with some care. For example in Fig. 8.1, a reflection coefficient R can be defined as:

$$R = \frac{A^+(t - z_0/c_0)}{A^-(t + z_0/c_0)} \qquad (8.19)$$

so that, using Eq. (8.16) and (8.17):

$$R = \frac{Z + 1}{Z - 1} \qquad (8.20)$$

While the impedance is a quantity which does not depend on any axis choice, R (as defined above) corresponds to an arbitrary choice where the 'reflected' wave is the wave A^+ progressing in the positive z direction.

For example, for an infinite duct (Table 8.1, case 1) towards $z = +\infty$, no wave is reflected from the right side and acoustic waves travel in the $z = +\infty$ direction without reflection: the A^- function is zero, $R = \infty$ and $Z = 1$. If the duct is infinite towards $z = -\infty$ (Table 8.1, case 2), all waves travel towards $z = -\infty$, the A^+ function is zero, $R = 0$ and $Z = -1$. If the duct is connected to a very large vessel where pressure is imposed ($p_1 = 0$), it has a reflection coefficient $R = -1$ and a zero impedance Z (Table 8.1, case 3). For an acoustically closed section (a wall for example), the acoustic velocity goes to zero and the reflection coefficient is $R = 1$ while the impedance Z is infinite (Table 8.1, case 4). In general, the reflection coefficients of the sections upstream and downstream of combustion chambers do not correspond to these ideal situations and must be either measured or predicted using more complex techniques (Beranek [47], Pierce [506], Doak [178]): for a nozzle terminating a combustion chamber for example, various theories provide acoustic impedances for choked or unchoked flow as a function of nozzle geometry and flow conditions (Tsien [657], Crocco et al. [157], Bell et al. [45], Candel [103], Vuillot [696]).

8.2.3   Harmonic waves and guided waves

Assuming harmonic waves, spatial and temporal variations may be decoupled by writing:

$$p_1 = \Re(p_\omega e^{-i\omega t}), \quad \vec{\mathbf{u}}_1 = \Re(\vec{\mathbf{u}}_\omega e^{-i\omega t}) \quad \text{and} \quad \rho_1 = \Re(\rho_\omega e^{-i\omega t}) \qquad (8.21)$$

where $i^2 = -1$ and p_ω and ρ_ω are complex numbers, $\vec{\mathbf{u}}_\omega$ is a complex vector and $\Re()$ designates the real part of a complex number. Using complex description of waves is convenient in acoustics to not only solve the wave equation but also to express results. For example, RMS (root-mean-square) values are characteristic of wave amplitudes: $p_{RMS} = (\overline{p_1^2})^{1/2}$ and may be obtained simply from their complex representation by writing $p_\omega = Ae^{i\phi}$. The average value of the squared pressure p_1 is then obtained by:

$$\overline{p_1^2} = \frac{1}{T} \int_T p_1^2 dt \qquad (8.22)$$

Configuration	Boundary condition	Reflection coefficient R	Impedance Z
(1): Infinite duct on the right side	Non reflecting	∞	1
(2): Infinite duct on the left side	Non reflecting	0	-1
(3): Duct terminating in large vessel	$p_1 = 0$	-1	0
(4): Duct terminating on a rigid wall	$u_1 = 0$	1	∞

Table 8.1: Reflection coefficients (R) and impedances (Z) of ideal one-dimensional ducts.

and may be expressed from p_ω as:

$$\overline{p_1^2} = \frac{1}{2}A^2 = \frac{1}{2}p_\omega p_\omega^* \tag{8.23}$$

where p_ω^* is the conjugate complex of p_ω.

In the same way, the time average product of two harmonic fields is expressed as:

$$\overline{ab} = \frac{1}{T}\int_T ab \ dt = \frac{1}{2}\Re\left(a_\omega b_\omega^*\right) \tag{8.24}$$

where b^* designates the conjugate complex of b.

For harmonic variations, the pressure and velocity equations (8.10) and (8.11) become:

$$- i\omega p_\omega + \rho_0 c_0^2 \nabla . \vec{\mathbf{u}}_\omega = 0 \tag{8.25}$$

$$- \rho_0 i\omega \vec{\mathbf{u}}_\omega + \nabla p_\omega = 0 \tag{8.26}$$

The isentropic relations remains:

$$p_\omega = c_0^2 \rho_\omega \tag{8.27}$$

while the wave equation becomes the Helmholtz equation:

$$\boxed{\nabla^2 p_\omega + k^2 p_\omega = 0} \tag{8.28}$$

where the wave number k is $k = \omega/c_0$. When waves travel in channels or in ducts (Fig. 8.2), they are called "guided waves".

The study of guided waves is essential to describe the propagation of transverse and longitudinal acoustic waves in all ducts going to or leaving the combustion chamber. For this presentation, rigid walls are assumed for all lateral channel walls. The solution is searched under the form of harmonic waves: $p(x, y, z, t) = p_\omega(x, y, z)e^{-i\omega t}$. Different analytical solutions are available depending on the geometry and on the mode shapes. The following sections present:

- pure longitudinal modes in constant cross section ducts (§ 8.2.4),

- pure longitudinal modes in variable cross section ducts (§ 8.2.5),

- longitudinal/transverse modes in rectangular ducts (§ 8.2.6),

- pure longitudinal modes in a series of constant cross section ducts (§ 8.2.7),

- the specific case of the double duct and the Helmholtz resonator (§ 8.2.8).

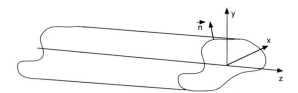

Figure 8.2: Guided waves in a constant cross section duct.

8.2.4   Longitudinal modes in constant cross section ducts

In a constant cross-section duct (Fig. 8.2), harmonic waves follow the Helmholtz equation (8.28):

$$\nabla^2 p_\omega + k^2 p_\omega = 0 \tag{8.29}$$

On the duct walls, the normal velocity component must vanish. Using Eq. (8.26):

$$\vec{n}.\nabla p_\omega = 0 \tag{8.30}$$

where $\vec{n}$ is the wall normal. Purely longitudinal waves which propagate in such a duct and satisfy this boundary condition have the form:

$$p_\omega(x, y, z) = Ae^{ik_z z} \tag{8.31}$$

Substituting p_ω in the Helmholtz equation (8.28) shows that $k_z^2 = k^2$ so that two solutions may be obtained:

- a wave traveling in the positive direction $p_\omega^+ = A^+ e^{ikz}$,

- a wave traveling in the negative direction $p_\omega^- = A^- e^{-ikz}$.

The pressure signal at a point of abscissa z is then:

$$p_1(z,t) = A^+ e^{i(kz-\omega t)} + A^- e^{i(-kz-\omega t)}$$

(8.32)

while the acoustic velocity is:

$$u_1(z,t) = \frac{1}{\rho_0 c_0} \left(A^+ e^{i(kz-\omega t)} - A^- e^{i(-kz-\omega t)} \right)$$

(8.33)

These modes correspond to the one-dimensional modes of § 8.2.2.

8.2.5 Longitudinal modes in variable cross section ducts

The previous analysis can be extended to longitudinal waves propagating in a duct of variable cross section $S(z)$, a configuration which is often used to describe the geometry of combustors. The duct is assumed to have a cylindrical section (Fig. 8.3 left) to simplify the derivation but the final result holds for any cross section (Fig. 8.3 right).

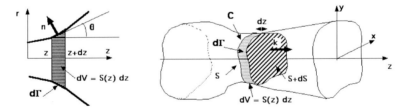

Figure 8.3: Longitudinal waves in a variable cross section duct.

Deriving quasi one-dimensional conservation equations in the duct of Fig. 8.3 requires some care (Nicoud and Wieczorek [470]). For any quantity f following a conservation equation with a flux F:

$$\frac{\partial \rho f}{\partial t} + \nabla . F = 0$$

(8.34)

an integration over the volume dV of Fig. 8.3 left leads to:

$$\frac{\partial}{\partial t} \int_{dV} \rho f dV + \int_{S+dS} F.\vec{k}ds - \int_S F.\vec{k}ds + \int_{d\Gamma} F.\vec{n}ds = 0$$

(8.35)

where $\vec{n} = (-sin\theta, cos\theta)$ is the normal vector to the duct wall and k the normal vector pointing in the z direction. The angle θ is linked to section changes by $2\pi r \tan\theta = dS/dz$. When dz goes to zero, this equation becomes:

$$S\frac{\partial\widehat{\rho f}}{\partial t} + \frac{\partial}{\partial z}(S\widehat{F}) + \int_C \frac{F}{cos\theta}.\vec{n}dc = 0 \qquad (8.36)$$

where the $\widehat{f}$ subscript indicates a spatial average of f over section S:

$$\widehat{f} = \frac{1}{\widehat{\rho}S}\int_S \rho f\, dS \qquad (8.37)$$

and C is the contour of volume dV in the z plane. The quasi one-dimensional assumption is used here to assume that $\widehat{\rho f} = \widehat{\rho}\widehat{f}$. This assumption is often justified because density has negligible gradients in the x-y plane of Fig. 8.3.

For the continuity equation, $f = 1$, $F = \rho u$ and the last term in Eq. (8.36) is zero (because $u = 0$ on walls) so that Eq. (8.2) can be integrated to obtain:

$$\frac{\partial\widehat{\rho}}{\partial t} + \frac{1}{S}\frac{\partial}{\partial z}(\widehat{\rho u}S) = 0 \qquad (8.38)$$

For the momentum equation in the z direction, $f = u$, $F = p + \rho u^2$, the last term in Eq. (8.36) is not zero (it is equal to $-2\pi r p \tan\theta = -pdS/dz$) and Eq.(8.3) leads to an integrated form of the momentum equation:

$$\frac{\partial(\widehat{\rho u})}{\partial t} + \frac{\partial(\widehat{\rho uu}+\widehat{p})}{\partial z} + \frac{\widehat{\rho u^2}}{S}\frac{dS}{dz} = 0 \qquad (8.39)$$

Eq. (8.38) and (8.39) can be combined to obtain a momentum equation where the section S does not appear any more:

$$\widehat{\rho}\frac{\partial\widehat{u}}{\partial t} + \widehat{\rho u}\frac{\partial\widehat{u}}{\partial z} = -\nabla\widehat{p} \qquad (8.40)$$

Note that the section S appears in Eq. (8.38) but not in (8.40).

These equations can be linearized around a mean state indexed 0 by writing:

$$\widehat{u} = \widehat{u}_0 + u_1 \quad \widehat{\rho} = \rho_0 + \rho_1 \quad \text{and} \quad \widehat{p} = p_0 + p_1 \qquad (8.41)$$

Density and pressure are usually assumed to be homogeneous in section S: $\widehat{p}_0 = p_0$ and $\widehat{\rho}_0 = \rho_0$. The mean velocity u_0 may change with x and y to account for no-slip walls but the velocity perturbation u_1 must be homogeneous in S. Retaining only the first order terms in Eq. (8.38) and (8.40), assuming negligible mean flow ($u_0 = 0$) and isentropic flow leads to :

$$\frac{1}{c_0^2}\frac{\partial p_1}{\partial t} + \rho_0\frac{1}{S}\frac{\partial}{\partial z}(Su_1) = 0 \qquad (8.42)$$

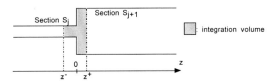

Figure 8.4: Jump conditions through a section change.

$$\rho_0 \frac{\partial u_1}{\partial t} + \frac{\partial p_1}{\partial z} = 0 \qquad (8.43)$$

A limiting case corresponds to two ducts (indexed j and $j+1$) connected by an abrupt section change (Fig. 8.4). Integrating the linearized continuity equation (8.42) and the momentum equation (8.43) between z^- and z^+ and having z^- and z^+ go to 0 provide the acoustic jump conditions through a section change from S_j to S_{j+1}:

$$\boxed{S_{j+1} u_1^{j+1} = S_j u_1^j} \quad \text{and} \quad \boxed{p_1^{j+1} = p_1^j} \qquad (8.44)$$

showing that the acoustic pressure p_1 is conserved through the interface while the acoustic velocity u_1 changes by a factor S_j/S_{j+1}: the unsteady volume flow $S_j u_1^j$ is conserved.

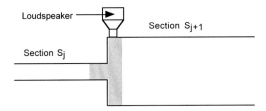

Figure 8.5: Jump conditions for a loudspeaker.

A direct extension[vi] of Eq. (8.44) is obtained when a loudspeaker is located at $z = 0$ (Fig. 8.5): loudspeakers can be described as a source of unsteady volume flow rate H (imposed by the movement of the membrane) and the jump condition (8.44) becomes:

$$S_{j+1} u_1^{j+1} = S_j u_1^j + H \quad \text{and} \quad p_1^{j+1} = p_1^j \qquad (8.45)$$

[vi]This result is useful to study active control of combustion where loudspeakers are usual actuators (McManus et al. [426]).

8.2.6   Longitudinal/transverse modes in rectangular ducts

For a rectangular duct, the previous results can be extended to consider not only longitudinal modes (depending only on z) but also modes having transverse structure (depending on x, y and z). These modes are searched as (Fig. 8.6):

$$\boxed{p_\omega(x,y,z) = A(x,y)e^{ik_z z}} \tag{8.46}$$

where the exponential term characterizes the propagation along the z direction while $A(x,y)$ describes the wave structure in planes normal to the main propagation axis z.

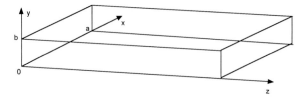

Figure 8.6: Guided wave in a rectangular cavity.

Substituting p_ω into the Helmholtz equation (8.28) gives:

$$\frac{\partial^2 A}{\partial x^2} + \frac{\partial^2 A}{\partial y^2} + (k^2 - k_z^2)A = 0 \tag{8.47}$$

It is convenient to introduce the transverse wave number $k_\perp$ such that $k_\perp^2 = k^2 - k_z^2$. The solution to the Helmholtz equation may be factored as $A(x,y) = X(x)Y(y)$ such that:

$$\frac{X''}{X} + \frac{Y''}{Y} + k_\perp^2 = 0 \tag{8.48}$$

The only solution to this equation is:

$$\frac{X''}{X} = -k_x^2 \quad \text{and} \quad \frac{Y''}{Y} = -k_y^2 \tag{8.49}$$

where k_x and k_y verify:

$$k_x^2 + k_y^2 = k_\perp^2 = k^2 - k_z^2 \tag{8.50}$$

Boundary conditions imposed by zero wall velocity (Eq. 8.30) are written (Fig. 8.6):

$$X'(0) = X'(a) = 0 \qquad Y'(0) = Y'(b) = 0 \tag{8.51}$$

The solution to Eq. (8.49) with boundary conditions (8.51) is:

$$X(x) = \cos(k_x x) \qquad Y(y) = \cos(k_y y) \tag{8.52}$$

where the wave numbers k_x and k_y must satisfy:

$$\sin(k_x a) = 0 \qquad \sin(k_y b) = 0 \tag{8.53}$$

Only a compact set of values (the "resonant" wave numbers) is possible for k_x and k_y:

$$k_x = m\pi/a \qquad k_y = n\pi/b \tag{8.54}$$

where m and n are positive integers $(m, n \geq 0)$. Finally the wave structure corresponding to a given mode (m, n) is:

$$A(x, y) = a_{mn} \cos\left(m\pi x/a\right) \cos\left(n\pi y/b\right) \tag{8.55}$$

and the pressure signal $p_1(x, y, z, t) = p_\omega(x, y, z)e^{-i\omega t}$ is for the (m, n) mode:

$$\boxed{p_1(x, y, z, t) = a_{mn} \cos\left(m\pi x/a\right) \cos\left(n\pi y/b\right) e^{i(k_z z - \omega t)}} \tag{8.56}$$

with

$$k = \omega/c_0 \quad \text{and} \quad k_z^2 = k^2 - (m\pi/a)^2 - (n\pi/b)^2 \tag{8.57}$$

This result must be used as follows: for an arbitrary pulsation ω (or frequency $f = \omega/2\pi$), a wave propagating in a rectangular duct of size a by b has a pressure distribution $p_1(x, y, z, t)$ given by Eq. (8.56). The pressure in a $x - y$ section is a superposition of harmonic waves of wave lengths $2a/m$ (resp. $2b/n$) in the x (resp. y) direction. Pressure is maximum on walls. Along z, pressure changes like $e^{ik_z z}$ where $k_z^2 = k^2 - (m\pi/a)^2 - (n\pi/b)^2$. The z wave number k_z can take purely real (if m and n are small) or purely imaginary values (if m and/or n are large):

- If k_z^2 is positive $(k^2 \geq (m\pi/a)^2 + (n\pi/b)^2)$, k_z is real and the pressure signal for the m, n mode can be expressed as:

$$\boxed{p_1(x, y, z, t) = a_{mn} \cos\left(m\pi x/a\right) \cos\left(n\pi y/b\right) e^{i(|k_z|z - \omega t)}} \tag{8.58}$$

The corresponding mode propagates into the duct along z without attenuation. This is always the case for the $(0, 0)$ mode for which $p_1(x, y, z, t) = a_{00}e^{i(|k_z|z - \omega t)}$ is the solution already identified in Section 8.2.4. If m and n are non zero, the mode structure in (x, y) planes has a transverse structure but propagates along the duct with no attenuation.

- On the other hand, if k_z^2 is negative $(k^2 < (m\pi/a)^2 + (n\pi/b)^2)$, k_z is pure imaginary and can be written:[vii] $k_z = i \mid k_z \mid$. The pressure signal in the duct is:

$$\boxed{p_1(x, y, z, t) = a_{mn} \cos\left(m\pi x/a\right) \cos\left(n\pi y/b\right) e^{-|k_z|z} e^{-i\omega t}} \tag{8.59}$$

[vii] The other solution $k_z = -i \mid k_z \mid$ corresponds to a non physical solution with exponential growth.

showing that the corresponding mode is exponentially attenuated and propagates only on a very short z length into the duct. The mode is "cut-off". Cut-off modes correspond to low oscillation frequencies (i.e. low wave numbers $k = \omega/c_0 = 2\pi f/c_0$) while high frequencies allow non-attenuated propagation. The cut-off wave number k_{mn}^c of mode (m, n) for a given duct is a function of the duct transverse sizes a and b and of the sound speed c_0. It is such that $k_z = 0$ or:

$$(k_{mn}^c)^2 = \left(m\frac{\pi}{a}\right)^2 + \left(n\frac{\pi}{b}\right)^2 \tag{8.60}$$

The cut-off frequency f_{mn}^c is linked to the cut off wave number k_{mn}^c by:

$$f_{mn}^c = k_{mn}^c \frac{c_0}{2\pi} = \frac{c_0}{2}\left[\left(\frac{m}{a}\right)^2 + \left(\frac{n}{b}\right)^2\right]^{\frac{1}{2}} \tag{8.61}$$

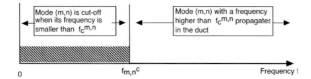

Figure 8.7: Propagation of mode (m,n) in a duct where the cut-off frequency is f_{mn}^c.

High-frequency waves with $f > f_{mn}^c$ propagate into the duct without attenuation (Fig. 8.7). Low frequency modes such that $f < f_{mn}^c$ are cut-off. As an example, in a duct of rectangular cross section filled with fresh gases (sound speed = 340 m/s) with $a = 0.1$ m and $b = 0.2$ m, cut-off frequencies are listed in Table 8.2. As a direct consequence, if such a duct is feeding a combustion chamber with premixed gases, a transverse mode is able to propagate through it to enter the combustion chamber when its frequency is higher than 850 Hz for the $(0, 1)$ mode, 1700 Hz for the $(1, 0)$ mode, etc. All longitudinal modes $(0, 0)$ propagate. Therefore, all oscillation modes going through the feeding pipe at frequencies smaller than 850 Hz must be associated with purely longitudinal modes.

m, n	$0, 0$	$0, 1$	$1, 0$	$1, 1$
Cut-off frequency f_{mn}^c (Hz)	0	850	1700	1900

Table 8.2: Cut-off frequencies f_{mn}^c of the first modes in a rectangular duct of section 0.1 by 0.2 m.

8.2.7   Longitudinal modes in a series of constant cross section ducts

Most combustion chambers are connected upstream and downstream with a series of ducts of variable sections. As shown above, all longitudinal modes (with $m = n = 0$) propagate through these ducts and may interact with the reacting flow in the combustor. Predicting wave propagation in these ducts is a crucial issue to build an acoustic description of a burner. This can be done as follows: consider a series of J connected ducts of section S_j and length $l_j = z_{j+1} - z_j$ (Fig. 8.8). The ducts are connected by $J - 1$ interfaces. In all ducts, the acoustic signal is the sum of two waves, one traveling left (indexed $^-$) and one traveling right (indexed $^+$).

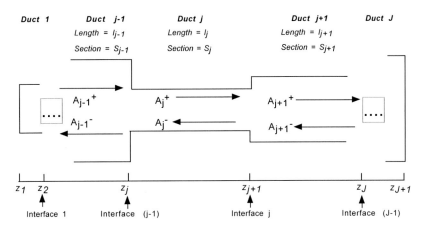

Figure 8.8: Propagation of longitudinal acoustic waves in connected ducts.

Assuming constant mean temperature in all ducts, Eq. (8.32) and (8.33) show that the acoustic pressure and velocity signals in duct j are:

$$p_1^j(z,t) = A_j^+ e^{ik(z-z_j)-i\omega t} + A_j^- e^{-ik(z-z_j)-i\omega t} \tag{8.62}$$

while the acoustic velocity is:

$$u_1^j(z,t) = \frac{1}{\rho_0 c_0} \left(A_j^+ e^{ik(z-z_j)-i\omega t} - A_j^- e^{-ik(z-z_j)-i\omega t} \right) \tag{8.63}$$

At interface j located at $z = z_{j+1}$, jump conditions are obtained by writing that pressure and acoustic flow rates are continuous as shown by Eq. (8.44):

$$p_1^j(z_{j+1},t) = p_1^{j+1}(z_{j+1},t) \quad \text{and} \quad S_j u_1^j(z_{j+1},t) = S_{j+1} u_1^{j+1}(z_{j+1},t) \tag{8.64}$$

so that

$$A_j^+ e^{ikl_j} + A_j^- e^{-ikl_j} = A_{j+1}^+ + A_{j+1}^- \tag{8.65}$$

$$S_j(A_j^+ e^{ikl_j} - A_j^- e^{-ikl_j}) = S_{j+1}(A_{j+1}^+ - A_{j+1}^-) \tag{8.66}$$

which relates the amplitudes of the wave in section $j+1$ to the amplitudes in section j through a transfer matrix T_j:

$$
\begin{pmatrix} A_{j+1}^+ \\ A_{j+1}^- \end{pmatrix} = T_j \begin{pmatrix} A_j^+ \\ A_j^- \end{pmatrix} \quad \text{with} \quad T_j = \frac{1}{2} \begin{bmatrix} e^{ikl_j}(1+\Gamma_j) & e^{-ikl_j}(1-\Gamma_j) \\ e^{ikl_j}(1-\Gamma_j) & e^{-ikl_j}(1+\Gamma_j) \end{bmatrix} \tag{8.67}
$$

where Γ_j is the area ratio between ducts j and $j+1$: $\Gamma_j = S_j/S_{j+1}$.

A global matrix G is then constructed to link wave amplitudes in the first ($j=1$) and last ($j=J$) sections:

$$
G = \prod_{j=1}^{J-1} T_j \quad \text{and} \quad \begin{pmatrix} A_J^+ \\ A_J^- \end{pmatrix} = G \begin{pmatrix} A_1^+ \\ A_1^- \end{pmatrix} \tag{8.68}
$$

To close the problem, boundary conditions must be specified at both ends of the rig. A usual technique is to specify reflection factors (or impedances, see Table 8.1) at the left side of section 1 and at the right side of section J:

$$
\frac{A_1^+}{A_1^-} = R_1 \quad \text{and} \quad \frac{A_J^+}{A_J^-}e^{2ikl_J} = R_J \tag{8.69}
$$

Eq. (8.68) and boundary conditions (8.69) constitute a linear system which has a non zero solution only if:

$$
R_J = \frac{G_{11}R_1 + G_{12}}{G_{21}R_1 + G_{22}}e^{2ikl_J} \tag{8.70}
$$

Solving Eq. (8.70) provides the eigenfrequencies of the complete duct. Having these frequencies, the phases and respective amplitudes of the acoustic modes in each section can be easily determined (Poinsot et al. [520, 521]), as summarized in Table 8.3.

8.2.8   The double duct and the Helmholtz resonator

A generic configuration of interest for combustors is the 'double duct' geometry (Fig. 8.9).[viii] For the moment, we will consider that temperature is the same in both ducts.[ix] The left boundary ($z = 0$) is supposed to be a hard wall with zero velocity fluctuations and a reflection coefficient $R_1 = 1$. The outlet section ($z = a_1 + a_2$) is an outlet with imposed pressure $R_2 = -1$.

This configuration has two sections (ducts) and one interface (at $z = a_1$). The global matrix G (Eq. (8.68)) is simply equal to the transfer matrix T (Eq. (8.67)) of the unique interface:

[viii]The equations presented here can be solved for generic 'double duct' configurations with or without temperature change using a tool available at *elearning.cerfacs.fr/combustion/tools/soundtube*.

[ix]The case where a flame is standing between Sections 1 and 2 will be fully treated in Section 8.4.2.

Specify left reflection coefficient	R_1
For each interface $j = 1$ to $J - 1$:	
- Evaluate section parameter	$\Gamma_j = \dfrac{S_j}{S_{j+1}}$
- Form transfer matrix T_j	$T_j = \dfrac{1}{2} \begin{bmatrix} e^{ikl_j}\left(1 + \Gamma_j\right) & e^{-ikl_j}\left(1 - \Gamma_j\right) \\ e^{ikl_j}\left(1 - \Gamma_j\right) & e^{-ikl_j}\left(1 + \Gamma_j\right) \end{bmatrix}$
Make global matrix G	$G = T_{J-1} \ldots T_2 T_1$
Specify right reflection coefficient	R_J
Solve for $\omega = kc_0$ in system:	$\begin{pmatrix} A_J^+ \\ A_J^- \end{pmatrix} = G \begin{pmatrix} A_1^+ \\ A_1^- \end{pmatrix}$
with boundary conditions:	$A_1^+/A_1^- = R_1$ and $A_J^+/A_J^- e^{2ikl_J} = R_J$
Knowing ω, find wave amplitudes:	$A_J^+/A_1^+ \quad A_J^-/A_1^+$ for $j = 1$ to J

Table 8.3: Procedure to compute the longitudinal eigenmodes of a series of J ducts separated by $J - 1$ interfaces. The reflection coefficients R_1 and R_J are complex numbers and must be known (from experiments for example). The sound speed c_0 is constant. The wave number k is $k = \omega/c_0$.

$$G = T = \frac{1}{2} \begin{bmatrix} e^{ika_1}\left(1 + \Gamma_1\right) & e^{-ika_1}\left(1 - \Gamma_1\right) \\ e^{ika_1}\left(1 - \Gamma_1\right) & e^{-ika_1}\left(1 + \Gamma_1\right) \end{bmatrix} \qquad (8.71)$$

where $\Gamma_1 = S_1/S_2$. Using the boundary conditions:

$$R_1 = \frac{A_1^+}{A_1^-} = 1 \quad \text{and} \quad R_2 = \frac{A_2^+}{A_2^-} e^{2ik_2 a_2} = -1 \qquad (8.72)$$

Eq. (8.70) can be recast as:

$$\boxed{\cos(ka_1)\cos(ka_2) - \Gamma_1 \sin(ka_1)\sin(ka_2) = 0} \qquad (8.73)$$

The double-duct equation (8.73) is useful to derive the eigenfrequencies, for example, of a combustor fed by a pipe. But the same double-duct configuration is also representative of another important acoustic device for combustion: the Helmholtz resonator (Kinsler et al. [347]). A Helmholtz device is a double-duct system in which the second duct (the neck) has a very small section S_2 (Fig. 8.10). Such systems oscillate at very low frequencies, so that ka_1

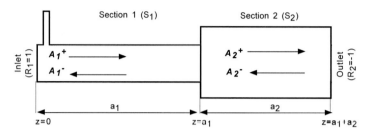

Figure 8.9: The double duct configuration.

is very small and Eq. (8.73) can be expanded to first order in ka_1 to give[x]:

$$k = \sqrt{\frac{1}{\Gamma_1 a_1 a_2}} \quad \text{or} \quad f_H = \frac{c_0}{2\pi}\sqrt{\frac{1}{\Gamma_1 a_1 a_2}} = \frac{c_0}{2\pi}\sqrt{\frac{S_2}{a_2 V_1}} \tag{8.74}$$

where $V_1 = S_1 a_1$ is the volume of the first duct. In practice, the length of the neck must be corrected to account for end effects: a correction length of the order of the neck radius is usually added to a_2 in Eq. (8.74).

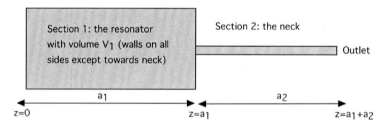

Figure 8.10: The Helmholtz resonator.

The reason why Helmholtz resonators are used in combustion chambers is that their damping coefficient for frequencies close to f_H is high: they inhibit pressure oscillations at f_H near the neck outlet. If they are installed on a combustion chamber (as shown in Fig. 8.11) they can damp a combustion instability created elsewhere in the combustor at f_H. Unfortunately, this property is satisfied only at the Helmholtz resonator frequency f_H so that these devices must be tuned for each oscillation frequency of the chamber.

---

[x]Eq. (8.74) can also be derived using a mechanical resonator analogy where the spring is the pressurized gas within the cavity, the mass is the gas within the neck, and the resistance is the acoustic radiation on the open end of the neck (Pierce [506], Kinsler et al. [347]).

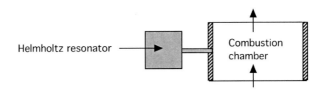

Figure 8.11: Helmholtz resonators as damping devices.

Fig. 8.12 displays the frequencies of the Helmholtz resonator (Eq. (8.74)) and of the quarter wave mode (numerical solution of Eq. (8.73)) as a function of the section ratio $\Gamma = S_1/S_2$ (Fig. 8.10). The values chosen for the application are: $c_0 = 830$ m/s (corresponding to a typical sound speed in burnt gases), $a_1 = 0.06$ m and $a_2 = 0.12$ m. For large values of Γ, both curves collapse confirming that a Helmholtz resonator oscillates simply at the quarter-wave frequency of the corresponding double duct system.

Another implication of Fig. 8.12 (illustrating a mistake which is often seen in the combustion community) is that the actual frequency of oscillation of the 'double duct' device displayed in Fig. 8.10 and computed either with Eq. (8.73) or with Eq. (8.74) can be significantly lower than the quarter-wave mode frequency f_Q of a constant section duct (dashed line in Fig. 8.12). For example, in a double duct combustor like Fig. 8.10, the total length of the device is $a_1 + a_2$ and the frequency f_Q of the quarter-wave mode at constant section is usually evaluated by:

$$f_Q = c_0/(4(a_1 + a_2)) \qquad (8.75)$$

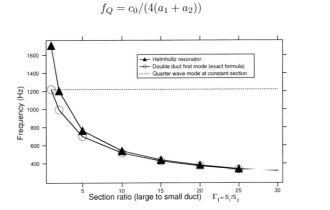

Figure 8.12: The frequencies of the Helmholtz resonator (Eq. (8.74)), the double-duct quarter-wave mode (Eq. (8.73)) of Fig. 8.10 and the quarter-wave mode (Eq. (8.75)) assuming constant section as a function of the section ratio $\Gamma = S_1/S_2$ between the volume V_1 and the neck.

Fig. 8.12 shows that f_Q (dashed line) is always higher than the real oscillation frequencies of the double duct (circles). Therefore, considering the total length $a_1 + a_2$ of a combustion chamber and evaluating the first quarter-wave frequency f_Q using the total length of the chamber can be misleading: the first acoustic mode frequency can be much lower than f_Q. When the section ratio Γ goes to large values (in other words when the geometry exhibits strong localized section restrictions, like injectors), the acoustic frequency goes to zero like $1/\Gamma^{1/2}$ as shown by Eq. (8.74). As a result, predicting the first longitudinal mode frequency in a combustor can be a difficult exercice and it is recommended that a one-dimensional acoustic solver be used (and not to approximate the quarter-wave formula like Eq. (8.75)) for this exercice.

8.2.9   Decoupling of longitudinal modes in combustors

When network codes or experiments are used to identify unstable modes in combustors, the analysis of the longitudinal modes often reveals that certain modes are 'decoupled': they can be recognized as acoustic modes of some limited parts of the combustor, apparently developing independently of the rest of the combustor. This phenomenon was illustrated analytically at the EM2C laboratory (Palies [487]) using a 'triple duct' configuration and this section presents some of the EM2C results. The reader is referred to the PhD thesis of Palies [487] for a detailed presentation and discussion.

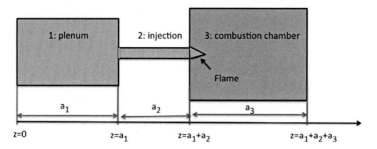

Figure 8.13: The three-duct configuration studied by Palies [487]: a plenum (1), an injection tube (2) and a combustion chamber (3).

The starting point of the analysis is that many combustor geometries can be described using a three-duct configuration (Fig. 8.13)[xi] where the temperature is constant in ducts 1 (the plenum) and 2 (the injection duct or the swirler) ($T_1 = T_2$) while it is higher in the combustion chamber (duct 3: the combustion chamber, $T_3 >> T_2$). Palies [487] derives the acoustic equations with corresponding jump conditions at $z = a_1$ and a_2, thereby solving analytically the system given in Table 8.7. This is done in a general case where the outlet

---

[xi]This configuration is an extension of the double-duct case described in Section 8.2.8 in which an additional volume (the combustion chamber) is added after the throat of the Helmholtz resonator.

impedance $(z = a_1 + a_2 + a_3)$ is set to Z while the inlet impedance $(z = 0)$ is infinite (velocity node, Palies [487]). We will present here only one specific case where the outlet is a pressure node $(Z = 0)$. For this case, a simple analytical form is found for the characteristic equation giving the eigenmodes when a parameter Θ called the coupling parameter, is small. This parameter is defined by:

$$\Theta = \frac{S_2}{S_3}\frac{\rho_3 c_3}{\rho_2 c_2} \simeq \frac{S_2}{S_3}(\frac{T_3}{T_2})^{1/2} \tag{8.76}$$

In this situation, the characteristic equation becomes:

$$\cos(k_3 a_3) * [\cos(k_1 a_1)\cos(k_1 a_2) - \Gamma_1 \sin(k_1 a_1)\sin(k_1 a_2)] = 0 \tag{8.77}$$

where $k_1 = k_2 = \omega/c_1$, $k_3 = \omega/c_3$ and $\Gamma_1 = S_1/S_2$.

Eq. 8.77 shows that the modes found in the configuration of Fig. 8.13 belong to two distinct families which are decoupled:

- The modes of the combustion chamber which satisfy $\cos(k_3 a_3) = 0$

- The modes of the double duct ensemble containing the plenum and the injection ducts, which satisfy $\cos(k_1 a_1)\cos(k_1 a_2) - \Gamma_1 \sin(k_1 a_1)\sin(k_1 a_2) = 0$ (this is exactly Eq. 8.73 derived for the double duct in the previous section).

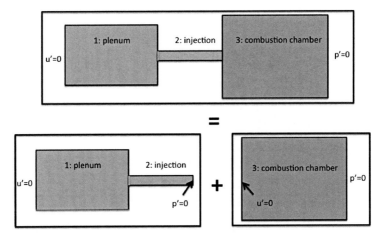

Figure 8.14: The three-duct configuration when modes are decoupled ($\Theta = \frac{S_2}{S_3}\frac{\rho_3 c_3}{\rho_2 c_2}$ small): the modes of the three-duct combustor of Fig. 8.13 correspond to union of the modes of the combustion chamber and of the double duct feeding it.

When Θ becomes small, the modes of the chamber and of the lines feeding it become decoupled and can be computed separately (Fig. 8.14). Note that the section where decoupling

takes place ($z = a_1 + a_2$) becomes a pressure node for the upstream ducts (1+2) and a velocity
node for the chamber. This can be interpreted simply as follows: when Θ is small, the section
$z = a_1 + a_2$ is essentially a wall and waves propagating in the combustion chamber reflect on
it as if it was a perfect wall ($u' = 0$). On the other hand, for waves propagating in duct 2, the
section $z = a_1 + a_2$ opens on a very large vessel (the combustion chamber 3) where pressure
does not change ($p' = 0$).

Conditions under which decoupling occur in practice are discussed in detail by Palies [487].
Understanding whether modes are decoupled or not is useful to analyze longitudinal modes:
in a decoupled situation, changing the length of the combustion chamber for example will have
no effect on modes if these modes correspond to the modes of the plenum and injection ducts
(and vice versa).

8.2.10 Multidimensional acoustic modes in cavities

A specific aspect of acoustics, which leads to certain combustion instabilities, is the existence
of multidimensional acoustic eigenmodes associated to high levels of oscillatory pressure and
velocity. For the general case of a cavity bounded by a surface A (rigid walls), eigenmodes are
obtained by solving the Helmholtz equation (8.28):

$$\nabla^2 p_\omega + k^2 p_\omega = 0 \tag{8.78}$$

On all cavity walls, velocity is zero and the pressure gradient normal to walls must be zero
(Eq. 8.26):

$$\vec{n}.\nabla p_\omega = 0 \quad \text{on} \quad A \tag{8.79}$$

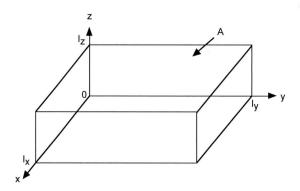

Figure 8.15: Configuration to study acoustic eigenmodes in a rectangular duct.

Only a set of eigenfunctions $p_\omega(x, y, z)$ (the acoustic modes of the cavity) satisfies the
Helmholtz equation with such boundary conditions. For complex configurations, numerical

solvers must be used to find the p_ω functions (Zikikout et al. [732], Benoit and Nicoud [46]). For simple geometrical configurations such as the rectangular cavity (Fig. 8.15), simple solutions may be obtained by searching for p_ω functions in the factored form $p_\omega(x, y, z) = X(x)Y(y)Z(z)$. Substituting into the Helmholtz equation (8.78) gives:

$$X''/X + Y''/Y + Z''/Z + k^2 = 0 \qquad (8.80)$$

The solution to this equation is conveniently written introducing three wave numbers k_x, k_y and k_z such that:

$$k^2 = k_x^2 + k_y^2 + k_z^2 \qquad (8.81)$$

The problem is then split along each direction:

$$X'' + k_x^2 X = 0 \quad Y'' + k_y^2 Y = 0 \quad Z'' + k_z^2 Z = 0 \qquad (8.82)$$

and boundary conditions (zero normal velocities) impose zero pressure gradients on walls:

$$\frac{dX}{dx}(x = 0 \text{ or } l_x) = \frac{dY}{dy}(y = 0 \text{ or } l_y) = \frac{dZ}{dz}(z = 0 \text{ or } l_z) = 0 \qquad (8.83)$$

The solution to these equations is:

$$X = \cos(k_x x) \quad Y = \cos(k_y y) \quad Z = \cos(k_z z) \qquad (8.84)$$

where boundary conditions (8.83) at $x = l_x$, $y = l_y$ and $z = l_z$ impose:

$$\sin(k_x l_x) = 0 \quad ; \quad \sin(k_y l_y) = 0 \quad ; \quad \sin(k_z l_z) = 0 \qquad (8.85)$$

so that:

$$k_x = n_x \pi / l_x \qquad k_y = n_y \pi / l_y \qquad k_z = n_z \pi / l_z \qquad (8.86)$$

The pressure amplitude and the instantaneous pressure in the cavity are:

$$p_\omega(x, y, z) = P \cos\left(n_x \pi x / l_x\right) \cos\left(n_y \pi y / l_y\right) \cos\left(n_z \pi z / l_z\right) \qquad (8.87)$$

$$\boxed{p_1(x, y, z, t) = p_\omega(x, y, z)e^{-i\omega t} = P \cos\left(n_x \pi x / l_x\right) \cos\left(n_y \pi y / l_y\right) \cos\left(n_z \pi z / l_z\right) e^{-i\omega t}} \qquad (8.88)$$

where $\omega = k c_0$ and $k^2 = \pi^2 \left[(n_x/l_x)^2 + (n_y/l_y)^2 + (n_z/l_z)^2\right]$.

The resonant frequency of the mode (n_x, n_y, n_z) is given by:

$$\boxed{f = \frac{k c_0}{2\pi} = \frac{c_0}{2} \left[\left(\frac{n_x}{l_x}\right)^2 + \left(\frac{n_y}{l_y}\right)^2 + \left(\frac{n_z}{l_z}\right)^2\right]^{\frac{1}{2}}} \qquad (8.89)$$

As an example, consider a combustion chamber geometry with a length $l_x = 1$ m and transverse sizes $l_y = 0.1$ m and $l_z = 0.2$ m. Table 8.4 summarizes the frequencies of the first

n_x, n_y, n_z	Identification	Frequency (Hz)
1, 0, 0	First longitudinal	422
2, 0, 0	Second longitudinal	845
3, 0, 0	Third longitudinal	1267
4, 0, 0	Fourth longitudinal	1690
0, 0, 1	First transverse along z	2112
1, 0, 1	First transverse in z - first longitudinal	2150
1, 1, 0	First transverse in y - first longitudinal	4240

Table 8.4: Frequencies of the first resonance modes in a typical laboratory combustion chamber: parallelepipedic box (1 m by 0.1 m by 0.2 m), sound speed: 840 m/s.

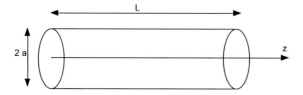

Figure 8.16: Configuration to study acoustic eigenmodes in a cylindrical duct.

modes. The cavity is filled with burnt gases at 2000 K, $\gamma = 1.25$ and the sound speed is approximately $c_0 \approx 840$ m/s. This case corresponds to a combustion chamber surrounded by rigid walls. The influence of inlets and outlets is ignored.

For a perfectly cylindrical cavity of radius a and length L (Fig. 8.16), similar derivations may be performed in cylindrical coordinates (r, θ, z) to determine the acoustic mode (m, n, q) where m, n and q are respectively the radial, tangential and longitudinal mode numbers:

$$p(r, \theta, z) = J_n(\pi \beta_{mn} r/a) \cos(q \pi z/L) \left(P e^{in\theta} + Q e^{-in\theta} \right) \qquad (8.90)$$

where J_n is the Bessel function of order n. The values of β_{mn} are the roots of $J_n'(\pi \beta_{mn}) = 0$ and are summarized in Table 8.5. The resonant frequencies are given by:

$$f_{mnq} = \frac{c}{2} \left[\left(\frac{\beta_{mn}}{a} \right)^2 + \left(\frac{q}{L} \right)^2 \right]^{\frac{1}{2}} \qquad (8.91)$$

For each cavity, there is an infinite number of acoustic eigenmodes but only the lowest ones are observed in combustion because high-frequency modes are damped by viscous effects (not included in the present analysis) more strongly than low frequency modes. In practical

Mode	m =0	m =1	m = 2	m =3
n=0	0	1.22	2.333	3.238
n=1	0.586	1.697	2.717	3.725
n=2	0.972	2.135	3.173	4.192

Table 8.5: Values of β_{mn} for resonant modes in cylindrical cavities.

combustion devices, observing acoustic modes between 100 and 5000 Hz is usual and these modes influence combustion significantly.

8.2.11 Azimuthal modes

A specific situation where the geometry of the combustor leads to the existence of a particular class of modes is the apparition of azimuthal modes in annular chambers. Many gas turbines exhibit combustion instabilities (Lieuwen and Yang [393]) and in systems using annular chambers, azimuthal oscillations are the most frequent and often the strongest unstable modes.

An azimuthal mode corresponds to a wave or a combinationof waves propagating along the azimuthal directions of the combustor (Fig. 8.17). To first order, it can be described by a combination of two simple one-dimensional waves propagating in opposite directions along θ, the angle measuring the azimuthal position.

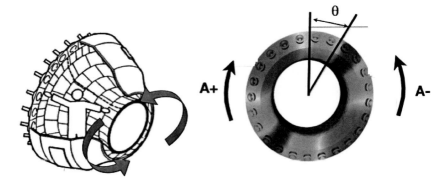

Figure 8.17: Azimuthal mode in an annular combustion chamber. Left: industrial gas turbine. Right: the two counter rotating modes M^+ (amplitude A^+) and M^- (amplitude A^-).

The structure of these azimuthal modes has been the subject of numerous recent studies (Krueger et al. [359], Stow and Dowling [628], Krebs et al. [357], Schuermans et al. [597], Evesque et al. [203], Staffelbach et al. [626], Schuermans et al. [598], Wolf et al. [713]). A simple way to begin their analysis is to assume that they are purely one-dimensional, propagate only along θ and that the mean swirl velocity is negligible so that they propagate exactly at the sound speed. In an annulus of radius R, the period and the pulsation of the first azimuthal modes are $T_{azi} = 2\pi R/c = 2\pi/\omega$ and $\omega = c/R$ respectively; higher-order modes will have periods equal to T_{azi}/n where n is the mode order.

Under these conditions, the general form of these modes corresponds to the superposition of a purely propagating wave called M^+ (amplitude A^+) turning in the clockwise direction on Fig. 8.17right and a purely propagating wave called M^- (amplitude A^-) turning in the opposite direction[xii]. Depending on the relative magnitudes of A^+ and A^-, three classes of modes can be defined:

- Turning modes (A^- or A^+ is zero): if only one of the two modes M^- and M^+ has a non-zero amplitude, the resulting pressure oscillation is turning along θ at the sound speed and the pressure perturbation can be written as $p' = \hat{p}e^{-i\omega t}$ where

$$\hat{p}(M^+) = A_+ e^{i\theta} \quad \text{or} \quad \hat{p}(M^-) = A_- e^{-i\theta} \tag{8.92}$$

The mode structure (ie the modulus and the argument (or the phase) of $\hat{p}$ versus θ) is displayed in Fig. 8.18 for the first azimuthal mode M^+ (period T_{azi}). The phase of $\hat{p}$ is equal to θ for M^+ and $-\theta$ for M^- and the modulus is constant for both modes.

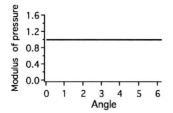 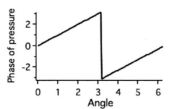

Figure 8.18: Structure of a purely turning azimuthal mode M^+: $A^- = 0$ and $A^+ = 1$. Left: modulus of pressure vs angular position θ, right: argument of pressure.

- Standing modes ($A^- = A^+$:) if the M^- and M^+ modes live simultaneously and have the same amplitude ($A^- = A^+ = A$), a standing mode is obtained. There are two independent standing modes called here S_1 andS_2. Their structures are shifted by ninety degrees. The pressure perturbation for a standing mode is obtained by combining the two turning modes (M^+ and M^-) amplitudes, for example for the S_1 mode:

$$\hat{p}(S_1) = A_+ e^{i\theta} + A_- e^{-i\theta} = 2A\cos(\theta) \tag{8.93}$$

[xii]A video illustration of these modes obtained by LES (Staffelbach et al. [626]) is available at *elearning.cerfacs.fr/combustion/illustrations/azimut*)

The structure of the first S_1 mode at T_{azi} is displayed in Fig. 8.19. The phase is either 0 or π and the modulus exhibits nodes and antinodes like for a standing mode in a straight duct. When a standing mode appears in a combustor, all sectors are not submitted to the same perturbations: burners located at pressure nodes for example, see no pressure oscillations but large azimuthal velocity perturbations.

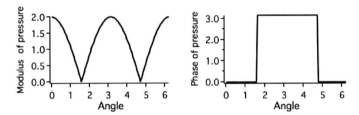

Figure 8.19: Structure of a standing azimuthal mode S_1 ($A^- = A^+ = 1$). Left: modulus of pressure vs angular position θ, right: argument of pressure.

- Mixed modes: when the M^- and M^+ modes exist simultaneously but have non equal amplitudes, a complex structure appears. For example, Fig. 8.20 displays the mode structure for $A^- = 0.5$ and $A^+ = 1$. Such a mode can be interpreted as a turning wave mode of amplitude $(A_- - A_+)$ superimposed on a standing wave of amplitude $2A_+$:

$$\hat{p} = A_+ e^{i\theta} + A_- e^{-i\theta} = 2A_+ cos(\theta) + (A_- - A_+)e^{-i\theta} \qquad (8.94)$$

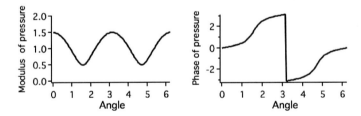

Figure 8.20: Structure of a mixed azimuthal mode ($A^- = 0.5$ and $A^+ = 1$). Left: modulus of pressure vs angular position θ, right: argument of pressure.

In general, there is no clear reason leading to a given set of values for A^- and A^+ in a given combustor for given operating conditions. Both turning and standing modes are observed in practice (Krebs et al. [357], Schuermans et al. [598]) and understanding why one class of modes is observed instead of the other is the topic of intense present research (Schuermans et al. [598], Staffelbach et al. [626], Moeck et al. [447]). The four modes (M^-, M^+, S_1 and

S_2) have the same frequency. This frequency is a degenerate eigenvalue of the wave equation solution. This implies that the corresponding eigenvectors can be any pair of independent vectors in the plane of the solutions: the (M^-, M^+) and the (S_1, S_2) are such pairs. Any of them can be used to generate all other eigenvectors. Recent theories point out two factors controlling the bifurcation from standing to turning modes:

- Non linearity: standing modes would be observed only at low amplitudes. At large amplitudes, only turning modes would survive because of non-linear effects (Schuermans et al. [598]).

- Non axisymmetry: turning modes would be observed only for perfectly axisymmetric combustors (Sensiau [608], Noiray et al. [474]). In other cases, standing or mixed modes would appear.

Measurements of the mode structure in annular chambers are difficult (Krebs et al. [357]) but recent LES of self-excited modes in full annular chambers can be used to investigate mode structures in such chambers: Fig. 8.21 shows pressure and temperature fields of the LES of Wolf et al. [713]. The pressure field (left) exhibits a structure corresponding to a standing (S_1) mode slightly perturbed by a turning mode (M_-) with a small amplitude (Eq. 8.94).

T/Tmean
2.60
2.05
1.50
0.95
0.40

Figure 8.21: LES of azimuthal mode in an annular combustion chamber [713]. Left: instantaneous pressure on combustor skin. Right: instantaneous temperature and velocity magnitude isocontours on a cylindrical plane passing through the burners axis. An animation of pressure and temperature fields can be found at *elearning.cerfacs.fr/combustion/illustrations/azimut/*.

The amplitudes A_+ and A_- can be adjusted to match the pressure perturbations structure measured in the LES: for $A_-/A_+ = 0.96$ a perfect fit between the simple expression   8.94

and the LES data is obtained (Fig. 8.22). This demonstrates that the self-excited mode appearing naturally in LES has a structure which corresponds very well to the simple model of Eq. 8.94 for an almost perfect standing mode but it does not explain why this is the case. Moreover, theoretical approaches (Noiray et al. [475]) suggest that long times might be needed before the final mode structure (turning or standing) is established: LES which can compute only a few hundred cycles might be unable to capture transitions at very long times (after thousands of cycles) and decide whether standing or turning modes appear after minutes or hours of operation. High turbulence levels could also force the mode to switch randomly from a standing to a turning structure.

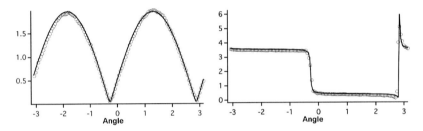

Figure 8.22: Analysis of pressure perturbations in the LES of Fig.8.21. Left: modulus of pressure vs angular position θ, bottom right: argument of pressure. The structure given by LES (solid line) is compared to the simple model (circles) of (Eq. 8.94) with $A^- = 0.96$ and $A^+ = 1$.

In most combustors, the situation is made more complex by the fact that, even though the configurations are axisymmetric, the swirl imposed in each burner makes one rotation direction preferential, leading to the existence of a mean swirling velocity in the combustor. For the two rotating modes, this induces an important difference between the corotating mode (the azimuthal mode turning in the direction of the swirl induced by the injectors) called here the "+" mode and the counter-rotating mode called the "-" mode. To first order, the + mode turns at a velocity $c + U$ where U is the mean swirl velocity and c the mean sound speed in the chamber while the − mode turns at $c - U$. The mean swirling velocity U is small compared to the sound speed c: average typical swirl velocities of 10 m/s are observed for example in the LES of Fig. 8.21. This allows to separate small and long time effects: the main high-frequency azimuthal mode is observed at a high frequency of the order of $c/2\pi R$ and it is modulated on a lower frequency (of the order of $U/2\pi R$). The pressure perturbation p' depends only on time and on the azimuthal position θ:

$$p' = \hat{p} e^{-i\omega t} = \left[A_+ e^{i(\theta - Ut/R)} + A_- e^{i(-\theta + Ut/R)} \right] e^{-i\omega t} \qquad (8.95)$$

The Ut/R terms are induced by the mean swirl convection at speed U. They change very slowly compared to the ωt term so that a structure can be defined for p' by observing it over a few periods of the short (acoustic) time: this structure then changes over long (convective) times. Typically, gas turbine experts observe standing wave modes (oscillating at hundreds of Hertz) where the pressure nodes are rotating very slowly (one full rotation in a few minutes to a few hours). The period required for a complete rotation of the structure is $2\pi R/U$ or T_{azi}/M_a where $M_a = U/c$ is the Mach number of the swirling flow component. This observation makes the analysis of azimuthal modes more complicated: a standing mode (observed over a few periods) can exhibit a structure which rotates slowly (with the swirl velocity). Such a mode is not a 'turning' mode where the pressure field rotates with the sound speed (like the M^+ and M^- modes): however, its global structure is turning at the swirl convection velocity.

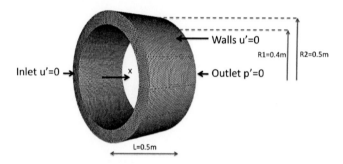

Figure 8.23: A simple annular combustion chamber(Sensiau [608]).

A second complexity of real combustor modes is that pure azimuthal modes are rarely observed. In most cases, coupled modes involving azimuthal and longitudinal components are found (Evesque and Polifke [202], Evesque et al. [203]). This is due to the fact that impedances imposed in the longitudinal direction lead to non constant values of $\hat{p}$ along the axial direction. Moreover, the frequencies of azimuthal and pure longitudinal modes are often found in the same range so that identifying a mode knowing only its frequency is usually impossible. A simple example (Sensiau [608]) is given in Fig. 8.23 for an annular domain filled with cold gases (sound speed=347 m/s). The inlet condition corresponds to a velocity node and the outlet to a pressure node.

For this chamber, the first pure longitudinal mode is found at 173 Hz and its structure is displayed in Fig. 8.24. The first azimuthal modes have a frequency of 213 Hz and the structures of the standing modes S_1 and S_2 are displayed in Fig. 8.25. Note that the structure of S_1 corresponds to the structure of S_2, shifted by 90 degrees. In an experiment exhibiting an unstable mode in the 200 Hz frequency range, the only method to know if the mode is longitudinal or azimuthal is to use multiple microphones installed along the azimuthal direction (Krebs et al. [357]), something which is often difficult in real combustors.

Finally, the number of modes found in real combustors is usually very high: for a typical industrial gas turbine, 20 to 30 acoustic modes can be found below 300 Hz. Identifying

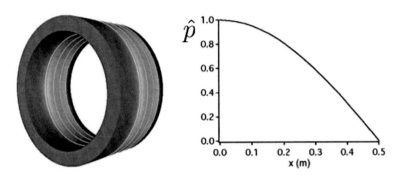

Figure 8.24: First longitudinal mode in the chamber of Fig. 8.23 (Sensiau [608]). Modulus of $\hat{p}$.

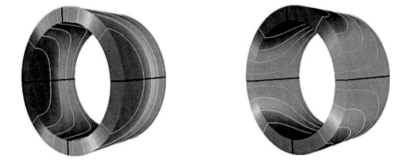

Figure 8.25: Standing modes S_1 and S_2 in the chamber of Fig. 8.23 (Sensiau [608]). Modulus of $\hat{p}$.

each of these modes and determining whether it is stable or not is a major challenge for thermoacoustics studies.

8.2.12   Acoustic energy density and flux

The notion of acoustic energy is useful to describe combustion instabilities. In the field of CFD, it also helps to understand the response of compressible codes to changes of boundary conditions. Its simplest derivation is given here for non-reacting flows. The extension to reacting flows is presented in Section 8.3.7.

The acoustic energy measures the total level of acoustic fluctuations in a given domain and corresponds to the linearized form of the mechanical energy (Landau and Lifchitz [364]) but a simpler derivation is presented here. Starting from Eq. (8.10) and (8.11):

$$\frac{1}{c_0^2}\frac{\partial p_1}{\partial t} + \rho_0 \nabla.\vec{u}_1 = 0 \tag{8.96}$$

$$\rho_0 \frac{\partial \vec{u}_1}{\partial t} + \nabla p_1 = 0 \tag{8.97}$$

Multiplying Eq. (8.96) by p_1/ρ_0, Eq. (8.97) by $\vec{u}_1$ and adding them gives:

$$\frac{\partial}{\partial t}\left(\frac{1}{2}\rho_0 \vec{u}_1^2 + \frac{1}{2}\frac{p_1^2}{\rho_0 c_0^2}\right) + \nabla.(p_1 \vec{u}_1) = 0 \tag{8.98}$$

The acoustic energy and flux are defined respectively by:

$$\boxed{e_1 = \frac{1}{2}\rho_0 \vec{u}_1^2 + \frac{1}{2}\frac{p_1^2}{\rho_0 c_0^2} \quad \text{and} \quad f_1 = p_1 \vec{u}_1} \tag{8.99}$$

Eq. (8.98) shows that the acoustic energy e_1 varies only because of the local acoustic flux f_1:

$$\boxed{\frac{\partial e_1}{\partial t} + \nabla.f_1 = 0} \tag{8.100}$$

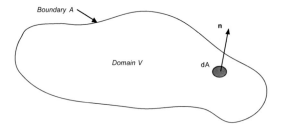

Figure 8.26: Integration domain for the acoustic energy equation (8.100).

This local energy balance may be integrated over a domain V (for example the computational domain in a CFD case) bounded by a surface A to yield (Fig. 8.26):

$$\frac{d}{dt}\int_V e_1 dV + \int_A f_1.\vec{n}dA = 0 \tag{8.101}$$

where $\int_V e_1 dV$ is the total acoustic energy present in the domain and $\vec{n}$ is the normal to the surface A. Eq. (8.101) shows that the changes in the total energy are only due to fluxes crossing the boundaries. These fluxes are locally expressed as $f_1.n = p_1\vec{u}_1.\vec{n}$.

Eq. (8.101) has simple implications for compressible CFD codes: the acoustic flux $p_1 \vec{u}_1 . \vec{n}$ is zero on all walls (where $\vec{u}_0 = \vec{u}_1 = 0$), on inlets where velocity is imposed ($\vec{u}_0 \neq 0$ but $\vec{u}_1 = 0$) and on outlets where pressure is imposed (p_0 is constant and $p_1 = 0$). As a consequence, in domains surrounded by walls and by constant velocity or pressure boundaries (Fig. 8.27), the acoustic energy, which is initially present in the computational domain, cannot escape through the boundaries. It is trapped in the domain and all flow variables oscillate indefinitely, preventing the convergence of the code towards steady state. Of course, using a dissipative algorithm (as done in most RANS codes) damps the acoustic energy (the present derivation is valid only for inviscid flows) but allowing acoustic waves to leave the computational box is mandatory in high-order steady or unsteady codes as demonstrated in Chapter 9. This explains why numerous efforts are still devoted to boundary conditions, not only for unsteady flows but also for steady flows (Rudy and Strikwerda [571, 572], Thompson [648], Giles [235], Nicoud [468], Poinsot and Lele [519], Baum et al. [40], Lodato et al. [403]).

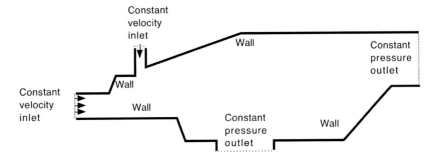

Figure 8.27: Example of computational domain surrounded by walls, constant velocity inlets or constant pressure outlets: the acoustic flux is zero on all boundaries, the total acoustic energy inside the domain is conserved and convergence to steady state is very slow.

The elements of acoustic theories derived here for non-reacting flows show that the acoustic energy of all acoustic eigenmodes is conserved: these modes are not damped but they cannot be amplified either and no strong aeroacoustic coupling should be expected if combustion is not present.[xiii] For reacting flows, as shown in Section 8.3, the acoustic energy of eigenmodes may be fed by unsteady combustion and increase enough to induce combustion instabilities.

[xiii]The analysis of Section 8.3 shows that combustion is actually not the only possible source of aeroacoustic coupling: vortices (without combustion) may also induce flow oscillations when they couple with acoustics as in a whistle (Tam and Block [637]).

8.3 Acoustics for reacting flows

Previous sections have described acoustic wave propagation in an isentropic non-reacting gas. For a reacting flow, the derivation of a wave equation is a more complex task and entropy variations must be included. A convenient way to derive this equation is to work with the logarithm of pressure as shown below.

8.3.1 An equation for the logarithm of P in reacting flows

The starting point is the Navier-Stokes equations expressed here in tensor form and using total derivatives defined by:

$$\frac{Df}{Dt} = \frac{\partial f}{\partial t} + \vec{u}.\nabla f$$

Two assumptions used in Section 8.2.1 remain useful for the derivation:

- H1 - zero volume forces ($f_k = 0$)
- H2 - zero volume heat sources ($\dot{\mathcal{Q}} = 0$).

The required equations are mass and momentum conservation like for non-reacting flows:

$$\frac{D\rho}{Dt} + \rho\nabla.\vec{u} = 0 \tag{8.102}$$

$$\rho\frac{D\vec{u}}{Dt} = -\nabla p + \nabla.\tau \tag{8.103}$$

Since the flow is not adiabatic anymore, the energy equation (1.67) is also required:

$$\rho C_p \frac{DT}{Dt} = \dot{\omega}'_T + \frac{Dp}{Dt} + \nabla(\lambda\nabla T) + \tau : \nabla\vec{u} - \left(\rho\sum_{k=1}^{N} C_{p,k}Y_k\vec{V}_k\right).\nabla T \tag{8.104}$$

where $\vec{V}_k$ is the diffusion velocity vector of species k.

Eq. (8.102) to (8.104) must be combined to derive a wave equation. A convenient method is to divide the energy equation (8.104) by $\rho C_p T$ and use the equation of state $p = \rho r T$ to obtain an equation for $\ln(p)$:

$$\boxed{\frac{1}{\gamma}\frac{D\ln(p)}{Dt} + \nabla.\vec{u} = \frac{1}{\rho C_p T}\left[\dot{\omega}'_T + \nabla(\lambda\nabla T) + \tau : \nabla\vec{u} - \left(\rho\sum_{k=1}^{N} C_{p,k}Y_k\vec{V}_k\right).\nabla T\right] + \frac{1}{r}\frac{Dr}{Dt}} \tag{8.105}$$

The momentum equation (8.103) may also be written as a function of $\ln(p)$:

$$\boxed{\frac{D\vec{u}}{Dt} + \frac{c_0^2}{\gamma}\nabla\ln(p) = \frac{1}{\rho}\nabla.\tau} \tag{8.106}$$

defining the local sound speed c_0 by: $c_0^2 = \gamma p/\rho$. Subtracting the material derivative of Eq. (8.105) from the divergence of Eq. (8.106) provides a wave equation for $\ln(p)$:

$$\nabla \cdot \left(\frac{c_0^2}{\gamma}\nabla \ln(p)\right) - \frac{D}{Dt}\left(\frac{1}{\gamma}\frac{D}{Dt}\ln(p)\right) = \nabla \cdot (\rho^{-1}\nabla.\tau) - \frac{D}{Dt}\left[\frac{D}{Dt}(\ln(r))\right] - \nabla\vec{u}:\nabla\vec{u}$$

$$- \frac{D}{Dt}\left[\frac{1}{\rho C_p T}\left(\dot{\omega}_T' + \nabla(\lambda\nabla T) + \tau:\nabla\vec{u} - \left(\rho\sum_{k=1}^{N}C_{p,k}Y_k\vec{V}_k\right).\nabla T\right)\right] \qquad (8.107)$$

For a non-reacting inviscid flow containing only one species, Eq. (8.107) reduces to the wave equation (8.12) derived in Section 8.2.

8.3.2 A wave equation in low Mach-number reacting flows

Two additional assumptions may be introduced to derive a simple wave equation in reacting flows:

- H6 - low-speed mean flow (already used in Section 8.2.1),
- H7 - identical molecular weights for all species.

These two assumptions are not very restrictive and bring many simplifications:

- $\dot{\omega}_T'$ can be replaced by $\dot{\omega}_T$ since all molecular weights are equal (see § 1.1.5).
- γ is constant and the mean pressure p_0 is also constant so that $\gamma p_0 = \rho_0 c_0^2$ is constant (which does not mean that ρ_0 and c_0 are constant).
- An order of magnitude analysis (Kotake [355]) indicates that the main source terms on the RHS of Eq. (8.107) are the chemical heat release term and the velocity perturbations leading to the simplified equation:

$$\boxed{\nabla \cdot \left(\frac{c_0^2}{\gamma}\nabla \ln(p)\right) - \frac{D}{Dt}\left(\frac{1}{\gamma}\frac{D}{Dt}\ln(p)\right) = -\frac{D}{Dt}\left(\frac{1}{\rho C_p T}\dot{\omega}_T\right) - \nabla\vec{u}:\nabla\vec{u}} \qquad (8.108)$$

- All convective derivatives are second order terms compared to time derivatives (Helley [282]). For example, consider the total derivative of a one-dimensional quantity f which oscillates harmonically: $f = e^{ikx-i\omega t}$:

$$\frac{Df}{Dt} = \frac{\partial f}{\partial t} + u\frac{\partial f}{\partial x} = (-i\omega + uik)f = -i\omega\left(1 - \frac{u}{c_0}\right)f = -i\omega(1-M)f \qquad (8.109)$$

since $k = \omega/c_0$. For small Mach numbers $M = u/c_0$, the second term in the expression of Df/Dt is negligible and Df/Dt can be approximated by $\partial f/\partial t$.

Eq. (8.108) then becomes:

$$\nabla \cdot \left(c_0^2 \nabla \ln(p)\right) - \frac{\partial^2}{\partial t^2} \ln(p) = -\frac{\partial}{\partial t}\left(\frac{1}{\rho C_v T}\dot{\omega}_T\right) - \gamma \nabla \vec{u} : \nabla \vec{u} \qquad (8.110)$$

This equation is not linearized yet and could describe waves of finite amplitude. Linearizing it as in Section 8.2.1, the pressure is written $p = p_0 + p_1$ with $p_1/p_0 << 1$ so that $\ln(p)$ is approximated by p_1/p_0. Eq. (8.110) becomes an equation for the pressure changes p_1:

$$\nabla \cdot \left(c_0^2 \nabla p_1\right) - \frac{\partial^2}{\partial t^2} p_1 = -(\gamma - 1)\frac{\partial \dot{\omega}_T}{\partial t} - \gamma p_0 \nabla \vec{u} : \nabla \vec{u} \qquad (8.111)$$

Table 8.6 compares the wave equation in non-reacting and reacting flows. For the non-reacting case, the $\nabla \vec{u} : \nabla \vec{u}$ term is retained and is responsible for turbulent flow noise. The main complexity brought by combustion is the variable sound speed c_0 which must be kept in the ∇ operator and the additional source term found on the RHS terms for the pressure equation with combustion. This source term is responsible for combustion noise and instabilities. The linearized form of Eq. (8.111) is sufficient to capture the growth of unstable modes but non-linear extensions are required to describe non-linear effects seen in many limit-cycles.

Non-reacting flows	$c_0^2 \nabla^2 p_1 - \dfrac{\partial^2 p_1}{\partial t^2}$	$=$	$-\gamma p_0 \nabla \vec{u} : \nabla \vec{u}$
Reacting flows	$\nabla . c_0^2 \nabla p_1 - \dfrac{\partial^2 p_1}{\partial t^2}$	$=$	$-\gamma p_0 \nabla \vec{u} : \nabla \vec{u} - (\gamma - 1)\dfrac{\partial \dot{\omega}_T}{\partial t}$

Table 8.6: Comparison of wave equations for non-reacting and reacting flows.

8.3.3   Acoustic velocity and pressure in low-speed reacting flows

Linearized equations for pressure and velocity perturbations are also needed for acoustic analysis. The equation for the acoustic velocity $\vec{u}_1$ is simplified from Eq. (8.103) using the assumptions of negligible viscous stresses and convective derivatives to yield:

$$\frac{\partial \vec{u}_1}{\partial t} = -\frac{1}{\rho_0}\nabla p_1 \qquad (8.112)$$

where ρ_0 can be a function of space.

The equation for pressure is obtained by first neglecting viscous terms and variations of molecular weights in Eq. (8.105). The term associated with diffusion velocities and the Dr/Dt term both vanish so that Eq. (8.105) simplifies to:

$$\frac{1}{\gamma}\frac{D \ln(p)}{Dt} + \nabla . \vec{u} = \frac{1}{\rho C_p T}\dot{\omega}_T \qquad (8.113)$$

To zero-th order (for the mean flow), this equation yields:

$$\nabla.\vec{u}_0 = \dot{\omega}_T^0/(\rho C_p T) \qquad (8.114)$$

where $\dot{\omega}_T^0$ is the mean reaction rate. Retaining first-order linear terms in Eq. (8.113) and neglecting spatial derivatives compared to time derivatives leads to (Crighton et al. [153], Helley [282]):

$$\boxed{\frac{1}{\gamma p_0} \frac{\partial p_1}{\partial t} + \nabla.\vec{u}_1 = \frac{\gamma - 1}{\gamma p_0} \dot{\omega}_T^1} \qquad (8.115)$$

where $\dot{\omega}_T^1$ is the unsteady heat release. For longitudinal waves propagating into a duct of variable cross section $S(z)$ (see Fig. 8.3) one-dimensional flow may be assumed so that Eq. (8.112) and (8.115) can be integrated along x and y to give:

$$\frac{\partial u_1}{\partial t} = -\frac{1}{\rho_0} \frac{\partial p_1}{\partial z} \qquad (8.116)$$

$$\frac{1}{\gamma p_0} \frac{\partial p_1}{\partial t} + \frac{1}{S} \frac{\partial}{\partial z}(S u_1) = \frac{\gamma - 1}{\gamma p_0} \dot{\omega}_T^1 \qquad (8.117)$$

8.3.4 Acoustic jump conditions for thin flames

The wavelengths associated with most longitudinal combustion oscillations are usually large compared to the size of the zone where combustion takes place. For example, for $f = 500$ Hz, the acoustic wavelength $\lambda_{ac} = c_0/f$ in burnt gases at 2000 K is of the order of 1.8 m while most flame zones (in efficient combustors) are of the order of 10 cm. In this case, flames can be supposed to be "compact" compared to acoustic wavelengths. For the present analysis, these flames become infinitely thin and jump conditions for acoustic quantities through a flame front can be derived from the previous equations. Consider the ideal thin flame model displayed in Fig. 8.28. In this model, the fresh gases are burnt in a zero-thickness flame located at $z = z_{j+1}$. Note that the duct section is also changing at $z = z_{j+1}$.

Integrating Eq. (8.116) and (8.117) from $z = z_{j+1}^-$ to $z = z_{j+1}^+$ and taking the limit where z_{j+1}^- and z_{j+1}^+ go to z_{j+1}:

$$[p_1]_{z_{j+1}^-}^{z_{j+1}^+} = 0 \qquad (8.118)$$

$$[S u_1]_{z_{j+1}^-}^{z_{j+1}^+} = \frac{\gamma - 1}{\gamma p_0} \dot{\Omega}_T^1 \qquad (8.119)$$

where $\dot{\Omega}_T^1 = \int_{z_{j+1}^-}^{z_{j+1}^+} S \dot{\omega}_T^1 dz$ is the total unsteady heat release produced by the flame.

The first condition shows that the acoustic pressure p_1 is continuous through the flame:

$$\boxed{p_1(z_{j+1}^-) = p_1(z_{j+1}^+)} \qquad (8.120)$$

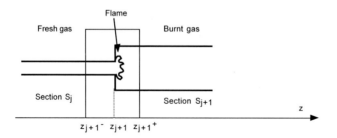

Figure 8.28: Jump conditions through a thin premixed flame.

while the second one shows that the acoustic velocity jump through the flame front is:

$$S_{j+1}u_1(z_{j+1}^+) - S_j u_1(z_{j+1}^-) = \frac{\gamma-1}{\rho_j c_j^2}\dot{\Omega}_T^1$$

(8.121)

where ρ_j and c_j are respectively the mean density and the sound speed in section j. In this expression, γp_0 was replaced by $\rho_j c_j^2$ which is conserved for all sections. Eq. (8.121) shows that a thin flame acts as a source of volume flow rate like a loudspeaker.[xiv]

A transfer matrix can also be derived for the interface of Fig. 8.28. Using the notations of Section 8.2.7, the acoustic waves in section j and $j+1$ are written:

$$p_1^j(z,t) = A_j^+ e^{ik_j(z-z_j)-i\omega t} + A_j^- e^{-ik_j(z-z_j)-i\omega t}$$

(8.122)

while the acoustic velocity is:

$$u_1^j(z,t) = \frac{1}{\rho_j c_j}\left(A_j^+ e^{ik_j(z-z_j)-i\omega t} - A_j^- e^{-ik_j(z-z_j)-i\omega t}\right)$$

(8.123)

where k_j, ρ_j and c_j are respectively the wave number, the mean density and the sound speed in section j.

The fluctuating heat release $\dot{\Omega}_T^1$ is also supposed to be harmonic:

$$\dot{\Omega}_T^1 = \Omega e^{-i\omega t}$$

(8.124)

[xiv]This result is somewhat surprising since one would expect the acoustic *mass* flow rate to be conserved and not the *volume* flow rate. This is due to the assumption of negligible convective terms compared to unsteady terms: the mean flow is neglected and the interface acts like a non-permeable membrane which transmits volume changes but not mass. More sophisticated analyses usually do not lead to simple analytical forms (Bloxsidge et al. [63], Dowling [184]). Note also that the continuity equation cannot be used simply to deduce these acoustic jump conditions if a flame is present: this equation cannot be linearized because the mean density gradients are large and the interface is moving. A more detailed discussion and validation of this result is given in *elearning.cerfacs.fr/combustion/illustrations/jump/*.

At the jth interface located at $z = z_{j+1}$ separating sections j and $j+1$, the jump conditions (8.120) and (8.121) yield:

$$p_1^{j+1}(z_{j+1}, t) = p_1^j(z_{j+1}, t) \quad \text{and} \quad S_{j+1} u_1^{j+1}(z_{j+1}, t) = S_j u_1^j(z_{j+1}, t) + \frac{\gamma - 1}{\rho_j c_j^2} \dot{\Omega}_T^1 \quad (8.125)$$

so that

$$A_j^+ e^{ik_j l_j} + A_j^- e^{-ik_j l_j} = A_{j+1}^+ + A_{j+1}^- \quad (8.126)$$

$$\frac{S_{j+1}}{\rho_{j+1} c_{j+1}}(A_{j+1}^+ - A_{j+1}^-) = \frac{S_j}{\rho_j c_j}(A_j^+ e^{ik_j l_j} - A_j^- e^{-ik_j l_j}) + \frac{\gamma - 1}{\rho_j c_j^2} \Omega \quad (8.127)$$

and the amplitudes of the wave in section $j + 1$ are linked to the amplitudes in section j by:

$$\begin{pmatrix} A_{j+1}^+ \\ A_{j+1}^- \end{pmatrix} = \frac{1}{2} \begin{bmatrix} e^{ik_j l_j}(1 + \Gamma_j) & e^{-ik_j l_j}(1 - \Gamma_j) \\ e^{ik_j l_j}(1 - \Gamma_j) & e^{-ik_j l_j}(1 + \Gamma_j) \end{bmatrix} \begin{pmatrix} A_j^+ \\ A_j^- \end{pmatrix} + \frac{\rho_{j+1} c_{j+1}}{2 S_{j+1}} \begin{pmatrix} \frac{\gamma-1}{\rho_j c_j^2} \Omega \\ -\frac{\gamma-1}{\rho_j c_j^2} \Omega \end{pmatrix} \quad (8.128)$$

where Γ_j is given by:

$$\Gamma_j = \frac{\rho_{j+1} c_{j+1}}{\rho_j c_j} \frac{S_j}{S_{j+1}} \quad (8.129)$$

Eq. (8.128) can also be recast as:

$$\boxed{\begin{pmatrix} A_{j+1}^+ \\ A_{j+1}^- \end{pmatrix} = T_j \begin{pmatrix} A_j^+ \\ A_j^- \end{pmatrix} + O_j} \quad (8.130)$$

with

$$\boxed{T_j = \frac{1}{2} \begin{bmatrix} e^{ik_j l_j}(1 + \Gamma_j) & e^{-ik_j l_j}(1 - \Gamma_j) \\ e^{ik_j l_j}(1 - \Gamma_j) & e^{-ik_j l_j}(1 + \Gamma_j) \end{bmatrix} \quad \text{and} \quad O_j = \frac{1}{2} \frac{\rho_{j+1} c_{j+1}}{S_{j+1}} \begin{pmatrix} \frac{\gamma-1}{\rho_j c_j^2} \Omega \\ -\frac{\gamma-1}{\rho_j c_j^2} \Omega \end{pmatrix}} \quad (8.131)$$

This form is more general than Eq. (8.67) because it incorporates variable density and reaction effects. The transfer matrix T_j links the waves amplitudes in section j to the amplitudes in section $j + 1$. The presence of a flame in the $(j + 1)^{th}$ duct appears through an additional O_j term in Eq. (8.130).

8.3.5 Longitudinal modes in a series of ducts with combustion

The previous relations may be used to determine one-dimensional resonant modes in a series of connected ducts with one or many flames (Fig. 8.29)[xv]. Transfer matrices T_j and source terms

---

[xv]To illustrate this section but also to avoid having to re derive the equations, readers can use the generic 'Soundtube' tool at *elearning.cerfacs.fr/combustion/tools/soundtube*. This tool solves the equations given below with or without active flame ($O_j = 0$) for simple combustors containing up to five connected ducts. Reflection coefficients at the mixing duct inlet and at the combustion chamber outlet are chosen by the user.

O_j can be estimated in each section of the duct and like for non-reacting flows, assembled from inlet to outlet to gather a global matrix.

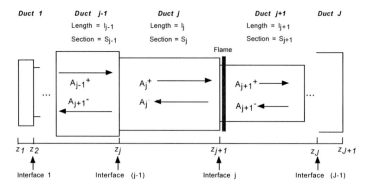

Figure 8.29: Decomposition of a combustor into one-dimensional sections.

The global matrix $G_{j,n}$ must now have two indices and is such that:

$$\begin{pmatrix} A_{j+1}^+ \\ A_{j+1}^- \end{pmatrix} = G_{j,1} \begin{pmatrix} A_1^+ \\ A_1^- \end{pmatrix} + \sum_{k=1}^{j-1} G_{j,k+1} O_k + O_j \qquad (8.132)$$

The matrix $G_{j,k}$ integrates all interfaces from k to j while the matrix $G_{j,1}$ integrates all interfaces from 1 to j:

$$G_{j,k+1} = T_j T_{j-1} \ldots T_{k+1} \quad \text{and} \quad G_{j,1} = T_j \ldots T_2 T_1 \qquad (8.133)$$

Writing the system (8.132) for the last section $j = J$ and knowing the boundary conditions:

$$\frac{A_1^+}{A_1^-} = R_1 \quad \text{and} \quad \frac{A_J^+}{A_J^-} e^{2ik_J l_J} = R_J \qquad (8.134)$$

leads to a linear system which has a non trivial (non-zero) solution only for a limited set of pulsations ω and associated mode shapes (determined by the wave amplitudes A_j^+ and A_j^- for $j = 1$ to J). The imaginary part ω_i of the pulsation ω determines the stability of the corresponding modes: if ω_i is positive, the mode is unstable and grows with time. The global procedure [xvi] is summarized in Table 8.7 for a geometry sketched in Fig. 8.29. Since the problem is linear, only scaled wave amplitudes may be obtained (such as A_J^+/A_1^+).

[xvi]Softwares solving these equations for thermoacoustics in a general framework may be found on the web: see for example the TaX library of TU Munich (Leandro et al. [373]) at *www.td.mw.tum.de/tum-td/en/forschung/infrastruktur/scientific_comp.*

Specify left reflection coefficient	R_1
For each interface $j = 1$ to $J - 1$:	
- Evaluate section parameter	$\Gamma_j = \frac{\rho_{j+1} c_{j+1} S_j}{\rho_j c_j S_{j+1}}$
- Form transfer matrix T_j	$T_j = \frac{1}{2} \begin{bmatrix} e^{ik_j l_j}\left(1 + \Gamma_j\right) & e^{-ik_j l_j}\left(1 - \Gamma_j\right) \\ e^{ik_j l_j}\left(1 - \Gamma_j\right) & e^{-ik_j l_j}\left(1 + \Gamma_j\right) \end{bmatrix}$
- Add source term O_j	$O_j = \frac{1}{2}\frac{\rho_{j+1}c_{j+1}}{S_{j+1}} \begin{pmatrix} \frac{\gamma - 1}{\rho_j c_j^2}\Omega \\ -\frac{\gamma - 1}{\rho_j c_j^2}\Omega \end{pmatrix}$ (if a flame is present)
- Make global matrices $G_{j,n}$	$G_{j,n} = T_j \dots T_{n+1} T_n$ (for $n = 1$ to j)
Specify right reflection coefficient	R_J
Solve for ω in system:	$\begin{pmatrix} A_J^+ \\ A_J^- \end{pmatrix} = G_{J-1,1}\begin{pmatrix} A_1^+ \\ A_1^- \end{pmatrix} + \sum_{k=1}^{J-2} G_{J-1,k+1}O_k + O_{J-1}$
with boundary conditions:	$A_1^+/A_1^- = R_1$ and $A_J^+/A_J^- e^{2ik_J l_J} = R_J$
Having ω, find wave amplitudes:	$A_J^+/A_1^+ \quad A_J^-/A_1^+$ for $j = 1$ to J

Table 8.7: Procedure to compute the longitudinal eigenmodes of a combustor at low speeds decomposed into J sections separated by $J - 1$ interfaces. The reflection coefficients R_1 and R_J are complex numbers and must be known (from experiments for example). Sound speeds c_j and densities ρ_j correspond to mean values. The product $\rho_j c_j^2$ is conserved in all sections: $\rho_j c_j^2 = \gamma p_0$. Wave numbers k_j are defined by $k_j = \omega/c_j$.

8.3.6   Three-dimensional Helmholtz tools

Longitudinal low-frequency modes described in the previous sections are not the only modes found in combustors: other modes, involving wave propagation in all directions can also appear. These modes generally have higher frequencies and can be even more dangerous than longitudinal modes. The azimuthal modes discussed in Section 8.2.11 are one example of such modes. Screech is another example: screech is a transverse mode observed in afterburners. It can destroy an engine in a few seconds (Rogers and Marble [565], Blackshear et al. [59]).

The signature of high-frequency transverse modes is that the pressure field exhibits oscillations which have a structure along the flow axis but also along the normal to the flow axis. The one-dimensional tool presented in the previous section cannot be used for such flows but the wave equation (8.111) is still valid:

$$\nabla \cdot \left(c_0^2 \nabla p_1 \right) - \frac{\partial^2}{\partial t^2} p_1 = -(\gamma - 1) \frac{\partial \dot{\omega}_T}{\partial t} - \gamma p_0 \nabla \vec{u} : \nabla \vec{u} \qquad (8.135)$$

Multidimensional tools have been developed to solve Eq. (8.135) along with the corresponding boundary conditions. Certain codes solve directly Eq. (8.135) in time domain (Pankiewitz and Sattelmayer [488]) but usually, it is solved in the frequency domain by assuming harmonic variations for pressure and local heat release perturbations:

$$p_1 = P'(x, y, z)\, e^{-i\omega t} \quad \text{and} \quad \dot{\omega}_T = \Omega'_T e^{-i\omega t} \quad \text{with} \quad i^2 = -1 \qquad (8.136)$$

The $\nabla \vec{u} : \nabla \vec{u}$ term in Eq. (8.135) is often neglected in combustion applications because the second term (due to the unsteady reaction rate) is larger. Introducing Eq. (8.136) into Eq. (8.135) leads to the Helmholtz equation where the unknown quantity is the pressure oscillation amplitude P' at frequency f and the heat release perturbation field Ω'_T:

$$\nabla \cdot \left(c_0^2 \nabla P' \right) + \omega^2 P' = i\omega(\gamma - 1)\Omega'_T \qquad (8.137)$$

This equation is the basis of three-dimensional Helmholtz codes (Nicoud et al. [471], Camporeale et al. [102]). Its resolution requires the field of sound speed (c_0) which is linked to the local composition and temperature: most codes use the mean sound speed field (obtained for example from a RANS or a time-averaged LES computation). It also requires a model for the unsteady reaction term Ω'_T. The solution of Eq. (8.137) provides two informations: (1) the eigenfrequencies ω_k and (2) the associated structure of all eigenmodes: $P'_k(x, y, z)$. At this point, two approaches of increasing complexity are found :

- First the effects of unsteady combustion can be neglected by setting $\Omega'_T = 0$, and finding the eigenmodes of the burner taking into account the presence of the flame through the mean temperature field, but neglecting the flame effect as an acoustic active element.

- In a second step the active effect of combustion can be included if a model for Ω'_T is provided. This is usually the difficult part of the approach (see Chapter 10).

Usual numerical techniques for solving Eq. (8.137) are based on finite element methods. An example of application is given for non active flames in Fig. 8.30: a model combustor with a cold inlet duct and a hot combustion chamber is computed using a Helmholtz solver (Nicoud et al. [471]). The length and diameter of the inlet pipe are 10 and 6 cm and the length and diameter of the combustion chamber are respectively 25 and 20 cm. The outlet is a small section tube imposing a zero-velocity section on the downstream wall of the combustion chamber so that all acoustic boundary conditions correspond to hard reflecting walls.

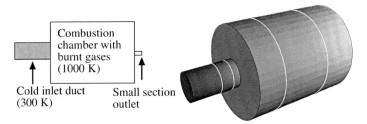

Figure 8.30: Computation of the modes of a dump combustor terminated by a contraction.

As an example of the output of Helmholtz solvers, the structures of two modes identified by solving Eq. (8.137) are displayed in Fig. 8.31: the first mode (left) at 727 Hz is a longitudinal one (which would also be recovered by the one-dimensional tools of the previous section). The second one (right) is a 1T-1L at 2211 Hz (first transverse - first longitudinal) which is invariant by rotation around the chamber axis. For this second mode, the axis of the combustion chamber is a velocity antinode which would have a strong effect on the flame in a reacting case because it would excite the jet issuing from the small section duct.

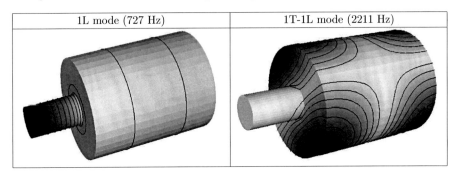

Figure 8.31: First two modes for the burner of Fig. 8.30. The acoustic pressure amplitude P' is plotted on the walls of the chamber. Dark regions correspond to pressure antinodes.

8.3.7   The acoustic energy balance in reacting flows

The acoustic energy in a reacting flow may be defined as in Section 8.2.12:

$$e_1 = \frac{1}{2}\rho_0 \vec{u}_1^2 + \frac{1}{2}\frac{p_1^2}{\rho_0 c_0^2} \tag{8.138}$$

where index 0 refers to mean values and index 1 to perturbations. Multiplying Eq. (8.115) by p_1, taking the scalar product of the momentum equation (8.112) by $\vec{u}_1$ yields:

$$\frac{\partial e_1}{\partial t} + \nabla \cdot f_1 = r_1 \quad \text{with} \quad r_1 = \frac{(\gamma - 1)}{\gamma p_0} p_1 \dot{\omega}_T^1 \quad \text{and} \quad f_1 = p_1 \vec{u}_1 \tag{8.139}$$

The RHS source term r_1 is a correlation between unsteady pressure p_1 and unsteady heat release $\dot{\omega}_T^1$. This term is due to combustion and can act as a source or a sink term for the acoustic energy.[xvii] When r_1 is positive, i.e. if the pressure oscillations (p_1) are in phase with the unsteady heat release ($\dot{\omega}_T^1$), r_1 acts as a source term for the acoustic energy and the instability is locally amplified. On the other hand, if unsteady heat release is maximum when pressure is minimum, the instability decreases. This qualitative criterion for combustion instability, first proposed by Rayleigh [548], seems a rather natural statement but many experiments do not actually support this result in a straightforward manner. The index r_1 changes with time and location: some regions excite the oscillation by burning in phase with pressure (positive r_1) while other regions damp the instability by burning out of phase with pressure (Poinsot et al. [521], Samaniego et al. [585]). The overall effect of flame/acoustics coupling can only be predicted by integrating Eq. (8.139) over space and time. If integrated first over the whole volume V of the combustor, it yields:

$$\frac{d}{dt}\int_V e_1 dV + \int_A f_1 \cdot \vec{n} dA = \int_V r_1 dV \quad \text{with} \quad f_1 = p_1 \vec{u}_1 \quad \text{and} \quad r_1 = \frac{(\gamma - 1)}{\gamma p_0} p_1 \dot{\omega}_T^1 \tag{8.140}$$

In Eq. (8.140), all terms are time dependent. To provide meaningful information on the growth of the instability, Eq. (8.140) must also be averaged over time. This can be done over a period of oscillation for harmonic oscillations (see Table 8.8 for notations):

$$p_1 = \Re(p_\omega(t)e^{-i\omega t}), \quad \vec{u}_1 = \Re(\vec{u}_\omega(t)e^{-i\omega t}) \quad \text{and} \quad \dot{\omega}_T^1 = \Re(\dot{w}_\omega(t)e^{-i\omega t}) \tag{8.141}$$

where $p_\omega(t)$, $\vec{u}_\omega(t)$ and $\dot{w}_\omega(t)$ are slowly varying functions of time. Whether these functions grow with time for a given pulsation ω will determine the stability of the combustor. Integrating Eq. (8.140) over a period of oscillation $\tau = 2\pi/\omega$ and dividing by τ (using averaging techniques introduced in § 8.2.3) gives:

[xvii]For a single-step reaction, as the heat release and the fuel reaction rate are linked by $\dot{\omega}_T = -Q\dot{\omega}_F$ (Eq. (2.17)), the RHS term becomes $r_1 = -\frac{(\gamma-1)}{\gamma}\frac{p_1}{p_0}Q\dot{\omega}_F^1$ where $\dot{\omega}_F^1$ is the perturbed fuel reaction rate.

$$\boxed{\frac{d}{dt}\mathcal{E}_1 + \mathcal{F}_1 = \mathcal{R}_1} \tag{8.142}$$

where $\mathcal{E}_1$ measures the period-averaged acoustic energy in the whole combustor:

$$\mathcal{E}_1 = \int_V E dV \quad \text{and} \quad E = \frac{1}{\tau}\int_0^\tau e_1 dt = \frac{1}{4\rho_0 c^2}p_\omega p_\omega^* + \frac{1}{4}\rho_0 \vec{\mathbf{u}}_\omega \vec{\mathbf{u}}_\omega^* \tag{8.143}$$

The period-averaged acoustic flux leaving the combustor is $\mathcal{F}_1$:

$$\mathcal{F}_1 = \int_A F.\vec{\mathbf{n}} dA \quad \text{and} \quad F = \frac{1}{\tau}\int_0^\tau f_1 dt = \frac{1}{\tau}\int_0^\tau p_1 \vec{\mathbf{u}}_1 dt = \frac{1}{2}\Re(p_\omega \vec{\mathbf{u}}_\omega^*) \tag{8.144}$$

And the average source term is $\mathcal{R}_1$:

$$\mathcal{R}_1 = \int_V R dV \quad \text{and} \quad R = \frac{1}{\tau}\int_0^\tau r_1 dt = \frac{(\gamma-1)}{\tau\gamma p_0}\int_0^\tau p_1 \dot{\omega}_T^1 dt = \frac{(\gamma-1)}{2\gamma p_0}\Re(p_\omega \dot{\omega}_\omega^*) \tag{8.145}$$

Flame/acoustic coupling is now represented in $\mathcal{R}_1$: the space-averaged integral (over V) of the period-averaged value of $p_\omega \dot{\omega}_\omega^*$ (unsteady pressure multiplied by unsteady heat release) must be positive to increase the acoustic energy of the oscillation.

Energy	Flux	Source term	Characteristic
e_1	f_1	r_1	local, instantaneous
E	F	R	local, period-averaged
$\mathcal{E}_1$	$\mathcal{F}_1$	$\mathcal{R}_1$	volume (or surface) averaged and period-averaged

Table 8.8: Definitions of acoustic energies, fluxes and source terms.

The growth rate of the acoustic energy g may be expressed by assuming that the perturbation amplitudes change slowly with time in comparison to acoustic times so that p_ω, $\vec{\mathbf{u}}_\omega$ and $\dot{\omega}_\omega$ functions may be written:

$$p_\omega(t) = P_1 e^{gt}, \quad \vec{\mathbf{u}}_\omega = \vec{U}_1 e^{gt} \quad \text{and} \quad \dot{\omega}_\omega = W_1 e^{gt} \tag{8.146}$$

where $gT \ll 1$. The energy balance equation (8.142) becomes:

$$\boxed{g = (\mathcal{R}_1 - \mathcal{F}_1)/(2\mathcal{E}_1)} \tag{8.147}$$

The growth rate g is the difference between the combustion source term $\mathcal{R}_1$ and the acoustic losses $\mathcal{F}_1$ at the boundaries. Eq. (8.147) can be interpreted as a generalized Rayleigh criterion. Combustion will be unstable if $g > 0$ which means that the instability criterion is (Table 8.11):

$$\mathcal{R}_1 > \mathcal{F}_1 \quad \text{with} \quad \mathcal{R}_1 = \frac{(\gamma-1)}{\tau\gamma p_0}\int_V \int_0^\tau p_1 \dot{\omega}_T^1 dt dV \quad \text{and} \quad \mathcal{F}_1 = \frac{1}{\tau}\int_A \int_0^\tau p_1 \vec{\mathbf{u}}_1 dt dA \tag{8.148}$$

This criterion is more complex and includes more acoustic effects than the classical Rayleigh criterion. More generally, instead of focusing on one such criterion, analyzing instabilities through budgets of acoustic energy as defined by Eq. (8.142) by post processing compressible LES of unstable combustors is the best method to understand combustion instabilities. An example of such analysis including the evaluation of all terms in Eq. (8.142) is given in § 10.4.

8.3.8   About energies in reacting flows

Is the acoustic energy relevant in reacting flows?

Even though Eq. (8.142) was rigorously derived, provides for the recovery of the Rayleigh criterion and can be verified using LES as shown in § 10.4, its relevance to combustion stability problems may be questioned:

- The acoustic energy has the same definition in non-reacting (see Eq. (8.99)) and reacting flows (Eq. (8.138)) and this is surprising: going from non-reacting to reacting flows means that an additional thermodynamic variable (enthalpy or entropy) is now changing; as a result, one should expect that a proper energy definition in reacting flows includes not only velocity ($\vec{u}_1$) and pressure (p_1) perturbations, but also entropy (s_1) changes.

- Implicitely, the derivation of the Rayleigh criterion assumes that combustion instability occurs if the acoustic energy grows. This is not necessarily the case: the acoustic energy in Eq. (8.138) is a quantity which can increase in a non-isentropic gas in the absence of any reaction or boundary term. Consider for example a flow where $\vec{u}_1$ and p_1 are both zero initially, but where the entropy is perturbed because of the presence of a hot spot. This hot spot will expand through heat diffusion: density will change. As a result, the fluid will move so that $\vec{u}_1$ will become non-zero and the acoustic energy which was initially zero will start increasing. Can knowledge of the acoustic energy be useful in determining whether the flow will be stable or not? In the present example, the acoustic energy grows but the flow is stable.

These two comments directly lead to the question of defining a proper 'fluctuating energy' in reacting flows as discussed in the next section.

Another energy for fluctuations including entropy changes

Determining what is an adequate quantity to measure fluctuations in reacting flows is a question which has been seldom addressed in the literature. A landmark paper by Chu [132] provides the right framework to answer it: according to Chu, a fluctuation energy should be "a positive quantity characterizing the mean level of fluctuations which, in the absence of heat transfer at boundaries and of work done by boundary or body forces and in the absence of heat and material sources, is a monotone non-increasing function of time". As shown in the previous example, the acoustic energy of Eq. (8.138) does not satisfy this criterion. But another form of energy which will be called here the 'fluctuation energy', does. This section describes the derivation of this energy in a more compact way than Chu. Non-linearized forms of this energy are also provided. To simplify the derivation, all species are supposed to have the same molar weight and heat capacities (see § 1.2.2). Molecular viscosity is neglected ($\tau = 0$) but thermal diffusion is conserved ($\lambda \neq 0$).

Taking the dot product of the momentum equation (1.35) with $\vec{u}$ gives an equation for $\vec{u}^2$:

$$\rho \frac{D\vec{u}^2/2}{Dt} + \nabla \cdot (p\vec{u}) = p\nabla \cdot \vec{u} \tag{8.149}$$

The pressure equation (1.81) can be used to express the divergence of velocity:

$$\frac{Dp}{Dt} = -\gamma p\nabla \cdot \vec{u} + (\gamma - 1)\left(\dot{\omega}_T + \nabla \cdot (\lambda\vec{\nabla}T)\right) \tag{8.150}$$

Using Eq. (8.150) to eliminate $\nabla \cdot \vec{u}$ in Eq. (8.149) leads to a non-linear form of the acoustic energy equation:

$$\rho \frac{D\vec{u}^2/2}{Dt} + \frac{1}{\rho c^2}\frac{Dp^2/2}{Dt} + \nabla \cdot (p\vec{u}) = \frac{\gamma - 1}{\gamma}\left(\dot{\omega}_T + \nabla \cdot (\lambda\vec{\nabla}T)\right) \tag{8.151}$$

Eq. (8.151) is exact (no linearization). Its linearization around the mean state (index 0)gives:

$$\frac{\partial e_1}{\partial t} + \nabla \cdot (p_1\vec{u}_1) = \frac{\gamma - 1}{\gamma p_0}p_1\left(\dot{\omega}_T^1 + \nabla \cdot (\lambda\vec{\nabla}T_1)\right) \tag{8.152}$$

which is simply the extension of the acoustic energy equation (8.139) including heat diffusion effects. To construct a fluctuation energy, the entropy contribution must now be defined by starting from the Gibbs equation:

$$Tds = C_v dT - \frac{p}{\rho^2}d\rho = de_s - \frac{p}{\rho^2}d\rho \tag{8.153}$$

Using the continuity equation, the state equation ($p = \rho r T$) as well as Eq. (1.63) yields:

$$\frac{Ds}{Dt} = \frac{r}{p}\left(\dot{\omega}_T + \nabla \cdot (\lambda\vec{\nabla}T)\right) \tag{8.154}$$

Multiplying Eq. (8.154) by ps/rC_p and adding it to Eq. (8.151) directly gives:

$$\boxed{\rho \frac{D\vec{u}^2/2}{Dt} + \frac{1}{\rho c^2}\frac{Dp^2/2}{Dt} + \frac{p}{rC_p}\frac{Ds^2/2}{Dt} + \nabla \cdot (p\vec{u}) = \frac{s+r}{C_p}\left(\dot{\omega}_T + \nabla \cdot (\lambda\vec{\nabla}T)\right)} \tag{8.155}$$

This exact equation can be linearized. Like pressure and velocity, entropy can be split into mean (s_0) and fluctuating (s_1) components. Since $Ds_0/Dt = \vec{u}_1 \cdot \vec{\nabla}s_0$, Eq. (8.154) gives:

$$\frac{Ds_1}{Dt} \approx \frac{r}{p}\left(\dot{\omega}_T^1 + \nabla \cdot (\lambda\vec{\nabla}T_1)\right) - \vec{u}_1 \cdot \vec{\nabla}s_0 \tag{8.156}$$

and

$$\frac{P}{rC_p}\frac{Ds^2/2}{Dt} \approx \frac{P_0}{rC_p}\frac{\partial s_1^2/2}{\partial t} + \frac{1}{C_p}\left(\dot{\omega}_T^1 + \nabla\cdot(\lambda\vec{\nabla}T_1)\right) + \frac{P_0}{rC_p}s_1\vec{u}_1\cdot\vec{\nabla}s_0 \qquad (8.157)$$

Finally, the linearized form of Eq. (8.155) becomes:

$$\boxed{\frac{\partial e_{\text{tot}}}{\partial t} + \nabla\cdot(p_1\vec{u}_1) = \frac{T_1}{T_0}\left(\dot{\omega}_T^1 + \nabla\cdot(\lambda\vec{\nabla}T_1)\right) - \frac{P_0}{rC_p}s_1\vec{u}_1\cdot\vec{\nabla}s_0} \qquad (8.158)$$

where the fluctuation energy e_{tot} now integrates pressure, velocity and entropy fluctuations:

$$\boxed{e_{\text{tot}} = \rho_0\vec{u}_1^2/2 + \frac{1}{\rho_0 c_0^2}p_1^2/2 + \frac{P_0}{rC_p}s_1^2/2} \qquad (8.159)$$

Equation (8.158) was first derived by Chu [132] except for the last term in $\vec{\nabla}s_0$ which vanishes when the mean flow entropy s_0 is uniform over space. It generalizes the acoustic energy form Eq. (8.139) to the case of entropy/acoustic fluctuations and degenerates naturally to it in isentropic flows.[xviii]

Constructing instability criteria from energy equations

At this point, two energies (Table 8.9) have been defined, leading to two energy equations (Table 8.10) and to different instability criteria (Table 8.11). These criteria were obtained by setting λ to zero and stating that the source terms due to combustion must be larger than the losses. The acoustic energy leads to a stability criterion (8.139) extending the Rayleigh criterion while the fluctuation energy equation (8.159) leads to a criterion (called here the Chu criterion) which is different (Table 8.11). Interestingly, the Rayleigh criterion predicts instability when pressure and heat release fluctuations are in phase while the Chu criterion requires temperature and heat release to be in phase for the instability to grow.

Acoustic energy	$e_1 = \rho_0\vec{u}_1^2/2 + \frac{1}{\rho_0 c_0^2}p_1^2/2$
Fluctuation energy	$e_{\text{tot}} = \rho_0\vec{u}_1^2/2 + \frac{1}{\rho_0 c_0^2}p_1^2/2 + \frac{P_0}{rC_p}s_1^2/2$

Table 8.9: Definitions of the acoustic energy and of the fluctuation energy.

A simple test to choose an energy form in flames

Since using acoustic of fluctuation energies leads to different instability criteria, the next question is to determine which of these two forms is the most adequate. This can be done by

---

[xviii]Another expression for e_{tot} is: $e_{\text{tot}} = \rho_0\vec{u}_1^2/2 + \frac{c_0^2}{\gamma\rho_0}\rho_1^2/2 + \frac{\rho_0 C_v}{T_0}T_1^2/2$.

Acoustic energy	$\frac{\partial e_1}{\partial t} + \nabla \cdot (p_1 \vec{u}_1)$	$=$	$\frac{\gamma-1}{\gamma p_0} p_1 \left(\dot{\omega}_T^1 + \nabla \cdot (\lambda \vec{\nabla} T_1) \right)$
Fluctuation energy	$\frac{\partial e_{tot}}{\partial t} + \nabla \cdot (p_1 \vec{u}_1)$	$=$	$\frac{T_1}{T_0} \left(\dot{\omega}_T^1 + \nabla \cdot (\lambda \vec{\nabla} T_1) \right) - \frac{p_0}{rC_p} s_1 \vec{u}_1 \cdot \vec{\nabla} s_0$

Table 8.10: Conservation equations for the acoustic energy and of the fluctuation energy.

Classical Rayleigh criterion	$\int_V \int_0^\tau p_1 \dot{\omega}_T^1 dt dV > 0$
Extended Rayleigh criterion	$\frac{(\gamma-1)}{\gamma p_0} \int_V \int_0^\tau p_1 \dot{\omega}_T^1 dt dV > \int_A \int_0^\tau p_1 \vec{u}_1 dt dA$
Chu criterion	$\frac{1}{T_0} \int_V \int_0^\tau (T_1 \dot{\omega}_T^1 dt - \frac{p_0 T_0}{rC_p} s_1 \vec{u}_1 \cdot \vec{\nabla} s_0) dt dV > \int_A \int_0^\tau p_1 \vec{u}_1 dt dA$

Table 8.11: Summary of criteria for combustion instability. V is the volume of the combustor, A its surface and τ is the averaging time (usually a multiple of the oscillation period).

considering a domain Ω with zero fluxes on boundaries and no combustion source term. A 'good' energy, according to Chu's definition [132] should only decrease in this situation and this decrease should be caused by dissipation. For clarity, the thermal diffusivity is assumed to be constant for this exercice and the gradients of the mean entropy s_0 are neglected. Starting from the equations of Table 8.10, integrating over the whole domain and setting $\dot{\omega}_T^1$ and all boundary fluxes to zero leads to the following equations:[xix]

$$\frac{\partial}{\partial t} \int_\Omega e_1 d\Omega = -\lambda \frac{\gamma-1}{\gamma p_0} \int_\Omega \nabla p_1 \cdot \nabla T_1 d\Omega$$

$$\frac{\partial}{\partial t} \int_\Omega e_{tot} d\Omega = -\frac{\lambda}{T_0} \int_\Omega (\nabla T_1)^2 d\Omega$$

Eq. (8.160) and (8.160) provide a better understanding of Chu's definition of a proper energy: if the flow is isentropic, pressure (p_1) and temperature (T_1) fluctuations are in phase and the RHS term of Eq. (8.160) is always negative so that the acoustic energy form e_1 is a proper estimate of energy. In all other cases, however, the RHS term of Eq. (8.160) can take any sign, increasing or decreasing the energy and thereby making the acoustic energy e_1 a quantity of limited interest. On the other hand, the RHS term of Eq. (8.160) is a truly dissipative term in all flows, even if they are not isentropic. This suggests that only the fluctuating energy e_{tot} should be used in flames. This has not been done yet but this derivation shows how much work remains to go in this field beyond the Rayleigh criterion.

[xix]Diffusive terms are written as follows: $T_1 \nabla \cdot (\lambda \vec{\nabla} T_1) = \lambda \nabla \cdot (T_1 \vec{\nabla} T_1) - \lambda (\nabla T_1)^2$.

8.4 Combustion instabilities

When acoustics and combustion get strongly coupled, oscillating regimes called combustion instabilities are observed[xx]. The mechanisms leading to instability are numerous and many of them are still unknown so that there is no reliable method to predict the occurrence and the characteristics of combustion instabilities without first firing the combustor. However, some insight may be gained on the mechanisms controlling the instability by using the tools developed in the previous sections.

8.4.1 Stable versus unstable combustion

Instability criteria of Table 8.11 state that combustion instability occurs if the combustion source terms overcome acoustic losses. These criteria are all linear and strictly valid only during the linear growth phase.[xxi] Fig. 8.32 shows the typical time evolution of pressure oscillations in a combustor where an instability is triggered at $t = 0$ (for example by changing the operating parameters or by using an active control device, Poinsot et al. [522] to start the instability on demand). First, linear oscillations appear. If the growth rate factor g given by Eq. (8.147) is positive, their amplitude grows exponentially: the source term $\mathcal{R}_1$ is larger than the acoustic losses $\mathcal{F}_1$. Amplitudes do not grow indefinitely: if the combustor does not explode or quench, a limit-cycle is reached in which non-linear effects are essential. Since the amplitude of this periodic regime is constant, the growth rate g must be zero. This can be due to an increase of the acoustic losses (increased $\mathcal{F}_1$) or to a phase change between unsteady pressure and heat release (decreased $\mathcal{R}_1$). An overshoot period is often observed during which the amplitude of pulsation is larger than the limit cycle amplitude (Poinsot et al. [522]) so that g is negative until a limit cycle is reached. Therefore, using the Rayleigh (or the Chu) criterion (Table 8.11) at the limit cycle does not necessarily bring valuable information because the instability is saturated: maps of Rayleigh criterion at the limit cycle usually show that certain regions of the combustor excite the instability while others damp it (Samaniego et al. [585]) and the overall result is unclear. Finally, the Rayleigh criterion being derived in a linear framework, its application to limit cycles could also be misleading.

In conclusion, it is necessary to understand the mechanisms creating the instability and not only their manifestation through Rayleigh-type criteria. This can be achieved experimentally by studying combustion instabilities during their initial linear phase; but the most logical approach is to use theoretical and numerical approaches as described below, to derive an exact solution of the problem, and not just a part of it like the Rayleigh criterion approach.

The methodology developed in the previous section can be used to predict the stability of a flame to longitudinal modes (as demonstrated in Section 8.4.2) if the concept of transfer functions is introduced (§ 8.4.3). The method is illustrated in the case of the Rijke tube

---

[xx]A tutorial on combustion instabilities, including a video of a simple experiment, a description of the equations and direct access to an on-line acoustic solver for unstable modes in a combustor is available at *elearning.cerfacs.fr/combustion/n7masterCourses/acoustic*.

[xxi]Section 10.4 shows that linear acoustic energy equations can actually be valid during limit cycles too.

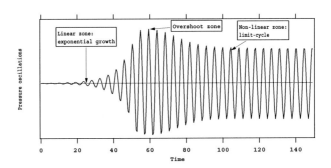

Figure 8.32: Growth of a combustion instability to limit cycle.

(Rijke [557, 558]) which is one of the simplest flame-acoustics resonators (§ 8.4.4). In this configuration, additional assumptions allow a fully analytical solution to be constructed. This simple solution highlights most of the physics of the problem and is used to emphasize the importance of the flame transfer function and the limits of n - τ models. Section 8.4.5 shows how LES can be used to compute flame transfer functions.

8.4.2 Interaction of longitudinal waves and thin flames

A classical model problem for combustion instabilities is the thin flame stabilized in a double-duct configuration (Fig. 8.33) because it allows a complete analytical solution of the stability problem under certain assumptions. It also illustrates many phenomena appearing in real devices such as mode hopping, influence of combustion delay on stability, etc.

The tools developed in Section 8.3 are sufficient to solve this problem. The first point is to recognize that all ducts connected to the combustion chamber participate in acoustic wave transmission and reflection and must be included in the analysis. The system must incorporate all elements until a proper acoustic condition can be set (a section where the impedance can be imposed with reasonable accuracy). Here this is the case as soon as the velocity perturbations u_1 are imposed to be zero at the inlet ($z = 0$) and the pressure perturbations p_1 are zero at the outlet ($z = a + b$).

Table 8.7 gathers the general methodology required for combustion instability analysis in a network of ducts. For the combustor displayed in Fig. 8.33 which contains only two duct sections (called 1 and 2), the problem is simpler and only has five unknowns: the four wave amplitudes A_1^+, A_1^-, A_2^+, A_2^- and the pulsation ω.

In this duct, a flame is stabilized at $z = a$. Section 1 is the portion of the duct upstream of the flame holder where the gases are cold and have a sound speed c_1 and a density ρ_1. Region 2 corresponds to the region downstream of the flame holder where the gases are hot and have a sound speed c_2 and a density ρ_2. Pressure is fixed at the outlet of the duct ($z = a + b$):

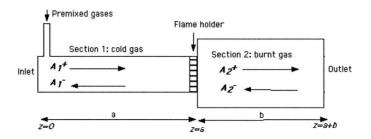

Figure 8.33: Model problem: a one-dimensional premixed combustor.

$p_1(a + b, t) = 0$ so that the reflection coefficient R_2 is -1. The upstream end of the duct is supposed to act like a rigid wall: $u_1(0, t) = 0$ so that the reflection coefficient R_1 is $+1$.

Using the notations of Table 8.7, this problem involves two sections and one interface (at $z = a$). The global matrix G_1 (equal to the transfer matrix T_1 of the unique interface) and the source term O_1 are:

$$
G_1 = T_1 = \frac{1}{2}
\begin{bmatrix}
e^{ik_1 a}(1 + \Gamma_1) & e^{-ik_1 a}(1 - \Gamma_1) \\
e^{ik_1 a}(1 - \Gamma_1) & e^{-ik_1 a}(1 + \Gamma_1)
\end{bmatrix}
\quad \text{and} \quad
O_1 = \frac{1}{2} \frac{\rho_2 c_2}{S_2}
\begin{pmatrix}
\frac{\gamma - 1}{\rho_1 c_1^2} \Omega \\
-\frac{\gamma - 1}{\rho_1 c_1^2} \Omega
\end{pmatrix}
\tag{8.160}
$$

where

$$
\Gamma_1 = (\rho_2 c_2 S_1)/(\rho_1 c_1 S_2)
\tag{8.161}
$$

System (8.160) must be solved for the wave amplitudes A_1^+, A_1^-, A_2^+, A_2^- and the pulsation ω using the additional boundary conditions:

$$
R_1 = A_1^+ / A_1^- = 1 \quad \text{and} \quad R_2 = e^{2ik_2 b} A_2^+ / A_2^- = -1
\tag{8.162}
$$

This can be done once a model for Ω, the unsteady combustion term, is chosen. Section 8.4.3 presents the most usual model for Ω, based on a time delay between acoustic perturbation at the flame holder and unsteady combustion.

8.4.3 Flame Fransfer Functions (FTF)

A model describing the response of the unsteady combustion term Ω is still needed to close the system given in Table 8.7. Determining $\Omega(A_1^+, A_1^-, A_2^+, A_2^-)$ or, in other words, the transfer function of the flame, is the crux of the problem. In general, there is no reason ensuring that Ω should depend on these amplitudes only: Ω might depend on other mechanisms in a more complex way, like local turbulence, chemical effects, or existence of coherent structures. But the assumption that a function $\Omega(A_1^+, A_1^-, A_2^+, A_2^-)$ exists, allows to build useful simple models which have been the basis of combustion instability studies since their introduction (Crocco [154, 155]).

Suppose that the oscillatory combustion is produced by perturbations of the velocity at the flame holder ($u_1(z = a, t)$) with a time delay τ. For example, when the velocity increases at the flame holder, a vortex is shed in the burnt gases and burns after a time τ. Such pictures are supported by experimental results (Smith and Zukoski [619], Poinsot et al. [521]). The simplest scaling law between $\dot{\Omega}_T^1$ and u_1 may be written for such a phenomenon:

$$\boxed{\frac{\gamma - 1}{\rho_1 c_1^2} \dot{\Omega}_T^1 = S_1 n u_1(a, t - \tau)} \qquad (8.163)$$

where n is called the interaction index and has no dimension[xxii]

If all variables are supposed to oscillate sinusoidally with time:

$$\frac{\gamma - 1}{\rho_1 c_1^2} \dot{\Omega}_T^1 = S_1 n e^{i\omega\tau} u_1(a) \qquad (8.165)$$

or, in terms of the unsteady harmonic combustion amplitude Ω:

$$\frac{\gamma - 1}{\rho_1 c_1^2} \Omega = \frac{n}{\rho_1 c_1} S_1 e^{i\omega\tau} (A_1^+ e^{ik_1 a} - A_1^- e^{-ik_1 a}) \qquad (8.166)$$

Substituting Ω in Eq. (8.160) and using the boundary condition (8.162) at the combustor inlet ($A_1^+ = A_1^-$) leads to the values of the wave amplitudes in the left duct A_2^+ and A_2^-:

$$A_2^+ = \left(\cos(k_1 a) + \Gamma_1 i \sin(k_1 a)(1 + n e^{i\omega\tau})\right) A_1^+ \qquad (8.167)$$

$$A_2^- = \left(\cos(k_1 a) - \Gamma_1 i \sin(k_1 a)(1 + n e^{i\omega\tau})\right) A_1^+ \qquad (8.168)$$

Using Eq. (8.167) and (8.168) to obtain A_2^+/A_2^- and the boundary condition (8.162) at the combustor outlet ($e^{2ik_2 b} A_2^+/A_2^- = -1$) gives an equation for the pulsation ω:

$$\boxed{\cos(k_1 a)\cos(k_2 b) - \Gamma_1 \sin(k_1 a)\sin(k_2 b)(1 + n e^{i\omega\tau}) = 0} \qquad (8.169)$$

where $k_1 = \omega/c_1$, $k_2 = \omega/c_2$ and Γ_1 is defined by Eq. 8.161.

[xxii]Equation 8.163 is the initial form of the Crocco model but many recent studies use a different interaction index N which does not require the introduction of scaling parameters like $(\gamma - 1)/\rho_1 c_1^2$ in Eq. 8.163:

$$\dot{\Omega}_T^1/\dot{\Omega}_T^0 = N u_1(a, t - \tau)/u_0(a) \qquad (8.164)$$

The N index is easier to use in practice than n but an advantage of n defined by Eq. 8.163 is that its magnitude can be determined in the low-frequency limit. In this case (ω going to zero), the flame reacts in a quasi steady fashion: all the fuel entering the flame burns and the unsteady reaction rate $\dot{\Omega}_T^1$ is simply $Q\dot{m}_F^1$ where Q is the heat of reaction and $\dot{m}_F^1$ is the unsteady fuel flow rate entering the burner. Expressing $\dot{m}_F^1$ as $S_1 \rho_1 u_1 Y_F^0$ where Y_F^0 is the fuel mass fraction in the fresh gas and substituting in Eq. 8.163 leads to the low-frequency limit value of n: $n = T_2/T_1 - 1$.

Solving Eq. (8.169) provides the real and imaginary parts of ω. If the imaginary part is positive, the solution (written as $e^{-i\omega t}$) is unstable and combustion instability is expected. The frequency of this instability is obtained from the real part of ω. In general, this resolution must be done numerically. However, it is instructive to study a simpler case using additional assumptions to understand the physics underlying this type of problem as done in Section 8.4.4.

8.4.4   Complete solution in a simplified case

A complete solution to Eq. (8.169) is obtained if specific values for the parameters are chosen. Assume: $a = b$ $c_1 = c_2 = c$ $S_1 = S_2$ $\rho_1 = \rho_2$. This configuration corresponds to a flame located in the center of a duct of length $2a$ and creating a negligible temperature jump (Fig. 8.34). In this case, $\Gamma_1 = 1$ and Eq. (8.169) reduces to:

$$\cos(2ka) - \sin^2(ka)ne^{i\omega\tau} = 0 \quad \text{or} \quad \cos(2ka) = ne^{i\omega\tau}/(2 + ne^{i\omega\tau}) \qquad (8.170)$$

or, assuming that $n << 1$:

$$\cos(2ka) = 0.5ne^{i\omega\tau} \qquad (8.171)$$

where $k = \omega/c$ is the same in fresh and burnt gas.

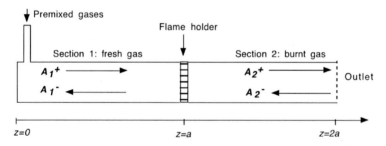

Figure 8.34: A simple Rijke tube: a flame stabilized in the middle of a duct of length $2a$.

The quarter-wave mode

Without combustion ($n = 0$), the first resonance frequency $\omega_0 = k_0 c$ is real (its imaginary part is equal to zero: $\Im(\omega_0) = 0$) and is given by:

$$\cos(2k_0 a) = 0 \quad \text{or} \quad k_0 a = \pi/4 \qquad (8.172)$$

This mode has a wavelength $\lambda = 2\pi c/\omega_0 = 8a$ which is four times the duct length and is called the quarter-wave mode. The mode structure is visualized by plotting the amplitudes of pressure and velocity fluctuations. For this simple case, the solution of the system (8.160) is:

$$A_1^+ = A_1^-; \quad A_2^+ = -iA_2^- = (1+i)A_1^+/\sqrt{2} \qquad (8.173)$$

and

$$p_1(z,t) = 2A_1^+ \cos(kz)e^{-i\omega t} \quad \text{or} \quad p_\omega(z) = 2A_1^+ \cos(kz) \qquad (8.174)$$

$$u_1(z,t) = 2iA_1^+ \sin(kz)e^{-i\omega t} = 2A_1^+ \sin(kz)e^{-i(\omega t - \frac{\pi}{2})} \quad \text{or} \quad u_\omega(z) = 2iA_1^+ \sin(kz) \quad (8.175)$$

Since the problem is linear, any amplitude A_1^+ can be used. The velocity fluctuation lags behind the pressure oscillations by $\pi/2$. It is maximum at the outlet of the burner ($z = 2a$) which is called a velocity antinode and zero at the inlet ($z = 0$) which is a velocity node. The pressure fluctuations are maximum at the burner inlet ($z = 0$) and zero at the outlet ($z = 2a$) (Fig. 8.35). In the absence of combustion, this mode is not amplified ($\Im(k_0) = 0$).

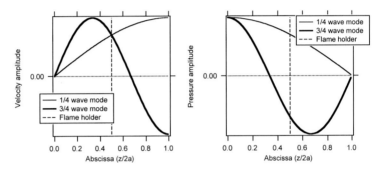

Figure 8.35: Acoustic modes in the simplified Rijke burner.

With combustion ($n > 0$), k may be expanded as $k = k_0 + k'$ using Eq. (8.171):

$$\Re(k') = -n/(4a) \; \cos(\omega_0\tau) \quad \text{and} \quad \Im(k') = -n/(4a) \; \sin(\omega_0\tau) \qquad (8.176)$$

The system is unstable (i.e. $\Im(k') > 0$) when $\sin(\omega_0\tau)$ is negative. In such cases, the acoustic oscillation at frequency k_0 which is present without combustion is amplified by the flame, leading to instability. Its frequency is slightly shifted from $\Re(k')$. The criterion for instability is therefore:

$$\sin(\omega_0\tau) < 0 \quad \text{or} \quad -\pi + 2p\pi < \omega_0\tau < 2p\pi \qquad (8.177)$$

where p is an integer. Rewriting this result as:

$$\boxed{(p - 1/2)\, T_0 < \tau < pT_0} \quad \text{with} \quad T_0 = \frac{2\pi}{\omega_0} = \frac{8a}{c} \qquad (8.178)$$

shows that a given acoustic mode becomes unstable with combustion if the time delay τ between unsteady heat release and inlet flow perturbations is more than half the acoustic mode period T_0 (modulus T_0). On the other hand, a flame with zero or small delays (less than $T_0/2$) is stable showing that minmizing combustion delays is a good strategy to control combustion instabilities.

The Rayleigh criterion derived in Section 8.3 can also be recovered from this result by evaluating the phase difference ϕ between unsteady pressure at the flame holder $p_1(z = a)$, given by Eq. (8.174), and unsteady heat release $\dot{\Omega}_T^1$, given by Eq. (8.165), where the velocity fluctuation is expressed using Eq. (8.175):

$$p_1(x = a, t) = \sqrt{2}A_1^+ e^{-i\omega t} \quad \text{and} \quad \dot{\Omega}_T^1 = \frac{\rho_1 c_1^2}{\gamma - 1} n e^{i\omega \tau} S_1 u_1(a) = \frac{\sqrt{2}A_1^+ S_1 c_1}{\gamma - 1} n e^{-i(\omega t - \omega \tau - \frac{\pi}{2})}$$

The phase difference between $p_1(x = a, t)$ and $\dot{\Omega}_T^1$ is:

$$\phi = \omega \tau + \pi/2 \tag{8.179}$$

According to the Rayleigh criterion, the instability grows if the phase ϕ between pressure and heat release ranges between $-\pi/2$ and $\pi/2$ (modulus 2π):

$$-\pi + 2p\pi < \omega\tau < 2p\pi \quad \text{or} \quad -T_0/2 + pT_0 < \tau < pT_0 \tag{8.180}$$

which is exactly the criterion obtained above. In this simple case, the Rayleigh criterion is equivalent to the complete model because combustion is concentrated in one section near the flame holder. In more complex cases, the Rayleigh criterion should be used with caution.

The three-quarter-wave mode and mode hopping

The quarter-wave mode is not the only acoustic mode of the duct. Another important mode is the three-quarter mode. Its wavenumber k_1 is given by:

$$\cos(2k_1 a) = 0 \quad \text{or} \quad k_1 a = 3\pi/4 \tag{8.181}$$

This mode has a wavelength $\lambda = 2\pi c/\omega_1 = 8a/3$. This second duct mode is called the three-quarter-wave mode (Fig. 8.35). As done for the quarter-wave mode at k_0, the corresponding oscillation frequency k may be expanded as $k = k_1 + k'$ using Eq. (8.171):

$$\Re(k') = n/(4a)\cos(\omega_1 \tau) \quad \text{and} \quad \Im(k') = n/(4a)\sin(\omega_1 \tau) \tag{8.182}$$

and instability is amplified if: $\sin(\omega_1 \tau) > 0$ or $2p\pi < \omega_1 \tau < \pi + 2p\pi$ or

$$\boxed{pT_1 < \tau < \frac{T_1}{2} + pT_1} \quad \text{with} \quad T_1 = \frac{2\pi}{\omega_1} = \frac{8a}{3c} \tag{8.183}$$

As displayed in Fig. 8.36, the stability conditions of the quarter-wave and the three quarter wave modes are:

$$\boxed{pT_0 < \tau < T_0/2 + pT_0} \quad \text{and} \quad \boxed{T_1/2 + pT_1 < \tau < T_1 + pT_1} \tag{8.184}$$

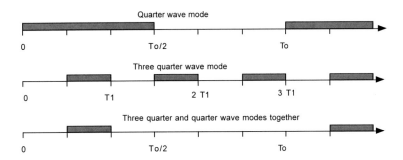

Figure 8.36: Stability domains (shaded regions) for the first two modes of the duct (quarter wave and three-quarter wave) and for their intersection: the abscissa is the time delay τ between velocity perturbations at the flame holder $u_1(a)$ and unsteady heat release $\dot{\Omega}_T^1$ (Eq. (8.163)).

Only a very small part of the τ domain provides stability for both the quarter-wave and the three-quarter wave modes. There are large overlapping zones between the instability domains of one mode and the instability domains of the other so that when one mode is stable, the other one is likely to be unstable: to stabilize the quarter-wave mode, one might try, for example, to decrease the time delay but doing so, the three-quarter wave mode may be triggered. Both modes are stable only in the region $T_0/6 < \tau < T_0/3$. But there, a higher-order (five-quarter) mode could be amplified. This phenomenon, called mode hopping, is commonly observed in combustors where frequencies vary discontinuously when operating conditions are changed: varying n and τ leads to the death of one mode but another one, at a different frequency, replaces the first one right away. Predicting which modes will be amplified requires to take into account more non-linear effects to predict dissipation for higher modes: the effects of the interaction index n must be accounted for as well as the acoustic losses inside the duct and at its ends. This leads to much more complex formulations. Although this result was obtained in a simplified case, it is typical of combustion instabilities in real devices:

- Multiple acoustic modes of the combustion chamber (including feeding lines), which have a constant acoustic energy without combustion, can be amplified with combustion. The frequencies of these modes are often shifted slightly from the frequencies of the purely acoustic modes but a simple acoustic computation of a combustion chamber [xxiii] usually predicts fairly well the unstable frequencies (Poinsot et al. [521]).

- Which acoustic mode is actually amplified by combustion is a more difficult question depending on the interaction index n, the time delay τ and the acoustic losses.

- All fluid mechanics complexities have been enclosed in the notion of a transfer function between flow and combustion, characterized by the interaction index n and the time

---

[xxiii]A tool to compute the modes of a combustor (Soundtube) containing different ducts is available at *elearning.cerfacs.fr/combustion/tools/soundtube.*

delay τ. How to obtain these quantities remains an open question. The next sections address this issue.

8.4.5   Vortices in combustion instabilities

To use the acoustic tools described above to predict combustion instabilities, obtaining information on the flame transfer function is crucial. To obtain this information, it is necessary to determine the flame response to perturbations induced by inlet conditions as postulated in Eq. (8.163). Typically, a perturbation of the inlet flow rate of the combustor induces a perturbation of the total reaction rate with an interaction index n and a time delay τ. Which mechanisms control n and τ and how to predict such mechanisms is the real difficulty of combustion instability studies. Many models (analytical or numerical) have been proposed for flame responses (Lieuwen [392]) in premixed burners[xxiv]: analytical or semi-analytical models based on thin flame approximations (Poinsot and Candel [518], Crighton et al. [153], Dowling [185], Birbaud et al. [55, 56]), numerical techniques (Barr [33], Kailasanath et al. [319], Truffin and Poinsot [656], Martin et al. [421]) or full LES techniques (Giauque et al. [233]) as described in Section 8.5.

One of the essential mechanisms controlling flame transfer functions is vortex formation and combustion after a certain delay. Vortex formation in combustion chambers has been known as one of the main sources of flame/acoustic coupling. The early studies of Reynst [553] already identify "whirls" as an essential source of combustion instabilities (Fig. 8.37). These vortices can be created by different mechanisms:

- hydrodynamic instabilities in sheared zones or

- strong acoustic waves.

Moreover, as shown by Ho and Huerre [296], hydrodynamic and acoustic modes can also get coupled and create vortices which are both hydrodynamically and acoustically excited.

If a vortex is formed in a combustor (Fig. 8.37), it can trap fresh gases which are convected and mixed with burnt products at later times. When this pocket of fresh gases burns downstream, nonsteady heat release takes place. This scenario matches the usual description of a time delay for combustion instabilities given in the previous section. The next sections discuss hydrodynamic modes and acoustic waves as vortex generators in the framework of combustion instabilities.

Note that, independently of the cause of generation (hydrodynamic or acoustic or both), an important feature of vortex formation during combustion instabilities is that they totally modify the flow structure: the flow during a combustion instability cannot be viewed as a "perturbation" around a stable state. Combustion gets organized in a different, intrinsically

---

[xxiv]For non-premixed flames, more mechanisms must be taken into account: the most important one comes from modulations of the equivalence ratio of the reactants (Lieuwen and Zinn [394], Altay et al. [7], Sheekrishna et al. [613]): pulsating the inlet flow (fuel or oxidizer feeding lines) leads to vortices as described here but also to the creation of rich and lean and pockets entering the combustor. These changes of equivalence ratio can also be the source of combustion oscillations which are not discussed here.

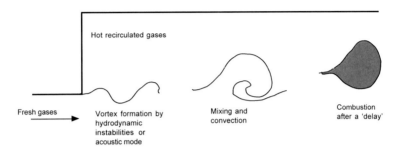

Figure 8.37: Delay introduced by the combustion of a vortex.

unsteady mode which is difficult to predict by considering only the stable flow and possible perturbations around this stable flow. This can make linear models difficult to apply with confidence for combustion instabilities since these models are essentially assuming that the perturbations around the mean flow are small, a property which is obviously not true in many combustion instability modes.

Vortices due to hydrodynamic instabilities

Vortices observed during combustion oscillations may be due to different sources. Hydrodynamic instabilities are one such possible mechanism. References in this field may be found in Drazin and Reid [186], Ho and Huerre [296], White [708]. Depending on the velocity profiles of the flow, instabilities may arise and grow, leading to the formation of large structures. The most unstable mode may have a two- but also three-dimensional structure: it controls the downstream structures (typically rollers (2D) or streamwise vortices (3D)). The frequency of these structures may be obtained from linear stability analysis if the mean profile may be assumed to be constant (parallel flow assumption) compared to the wavelength of the unstable mode. A typical result of linear stability theory for constant density flows is that the Strouhal number S_t associated to the frequency f_h of the most amplified mode is:

$$\boxed{S_t = \frac{f_h \theta}{(U_1 - U_2)} - 0.031} \tag{8.185}$$

where θ is the momentum thickness of the velocity profile (Schlichting [591], Ho and Huerre [296]) and $U_1 - U_2$ is the velocity difference between both streams. Various difficulties are encountered when linear stability analysis is used in the framework of combustion instabilities:

- Unlike acoustic eigenmodes which have discrete resonant frequencies, hydrodynamic instabilities are amplified over a wide range of frequencies. They can also shift frequency through vortex merging (Ho and Huerre [296]). This makes their identification delicate.

- The input data for hydrodynamic stability analysis is mean profiles of velocity and density. Where to extract these profiles in a combustion chamber is not necessarily obvious and influences results. If mean profiles change rapidly, the linear analysis becomes difficult as the choice of the mean profile becomes dubious. More sophisticated analyses are possible but become rapidly complex.

- Density gradients strongly affect the stability of shear flows (White [708]). This effect has been studied in high-speed compressible flows (Betchov and Criminale [48]) and to a lesser extent in reacting flows where the large density gradients through the flame front significantly change linear stability characteristics (Trouve et al. [653], Planché and Reynolds [515]). The most amplified frequency can be shifted compared to a case with the same velocity gradient but without density gradient. In practical situations, uncertainties on the mean velocity and density profiles (and on their derivatives) are so large that the result of the stability analysis can change by orders of magnitude.

- Finally, coupling between acoustic and hydrodynamic modes may occur through nonlinear mechanisms: acoustic and hydrodynamic frequencies do not have to match to create a resonance. In some cases, the coincidence of a multiple of the hydrodynamic frequency with an acoustic frequency (Rogers and Marble [565]) may be sufficient to create an instability. This is true even without combustion, for example in the case of cavity noise (Powell [540], Rossiter [568], Lucas and Rockwell [406], Ohring [479], Desvigne [176]). Such couplings can be achieved in so many ways that a priori prediction is almost impossible.

Vortices due to acoustic waves: mushrooms and ring vortices

Hydrodynamic instabilities are not the only source of vortices in a combustion chamber. By inducing large velocity variations of the inlet flow rate, acoustic waves create vortices on inlet jets by a mechanism similar to vortices formed in impulsively started flows (Keller et al. [333], Poinsot et al. [521], Buechner et al. [96]). These vortices appear only for sufficiently large oscillation amplitudes of the inlet speed i.e. for strong combustion instabilities. They have the shape of mushrooms for two-dimensional jets and of rings for circular jets.

As an example, Fig. 8.38 shows a rectangular combustion device used to study turbulent combustion (Poinsot et al. [521]). In the absence of instability, a typical turbulent reacting jet stabilized by recirculating gases is observed: the left view of Fig. 8.39 displays a Schlieren visualization of a stable regime where no large scale vortex is created. If the equivalence ratio is changed, the flame exhibits strong instabilities at various frequencies. For the most unstable regime, the right view of Fig. 8.39 shows the formation of very large mushroom vortices at 530 Hz. These vortices increase the combustion efficiency by 50 percent (the mean flame is much shorter) and decrease the lifetime of the combustion chamber by a large factor. Hydrodynamic instabilities also exist in this flame but their effect is dominated by the vortices created at 530 Hz by the large velocity excursions in the inlet section of the combustor.

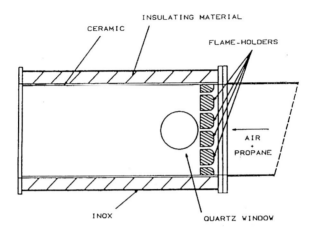

Figure 8.38: Experimental burner of Poinsot et al. [521] (Reprinted with permission by Cambridge University Press): premixed propane - air turbulent flames are stabilized in a dump combustor.

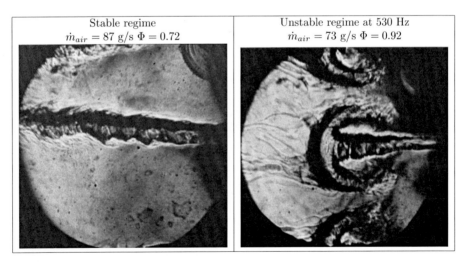

Figure 8.39: Comparison of a stable and an unstable regime in the premixed dump combustor displayed in Fig. 8.38. Schlieren views of the central jet through the quartz window of Fig. 8.38. Flow: right to left (Poinsot et al. [521]).

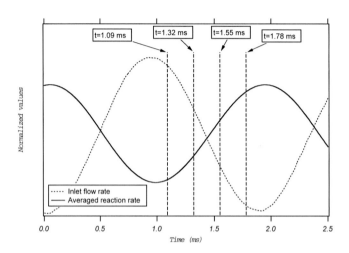

Figure 8.40: Phase average variations of inlet flow rate and integrated reaction rate, observed through the quartz window of Fig.8.38 for an unstable regime: equivalence ratio = 0.92, air flow rate = 73 g/s (Poinsot et al. [521]).

For the unstable regime presented on Fig. 8.39, the evolution of the velocity in the slots and of the phase averaged reaction rate as observed in the quartz window of Fig. 8.38 is displayed in Fig. 8.40 while Fig. 8.41 displays the Schlieren view and phase averaged fields of reaction rates (chemiluminescence of OH radical) at four instants during the cycle.

The vortex is formed at the moment of maximum acceleration in the inlet slots (just before $t = 1.09$ ms on Fig. 8.41). The vorticity created during this velocity surge wraps the flame as evidenced in Fig. 8.41 and traps fresh gases within the vortices. When these vortices interact with vortices issuing from neighboring slots, very intense turbulence is created (at $t = 1.55$ and 1.78 ms) leading to large combustion rates. These rates and the phase at which they are produced are the source of acoustic energy needed to sustain the instability.

This example illustrates the difficulty of predicting flame transfer functions (FTF) when the combustor is submitted to an intense oscillation: the mushroom vortex appears only for high levels of oscillation and the interaction between neighboring slot vortices is a key parameter of the feedback processes. These two mechanisms can not be predicted by a linear stability analysis: in the absence of combustion instability, no large-scale vortex is ever formed. The only way to solve this problem is to use LES (Large Eddy Simulation) techniques. Such methods have been used as research tools since the 1990s and are specifically discussed in Section 8.5. The fact that FTFs depend not only on the oscillation frequency but also on the amplitude of the oscillation must also be included in the acoustic models (Noiray et al. [473], Boudy et al. [76]) and makes them much more complex.

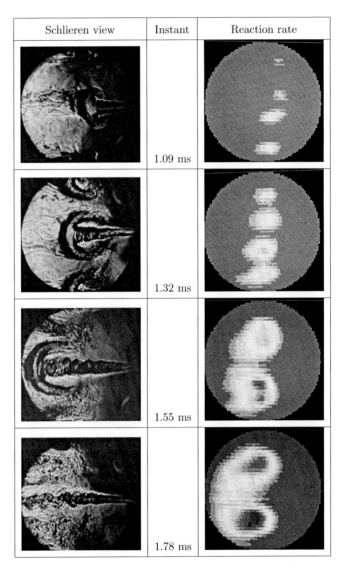

Figure 8.41: Schlieren views and phase averaged fields of reaction rates at four instants of a 530 Hz cycle (Poinsot et al. [521]) in the combustor of Fig. 8.38. Flow: right to left.

8.5   Large eddy simulations of combustion instabilities

A central difficulty to study combustion instability is that the vortices created during instabilities are usually never observed in stable regimes. It is difficult to anticipate their shape, frequency and effects before they actually appear. Improving predictive capacities for combustion instabilities requires numerical methods which can compute large-scale vortices in reacting flows: LES is one such method and is discussed in this section.

8.5.1   Introduction

The Large Eddy Simulation (LES) techniques described in Chapters 4 to 6 have become standard numerical tools to study combustion instabilities (Schmitt et al. [594], Selle et al. [603], Wolf et al. [712]) for various reasons: first, LES are intrinsically unsteady and this is mandatory to predict combustion instabilities: RANS codes are not adapted for such computations. Second, experiments show that very large scale structures (as seen on Fig. 8.41) control combustion instabilities: for these scales, LES should perform better than for "stable" turbulent combustion where an extended range of eddies has to be resolved to characterize the turbulence/chemistry interaction. Despite these advantages, many issues must be addressed before using LES for combustion instabilities:

- LES models must be available both for the flow and for the flow/chemistry interaction (see Chapters 4 to 6). In many engines, this requires handling complex fuels and complex combustion regimes (partially premixed, two-phase flow).

- The models for flow and combustion must be implemented in CFD codes able to handle complex geometries. This usually implies using unstructured or hybrid meshes (Gourdain et al. [250]) and using models (Pitsch [512]) which are not, by construction, limited to simple configurations (requiring for example averaging over certain space dimensions).

- Boundary conditions treatments in the LES code must be able to handle acoustic waves properly: the capacity to simulate various acoustic impedances at inlets and outlets is mandatory (see Chapter 9). Turbulence must also be injected at inlets (Prosser [545], Guezennec and Poinsot [256]).

- Using LES for a complete combustor (including compressor and turbine for example) will remain too expensive for a long time (Gourdain et al. [251], Moin and Apte [449], Mahesh et al. [414]). LES have to be used only for the combustion chamber and coupled to other simpler tools upstream and downstream of the chamber, typically one-dimensional codes to describe wave propagation or (U)RANS codes for turbomachinery computations (see for example recent progress at Stanford *www.stanford.edu/group/cits/about*).

This section focusses on theoretical background and general issues in this new field. Large eddy simulations have been used only since the 1990s to study these problems and even though their potential has been demonstrated, few complete studies are available to date: examples of recent progress with LES are presented in Chapter 10.

8.5.2 LES strategies to study combustion instabilities

To understand the various strategies used to study combustion instabilities with LES, the difference between flow amplificators (or convectively unstable flows) and flow resonators (or absolutely unstable) as defined by Ho and Huerre [296] must be first recalled. In flow amplificators (Fig. 8.42 left), any perturbation induced locally in the flow at time $t = t_0$ propagates downstream and is eventually washed away at later times. In a resonator, a perturbation at time $t = t_0$ propagates in all directions and is not dissipated (Fig. 8.42 right): if boundary conditions do not damp these perturbations, a mechanism for self-sustained oscillation is created. A flow system can be a resonator only if some mechanism is able to propagate information not only downstream but also upstream. This upstream propagation can be produced by acoustics (if the flow is subsonic) or by the flow itself in recirculating regions. Combustors are obviously good resonator candidates: (1) flows are subsonic and confined; acoustic waves are only weakly damped and (2) recirculating flow is used in most combustors for flame stabilization.

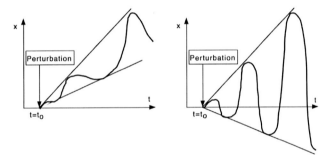

Figure 8.42: Amplificators (left) and resonators (right) response to a perturbation at time $t = t_0$ (Ho and Huerre [296]): the perturbation is convected away in an amplificator (left) but it propagates upstream and downstream in a resonator, leading to resonance (right).

The mechanisms controlling instabilities (acoustics, vortices, unsteady combustion) were beyond the capabilities of RANS codes but they can be studied using LES as shown by the fast developments of these methods since 2005. There are two main paths to use LES to predict unstable combustion in a burner:

- Forced response (amplificators): if the feedback loop leading to instability is inhibited (Fig. 8.43a), the flow becomes stable. It can then be excited in a forced controlled mode to measure its transfer function. This procedure is often called 'system identification'.

- Self-excited modes (resonators): if the feedback loop (especially acoustic waves) cannot be inhibited (Fig. 8.43b), the flow will resonate on it own. It cannot be studied as an amplificator and no external forcing can be applied because the flow is dominated by its own instability mode.

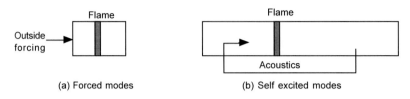

(a) Forced modes   (b) Self excited modes

Figure 8.43: Self-excited and forced strategies to compute flame instabilities.

Forced modes and system identification: Flame Transfer Functions

Relationships between unsteady heat release and inlet velocity perturbations used for Flame Transfer Functions in linear stability models (see § 8.4.3) can be established by forcing a combustor with controlled excitations and measuring the time delay between flow rate oscillations and unsteady reaction rate (Paschereit et al. [490], Noiray et al. [473]). A prerequisite condition for forcing is that a relatively "stable" baseline regime is attained upon which forcing is subsequently applied. In experiments, one method is to take flames out of the chamber and let them burn in free space, thereby suppressing most acoustic coupling modes. Computationally, this is not the way to go as "free space" computations are even more demanding in terms of specifying and implementing boundary conditions. A possible method is to use non reflecting boundary conditions (§ 9.4.2, 9.4.3 and § 9.4.4) and limit the computational domain to the minimum size (usually the combustion chamber itself) so that possible resonant frequencies are not "tuned" anymore and the combustor remains stable. Even in this case, specifying boundary conditions in a compressible simulation is a difficult task and false resonant modes can be obtained (Kaufmann et al. [326], Selle et al. [602]) even for laminar flames.[xxv]

Information obtained by forcing is a building block of acoustic models which try to predict the behavior of the combustor by decomposing it into acoustic elements as shown in Section 8.4.4. The burner itself is seen as one such part and LES is used to determine its transfer function. The actual occurrence and the characteristics of combustion oscillation modes are then determined by the acoustic code (generally a one-dimensional code as described in § 8.3).

Forced modes are rather fast to compute because the computational domain is smaller and less cycles are required to obtain the forced response. They cannot predict transverse acoustic modes because these modes are created inside the chamber itself. An example of flame response to longitudinal forcing computed by LES is given in § 10.3.4.

[xxv]Examples of the effects of inlet boundary conditions on a forced laminar flame can be found at *elearning.cerfacs.fr/combustion/illustrations/UPFILM* (inlet boundary condition leading to false numerical resonance) and *elearning.cerfacs.fr/combustion/illustrations/STABLEFILM/* (proper inlet boundary condition leading to harmonic regime). The flame is forced by acoustic waves injected at the inlet (Kaufmann et al. [326], Truffin and Poinsot [656]).

Self-excited modes: the 'brute-force' approach

A second method is to use LES to compute the entire combustor geometry as a resonator including inlets and outlets, far enough upstream and downstream to stop at places where well-defined acoustic boundary conditions can be set: the LES code should then exhibit self-excited modes (limit cycles) exactly like the experiment, providing the right frequency but also the mode amplitude. Since LES does not require assumptions on linearity, mode coupling will also be captured by LES as well as saturation effects at the limit cycle.

The advantage of self-excited computations is to be similar to experiments: they capture any mode as soon as it gets amplified. Transverse modes, for example, are naturally captured. However, self-excited modes may require long computing times due to the large computational domain: limit cycles must be computed over many periods to reach converged states. More-over, many combustors exhibit hysteresis phenomena and long transition times from stable to unstable operation. Having to wait a few minutes for a burner to reach a steady and re-producible limit-cycle in an experiment is usual. Computing the thousands of cycles required for such a transition is out of reach of present computers. The example of § 10.4 shows LES results of self-excited modes for which 50 cycles can be computed. Typical CPU ressources available since 2010 allow to compute hundreds of unstable cycles but not thousands.

Such computations also rely heavily on the precision of all sub-models and on the boundary conditions: if one boundary condition is not accurately prescribed, no limit cycle or the wrong one will be obtained. Considering the high costs of LES, this is a major drawback: in gas turbines for example, where impedances upstream and downstream of the combustion chamber are controlled by the compressor and the turbine respectively, performing self-excited LES can be hazardous because these impedances are usually unknown and complex. Moreover, these impedances may have non zero imaginary parts, implying time delays which can not be included easily in an LES because this would require keeping track of waves leaving the domain to reinject them at later times. Despite these difficulties, LES of self-excited modes in full gas turbines combustion chambers (including all sectors) have started to appear in 2010 (Staffelbach et al. [626], Fureby [222], Wolf et al. [713]).

An additional difficulty is that self-excited modes may depend on initial conditions. Some combustors are non-linearly unstable: an initial perturbation must be added to the flow to start oscillating. Determining numerically which type of initial condition is adequate for testing stability is a difficult task because of the large number of cases to investigate.

Successful computations of both self-excited (Baum and Levine [37], Kailasanath et al. [319], Selle et al. [601]) and forced modes (Poinsot et al. [527], Polifke et al. [529], Giauque et al. [233]) may be found in the literature indicating that both strategies may be valid. However, depending on the exact geometry of the burner, one technique usually proves superior over the other. Examples of self-excited modes computed with LES are given in § 10.3.5 for high-frequency modes and § 10.4 for low-frequency modes.

Chapter 9

Boundary conditions

9.1 Introduction

The formulation of boundary conditions is often seen as a small and non critical part of simulations, compared to the method used within the computation domain. Multiple recent studies, however, demonstrate that deriving adequate boundary conditions for reacting flows is a critical issue in many codes, especially for recent methods solving the unsteady Navier Stokes equations (Direct Numerical Simulations and Large Eddy Simulations). For such applications, many numerical schemes can provide high-order precision and low numerical dissipation (Lele [378], Carpenter et al. [114], Sengupta [606], Moureau et al. [456], Moin and Apte [449], Moureau et al. [458]) but their precision and their potential applications are constrained by the quality of boundary conditions which become critical elements for the simulation fidelity. DNS are often performed with periodic boundary conditions. This is the only situation where the problem can be closed exactly at the boundary: assuming periodicity, the computation domain is folded on itself and no boundary condition is actually required. Periodicity assumptions considerably limit the field of application of these simulations. Non-periodic simulations including flow inlets and outlets are needed in all practical cases. The new constraints imposed on boundary condition formulations by high-order unsteady simulations are the following:

- Unsteady simulations of compressible flows (LES or DNS) require an accurate control of wave reflections from the computational domain boundaries. This is not the case when Navier-Stokes codes are used only to compute steady states. In these situations waves are simply eliminated by numerical dissipation and no one is interested in the unsteady behavior of boundaries as long as a final steady state can be reached. As LES and DNS algorithms strive to minimize numerical viscosity, acoustic waves must be controlled by another mechanism such as better non-reflecting or absorbing boundary conditions.

- Non-dissipative high-order schemes needed for unsteady simulations propagate (in addition to acoustic waves) numerical waves (wiggles) on long distances and times (Vichnevetsky and Bowles [687], Lele [378], Sengupta [606]). These waves interact with boundary conditions and may lead to major problems. Even in cases where physical waves are not able to propagate upstream from the outlet, numerical waves may do so and interact with the flow. For example, numerical coupling mechanisms between inlet and outlet boundaries can lead to non-physical oscillations for the one-dimensional advection equation (Vichnevetsky and Bowles [687]) as well as for two-dimensional incompressible (Buell and Huerre [97]) or compressible (Poinsot and Lele [519]) flow formulations.

- Acoustic waves are strongly coupled to many mechanisms encountered in turbulent reacting flows (Chapter 8). For example, the numerical simulation of combustion instabilities requires an accurate control of the behavior of the computation boundaries. For those boundaries, usual boundary conditions (such as imposed velocity or pressure) but also acoustic conditions (such as imposed impedance or amplitude of incoming acoustic wave) must be correctly prescribed (see Chapter 10).

- A basic difficulty for boundary conditions in Navier-Stokes codes is the lack of complete theoretical background: exact boundary conditions ensuring well-posedness can be derived for Euler equations (Kreiss [358], Higdon [285, 286], Engquist and Majda [200], Gustafsson and Sundstrøm [262]), but the problem is much more complex for Navier-Stokes equations. Determining if a given set of boundary conditions applied to Navier-Stokes equations leads to a well-posed problem can only be assessed in certain simple cases (Gustafsson and Sundstrøm [262]).

- Discretization and implementation of boundary conditions require more than the knowledge of the conditions ensuring well-posedness of the original Navier-Stokes equations. "Numerical" boundary conditions (such as extrapolation of some variables) have to be added to the original set of conditions. The computational results depend not only on the original equations and the physical boundary conditions but also on the numerical scheme and on the numerical conditions used at the boundaries.

This chapter presents a method called NSCBC which is typical of many recent boundary conditions techniques developed for the compressible Navier-Stokes equations:

- It reduces to Euler boundary conditions when viscous terms vanish. It is valid both for Euler and Navier-Stokes equations. It allows a control of waves crossing boundaries.

- No extrapolation procedure is used.

- The number of boundary conditions specified for the Navier-Stokes equations corresponds to theoretical results (Strikwerda [631], Dutt [194]).

The presentation focuses on reacting flows but simplification for non-reacting flows is straightforward. It is also limited to explicit codes, but the method may be extended to implicit formulations. A first necessary step is to revisit the compressible Navier-Stokes equations in terms of usual simplifications found in combustion codes because these assumptions change the type of boundary conditions treatment (§ 9.2). Section 9.3 then describes the theory and its implementation for Euler and Navier-Stokes equations. Section 9.4 provides examples of implementation for different boundary conditions (subsonic inflow with or without turbulence injection, subsonic outflow, non-reflecting boundaries, slip wall, no-slip wall). Section 9.5 concentrates on test results for stationary non-reacting flows. Section 9.6 presents results obtained for stationary reacting flows. Section 9.7 gives examples of applications for unsteady flows and emphasizes the importance of numerical waves in unsteady flows. Finally, Section 9.8 provides examples of viscous flow computations at low Reynolds number (Poiseuille flow).

9.2 Classification of compressible Navier-Stokes equations

There are many formulations for the 'Navier-Stokes' equations: in combustion, the full equations of Chapter 1 are not systematically used and simplified sets are often preferred (as discussed for example in § 4.6.2 for DNS), so that 'solving the Navier-Stokes equations in a reacting flow' may actually designate many different sets of equations.

This chapter discusses only fully compressible formulations in which acoustics are explicitly resolved. Even in this case, additional choices must be made: they depend mainly on the state equation. If all species are supposed to have identical molecular weights ($W_k = W_1$), then the mean molecular weight W is equal to W_1 and the state equation is simply $p = \rho(R/W_1)T$. The heat capacity C_p is also assumed to be constant. This leads to a first class of codes called 'Identical-species state equation (ISSE)' here because the state equation corresponds to a gas in which all species would be identical in terms of equation of state (Table 9.1). This assumption is false but can still be used with reasonable accuracy in certain cases: for example, in flames using air as oxidizer, the local composition corresponds mainly to nitrogen so that assuming that W does not change is acceptable. Using ISSE leads to a partial decoupling of flow and combustion: only temperature changes directly affect the flow field. Mass fractions variations do not modify the density or the velocity field.

A second level of modeling (MSSE for 'multi species state equations') is to use the full equations of Chapter 1 and take into account the changes of W with the local mass fractions given by Eq. (1.5). In terms of boundary conditions this has multiple implications: the density and the sound speed change with temperature as well as with species concentrations, leading to more complex formulations near the boundaries. Finally, in ISSE or MSSE the state equation for each gas remains the perfect gas equation (1.4); for certain cases (rocket combustion for example) even the perfect gas equation assumption must be replaced by real gas formulations (RGSE for 'real gas state equations') leading to other boundary condition formulations.

For the sake of simplicity and because the basis of the method does not depend on the details of the equation of state, this presentation is limited to ISSE equations. Table 9.1 indicates where to find extensions to MSSE and RGSE. There has been numerous improvements of the initial NSCBC technique in the last twenty years (Baum et al. [40], Okong'o and Bellan [480], Sutherland and Kennedy [633], Yoo and Im [725], Prosser [545], Lodato et al. [403], Guezennec and Poinsot [256]) and they are pointed out in this chapter. The core of the method remains the same and this chapter focuses on its basic elements.

ISSE Identical-species state equation	MSSE Multi species state equation	RGSE Real gas state equation
A mixture of N 'identical' gases	A mixture of N perfect gases	One single real gas
C_p and W are constant	C_p and W depend on the Y_k and on T	N/A
This chapter Poinsot and Lele [519] Prosser [545] Thompson [648] Giles [235] Grappin et al. [252]	Baum et al. [40] Moureau et al. [456] Guezennec and Poinsot [256] Pakdee and Mahalingam [486] Yoo and Im [725]	Okong'o and Bellan [480] Schmitt et al. [595]

Table 9.1: Compressible Navier-Stokes formulations for boundary conditions.

9.3 Description of characteristic boundary conditions

An appealing technique for specifying boundary conditions for hyperbolic systems is to use relations based on the analysis of the different waves crossing the boundary. This method has been extensively studied for Euler equations (Kreiss [358], Engquist and Majda [200], Hirsch [294]) and is referred to as Euler Characteristic Boundary Conditions (ECBC). The principle of the present method is to extend the ECBC analysis to the Navier-Stokes equations and is called Navier-Stokes Characteristic Boundary Conditions (NSCBC), even if the concept of "characteristic lines" becomes questionable for Navier-Stokes equations. Section 9.3.1 presents the principles of the approach while its applications for a reacting flow are described in Section 9.3.2. A central issue in characteristic methods is the evaluation of waves crossing the boundary and Section 9.3.3 shows a simple approximation for these waves. Practical implementation is presented in Section 9.3.4 for the Euler equations and 9.3.5 for the Navier-Stokes equations. Finally, the treatment of edges and corners is discussed in Section 9.3.6.

9.3.1 Theory

The reader is referred to the papers of Kreiss [358] or Engquist and Majda [200] for a description of the mathematical background of the "Euler" boundary conditions. Different levels of complexity may be incorporated in ECBC methods. For example, some of the variables on the boundaries can be extrapolated while some others are obtained from a partial set of characteristic relations (Rudy and Strikwerda [571, 572], Nicoud [468]). However, it seems reasonable

Boundary type:	EULER Non-reacting	NAVIER STOKES Non-reacting	NAVIER STOKES Reacting
Supersonic inflow	5	5	$5 + N$
Subsonic inflow	4	5	$5 + N$
Supersonic outflow	0	4	$4 + N$
Subsonic outflow	1	4	$4 + N$

Table 9.2: Number of physical boundary conditions required for well-posedness (three-dimensional flow). N is the number of reacting species.

to avoid any kind of extrapolation and use conditions obtained by characteristic relations. The method is first described for the Euler equations (§ 9.3.4). Modifications required for the Navier-Stokes equations are given in Section 9.3.5. The following presentation focuses on explicit finite difference algorithms but can be extended to other numerical methods.

In a first step, two classes of boundary conditions must be distinguished:

- physical boundary conditions,

- soft or numerical boundary conditions.

Physical boundary conditions specify the known physical behavior of one or more of the dependent variables at the boundaries. For example, specification of the inlet longitudinal velocity on a boundary is a physical boundary condition. These conditions are independent of the numerical method used to solve the relevant equations. The number of necessary and sufficient physical boundary conditions for well-posedness should match theoretical results (Oliger and Sundstrom [481], Dutt [194], Strikwerda [631]), as summarized in Table 9.2. To build Navier-Stokes boundary conditions, the approach used in the NSCBC method is to take conditions corresponding to Euler conditions (the *ECBC conditions*) and to supply additional relations (the *"viscous" conditions*). The term "viscous" is used here to describe processes specific to Navier-Stokes, i.e. viscous dissipation, thermal diffusion and species diffusion. For example, a three-dimensional reacting viscous subsonic outflow with one species ($N = 1$) requires five "physical" boundary conditions : one of them is the ECBC relation obtained for Euler equations and it must be completed by four "viscous" conditions.

Knowing the physical boundary conditions to impose is not enough to solve the problem numerically. When the number of physical boundary conditions is lower than the number of primitive variables (this is always the case for an outflow, for example), variables which are not specified must be obtained by another method. A usual technique is to introduce "numerical" conditions. A boundary condition is called "numerical" when no explicit physical law fixes one of the dependent variables, but the numerical implementation requires to specify something about this variable. Numerical boundary conditions appear to be needed for the numerical method while not being explicitly given by the physics of the problem. In fact, the flow outside the computational domain imposes these conditions and no arbitrary numerical procedure (such as extrapolation) should be used to construct these numerical boundary conditions. Variables which are not imposed by physical boundary conditions must be computed on the boundaries by solving the same conservation equations as in the domain. For example, fixing the velocity and the temperature at the inlet of a one-dimensional duct for an inviscid flow computation comprise two "physical" boundary conditions which require a "numerical" boundary condition for the inlet pressure for subsonic flows. Extrapolation of outlet pressure from pressure values inside the domain may be used but the compatibility of these methods with the original set of physical boundary conditions is unclear: extrapolation acts as an additional physical condition, imposing a zero pressure gradient and therefore overspecifying the boundary conditions. The NSCBC method is based on a more natural technique: compute pressure on the boundary by using the equation of energy conservation on the boundary itself.

Additional difficulties are associated with numerical boundary conditions:

- Near boundaries, the accuracy of the spatial derivatives used in the conservation equations decreases. Typically, centered differences have to be replaced by one-sided differencing because grid points are available only on the interior side of the boundary.

- It is well known that one-sided derivatives lead to stable finite difference schemes when they are performed in the opposite direction of the traveling waves (upwind differencing), but also to unconditionally unstable schemes in the other case (downwind differencing). Near boundaries, waves propagating information from the outside to the inside of the computational domain must be identified and should not be computed using one-sided differencing. Failing to do so leads to downwind differencing of incoming waves and numerical instability. In other words, waves propagating outward can be computed from the internal points while waves entering the domain must be specified by boundary conditions.

9.3.2   Reacting Navier-Stokes equations near a boundary

As an example, the method is first derived using the ISSE assumptions (§ 9.2):

- H1 - All gases have the same constant heat capacity ($C_{pk} = C_p$) and γ is constant. The variations of the mean molecular weight W defined by Eq. (1.5) are neglected.

- H2 - Volume forces are neglected ($f_k = 0$) like volume heat sources ($\dot{\mathcal{Q}} = 0$).

- H3 - The Hirschfelder and Curtis approximation (1.45) is used for diffusion velocities. No correction velocity is needed because of assumption H1.

Under these assumptions, the fluid dynamics equations derived in Chapter 1 are written (with summation convention):

$$\frac{\partial \rho}{\partial t} + \frac{\partial}{\partial x_i}(\rho u_i) = 0 \qquad (9.1)$$

$$\frac{\partial(\rho E)}{\partial t} + \frac{\partial}{\partial x_i}[u_i(\rho E + p)] = -\frac{\partial}{\partial x_i}(q_i) + \frac{\partial}{\partial x_i}(u_i \tau_{ij}) + \dot{\omega}_T \tag{9.2}$$

$$\frac{\partial(\rho u_j)}{\partial t} + \frac{\partial}{\partial x_i}(\rho u_i u_j) + \frac{\partial p}{\partial x_j} = \frac{\partial \tau_{ij}}{\partial x_i} \quad \text{for} \quad i = 1, 3 \tag{9.3}$$

$$\frac{\partial(\rho Y_k)}{\partial t} + \frac{\partial}{\partial x_i}(\rho u_i Y_k) = \frac{\partial}{\partial x_i}(M_{ki}) - \dot{\omega}_k \quad \text{for} \quad k - 1, N \tag{9.4}$$

where E is the total energy (without chemical term) defined in Table 1.4:

$$E = e_s + \frac{1}{2}u_k u_k = \int_0^T C_v dT + \frac{1}{2}u_k u_k = C_v T + \frac{1}{2}u_k u_k \tag{9.5}$$

The molecular fluxes of heat (q_i) and of species (M_{ki}) in direction i are defined by:

$$q_i = -\lambda \frac{\partial T}{\partial x_i} \quad \text{and} \quad M_{ki} = \rho D_k \frac{W_k}{W}\frac{\partial X_k}{\partial x_i} = \rho D_k \frac{\partial Y_k}{\partial x_i} \tag{9.6}$$

Consider a boundary located at $x_1 = L$ (Fig. 9.1). Terms in the x_1 direction can be recast in terms of waves propagating in the x_1 direction to obtain:

$$\frac{\partial \rho}{\partial t} + d_1 + \frac{\partial}{\partial x_2}(\rho u_2) + \frac{\partial}{\partial x_3}(\rho u_3) = 0 \tag{9.7}$$

$$\frac{\partial(\rho E)}{\partial t} + \frac{1}{2}\left(\sum_{k=1}^3 u_k^2\right)d_1 + \frac{d_2}{\gamma - 1} + \rho u_1 d_3 + \rho u_2 d_4 + \rho u_3 d_5$$

$$+ \frac{\partial}{\partial x_2}[u_2(\rho e_s + p)] + \frac{\partial}{\partial x_3}[u_3(\rho e_s + p)] = \frac{\partial}{\partial x_i}\left(\lambda \frac{\partial T}{\partial x_i}\right) + \frac{\partial}{\partial x_i}(u_i \tau_{ij}) + \dot{\omega}_T \tag{9.8}$$

$$\frac{\partial(\rho u_1)}{\partial t} + u_1 d_1 + \rho d_3 + \frac{\partial}{\partial x_2}(\rho u_2 u_1) + \frac{\partial}{\partial x_3}(\rho u_3 u_1) = \frac{\partial \tau_{1j}}{\partial x_j} \tag{9.9}$$

$$\frac{\partial(\rho u_2)}{\partial t} + u_2 d_1 + \rho d_4 + \frac{\partial}{\partial x_2}(\rho u_2 u_2) + \frac{\partial}{\partial x_3}(\rho u_3 u_2) + \frac{\partial p}{\partial x_2} = \frac{\partial \tau_{2j}}{\partial x_j} \tag{9.10}$$

$$\frac{\partial(\rho u_3)}{\partial t} + u_3 d_1 + \rho d_5 + \frac{\partial}{\partial x_2}(\rho u_2 u_3) + \frac{\partial}{\partial x_3}(\rho u_3 u_3) + \frac{\partial p}{\partial x_3} = \frac{\partial \tau_{3j}}{\partial x_j} \tag{9.11}$$

$$\frac{\partial(\rho Y_k)}{\partial t} + Y_k d_1 + \rho d_{5+k} + \frac{\partial}{\partial x_2}(\rho u_2 Y_k) + \frac{\partial}{\partial x_3}(\rho u_3 Y_k) = \frac{\partial}{\partial x_j}(M_{kj}) - \dot{\omega}_k \quad \text{for} \quad k = 1, N \tag{9.12}$$

The different terms of the system of equations (9.7) to (9.12) contain derivatives normal to the x_1 boundary (d_1 to d_{5+k}), derivatives parallel to the x_1 boundary, and local viscous and reaction terms.

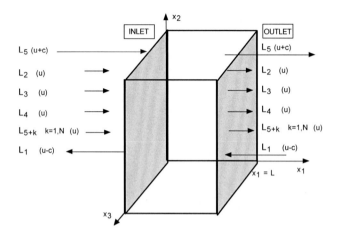

Figure 9.1: Boundary conditions located on the x_1 axis.

The vector **d** is given by characteristic analysis:[i]

$$
\mathbf{d} =
\begin{pmatrix}
d_1 \\
d_2 \\
d_3 \\
d_4 \\
d_5 \\
d_{5+k}
\end{pmatrix}
=
\begin{pmatrix}
\dfrac{1}{c^2}\left[L_2 + \dfrac{1}{2}(L_5 + L_1) \right] \\
\dfrac{1}{2}(L_5 + L_1) \\
\dfrac{1}{2\rho c}(L_5 - L_1) \\
L_3 \\
L_4 \\
L_{5+k}
\end{pmatrix}
=
\begin{pmatrix}
\dfrac{\partial(\rho u_1)}{\partial x_1} \\
\rho c^2 \dfrac{\partial u_1}{\partial x_1} + u_1 \dfrac{\partial p_1}{\partial x_1} \\
u_1 \dfrac{\partial u_1}{\partial x_1} + \dfrac{1}{\rho}\dfrac{\partial p_1}{\partial x_1} \\
u_1 \dfrac{\partial u_2}{\partial x_1} \\
u_1 \dfrac{\partial u_3}{\partial x_1} \\
u_1 \dfrac{\partial Y_k}{\partial x_1}
\end{pmatrix}
\tag{9.13}
$$

where the L_i's are the amplitudes of characteristic waves associated with each characteristic velocity λ_i:

$$
\boxed{\lambda_1 = u_1 - c \quad ; \quad \lambda_2 = \lambda_3 = \lambda_4 = \lambda_{5+k} = u_1 \quad ; \quad \lambda_5 = u_1 + c}
\tag{9.14}
$$

---

[i]The decomposition of normal terms into d_i and L_i terms is given here without demonstration. It can be recovered using a wave analysis of the Euler equations (Thompson [648]). For practical purposes, it is sufficient to accept that Eq. (9.7) to (9.12) are equivalent to the initial Navier-Stokes equations while isolating terms (d_i and L_i) which control waves.

where c is the local speed of sound given by $c^2 = \gamma p / \rho$. λ_1 and λ_5 are the velocities of sound waves moving in the negative and positive x_1 directions respectively; λ_2 is the velocity for entropy advection while λ_3 and λ_4 are the velocities at which u_2 and u_3 are advected in the x_1 direction. λ_{5+k} is the velocity at which the species k is advected in the x_1 direction ($k = 1, N$). The L_i's are given by:

$$L_1 = \lambda_1 \left(\frac{\partial p}{\partial x_1} - \rho c \frac{\partial u_1}{\partial x_1} \right) \tag{9.15}$$

$$L_2 = \lambda_2 \left(c^2 \frac{\partial \rho}{\partial x_1} - \frac{\partial p}{\partial x_1} \right) \tag{9.16}$$

$$L_3 = \lambda_3 \frac{\partial u_2}{\partial x_1} \quad \text{and} \quad L_4 = \lambda_4 \frac{\partial u_3}{\partial x_1} \tag{9.17}$$

$$L_5 = \lambda_5 \left(\frac{\partial p}{\partial x_1} + \rho c \frac{\partial u_1}{\partial x_1} \right) \tag{9.18}$$

$$L_{5+k} = \lambda_{5+k} \frac{\partial Y_k}{\partial x_1} \quad \text{for} \quad k = 1, N \tag{9.19}$$

A simple physical interpretation of the L_i's can be given by considering the linearized Navier-Stokes equations for one-dimensional inviscid acoustic waves (§ 8.2). Consider the upstream-propagating wave associated with the velocity $\lambda_1 = u_1 - c$. If p' and u' are the pressure and velocity perturbations, the wave amplitude $A_1 = p' - \rho c u'$ is conserved along the characteristic line $x + \lambda_1 t = constant$ so that:

$$\frac{\partial A_1}{\partial t} + \lambda_1 \frac{\partial A_1}{\partial x_1} = 0 \quad \text{or} \quad \frac{\partial A_1}{\partial t} + L_1 = 0.$$

At a given location, L_1 represents the opposite of the time variation of the wave amplitude A_1. By analogy, L_i is called the amplitude variation of the ith characteristic wave crossing the boundary. The principle of the NSCBC method is to advance the solution in time on the boundaries by using the system of equations (9.7) to (9.12). In this system, most quantities can be estimated using interior points and values at previous time steps: terms involving derivatives along x_2 or x_3 are obtained on the boundaries with the same approximation as in the interior since they do not require any derivatives normal to the boundary. The only quantities requiring a more careful approach are the d_i's which depend on the amplitude variations L_i. The L_i corresponding to information propagating from the inside of the domain to the outside may be calculated using one-sided differences so that the only missing information is the amplitude variations L_i of waves propagating into the domain from the outside.

At this point, two different types of problems must be distinguished: (1) those where some information is known about the outside domain so that the L_i of the incoming waves can be evaluated and (2) those where such information is not available.

- In certain problems, simplified methods may be used to describe the solution between the boundary and infinity (Fig. 9.2). For example, the self-similar solution for a boundary

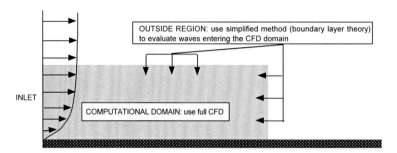

Figure 9.2: Waves propagating into the domain from the outside.

layer can provide satisfactory estimates of gradients at the upper side and at the outlet of the computation domain. The incoming L_i may be estimated from these gradients using equations (9.15) to (9.19). A precise method to impose boundary conditions for such problems is therefore to specify the amplitude variations of the incoming waves. However, such formulations for boundary conditions impose only values for derivatives and no constraint for the mean values (for example, the mean pressure). Using only these exact values for the incoming waves may lead to a drift of mean quantities (see § 9.4.4) such as pressure.

- In most cases, however, no information of this type is available and exact values of the incoming wave amplitude variations cannot be obtained. A proper approximation for the incoming wave amplitude variations has to be provided as described now.

9.3.3   The Local One Dimensional Inviscid (LODI) relations

There is no exact method to specify the values L_i of the incoming waves for multi-dimensional Navier-Stokes equations. However this can be done for one-dimensional inviscid equations. The NSCBC approach is to infer values for the wave amplitude variations in the viscous multi-dimensional case by examining a local one-dimensional inviscid (LODI) problem.

At each point on the boundary such a LODI system can be constructed from the the system of equations (9.7) to (9.12), neglecting transverse, viscous, and reaction terms. The relations obtained by this method are not "physical" conditions and are used only to specify the amplitudes of the waves crossing the boundary.

The LODI system can be cast in many different forms depending on the choice of variables. In terms of primitive variables, this LODI system is:

$$\frac{\partial \rho}{\partial t} + \frac{1}{c^2}\left[L_2 + \frac{1}{2}\left(L_5 + L_1 \right) \right] = 0 \qquad (9.20)$$

$$\frac{\partial p}{\partial t} + \frac{1}{2}\left(L_5 + L_1\right) = 0 \tag{9.21}$$

$$\frac{\partial u_1}{\partial t} + \frac{1}{2\,\rho c}\left(L_5 - L_1\right) = 0 \tag{9.22}$$

$$\frac{\partial u_2}{\partial t} + L_3 = 0 \tag{9.23}$$

$$\frac{\partial u_3}{\partial t} + L_4 = 0 \tag{9.24}$$

$$\frac{\partial Y_k}{\partial t} + L_{5+k} = 0 \tag{9.25}$$

The previous relations may be combined to express the time derivatives of all other quantities of interest. For example, the time derivatives of the temperature T, the flow rate ρu_1, the entropy s, or the stagnation enthalpy H are:

$$\frac{\partial T}{\partial t} + \frac{T}{\gamma p}\left[-L_2 + \frac{1}{2}(\gamma - 1)\left(L_5 + L_1\right)\right] = 0 \tag{9.26}$$

$$\frac{\partial \rho u_1}{\partial t} + \frac{1}{c}\left[\mathcal{M}L_2 + \frac{1}{2}\left\{(\mathcal{M} - 1)L_1 + (\mathcal{M} + 1)L_5\right\}\right] = 0 \tag{9.27}$$

$$\frac{\partial s}{\partial t} - \frac{1}{(\gamma - 1)\rho T}L_2 = 0 \tag{9.28}$$

$$\frac{\partial H}{\partial t} + \frac{1}{(\gamma - 1)\rho}\left[-L_2 + \frac{\gamma - 1}{2}\left\{(1 - \mathcal{M})L_1 + (1 + \mathcal{M})L_5\right\}\right] = 0 \tag{9.29}$$

where $H = E + p/\rho = u_1^2/2 + C_p T$, $s = C_v \ln(p/\rho^\gamma)$ and $\mathcal{M}$ is the Mach number: $\mathcal{M} = u_1/c$.

Other LODI relations may be useful when boundary conditions are imposed in terms of gradients. All gradients normal to the boundary may be expressed as functions of the L_i:

$$\frac{\partial \rho}{\partial x_1} = \frac{1}{c^2}\left[\frac{L_2}{u_1} + \frac{1}{2}\left(\frac{L_5}{u_1 + c} + \frac{L_1}{u_1 - c}\right)\right] \tag{9.30}$$

$$\frac{\partial p}{\partial x_1} = \frac{1}{2}\left(\frac{L_5}{u_1 + c} + \frac{L_1}{u_1 - c}\right) \tag{9.31}$$

$$\frac{\partial u_1}{\partial x_1} = \frac{1}{2\rho c}\left(\frac{L_5}{u_1 + c} - \frac{L_1}{u_1 - c}\right) \tag{9.32}$$

$$\frac{\partial T}{\partial x_1} = \frac{T}{\gamma p}\left[-\frac{L_2}{u_1} + \frac{1}{2}(\gamma - 1)\left(\frac{L_5}{u_1 + c} + \frac{L_1}{u_1 - c}\right)\right] \tag{9.33}$$

Most physical boundary conditions have a corresponding LODI relation. For example, imposing a constant entropy on a boundary requires setting $L_2 = 0$ to satisfy equation (9.28). Imposing a constant inlet pressure corresponds to setting $L_5 = -L_1$ (from Eq. (9.21)).

Values derived for the wave amplitude variations through LODI relations are approximate because the complete Navier-Stokes equations involve viscous and parallel terms. But boundary variables are time advanced using the system of equations (9.7) to (9.12) and viscous, parallel and reaction terms are effectively taken into account at this stage. The LODI relations are used only to estimate the incoming wave amplitude variations L_i to introduce in the system of conservation equations (9.7) to (9.12): some approximation at this level can be tolerated as long as the choice is compatible with the imposed physical conditions.[ii]

9.3.4   The NSCBC strategy for the Euler equations

The NSCBC procedure involves three steps for the Euler equations. The case of a subsonic outlet boundary where pressure is specified is used as an example in Fig. 9.3 to illustrate the method. At a given boundary:

- **Step 1.** For each ECBC physical boundary condition imposed on this boundary, eliminate the corresponding conservation equations from the system of equations (9.7) to (9.12). In the example of Fig. 9.3, the outlet pressure p is specified and there is no need to use the energy equation (9.8).

- **Step 2.** For each conservation equation eliminated in Step 1, use the corresponding LODI relation to express the unknown L_i (corresponding to incoming waves) as a function of the known L_i (corresponding to outgoing waves). For the example of Fig 9.3, Fig. 9.1 shows that the only incoming wave is L_1 and the LODI relation (9.21) suggests that:

$$\boxed{L_1 = -L_5} \tag{9.35}$$

  is a physically meaningful choice. The amplitude variation L_5 of the wave leaving the domain through the outlet (Fig. 9.1) may be computed from interior points and one-sided derivatives. The amplitude variation L_1 of the acoustic wave entering the domain through the outlet at a velocity $\lambda_1 = u_1 - c$ is not estimated using any mesh point values but given by equation (9.35).

- **Step 3.** Use the remaining conservation equations of system (9.7) to (9.12) combined with the values of the L_i obtained from step 2 to compute all variables which are not given by ECBC boundary conditions. In the case of the constant pressure outlet of Fig. 9.3, density, velocities, and reactant mass fraction are obtained through the corresponding balance equations (9.7) and (9.9) to (9.12) where Eq. (9.35) has been used to specify L_1.

Step 2 is the key part of the NSCBC method. Using the conservation equations written on the boundary as well as some reasonable information on the amplitude of incoming waves

---

[ii] Using LODI relations alone may also provide a simple but approximate method to derive boundary conditions. For example, the assumption of non-reflection for an outlet is equivalent to imposing $L_1 = 0$. Combining equations (9.21) and (9.22) to eliminate L_5, leads to the well-known relation:

$$\frac{\partial p}{\partial t} - \rho c \frac{\partial u_1}{\partial t} = 0 \tag{9.34}$$

which has been used by many authors to build non-reflecting conditions (Hedstrom [280], Rudy and Strikwerda [572]) and is the first approximation of Engquist and Majda [200].

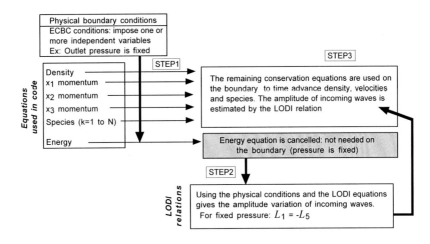

Figure 9.3: NSCBC implementation for Euler equations on a fixed pressure outlet.

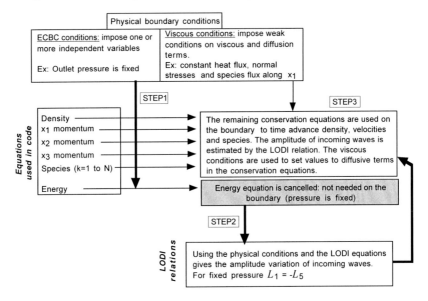

Figure 9.4: NSCBC implementation for Navier-Stokes equations on a fixed pressure outlet.

(suggested by the LODI relations) removes the ambiguity of having to choose some "numerical" conditions. Note that the time advancement of Step 3 includes parallel terms to obtain the solution at the next time step. The complete set of equations (9.7) to (9.12) with LODI relations like (9.35) would not satisfy the physical boundary conditions which were imposed. Step 1 is necessary to discard equations in the system (9.7) to (9.12) which have to be replaced by physical boundary conditions.

9.3.5   The NSCBC strategy for Navier-Stokes equations

Navier-Stokes equations require more boundary conditions than Euler equations. In the NSCBC method, complete Navier-Stokes boundary conditions are obtained by using Euler inviscid boundary conditions (ECBC conditions) and supplementing them with additional (viscous) conditions. These additional conditions must have a negligible effect when the viscosity goes to zero and their implementation is not done at the same level as the ECBC conditions. In the NSCBC procedure, viscous conditions are applied only during Step 3 by specifying viscous and diffusion terms in the conservation equations involving normal derivatives. Therefore, viscous conditions are not strictly enforced by the NSCBC approach. They are only used to modify the balance equations during Step 3. Fig. 9.4 shows the complete NSCBC procedure for a viscous subsonic outlet with specified pressure. Steps 1 and 2 are the same for Euler (Fig. 9.3) and Navier-Stokes equations (Fig. 9.4).

The choice of viscous conditions compatible with ECBC conditions has not been discussed yet. In the NSCBC method, the number and the choices of physical boundary conditions (ECBC and viscous) match theoretical results (Strikwerda [631], Oliger and Sundstrom [481]). Tables 9.3 and 9.4 summarize the physical conditions for a three-dimensional reacting flow. Table 9.3 corresponds to inlets and Table 9.4 to walls and outlets. Only subsonic flows are considered. The case of Euler equations is also displayed in the left column of each table to allow comparison with Navier-Stokes.

For inflow conditions, four possibilities are listed in Table 9.3. Imposing u_1, u_2, u_3, T and Y_k (Case SI-1) does not require more conditions for Navier-Stokes than for Euler equations (only $4 + N$, where N is the number of chemical species): the only remaining unknown is the density ρ which can be obtained through the continuity equation where no viscous term appears even for the Navier-Stokes equations. In general, $5 + N$ conditions should be necessary as suggested by Strikwerda. For example, condition SI-2 is well posed for Euler equations (Oliger and Sundstrom [481]) and an additional viscous condition is provided for Navier-Stokes equations: the normal stress is constant along the normal to the boundary (Dutt [194]). Most tests presented later in this chapter are performed with inflow conditions SI-1. Condition SI-2 gives results similar to SI-1.

Condition SI-3 is the only one for which a well-posedness proof for Navier-Stokes has been given (Oliger and Sundstrom [481]). However, a compatible numerical condition for this case is difficult to find. SI-4 is the non-reflecting inlet treatment used for the NSCBC method. For the inviscid case, it fixes relations on the wave amplitude variations. Conditions SI-3 and SI-4 are equivalent for one-dimensional cases: they both express entropy conservation and the

	Euler		Navier -Stokes with N species			
	ECBC Conditions	Total Nbr	ECBC Conditions	Viscous Conditions	Reaction Condition	Total Nbr
SI-1	u_i, T, Y_k imposed		u_i, T, Y_k imposed	No	No	
		4+N	4+N	0	0	4+N
SI-2	u_i, ρ, Y_k imposed		u_i, ρ, Y_k imposed	$\dfrac{\partial \tau_{11}}{\partial x_1} = 0$	No	
		4+N	4+N	1	0	5+N
SI-3	$u_1 - 2\frac{c}{\gamma-1}, u_2,$ u_3, s, Y_k imposed		$u_1 - 2\frac{c}{\gamma-1}, u_2,$ u_3, s, Y_k imposed	$\dfrac{\partial \tau_{11}}{\partial x_1} = 0$	No	
		4+N	4+N	1	0	5+N
SI-4	No reflected wave		No reflected wave	$\dfrac{\partial \tau_{11}}{\partial x_1} = 0$	No	
		4+N	4+N	1	0	5+N

Table 9.3: Physical boundary conditions for three-dimensional reacting flows. Subsonic inflow. The total number of species is N. The boundary is normal to the x_1 axis.

non-reflection of acoustic waves at the inlet section (this can be easily deduced from the LODI relations of Section 9.3.3). However, the principle of their implementation is quite different: SI-3 tries to enforce relations between primitive variables while SI-4 only fixes the waves amplitude variations through the boundary. For multi-dimensional flows, the implementation of SI-4 using NSCBC is straightforward but no satisfactory method could be found for SI-3.

Outflow conditions are listed in Table 9.4. Both perfectly (B2) and partially (B3) non-reflecting conditions are discussed. For the reacting Navier-Stokes equations, $3+N$ conditions have to be added to the Euler boundary conditions as suggested by Strikwerda [631]. One good choice is proposed by Dutt [194]: the tangential viscous stresses (τ_{12} and τ_{13} for a boundary at $x_1 = a$) are imposed (along x_1) as well as the normal heat flux ($q_1 = -\lambda \partial T/\partial x_1$) through the boundary. For reacting flows, the molecular diffusion fluxes of each species k through the boundary $M_{k1} = \rho D \partial Y_k/\partial x_1$ are also supposed to be constant. These conditions relax smoothly to the inviscid conditions when the viscosity and the conductivity go to zero. They are implemented numerically by setting the derivatives along x_1 of τ_{12}, τ_{13}, q_1 and M_{k1} to zero on the boundary in the system of equations (9.7) to (9.12).

		Euler		Navier-Stokes with N species			
		ECBC Condition	Total Nbr	ECBC Conditions	Viscous Conditions	Reaction Condition	Total Nbr
B2	Perfectly non reflecting outflow	No reflection		No reflection	$\frac{\partial \tau_{12}}{\partial x_1} = 0$ $\frac{\partial \tau_{13}}{\partial x_1} = 0$ $\frac{\partial q_1}{\partial x_1} = 0$	$\frac{\partial M_{k1}}{\partial x_1} = 0$	
			1	1	3	N	4+N
B3	Partially non reflecting outflow	P infinity imposed		P at infinity imposed	$\frac{\partial \tau_{12}}{\partial x_1} = 0$ $\frac{\partial \tau_{13}}{\partial x_1} = 0$ $\frac{\partial q_1}{\partial x_1} = 0$	$\frac{\partial M_{k1}}{\partial x_1} = 0$	
		1		1	3	N	4+N
B4	Subsonic reflecting outflow	P outlet imposed		P outlet imposed	$\frac{\partial \tau_{12}}{\partial x_1} = 0$ $\frac{\partial \tau_{13}}{\partial x_1} = 0$ $\frac{\partial q_1}{\partial x_1} = 0$	$\frac{\partial M_{k1}}{\partial x_1} = 0$	
		1		1	3	N	4+N
NSW	Isothermal no slip wall			$u_i = 0$ T imposed		$M_{k1} = 0$	
				4	0	N	4+N
ASW	Adiabatic slip wall			Zero normal velocity	$q_1 = 0$	$M_{k1} = 0$	
				3	1	N	4+N

Table 9.4: Physical boundary conditions for three-dimensional reacting flows: subsonic outflow and walls. The total number of species is N. The boundary is perpendicular to the x_1 axis.

9.3.6   Edges and corners

The treatment of corners in two-dimensional situations and of edges and corners in three-dimensional situations requires extensions of the NSCBC procedure. For edges, a second direction (for example x_2) has to be treated using characteristic relations. Terms of the type $\partial/\partial x_2$ on the left hand side of the system of equations (9.7) to (9.12) are replaced by characteristic wave amplitude variations estimated for the x_2 direction. A second LODI system, relative to the x_2 direction is used to infer the values of the different waves along x_2. Viscous and reaction terms are simply corrected for viscous conditions and added as for the usual boundaries. The extension to corners in three dimensions is straightforward.

The NSCBC approach for edges and corners requires compatibility conditions to be satisfied at these locations: recent work by Lodato et al. [403] show how to derive these relations. However, certain combinations of boundary conditions may simply be impossible to satisfy: for example, a no-slip wall cannot intersect an outlet section where pressure is imposed because pressure is a floating quantity on a wall. Compatibility conditions may be ignored but this leads to numerical instability. A general definition of possible combinations of boundary conditions for edges and corners remains to be given and appears to be even more difficult than the usual studies of well-posedness.

9.4   Examples of implementation

Although all recent methods developed for Euler boundary conditions emphasize the importance of characteristic lines, many differences appear in the practical implementation of the characteristic relations and the choice of numerical conditions, especially in multi-dimensional flows. The situation is even more complex for Navier-Stokes cases. It is useful to go into more details by presenting the practical implementation of the NSCBC method in the following typical situations:

- A subsonic inflow (§ 9.4.1) with fixed velocities (SI-1)

- A subsonic non-reflecting inflow with constant velocities (§ 9.4.2) (SI-4)

- A subsonic non-reflecting inflow (§ 9.4.3) with vorticity injection (SI-4)

- Non-reflecting outflows (§ 9.4.4) (B2 and B3)

- A subsonic reflecting outflow (§ 9.4.5) (B4)

- An isothermal no-slip wall (§ 9.4.6) (NSW)

- An adiabatic slip wall (§ 9.4.7) (ASW)

Notations are displayed in Fig. 9.1: section $x_1 = 0$ corresponds to the inlet and $x_1 = L$ to the outlet boundaries. Supersonic cases are not discussed here because they are usually simpler than subsonic cases. For simplicity, only one species is considered: $N = 1$.

9.4.1   A subsonic inflow with fixed velocities and temperature (SI-1)

The simplest "physical" inflow conditions correspond to a situation where all components of velocity u_1, u_2 and u_3 as well as the temperature T and the mass fraction Y_k ($k = 1$ to N) are constant (over time) and imposed at $x_1 = 0$ (Case SI-1 in Table 9.3). For a subsonic reacting three-dimensional flow, $4 + N$ characteristic waves are entering the domain (Fig. 9.1): L_2, L_3, L_4, L_5 and L_{5+k} while one of them (L_1) is leaving the domain at the speed $\lambda_1 = u_1 - c$. Therefore, the density ρ (or the pressure p) has to be determined by the flow itself. Five physical boundary conditions (for u_1, u_2, u_3, T and Y_1) and one numerical boundary condition (for ρ) are required. No viscous relation is needed. To advance the solution in time on the boundary, the amplitudes L_i of the different waves crossing the boundary must be determined. Only one of these waves (L_1) is leaving the domain and may be computed from interior points. The others are given by the NSCBC procedure, as follows:

Step 1. The inlet velocities u_1, u_2 and u_3 are fixed, therefore equations (9.9), (9.10) and (9.11) are not needed. The inlet temperature is fixed and the energy equation (9.8) is not needed any more. The reactant mass fraction Y_1 are imposed and Eq. (9.12) is also eliminated. The only remaining equation is the continuity equation (9.7). L_1 can be determined at this step.

Step 2. As the inlet velocity u_1 is fixed, LODI relation (9.22) suggests the following expression for the acoustic wave L_5 entering the domain:

$$\boxed{L_5 = L_1} \tag{9.36}$$

As the inlet temperature is fixed, LODI relation (9.26) gives an estimate of the entropy wave amplitude L_2:

$$\boxed{L_2 = \frac{1}{2}(\gamma - 1)(L_5 + L_1) = (\gamma - 1)L_1} \tag{9.37}$$

using equation (9.36). LODI relations (9.23), (9.24) and (9.25) show that:

$$\boxed{L_3 = L_4 = L_{5+k} = 0} \tag{9.38}$$

Step 3. The density ρ is obtained from Eq. (9.7):

$$\frac{\partial \rho}{\partial t} + d_1 + \frac{\partial}{\partial x_2}(\rho u_2) + \frac{\partial}{\partial x_3}(\rho u_3) = 0 \tag{9.39}$$

where d_1 is given by equation (9.13):

$$\boxed{d_1 = \frac{1}{c^2}\left[L_2 + \frac{1}{2}(L_5 + L_1)\right] = \frac{1}{c^2}\gamma L_1} \tag{9.40}$$

and L_1 has been determined at Step 1, L_2 and L_5 at step 2. Only $4 + N$ ECBC conditions and no viscous condition are used while Strikwerda [631] claims that $5 + N$ physical conditions should be necessary. The present choice however is special as the only unknown variable (ρ) is obtained by the continuity equation for both Euler and Navier-Stokes equations.

9.4.2   A subsonic non-reflecting inflow with constant velocities (SI-4)

Strictly imposing inlet velocities in a compressible computation as done in Section 9.4.1 may not be adequate if acoustic waves travel upstream and interact with the inlet section. As shown in Chapter 8, a fixed velocity section leads to a full reflection of incident acoustic waves. In an experiment, an inlet section is obviously not necessarily a velocity node for acoustic waves and a boundary condition able to maintain a "target" velocity (u^t, v^t, w^t) and a "target" temperature T^t while acting at the same time as a partially non-reflecting section is often a useful property. In this case, the inlet velocities and temperature will not be strictly equal to their target values but will remain close to them.

This can be achieved simply by setting the following waves expressions at the inlet:

$$\mathrm{L}_3 = \sigma_3(v - v^t) \quad \mathrm{L}_4 = \sigma_4(w - w^t) \quad \mathrm{L}_5 = \sigma_5(u - u^t) \quad \mathrm{L}_2 = \sigma_2(T - T^t) \qquad (9.41)$$

The relaxation parameters σ_i must be chosen to match the impedance of the inlet section. For zero or for low values of these coefficients, the inlet behaves as a perfectly non-reflecting section: acoustic waves propagating towards the inlet are not reflected but the target velocities are not maintained; as the computation goes on, drifts of inlet velocities will appear. For large σ_i parameters, the target velocities are strictly maintained but the inlet section is reflecting as discussed in Section 9.4.1. For intermediate values of the σ_i parameters, the mean values of the inlet velocities and temperature oscillate around the target values but still allow acoustic waves to propagate through the inlet with little amounts of reflection. The σ_i coefficients characterize the response of the entire system feeding the inflow and must be adapted to each case.

9.4.3   A subsonic non-reflecting inflow with vorticity injection

The issue discussed in Section 9.4.2 becomes more critical when the objective is not only to maintain the inlet speed around a fixed value but also to inject an unsteady vorticity signal in the same section. Injecting turbulence while maintaining a low level of reflection on an inlet is required in many cases: for simulations of jet noise (Bogey and Bailly [66, 67], Desvigne [176]) or of instabilities in combustors (Prière et al. [543], Schmitt et al. [594], Wolf et al. [713]), the flow entering the computational domain must contain a resolved turbulent component (generated to satisfy proper spectra and energy distribution) but simultaneously, acoustic waves propagating back to the inlet must not reflect on this boundary (Fig. 9.5): if acoustic waves generated in the combustor reflect on the inlet and interact again with the flow, the whole system can enter a state of self-sustained oscillations.

For such problems, there is a difficult trade-off between strictly imposing the unsteady inlet signal and letting acoustic waves propagate through the inlet without reflection[iii]: for example, imposing the velocity $u(x, y, z, t)$ in an inlet plane to be exactly equal at each instant to a

---

[iii]This difficulty is a specificity of fully compressible codes: in incompressible or low-Mach number formulations, the problem does not appear since acoustic waves are not computed. This is an obvious disadvantage of compressible codes and a real problem in flows which definitely require compressible solvers.

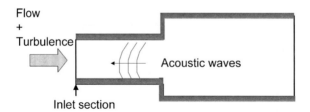

Figure 9.5: 'Non-reflecting' inlet: turbulence must be injected but acoustic waves must be able to leave the domain through the inlet with limited acoustic reflections (Guezennec and Poinsot [256]).

'target' value $U^t(x, y, z, t)$ (corresponding to the instantaneous turbulent signal to be injected) will obviously ensure that the proper inlet turbulent flow is injected at the inlet but it will also reflect acoustic waves totally since the inlet velocity will not depend on outgoing waves. On the other hand, any attempt to make the inlet section perfectly non-reflecting might lead to an inlet velocity drifting away from the target field.

Following the low-Mach number analysis of Prosser [544, 545], Guezennec and Poinsot [256] proposed a direct extension of NSCBC (called VFCBC) to inject vorticity fluctuations. If the target velocity[iv] is U^t, corresponding to a vortical flow (vortices, homogeneous isotropic turbulence...), the wave amplitudes should be imposed as follows:

$$\mathcal{L}_3 = \sigma_3(v - \bar{v}^t) \quad \mathcal{L}_4 = \sigma_4(w - \bar{w}^t) \quad \mathcal{L}_2 = \sigma_2(T - \bar{T}^t) \qquad (9.42)$$

$$\mathcal{L}_5 = \sigma_5(u - \bar{u}^t) - \rho c \frac{\partial U^t}{\partial t} \qquad (9.43)$$

where the $\bar{}$ symbol corresponds to a time average of the components of the target velocity U^t components. Note that Eq. 9.43 is not an obvious result: to inject a purely acoustic signal (associated to no vorticity), this equation should be written $\mathcal{L}_5 = -2\rho c \partial U^t/\partial t$. The reasons for this factor-of-two difference are discussed and validated through various examples by Guezennec and Poinsot [256].

9.4.4   Subsonic non-reflecting outflows (B2 and B3)

As demonstrated in Chapter 8, the existence of acoustic waves in a compressible computation where reflecting boundary conditions are used, can lead to very long convergence times. Using non-reflecting boundary conditions to allow acoustic waves to leave the domain is very appealing but requires some caution. First, building a perfectly non-reflecting condition might not lead to a well-posed problem: consider a ducted flow (Fig. 9.6) with inlet boundary conditions described in the previous section, i.e. imposed inlet velocities and temperature. For

---

[iv]The target unsteady signal U^t must be generated separately, corresponding either to vortices entering the domain or to a synthetic turbulent flow (Celik et al. [116], Kraichnan [356]).

"perfectly non-reflecting" boundary conditions on the outlet of the domain, how does the flow know what the mean pressure should be ? Physically, this information is conveyed by waves reflected through the outlet into the domain by the outside flow (where the static pressure p_∞ at infinity is specified): if the local pressure p on the outlet is different from p_∞, a reflected wave is produced to bring p closer to p_∞. With perfectly non-reflecting boundary conditions this information is not fed back into the computation: the problem might be ill-posed, leading to a drifting value of the mean pressure (Rudy and Strikwerda [571, 572], Keller and Givoli [332]). Corrections may be added to the treatment of boundary conditions to make them only partially non-reflecting and control the mean pressure level. This is the principle of the treatment proposed in the NSCBC approach (Condition B3).

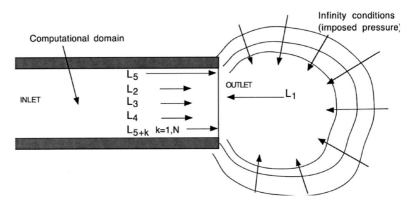

Figure 9.6: The role of infinity conditions to fix the mean pressure in a computational box.

For a subsonic outlet (Fig. 9.1), five characteristic waves, L_2, L_3, L_4, L_5 and L_6 leave the domain while only one (L_1) is entering it at the speed $\lambda_1 = u_1 - c$. Information on the mean static pressure at infinity p_∞ must be added to the boundary conditions so that the problem remains well-posed. A convenient way to achieve this is to link the amplitude variation L_1 of the incoming wave to the pressure difference $p - p_\infty$ as shown below:

Step 1. Only one physical boundary condition is imposed: the pressure at infinity is fixed. This condition does not fix any of the dependent variables on the boundary and all conservation equations must be kept in the system of equations (9.7) to (9.12).

Step 2. The amplitude of the incoming wave L_1 is fixed at:

$$\boxed{L_1 = K(p - p_\infty)} \qquad (9.44)$$

If the outlet pressure is not close to p_∞, reflected waves enter the domain through the outlet to bring the mean pressure back to a value close to p_∞. When $K = 0$, Eq. (9.44) sets the amplitude of reflected waves to 0 and is a perfectly non-reflecting condition. The form of the constant K was proposed by Rudy and Strikwerda [571]:

$$K = \sigma(1 - \mathcal{M}^2)c/L \qquad (9.45)$$

where $\mathcal{M}$ is the maximum Mach number in the flow, L is a characteristic size of the domain and σ is a constant. Small σ values lead to possible drifts of the mean pressure while large σ induce high reflection levels of the boundary. Indeed, Selle et al. [602] show that the reflection coefficient $R(\omega)$ of a boundary where Eq. (9.44) is used has a magnitude equal to $R(\omega) = 1/(1 + (2\omega/K)^2)^{1/2}$. Large σ (or K) values produce values of $R(\omega)$ close to unity and must be avoided. The final scaling proposed in Selle et al. [602] to avoid both mean pressure drifts and large reflection coefficients is $0.1 < \sigma < \pi$.[v]

Some problems are simple enough to allow the determination (through an asymptotic method for example) of an exact value L_1^{exact} of L_1. Then Eq. (9.44) should be written:

$$\boxed{\text{L}_1 = K(p - p_\infty) + \text{L}_1^{exact}} \qquad (9.46)$$

The second term ensures an accurate matching of derivatives between both sides of the boundary while the first term keeps the mean values around p_∞. In practice, Eq. (9.44) can often be used directly without an additional term. For a viscous flow (Table 9.4), constant tangential stresses τ_{12} and τ_{13}, a constant normal heat flux q_1 and a constant flux species M_{11} through the boundary $x_1 = L$ are imposed.

Step 3. All the L_i with $i \neq 1$ may be estimated from interior points. L_1 is given by Eq. (9.44) and the system of equations (9.7) to (9.12) is used to advance the solution in time on the boundary.

9.4.5   A subsonic reflecting outflow (B4)

For certain cases, enforcing a total reflection of waves at the boundary may be of interest. Imposing an ECBC condition at an outlet (constant pressure or constant velocity, for example) induces a total reflection of waves. This is done here for the case of a constant outlet static pressure (condition B4).

Step 1. As the pressure at the outlet is fixed, energy equation (9.8) is not needed.

Step 2. LODI relation (9.21) suggests that the amplitude of the reflected wave should be: $\text{L}_1 = -\text{L}_5$. According to Table 9.4, constant tangential stresses and a constant normal heat flux are also imposed. Constant species diffusion flux is imposed for reactive flow.

Step 3. All the L_i with $i \neq 1$ may be estimated from interior points. L_1 is given by $\text{L}_1 = -\text{L}_5$ and the system of equations (9.7) to (9.12) is used to obtain u_1, u_2, u_3, ρ and Y_1 on the boundary at the next time step.

---

[v]This range is consistent with other results obtained by Rudy and Strikwerda [571, 572] who derived an optimal value for σ around 0.27 to ensure well posedness but found out that $\sigma = 0.58$ provided better results in practice.

9.4.6   An isothermal no-slip wall (NSW)

At an isothermal no-slip wall (NSW), all velocity components vanish and the temperature is imposed. No relation is imposed on the stresses or on the heat fluxes. Only the reactant species flux M_{11} is set to zero.

Step 1. As velocities u_1, u_2 and u_3 are fixed, Eq. (9.9), (9.10) and (9.11) are not needed. As the temperature is imposed, the energy equation (9.8) is also discarded.

Step 2. The LODI relation (9.22) suggests that the amplitude of the reflected wave should be $L_1 = L_5$. The characteristic amplitudes L_2, L_3, L_4 and L_6 are zero because the normal velocity u_1 is zero (see Eq. (9.13) and Eq. (9.16) to (9.19)).

Step 3. Computing the value of L_5 from interior points, L_1 is obtained by $L_1 = L_5$ in the system of equations (9.7) to (9.12). The density ρ is obtained from integration of Eq. (9.7) and the reactant mass fraction Y_1 from Eq. (9.12).

Note that the implementation of a zero reactant flux M_1 on the wall during Step 3 requires a special estimate of the reactant flux derivative $\partial M_{11}/\partial x_1$ appearing in the conservation equation (9.12). For a second-order scheme, the simplest estimate of this flux, taking into account the zero value of $M_{11} \mid_{x_1=L}$ is:

$$\frac{\partial M_{11}}{\partial x_1} \mid_{x_1=L} = -\frac{1}{\Delta x_1} M_{11} \mid_{x_1=(L-\Delta x_1)} \qquad (9.47)$$

where Δx_1 is the mesh size near the boundary.

9.4.7   An adiabatic slip wall (ASW)

Adiabatic slip walls are characterized by only one ECBC condition: the normal velocity at the wall is zero. The viscous relations correspond to zero reactant diffusion flux through the wall, zero tangential stresses and a zero heat flux through the adiabatic wall. The reactant diffusion flux through the wall M_{11} is also set to zero. As the normal velocity is zero, the amplitudes L_2, L_3, L_4 and L_6 are zero (from Eq. (9.16), (9.17) and (9.19)). One wave L_5 is leaving the computation domain through the wall while a reflected wave L_1 is entering the domain (the wall is located at $x_1 = L$ on Fig. 9.1):

Step 1. The velocity u_1 normal to the wall is zero and equation (9.9) is not needed.

Step 2. The LODI relation (9.22) suggests that the amplitude of the reflected wave should be: $L_1 = L_5$.

Step 3. L_5 is computed from interior points and L_1 is set to L_5. The derivatives along x_1 of the reactant diffusion flux M_1, of the tangential viscous stresses τ_{12}, τ_{13} and of the normal heat flux q_1 at the wall are computed using the viscous conditions at the wall: $M_1 = 0$, $q_1 = 0$, $\tau_{12} = \tau_{13} = 0$ as indicated in the previous section for M_{11}. Remaining variables (ρ, u_2, u_3, T and Y_1) are obtained by integration of Eq. (9.7) to (9.12) without Eq. (9.9).

9.5   Application to steady non-reacting flows

The first example of validation corresponds to a non-reacting confined steady laminar shear
layer (Fig. 9.7b). Although all computations presented are time-dependent, steady-state solutions provide interesting test cases. For these tests, a high-order finite difference algorithm
(Lele [378]) is used (third-order accurate in time and sixth-order in space). Using a high-order
scheme for these tests is necessary to isolate the effects of boundary conditions: low-order
schemes smooth out problems introduced by boundaries and hide possible deficiencies. The
NSCBC method is used for inlets and walls in all tests.

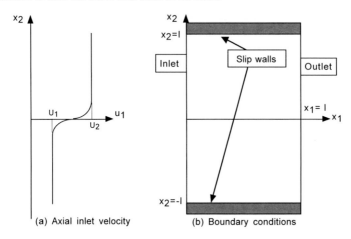

(a) Axial inlet velocity   (b) Boundary conditions

Figure 9.7: Boundary conditions for a confined shear layer.

Lateral boundaries ($x_2 = -l$ and $x_2 = l$) are adiabatic slip-walls (ASW). In the inlet
($x_1 = 0$), the temperature is constant ($T = T_{in}$), the transverse velocity u_2 is zero and the
axial velocity u_1 is imposed using a hyperbolic tangent profile (Fig. 9.7a):

$$u_1(0, x_2, t) = \frac{U_1 + U_2}{2} + \frac{U_2 - U_1}{2} \tanh\left(\frac{x_2}{2\theta}\right) \qquad (9.48)$$

where U_1 and U_2 are the far field velocities on each side of the shear layer and θ is the inlet
momentum thickness. Inlet pressure and density are obtained through the NSCBC procedure
SI-1 described in Section 9.4.1. The initial conditions consist of setting at every location x_1
of the flow the same velocity and temperature profiles as the ones chosen for the inlet section.

Four different sets of boundary conditions for the outlet section ($x_1 = l$) are tested for the
non-reacting ducted shear layer:

- B1: Condition B1 is the method proposed by Rudy and Strikwerda [571] and based
  on partial use of extrapolation (for velocities and density) and Riemann invariants (for

pressure). It is chosen here as a reference technique because multiple codes use this extrapolation approach. The pressure is obtained from the non-reflecting condition:

$$\frac{\partial p}{\partial t} - \rho c \frac{\partial u_1}{\partial t} + K(p - p_\infty) = 0 \tag{9.49}$$

where the term $K(p - p_\infty)$ is similar to the correction term introduced in the NSCBC formulation in Section 9.4.4: $K = \sigma'(1 - \mathcal{M}^2)c/L$ with $\sigma' = 0.58$. The main differences between this approach and the NSCBC method are the use of extrapolation (for velocities and densities) and the introduction of a corrective term $K(p-p_\infty)$ in the energy equation for the reference method while the NSCBC method does not use extrapolation and introduces a correction on the incoming wave amplitude L_1 (Eq. 9.44).

- B2: Condition B2 is the NSCBC formulation with $\sigma = 0$. It corresponds to perfectly non-reflecting boundary conditions (§ 9.4.4).

- B3: Formulation B3 is the corrected non-reflecting NSCBC formulation with $\sigma \neq 0$ (§ 9.4.4).

- B4: Condition B4 corresponds to a reflecting outlet maintained at a constant static pressure p_∞ with a NSCBC procedure described in Section 9.4.5.

The parameters for the computation are the following (velocities are normalized by the sound speed c and lengths by the half width of the duct L): $U_2/c = 0.9$, $U_1/c = 0.81$, $Re = U_2 L/\nu = 2000$ and $\theta/L = 0.025$.

Figures 9.8 to 9.11 display the time variations of the inlet and outlet flow rates (normalized by the initial inlet density ρ_{in}, the sound speed c and the duct half width L). A reduced time ct/L of 50 allows more than 40 travels at the mean convection speed $(U_1 + U_2)/(2c) = 0.85$ between inlet and outlet and is long enough for the flow to reach steady state.

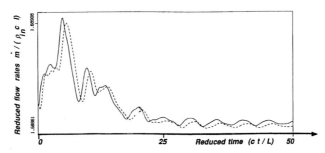

Figure 9.8: Flow rates with outlet condition B1 (extrapolation at outlet) + condition (9.49) for pressure with $\sigma' = 0.58$ (———: inlet, - - - -: outlet).

Figure 9.8 shows results obtained using boundary conditions B1. This condition allows waves to be transmitted at the outlet and works well until a reduced time of 30. If the computation is continued, no steady state is obtained. The inlet and outlet flow rates oscillate. The amplitude of these oscillations is a function of the initial condition and of the waves generated at the beginning of the computation.[vi]

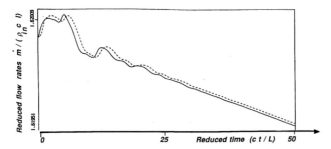

Figure 9.9: Flow rates with outlet condition B2: perfectly non-reflecting NSCBC procedure with $\sigma = 0$ (——— : inlet, - - - - : outlet).

Figure 9.9 presents the results obtained with the perfectly non-reflecting condition B2. In this case, waves are rapidly eliminated but the solution does not converge. Although the pressure and temperature fields are smooth and correspond to reasonable results, the mean pressure in the domain decreases linearly. The inlet and outlet flow rates which depend on the mean pressure decrease too and no steady state is reached. The Navier-Stokes equations with perfectly non-reflecting conditions are ill-posed in this case because nothing controls the mean pressure level in the box.

Figure 9.10 displays the results corresponding to the corrected non-reflecting condition B3 with a parameter $\sigma = 0.15$. In this case, waves are eliminated and the solution reaches steady state after a reduced time $ct/L = 25$. The mean pressure reaches a constant value and the inlet and outlet flow rates become equal. The influence of the constant σ is weak. For the present test case, $\sigma = 0.15$ was used. Values of this parameter equal to 0.08, 0.15 and 0.25 were tested: $\sigma = 0.08$ produced a drifting solution similar to the one obtained for $\sigma = 0$ (Fig. 9.9) while the two other values yielded satisfactory and almost identical results. Increasing σ beyond certain limits (here $\sigma \simeq 0.7$) leads to large flow oscillations. The optimum value of σ is close to the optimal value of σ' (Eq. 9.49) derived analytically by Rudy and Strikwerda.

Finally, the behavior of the solution for a reflecting outlet (condition B4) is illustrated in Fig. 9.11. In this case, no steady state is reached because the first longitudinal acoustic mode of the system cannot leave the domain. This mode is damped only by viscous dissipation and would still be present after a longer time. Its period t_o can be evaluated using the duct length

---

[vi]Rudy and Strikwerda did not observe these problems in their computation of a boundary layer over a flat plate but they were using a MacCormack scheme which introduces artificial dissipation and allows the code to damp the oscillations appearing on Fig. 9.8. When a non-dissipative code is used, the errors due to the extrapolation procedure at the outlet boundary are never damped.

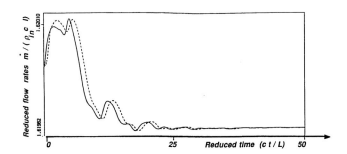

Figure 9.10: Flow rates with outlet condition B3: non-reflecting NSCBC procedure with pressure correction ($\sigma = 0.15$) (———: inlet, - - - -: outlet).

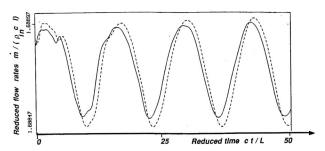

Figure 9.11: Flow rates with outlet condition B4: NSCBC procedure with imposed outlet pressure. (———: inlet, - - - -: outlet).

L and the mean Mach number $\mathcal{M} = 0.85$ by: $ct_o/L = 4/(1 - \mathcal{M}^2) \simeq 14$. Such a scenario was described in Section 8.2.12: the acoustic energy is conserved because its flux is zero on all boundaries.

Figures 9.8 to 9.11 show that the existence of a steady state solution depends on the boundary conditions used for the outlet section. Although the oscillation displayed in Fig. 9.8 for the reference method or the drift in the mean values encountered for the perfectly non reflecting NSCBC method in Fig. 9.9 are small, these effects are a clear manifestation of the inadequacy of these treatments. Furthermore, even a correct treatment of the outflow condition like condition B4 in Fig. 9.11 may not lead to a steady state if reflections are allowed on the boundary.

9.6   Application to a steady laminar flame

The second test case is a reacting steady layer (Fig. 9.12): the upper side of the layer feeds burnt hot gases and the lower side fresh premixed reactants. A premixed flame propagates towards the fresh flow at the laminar flame speed.

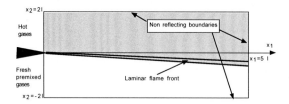

Figure 9.12: Reacting shear layer: configuration and boundary conditions.

The inlet axial velocity profile is constant (Fig. 9.13a). Transverse inlet velocities are set to zero. Temperature and reactant mass fraction profiles are shown in Fig. 9.13b and 9.13c. They correspond to a laminar flame propagating from the upper to the lower wall: combustion begins right after the inlet and the flame propagate towards the fresh gases at a constant angle.

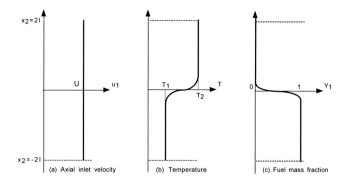

Figure 9.13: Reacting shear layer: inlet profiles.

A single one-step reaction similar to Eq. (2.37) is used to describe chemistry. The computation parameters are the following:

$$Le = 1 \quad \alpha = 0.6 \quad \beta = 8 \quad U/c_1 = 0.2 \quad R_e = Ul/\nu_1 = 230 \tag{9.50}$$

where α and β characterize the heat release and the activation energy respectively (Eq. 2.38). The preexponential factor Λ is chosen to give a laminar flame speed $s_l^0/c_1 = 0.01$. The initial field is obtained by setting the same profiles in the domain and in the inlet. At $t = 0$, the flame is sitting on the centerline of the domain and starts propagating towards the fresh gases.

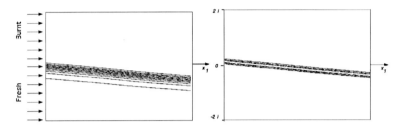

Figure 9.14: Reacting layer with outlet condition B3: temperature (left) and reaction rate (right).

At the inlet, velocities and temperature are fixed using the SI-1 technique (§ 9.4.1). For the three other frontiers (lateral and outlet), the boundary conditions B1 (the reference method) or B3 (the partially non-reflecting NSCBC method) presented in Section 9.4 are applied to set non-reflecting boundaries.

With the NSCBC procedure B3, a steady state is reached after a reduced time equal to 60 (Fig. 9.14a), corresponding roughly to three convective travel times from inlet to outlet. No numerical instability arises and the flame crosses the outlet boundary without any perturbation. The reaction rate field exhibits the same behavior (Fig. 9.14b). Finally Fig. 9.15 gives the longitudinal and transverse velocity fields. All velocities have been normalized by the inlet flow speed U_1. The flame generates its own shear because of density gradients through the flame front. The maximum longitudinal speed reaches $1.08U_1$.

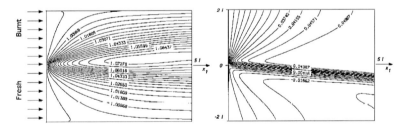

Figure 9.15: Reacting layer with outlet condition B3: longitudinal (left) and transverse (right) velocity fields.

Performing this computation with the reference method B1 leads to different results (Fig. 9.16): a steady state is also obtained but velocity profiles exhibit instabilities and strong gradients near the downstream boundary. No numerical divergence is observed because of the

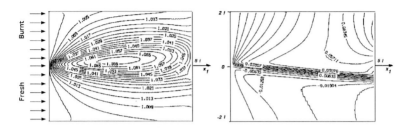

Figure 9.16: Reacting layer with outlet condition B1: longitudinal (left) and transverse (right) velocity fields.

low Reynolds number of this flow ($R_e = 230$) which induces enough dissipation to damp the numerical instability. However, the quality of the solution is poor.

9.7 Unsteady flows and numerical waves control

9.7.1 Physical and numerical waves

Numerical codes propagate waves like fluids do in the real world: acoustics, vortices, entropy spots are all 'waves' which must be captured by simulations. This section shows that numerical simulations face two difficulties to compute waves and that these difficulties are connected to boundary conditions treatments :

- Most codes do not propagate waves at the right speed, introducing 'dispersion' errors which grow rapidly when the spatial order of the scheme is low.

- Non-physical ('ghost') waves which do not exist in the real world, are created by the solver because of the space discretization. These ghost waves are especially sensitive to boundary conditions.

Let us first study the speed at which codes propagate waves by studying the case of a simple inviscid convection equation in one dimension at velocity V:

$$\frac{\partial f}{\partial t} + V \frac{\partial f}{\partial x} = 0 \qquad (9.51)$$

If the initial condition to this equation is $f(x, t = 0) = A \exp(ikx)$, the solution at all times is a convection without deformation at speed V : $f(x,t) = A \exp(ik(x - Vt))$.

If this equation is discretized on a regular grid with mesh spacing Δx, using a second-order spatial differencing scheme ($\partial f/\partial x_j = (f_{j+1} - f_{j-1})/(2\Delta x)$) and a perfect time advancement, its solution can be written analytically by expressing it as $f(x,t) = F \exp(ikx)$ where F is a function of time which must satisfy Eq. (9.51):

$$F'e^{ikx} + VF\frac{e^{ik(x+\Delta x)} - e^{ik(x-\Delta x)}}{2\Delta x} = 0 \tag{9.52}$$

which leads (after using the initial condition $f(x, t = 0) = A\exp(ikx)$) to:

$$F(t) = Ae^{-iV\frac{sin(k\Delta x)}{\Delta x}t} \quad \text{so that} \quad f(t) = Ae^{ik(x-V\frac{sin(k\Delta x)}{k\Delta x}t)} \tag{9.53}$$

Eq. (9.53) shows that the discretized solution will correspond to wave propagation (like the exact solution) but at a speed $V(k)$ which is not equal to the true convection speed V. For the second-order centered scheme considered here, $V(k)$ is not constant. It depends on the spatial wavenumber k:

$$\boxed{V(k) = V\frac{sin(k\Delta x)}{k\Delta x}} \tag{9.54}$$

so that, even though the true equation propagates all waves at speed V, the numerical solver propagates waves at speeds which depend on their wavenumber: the computed flow is 'dispersive' (while the physical problem was not). Fig. 9.17 shows the variation of $V(k)$ vs wavenumber k (left picture) and vs the number of points used to discretize one spatial period at wavenumber k: $N_{period} = 2\pi/(k\Delta x)$ (right picture). Even when 10 points are used to discretize one wave length, the error on the wave velocity is still large (10 percent). Note however that this scheme which is centered in space, introduces no dissipation: in Eq. (9.53), the amplitude A of the initial signal is conserved. The introduction of any upwinding procedure or artificial viscosity would also introduce additional dissipation, another undesired property. In LES, there are always scales (vortices usually) with wavelengths of the order of the mesh size: for these scales, significant errors on propagation must be expected when low-order spatial schemes are used.

The fact that a second-order discretization leads to a dispersive flow is a major problem for high fidelity simulations: vortices, acoustic waves, entropy waves will not propagate at the right physical speed. This classical result is one reason leading to high-order schemes which offer much better dispersion characteristics (Lele [378], Sengupta [606]).

Vichnevetsky and Bowles [687] show that the dispersive nature of the discretized equations has another implication: since all waves travel at different speeds, wave packets can also propagate and lead to non-physical ('ghost') waves, which exist only in the numerical solver. Wave packets are short wavelength oscillations (corresponding to a high wavenumber k) modulated by a long wavelength envelope (small wavenumber γ) (Fig, 9.18 left). They are often identified as "wiggles" during a computation and most CFD users try to kill them by adding viscosity (artificial or turbulent) because they can affect significantly the precision of the code. In the worst cases, they lead to complete divergence. But they can also be present and change results without clear warning to users as shown below.

A complete theoretical background on numerical waves may be found in the work of Vichnevetsky and Bowles [687] and Vichnevetsky [686]. Only the most important results are summarized here. Let us first recall the derivation of the group velocity of a wave packet [687]. Consider a wave packet solution to Eq. 9.51 consisting of a sinusoidal high-frequency content

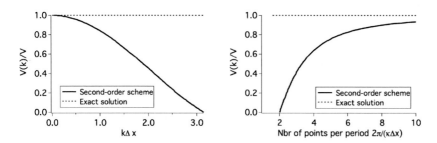

Figure 9.17: Ratio of the speed $V(k)$ at which waves propagate in a second-order solver to physical speed V for the convection equation (9.51). Left: $V(k)/V$ as a function of $k\Delta x$. Right: $V(k)/V$ as a function of the number of points used to discretize one spatial period ($N_{period} = 2\pi/(k\Delta x)$).

at wavenumber k, modulated by a low frequency envelope ϕ: $f = \phi(x,t)\exp(ikx)$ (Fig, 9.18 left). The envelope $\phi(x,t=0)$ can be expanded into Fourier series: $\phi = \sum_{\gamma} a_{\gamma}\exp(i\gamma x)$ so that the initial function is:

$$f(x,t=0) = \sum_{\gamma} a_{\gamma}e^{i(\gamma+k)x} \tag{9.55}$$

where $\gamma \ll k$. Since the propagation velocity of each sinusoidal component is given by Eq. (9.54), the numerical solution at time t can be written:

$$f(x,t) = \sum_{\gamma} a_{\gamma}e^{i(\gamma+k)(x-V(\gamma+k)t)} \tag{9.56}$$

where $V(\gamma + k)$ is given by Eq. (9.54). Since γ is small compared to k, Eq. (9.56) can be linearized to obtain a simple expression for $f(x,t)$:

$$f(x,t) = \sum_{\gamma} a_{\gamma}e^{i\gamma(x-\mathcal{V}_g t)}e^{ik(x-V(k)t)} \tag{9.57}$$

where $\mathcal{V}_g$ is the group velocity given by:

$$\boxed{\mathcal{V}_g = \frac{d}{dk}(kV(k))} \tag{9.58}$$

Eq. (9.56) shows that the numerical solution corresponds to the propagation at speed $V(k)$ of the sinusoidal function at wavenumber k and of its envelope at speed $\mathcal{V}_g$ without deformation. For a second-order scheme, $V(k)$ is simply given by Eq. (9.54) so that the group velocity is $\mathcal{V}_g = V\cos(k\Delta x)$. It is *negative* for all wave packets with $k\Delta x < \pi/2$ or equivalently with less than 4 points per wavelength (Fig. 9.18 right). In other words, all wave packets for

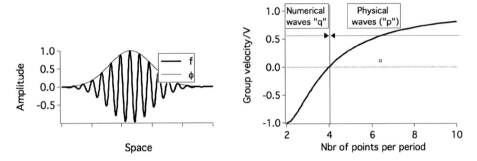

Figure 9.18: Left: a wave packet. Right: the group velocity of wave packets as a function of the number of discretization points used per period N_{period} of the high-wavenumber component for a second-order centered spatial scheme.

which the sinusoidal signal is resolved with less than 4 points per wavelength will propagate in the wrong direction. Acoustic waves will propagate at a speed equal to the sound speed but in the opposite direction compared to real well-resolved waves. Obviously, this will lead to totally erroneous results.

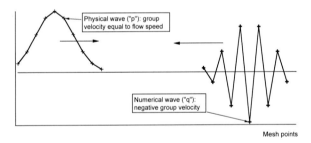

Figure 9.19: Physical and numerical waves in centered schemes.

Vichnevetsky and Bowles [687] use the change of sign of the group velocity V_g to define physical and numerical waves (Fig. 9.19):

- Physical "p" waves have a positive group velocity, long wavelengths and correspond to valid physical solutions of the Navier-Stokes equations.

- Numerical "q" waves have have a negative group velocity, short wavelengths (typically smaller than four times the mesh size). They are artefacts caused by the discretization and they propagate at high speeds, usually against the physical velocity direction because, in general, $\mathcal{V}_g/V$ becomes negative for small wavelengths.

Spatial scheme	Group velocity / physical velocity ($\mathcal{V}_g/V$)
Second-order	-1
Compact fourth-order	-3
Compact sixth-order	-13/3
Spectral	$-\infty$

Table 9.5: Group velocity of wiggles ($N_{period} = 2$ or $k\Delta x = \pi$) for typical (centered) schemes with perfect time advancement (Vichnevetsky and Bowles [687], Baum [38]).

The most negative value of $\mathcal{V}_g/V$ is reached for "saw-teeth" oscillations (also called "wiggles") which have a wavelength equal to $2\Delta x$: the right picture of Fig. 9.18 shows that a second-order central scheme leads to a minimum group velocity $\mathcal{V}_g$ given by $\mathcal{V}_g = -V$ when $N_{period} = 2$. Increasing the accuracy of the scheme increases the magnitude of $\mathcal{V}_g$ for wiggles (Table 9.5). The modulus of this group velocity may then be much higher than the advection speed V. In a one-dimensional compressible flow, "q" waves can appear on any of the three waves traveling in the fluid: the convective wave ($V = u$) or the two sound waves ($V = u \pm c$). "q" waves associated with the sound speed travel very fast (Table 9.5): with a sixth-order spatial scheme, their group velocity is $-13/3c$. Such waves can propagate upstream even in a supersonic flow.

9.7.2   Influence of boundary conditions on numerical waves

Avoiding "q" waves in simulations is the overarching problem for most developers of DNS and LES codes. Numerical "q" waves may be generated in two ways (Vichnevetsky and Bowles [687], Vichnevetsky and Pariser [688]):

- Initial conditions may contain steep gradients and therefore high frequency modes. Starting a DNS or LES computation with steep gradients leads to the formation of "q" waves which are not dissipated at later times.

- Numerical waves can also be induced by boundary conditions. Approximate boundary conditions in compressible solvers are a strong source of intense numerical waves when physical waves reach these boundaries.

Vichnevetsky and Bowles [687] or Baum [38] show how "q" waves can be generated at boundaries when "p" waves reach them and vice versa. They also compute reflection coefficients of any type of wave into another type, depending on the schemes used near the boundaries for differencing. As an example, Fig. 9.20 shows the propagation of a right traveling acoustic wave in a stagnant flow: the initial condition (Fig. 9.20a) corresponds to a purely propagating acoustic pulse for which the pressure perturbation p_1 and the velocity perturbation u_1 are linked by $p_1 = \rho c u_1$ (see § 8.2.2). A second-order scheme is used for spatial differencing for which the group velocity $\mathcal{V}_g$ of the "q" waves is exactly $\mathcal{V}_g = -V$ (Table 9.5). Here V is the sound speed because the initial condition corresponds to an acoustic pulse.

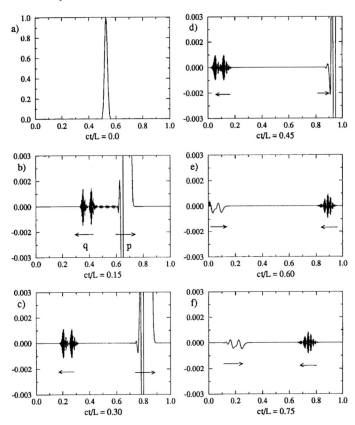

Figure 9.20: Acoustic wave propagating in a box of size L. The initial pulse (a) propagates in the right direction (Baum [38]). The y scale of pictures b) to f) is magnified by 300 to visualize wiggles.

The initial pulse is too steep for the mesh and "q" waves are generated immediately (Fig. 9.20b). These waves travel left at the group velocity (equal to $-c$) while the main acoustic wave travels right at a speed $V(k)$ close to the sound speed c (Fig. 9.20c). Both waves reach the boundaries of the computational domain ($x = 0$ and $x/L = 1$) at a reduced time $ct/L = 0.5$ and create reflected waves (Fig. 9.20e). Boundaries are supposed to be perfectly non reflecting. As predicted by theory (Vichnevetsky and Bowles [687], Baum [38]), at the domain outlet, the physical wave leaves the domain but creates a reflected "q" wave of non negligible amplitude which propagates back into the domain (Fig. 9.20f). At the inlet, the "q" wave generated by the initial condition reflects into a physical "p" wave propagating now into the domain at speed c (Fig. 9.20e). With adequate boundary conditions, the level of reflection of "p to q" and "q to p" waves may be small, but is never zero.

The existence of numerical waves in fluid computations is often hidden by the large values of artificial and turbulent viscosity used in most RANS codes which dissipate wiggles. For LES or DNS, artificial viscosity is small or zero and turbulent viscosity is reduced to minimum levels (zero in DNS). Then, numerical waves become an issue and boundary conditions have to be considered much more precisely because they play a significant role on the evolution of numerical waves.

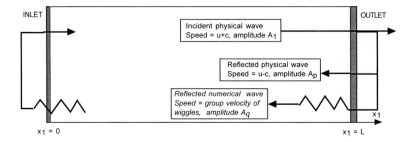

Figure 9.21: Reflection of physical and numerical waves on boundaries.

The reflection of a physical wave (picture 9.20d) on the right side of the domain into a "q" wave propagating left (picture 9.20e) and the reverse mechanism taking place on the left side of the domain (reflection of the "q" wave into a physical "p" wave propagating into the domain) may lead to an entirely numerical resonance as shown by Buell and Huerre [97] or Poinsot and Lele [519] which can exist in any flow (even supersonic because wave packets can travel faster than sound). The strength of this feedback is determined by the amplitude of the numerical wave. This amplitude is fixed by the initial conditions and the quality of the boundary condition treatment: approximate treatments of boundary conditions lead to large numerical reflected waves. Accurate LES and DNS codes must address this issue by limiting the steepness of the initial fields and improving the precision of boundary conditions.

The example of Fig. 9.20 suggests that two reflection coefficients must be used to characterize a given boundary condition treatment (Fig. 9.21): the reflection coefficient of physical waves A_p/A_1 and the reflection coefficient of numerical waves A_q/A_1 (A_1 is the amplitude of the incident physical wave). An adequate boundary condition treatment should minimize the amplitude of the numerical reflected waves in any case: $A_q/A_1 \ll 1$. An adequate *non-reflecting* boundary condition treatment should minimize both the amplitude of numerical *and* physical reflected waves: $A_q/A_1 \ll 1$ and $A_p/A_1 \ll 1$.

9.7.3 Vortex/boundary interactions

The previous section has demonstrated the need for adequate boundary conditions to avoid numerical waves. The quality of a given boundary condition may be studied by considering simple waves leaving the computation domain through an outlet boundary. The transmission of one-dimensional acoustic waves through a non-reflecting boundary is a well-known test and the NSCBC method allows complete transmission with very small levels of physical and numerical reflections: A_q/A_1 is of the order of 10^{-3} (see Fig. 9.20). This section presents a case which is more typical of unsteady flows: a vortex superimposed on a supersonic plug flow and propagating through a non-reflecting boundary (Fig. 9.22).[vii] The velocity field of the vortex is initialized at $t = 0$ using the stream function ψ for an incompressible non-viscous vortex in cylindrical coordinates (the coordinate origin is located on the vortex center):

$$\begin{pmatrix} u_1 \\ u_2 \end{pmatrix} = \begin{pmatrix} u_0 \\ 0 \end{pmatrix} + 1/\rho \begin{pmatrix} \dfrac{\partial \psi}{\partial x_2} \\ -\dfrac{\partial \psi}{\partial x_1} \end{pmatrix} \quad \text{and} \quad \psi = C \exp\left(-\frac{x_1{}^2 + x_2{}^2}{2R_c{}^2}\right) \qquad (9.59)$$

C determines the vortex strength. R_c is the vortex radius. This vortex has a central core of vorticity with the sign of C surrounded by a region of opposite vorticity. This structure is useful for numerical simulations because the total circulation is zero for $r > 2R_c$ and the influence of the vortex is limited to a small zone around it: no correction is required initially for boundary values (Rutland and Ferziger [578]).

The pressure field is initialized as:

$$p - p_\infty = \rho \frac{C^2}{R_c{}^2} \exp\left(-\frac{x_1{}^2 + x_2{}^2}{2R_c{}^2}\right) \qquad (9.60)$$

The mean flow characteristics used for this case are the following:

$$\mathcal{M} = u_0/c = 1.1, \qquad Re = u_0 l/\nu = 10000 \qquad (9.61)$$

The vortex is initially located in the center of the domain ($x_1 = 0, x_2 = 0$) and is defined by its radius R_c and its strength C:

$$R_c/l = 0.15 \qquad C/(cl) = -0.0005 \qquad (9.62)$$

Inlet and lateral boundaries are treated using the perfectly non reflecting NSCBC procedure. Two sets of boundary conditions are used for the outlet:

- B1: Reference method for non-reflecting conditions (Rudy and Strikwerda [571]).

[vii]The case of a subsonic mean flow gives similar results. The present example is chosen to show that even a supersonic flow can be submitted to this type of problem. A systematic comparison of subsonic vortex convection in periodic domains computed with various high-fidelity codes can be found at *elearning.cerfacs.fr/numerical/benchmarks/vortex2d/* .

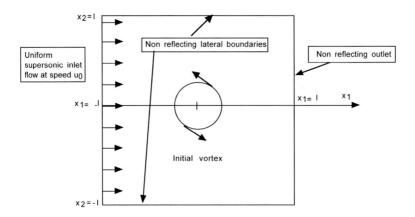

Figure 9.22: Test of outlet boundary condition: vortex convected at supersonic speed.

- B3: Non-reflecting NSCBC conditions with $\sigma = 0.15$.

Fig. 9.23 shows the vorticity and longitudinal velocity fields computed using conditions B1 and B3 at the initial time $ct/l = 0$ and at $ct/l = 1$ and 2. Dashed lines correspond to negative values of the isolines while solid lines indicate positive values. The longitudinal velocity u_1 is plotted as $(u_1 - u_0)/u_0$ so that dashed lines correspond to flow locally slower than the mean speed u_0, while solid lines reveal flow faster than u_0. In Fig. 9.23, the initial vortex is turning counterclockwise. The central core of negative vorticity is surrounded by a ring of positive vorticity. The vortex is convected downstream at the mean flow speed $u_0/c = 1.1$. The maximum speed induced initially by the vortex is $0.0018u_0$.

After a reduced time $ct/l \simeq 1$, the vortex leaves the computation domain. Condition B1 does not allow the vortex to leave the domain without creating instability. The initial structure of the vorticity field is modified: the vorticity is not continuous at the outlet. The longitudinal velocity contour also exhibits numerical instabilities ("q" waves) which are characteristic of an incompatibility between the vortical flow and the boundary conditions treatment. These numerical waves propagate upstream at the group velocity $V_g = -13/3c$ (see Table 9.5), are reflected on the upstream section and induce inlet perturbations and later the formation of a new vortex at the inlet. At $ct/l = 2$, this new structure is near the center of the computation domain and convected downstream. It is now turning clockwise and its maximum vorticity is around 0.15 times the initial maximum vorticity. Although the flow is supersonic, condition B1 creates a numerical feedback between inlet and outlet.

Fig. 9.23 also displays results obtained with the non-reflecting NSCBC procedure B3. When the vortex leaves the domain at a reduced time $ct/l = 1$, the vorticity field is preserved and the longitudinal velocity field is smooth. The amplitude of the reflected numerical waves is low and no noticeable perturbation appears on the inlet section. At later times ($ct/l = 2$), the

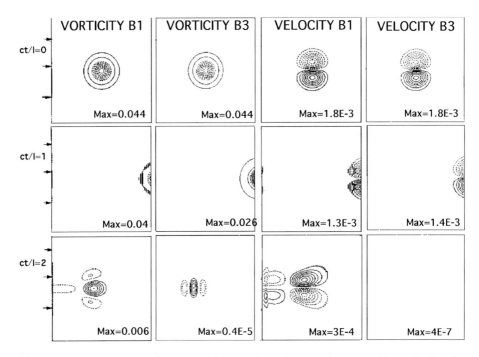

Figure 9.23: Vortex convected at supersonic speed through an outlet: computations with the reference method B1 and with non reflecting NSCBC method B3 (§ 9.5). Vorticity fields and excess axial velocity fields $(u_1 - u_0)/u_0$. Dashed lines correspond to negative values, solid lines to positive values.

original vortex has disappeared and the only perturbation generated at the inlet corresponds to a vortex with a maximum vorticity which is 10^{-4} times the initial maximum vorticity.

This test confirms the importance of the downstream boundary condition on the global result. The mechanism evidenced here is also found in incompressible codes: similar results are obtained by Vichnevetsky and Pariser [688] for the simple advection equation where no physical information can travel upstream and by Buell and Huerre [97] for an incompressible flow. This "numerical resonance" is entirely due to the boundary condition treatment. It is generally ignored in RANS codes because the high levels of turbulent and numerical viscosity present in these solvers kill wiggles rapidly. In modern DNS and LES codes which have limited dissipation, it must be carefully monitored.

9.8   Application to low Reynolds number flows

The last example (Poiseuille flow) is a low Reynolds number flow with isothermal no-slip walls (Fig. 9.24). The geometry corresponds to a two-dimensional domain of half-width l and length $L/l = 10$. The inflow conditions are:

$$u_1(0, x_2, t) = u_0 \left[\cos \left(\frac{\pi}{2} \frac{x_2}{l} \right) \right]^2 ; \quad u_2(0, x_2, t) = 0; \quad T(0, x_2, t) = T_0 \quad (9.63)$$

where u_0 is the inlet maximum speed. The Reynolds number is $Re = u_0 l / \nu = 15$. The Mach number is $u_0/c = 0.1$. The total volumetric inlet flow rate $\dot{m}_{in}$ is imposed: $\dot{m}_{in} = u_0 l$. The lateral boundary conditions ($x_2 = \pm l$) correspond to constant temperature (T_0) no-slip walls. Non-reflecting boundary conditions are imposed at the duct outlet ($x_1 = L$).

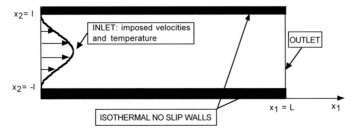

Figure 9.24: Poiseuille flow configuration.

Inlet conditions (9.63) impose the total volumetric flow rate $\dot{m}_{in}$. If density remains approximately constant along the duct ($\rho \simeq \rho_0$), an analytic form of the solution similar to the incompressible solution derived by Schlichting [591] is found.[viii] The pressure gradient along the duct is:

$$\frac{\partial p}{\partial x_1}^{exact} = -\frac{3}{2} \mu \frac{\dot{m}_{in}}{l^3} = -1.5 Re^{-1} \frac{\rho_0 u_o^2}{l} \quad (9.64)$$

The exact velocity field is independent of x_1 and t and given by:

$$u_1(x_1, x_2, t) = -\frac{1}{2\mu} \frac{\partial p}{\partial x_1}^{exact} (l^2 - x_2^2) \quad \text{or} \quad u_1(x_1, x_2, t) = \frac{3}{4} \frac{\dot{m}_{in}}{l} (1 - \frac{x_2^2}{l^2}) \quad (9.65)$$

The exact temperature field can also be obtained by integrating the energy equation (1.67) where x_1 gradients are neglected except for pressure:

$$T(x_1, x_2, t) = T_0 - \frac{\mu u_m^2}{\lambda} \left[\frac{1}{2} + \frac{1}{2} \left(\frac{x_2}{l} \right)^4 - \left(\frac{x_2}{l} \right)^2 \right] \quad (9.66)$$

[viii]This solution is valid if the total pressure loss between the duct inlet and outlet is small compared to the mean pressure, i.e. if: $L/l \ Re^{-1} \mathcal{M}^2 \ll 1$. This parameter is 0.007 for this computation and the incompressible solution can be considered as an exact solution.

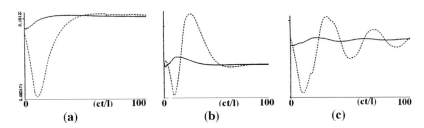

Figure 9.25: Time evolutions of inlet (——) and outlet (----) flow rates (normalized by ρcl) for a Poiseuille flow computation with three outlet boundary conditions: (a) outlet condition B1, (b) non reflecting NSCBC B3 and (c) fixed outlet pressure NSCBC method B4.

where u_m is the maximum velocity on the axis:

$$u_m = -\frac{l^2}{2\mu}\frac{\partial p}{\partial x_1}^{exact} = \frac{3}{4}\frac{\dot{m}_{in}}{l} \tag{9.67}$$

Note that the temperature in the tube is lower than the wall temperature because pressure decreases with x_1. This result is different from the one derived by Schlichting [591] (page 84) who neglected pressure variations in the energy equation.

The computation was performed using three conditions for the outlet:

- the reference method B1 of Rudy and Strikwerda,

- the non-reflecting NSCBC formulation B3 with $\sigma = 0.15$ (§ 9.4.4),

- the formulation B4 with a constant outlet pressure p_∞ (§ 9.4.5).

In all cases the isothermal no-slip walls were computed using the NSCBC procedure NSW described in Section 9.4.7. For the Poiseuille flow, an exact value may be found from Eq. (9.15) for the incoming wave at the outlet:

$$L_1^{exact} = \lambda_1 \frac{\partial p}{\partial x_1}^{exact} \tag{9.68}$$

This value was used for the NSCBC method B3 as indicated in Section 9.4.4.

All methods converge to steady state. Fig. 9.25 gives the time variations of the inlet and outlet flow rates for the outlet condition B1 (Fig. 9.25a), the non-reflecting NSCBC condition B3 (Fig. 9.25b) and the reflecting NSCBC condition B4 (Fig. 9.25c). Since the flow is very viscous, the acoustic modes generated by a downstream reflecting end B4 are damped rapidly and Fig. 9.25c shows that a steady state is reached with formulation B4 after a reduced time of 160.

Fig. 9.26 displays steady state fields for the reference method while results obtained with the NSCBC methods B3 and B4 are presented on Fig. 9.28 (left and right respectively). The x_2 coordinate has been dilated by a factor of three. The plotted fields are:

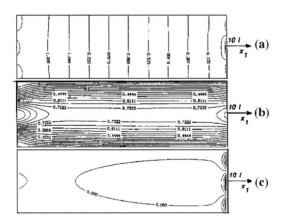

Figure 9.26: Steady state pressure (a), velocity (b) and temperature (c) for the Poiseuille flow with outlet condition B1.

- (a) the pressure difference $(100(p - p_\infty)/p_\infty)$,

- (b) the longitudinal velocity (u_1/u_0) and

- (c) the temperature difference between the inlet section (T_0) and a given point in the flow $(100(T - T_0)/T_0)$.

The comparison between the exact velocity and temperature profiles (Eq. (9.65) and (9.66)) and the computed values is given in Fig. 9.27 for the NSCBC method B3. The agreement is quite good although the duct seems slightly too short to reach the thermally established regime. The outlet condition B1 does not correctly handle the outlet conditions (Fig. 9.26): strong pressure and temperature gradients are produced near the outflow and the velocity profile is incorrect (Fig. 9.26b).

The non-reflecting NSCBC method B3 provides accurate results (left picture on Fig. 9.28a): the pressure gradient is constant in most of the duct. This gradient is $0.998(\partial p^{exact}/\partial x_1)$. No boundary layer behavior is observed in the longitudinal velocity profiles (Fig. 9.28b, left) or in the temperature field (Fig. 9.28c,left). Note that the outlet pressure is not exactly equal to p_∞: a small reflected wave is entering the domain through this section.

The reflecting formulation B4 also gives accurate results. There is no drift of the mean values after the acoustic waves are damped and the velocity profiles are correct (right picture in Fig. 9.28b). However a small perturbation in the temperature profiles near the outlet is observed (Fig. 9.28c right). This behavior might be due to the corner treatment as indicated in Section 9.3.6 for which this configuration creates compatibility problems.

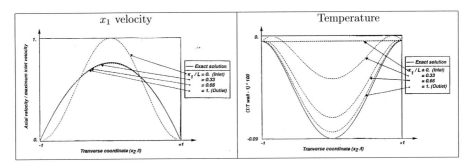

Figure 9.27: Poiseuille flow: comparison between numerical results using method B3 NSCBC formulation and the analytical solution.

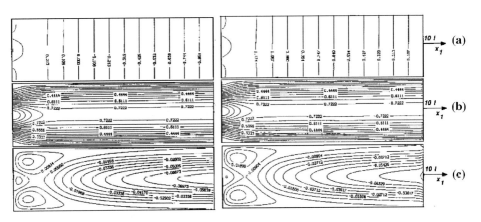

Figure 9.28: Steady state pressure (a), velocity (b) and temperature (c) fields. Left : the Poiseuille flow with outlet NSCBC condition B3 ($\sigma = 0.15$). Right: with outlet NSCBC condition B4.

Chapter 10

Examples of LES applications

10.1 Introduction

All previous chapters have discussed methods and issues linked to simulations of combustors. To illustrate how these techniques are used in practice, this chapter presents examples of applications to complex geometry combustors. For each case, the presentation shows how the tools described in the previous chapters (Large Eddy Simulation techniques, acoustic analysis, etc.) can be used together with experiments in real combustors.[i]

The examples which follow (Lartigue [365], Selle [600], Selle et al. [601], Martin et al. [420]) gather the specificities of most modern high-power combustion chambers, especially of gas turbines: the flame is stabilized by strongly swirled flows (see § 6.2), the Reynolds numbers are large, the flow field sensitivity to boundary conditions is high, intense acoustic/combustion coupling can lead to self-sustained oscillations (see § 8.5.2).

Swirl is a new and essential additional phenomenon in these examples: as discussed in Chapter 6, it is required to stabilize combustion in high-speed burners. It also creates specific flow patterns (a Central Toroidal Recirculation Zone called CTRZ) and instabilities (the Precessing Vortex Core called PVC)[ii].

Table 10.1 summarizes the chapter organization and the objectives of each section. Three swirled configurations will be described. The first one is a small-scale laboratory combustor using an aeroengine gas turbine burner (power: 30 kW) while the second one corresponds to a larger chamber (power : 500 kW) equipped with an industrial gas turbine burner. The last one is a laboratory-scale staged burner in which self-excited instabilities can be easily triggered by changing the outlet acoustic boundary conditions. In staged combustors, fuel and air are premixed but they are introduced into the chamber at different locations and

---

[i]RANS (Reynolds Averaged Navier Stokes) techniques presented in Chapter 4 will not be discussed here because they are now standard tools in most commercial codes.

[ii]See examples of swirled flows and PVC unstable modes in reacting flows at *www.cerfacs.fr/cfd/Gallery/movies/ev7_cool.mov* or *PVC_film_new.mov*. See also a simple non reacting swirling example in a dump geometry at *www.cerfacs.fr/cfd/Gallery/movies/expansion_swirl_flow.mpg*

different equivalence ratios so that partially premixed flames are found inside the burner. All combustors are operated at atmospheric pressure.

These case studies illustrate various phenomena discussed in the other chapters: the mean structures of the cold and reacting flows are compared to demonstrate the influence of combustion (§ 10.3.3); comparison of mean LES fields and experimental data (§ 10.2.3) confirm the predictive capacities of LES methods described in Chapter 4 to 6; unsteady combustion (§ 8.5) is also discussed through specific examples: for Case 2, the flame response to low frequency external acoustic forcing is presented (§ 10.3.4) and a self-excited high-frequency mode is discussed (§ 10.3.5); for Case 3 a self-excited low-frequency mode is studied and controlled through acoustic boundary conditions to close the budget of acoustic energy developed in § 8.3.7. The use of Helmholtz solvers (§ 8.3.6) to obtain the structure of acoustic modes is also illustrated in cases 1 and 2.

All LES models used in this chapter have been described in previous chapters. The flame/turbulence interaction model is the thickened flame model (§ 5.4.3) and boundary conditions are specified using the NSCBC method of Chapter 9. The turbulence model is the Smagorinski model (Eq. (4.64)) or the Wale model (Nicoud and Ducros [469]).

Case	Topic	Combustion
1	Swirling flow patterns without combustion	None
	Comparison LES / measurements	§ 10.2.2
1	Reacting flow field	Stable regime
	Comparison LES / measurements / acoustic codes	§ 10.2.3
2	Reacting flow field	Low-frequency forced mode
	Comparison LES / measurements / acoustic codes	§ 10.3.4
2	Reacting flow field	High-frequency self-excited mode
	Comparison LES / Acoustic codes	§ 10.3.5
3	Reacting flow field	Low-frequency self-excited mode
	Closure of the acoustic energy equation	§ 10.4

Table 10.1: Organization of chapter.

10.2   Case 1: small scale gas turbine burner

The first example presents typical cold flow fields with swirl (§ 10.2.2), as well as reacting flow fields (§ 10.2.3), and compares them with experimental data. This test case has been very widely used since 2005 to validate multiple LES solvers (Roux et al. [570], Roux [569], Moureau et al. [458]) because of the wide range of diagnostics and regimes studied experimentally at DLR during and after the European PRECCINSTA project (Meier et al. [430], Weigand et al. [699]). [iii]

[iii] A convenient method to visualize the flow in the PRECCINSTA combustor is to look at the movie produced by Moureau et al. [458] available at *elearning.cerfacs.fr/combustion/illustrations/moureau-short.*

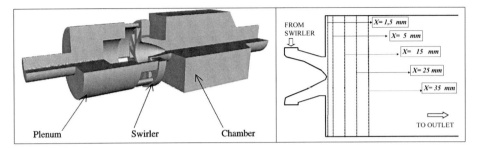

Figure 10.1: Configuration for Case 1 (left). Location of cuts for velocity profiles (right).

10.2.1 Configuration and boundary conditions

The burner of Case 1 uses a swirled injector (Fig. 10.1) where swirl is produced by tangential injection downstream of a plenum. A central hub contributes to flame stabilization. In the experiment methane is injected through holes located in the swirler but mixing is fast so that perfect premixing is assumed for computations. Experiments include LDV (Laser Doppler Velocimetry) measurements for the cold flow as well as a study of various combustion regimes. The dimensions of the combustion chamber are 86 mm × 86 mm × 110 mm.

For LES, the critical question of boundary conditions is avoided in Case 1 by extending the computational domain upstream and downstream of the chamber: the swirlers and the plenum are fully meshed and computed and even a part of the outside atmosphere (not shown on Fig. 10.1 for clarity) is meshed to avoid having to specify a boundary condition at the chamber outlet. This procedure is applicable only for certain configurations: a real gas turbine combustion chamber is surrounded by more complex passages for air or by moving parts (the blades of the turbine for example) for which specifying boundary conditions remains much more difficult.

10.2.2 Non reacting flow

Average fields

LES and experimental LDV profiles (measured at DLR Stuttgart) are compared at various sections of the combustion chamber (Fig. 10.1) for average axial (Fig. 10.2), azimuthal (Fig. 10.4), RMS axial (Fig. 10.3) and RMS azimuthal velocities (Fig. 10.5).[iv] All mean and RMS velocity profiles are correctly predicted (Lartigue [365]). Considering that this computation has no boundary condition which can be tuned to fit the velocity profiles, these results demonstrate the predictive capacity of LES in such swirling flows (RANS models are usually not well suited to swirling flows). A large central toroidal recirculation zone (evidenced through

---

[iv]Only the resolved part of the LES RMS fluctuations is taken into account (first RHS term in Eq. (4.93)).

negative values of the mean axial velocity) develops on the chamber axis. This CTRZ begins at x=2 mm downstream of the hub and is still observed at x=35mm.

Structure of unsteady swirling non reacting flows

RMS fluctuations in both LES and experimental results (Fig. 10.3 and 10.5) are large around the axis, close to the injector nozzle (of the order of 20 m/s at $x = 1.5$ mm). These oscillations are typical of most swirled burners. They may be due to a very intense turbulent field, an acoustic mode of the chamber (§ 8.2.6) or an hydrodynamic instability (§ 8.4.5).

First, it is unlikely that random turbulent fluctuations can reach such high values: on the burner axis, Fig. 10.2 and 10.4 show that the mean axial velocity is of the order of 5 m/s and that velocity gradients are not very large. Such a mean flow field cannot explain how the RMS velocity observed on Fig. 10.3 on the axis could be 4 times larger than the mean velocity. Furthermore, spectral analysis of velocity signals in this region reveals that a 540 Hz peak dominates the signal confirming that the source of fluctuations is either acoustic or hydrodynamic. A useful second step is to compute all acoustic eigenmodes of the rig using a Helmholtz solver (§ 8.3.6). Using the exact geometry of the burner the acoustic eigenmodes of the combustor obtained with such an Helmholtz solver are given in Table 10.2 and none of them matches the 540 Hz frequency. The first mode (172 Hz) is observed neither in LES nor in experiments: this mode is stable. The second mode (363 Hz) is indeed identified in experiments (around 320 Hz) and in LES (around 360 Hz) but only in the plenum and the exhaust pipe. No acoustic mode is identified around 500 Hz. This analysis shows that acoustics are not responsible for the large RMS fluctuations on the burner axis. Finally, the existence of a large-scale hydrodynamic structure can be investigated in the LES by plotting an isosurface of low pressure (Fig. 10.6): this diagnostic evidences a large spiral structure rotating around the burner axis at a frequency of 540 Hz. Experimental wall pressure measurements performed inside the chamber also reveal a dominant frequency around 510 Hz. This large hydrodynamic structure called PVC (Precessing Vortex Core, see § 6.2.3) is the actual source of the axis fluctuations observed in Fig. 10.3 and 10.5.

Mode number	Mode name	Cold flow (Hz)	Reacting flow (Hz)
(1)	Quarter wave	172	265
(2)	Three quarter wave	363	588
(3)	Five quarter wave	1409	1440

Table 10.2: Longitudinal modes of Case 1 predicted by a Helmholtz solver.

Coexistence of acoustic modes and Precessing Vortex Core

The previous section shows that two modes control the cold flow structure in Case 1:

- a low amplitude acoustic mode (360 Hz) everywhere in the device and

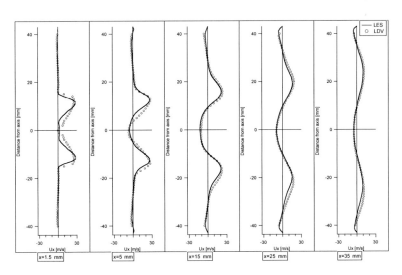

Figure 10.2: Average axial velocity profiles. Circles: LDV; solid line: LES.

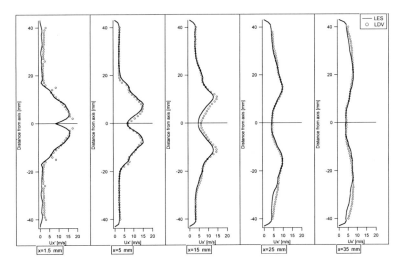

Figure 10.3: RMS axial velocity profiles. Circles: LDV; solid line: LES.

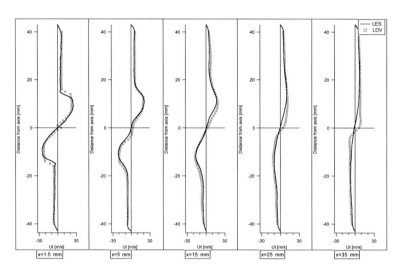

Figure 10.4: Average tangential velocity profiles. Circles: LDV; solid line: LES.

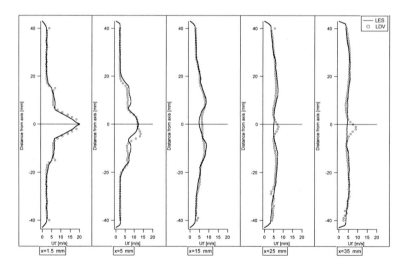

Figure 10.5: RMS tangential velocity profiles. Circles: LDV; solid line: LES.

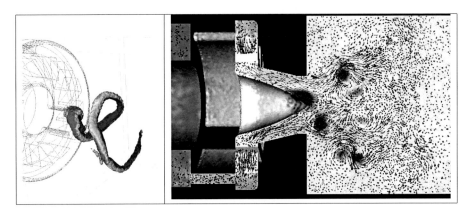

Figure 10.6: Visualization of the PVC mode in Case 1 using an isosurface of low pressure (left) and a field of pressure (gray scale) and velocity vectors in the central plane (right) (Lartigue [365]).

- a strong hydrodynamic mode (540 Hz) due to the PVC at the burner exit ($0 < x < 5$ cm).

These two modes actually coexist but do not interact. Their respective traces can be found in an analysis of RMS pressure fluctuations (P' defined by Eq. (8.136)) because both acoustic and hydrodynamic fluctuations induce pressure perturbations: P' profiles along the burner axis[v], computed both with LES and the Helmholtz solver, are presented in Fig. 10.7. The two codes give similar results in the plenum and in the exhaust, indicating the acoustic nature of the pressure fluctuations in these regions. However, in the swirler and in the first half of the chamber where the PVC is found, the pressure fluctuations given by LES are much larger than the acoustic predictions, because they also contain the effects of the PVC.

The PVC acts acoustically like a rotating solid placed in the flow and partially blocking the swirler exhaust. Such a moving solid acts like an acoustic dipole (Pierce [506], Kinsler et al. [347]) which radiate weakly: the PVC modifies the pressure field in the chamber but does not affect the pressure field upstream and downstream: this explains why the acoustic mode at 360 Hz is visible and unaffected in the plenum and the exhaust.

10.2.3 Stable reacting flow

This section presents results for a stable reacting regime corresponding to an equivalence ratio of 0.75, an air flow rate of 12 g/s, and a thermal power of 27 kW (Lartigue [365]). A snapshot of an instantaneous temperature isosurface (Fig. 10.8) reveals a very compact flame located close to the burner nozzle exit. No comparison is possible with experiments here because temperatures were not measured. The velocity fields, however, were investigated in detail

---

[v]Since the acoustic mode structure is longitudinal, P' can be plotted along the burner axis x.

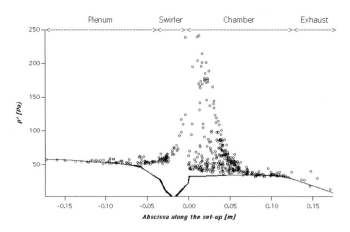

Figure 10.7: Pressure fluctuations amplitude measured in the LES (——) and predicted by the acoustic code (o) for the non-reacting flow in Case 1 (Lartigue [365]).

using LDV and are presented in Figs. 10.9 (mean axial velocity), 10.10 (RMS axial velocity), 10.11 (mean tangential velocity) and 10.12 (RMS tangential velocity). The overall agreement between mean LES results and experimental data is good.

Although this regime is considered as a 'stable' case some acoustic activity exists in the burner: two acoustic modes are found experimentally around 300 Hz and 570 Hz and the overall sound level inside the combustor reaches 500 Pa in the LES (more than 140 db). To identify the nature of these modes, the Helmholtz solver was used with the average temperature field given by LES to identify acoustic eigenmodes with combustion. Table 10.2 confirms that the two frequencies observed in experiments are the two first acoustic modes of the combustor. In LES, a single frequency is observed at 520 Hz, which is close to the second acoustic mode of Table 10.2. To check that the 520 Hz mode found by LES is indeed acoustic the field of unsteady pressure given by LES is compared to the modal structure predicted by the Helmholtz solver for the 588 Hz mode (Fig. 10.13). Even though the LES signal contains all modes its shape is clearly close to the structure of the second acoustic mode predicted by the Helmholtz solver. Another major effect of combustion revealed by LES is to damp the PVC observed in the cold flow. The agreement of Fig. 10.13 confirms that the unsteady activity for this reacting regime is controlled everywhere by the acoustic field even though no strong combustion instability is observed.

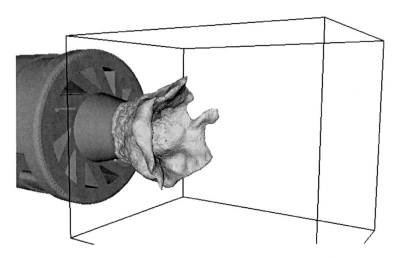

Figure 10.8: Instantaneous 1250 K isosurface (LES data).

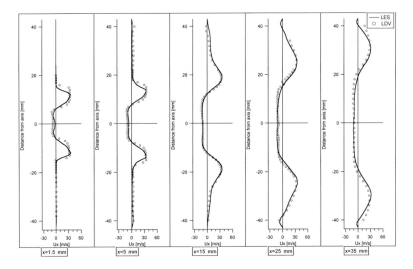

Figure 10.9: Mean axial velocity in the central plane. Circles: LDV; solid line: LES.

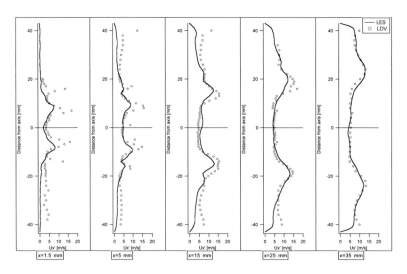

Figure 10.10: RMS axial velocity in the central plane. Circles: LDV; solid line: LES.

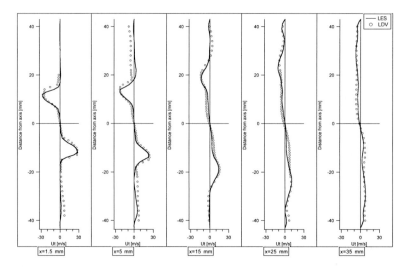

Figure 10.11: Mean tangential velocity in the central plane. Circles: LDV; solid line: LES.

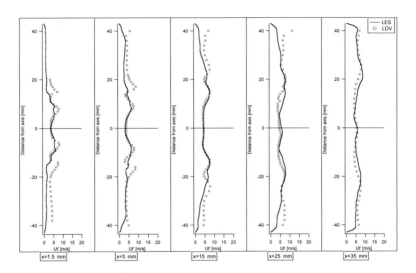

Figure 10.12: RMS tangential velocity in the central plane. Circles: LDV; solid line: LES.

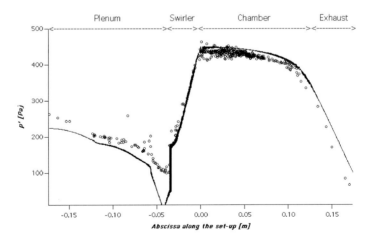

Figure 10.13: Pressure fluctuations amplitude predicted by LES (———) and Helmholtz solver (o) for the reacting flow in Case 1.

10.3   Case 2: large-scale gas turbine burner

10.3.1   Configuration

The second example is a burner corresponding to a large-scale industrial gas turbine and installed on a square cross-section chamber at University of Karlsruhe (Selle et al. [601]). Fig. 10.14 shows the main features of the burner: a central axial swirler (colored in dark) injects and swirls air. The main part of the combustion air as well as fuel (through holes located on both sides of the vanes used for swirling) is injected by the diagonal swirler. Perfectly mixed gases enter the diagonal swirler while pure air enters the axial swirler: the flame inside the chamber burns in a partially premixed regime. The burner is fired with natural gas (assumed to be mostly methane) and the air is pre-heated to 673 K. The thermal power is 420 kW and the mean equivalence ratio Φ is 0.5.

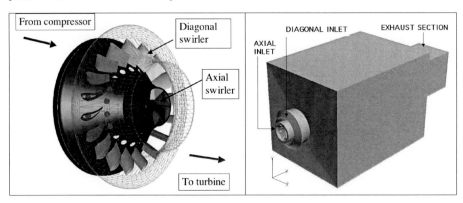

Figure 10.14: Configuration for Case 2: burner (left) and combustion chamber (right).

10.3.2   Boundary conditions

Specifying boundary conditions is a difficult exercice in LES: mean and turbulent velocity profiles must be imposed somewhere upstream of the combustion chamber and acoustic boundary conditions (typically impedances) must be specified for all inlets or outlets (see Chapter 9). For Case 1, the difficulty was avoided by finding a section (upstream of the plenum) where the velocity profile was known and the acoustic impedance corresponded to a non reflecting inlet. At the combustor outlet, a part of the surrounding atmosphere was also computed so that the outlet behavior was explicitly computed by the LES solver and did not need any acoustic condition. This 'ideal' situation is not often found. In Case 2, for example, the burner is larger and no simple inlet section can be identified experimentally so that Case 2 cannot be computed from inlet to exhaust: the computation of the *axial swirler* for Case 2 begins upstream of the vanes ('Axial inlet 'Section in Fig. 10.14 right) which are included in the mesh; for the *diagonal swirler*, however, ('Diagonal inlet' section in Fig. 10.14 right), the problem is more difficult and typical of gas turbines since full computation of this part of the burner would require also a full computation of all vanes placed in the passage. This was not done here: inlet conditions were specified just downstream of these vanes and adjusted to match the first measurement section data in the burner under non-reacting cases. This adjustment procedure of boundary conditions is a major difficulty for such LES and a source of uncertainties. Note also that most of the turbulence in such configurations is generated by the flow within the chamber so that injecting turbulence in the inlets is not needed: steady velocity fields are imposed in both swirler inlets.

10.3.3 Comparison of cold and hot flow structures

Typical velocity fields in swirled burners have already been displayed for Case 1: since they are similar for Case 2, they will not be repeated here (Selle et al. [601]). However, the comparison of the flow structure with and without combustion for Case 2 is instructive. Fig. 10.15 shows

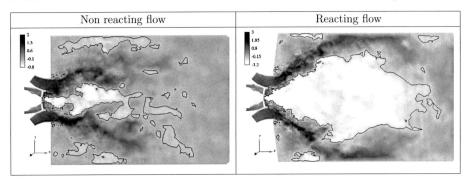

Figure 10.15: Comparison of cold (left) and reacting (right) instantaneous flow for Case 2 (axial velocity field displayed in central plane of the combustor). Black lines limit backflow regions (Selle [600]).

the fields of axial velocity with black lines indicating zero values of this velocity. Within closed contours of this line, the flow is going backwards. With combustion the size of this backflow zone is much larger: the flow issuing from the burner spreads much more and the size of the CTRZ is larger so that the quantity of recirculating burnt gases providing flame stabilization is very large. The maximum positive axial velocity reached within the chamber (usually at the burner throat) is also larger with combustion: it changes from 2 U_{bulk} for cold flow to 3 U_{bulk} with combustion.[vi] The backflow intensity within the CTRZ is also higher with combustion

---

[vi]The bulk velocity U_{bulk} is defined by $U_{bulk} = \dot{V}/\pi R^2$ where $\dot{V}$ is the total volume flow rate through the burner and R is the burner nozzle exit diameter.

(from -0.8 to $-1.2U_{bulk}$) indicating that combustion increases not only the size but also the strength of the recirculation zone.

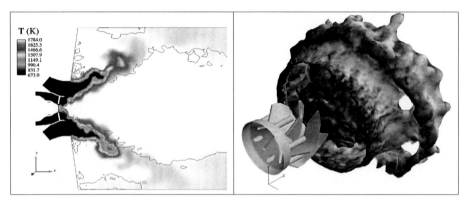

Figure 10.16: Temperature field in the chamber central plane (left) and isosurface of temperature $T = 1000$ K (right) for Case 2 (instantaneous values).

Fig. 10.16 shows the temperature field in the central plane of the burner (left) and a 1000 K isosurface (instantaneous fields). The hot gases recirculated in the CTRZ reach the axial swirler exit, confirming their essential role for flame stabilization. The flame surface (right) shows very large flame motions which will be analyzed in § 10.3.5.

10.3.4   A low-frequency forced mode

This section shows a computation of the forced response of the burner of Fig. 10.14 mounted on a circular combustion chamber (Lohrmann et al. [404]). As discussed in Chapter 8, the identification of a burner response to acoustic perturbations is an essential ingredient of acoustic approaches for combustor stability (Crocco [156], Hsiao et al. [298], Paschereit et al. [489], Polifke et al. [529]). To evaluate this response the usual procedure is to force the burner using loudspeakers or rotating valves and measure the perturbation of the heat release (typically the time delay between the ingoing unsteady flow rate and the total unsteady heat release). Because of the cost of such experiments, performing the same task with LES has obvious advantages. However the numerical procedure to introduce acoustic waves in a computation may lead to numerical artifacts (Poinsot and Lele [519], Selle et al. [602]) as discussed in Chapter 9. Kaufmann et al. [327] and Ducruix and Candel [193] show that a proper method to excite a combustion chamber is to pulsate the ingoing acoustic wave and not the local inlet velocity. This procedure was retained here.

The reacting case corresponds to a global equivalence ratio of 0.51, air flow rate of 180 g/s, a Reynolds number of 120000 (based on bulk velocity and burner diameter) and power

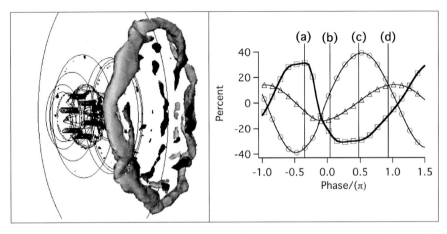

Figure 10.17: Left: visualization of ring structure (vortex criterion of Hussain and Jeong [301]) induced by inlet acoustic forcing (instant (c) of the cycle). Right: heat release (—□—), inlet normal velocity (○) and fuel mass (△) fluctuations normalized by their mean values. (a) to (d) refer to the snapshots of Fig. 10.18 (Selle [600]).

of 277 kW. The forcing frequency is 120 Hz.[vii] The first effect of forcing is to create a large toroidal ring vortex starting at the lips of the burner and growing when propagating downstream. This vortex is visualized in Fig. 10.17 using the vortex criterion of Hussain and Jeong [301] which is based on the invariants of the deformation tensor.

The ring vortex has a direct effect on the global heat released inside the combustor: Fig. 10.17 compares time evolutions of total heat release, diagonal inlet velocity and total mass of fuel in the chamber. While the inlet velocity (circles) and the enclosed fuel mass (triangles) oscillate sinusoidally, the total heat release (squares) exhibits more nonlinearities, decreasing very rapidly between times a) and b). Fig. 10.18 displays the flame surface for four phases of the cycle ($\phi = 0$, $\pi/2$, π and $3\pi/2$): the flame perturbations are shaped by the ring vortex. While the inlet velocity (triangle) oscillates between 0.85 and 1.15 times its mean value, the total heat release varies from 0.7 to 1.3 times its mean value (Fig. 10.17) in opposite phase to the inlet velocity. The mass of fuel enclosed in the chamber (triangles) changes even more indicating that the flame undergoes strong displacements with phases of rapid expansion (between instants c and d on Fig 10.18 for example) during which the ring vortex created by the forcing stretches the flame front . Later in the cycle, the flame shrinks rapidly (between instants a and b on Fig. 10.18) when the fresh gases injected previously burn

---

[vii]Animations of the complete instability sequence (growth, limit cycle and decay) can be found at *www.cerfacs.fr/cfd/Gallery/movies/Buechner.mov*.

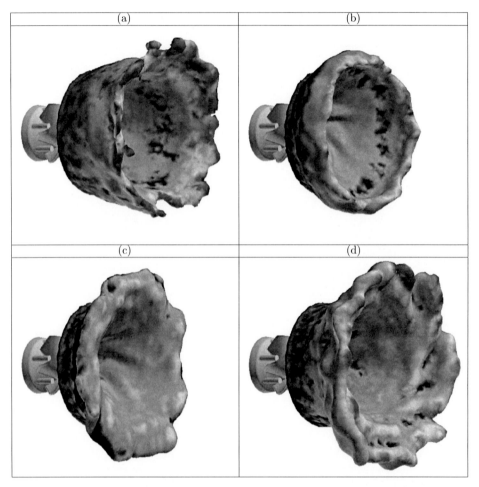

Figure 10.18: Temperature iso-surface (1000 K) for four phases ($\phi = 0$, $\pi/2$, π and $3\pi/2$) of a forced cycle at 120 Hz: (a) to (d) refer to Fig. 10.17. The vortex ring formed at the burner exit induces the mushroom-shape response of the flame. The minimum flame surface is reached after instant (b) while the maximum surface is reached at time (a) leading to changes in total reaction rate of 0.7 to 1.3 times the mean value (Selle [600]).

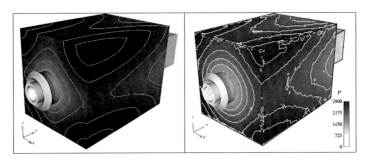

Figure 10.19: 1200 Hz turning mode of Eq. (10.1). Left: Helmholtz result. Right: LES result.

out. The time delay between velocity and total heat release oscillations is the time τ used in acoustic approaches described in § 8.4.3.

10.3.5   A high-frequency self-excited mode

Low-frequency modes are not the only product of flame/acoustics interactions. Higher order acoustic modes of the chamber can also interact with the flame front. The joint usage of LES and Helmholtz solvers helps to understand the structure of these modes as shown here for a high-frequency mode in Case 2. The LES of this combustor exhibits a natural unstable mode at 1200 Hz which is visible in the wall pressure traces. The structure of this mode is visualized by plotting the pressure amplitude P' defined by Eq. (8.136) on the chamber walls (Fig. 10.19 right). When the Helmholtz solver described in § 8.3.6 is applied to this geometry, two eigenmodes are found at the same frequency 1220 Hz. These modes correspond to the transverse modes $(1,0,1)$ and $(1,1,0)$ of the chamber. Their structure is displayed in Fig. 10.20 which shows the RMS wall pressure P' on the walls. Modes $(1,0,1)$ and $(1,1,0)$ are at the same frequency because the chamber is square: they can be combined to produce a 'turning mode' given by:

$$p'_{turning}(x,y,z,t) = P'_{1,0,1}(x,y,z)cos(\omega t) + P'_{1,1,0}(x,y,z)cos(\omega t - \pi/2) \qquad (10.1)$$

This mode rotates around the axis of the combustion chamber.[viii] The resulting average structure is displayed in Fig. 10.19 right and matches the structure measured in the LES (Fig. 10.19 right): the 1200 Hz mode seen in the LES is a turning mode which is a linear combination of the $(1,0,1)$ and $(1,1,0)$ modes. This turning mode controls the flame shape as shown in Fig. 10.21 for four instants during one 1200 Hz cycle: the acoustic velocity induced by the turning mode at the lips of the diagonal swirler creates an helicoidal perturbation which is convected downstream and slices flame elements when it reaches the flame extremities.

[viii]See animations of flame position and pressure fields on *www.cerfacs.fr/cfd/Gallery/movies/flame-ITS.mov, P_traces_longi-ITS.mov* and *P_traces_trans-ITS.mov.*.

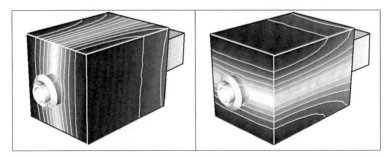

Figure 10.20: Structure of the two transverse modes at 1200 Hz: (1,0,1): left and (1,1,0): right (Selle [600]). The pressure amplitude P' (Eq. (8.136)) is plotted on the walls.

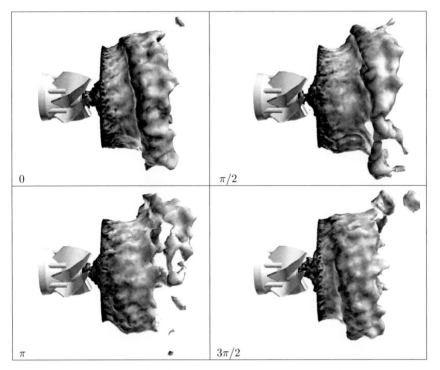

Figure 10.21: Isosurfaces of temperature $T = 1000$ K for four phases of the 1200 Hz cycle.

10.4 Case 3: self-excited laboratory-scale burner

10.4.1 Configuration

The geometry of Case 3 is displayed in Fig. 10.22. Swirled premixed (propane and air) gases are introduced tangentially into a long cylindrical duct feeding the combustion chamber. The tangential injection creates the swirl required for stabilization. A specification of the present

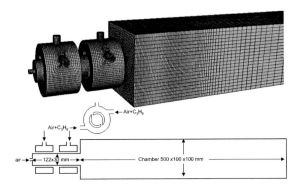

Figure 10.22: Case 3 configuration: a staged swirled combustor.

set-up is that the injection duct is split into two parts to allow staged combustion: the equivalence ratio of the first part (called ϕ_1) can differ from the second part (called ϕ_2). Staged combustion is used in certain burners to control emissions and instabilities. The air flow rates in each section are equal to half the total air flow rate $\dot{m}_{air}$ and the equivalence ratio modulation is obtained by splitting the propane flow rates in different proportions for each section. The global equivalence ratio defined by Eq. (1.33) of the burner ϕ_g is $\phi_g = s\dot{m}_F/\dot{m}_O$ where s is the stoichiometric ratio and $\dot{m}_O$ is the oxygen flow rate ($\dot{m}_O = Y_{ox} * \dot{m}_{air}$). The parameter α used to characterize staging measures the fraction of fuel injected into the first injection section: $\alpha = \dot{m}_F^1/\dot{m}_F$. The equivalence ratios ϕ_1, ϕ_2 and α are linked by $\phi_1 = 2\alpha\phi_g$ and $\phi_2 = 2(1-\alpha)\phi_g$. One specific regime exhibiting large oscillations when the outlet section is acoustically closed is studied here (Table 10.3).

Total flow rate (kg/s)	Mean equivalence ratio	α	ϕ_1	ϕ_2
22.10^{-3}	0.8	0.3	0.5	1.16

Table 10.3: Flow parameters for combustion cases.

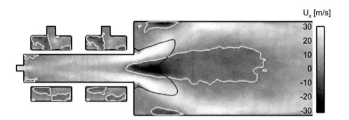

Figure 10.23: Mean axial velocity, white line: $u_x = 0$, black line: T = 1500 K for stable combustion.

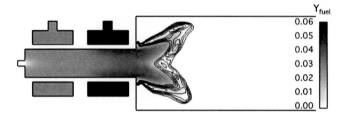

Figure 10.24: Mean fuel mass fraction field, black lines: iso-reaction rate for stable combustion.

10.4.2   Stable flow

When the combustor outlet is non-reflecting, the flame is stable. The mean axial velocity and fuel mass fraction fields are displayed in Fig. 10.23 and 10.24 (Martin et al. [420]): the central recirculation zone (marked by a white line in Fig. 10.23) is filled by burnt gases which provide flame stabilization. Fuel staging is also apparent in Fig. 10.24.

10.4.3   Control through acoustic conditions at the outlet

It is well known experimentally that combustion instabilities are modified when the impedance of the inlet or outlet ducts are changed. This can also be observed in a compressible LES: here the level of reflection of the outlet boundary is controlled by changing the relaxation coefficient σ of the wave correction (Selle et al. [602]) which determines the amplitude of the incoming wave entering the computational domain (Eq. (9.45)). For small values of σ, the pressure p remains around its target value p_t while letting acoustic waves go out without reflection: the outlet is non reflecting. When large values of σ are specified, the outlet pressure remains strictly equal to p_t and the outlet becomes totally reflecting.

The combustion chamber reacts strongly to changes in outlet impedance: for non-reflecting outlet, the flow is stable as seen in § 10.4.2 and it becomes unstable when the outlet becomes reflecting. To analyse this instability, the following scenario is utilized (Martin et al. [420]):

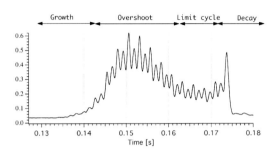

Figure 10.25: Evolution of the acoustic energy vs time for Case 3.

- Starting from a stable flame and a reduced level of fluctuations, the outlet impedance is changed to become reflecting at time $t = 0.127s$. This is obtained by increasing the σ coefficient for the outlet section (Fig. 10.25).

- At time $t = 0.173s$, the outlet impedance is switched again to a non-reflecting condition and the instability disappears[ix]

During these phases, the total acoustic energy $\mathcal{E}_1$ in the combustor defined by Eq. (8.143) is extracted from LES. Fig. 10.25 shows that it first grows, becomes maximum and then decreases slightly to reach a limit cycle at a frequency of 360 Hz mode which is one of the acoustic modes of the combustor (Martin et al. [420]). After $t = 0.173$ s, when the outlet becomes non reflecting again, it decays rapidly.

When the limit cycle is reached, the combustor is submitted to a strong oscillation where the flame periodically contracts on the exit of the burner before expanding through most of the combustion chamber (Fig. 10.26) and shrinking again. Snapshots corresponding to a full cycle are displayed in Fig. 10.26 at instants indicated on Fig. 10.27. The vortex criterion of Hussain and Jeong [301] is used to visualize the vortex rings formed at the burner exit. These vortices form a well-defined ring only after their birth (instants 1 to 3) and they degenerate after instant 4 into small scale turbulence. They are created when the inlet acceleration at the burner exit is maximum (just before instant 1). Fig. 10.27 also confirms the intensity of the oscillation: the total reaction rate oscillates between 0.5 and 1.7 times its mean value; the inlet velocity also changes between 0.5 and 1.6 times its mean value: as discussed in § 8.2.2, these fluctuating velocities are much larger than typical turbulent velocities and influence the combustion process more than small-scale turbulent motions.

During the evolution of the instability, the budget of acoustic energy given in Eq. (8.142) can be closed using time- and space-resolved LES data: Fig. 10.28 displays the evolutions of the time derivative of the total acoustic energy $\mathcal{E}_1$ and of the RHS source term $\mathcal{R}_1 - \mathcal{F}_1$. The budget closes well suggesting that both the LES and the linearized acoustic energy equation (8.142)

[ix]Animations of the complete instability sequence (growth, limit cycle and decay) can be found at *www.cerfacs.fr/cfd/Gallery/movies/ECPMod_insta3D.mov*.

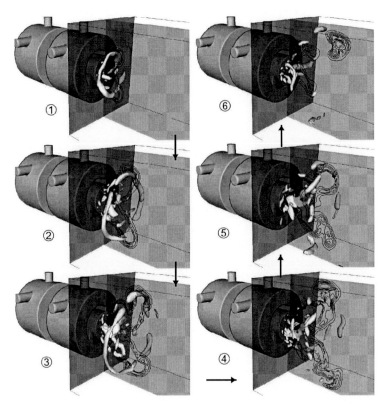

Figure 10.26: Limit cycle for Case 3. Isosurface: Q vortex criterion; black lines: iso-reaction rate.

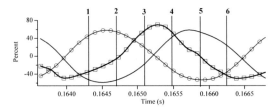

Figure 10.27: Chamber pressure (———), burner inlet velocity (o) and total heat release (—□—) fluctuations normalized by mean values during one period of the limit cycle.

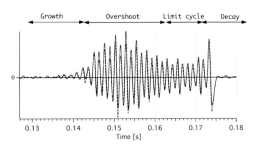

Figure 10.28: Budget of the acoustic energy equation for Case 3: $d\mathcal{E}_1/dt$ (solid); $\mathcal{R}_1 - \mathcal{F}_1$ (dotted).

are correct. Finally, since the budget closes correctly, each term in the budget equation can be analyzed. Fig. 10.29 shows that the Rayleigh source term $\mathcal{R}_1$ defined by Eq. (8.145) is actually not dominant. It is indeed positive and driving the instability most of the time even though it may take negavive values for limited times. But the acoustic losses term $\mathcal{F}_1$ given by Eq. (8.144) is also large and provides almost all the damping of the acoustic energy $\mathcal{E}_1$ at the limit cycle. This result shows that the amplitude of the limit cycle is controlled mainly by acoustic losses, as expected from the direct observation that changes in acoustic boundary conditions at the outlet could control the oscillation amplitude.This example shows how LES can be used together with budgets of acoustic energy to understand combustion instabilities in combustors. It also demonstrates the importance of acoustics in combustion oscillations and points out an important implication for experimental studies: if acoustic impedances upstream and downstream of the burner are important, it is difficult to take a given burner out of a real gas turbine for example to test it in a laboratory environment where it will be installed in a different set-up. Since acoustic boundary conditions will differ, what will be learned in the laboratory may not be relevant for the full combustor in its real environment.

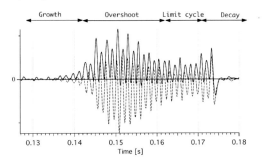

Figure 10.29: RHS terms in the acoustic energy equation for Case 3: $\mathcal{R}_1$ (solid); $\mathcal{F}_1$ (dotted).

Bibliography

[1] W. Abdal-Masseh, D. Bradley, P. Gaskell, and A. Lau. Turbulent premixed swirling combustion: direct stress, strained flamelet modelling and experimental investigation. *Proc. Combust. Inst.*, 23:825–833, 1990.

[2] R. G. Abdel-Gayed and D. Bradley. Combustion regimes and the straining of turbulent premixed flames. *Combust. Flame*, 76:213–218, 1989.

[3] R. G. Abdel-Gayed, D. Bradley, M. N. Hamid, and M. Lawes. Lewis number effects on turbulent burning velocity. *Proc. Combust. Inst.*, 20:505–512, 1984.

[4] R. G. Abdel-Gayed, D. Bradley, and A. K. C. Lau. The straining of premixed turbulent flames. *Proc. Combust. Inst.*, 22:731–738, 1988.

[5] K. Akselvoll and P. Moin. Large eddy simulation of a backward facing step flow. In W. Rodi and F. Martelli, editors, *Proc. of the 2nd International Symposium on Eng. Turb. Modelling and Exp.*, volume 2, pages 303–313. Elsevier, 1993.

[6] T. Alshaalan and C. J. Rutland. Turbulence, scalar transport and reaction rates in flame wall interaction. *Proc. Combust. Inst.*, 27:793–799, 1998.

[7] H. M. Altay, R. L. Speth, D. E. Hudgins, and A. F. Ghoniem. The impact of equivalence ratio oscillations on combustion dynamics in a backward-facing step combustor. *Combust. Flame*, 156(11):2106–2116, 2009.

[8] S. L. Aly and C. E. Hermance. A two-dimensional theory of laminar flame quenching. *Combust. Flame*, 40:173–185, 1981.

[9] J. Amaya, O. Cabrit, D. Poitou, B. Cuenot, and M. El Hafi. Unsteady coupling of Navier-Stokes and radiative heat transfer solvers applied to an anisothermal multicomponent turbulent channel flow. *J. Quant. Spect. and Radiative Transfer*, 111(2):295–301, January 2010.

[10] D. A. Anderson. *Computational Fluid Mechanics and Heat Transfer*. Hemisphere Publishing Corporation, New York, 1984.

[11] C. Angelberger. *Contributions a la modélisation de l'interaction flamme-paroi et des flux parietaux dans les moteurs a allumage commande.* Phd thesis, INP, Toulouse, 1997.

[12] C. Angelberger, T. Poinsot, and B. Delhaye. Improving near-wall combustion and wall heat transfer modelling in si engine computations. In SAE Paper 972881, editor, *Int. Fall Fuels & Lub. Meeting & Exposition*, Tulsa, 1997.

[13] C. Angelberger, D. Veynante, F. Egolfopoulos, and T. Poinsot. Large eddy simulations of combustion instabilities in premixed flames. In *Proc. of the Summer Program*, pages 61–82. Center for Turbulence Research, NASA Ames/Stanford Univ., 1998.

[14] W. T. Ashurst. Vortex simulation of unsteady wrinkled laminar flames. *Combust. Sci. Tech.*, 52:325–331, 1987.

[15] W. T. Ashurst. Geometry of premixed flames in three-dimensional turbulence. In *Proc. of the Summer Program*, pages 245–253. Center for Turbulence Research, NASA Ames/Stanford Univ., 1990.

[16] W. T. Ashurst. Flame propagation through swirling eddies, a recursive pattern. *Combust. Sci. Tech.*, 92:87–103, 1993.

[17] W. T. Ashurst and P. K. Barr. Stochastic calculation of laminar wrinkled flame propagation via vortex dynamics. *Combust. Sci. Tech.*, 34:227–256, 1983.

[18] W. T. Ashurst and P. A. McMurtry. Flame generation of vorticity: vortex dipoles from monopoles. *Combust. Sci. Tech.*, 66:17–37, 1989.

[19] W. T. Ashurst, A. R. Kerstein, R. M. Kerr, and C. H. Gibson. Alignment of vorticity and scalar gradient with strain in simulated Navier-Stokes turbulence. *Phys. Fluids*, 30:2343–2353, 1987.

[20] W. T. Ashurst, N. Peters, and M. D. Smooke. Numerical simulation of turbulent flame structure with non-unity lewis number. *Combust. Sci. Tech.*, 53:339–375, 1987.

[21] K. T. Aung, M. I. Hassan, and G. M. Faeth. Flame/stretch interactions of laminar premixed hydrogen/air flames at normal temperature and pressure. *Combust. Flame*, 109:1–24, 1997.

[22] K. T. Aung, M. I. Hassan, and G. M. Faeth. Effects of pressure and nitrogen dilution on flame stretch interactions of laminar premixed hydrogen air flames. *Combust. Flame*, 112(1):1–15, 1998.

[23] P. Auzillon, B. Fiorina, R. Vicquelin, N. Darabiha, O. Gicquel, and D. Veynante. Modeling chemical flame structure and combustion dynamics in LES. *Proc. Combust. Inst.*, 33(1):1331 – 1338, 2011.

[24] P. Auzillon, O. Gicquel, N. Darabiha, D. Veynante, and B. Fiorina. A filtered tabulated chemistry model for LES of partially-premixed flames. In *3rd ICDERS Conference*, UC Irvine (USA), July 24-29, 2011.

[25] P. Bailly, D. Garréton, O. Simonin, P. Bruel, M. Champion, B. Deshaies, S. Duplantier, and S. Sanquer. Experimental and numerical study of a premixed flame stabilized by a rectangular section cylinder. *Proc. Combust. Inst.*, 26:923 – 930, 1996.

[26] G. Balarac, H. Pitsch, and V. Raman. Development of a dynamic model for the subfilter scalar variance using the concept of optimal estimators. *Phys. Fluids*, 20(3), 2008.

[27] J. Bardina, J.H. Ferziger, and W.C. Reynolds. Improved subgrid scales models for large eddy simulations. In *AIAA 13th Fluid & Plasma Dyn. Conf.*, Snowmass, Colorado, 1980. AIAA Paper 80-1357.

[28] J. Bardina, J. H. Ferziger, and W. C. Reynolds. Improved turbulence models based on large-eddy simulation of homogeneous, incompressible, turbulent flows. Technical Report TF-19, Department of Mechanical Engineering, Stanford University, 1983.

[29] R. S. Barlow. Laser diagnostics and their interplay with computations to understand turbulent combustion. *Proc. Combust. Inst.*, 31:49–75, 2006.

[30] R. S. Barlow and J. Y. Chen. On transient flamelets and their relationship to turbulent methane-air jet flames. *Proc. Combust. Inst.*, 24:231–237, 1992.

[31] R. S. Barlow and J.H. Franck. Effects of turbulence on species mass fractions in methane/air jet flames. *Proc. Combust. Inst.*, 27:1087–1095, 1998.

[32] R. S. Barlow, G. J. Fiechtner, C. D. Carter, and J.-Y. Chen. Experiments on the scalar structure of turbulent co/h2/n2 jet flames. *Combust. Flame*, 120(4):544–569, 2000.

[33] P. K. Barr. Acceleration of a flame by flame vortex interactions. *Combust. Flame*, 82: 111–125, 1990.

[34] M. Barrère. Modeles de combustion. *Revue Générale de Thermique*, 148:295–308, 1974.

[35] M. Barrère and F. A. Williams. Comparison of combustion instabilities found in various types of combustion chambers. *Proc. Combust. Inst.*, 12:169–181, 1968.

[36] H. Barths, C. Hasse, G. Bikas, and N. Peters. Simulation of combustion in direct injection diesel engines using a eulerian particle flamelet model. *Proc. Combust. Inst.*, 28(1):1161–1168, 2000.

[37] J. D. Baum and J. N. Levine. Numerical techniques for solving nonlinear instability problems in solid rocket motors. *AIAA Journal*, 20:955–961, 1982.

[38] M. Baum. *Etude de l'allumage et de la structure des flammes turbulentes*. Phd thesis, Ecole Centrale Paris, 1994.

[39] M. Baum, T. Poinsot, D. Haworth, and N. Darabiha. Using direct numerical simulations to study $H_2/O_2/N_2$ flames with complex chemistry in turbulent flows. *J. Fluid Mech.*, 281:1–32, 1994.

[40] M. Baum, T. J. Poinsot, and D. Thévenin. Accurate boundary conditions for multicomponent reactive flows. *J. Comput. Phys.*, 116:247–261, 1994.

[41] H. Becker, P. Monkhouse, J. Wolfrum, R. Cant, K. Bray, R. Maly, and W. Pfister. Investigation of extinction in unsteady flows in turbulent combustion by 2D LIF of OH radicals and flamelet analysis. In *23rd Symp. (Int.) on Combustion*, pages 817–823. The Combustion Institute, Pittsburgh, 1990.

[42] B. Bédat, F. Egolfopoulos, and T. Poinsot. Direct numerical simulation of heat release and nox formation in turbulent non premixed flames. *Combust. Flame*, 119(1/2):69–83, 1999.

[43] J. M. Beer and N. A. Chigier. *Combustion aerodynamics*. Krieger, Malabar, Florida, 1983.

[44] J.B. Bell, M.S. Day, J.F. Grcar, M.J. Lijewskia, J. F. Driscoll, and S.A. Filatyev. Numerical simulation of a laboratory-scale turbulent slot flame. *Proc. Combust. Inst.*, 31: 1299–1307, 2007.

[45] W. Bell, B. Daniel, and B. Zinn. Experimental and theoretical determination of the admittances of a family of nozzles subjected to axial instabilities. *J. Sound Vib.*, 30(2): 179–190, 1973.

[46] L. Benoit and F. Nicoud. Numerical assessment of thermo-acoustic instabilities in gas turbines. *Int. J. Numer. Meth. Fluids*, 47(8-9):849–855, 2005.

[47] L. L. Beranek. *Acoustics*. McGraw Hill, New York, 1954.

[48] R. Betchov and W. O. Criminale. *Stability of parallel flows*. Academic Press, New York, 1963.

[49] R. W. Bilger. Turbulent flows with non-premixed reactants. In P.A. Libby and F.A. Williams, editors, *Turbulent reacting flows*. Springer Verlag, Berlin, 1980.

[50] R. W. Bilger. The structure of turbulent non premixed flames. In *22nd Symp. (Int.) on Combustion*, pages 475–488. The Combustion Institute, Pittsburgh, 1988.

[51] R. W. Bilger. Turbulent diffusion flames. *Ann. Rev. Fluid Mech*, 21:101, 1989.

[52] R. W. Bilger. Conditional moment closure for turbulent reacting flow. *Phys. FluidsA*, 5(22):436–444, 1993.

[53] R. W. Bilger, S. H. Starner, and R. J. Kee. On reduced mechanisms for methane-air combustion in nonpremixed flames. *Combust. Flame*, 80:135–149, 1990.

[54] M. Bini and Jones. W. P. Large-Eddy Simulation of particle laden turbulent flows. *J. Fluid Mech.*, 614:207–252, 2008.

[55] A. L. Birbaud, D. Durox, S. Ducruix, and S. Candel. Dynamics of confined premixed flames submitted to upstream acoustic modulations. *Proc. Combust. Inst.*, 31:1257–1265, 2007.

[56] A.L. Birbaud, S. Ducruix, D. Durox, and S. Candel. The nonlinear response of inverted V flames to equivalence ratio nonuniformities. *Combust. Flame*, 154(3):356–367, 2008.

[57] F. Bisetti, J.-Y. Chen, E.R. Hawkes, and J. H. Chen. Probability density function treatment of turbulence/chemistry interactions during the ignition of a temperature-stratified mixture for application to HCCI engine modeling. *Combust. Flame*, 155(4): 571–584, 2008.

[58] E. S. Bish and W. J. A. Dahm. Strained dissipation and reaction layer analyses of nonequilibrium chemistry in turbulent reaction flows. *Combust. Flame*, 100(3):457–464, 1995.

[59] P. L. Blackshear, W. U. Rayle, and L. K. Tower. Study of screeching combustion in a 6-in simulated afterburner. Technical Report TN 3567, NACA, 1955.

[60] R. J. Blint. The relationship of the laminar flame width to flame speed. *Combust. Sci. Tech.*, 49:79–92, 1986.

[61] R. J. Blint and J. H. Bechtel. Flame-wall interface: theory and experiment. *Combust. Sci. Tech.*, 27:87–95, 1982.

[62] R. J. Blint and J. H. Bechtel. Hydrocarbon combustion near a cooled wall. In *Int. Congress and Exposition*, page SAE Paper 820063, Detroit, 1982.

[63] G. Bloxsidge, A. Dowling, N. Hooper, and P. Langhorne. Active control of reheat buzz. *AIAA Journal*, 26:783–790, 1988.

[64] M. Boger and D. Veynante. Large eddy simulations of a turbulent premixed v-shape flame. In C. Dopazo, editor, *Advances in Turbulence VIII*, pages 449 – 452. CIMNE, Barcelona, Spain, 2000.

[65] M. Boger, D. Veynante, H. Boughanem, and A. Trouvé. Direct numerical simulation analysis of flame surface density concept for large eddy simulation of turbulent premixed combustion. In *27th Symp. (Int.) on Combustion*, pages 917–927, Boulder, 1998. The Combustion Institute, Pittsburgh.

[66] C. Bogey and C. Bailly. Effects of inflow conditions and forcing on subsonic jet flows and noise. *AIAA Journal*, 43(5):1000–1007, 2005.

[67] C. Bogey and C. Bailly. Computation of a high Reynolds number jet and its radiated noise using large eddy simulation based on explicit filtering. *Computers and Fluids*, 35: 1344–1358, 2006.

[68] M. Boileau, S. Pascaud, E. Riber, B. Cuenot, L.Y.M. Gicquel, T. Poinsot, and M. Cazalens. Investigation of two-fluid methods for Large Eddy Simulation of spray combustion in Gas Turbines. *Flow, Turb. and Combustion*, 80(3):291–321, 2008.

[69] M. Boileau, G. Staffelbach, B. Cuenot, T. Poinsot, and C. Bérat. LES of an ignition sequence in a gas turbine engine. *Combust. Flame*, 154(1-2):2–22, 2008.

[70] R. Borghi. *Réactions chimiques en milieu turbulent*. Phd thesis, Université Pierre et Marie Curie - Paris 6, 1978.

[71] R. Borghi. Mise au point sur la structure des flammes turbulentes. *Journal de chimie physique*, 81:361–370, 1984.

[72] R. Borghi. Turbulent combustion modelling. *Prog. Energy Comb. Sci.*, 14(4):245–292, 1988.

[73] R. Borghi and M. Destriau. *Combustion and Flames, chemical and physical principles*. Editions TECHNIP, 1998.

[74] G. Boudier, L. Y. M. Gicquel, T. Poinsot, D. Bissières, and C. Bérat. Comparison of LES, RANS and experiments in an aeronautical gas turbine combustion chamber. *Proc. Combust. Inst.*, 31:3075–3082, 2007.

[75] P. Boudier, S. Henriot, T. Poinsot, and T. Baritaud. A model for turbulent flame ignition and propagation in spark ignition engines. In The Combustion Institute, editor, *Twenty-Fourth Symposium (International) on Combustion*, pages 503–510, 1992.

[76] F. Boudy, D. Durox, T. Schuller, G. Jomaas, and S. Candel. Describing function analysis of limit cycles in a multiple flame combutor. In GT2010-22372, editor, *ASME Turbo expo*, Glasgow, UK, June 2010.

[77] H. Boughanem and A. Trouvé. The occurrence of flame instabilities in turbulent premixed combustion. In *27th Symp. (Int.) on Combustion*, pages 971–978, Boulder, 1998. The Combustion Institute, Pittsburgh.

[78] D. Bradley, L.K. Kwa, A.K.C. Lau, M. Missaghi, and S.B. Chin. Laminar flamelet modeling of recirculating premixed methane and propane-air combustion. *Combust. Flame*, 71(2):109 – 122, 1988.

[79] D. Bradley, P.H. Gaskell, and A.K.C. Lau. A mixedness-reactedness flamelet model for turbulent diffusion flames. In *Twenty-third Symposium (International) on Combustion*, pages 685 – 692. The Combustion Institute, 1990.

[80] D. Bradley, P. H. Gaskell, and X. J. Gu. Burning velocities, markstein lengths, and flame quenching for spherical methane-air flames: a computational study. *Combust. Flame*, 104(1/2):176–198, 1996.

[81] P. Bradshaw. Compressible turbulent shear layers. *Ann. Rev. Fluid Mech*, 9:33–54, 1977.

[82] P. Bradshaw, T. Cebeci, and J. H. Whitelaw. *Calculation methods for turbulent flows*. Academic Press, New York, 1981.

[83] K. N. C. Bray. *Turbulent flows with premixed reactants in turbulent reacting flows*, volume 44 of *Topics in applied physics*. Springer Verlag, New York, 1980.

[84] K. N. C. Bray. Studies of the turbulent burning velocity. *Proc. R. Soc. Lond. A*, 431: 315–335, 1990.

[85] K. N. C. Bray and R. S. Cant. Some applications of Kolmogorov's turbulence research in the field of combustion. *Proc. R. Soc. Lond. A. A.N. Kolmogorov Special Issue*, 434 (1890):217–240, 1991.

[86] K. N. C. Bray and P. A. Libby. Passage times and flamelet crossing frequencies in premixed turbulent combustion. *Combust. Sci. Tech.*, 47:253, 1986.

[87] K. N. C. Bray and J. B. Moss. A unified statistical model of the premixed turbulent flame. *Acta Astronautica*, 4:291 – 319, 1977.

[88] K. N. C. Bray and N. Peters. Laminar flamelets in turbulent flames. In P.A. Libby and F.A. Williams, editors, *Turbulent Reacting Flows*, pages 63–113, London, 1994. Academic Press.

[89] K. N. C. Bray, P. A. Libby, and J. B. Moss. Flamelet crossing frequencies and mean reaction rates in premixed turbulent combustion. *Combust. Sci. Tech.*, 41(3-4):143–172, 1984.

[90] K. N. C. Bray, M. Champion, and P. A. Libby. The interaction between turbulence and chemistry in premixed turbulent flames. In R. Borghi and S.N.B. Murthy, editors, *Turbulent Reactive Flows*, volume 40, pages 541–563. Lecture notes in engineering, Springer Verlag, 1989.

[91] G. Bruneaux, K. Akselvoll, T. Poinsot, and J. H. Ferziger. Simulation of a turbulent flame in a channel. In *Proc. of the Summer Program*, pages 157–174. Center for Turbulence Research, NASA Ames/Stanford Univ., 1994.

[92] G. Bruneaux, K. Akselvoll, T. Poinsot, and J. Ferziger. Flame-wall interaction in a turbulent channel flow. *Combust. Flame*, 107(1/2):27–44, 1996.

[93] G. Bruneaux, T. Poinsot, and J. H. Ferziger. Premixed flame-wall interaction in a turbulent channel flow: budget for the flame surface density evolution equation and modelling. *J. Fluid Mech.*, 349:191–219, 1997.

[94] J. Buckmaster and A. Crowley. The fluid mechanics of flame tips. *J. Fluid Mech.*, 131: 341, 1984.

[95] J. Buckmaster and G. Ludford. *Theory of laminar flames*. Cambridge University Press, 1982.

[96] H. Buechner, C. Hirsch, and W. Leuckel. Experimental investigations on the dynamics of pulsated premixed axial jet flames. *Combust. Sci. Tech.*, 94:219–228, 1993.

[97] J. Buell and P. Huerre. Inflow outflow boundary conditions and global dynamics of spatial mixing layers. In *Proc. of the Summer Program*, pages 19–27. Center for Turbulence Research, NASA Ames/Stanford Univ., 1988.

[98] S. P. Burke and T. E. W. Schumann. Diffusion flames. *Industrial and Engineering Chemistry*, 20(10):998–1005, 1928.

[99] W. Bush and F. Fendell. Asymptotic analysis of laminar flame propagation for general lewis numbers. *Combust. Sci. Tech.*, 1:421, 1970.

[100] T. D. Butler and P. J. O'Rourke. A numerical method for two-dimensional unsteady reacting flows. *Proc. Combust. Inst.*, 16(1):1503 – 1515, 1977.

[101] W. H. Calhoon and S. Menon. Subgrid modeling for large eddy simulations. In *AIAA 34th Aerospace Science Meeting, AIAA Paper 96-0516*, Reno, Nevada, 1996.

[102] SM Camporeale, B Fortunato, and G Campa. A finite element method for three-dimensional analysis of thermo-acoustic combustion instability. *Journal of engineering for gas turbines and power*, 133(1), 2011.

[103] S. Candel. Acoustic conservation principles, application to plane and modal propagation in nozzles and diffusers. *J. Sound Vib.*, 41:207–232, 1975.

[104] S. Candel. *Mécanique des Fluides*. Dunod, Paris, 1995.

[105] S. Candel, D. Veynante, F. Lacas, E. Maistret, N. Darabiha, and T. Poinsot. Coherent flame model: applications and recent extensions. In B. Larrouturou, editor, *Advances in combustion modeling. Series on advances in mathematics for applied sciences*, pages 19–64. World Scientific, Singapore, 1990.

[106] S. Candel, D. Veynante, F. Lacas, N. Darabiha, M. Baum, and T. Poinsot. A review of turbulent combustion modeling. *ERCOFTAC Bulletin*, 20:9–16, 1994.

[107] S. Candel, C. Huynh., and T. Poinsot. Some modeling methods of combustion insta-bilities. In *Unsteady combustion*, pages 83–112. Nato ASI Series, Kluwer Academic Publishers, Dordrecht, 1996.

[108] S. Candel, D. Durox, S. Ducruix, A.L. Birbaud, N. Noiray, and T. Schuller. Flame dynamics and combustion noise : progress and challenges. *Int. J. Aeroacoustics*, 8: 1–56, 2009.

[109] S. M. Candel and T. Poinsot. Flame stretch and the balance equation for the flame surface area. *Combust. Sci. Tech.*, 70:1–15, 1990.

[110] S. M. Candel, E. Maistret, N. Darabiha, T. Poinsot, D. Veynante, and F. Lacas. Exper-imental and numerical studies of turbulent ducted flames. In *Marble Symposium*, pages 209–236, Caltech, 1988.

[111] R. S. Cant and K. N. C. Bray. Strained laminar flamelet calculations of premixed turbulent combustion in a closed vessel. In *22nd Symp. (Int.) on Combustion*, pages 791–799. The Combustion Institute, Pittsburgh, 1988.

[112] R. S. Cant, S. B. Pope, and K. N. C. Bray. Modelling of flamelet surface to volume ratio in turbulent premixed combustion. In *23rd Symp. (Int.) on Combustion*, pages 809–815, Orleans, 1990. The Combustion Institute, Pittsburgh.

[113] R. S. Cant, C. J. Rutland, and A. Trouvé. Statistics for laminar flamelet modeling. In *Proc. of the Summer Program*, pages 271–279. Center for Turbulence Research, Stanford Univ./NASA-Ames, 1990.

[114] M. H. Carpenter, D. Gottlieb, and S. Abarbanel. Time stable boundary conditions for finite difference schemes solving hyperbolic systems: methodology and application to high order schemes. *J. Comput. Phys.*, 111:220–236, 1994.

[115] R. J. Cattolica, P. K. Barr, and N. N. Mansour. Propagation of a premixed flame in a divided-chamber combustor. *Combust. Flame*, 77:101–121, 1989.

[116] I. Celik, I. Yavuz, and A. Smirnov. Large eddy simulations of in-cylinder turbulence for internal combustion engines: a review. *Int. J. Engine Research*, 2(2):119–148, 2001.

[117] F. Charlette, C. Meneveau, and D. Veynante. A power-law flame wrinkling model for LES of premixed turbulent combustion. Part II: Dynamic formulation. *Combust. Flame*, 131(1/2):181 – 197, 2002.

[118] F. Charlette, D. Veynante, and C. Meneveau. A power-law wrinkling model for LES of premixed turbulent combustion: Part I - non-dynamic formulation and initial tests. *Combust. Flame*, 131:159–180, 2002.

[119] H. C. Chen, S. Chen, and R. H. Kraichnan. Probability distribution of a stochastically advected scalar field. *Phys. Rev. Lett.*, 63:2657, 1989.

[120] J. H. Chen, A. Choudhary, B. deSupinski, M. DeVries, E. R. Hawkes, S. Klasky, W. K. Liao, K. L. Ma, J. Mellor-Crummey, N. Podhorszki, R. Sankaran, S. Shende, and C. S. Yoo. Terascale direct numerical simulations of turbulent combustion using s3d. *Comput. Sci. Disc.*, 2(015001), 2009.

[121] J.H. Chen. Petascale direct numerical simulation of turbulent combustion - fundamental insights towards predictive models. *Proc. Combust. Inst.*, 33(1):99–123, Jan 2011.

[122] M. Chen, K. Kontomaris, and J. B. McLaughlin. Direct numerical simulation of droplet collisions in a turbulent channel flow. part I: collision algorithm. *Int. J. Multiphase Flow*, pages 1079–1103, 1998.

[123] M. Chen, M. Herrmann, and N. Peters. Flamelet modeling of lifted turbulent methane/air jet diffusion flames. *Proc. Combust. Inst.*, 28:167–174, 2000.

[124] Z. Chen. On the extraction of laminar flame speed and Markstein length from outwardly propagating spherical flames. *Combust. Flame*, 158(2):291–300, 2011.

[125] R. K. Cheng and I. G. Shepherd. Intermittency and conditional velocities in premixed conical turbulent flames. *Combust. Sci. Tech.*, 52:353–375, 1987.

[126] R. K. Cheng and I. G. Shepherd. The influence of burner geometry on premixed turbulent flame propagation. *Combust. Flame*, 85:7–26, 1991.

[127] R. K. Cheng, J. A. Wehrmeyer, and R. W. Pitz. Simultaneous temperature and multi-species measurement in a lifter hydrogen diffusion flame. *Combust. Flame*, 91:323–345, 1992.

[128] W. K. Cheng and J. A. Diringer. Numerical modelling of SI engine combustion with a flame sheet model. In *Int. Congress and Exposition*, page SAE Paper 910268, Detroit, 1991.

[129] C. C. Chieng and B. E. Launder. On the calculation of turbulent heat transport downstream from an abrupt pipe expansion. *Numer. Heat Transfer*, 3:189–207, 1980.

[130] P. Cho, C. K. Law, R. K. Cheng, and I. G. Shepherd. Velocity and scalar fields of turbulent premixed flames in stagnation flow. In *22nd Symp. (Int.) on Combustion*, pages 739–745. The Combustion Institute, Pittsburgh, 1988.

[131] C. R. Choi and K. Y. Huh. Development of a coherent flamelet model for a spark ignited turbulent premixed flame in a closed vessel. *Combust. Flame*, 114(3/4):336–348, 1998.

[132] B. T. Chu. On the energy transfer to small disturbances in fluid flow (part i). *Acta Mechanica*, pages 215–234, 1965.

[133] S. H. Chung and C. K. Law. An invariant derivation of flame stretch. *Combust. Flame*, 55:123–125, 1984.

[134] H. Ciofalo and M. W. Collins. $k-\epsilon$ predictions of heat transfer in turbulent recirculating flows using an improved wall treatment. *Numerical Heat Transfer*, B-15:21–47, 1989.

[135] R. A. Clark, J. H. Ferziger, and W. C. Reynolds. Evaluation of subgrid-scale models using an accurately simulated turbulent flow. *J. Fluid Mech.*, 91:1–16, 1979.

[136] P. Clavin. Dynamic behavior of premixed flame fronts in laminar and turbulent flows. *Prog. Energy Comb. Sci.*, 11:1–59, 1985.

[137] P. Clavin. Dynamics of combustion fronts in premixed gases: from flames to detonations. *Proc. Combust. Inst.*, 28:569–586, 2000.

[138] P. Clavin and P. Garcia. The influence of the temperature dependence of diffusivities on the dynamics of flame fronts. *J. Mécanique*, 2:245–263, 1983.

[139] P. Clavin and G. Joulin. Premixed flames in large scale and high intensity turbulent flow. *J. Physique Lettres*, 44:L1–L12, 1983.

[140] P. Clavin and A. Li nán. Theory of gaseous combustion. an introductive course. *NATO ASI Ser. B*, 116:291–338, 1984.

[141] P. Clavin and F. A. Williams. Effects of molecular diffusion and of thermal expansion on the structure and dynamics of premixed flames in turbulent flows of large scales and low intensity. *J. Fluid Mech.*, 116:251–282, 1982.

[142] C. W. Clendening, W. Shackleford, and R. Hilyard. Raman scatterring measurement in a side wall quench layer. In *18th Symp. (Int.) on Combustion*, pages 1583–1589. The Combustion Institute, Pittsburgh, 1981.

[143] C. M. Coats. Coherent structures in combustion. *Prog. Energy Comb. Sci.*, 22:427 – 509, 1996.

[144] P.J. Coelho. Numerical simulation of the interaction between turbulence and radiation in reacting flows. *Prog. Energy Comb. Sci.*, 33:311 – 383, 2007.

[145] P.J. Coelho. Approximate solutions of the filtered radiative transfer equation in large eddy simulation of turbulent reactive flows. *Combust. Flame*, 156:1099 – 1110, 2009.

[146] O. Colin and K. Truffin. A spark ignition model for large eddy simulation based on an FSD transport equation (ISSIM-LES). *Proc. Combust. Inst.*, 33(2):3097–3104, 2011.

[147] O. Colin, F. Ducros, D. Veynante, and T. Poinsot. A thickened flame model for large eddy simulations of turbulent premixed combustion. *Phys. Fluids*, 12(7):1843–1863, 2000.

[148] T. Colonius, S. Lele, and P. Moin. Boundary conditions for direct computation of aerodynamic sound generation. *AIAA Journal*, 31(9):1574–1582, 1993.

[149] A. W. Cook. Determination of the constant coefficient in scale similarity models of turbulence. *Phys. FluidsA*, 9(5):1485 – 1487, 1997.

[150] A. W. Cook and W. K. Bushe. A subgrid-scale model for the scalar dissipation rate in non premixed combustion. *Phys. FluidsA*, 11(3):746 – 748, 1999.

[151] A. W. Cook and J. J. Riley. A subgrid model for equilibrium chemistry in turbulent flows. *Phys. FluidsA*, 6(8):2868 – 2870, 1994.

[152] A. W. Cook and J. J. Riley. Subgrid scale modeling for turbulent reacting flows. *Combust. Flame*, 112:593 – 606, 1998.

[153] D. G. Crighton, A. P. Dowling, J. E. Ffowcs Williams, M. Heckl, and F. Leppington. *Modern methods in analytical acoustics*. Lecture Notes. Springer Verlag, New-York, 1992.

[154] L. Crocco. Aspects of combustion instability in liquid propellant rocket motors. Part I. *J. American Rocket Society*, 21:163–178, 1951.

[155] L. Crocco. Aspects of combustion instability in liquid propellant rocket motors. part II. *J. American Rocket Society*, 22:7–16, 1952.

[156] L. Crocco. Research on combustion instability in liquid propellant rockets. In *12th Symp. (Int.) on Combustion*, pages 85–99. The Combustion Institute, Pittsburgh, 1969.

[157] L. Crocco, R. Monti, and J. Grey. Verification of nozzle admittance theory by direct measurement of the admittance parameter. *ARS Journal*, 31(6):771–775, 1961.

[158] B. Cuenot and T. Poinsot. Effects of curvature and unsteadiness in diffusion flames. implications for turbulent diffusion flames. *Proc. Combust. Inst.*, 25:1383–1390, 1994.

[159] B. Cuenot and T. Poinsot. Asymptotic and numerical study of diffusion flames with variable lewis number and finite rate chemistry. *Combust. Flame*, 104:111–137, 1996.

[160] F. E. C. Culick and P. Kuentzmann. *Unsteady Motions in Combustion Chambers for Propulsion Systems*. NATO Research and Technology Organization, 2006.

[161] F. Dabireau, B. Cuenot, O. Vermorel, and T. Poinsot. Interaction of H2/O2 flames with inert walls. *Combust. Flame*, 135(1-2):123–133, 2003.

[162] T. Daguse, T. Croonenbroek, N. Darabiha, J. C. Rolon, and A. Soufiani. Study of radiative effects on laminar counterflow H2/O2/N2 diffusion flames. *Combust. Flame*, 106:271–287, 1996.

[163] N. Darabiha. Transient behaviour of laminar counterflow hydrogen-air diffusion flames with complex chemistry. *Combust. Sci. Tech.*, 86:163–181, 1992.

[164] N. Darabiha and S. Candel. The influence of the temperature on extinction and ignition limits of strained hydrogen-air diffusion flames. *Combust. Sci. Tech.*, 86:67–85, 1992.

[165] N. Darabiha, S. Candel, and F. E. Marble. The effect of strain rate on a premixed laminar flame. *Combust. Flame*, 64:203–217, 1986.

[166] N. Darabiha, V. Giovangigli, A. Trouvé, S. M. Candel, and E. Esposito. Coherent flame description of turbulent premixed ducted flames. In R. Borghi and S.N.B. Murthy, editors, *Turbulent Reactive Flows. Lecture notes in engineering*, volume 40, pages 591–637. Springer, 1987.

[167] H. Davy. Some researches on flame. *Phil. Trans.*, page **45**, 1817.

[168] S.M. De Bruyn Kops, J.J. Riley, G. Kosaly, and A.W. Cook. Investigation of modeling for non-premixed turbulent combustion. *Flow, Turb. and Combustion*, 60(1):105–122, 1998.

[169] L. P. H. de Goey, J. A. van Oijen, H. Bongers, and G. R. A. Groot. New flamelet based reduction methods: the bridge between chemical reduction techniques and flamelet methods. In *European Combustion Meeting*, Orléans (France), 2003.

[170] J. E. Dec and J. O. Keller. Pulse combustor tail-pipe heat-transfer dependence on frequency, amplitude, and mean flow rate. *Combust. Flame*, 77(3-4):359–374, 1989.

[171] J. E. Dec and J. O. Keller. Time-resolved gas temperatures in the oscillating turbulent flow of a pulse combustor tail pipe. *Combust. Flame*, 80(3-4):358–370, 1990.

[172] A. Delataillade, F. Dabireau, B. Cuenot, and T. Poinsot. Flame/wall interaction and maximum heat wall fluxes in diffusion burners. *Proc. Combust. Inst.*, 29:775–780, 2002.

[173] A. Dervieux, B. Larrouturou, and R. Peyret. On some adaptive numerical approaches of thin flame propagation problems. *Combust. Flame*, 17(1):39–60, 1989.

[174] B. Deshaies and P. Cambray. The velocity of a premixed flame as a function of the flame stretch: an experimental study. *Combust. Flame*, 82:361–375, 1990.

[175] P. E. DesJardin and S. H. Frankel. Large eddy simulation of a nonpremixed reacting jet: application and assessment of subgrid-scale combustion models. *Phys. FluidsA*, 10 (9):2298 – 2314, 1998.

[176] D. Desvigne. *Bruit rayonne par un ecoulement subsonique affleurant une cavite cylindrique : caracterisation experimentale et simulation numerique directe par une approche multidomaine d'ordre eleve.* Phd thesis, Ecole Centrale Lyon, 2010.

[177] R. Diwakar. Assessment of the ability of a multidimensional computer code to model combustion in a homogeneous-charge engine. In *SAE Paper 840230*, 1984.

[178] P. E. Doak. Fundamentals of aerodynamic sound theory and flow duct acoustics. *J. Sound Vib.*, 28:527–561, 1973.

[179] J. W. Dold. Flame propagation in a nonuniform mixture: analysis of a slowly varying triple flame. *Combust. Flame*, 76:71–88, 1989.

[180] P. Domingo and K. N. C. Bray. Laminar flamelet expressions for pressure fluctuation terms in second moment models of premixed turbulent combustion. *Combust. Flame*, 121(4):555–574, 2000.

[181] P. Domingo and L. Vervisch. Triple flames and partially premixed combustion in autoignition of non-premixed mixtures. In *26th Symp. (Int.) on Combustion*, pages 233–240. The Combustion Institute, Pittsburgh, 1996.

[182] C. Dopazo. Recent developments in pdf methods. In P. A. Libby and F. A. Williams, editors, *Turbulent Reacting Flows*, pages 375 – 474. Academic, London, 1994.

[183] D. R. Dowdy, D. B. Smith, and S. C. Taylor. The use of expanding spherical flames to determine burning velocities and stretch effects in hydrogen/air mixtures. In *23rd Symp. (Int.) on Combustion*, pages 325–332. The Combustion Institute, Pittsburgh, 1990.

[184] A. P. Dowling. The calculation of thermoacoustic oscillations. *J. Sound Vib.*, 180(4):557–581, 1995.

[185] A. P. Dowling. A kinematic model of ducted flame. *J. Fluid Mech.*, 394:51–72, 1999.

[186] P. G. Drazin and W. H. Reid. *Hydrodynamic stability*. Cambridge University Press, London, 1981.

[187] J. F. Driscoll, D. Sutkus, W. L. Roberts, M. Post, and L. P. Goss. The strain exerted by a vortex on a flame - determined from velocity images. *Combust. Sci. Tech.*, 96:213–229, 1994.

[188] J. M. Duclos and O. Colin. Arc and kernel tracking ignition model for 3D spark ignition engine calculations. In *Fifth Int. Symp. on Diagnostics, Modelling of Combustion in Internal Combustion Engines (COMODIA)*, pages 343–350, Nagoya, Japan, 2001.

[189] J. M. Duclos, D. Veynante, and T. Poinsot. A comparison of flamelet models for premixed turbulent combustion. *Combust. Flame*, 95:101–117, 1993.

[190] J. M. Duclos, G. Bruneaux, and T. Baritaud. 3d modelling of combustion and pollutants in a 4 valve SI engine: effect of fuel and residuals distribution and spark location. In SAE Paper 961964, editor, *Int. Fall Fuels and Lubricants Meeting and Exposition*, San Antonio, 1996.

[191] J.-M. Duclos, M. Zolver, and T. Baritaud. 3d modeling of combustion for DI-SI engines. *Oil and Gas Science Tech.- Rev de l'IFP*, 54(2):259–264, 1999.

[192] F. Ducros, P. Comte, and M. Lesieur. Large-eddy simulation of transition to turbulence in a boundary layer developing spatially over a flat plate. *J. Fluid Mech.*, 326:1–36, 1996.

[193] S. Ducruix and S. Candel. External flow modulation in computational fluid dynamics. *AIAA Journal*, 42(8):1550–1558, 2004.

[194] P. Dutt. Stable boundary conditions and difference schemes for navier stokes equations. *J. Numer. Anal.*, 25:245–267, 1988.

[195] C. Duwig. Study of a filtered flamelet formulation for large eddy simulation of premixed turbulent flames. *Flow, Turb. and Combustion*, 79(4):433–454, 2007. ISSN 1386-6184. doi: {10.1007/s10494-007-9107-1}.

[196] T. Echekki and J. H. Chen. Unsteady strain rate and curvature effects in turbulent premixed methane-air flames. *Combust. Flame*, 106:184–202, 1996.

[197] T. Echekki and J. Ferziger. A simplified reaction rate model and its application to the analysis of premixed flames. *Combust. Sci. Tech.*, 89:293–351, 1993.

[198] E. Effelsberg and N. Peters. Scalar dissipation rates in turbulent jets and jet diffusion flames. In *22nd Symp. (Int.) on Combustion*, pages 693–700. The Combustion Institute, Pittsburgh, 1988.

[199] F. Egolfopoulos and C. K. Law. Further considerations on the determination of laminar flame speeds with the counterflow twin flame technique. In *25th Symp. (Int.) on Combustion*, pages 1341–1347. The Combustion Institute, Pittsburgh, 1994.

[200] B. Engquist and A. Majda. Absorbing boundary conditions for the numerical simulation of waves. *Math. Comput.*, 31(139):629–651, 1977.

[201] A. Ern and V. Giovangigli. *Multicomponent Transport Algorithms*. Lecture Notes in Physics. Springer Verlag, Heidelberg, 1994.

[202] S. Evesque and W. Polifke. Low-order acoustic modelling for annular combustors: Validation and inclusion of modal coupling. In *International Gas Turbine and Aeroengine Congress & Exposition, ASME Paper*, volume GT-2002-30064, 2002.

[203] S. Evesque, W. Polifke, and C. Pankiewitz. Spinning and azimuthally standing acoustic modes in annular combustors. In *9th AIAA/CEAS Aeroacoustics Conference*, volume AIAA paper 2003-3182, 2003.

[204] O. A. Ezekoye, R. Greif, and D. Lee. Increased surface temperature effects on wall heat transfer during unsteady flame quenching. In *24th Symp. (Int.) on Combustion*, pages 1465–1472. The Combustion Institute, Pittsburgh, 1992.

[205] P. W. Fairchild, R. D. Fleeter, and F. E. Fendell. Raman spectroscopy measurement of flame quenching in a duct type crevice. In *20th Symp. (Int.) on Combustion*, pages 85–90. The Combustion Institute, Pittsburgh, 1984.

[206] A. Favre. Statistical equations of turbulent gases. In *Problems of hydrodynamics and continuum mechanics*, pages 231–266. SIAM, Philadelphia, 1969.

[207] E. Fernandez, V. Kurdyumov, and A. Linan. Diffusion flame attachment and lift-off in the near wake of a fuel injector. *Proc. Combust. Inst.*, 28:2125–2131, 2000.

[208] E. Fernández-Tarrazo, A. L. Sánchez, A. Liñán, and F. A. Williams. A simple one-step chemistry model for partially premixed hydrocarbon combustion. *Combust. Flame*, 147 (1-2):32–38, 2006.

[209] J. Ferziger. Large eddy simulation: an introduction and perspective. In O. Métais and J. Ferziger, editors, *New tools in turbulence modelling*, pages 29 – 47. Les Editions de Physique - Springer Verlag, 1997.

[210] J. H. Ferziger and M. Perić. *Computational Methods for Fluid Dynamics*. Springer Verlag, Berlin, Heidelberg, New York, 1997.

[211] F. Fichot, F. Lacas, D. Veynante, and S. Candel. One-dimensional propagation of a premixed turbulent flame with the coherent flame model. *Combust. Sci. Tech.*, 48: 1–26, 1993.

[212] F. Fichot, B. Delhaye, D. Veynante, and S. M. Candel. Strain rate modelling for a flame surface density equation with application to non-premixed turbulent combustion. In *25th Symp. (Int.) on Combustion*, pages 1273–1281. The Combustion Institute, Pittsburgh, 1994.

[213] B. Fiorina, R. Baron, O. Gicquel, D. Thévenin, S. Carpentier, and N. Darabiha. Modelling non-adiabatic partially premixed flames using flame-prolongation of ILDM. *Combust. Theory and Modelling*, 7(3):449–470, 2003.

[214] B. Fiorina, O. Gicquel, L. Vervisch, S. Carpentier, and N. Darabiha. Premixed turbulent combustion modeling using a tabulated detailed chemistry and PDF. *Proc. Combust. Inst.*, 30(1):867–874, 2005.

[215] B. Fiorina, O. Gicquel, and D. Veynante. Turbulent flame simulation taking advantage of tabulated chemistry self-similar properties. *Proc. Combust. Inst.*, 32:1687–1694, 2009.

[216] B. Fiorina, R. Vicquelin, P. Auzillon, N. Darabiha, O. Gicquel, and D. Veynante. A filtered tabulated chemistry model for LES of premixed combustion. *Combust. Flame*, 157(3):465–475, 2010.

[217] C. G. Fotache, H. Wang, and C. K. Law. Ignition of ethane, propane and butane in counterflow jets of cold fuel versus hot air under variable pressures. *Combust. Flame*, 117(4):777–794, 1999.

[218] R. O. Fox, J. C. Hill, F. Gao, R. D. Moser, and M. M. Rodgers. Stochastic modeling of turbulent reacting flows. In *Proc. of the Summer Program*, pages 403–424. Center for Turbulence Research, NASA Ames/Stanford Univ., 1992.

[219] R.O. Fox. *Computational models for turbulent reacting flows*. Cambridge University Press, 2003.

[220] B. Franzelli, E. Riber, M. Sanjosé, and T. Poinsot. A two-step chemical scheme for Large-Eddy Simulation of kerosene-air flames. *Combust. Flame*, 157(7):1364–1373, 2010.

[221] M. Frenklach, H. Wang, M. Goldenberg, G. P. Smith, D. M. Golden, C. T. Bowman, R. K. Hanson, W. C. Gardiner, and V. Lissianki. GRI-mech: an optimized detailed chemical reaction mechanism for methane combustion. Technical Report GRI-Report GRI-95/0058, Gas Research Institute, 1995.

[222] C. Fureby. LES of a multi-burner annular gas turbine combustor. *Flow, Turb. and Combustion*, 84:543–564, 2010.

[223] C. Fureby and C. Løfstrøm. Large eddy simulations of bluff body stabilized flames. In *25th Symp. (Int.) on Combustion*, pages 1257 – 1264. The Combustion Institute, Pittsburgh, 1994.

[224] C. Fureby and S. I. Møller. Large eddy simulations of reacting flows applied to bluff body stabilized flames. *AIAA Journal*, 33(12):2339, 1995.

[225] D. Galley, S. Ducruix, F. Lacas, and D. Veynante. Mixing and stabilization study of a partially premixed swirling flame using laser induced fluorescence. *Combust. Flame*, 158:155–171, 2011.

[226] F. Gao and E.E. O'Brien. A large-eddy simulation scheme for turbulent reacting flows. *Phys. Fluids*, 5(6):1282–1284, 1993.

[227] A. Garmory and E. Mastorakos. Capturing localised extinction in sandia flame f with les-cmc. *Proc. Combust. Inst.*, 33(1):1673 – 1680, 2011.

[228] M. Germano, U. Piomelli, P. Moin, and W. Cabot. A dynamic subgrid-scale eddy viscosity model. *Phys. Fluids*, 3(7):1760–1765, 1991.

[229] M. Germano, A. Maffio, S. Sello, and G. Mariotti. On the extension of the dynamic modelling procedure to turbulent reacting flows. In J. P. Chollet, P. R. Voke, and L. Kleiser, editors, *Direct and Large Eddy Simulation II*, pages 291 – 300. Kluwer Academic Publishers, 1997.

[230] B.J. Geurts. *Elements of Direct and Large-Eddy Simulation.* Edwards Inc., Philadelphia, PA, U.S.A., 2004.

[231] S. Ghosal and P. Moin. The basic equations for the large eddy simulation of turbulent flows in complex geometry. *J. Comput. Phys.*, 118:24 – 37, 1995.

[232] S. Ghosal and L. Vervisch. Theoretical and numerical investigation of a symmetrical triple flame using a parabolic flame type approximation. *J. Fluid Mech.*, 415:227–260, 2000.

[233] A. Giauque, L. Selle, T. Poinsot, H. Buechner, P. Kaufmann, and W. Krebs. System identification of a large-scale swirled partially premixed combustor using LES and measurements. *J. Turb.*, 6(21):1–20, 2005.

[234] O. Gicquel, N. Darabiha, and D. Thévenin. Laminar premixed hydrogen/air counterflow flame simulations using flame prolongation of ILDM with differential diffusion. *Proc. Combust. Inst.*, 28:1901–1908, 2000.

[235] M. Giles. Non-reflecting boundary conditions for euler equation calculations. *AIAA Journal*, 28(12):2050–2058, 1990.

[236] V. Giovangigli. *Structure et extinction de flammes laminaires prémélangées.* Phd thesis, Paris VI, 1988.

[237] V. Giovangigli. *Multicomponent Flow Modeling.* Modeling and Simulation in Science, Engineering and Technology. Birkhauser, Boston, 1999.

[238] V. Giovangigli and M. Smooke. Calculation of extinction limits for premixed laminar flames in a stagnation point flow. *J. Comput. Phys.*, 68(2):327–345, 1987.

[239] V. Giovangigli and M. Smooke. Extinction of strained premixed laminar flames with complex chemistry. *Combust. Sci. Tech.*, 53:23–49, 1987.

[240] V. Giovangigli and M. Smooke. Application of continuation methods to laminar premixed flames. *Combust. Sci. Tech.*, 87:241–256, 1993.

[241] S. S. Girimaji and S. B. Pope. Propagating surfaces in isotropic turbulence. *J. Fluid Mech.*, 234:247–277, 1992.

[242] S. S. Girimaji and Y. Zhou. Analysis and modeling of subgrid scalar mixing using numerical data. *Phys. FluidsA*, 8(5):1224–1236, 1996.

[243] P. Givi. Model-free simulations of turbulent reactive flows. *Prog. Energy Comb. Sci.*, 15:1–107, 1989.

[244] P. Givi. Spectral and random vortex methods in turbulent reacting flows. In F. Williams and P. Libby, editors, *Turbulent Reacting Flows*, pages 475–572. Academic Press, 1994.

[245] I. Glassman. *Combustion*. Academic Press, New York, 1987.

[246] R. Goncalves dos Santos, M. Lecanu, S. Ducruix, O. Gicquel, E. Iacona, and D. Veynante. Coupled large eddy simulations of turbulent combustion and radiative heat transfer. *Combust. Flame*, 152(3):387 – 400, 2008.

[247] F. Gouldin, K. Bray, and J. Y. Chen. Chemical closure model for fractal flamelets. *Combust. Flame*, 77:241, 1989.

[248] F. C. Gouldin. Combustion intensity and burning rate integral of premixed flames. In *26th Symp. (Int.) on Combustion*, pages 381 – 388. The Combustion Institute, Pittsburgh, 1996.

[249] F.C. Gouldin. An application of fractals to modeling premixed turbulent flames. *Combust. Flame*, 68(3):249 – 266, 1987.

[250] N Gourdain, L Gicquel, M Montagnac, O Vermorel, M Gazaix, G Staffelbach, M Garcia, JF Boussuge, and T Poinsot. High performance parallel computing of flows in complex geometries: I. methods. *Comput. Sci. Disc.*, 2:015003, 2009.

[251] N Gourdain, L Gicquel, M Montagnac, O Vermorel, M Gazaix, G Staffelbach, M Garcia, JF Boussuge, and T Poinsot. High performance parallel computing of flows in complex geometries: II - applications. *Comput. Sci. Disc.*, 2:015004, 2009.

[252] R. Grappin, J. Léorat, and A. Buttighoffer. Alfvén wave propagation in the high solar corona. *Astron. and Astrophys.*, 362:342–358, 2000.

[253] G.R.A. Groot and L.P.H. De Goey. A computational study on propagating spherical and cylindrical premixed flames. *Proc. Combust. Inst.*, 29(2):1445–1451, 2002.

[254] A. Gruber, R. Sankaran, E. R. Hawkes, and J. Chen. Turbulent flame–wall interaction: a direct numerical simulation study. *J. Fluid Mech.*, 658:5–32, 2010.

[255] X. J. Gu, M. Z. Haq, M. Lawes, and R. Woolley. Laminar burning velocity and markstein lengths of methane-air mixtures. *Combust. Flame*, 121:41–58, 2000.

[256] N. Guezennec and T. Poinsot. Acoustically nonreflecting and reflecting boundary conditions for vorticity injection in compressible solvers. *AIAA Journal*, 47:1709–1722, 2009.

[257] L. Guichard. *Développement d'outils numériques dédiés a l'étude de la combustion turbulente*. Phd thesis, Université de Rouen, 1999.

[258] O. Gulder. Turbulent premixed flame propagation models for different combustion regimes. In *23rd Symp. (Int.) on Comb.*, pages 743–835, Orleans, 1990. The Combustion Institute, Pittsburgh.

[259] O. L. Gulder and G. J. Smallwood. Inner cutoff scale of flame surface wrinkling in turbulent premixed flames. *Combust. Flame*, 103:107–114, 1995.

[260] O.L. Gulder. Turbulent premixed combustion modelling using fractal geometry. *Proc. Combust. Inst.*, 23:835–842, 1991.

[261] A. K. Gupta, D. G. Lilley, and N. Syred. *Swirl flows.* Abacus Press, 1984.

[262] B. Gustafsson and A. Sundstrøm. Incompletely parabolic problems in fluid dynamics. *SIAM J. Appl. Math.*, 35(2):343–357, 1978.

[263] E. Gutheil. The effect of multi dimensional pdfs on the turbulent reaction rate in turbulent reactive flows at moderate Damkohler numbers. *Physico chemical Hydrodynamics*, 9(3/4):525–535, 1987.

[264] B. Hakberg and A. D. Gosman. Analytical determination of turbulent flame speed from combustion models. In *20th Symp. (Int.) on Combustion*, pages 225–232. The Combustion Institute, Pittsburgh, 1984.

[265] M. Hallback, A. V. Johansson, and A. D. Burden. The basics of turbulence modelling. In H. Hallback, D.S. Henningson, A.V. Johansson, and P.H. Alfredsson, editors, *Turbulence and Transition Modelling*, pages 81 – 154. Kluwer Academic Publishers, 1996.

[266] F. Halter, C. Chauveau, I. Gokalp, and D. Veynante. Analysis of flame surface density measurements in turbulent premixed combustion. *Combust. Flame*, 156(3):657 – 664, 2009.

[267] F. Halter, T. Tahtouh, and C. Mounaïm-Rousselle. Nonlinear effects of stretch on the flame front propagation. *Combust. Flame*, 157(10):1825 – 1832, 2010.

[268] Z. Han, R. D. Reitz, F. E. Corcione, and G. Valentino. Interpretation of $k - \epsilon$ computed turbulence length scale predictions for engine flows. In *26th Symp. (Int.) on Combustion*, pages 2717–2723. The Combustion Institute, Pittsburgh, 1996.

[269] Y. Hardalupas, M. Tagawa, and A. M. K. P. Taylor. Characteristics of countergradient heat transfer in nonpremixed swirling flame. In R.J. Adrian, editor, *Developments in Laser Techniques and Applications to Fluid Mechanics*, page 159. Springer, Berlin, 1996.

[270] D. J. Harrje and F. H. Reardon. Liquid propellant rocket instability. Technical Report Report SP-194, NASA, 1972.

[271] C. Hasse, M. Bollig, N. Peters, and H. A. Dwyer. Quenching of laminar isooctane flames at cold walls. *Combust. Flame*, 122:117–129, 2000.

[272] E. R. Hawkes and S. R. Cant. A flame surface density approach to large eddy simulation of premixed turbulent combustion. In *28th Symp. (Int.) on Combustion*, pages 51–58. The Combustion Institute, Pittsburgh, 2000.

[273] E.R. Hawkes, R. Sankaran, J.H. Chen, S.A. Kaiser, and J.H. Franck. Analysis of lower-dimensional approximations to the scalar dissipation rate using direct numerical simulations of plane jet flames. *Proc. Combust. Inst.*, 32:1455 – 1463, 2009.

[274] E.R. Hawkes, R. Sankaran, and J.H. Chen. Estimates of the three-dimensional flame surface density and every term in its transport equation from two-dimensional measurements. *Proc. Combust. Inst.*, 33(1):1447 – 1454, 2011.

[275] D. Haworth, B. Cuenot, T. Poinsot, and R. Blint. Numerical simulation of turbulent propane-air combustion with non homogeneous reactants. *Combust. Flame*, 121:395–417, 2000.

[276] D. C. Haworth and T. J. Poinsot. The influence of Lewis number and nonhomogeneous mixture on premixed turbulent flame structure. In *Proc. of the Summer Program*, pages 281–298. Center for Turbulence Research, Stanford Univ./NASA-Ames, 1990.

[277] D. C. Haworth and T. J. Poinsot. Numerical simulations of Lewis number effects in turbulent premixed flames. *J. Fluid Mech.*, 244:405–436, 1992.

[278] D. C. Haworth, M. C. Drake, S. B. Pope, and R. J. Blint. The importance of time-dependent flame structures in stretched laminar flamelet models for turbulent jet diffusion flames. In *22nd Symp. (Int.) on Combustion*, pages 589–597. The Combustion Institute, Pittsburgh, 1988.

[279] D.C. Haworth. Progress in probability density function methods for turbulent reacting flows. *Prog. Energy Comb. Sci.*, 36(2):168–259, 2011.

[280] G. W. Hedstrom. Non reflecting boundary conditions for nonlinear hyperbolic systems. *J. Comput. Phys.*, 30:222–237, 1979.

[281] J. Hélie and A. Trouve. A modified coherent flame model to describe flame propagation in mixture with variable composition. In *28th Symp. (Int.) on Combustion*, pages 193–202. The Combustion Institute, Pittsburgh, 2000.

[282] P. Le Helley. *Etude theorique et experimentale des instabilites de combustion et de leur controle dans un bruleur premelange*. Phd thesis, Ecole Centrale de Paris, 1994.

[283] J. R. Herring, S. A. Orszag, and R. H. Kraichnan. Decay of two-dimensional homogeneous turbulence. *J. Fluid Mech.*, 66:417–444, 1974.

[284] J. B. Heywood. *Internal combustion engine fundamentals*. McGraw and Hill Series in Mechanical Engineering. McGraw-Hill, New-York, 1988.

[285] R. L. Higdon. Initial-boundary value problems for linear hyperbolic systems. *SIAM Review*, 28:177–217, 1986.

[286] R. L. Higdon. Numerical absorbing boundary conditions for the wave equation. *Math. of Comp.*, 49(179):65–90, 1987.

[287] R. Hilbert and D. Thévenin. Autoignition of turbulent non-premixed flames investigated using direct numerical simulations. *Combust. Flame*, 128(1/2):22 – 37, 2002.

[288] R. Hilbert, F. Tap, D. Veynante, and D. Thévenin. A new modeling approach for the autoignition of a non-premixed turbulent flame using dns. *Proc. Combust. Inst.*, 29: 2079 – 2086, 2002.

[289] R. Hilbert, F. Tap, H. El-Rabii, and D. Thévenin. Impact of detailed chemistry and transport models on turbulent combustion simulations. *Prog. Energy Comb. Sci.*, 30 (1):61–117, 2004.

[290] M. Hilka. *Simulation numérique directe et modélisation de la pollution des flammes turbulentes*. Phd thesis, Ecole Centrale Paris, 1998.

[291] M. Hilka, D. Veynante, M. Baum, and T. Poinsot. Simulation of flame vortex interactions usind detailed and reduced chemical kinetics. In *10th Symp. on Turbulent Shear Flows*, pages 19–19, Penn State, 1995.

[292] M. Hilka, M. Baum, T. Poinsot, and D. Veynante. Simulation of turbulent combustion with complex chemistry. In T. J. Poinsot, T. Baritaud, and M. Baum, editors, *Direct numerical simulation for turbulent reacting flows (Rapport du Centre de Recherche sur la Combustion Turbulente)*, pages 201–224. Editions TECHNIP, Rueil Malmaison, 1996.

[293] J. O. Hinze. *Turbulence*. McGraw-Hill, New-York, 1975.

[294] C. Hirsch. *Numerical Computation of Internal and External Flows*. John Wiley, New York, 1988.

[295] J. O. Hirschfelder, C. F. Curtiss, and R. B. Bird. *Molecular theory of gases and liquids*. John Wiley & Sons, New York, 1969.

[296] C. M. Ho and P. Huerre. Perturbed free shear layers. *Ann. Rev. Fluid Mech*, 16:365, 1984.

[297] H. C. Hottel and W. R. Hawthorne. Diffusion in laminar flame jets. In *3rd Symposium on Combustion, Flame and Explosion Phenomena*, pages 254 – 266. The Combustion Institute, Pittsburgh, 1949.

[298] G. Hsiao, R. Pandalai, H. Hura, and H. Mongia. Combustion dynamic modelling for gas turbine engines. In *AIAA Paper 98-3380*, 1998.

[299] W. M. Huang, S. R. Vosen, and R. Greif. Heat transfer during laminar flame quenching, effect of fuels. In *21st Symp. (Int.) on Combustion*, pages 1853–1860. The Combustion Institute, Pittsburgh, 1986.

[300] Y. Huang and V. Yang. Dynamics and stability of lean-premixed swirl-stabilized combustion. *Prog. Energy Comb. Sci.*, 35(4):293–364, 2011.

[301] F. Hussain and J. Jeong. On the identification of a vortex. *J. Fluid Mech.*, 285:69–94, 1995.

[302] M. Ihme, H. Pitsch, and H. Bodony. Radiation of noise in turbulent flames. *Proc. Combust. Inst.*, 32:1545–1554, 2009.

[303] H. G. Im, T. S. Lund, and J. H. Ferziger. Large eddy simulation of turbulent front propagation with dynamic subgrid models. *Phys. FluidsA*, 9(12):3826 – 3833, 1997.

[304] S. Ishizuka and C. K. Law. An experimental study of extinction and stability of stretched premixed flames. In *19th Symp. (Int.) on Combustion*, pages 327–335. The Combustion Institute, Pittsburgh, 1982.

[305] S. Ishizuka, K. Miyasaka, and C. K. Law. Effects of heat loss, preferential diffusion, and flame stretch on flame front instability and extinction of propane/air mixtures. *Combust. Flame*, 45:293–308, 1982.

[306] F. Jaegle, J.-M. Senoner, M. Garcia, F. Bismes, R. Lecourt, B. Cuenot, and T. Poinsot. Lagrangian and eulerian simulations of evaporating fuel spray in an aeronautical multi-point injector. *Proc. Combust. Inst.*, 33:2099–2107, 2011.

[307] J. Janicka and A. Sadiki. Large eddy simulation for turbulent combustion. *Proc. Combust. Inst.*, 30:537–547, 2004.

[308] J. Jarosinski. A survey of recent studies on flame extinction. *Combust. Sci. Tech.*, 12: 81–116, 1986.

[309] J. Jarosinski, J. Lee, and R. Knystautas. Interaction of a vortex ring and a laminar flame. In *22nd Symp. (Int.) on Combustion*, pages 505–514. The Combustion Institute, Pittsburgh, 1988.

[310] M. Jennings. Multi-dimensional modeling of turbulent premixed charge combustion. In *Int. Congress and Exposition*, page SAE Paper 920589, Detroit, 1992.

[311] C. Jiménez, B. Cuenot, T. Poinsot, and D. Haworth. Numerical simulation and modeling for lean stratified propane-air flames. *Combust. Flame*, 128(1-2):1–21, 2002.

[312] J. Jiménez, A. A. Wray, P. G. Saffman, and R. S. Rogallo. The structure of intense vorticity in isotropic turbulence. *J. Fluid Mech.*, 255:65–90, 1993.

[313] J. Jiménez, A. Li nán, M. Rogers, and F. Higuera. A priori testing of sub grid models for chemically reacting nonpremixed turbulent shear flows. *J. Fluid Mech.*, 349:149–171, 1997.

[314] R. W. Johnson and B. E. Launder. Discussion of on the calculation of turbulent heat transport downstream from an abrupt pipe expansion. *Numerical Heat Transfer*, 5: 189–212, 1982.

[315] W. P. Jones and B. E. Launder. The prediction of laminarization with a 2-equation model of turbulence. *Int. J. Heat and Mass Transfer*, 15:301, 1972.

[316] W. P. Jones and R. P. Lindstedt. Global reaction schemes for hydrocarbon combustion. *Combust. Flame*, 73:222–233, 1988.

[317] G. Joulin and T. Mitani. Linear stability of two-reactant flames. *Combust. Flame*, 40: 235–246, 1981.

[318] T. Just. Multichannel reactions in combustion. *Proc. Combust. Inst.*, 25:687–704, 1994.

[319] K. Kailasanath, J. H. Gardner, E. S. Oran, and J. P. Boris. Numerical simulations of unsteady reactive flows in a combustion chamber. *Combust. Flame*, 86:115–134, 1991.

[320] S. Kalamatianos, Y. K. Park, and D. G. Vlachos. Two-parameter continuation algorithms for sensitivity analysis, parametric dependence, reduced mechanisms, and stability criteria of ignition and extinction. *Combust. Flame*, 112(1/2):45–61, 1998.

[321] P. A. M. Kalt. *Experimenal investigation of turbulent scalar flux in premixed flames*. Phd thesis, University of Sydney, 1999.

[322] A. R. Karagozian and F. E. Marble. Study of a diffusion flame in a stretched vortex. *Combust. Sci. Tech.*, 46:65–84, 1986.

[323] V. Karpov, A. Lipatnikov, and V. Zimont. A test of an engineering model of premixed turbulent combustion. In *26th Symp. (Int.) on Combustion*, pages 249–257. The Combustion Institute, Pittsburgh, 1996.

[324] V. R. Katta and W. M. Roquemore. Role of inner and outer structures in transitional jet diffusion flame. *Combust. Flame*, 92:274–282, 1993.

[325] V. R. Katta and W. M. Roquemore. Simulation of dynamic methane jet diffusion flames using finite rate chemistry models. *AIAA Journal*, 36(11):2044–2054, 1998.

[326] A. Kaufmann, F. Nicoud, and T. Poinsot. Flow forcing techniques for numerical simulation of combustion instabilities. *Combust. Flame*, 131:371–385, 2002.

[327] A. Kaufmann, O. Simonin, T. Poinsot, and J. Hélie. Dynamics and dispersion in Eulerian-Eulerian DNS of two-phase flows. In *Proc. of the Summer Program*, pages 381–392. Center for Turbulence Research, NASA Ames/Stanford Univ., 2002.

[328] W. M. Kays and M. E. Crawford. *Convective Heat and Mass Transfer*. McGraw Hill, 1993.

[329] R. J. Kee, J. Warnatz, and J. A. Miller. A fortran computer code package for the evaluation of gas phase viscosities, conductivities, and diffusion coefficients. Technical Report SAND83-8209, Sandia National Laboratories, 1983.

[330] R. J. Kee, J. F. Grcar, M. D. Smooke, and J. A. Miller. Premix: A fortran program for modeling steady laminar one-dimensional flames. Technical Report SAND85-8240, Sandia National Laboratories, 1985.

[331] R. J. Kee, F. M. Rupley, and J. A. Miller. Chemkin-ii: A fortran chemical kinetics package for the analysis of gas-phase chemical kinetics. Technical Report SAND89-8009B, Sandia National Laboratories, 1989.

[332] J. O. Keller and D. Givoli. Exact non-reflecting boundary conditions. *J. Comput. Phys.*, 82(1):172–192, 1989.

[333] J. O. Keller, L. Vaneveld, D. Korschelt, G. L. Hubbard, A. F. Ghoniem, J. W. Daily, and A. K. Oppenheim. Mechanism of instabilities in turbulent combustion leading to flashback. *AIAA Journal*, 20:254–262, 1981.

[334] J. O. Keller, T. T. Bramlette, P. K. Barr, and J. R. Alvarez. NOx and CO emissions from a pulse combustor operating in a lean premixed mode. *Combust. Flame*, 99(3-4): 460–466, 1994.

[335] A.P. Kelley and C.K. Law. Nonlinear effects in the extraction of laminar flame speeds from expanding spherical flames. *Combust. Flame*, 156:1844–1851, 2009.

[336] R. M. Kerr. Higher order derivative correlation and the alignment of small scale structures in isotropic numerical turbulence. *J. Fluid Mech.*, 153:31–58, 1985.

[337] A. R. Kerstein. A linear eddy model of turbulent scalar transport and mixing. *Combust. Sci. Tech.*, 60:391, 1988.

[338] A. R. Kerstein. Linear-Eddy modeling of turbulent transport: Part II. Application to shear layer mixing. *Combust. Flame*, 75(3 - 4):397 – 413, 1989.

[339] A. R. Kerstein. Linear-eddy modelling of turbulent transport. part 3. mixing and differential molecular diffusion in round jets. *J. Fluid Mech.*, 216:411 – 435, 1990.

[340] A. R. Kerstein. Linear-eddy modelling of turbulent transport. part 6. microstructure of diffusive scalar mixing fields. *J. Fluid Mech.*, 231:361 – 394, 1991.

[341] A. R. Kerstein. Linear eddy modeling of turbulent transport. part 4: structure of diffusion flames. *Combust. Sci. Tech.*, 81:75 – 96, 1992.

[342] A. R. Kerstein, W. Ashurst, and F. A. Williams. Field equation for interface propagation in an unsteady homogeneous flow field. *Phys. Rev. A*, 37(7):2728–2731, 1988.

[343] K. Khose-Hoinghaus and J.K Jeffries. *Applied combustion diagnostics*. Taylor & Francis, 2002.

[344] T. M. Kiehne, R. D. Matthews, and D. E. Wilson. The significance of intermediate hydrocarbons during wall quench of propane flames. In *21st Symp. (Int.) on Combustion*, pages 1583–1589. The Combustion Institute, Pittsburgh, 1986.

[345] J. Kim, P. Moin, and R. Moser. Turbulence statistics in fully developed channel flow at low Reynolds number. *J. Fluid Mech.*, 177:133–166, 1987.

[346] S. W. Kim. Calculations of divergent channel flows with a multiple-time-scale turbulence model. *AIAA Journal*, 29(4):547–554, 1991.

[347] L. E. Kinsler, A. R. Frey, A. B. Coppens, and J. V. Sanders. *Fundamental of Acoustics*. John Wiley, 1982.

[348] P. N. Kioni, B. Rogg, K. N. C. Bray, and A. Linan. Flame spread in laminar mixing layers: the triple flame. *Combust. Flame*, 95:276, 1993.

[349] P. N. Kioni, K. N. C. Bray, D. A. Greenhalgh, and B. Rogg. Experimental and numerical study of a triple flame. *Combust. Flame*, 116:192–206, 1998.

[350] A. Y. Klimenko. Multicomponent diffusion of various admixtures in turbulent flow. *Fluid Dynamics*, 25(3):327 – 334, 1990.

[351] A. Y. Klimenko and R. W. Bilger. Conditional moment closure for turbulent combustion. *Prog. Energy Comb. Sci.*, 25(6):595 – 687, 1999.

[352] R. Knikker, D. Veynante, and C. Meneveau. A priori testing of a similarity model for large eddy simulations of turbulent premixed combustion. *Proc. Combust. Inst.*, 29: 2105 – 2111, 2002.

[353] R. Knikker, D. Veynante, and C. Meneveau. A dynamic flame surface density model for large eddy simulation of turbulent premixed combustion. *Phys. Fluids*, 16:L91–L94, 2004.

[354] A. N. Kolmogorov. The local structure of turbulence in incompressible viscous fluid for very large reynolds numbers. *C. R. Acad. Sci., USSR*, 30:301, 1941.

[355] S. Kotake. On combustion noise related to chemical reactions. *J. Sound Vib.*, 42: 399–410, 1975.

[356] R.H. Kraichnan. Diffusion by a random velocity field. *Phys. Fluids*, 13:22–31, 1970.

[357] W. Krebs, P. Flohr, B. Prade, and S. Hoffmann. Thermoacoustic stability chart for high intense gas turbine combustion systems. *Combust. Sci. Tech.*, 174:99–128, 2002.

[358] H.-O. Kreiss. Initial boundary value problems for hyperbolic systems. *Commun. Pure Appl. Math.*, 23:277–298, 1970.

[359] U. Krueger, J. Hueren, S. Hoffmann, W. Krebs, P. Flohr, and D. Bohn. Prediction and measurement of thermoacoustic improvements in gas turbines with annular combustion systems. In ASME Paper, editor, *ASME TURBO EXPO*, Munich, Germany, 2000.

[360] G. Kuenne, A. Ketelheun, and J. Janicka. LES modeling of premixed combustion using a thickened flame approach coupled with fgm tabulated chemistry. *Combust. Flame*, 158(9):1750 – 1767, 2011.

[361] K. K. Kuo. *Principles of combustion.* John Wiley & Sons, Inc., Hoboken, New Jersey, 2005 Second Edition.

[362] P. Laffitte. *La propagation des flammes dans les mélanges gazeux.* Hermann et Cie, Actualités scientifiques et industrielles, PARIS, 1939.

[363] H. Lahjaily, M. Champion, D. Karmed, and P. Bruel. Introduction of dilution in the bml model: application to a stagnating turbulent flame. *Combust. Sci. Tech.*, 135:153 – 173, 1998.

[364] L. Landau and E. Lifchitz. *Fluid Mechanics. Vol. 6 (2nd ed.).* Butterworth-Heinemann, 1987.

[365] G. Lartigue. *Simulation aux grandes échelles de la combustion turbulente.* Phd thesis, INP Toulouse, 2004.

[366] B. E. Launder. Advanced turbulence models for industrial applications. In H. Hallback, D.S. Henningson, A.V. Johansson, and P.H. Alfredsson, editors, *Turbulence and Transition Modelling*, pages 193 – 192. Kluwer Academic Publishers, 1996.

[367] A. M. Laverdant and S. Candel. Computation of diffusion and premixed flames rolled up in vortex structures. *J. Prop. Power*, 5:134–143, 1989.

[368] A. M. Laverdant and S. M. Candel. A numerical analysis of a diffusion flame-vortex interaction. *Combust. Sci. Tech.*, 60:79–96, 1988.

[369] C. K. Law. Dynamics of stretched flames. In *22nd Symp. (Int.) on Combustion*, pages 1381–1402. The Combustion Institute, Pittsburgh, 1988.

[370] C. K. Law and C. J. Sung. Structure, aerodynamics and geometry of premixed flamelets. *Prog. Energy Comb. Sci.*, 26:459–505, 2000.

[371] C. K. Law, D. L. Zhu, and G. Yu. Propagation and extinction of stretched premixed flames. In *21st Symp. (Int.) on Combustion*, pages 1419–1426. The Combustion Institute, Pittsburgh, 1986.

[372] C.K. Law, G. Jomaas, and J.K. Bechtold. Cellular instabilities of expanding hydrogen/propane spherical flames at elevated pressures: theory and experiment. *Proc. Combust. Inst.*, 30(1):159–167, 2005.

[373] R. Leandro, A. Huber, and W. Polifke. taxmanual. Technical report, TU München, 2010.

[374] G. Lecocq, S. Richard, O. Colin, and L. Vervisch. Hybrid presumed pdf and flame surface density approaches for large-eddy simulation of premixed turbulent combustion: Part 1: Formalism and simulation of a quasi-steady burner. *Combust. Flame*, 158(6): 1201 – 1214, 2011.

[375] T. W. Lee, J. Lee, D. Nye, and D. Santavicca. Local response and surface properties of premixed flames during interactions with kármán vortex streets. *Combust. Flame*, 94: 146–160, 1993.

[376] J.-Ph. Légier. *Simulations numériques des instabilités de combustion dans les foyers aéronautiques.* Phd thesis, INP Toulouse, 2001.

[377] J.-Ph. Légier, B. Varoquié, F. Lacas, T. Poinsot, and D. Veynante. Large eddy simulation of a non-premixed turbulent burner using a dynamically thickened flame model. In A. Pollard Eds and S. Candel, editors, *IUTAM Symposium on Turbulent Mixing and Combustion*, pages 315 – 326. Kluwer Academic Publishers, 2002.

[378] S.K. Lele. Compact finite difference schemes with spectral like resolution. *J. Comput. Phys.*, 103:16–42, 1992.

[379] A. Leonard and J. Hill. Direct numerical simulation of turbulent flows with chemical reaction. *J. Sci. Comput.*, 3(1):25–43, 1988.

[380] M. Lesieur. *Turbulence in fluids.* Fluid Mechanics and its applications. Kluwer Academic Publishers, 1990.

[381] M. Lesieur. Recent approaches in large-eddy simulations of turbulence. In O. Métais and J. Ferziger, editors, *New tools in turbulence modelling*, pages 1 – 28. Les Editions de Physique - Springer Verlag, 1997.

[382] M. Lesieur and O. Metais. New trends in large-eddy simulations of turbulence. *Ann. Rev. Fluid Mech*, 28:45 – 82, 1996.

[383] B. Lewis and G. Von Elbe. *Combustion, Flames and Explosions of Gases.* Academic Press, New York, third edition, 1987.

[384] M. Leyko, F. Nicoud, and T. Poinsot. Comparison of direct and indirect combustion noise mechanisms in a model combustor. *AIAA Journal*, 47(11):2709–2716, 2009.

[385] P. Libby and F. Williams. Premixed flames with general rates of strain. *Combust. Sci. Tech.*, 54:237, 1987.

[386] P. A. Libby and K. N. C. Bray. Countergradient diffusion in premixed turbulent flames. *AIAA Journal*, 19:205–213, 1981.

[387] P. A. Libby and F. A. Williams. Structure of laminar flamelets in premixed turbulent flames. *Combust. Flame*, 44:287, 1982.

[388] P. A. Libby and F. A. Williams. Strained premixed laminar flames under non-adiabatic conditions. *Combust. Sci. Tech.*, 31:1–42, 1983.

[389] P. A. Libby and F. A. Williams. Turbulent combustion: fundamental aspects and a review. In *Turbulent Reacting Flows*, pages 2–61. Academic Press London, 1994.

[390] P. A. Libby, K. N. C. Bray, and J. B. Moss. Effects of finite reaction rate and molecular transport in premixed turbulent combustion. *Combust. Flame*, 34:285–301, 1979.

[391] P. A. Libby, A. Linan, and F. A. Williams. Strained premixed laminar flames with non-unity lewis number. *Combust. Sci. Tech.*, 34:257, 1983.

[392] T. Lieuwen. Modeling premixed combustion-acoustic wave interactions: A review. *J. Prop. Power*, 19(5):765–781, 2003.

[393] T. Lieuwen and V. Yang. Combustion instabilities in gas turbine engines. operational experience, fundamental mechanisms and modeling. In *AIAA Prog. in Astronautics and Aeronautics*, volume 210, 2005.

[394] T. Lieuwen and B. T. Zinn. The role of equivalence ratio oscillations in driving combustion instabilities in low nox gas turbines. *Proc. Combust. Inst.*, 27:1809–1816, 1998.

[395] S. K. Liew, K. N. C. Bray, and J. B. Moss. A stretched laminar flamelet model of turbulent nonpremixed combustion. *Combust. Flame*, 56:199–213, 1984.

[396] D. O. Lignell, J. H. Chen, P. J. Smith, T. Lu, and C. K. Law. The effect of flame structure on soot formation and transport in turbulent nonpremixed flames using direct numerical simulation. *Combust. Flame*, 151(1-2):2–28, 2007.

[397] A. Linan. The asymptotic structure of counterflow diffusion flames for large activation energies. *Acta Astronautica*, 1:1007, 1974.

[398] A. Linan and A. Crespo. An asymptotic analysis of unsteady diffusion flames for large activation energies. *Combust. Sci. Tech.*, 14:95–117, 1976.

[399] A. Linan and F. A. Williams. *Fundamental aspects of combustion*. Oxford University Press, 1993.

[400] A. Linan, P. Orlandi, R. Verzicco, and F. J. Higuera. Effects of non-unity Lewis numbers in diffusion flames. In *Proc. of the Summer Program*, pages 5–18. Center for Turbulence Research, NASA Ames/Stanford Univ., 1994.

[401] A. Lipatnikov and J. Chomiak. Dependence of heat release on the progress variable in premixed turbulent combustion. *Proc. Combust. Inst.*, 28:227 – 234, 2000.

[402] F. C. Lockwood and A. S. Naguib. The prediction of the fluctuations in the properties of free round-jet, turbulent diffusion flames. *Combust. Flame*, 24:109–124, 1975.

[403] G. Lodato, P. Domingo, and Vervisch L. Three-dimensional boundary condtions for direct and large-eddy simulation of compressible viscous flow. *J. Comput. Phys.*, 227 (10):5105–5143, 2008.

[404] M. Lohrmann, H. Buechner, and N. Zarzalis. Flame transfer function characteristics of swirled flames for gas turbine applications. In ASME Paper 2003-GT-38113, editor, *ASME Turbo expo*, Atlanta, 2003.

[405] J. H. Lu, O. Ezekoye, R. Greif, and F. Sawyer. Unsteady heat transfer during side wall quenching of a laminar flame. In *23rd Symp. (Int.) on Combustion*, pages 441–446. The Combustion Institute, Pittsburgh, 1990.

[406] L. Lucas and D. Rockwell. Self-excited jet: upstream modulation and multiple frequencies. *J. Fluid Mech.*, 147:333–352, 1984.

[407] O. Lucca-Negro and T. O'Doherty. Vortex breakdown: a review. *Prog. Energy Comb. Sci.*, 27:431–481, 2001.

[408] K. H. Luo. On local countergradient diffusion in turbulent diffusion flames. In *28th Symp. (Int.) on Combustion*, pages 489–498. The Combustion Institute, Pittsburgh, 2000.

[409] K. H. Luo and K. N. C. Bray. Combustion induced pressure effects in supersonic diffusion flame. In *27th Symp. (Int.) on Combustion*, pages 2165 – 2171. The Combustion Institute, Pittsburgh, 1998.

[410] A. E. Lutz, R. J. Kee, and J. A. Miller. Senkin: A fortran program for predicting homogeneous gas phase kinetics with sensitivity analysis. Technical Report SAND87-8248, Sandia National Laboratories, 1991.

[411] U. Maas and S. B. Pope. Implementation of simplified chemical kinetics based on low-dimensional manifolds. *Proc. Combust. Inst.*, 24:719–729, 1992.

[412] U. Maas and S. B. Pope. Simplifying chemical kinetics: intrinsic low-dimensional manifolds in composition space. *Combust. Flame*, 88:239–264, 1992.

[413] B. F. Magnussen and B. H. Mjertager. On mathematical modeling of turbulent combustion. In *16th Symp. (Int.) on Combustion*, pages 719–727. The Combustion Institute, Pittsburgh, 1976.

[414] K. Mahesh, G. Constantinescu, S. Apte, G. Iaccarino, F. Ham, and P. Moin. Large eddy simulation of reacting turbulent flows in complex geometries. In *ASME J. Appl. Mech.*, volume 73, pages 374–381, 2006.

[415] E. Maistret, E. Darabiha, T. Poinsot, D. Veynante, F. Lacas, S. Candel, and E. Esposito. Recent developments in the coherent flamelet description of turbulent combustion. In A. Dervieux and B. Larrouturou, editors, *Numerical Combustion*, volume 351, pages 98–117, Antibes, 1989. Springer Verlag, Berlin.

[416] G. M. Makhviladze and V. I. Melikov. Flame propagation in a closed channel with cold side wall. *UDC, Plenum Publishing Corporation*, 536.46:176–183. Translated from Fizika Goreniya i Vzryva, 2, 49–58, 1991, 1991.

[417] T. Mantel and R. Borghi. A new model of premixed wrinkled flame propagation based on a scalar dissipation equation. *Combust. Flame*, 96(4):443–457, 1994.

[418] T. Mantel, J.-M. Samaniego, and C. T. Bowman. Fundamental mechanisms in premixed turbulent flame propagation via vortex-flame interactions - part ii: numerical simulation. *Combust. Flame*, 118(4):557–582, 1999.

[419] F. E. Marble and J. E. Broadwell. The coherent flame model for turbulent chemical reactions. Technical Report Tech. Rep. TRW-9-PU, Project Squid, 1977.

[420] C. Martin, L. Benoit, F. Nicoud, and T. Poinsot. Analysis of acoustic energy and modes in a turbulent swirled combustor. In *Proc. of the Summer Program*, pages 377–394. Center for Turbulence Research, NASA Ames/Stanford Univ., 2004.

[421] C. Martin, L. Benoit, Y. Sommerer, F. Nicoud, and T. Poinsot. LES and acoustic analysis of combustion instability in a staged turbulent swirled combustor. *AIAA Journal*, 44(4):741–750, 2006.

[422] E. Mastorakos, T. A. Baritaud, and T. J. Poinsot. Numerical simulations of autoignition in turbulent mixing flows. *Combust. Flame*, 109:198 – 223, 1997.

[423] E. Mastorakos, A. Pires Da Cruz, T. A. Baritaud, and T. J. Poinsot. A model for the effects of mixing on the autoignition of turbulent flows. *Combust. Sci. Tech.*, 125:243 – 282, 1997.

[424] M. Matalon and B. J. Matkowsky. Flames as gasdynamic discontinuities. *J. Fluid Mech.*, 124:239, 1982.

[425] F. Mathey and J. P. Chollet. Subgrid-scale model of scalar mixing for large eddy simulation of turbulent flows. In J. P. Chollet, P. R. Voke, and L. Kleiser, editors, *Direct and Large Eddy Simulation II*, pages 103 – 114. Kluwer Academic Publishers, 1997.

[426] K. McManus, T. Poinsot, and S. Candel. A review of active control of combustion instabilities. *Prog. Energy Comb. Sci.*, 19:1–29, 1993.

[427] P. A. McMurthy, S. Menon, and A. R. Kerstein. A linear eddy subgrid model for turbulent reacting flows: application to hydrogen-air combustion. In *24th Symp. (Int.) on Combustion*, pages 271 – 278. The Combustion Institute, Pittsburgh, 1992.

[428] P. A. McMurthy, T. C. Gansauge, A. R. Kerstein, and S. K. Krueger. Linear eddy simulations of mixing in a homogeneous turbulent flow. *Phys. FluidsA*, 5(4):1023 – 1034, 1993.

[429] J. P. Meeder and F. T. M. Nieuwstadt. Subgrid-scale segregation of chemically reactive species in a neutral boundary layer. In J. P. Chollet, P. R. Voke, and L. Kleiser, editors, *Direct and Large Eddy Simulation II*, pages 301 – 310. Kluwer Academic Publishers, 1997.

[430] W. Meier, P. Weigand, X.R. Duan, and R. Giezendanner-Thoben. Detailed characterization of the dynamics of thermoacoustic pulsations in a lean premixed swirl flame. *Combust. Flame*, 150(1-2):2–26, 2007.

[431] C. Meneveau and J. Katz. Scale-invariance and turbulence models for large eddy simulation. *Ann. Rev. Fluid Mech*, 32:1–32, 2000.

[432] C. Meneveau and T. Poinsot. Stretching and quenching of flamelets in premixed turbulent combustion. *Combust. Flame*, 86:311–332, 1991.

[433] C. Meneveau and K. R. Sreenivasan. Measurement of $f(\alpha)$ from scaling of histograms and applications to dynamical systems and fully developed turbulence. *Phys. Lett. A*, 137:103, 1989.

[434] C. Meneveau and K. R. Sreenivasan. The multifractal nature of the turbulent energy dissipation. *J. Fluid Mech.*, 24:429–484, 1991.

[435] C. Meneveau, T. Lund, and W. Cabot. A lagrangian dynamic subgrid-scale model of turbulence. *J. Fluid Mech.*, 319:353, 1996.

[436] S. Menon and A. R. Kerstein. Stochastic simulation of the structure and propagation rate of turbulent premixed flames. In *24th Symp. (Int.) on Combustion*, pages 443–450. The Combustion Institute, Pittsburgh, 1992.

[437] S. Menon, P. A. McMurthy, and A. R. Kerstein. A linear eddy mixing model for large eddy simulation of turbulent combustion. In B. Galperin and S.A. Orzag, editors, *Large eddy simulation of complex engineering and geophysical flows*, pages 87 – 314. Cambridge University Press, 1993.

[438] S. Menon, P. A. McMurthy, A. R. Kerstein, and J. Y. Chen. Prediction of NOx production in a turbulent hydrogen-air jet flame. *J. Prop. Power*, 10(2):161–168, 1994.

[439] M. Metghalchi and J. C. Keck. Laminar burning velocity of propane-air mixtures at high temperature and pressure. *Combust. Flame*, 38:143–154, 1980.

[440] J.B. Michel, O. Colin, and D. Veynante. Modeling ignition and chemical structure of partially premixed turbulent flames using tabulated chemistry. *Combust. Flame*, 152: 80–99, 2008.

[441] D. Mikolaitis. The interaction of flame curvature and stretch. Part I: the concave premixed flame. *Combust. Flame*, 57:25–31, 1984.

[442] H. P. Miller, R. Mitchell, M. Smooke, and R. Kee. Towards a comprehensive chemical kinetic mechanism for the oxidation of acetylene: comparison of model predictions with results from flame and shock tube experiments. In *19th Symp. (Int.) on Combustion*, pages 181–196. The Combustion Institute, Pittsburgh, 1982.

[443] T. Mitani. Propagation velocities of two-reactant flames. *Combust. Sci. Tech.*, 21:175, 1980.

[444] Y. Mizobuchi, S. Tachibana, J. Shinjo, S. Ogawa, and T. Takeno. A numerical analysis of the structure of a turbulent hydrogen jet-lifted flame. *Proc. Combust. Inst.*, 29:2009 – 2015, 2002.

[445] Y. Mizobuchi, J. Shinjo, S. Ogawa, and T. Takeno. A numerical study on the formation of diffusion flame islands in a turbulent hydrogen jet-lifted flame. *Proc. Combust. Inst.*, 30:611 – 619, 2005.

[446] J.P. Moeck, M. Oevermann, R. Klein, C. Paschereit, and H. Schmidt. A two-way coupling for modeling thermoacoustic instabilities in a flat flame rijke tube. *Proc. Combust. Inst.*, 32:1199–1207, 2009.

[447] J.P. Moeck, M. Paul, and C. Paschereit. Thermoacoustic instabilities in an annular flat rijke tube. In *ASME Turbo Expo 2010 GT2010-23577*, 2010.

[448] R. K. Mohammed, M. A. Tanoff, M. D. Smooke, A. M. Schaffer, and M. B. Long. Computational and experimental study of a forced, time varying, axisymmetric, laminar diffusion flame. In *27th Symp. (Int.) on Combustion*, pages 693–702. The Combustion Institute, Pittsburgh, 1998.

[449] P. Moin and S. V. Apte. Large-eddy simulation of realistic gas turbine combustors. *AIAA Journal*, 44(4):698–708, 2006.

[450] P. Moin and J. Kim. Numerical investigation of turbulent channel flow. *J. Fluid Mech.*, 118:341–377, 1982.

[451] P. Moin, K. D. Squires, W. Cabot, and S. Lee. A dynamic subgrid-scale model for compressible turbulence and scalar transport. *Phys. Fluids*, A 3(11):2746–2757, 1991.

[452] C. J. Montgomery, G. Kosály, and J. J. Riley. Direct numerical solution of turbulent nonpremixed combustion with multistep hydrogen-oxygen kinetics. *Combust. Flame*, 109:113–144, 1997.

[453] P. Moreau. Experimental determination of probability density functions within a turbulent high velocity premixed flame. In *18th Symp. (Int.) on Combustion*, pages 993 – 1000. The Combustion Institute, Pittsburgh, 1981.

[454] A. S. Morgans and S. R. Stow. Model-based control of combustion instabilities in annular combustors. *Combust. Flame*, 150(4):380–399, 2007.

[455] P. M. Morse and K. U. Ingard. *Theoretical acoustics*, volume 332. Princeton University Press, 1968.

[456] V. Moureau, G. Lartigue, Y. Sommerer, C. Angelberger, O. Colin, and T. Poinsot. Numerical methods for unsteady compressible multi-component reacting flows on fixed and moving grids. *J. Comput. Phys.*, 202(2):710–736, 2005.

[457] V. Moureau, P. Domingo, L. Vervisch, and D. Veynante. DNS analysis of a Re=40000 swirl burner. In NASA Ames/Stanford Univ. Center for Turbulence Research, editor, *Proc. of the Summer Program*, pages 209–298, 2010.

[458] V. Moureau, P. Domingo, and L. Vervisch. From large-eddy simulation to direct numerical simulation of a lean premixed swirl flame: Filtered laminar flame-pdf modeling. *Combust. Flame*, 158(7):1340–1357, 2011.

[459] V. R. Moureau, O. V. Vasilyev, C. Angelberger, and T. J. Poinsot. Commutation errors in Large Eddy Simulations on moving grids: Application to piston engine flows. In *Proc. of the Summer Program*, pages 157–168, Center for Turbulence Research, NASA AMES/Stanford University, USA, 2004.

[460] C. Mueller, J. F. Driscoll, D. Reuss, M. Drake, and M. Rosalik. Vorticity generation and attenuation as vortices convect through a premixed flame. *Combust. Flame*, 112: 342–358, 1998.

[461] B. D. Mugridge. Combustion driven oscillations. *J. Sound Vib.*, 70:437–452, 1980.

[462] C. M. Muller, H. Breitbach, and N. Peters. Partially premixed turbulent flame propagation in jet flames. In *25th Symp. (Int.) On Combustion*, pages 1099 – 1106. The Combustion Institute, Pittsburgh, 1994.

[463] L. Muniz and M. G. Mungal. Instantaneous flame-stabilization velocities in lifted-jet diffusion flames. *Combust. Flame*, 111(1-2):16–31, 1997.

[464] S. Navarro-Martinez and A. Kronenburg. LES-CMC simulations of a turbulent bluff-body flame. *Proc. Combust. Inst.*, 31:1721–1728, 2007.

[465] S. Navarro-Martinez and A. Kronenburg. LES-CMC simulations of a lifted methane flame. *Proc. Combust. Inst.*, 32(1):1509 – 1516, 2009.

[466] C. Nicoli and P. Clavin. Effect of variable heat loss intensities on the dynamics of a premixed flame front. *Combust. Flame*, 68:69–71, 1987.

[467] F. Nicolleau. *Processus fractals et reaction chimique en milieux turbulents*. Phd thesis, Ecole Centrale Lyon, 1994.

[468] F. Nicoud. Defining wave amplitude in characteristic boundary conditions. *J. Comput. Phys.*, 149(2):418–422, 1998.

[469] F. Nicoud and F. Ducros. Subgrid-scale stress modelling based on the square of the velocity gradient. *Flow, Turb. and Combustion*, 62(3):183–200, 1999.

[470] F. Nicoud and K. Wieczorek. About the zero mach number assumption in the calculation of thermoacoustic instabilitie. *Int. J. Spray and Combustion Dynamic*, 1:67–112, 2009.

[471] F. Nicoud, L. Benoit, C. Sensiau, and T. Poinsot. Acoustic modes in combustors with complex impedances and multidimensional active flames. *AIAA Journal*, 45:426–441, 2007.

[472] F. T. M. Nieuwstadt and J. P. Meeder. Large-eddy simulation of air pollution dispersion: a review. In *New tools in turbulence modelling*, pages 264 – 280. Les Editions de Physique - Springer Verlag, 1997.

[473] N. Noiray, D. Durox, T. Schuller, and S. Candel. A unified framework for nonlinear combustion instability analysis based on the flame describing function a unified framework for nonlinear combustion instability analysis based on the flame describing function. *J. Fluid Mech.*, 615:139–167, 2008.

[474] N. Noiray, M. Bothien, and B. Schuermans. Analytical and numerical analysis of staging concepts in annular gas turbines. In *n3l - Int'l Summer School and Workshop on Non-normal and non linear effects in aero and thermoacoustics*, 2010.

[475] N. Noiray, M. Bothien, and B. Schuermans. Investigation of azimuthal staging concepts in annular gas turbines. *Combust. Theory and Modelling*, pages 585–606, 2011.

[476] K. Nomura. *Small scale structure of turbulence in a non premixed reacting flow with and without energy release*. Phd thesis, Irvine, 1994.

[477] K. K. Nomura and S. E. Elgobashi. Mixing characteristics of an inhomogeneous scolar in isotropic and homogeneous sheared turbulence. *Phys. Fluids*, 4:606–625, 1992.

[478] E. O'Brien. The pdf approach to reacting turbulent flows. In P.A. Libby and F.A. Williams, editors, *Turbulent Reacting Flows, Topics in Applied Physics*, volume 44. Academic Press London, 1980.

[479] S. Ohring. Calculations of edgetone flow with forced longitudinal oscillations. *J. Fluid Mech.*, 184:505–531, 1987.

[480] N. Okong'o and J. Bellan. Consistent boundary conditions for multicompoment real gas mixtures based on characteristic waves. *J. Comput. Phys.*, 176:330–344, 2002.

[481] J. Oliger and A. Sundstrom. Theoretical and practical aspects of some initial boundary value problems in fluid dynamics. *SIAM J. Appl. Math.*, 35:419–446, 1978.

[482] E. S. Oran and J. P. Boris. Computing turbulent shear flows - a convenient conspiracy. *Comput. Phys.*, September/October(7):523–533, 1993.

[483] E. S. Oran and J. P. Boris. *Numerical simulation of reactive flow. 2nd edition.* Cambridge University Press, New-York, 2001.

[484] I. Orlanski. A simple boundary condition for unbounded hyperbolic flows. *J. Comput. Phys.*, 21:251–269, 1976.

[485] S. Osher and J. Sethian. Fronts propagating with curvature dependent speed: algorithms based on Hamilton-Jacobi formulations. Technical Report 87-66, ICASE, 1987.

[486] W. Pakdee and S. Mahalingam. An accurate method to implement boundary conditions for reacting flows based on characteristic analysis. *Combust. Theory and Modelling*, 7: 705–729, 2003.

[487] P. Palies. *Dynamique et instabilites de combustion de flammes swirlees.* Phd thesis, Ecole Centrale Paris, 2010.

[488] C. Pankiewitz and T. Sattelmayer. Time domain simulation of combustion instabilities in annular combustors. *ASME Journal of Engineering for Gas Turbines and Power*, 125 (3):677–685, 2003.

[489] C. O. Paschereit, P. Flohr, and B. Schuermans. Prediction of combustion oscillations in gas turbine combustors. In AIAA Paper 2001-0484, editor, *39th AIAA Aerospace Sciences Meeting and Exhibit*, Reno, NV, 2001.

[490] C. O. Paschereit, W. Polifke, B. Schuermans, and O. Mattson. Measurement of transfer matrices and source terms of premixed flames. *J. Eng. Gas Turb. and Power*, 124: 239–247, 2002.

[491] G. Patnaik and K. Kailasanath. Effect of gravity on the stability and structure of lean hydrogen - air flames. In *23rd Symp. (Int.) on Combustion*, pages 1641–1647. The Combustion Institute, Pittsburgh, 1991.

[492] G. Patnaik and K. Kailasanath. Simulation of multidimensional burner-stabilized flames. In AIAA Paper 93-0241, editor, *31st AIAA Aerospace Sciences Meeting*, Reno, 1993.

[493] G. Patnaik and K. Kailasanath. A computational study of local quenching in flame vortex interactions with radiative losses. In *27th Symp. (Int.) on Combustion*, pages 711 – 717. The Combustion Institute, Pittsburgh, 1998.

[494] G. Patnaik, K. Kailasanath, K. Laskey, and E. Oran. Detailed numerical simulations of cellular flames. In *22nd Symp. (Int.) on Combustion*, pages 1517–1526. The Combustion Institute, Pittsburgh, 1988.

[495] P. Paul and J. Warnatz. A reevaluation of the means used to calculate transport properties of reacting flows. In *27th Symp. (Int.) on Combustion*, pages 495–504. The Combustion Institute, Pittsburgh, 1998.

[496] R.N. Paul and K.N.C. Bray. Study of premixed turbulent combustion including landau–darrieus instability effects. *Proc. Combust. Inst.*, 26:259 – 266, 1996.

[497] P. Pelce and P. Clavin. Influence of hydrodynamics and diffusion upon stability limits of laminar premixed flames. *J. Fluid Mech.*, 124:219, 1982.

[498] N. Peters. Laminar diffusion flamelet models in non-premixed turbulent combustion. *Prog. Energy Comb. Sci.*, 10:319–339, 1984.

[499] N. Peters. Numerical and asymptotic analysis of systematically reduced reaction schemes for hydrocarbon flames. In B. Larrouturou R. Glowinsky and R. Temam, editors, *Numerical simulation of combustion phenomena*, volume 241, pages 90–109. Springer-Verlag, Berlin, 1985.

[500] N. Peters. Laminar flamelet concepts in turbulent combustion. In *21st Symp. (Int.) on Combustion*, pages 1231–1250. The Combustion Institute, Pittsburgh, 1986.

[501] N. Peters. The turbulent burning velocity for large-scale and small-scale turbulence. *J. Fluid Mech.*, 384:107 – 132, 1999.

[502] N. Peters. *Turbulent combustion*. Cambridge University Press, 2001.

[503] S. Pfadler, J. Kerl, F. Beyrau, A. Leipertz, A. Sadiki, J. Scheuerlein, and F. Dinkelacker. Direct evaluation of the subgrid scale scalar flux in turbulent premixed flames with conditioned dual-plane stereo PIV. *Proc. Combust. Inst.*, 32(2):1723–1730, 2009.

[504] H. Phillips. Flame in a buoyant methane layer. In *10th Symp. (Int.) on Combustion*, pages 1277–1283. The Combustion Institute, Pittsburgh, 1965.

[505] J. Piana, D. Veynante, S. Candel, and T. Poinsot. Direct numerical simulation analysis of the g-equation in premixed combustion. In J. P. Chollet, P. R. Voke, and L. Kleiser, editors, *Direct and Large Eddy Simulation II*, pages 321–330. Kluwer Academic Publishers, 1997.

[506] A. D. Pierce. *Acoustics: an introduction to its physical principles and applications.* McGraw Hill, New York, 1981.

[507] C. D. Pierce and P. Moin. A dynamic model for subgrid scale variance and dissipation rate of a conserved scalar. *Phys. Fluids*, 10(12):3041–3044, 1998.

[508] C. D. Pierce and P. Moin. Progress-variable approach for large eddy simulation of non-premixed turbulent combustion. *J. Fluid Mech.*, 504:73–97, 2004.

[509] U. Piomelli. Large-eddy simulation: achievements and challenges. *Prog. Aerospace Sci.*, 35:335–362, 1999.

[510] U. Piomelli and J. R. Chasnov. Large eddy simulations: theory and applications. In H. Hallback, D.S. Henningson, A.V. Johansson, and P.H. Alfredsson, editors, *Turbulence and Transition Modelling*, pages 269 – 336. Kluwer Academic Publishers, 1996.

[511] J. Piquet. *Turbulent flows, models and physics.* Springer-Verlag, 1999.

[512] H. Pitsch. Large eddy simulation of turbulent combustion. *Ann. Rev. Fluid Mech*, 38: 453–482, 2006.

[513] H. Pitsch and N. Peters. A consistent flamelet formulation for non-premixed combustion considering differential diffusion effects. *Combust. Flame*, 114:26–40, 1998.

[514] H. Pitsch and N. Peters. Unsteady flamelet modeling of turbulent hydrogen-air diffusion flames. In *27th Symp. (Int.) on Combustion*, pages 1057–1064. The Combustion Institute, Pittsburgh, 1998.

[515] O. H. Planché and W. C. Reynolds. Heat release effect on mixing in supersonic reacting free shear layers. In *30th Aerospace Sciences Meeting & Exhibit*, pages AIAA Paper 92–0092, Washington DC, 1992.

[516] T. Plessing, P. Terhoeven, N. Peters, and M. Mansour. An experimental and numerical study of a laminar triple flame. *Combust. Flame*, 115:335–353, 1998.

[517] T. Poinsot. Comments on 'flame stretch interactions of laminar premixed hydrogen air flames at normal temperature and pressure' by Aung et al. *Combust. Flame*, 113: 279–284, 1998.

[518] T. Poinsot and S. Candel. A nonlinear model for ducted flame combustion instabilities. *Combust. Sci. Tech.*, 61:121–153, 1988.

[519] T. Poinsot and S. Lele. Boundary conditions for direct simulations of compressible viscous flows. *J. Comput. Phys.*, 101(1):104–129, 1992. doi: 10.1016/0021-9991(92) 90046-2.

[520] T. Poinsot, T. Le Chatelier, S. Candel, and E. Esposito. Experimental determination of the reflection coefficient of a premixed flame in a duct. *J. Sound Vib.*, 107:265–278, 1986.

[521] T. Poinsot, A. Trouvé, D. Veynante, S. Candel, and E. Esposito. Vortex driven acoustically coupled combustion instabilities. *J. Fluid Mech.*, 177:265–292, 1987.

[522] T. Poinsot, D. Veynante, F. Bourienne, S. Candel, E. Esposito, and J. Surjet. Initiation and suppression of combustion instabilities by active control. In *22nd Symp. (Int.) on Combustion*, pages 1363–1370. The Combustion Institute, Pittsburgh, 1988.

[523] T. Poinsot, D. Veynante, and S. Candel. Quenching processes and premixed turbulent combustion diagrams. *J. Fluid Mech.*, 228:561–605, 1991.

[524] T. Poinsot, T. Echekki, and M. G. Mungal. A study of the laminar flame tip and implications for premixed turbulent combustion. *Combust. Sci. Tech.*, 81(1-3):45–73, 1992.

[525] T. Poinsot, D. Haworth, and G. Bruneaux. Direct simulation and modelling of flame-wall interaction for premixed turbulent combustion. *Combust. Flame*, 95(1/2):118–133, 1993.

[526] T. Poinsot, S. Candel, and A. Trouvé. Application of direct numerical simulation to premixed turbulent combustion. *Prog. Energy Comb. Sci.*, 21:531–576, 1996.

[527] T. Poinsot, C. Angelberger, F. Egolfopoulos, and D. Veynante. Large eddy simulations of combustion instabilities. In *1st Int. Symp. On Turbulence and Shear Flow Phenomena*, pages 1-6, Santa Barbara, Sept 12-15., 1999.

[528] T. J. Poinsot, D. Veynante, and S. Candel. Diagrams of premixed turbulent combustion based on direct simulation. In *23rd Symp. (Int.) on Combustion*, pages 613–619. The Combustion Institute, Pittsburgh, 1990.

[529] W. Polifke, A. Poncet, C. O. Paschereit, and K. Doebbeling. Reconstruction of acoustic transfer matrices by instationnary computational fluid dynamics. *J. Sound Vib.*, 245 (3):483–510, 2001.

[530] S. Pope. The evolution of surfaces in turbulence. *Int. J. Engng. Sci.*, 26(5):445–469, 1988.

[531] S. Pope and W. Cheng. The stochastic flamelet model of turbulent premixed combustion. In *22nd Symp. (Int.) on Combustion*, pages 781–789. The Combustion Institute, Pittsburgh, 1988.

[532] S. B. Pope. Pdf methods for turbulent reactive flows. *Prog. Energy Comb. Sci.*, 19(11): 119–192, 1985.

[533] S. B. Pope. Computations of turbulent combustion: progress and challenges. In *23rd Symp. (Int.) on Combustion*, pages 591–612. The Combustion Institute, Pittsburgh, 1990.

[534] S. B. Pope. Computationally efficient implementation of combustion chemistry using in situ adaptive tabulation. *Combust. Theory and Modelling*, 1:41–63, 1997.

[535] S. B. Pope. *Turbulent flows*. Cambridge University Press, 2000.

[536] S. B. Pope. Ten questions concerning the large-eddy simulation of turbulent flows. *New Journal of Physics*, 6:35, 2004.

[537] S. B. Pope, P. K. Yeung, and S. S. Girimaji. The curvature of material surfaces in isotropic turbulence. *Phys. Fluids A*, 12:2010–2018, 1989.

[538] P. Popp and M. Baum. An analysis of wall heat fluxes, reaction mechanisms and unburnt hydrocarbons during the head-on quenching of a laminar methane flame. *Combust. Flame*, 108(3):327 – 348, 1997.

[539] P. Popp, M. Smooke, and M. Baum. Heterogeneous/homogeneous reactions and transport coupling during flame-wall interaction. *Proc. Combust. Inst.*, 26:2693–2700, 1996.

[540] A. Powell. On the edgetone. *J. Acous. Soc. Am.*, 33:395–409, 1961.

[541] L. Prandtl. Investigations on turbulent flow. *Zeitschrift fur angewandte Mathematik und Mechanik*, 5:136, 1925.

[542] E. W. Price. Recent advances in solid propellant combustion instability. In *12th Symp. (Int.) on Combustion*, pages 101–113. The Combustion Institute, Pittsburgh, 1969.

[543] C. Prière, L. Y. M. Gicquel, P. Gajan, A. Strzelecki, T. Poinsot, and C. Bérat. Experimental and numerical studies of dilution systems for low emission combustors. *AIAA Journal*, 43(8):1753–1766, 2005.

[544] R. Prosser. Improved boundary conditions for the direct numerical simulation of turbulent subsonic flows i: Inviscid flows. *J. Comput. Phys.*, 207:736–768, 2005.

[545] R. Prosser. Towards improved boundary conditions for the DNS and LES of turbulent subsonic flows. *J. Comput. Phys.*, 222:469–474, 2007.

[546] A. A. Putnam. *Combustion driven oscillations in industry*. American Elsevier, J.M. Beer editor, Fuel and Energy Science Series, 1971.

[547] A. A. Putnam and L. Faulkner. An overview of combustion noise. *J. Energy*, 7(6): 458–469, 1983.

[548] L. Rayleigh. The explanation of certain acoustic phenomena. *Nature*, July 18:319–321, 1878.

[549] P. H. Renard, D. Thévenin, J. C. Rolon, and S. Candel. Dynamics of flame/vortex interactions. *Prog. Energy Comb. Sci.*, 26:225–282, 2000.

[550] J. Réveillon. *Simulation dynamique des grandes structures appliquée aux flammes turbulentes non-prémélangées.* Phd thesis, Université de Rouen, 1996.

[551] J. Réveillon and L. Vervisch. Response of the dynamic LES model to heat release induced effects. *Phys. FluidsA*, 8(8):2248 – 2250, 1996.

[552] W. C. Reynolds and H. C. Perkins. *Engineering thermodynamics.* McGraw-Hill, 1977.

[553] F. H. Reynst. *Pulsating combustion.* edited by M. Thring, Pergamon press, New-York, 1961.

[554] G. Ribert, M. Champion, O. Gicquel, N. Darabiha, and D. Veynante. Modeling nonadiabatic turbulent premixed reactive flows including tabulated chemistry. *Combust. Flame*, 141(3):271 – 280, 2005.

[555] G. Ribert, O. Gicquel, N. Darabiha, and D. Veynante. Tabulation of complex chemistry based on self-similar behaviour of laminar premixed flames. *Combust. Flame*, 146:649 – 664, 2006.

[556] S. Richard, O. Colin, O. Vermorel, A. Benkenida, C. Angelberger, and D. Veynante. Towards large eddy simulation of combustion in spark ignition engines. *Proc. Combust. Inst.*, 31:3059–3066, 2007.

[557] P. L. Rijke. Notice of a new method of causing a vibration of the air contained in a tube open at both ends. *Phil. Mag.*, 17:419–422, 1859.

[558] P. L. Rijke. Notiz uber eine neue art, die in einer an beiden enden offenen rohre enthaltene luft in schwingungen zu ersetzen. *Annalen der Physik*, 107:339, 1859.

[559] P. J. Roache. *Computational fluid dynamics.* Hermosa Publishers, Albuquerque, 1972.

[560] W. L. Roberts and J. F. Driscoll. A laminar vortex interacting with a premixed flame: measured formation of pockets of reactants. *Combust. Flame*, 87:245–256, 1991.

[561] W. L. Roberts, J. F. Driscoll, M. C. Drake, and J. Ratcliffe. Fluorescence images of the quenching of a premixed flame during an interaction with a vortex. In *24th Symp. (Int.) on Combustion*, pages 169–176. The Combustion Institute, Pittsburgh, 1992.

[562] W. L. Roberts, J. F. Driscoll, M. C. Drake, and L. P. Goss. Images of the quenching of a flame by a vortex: to quantify regimes of turbulent combustion. *Combust. Flame*, 94:58–69, 1993.

[563] V. Robin, A. Mura, M. Champion, and P. Plion. A multi-dirac presumed pdf model for turbulent reactive flows with variable equivalence ratio. *Combust. Sci. Tech.*, 178 (10-11):1843 – 1870, 2006.

[564] M. Roger, C.B. da Silva, and P.J. Coelho. Analysis of the turbulence-radiation interactions for large eddy simulations of turbulent flows. *Int. J. Heat Mass Transfer*, 52:2243 – 2254, 2009.

[565] D. E. Rogers and F. E. Marble. A mechanism for high frequency oscillations in ramjet combustors and afterburners. *Jet Propulsion*, 26:456–462, 1956.

[566] B. Rogg. Modelling and numerical simulation of premixed turbulent combustion in a boundary layer. In *7th Symposium on Turbulent Shear Flows*, pages 26.1.1–26.1.6, Stanford, 1989.

[567] P.D. Ronney and G.I. Sivashinsky. A theoretical study of propagation and extinction of nonsteady spherical flame fronts. *SIAM Journal on Applied Mathematics*, pages 1029–1046, 1989.

[568] J.E. Rossiter. Wind-tunnel experiments on the flow over rectangular cavities at subsonic and transonic speeds. Technical Report Technical Report 3438, Aeronautical Research Council Reports and Memoranda, 1964.

[569] S. Roux. *Influence de la modélisation du mélange air/carburant et de l'étendue du domaine de calcul dans la simulation aux grandes échelles des instabilités de combustion. Application à des foyers aéronautiques.* Phd thesis, INP Toulouse, 2008.

[570] S. Roux, G. Lartigue, T. Poinsot, U. Meier, and C. Bérat. Studies of mean and unsteady flow in a swirled combustor using experiments, acoustic analysis and large eddy simulations. *Combust. Flame*, 141:40–54, 2005.

[571] D. H. Rudy and J. C. Strikwerda. A non-reflecting outflow boundary condition for subsonic Navier Stokes calculations. *J. Comput. Phys.*, 36:55–70, 1980.

[572] D. H. Rudy and J. C. Strikwerda. Boundary conditions for subsonic compressible Navier Stokes calculations. *Comput. Fluids*, 9:327–338, 1981.

[573] G. R. Ruetsch and M. R. Maxey. Small scale features of vorticity and passive scalar fields in homogeneous isotropic turbulence. *Phys. Fluids A*, 3:1587–1597, 1991.

[574] G. R. Ruetsch, L. Vervisch, and A. Linan. Effects of heat release on triple flames. *Phys. Fluids*, 7(6):1447–1454, 1995.

[575] A. Ruiz and L. Selle. Simulation of a turbulent supercritical hydrogen/oxygen flow behind a splitter plate: cold flow and flame stabilization. Seventh Mediterranean Combustion Symposium, September 2011.

[576] C. J. Rutland and R. S. Cant. Turbulent transport in premixed flames. In *Proc. of the Summer Program*, pages 75–94. Center for Turbulence Research, NASA Ames/Stanford Univ., 1994.

[577] C. J. Rutland and J. Ferziger. Interaction of a vortex and a premixed flame. In AIAA Paper 89-0127, editor, *27th AIAA Aerospace Sciences Meeting*, Reno, 1989.

[578] C. J. Rutland and J. Ferziger. Simulation of flame-vortex interactions. *Combust. Flame*, 84:343–360, 1991.

[579] C. J. Rutland and A. Trouvé. Pre-mixed flame simulations for non-unity Lewis numbers. In *Proc. of the Summer Program*, pages 299–309. Center for Turbulence Research, NASA Ames/Stanford Univ., 1990.

[580] C. J. Rutland and A. Trouvé. Direct simulations of premixed turbulent flames with nonunity lewis number. *Combust. Flame*, 94(1/2):41–57, 1993.

[581] P. Sagaut. *Large Eddy Simulation for incompressible flows*. Scientific computation series. Springer-Verlag, 2000.

[582] R. Said and R. Borghi. A simulation with a "cellular automaton" for turbulent combustion modelling. In *22nd Symp. (Int.) on Combustion*, pages 569 – 577. The Combustion Institute, 1988.

[583] J.-M. Samaniego. An experimental study of the interaction of a two-dimensional vortex with a plane laminar premixed flame. In *Western States Section Fall Meeting*, pages Paper 93–061, Menlo Park, 1993. The Combustion Institute, Pittsburgh.

[584] J.-M. Samaniego and T. Mantel. Fundamental mechanisms in premixed turbulent flame propagation via vortex flame interactions. part i: experiment. *Combust. Flame*, 118(4): 537–556, 1999.

[585] J.-M. Samaniego, B. Yip, T. Poinsot, and S. Candel. Low-frequency combustion instability mechanism in a side-dump combustor. *Combust. Flame*, 94(4):363–381, 1993.

[586] R. Sankaran, E. Hawkes, J. Chen, T. Lu, and C. K. Law. Structure of a spatially developing turbulent lean methane–air bunsen flame. *Proc. Combust. Inst.*, 31:1291–1298, 2007.

[587] F. Sarghini, U. Piomelli, and E. Balaras. Scale-similar models for large-eddy simulations. *Phys. Fluids A*, 11(6):1596 – 1607, 1999.

[588] S. Sarkar, G. Erlebacher, M. Y. Hussaini, and H. O. Kreiss. The analysis and modelling of dilatational terms in compressible turbulence. *J. Fluid Mech.*, 227:473–491, 1991.

[589] J. Sato. Effects of Lewis number on extinction behavior of premixed flames in stagnation flow. In *19th Symp. (Int.) on Combustion*, pages 1541–1548. The Combustion Institute, Pittsburgh, 1982.

[590] R. W. Schefer and P. Goix. Mechanisms of flame stabilization in turbulent lifted-jet flames. *Combust. Flame*, 112:559–570, 1998.

[591] H. Schlichting. *Boundary layer theory*. McGraw-Hill, New York, 1955.

[592] J.U. Schluter, H. Pitsch, and P. Moin. Large eddy simulation inflow conditions for coupling with Reynolds-averaged flow solvers. *AIAA Journal*, 42(3):478–484, 2004.

[593] J.U. Schluter, X. Wu, S. Kim, S. Shankaran, J.J. Alonso, and H. Pitsch. A framework for coupling Reynolds-averaged with large-eddy simulations for gas turbine applications. *J. Fluids Eng.*, 127(4):806–815, 2005.

[594] P. Schmitt, T. Poinsot, B. Schuermans, and K. P. Geigle. Large-eddy simulation and experimental study of heat transfer, nitric oxide emissions and combustion instability in a swirled turbulent high-pressure burner. *J. Fluid Mech.*, 570:17–46, 2007.

[595] T. Schmitt, L. Selle, A. Ruiz, and B. Cuenot. Large-eddy simulation of supercritical-pressure round jets. *AIAA Journal*, 48(9):2133–2144, September 2010.

[596] T. Schmitt, Y. Méry, M. Boileau, and S. Candel. Large-eddy simulation of methane/oxygen flame under transcritical conditions. *Proc. Combust. Inst.*, 33, 2011.

[597] B. Schuermans, V. Bellucci, and C. Paschereit. Thermoacoustic modeling and control of multiburner combustion systems. In *International Gas Turbine and Aeroengine Congress & Exposition, ASME Paper*, volume 2003-GT-38688, 2003.

[598] B. Schuermans, C. Paschereit, and P. Monkewitz. Non-linear combustion instabilities in annular gas-turbine combustors. In *44th AIAA Aerospace Sciences Meeeting and Exhibit*, volume AIAA paper 2006-0549, 2006.

[599] G. Searby and J. Quinard. Direct and indirect measurements of Markstein numbers of premixed flames. *Combust. Flame*, 82:298–311, 1990.

[600] L. Selle. *Simulation aux grandes échelles des interactions flamme-acoustique dans un écoulement vrillé*. Phd thesis, INP Toulouse, 2004.

[601] L. Selle, G. Lartigue, T. Poinsot, R. Koch, K.-U. Schildmacher, W. Krebs, B. Prade, P. Kaufmann, and D. Veynante. Compressible large-eddy simulation of turbulent combustion in complex geometry on unstructured meshes. *Combust. Flame*, 137(4):489–505, 2004.

[602] L. Selle, F. Nicoud, and T. Poinsot. The actual impedance of non-reflecting boundary conditions: implications for the computation of resonators. *AIAA Journal*, 42(5):958–964, 2004.

[603] L. Selle, L. Benoit, T. Poinsot, F. Nicoud, and W. Krebs. Joint use of compressible large-eddy simulation and Helmholtz solvers for the analysis of rotating modes in an industrial swirled burner. *Combust. Flame*, 145(1-2):194–205, 2006.

[604] L. Selle, T. Poinsot, and B. Ferret. Experimental and numerical study of the accuracy of flame-speed measurements for methane/air combustion in a slot burner. *Combust. Flame*, 158(1):146–154, 2011.

[605] A. Sengissen, A. Giauque, G. Staffelbach, M. Porta, W. Krebs, P. Kaufmann, and T. Poinsot. Large eddy simulation of piloting effects on turbulent swirling flames. *Proc. Combust. Inst.*, 31:1729–1736, 2007.

[606] T. K. Sengupta. *Fundamentals of Computational Fluid Dynamics*. Universities Press, Hyderabad (India), 2004.

[607] T. K. Sengupta, G. Ganerwal, and A. Dipankar. High accuracy compact schemes and Gibbs' phenomenon. *J. Sci. Comput.*, 21(3):253–268, 2004.

[608] C. Sensiau. *Simulations numériques des instabilités thermoacoustiques dans les chambres de combustion aéronautiques - TH/CFD/08/127*. PhD thesis, Université de Montpellier II, - Institut de Mathématiques et de Modélisation de Montpellier, France, 2008.

[609] K. Seshadri. Multistep asymptotic analyses of flame structures (plenary lecture). *Proc. Combust. Inst.*, 26:831–846, 1996.

[610] K. Seshadri and N. Peters. Asymptotic structure and extinction of methane-air diffusion flames. *Combust. Flame*, 73:23–44, 1988.

[611] K. Seshadri, N. Peters, and F. A. Williams. Asymptotic analyses of stoichiometric and lean hydrogen-air flames. *Combust. Flame*, 96(4):407–427, 1994.

[612] Z.-S. She, E. Jackson, and S. A. Orszag. Intermittent vortex structures in homogeneous isotropic turbulence. *Nature*, 344:226–228, 1990.

[613] S. Sheekrishna, S. Hemchandra, and T. Lieuwen. Premixed flame response to equivalence ratio perturbations. *Combust. Theory and Modelling*, 14(5):681 – 714, 2010.

[614] I. G. Shepherd, J. B. Moss, and K. N. C. Bray. Turbulent transport in a confined premixed flame. In *19th Symp. (Int.) on Combustion*, pages 423–431. The Combustion Institute, Pittsburgh, 1982.

[615] M. A. Singer and S. B. Pope. Exploiting ISAT to solve the equations of reacting flow. *Combust. Theory and Modelling*, 8(2):361 383, 2004.

[616] G. I. Sivashinsky. Instabilities, pattern formation, and turbulence in flames. *Ann. Rev. Fluid Mech*, 15:179–199, 1983.

[617] J. Smagorinsky. General circulation experiments with the primitive equations: 1. the basic experiment. *Mon. Weather Rev.*, 91:99–164, 1963.

[618] V. Smiljanovski, V. Moser, and R. Klein. A capturing-tracking hybrid scheme for deflagration discontinuities. *Combust. Theory and Modelling*, 1(2):183 – 215, 1997.

[619] D. A. Smith and E. E. Zukoski. Combustion instability sustained by unsteady vortex combustion. In *21st Joint Propulsion Conference*, pages AIAA paper 85–1248, Monterey, 1985.

[620] T. Smith and S. Menon. Model simulations of freely propagating turbulent premixed flames. In *26th Symp. (Int.) on Combustion*, pages 299–306. The Combustion Institute, Pittsburgh, 1996.

[621] M. D. Smooke. *Reduced kinetic mechanisms and asymptotic approximations of methane-air flames*, volume 384 of *Lecture Notes in Physics*. Springer-Verlag, Berlin, 1991.

[622] A. Soufiani and E. Djavdan. A comparison between weighted sum of gray gases and statistical narrow-band radiation models for combustion applications. *Combust. Flame*, 97(2):240–250, 1994.

[623] D. B. Spalding. Mixing and chemical reaction in steady confined turbulent flames. In *13th Symp. (Int.) on Combustion*, pages 649–657. The Combustion Institute, Pittsburgh, 1971.

[624] D. B. Spalding. Development of the eddy-break-up model of turbulent combustion. In *16th Symp. (Int.) on Combustion*, pages 1657–1663. The Combustion Institute, 1976.

[625] E. F. Spina, A. J. Smits, and S. K. Robinson. The physics of supersonic turbulent boundary layers. *Ann. Rev. Fluid Mech*, 26:287–319, 1994.

[626] G. Staffelbach, L.Y.M. Gicquel, G. Boudier, and T. Poinsot. Large eddy simulation of self-excited azimuthal modes in annular combustors. *Proc. Combust. Inst.*, 32:2909–2916, 2009.

[627] A. Stoessel, M. Hilka, and M. Baum. 2D direct numerical simulation of turbulent combustion on massively parallel processing platforms. In *1994 EUROSIM Conference on Massively Parallel Computing*, pages 793–800, Delft, 1994. Elsevier Science B.V.

[628] S. R. Stow and A. P. Dowling. Thermoacoustic oscillations in an annular combustor. In *ASME Paper*, New Orleans, Louisiana, 2001.

[629] W. Strahle. Combustion noise. *Prog. Energy Comb. Sci.*, 4:157–176, 1978.

[630] W. Strahle. A more modern theory of combustion noise. In C. Casci and C. Bruno, editors, *Recent Advances in the Aerospace Sciences*, pages 103–114. Plenum Press, New York, 1985.

[631] J. C. Strikwerda. Initial boundary value problem for incompletely parabolic systems. *Commun. Pure Appl. Math.*, 30:797, 1977.

[632] D. R. Stull and H. Prophet. JANAF thermochemical tables, 2nd Edition. Technical Report NSRDS-NBS 37, US National Bureau of Standards, 1971.

[633] J. Sutherland and C. Kennedy. Improved boundary conditions for viscous, reacting, compressible flows. *J. Comput. Phys.*, 191:502–524, 2003.

[634] N. Swaminathan and R. W. Bilger. Assessment of combustion submodels for turbulent nonpremixed hydrocarbon flames. *Combust. Flame*, 116(4):519–545, 1999.

[635] N. Syred. A review of oscillation mechanims and the role of the precessing vortex core in swirl combustion systems. *Prog. Energy Comb. Sci.*, 32(2):93–161, 2006.

[636] S. E. El Tahry, C. J. Rutland, and J. Ferziger. Structure and propagation speeds of turbulent premixed flames - a numerical study. *Combust. Flame*, 83:155–173, 1991.

[637] C. Tam and P. Block. On the tones and pressure oscillations over rectangular cavities. *J. Fluid Mech.*, 89(2):373–399, 1978.

[638] M. Tanahashi, Y. Nada, M. Fujimura, and T. Miyauchi. Fine scale structure of H2-air turbulent premixed flames. In S. Banerjee Eds and J.Eaton, editors, *1st International Symposium on Turbulence and Shear Flow*, pages 59–64, Santa Barbara, Sept 12-15., 1999.

[639] M. Tanahashi, T. Saito, M. Shimamura, and T. Miyauchi. Local extinction and NOx formation in methane-air turbulent premixed flames. In *2nd Asia-Pacific Conference on Combustion*, pages 500–503, Tainan, Taiwan, 1999. The Combustion Institute, Pittsburgh.

[640] J.C. Tannehill, D.A. Anderson, and R.H. Pletcher. *Computational Fluid Mechanics and Heat Transfer*. Taylor & Francis, 1997.

[641] B. Tao, J. Katz, and C. Meneveau. Statistical geometry of subgrid-scale stresses determined from holographic partcile image velocimetry measurements. *J. Fluid Mech.*, 457:35–78, 2002.

[642] F. Tap and D. Veynante. Simulation of flame lift-off on a diesel jet using a generalized flame surface density modelling approach. *Proc. Combust. Inst.*, 30:in press, 2004.

[643] F. Tap, R. Hilbert, D. Thévenin, and D. Veynante. A generalized flame surface density modelling approach for the auto-ignition of a turbulent non-premixed system. *Combust. Theory and Modelling*, 8:165 – 193, 2004.

[644] H. Tennekes and J. L. Lumley. *A first course in turbulence*. M.I.T. Press, Cambridge, 1972.

[645] D. Thevenin. Three-dimensional direct simulations and structure of expanding turbulent methane flames. *Proc. Combust. Inst.*, 30:in press, 2004.

[646] D. Thevenin, P. H. Renard, C. Rolon, and S. Candel. Extinction processes during a non-premixed flame vortex interaction. In *27th Symp. (Int.) on Combustion*, pages 719–726. The Combustion Institute, Pittsburgh, 1998.

[647] D. Thevenin, P. H. Renard, G. Fiechtner, J. Gord, and J. C. Rolon. Regimes of non-premixed flame/vortex interaction. In *28th Symp. (Int.) on Combustion*, pages 2101–2108. The Combustion Institute, Pittsburgh, 2000.

[648] K. W. Thompson. Time dependent boundary conditions for hyperbolic systems. *J. Comput. Phys.*, 68:1–24, 1987.

[649] J.H. Tien and M. Matalon. On the burning velocity of stretched flames. *Combust. Flame*, 84(3-4):238–248, 1991.

[650] A. Triantafyllidis, E. Mastorakos, and R. Eggels. Large eddy simulations of forced ignition of a non-premixed bluff-body methane flame with conditional moment closure. *Combust. Flame*, 156(12):2328 – 2345, 2009.

[651] A. Trouve. Simulation of flame-turbulence interactions in premixed combustion. In *Annual Research Briefs*, pages 273–286. Center for Turbulence Research, NASA Ames/Stanford Univ., 1991.

[652] A. Trouvé and T. Poinsot. The evolution equation for the flame surface density. *J. Fluid Mech.*, 278:1–31, 1994.

[653] A. Trouve, S. Candel, and J. W. Daily. Linear stability of the inlet jet in a ramjet combustor. In *26th Aerospace Sciences Meeting*, pages AIAA paper 88–0149, Reno, 1988.

[654] A. Trouvé, D. Veynante, K. N. C. Bray, and T. Mantel. The coupling between flame surface dynamics and species mass conservation in premixed turbulent combustion. In *Proc. of the Summer Program*, pages 95–124. Center for Turbulence Research, NASA Ames/Stanford Univ., 1994.

[655] J. M. Truffaut and G. Searby. Experimental study of the darrieus-landau instability on an inverted-'V' flame, and measurement of the Markstein number. *Combust. Sci. Tech.*, 149(1-6):35–52, 1999.

[656] K. Truffin and T. Poinsot. Comparison and extension of methods for acoustic identification of burners. *Combust. Flame*, 142(4):388–400, 2005.

[657] H. S. Tsien. The transfer functions of rocket nozzles. *J. American Rocket Society*, 22 (3):139–143, 1952.

[658] A. Upatnieks, J. F. Driscoll, C. Rasmussen, and S. Ceccio. Liftoff of turbulent jet flames - assessment of edge flame and other concepts using cinema-piv. *Combust. Flame*, 138: 259–272, 2004.

[659] T. Upton, D. Verhoeven, and D. Hudgins. High-resolution computed tomography of a turbulent reacting flow. *Exp. Fluids*, 50:125–134, 2011.

[660] C. M. Vagelopoulos and F. Egolfopoulos. Direct experimental determination of laminar flame speeds. In *27th Symp. (Int.) on Combustion*, pages 513–519. The Combustion Institute, Pittsburgh, 1998.

[661] F. van der Bos, B. Tao, C. Meneveau, and J. Katz. Effects of small-scale turbulent motions on the filtered velocity gradient tensor as deduced from holographic partilce image velocimetry measurements. *Phys. Fluids*, 14(7):2456 – 2474, 2002.

[662] E. van Kalmthout. *Stabilisation et modelisation des flammes turbulentes non premelangees. Etude theorique et simulations directes.* Phd thesis, Ecole Centrale de Paris, 1996.

[663] E. van Kalmthout and D. Veynante. Analysis of flame surface density concepts in non-premixed turbulent combustion using direct numerical simulation. In *11th Symp. on Turbulent Shear Flows*, pages 21–7, 21–12, Grenoble, France, 1997.

[664] E. van Kalmthout and D. Veynante. Direct numerical simulation analysis of flame surface density models for non premixed turbulent combustion. *Phys. Fluids A*, 10(9): 2347 – 2368, 1998.

[665] E. van Kalmthout, D. Veynante, and S. Candel. Direct numerical simulation analysis of flame surface density in non-premixed turbulent combustion. In *26th Symp. (Int.) on Combustion*, pages 35–42. The Combustion Institute, Pittsburgh, 1996.

[666] J. A. van Oijen, F. A. Lammers, and L. P. H. de Goey. Modeling of premixed laminar flames using flamelet generated manifolds. *Combust. Sci. Tech.*, 127:2124–2134, 2001.

[667] B. Varoquié, J.-P. Légier, F. Lacas, D. Veynante, and T. Poinsot. Experimental analysis and large eddy simulation to determine the response of non-premixed flame submitted to acoustic forcing. *Proc. Combust. Inst.*, 29:1965–1970, 2002.

[668] O. Vermorel. Flame wall interaction of h2-o2 flames. Technical Report STR/CFD/99/44, CERFACS, 1999.

[669] O. Vermorel, S. Richard, O. Colin, C. Angelberger, A. Benkenida, and D. Veynante. Towards the understanding of cyclic variability in a spark ignited engine using multi-cycle LES. *Combust. Flame*, 156(8):1525–1541, 2009.

[670] L. Vervisch and T. Poinsot. Direct numerical simulation of non premixed turbulent flames. *Ann. Rev. Fluid Mech*, 30:655–692, 1998.

[671] L. Vervisch and D. Veynante. Interlinks between approaches for modeling turbulent flames. *Proc. Combust. Inst.*, 28:175–183, 2000.

[672] L. Vervisch, E. Bidaux, K. N. C. Bray, and W. Kollmann. Surface density function in premixed turbulent combustion modeling, similarities between probability density function and flame surface approaches. *Phys. Fluids A*, 7(10):2496, 1995.

[673] L. Vervisch, R. Hauguel, P. Domingo, and M. Rullaud. Three facets of turbulent combustion modelling: DNS of premixed V-flame, LES of lifted nonpremixed flame and
RANS of jet flame. *J. Turb.*, 5:004, 2004.

[674] D. Veynante and R. Knikker. Comparison between LES results and experimental data
in reacting flows. *J. Turb.*, 7(35):1–20, 2006.

[675] D. Veynante and T. Poinsot. Effects of pressure gradients on turbulent premixed flames.
J. Fluid Mech., 353:83–114, 1997.

[676] D. Veynante and T. Poinsot. Large eddy simulation of combustion instabilities in turbulent premixed burners. In *Annual Research Briefs*, pages 253–274. Center for Turbulence
Research, NASA Ames/Stanford Univ., 1997.

[677] D. Veynante and T. Poinsot. Reynolds averaged and large eddy simulation modeling
for turbulent combustion. In O. Métais and J. Ferziger, editors, *New tools in turbulence
modelling. Lecture 5*, pages 105–135. Les editions de Physique, Springer, 1997.

[678] D. Veynante and L. Vervisch. Turbulent combustion modeling. *Prog. Energy Comb.
Sci.*, 28:193 – 266, 2002.

[679] D. Veynante, S. Candel, and J.-P. Martin. Coherent flame modelling of chemical reaction
in a turbulent mixing layer. In J. Warnatz and W. Jager, editors, *Complex Chemical
Reactions*, pages 386–398. Springer Verlag, Heidelberg, 1987.

[680] D. Veynante, F. Lacas, E. Maistret, and S. Candel. Coherent flame model in non
uniformly premixed turbulent flames. In *7th Symposium on Turbulent Shear Flows*,
pages 26.2.1–26.2.6, Stanford, 1989.

[681] D. Veynante, J. M. D. Duclos, and J. Piana. Experimental analysis of flamelet models for
premixed turbulent combustion. In *25th Symp. (Int.) on Combustion*, pages 1249–1256.
The Combustion Institute, Pittsburgh, 1994.

[682] D. Veynante, J. Piana, J. M. Duclos, and C. Martel. Experimental analysis of flame
surface density model for premixed turbulent combustion. In *26th Symp. (Int.) on
Combustion*, pages 413–420, Naples, 1996. The Combustion Institute, Pittsburgh.

[683] D. Veynante, A. Trouvé, K. N. C. Bray, and T. Mantel. Gradient and counter-gradient
scalar transport in turbulent premixed flames. *J. Fluid Mech.*, 332:263–293, 1997.

[684] D. Veynante, B. Fiorina, P. Domingo, and L. Vervisch. Using self-similar properties of
turbulent premixed flames to downsize chemical tables in high-performance numerical
simulations. *Combust. Theory and Modelling*, 12(6):1055–1088, 2008.

[685] D. Veynante, G. Lodato, P. Domingo, L. Vervisch, and E.R. Hawkes. Estimation of
three-dimensional flame surface densities from planar images in turbulent premixed combustion. *Exp. Fluids*, 49(1):267–278, 2010.

[686] R. Vichnevetsky. Invariance theorems concerning reflection at numerical boundaries. Technical Report 08544, Princeton University, Dept of Mech. and Aerospace Eng., 1982.

[687] R. Vichnevetsky and J. B. Bowles. *Fourier analysis of numerical approximations of hyperbolic equations*. SIAM Studies in Applied Mechanics, Philadelphia, 1982.

[688] R. Vichnevetsky and E. C. Pariser. Nonreflecting upwind boundaries for hyperbolic equations. *Num. Meth. for Partial Diff. Equations*, 2:1–12, 1986.

[689] R. Villasenor, J. Y. Chen, and R. W. Pitz. Modeling ideally expanded supersonic turbulent jet flows with nonpremixed H2-air combustion. *AIAA Journal*, 30(2):395–402, 1992.

[690] A. Vincent and M. Meneguzzi. The spatial structure and statistical properties of homogeneous turbulence. *J. Fluid Mech.*, 225:1–25, 1991.

[691] T. von Kármán and G. Millan. Thermal theory of laminar flame front near cold wall. In *Fourth Symp. (Int.) on Combustion*, pages 173–177, Munich, 1953. The Combustion Institute, Pittsburgh.

[692] S. R. Vosen, R. Greif, and C. K. Westbrook. Unsteady heat transfer during laminar flame quenching. In *20th Symp. (Int.) on Combustion*, pages 76–83. The Combustion Institute, Pittsburgh, 1984.

[693] A. W. Vreman. An eddy-viscosity subgrid-scale model for turbulent shear flow: algebraic theory and applications. *Phys. Fluids*, 16(10):3670–3681, October 2004.

[694] B. Vreman, B. Geurts, and H. Kuerten. On the formulation of the dynamic mixed subgrid-scale model. *Phys. Fluids*, 6(12):4057–4059, 1994.

[695] B. Vreman, B. Geurts, and H. Kuerten. Large-eddy simulation of the turbulent mixing layer. *J. Fluid Mech.*, 1997.

[696] F. Vuillot. Acoustic mode determination in solid rocket motor stability analysis. *J. Prop. Power*, 3(4):381–384, 1987.

[697] G. Wang, M. Boileau, and D. Veynante. Implementation of a dynamic thickened flame model for large eddysimulations of turbulent premixed combustion. *Combust. Flame*, 158(11):2199–2213, 2011.

[698] K. Wang, G. Ribert, P. Domingo, and L. Vervisch. Self-similar behavior and chemistry tabulation of burnt-gas diluted premixed flamelets including heat-loss. *Combust. Theory and Modelling*, 14(4):541–570, 2010.

[699] P. Weigand, W. Meier, X.R. Duan, W. Stricker, and M. Aigner. Investigations of swirl flames in a gas turbine model combustor: I. flow field, structures, temperature, and species distributions. *Combust. Flame*, 144(1-2):205–224, January 2006.

[700] E. Well. An unpublished letter by Davy on the safety-lamp. *Annals of Science*, 6(3): 306–307, 1950.

[701] H. G. Weller, G. Tabor, A. D. Gosman, and C. Fureby. Application of a flame-wrinkling LES combustion model to a a turbulent mixing layer. In *27th Symp. (Int.) on Combustion*, pages 899 – 907. The Combustion Institute, Pittsburgh, 1998.

[702] C. Westbrook and F. Dryer. Simplified reaction mechanism for the oxidation of hydrocarbon fuels in flames. *Combust. Sci. Tech.*, 27:31–43, 1981.

[703] C. Westbrook, Y. Mizobuchi, T. Poinsot, P. J. Smith, and J. Warnatz. Computational combustion (plenary lecture). *Proc. Combust. Inst.*, 30:125–157, 2004.

[704] C. K. Westbrook. Hydrogen oxydation kinetics in gaseous detonation. *Combust. Sci. Tech.*, 29:67 – 81, 1982.

[705] C. K. Westbrook, A. A. Adamczyk, and G. A. Lavoie. A numerical study of laminar flame wall quenching. *Combust. Flame*, 40:81–99, 1981.

[706] R. V. Wheeler. The inflammation of mixtures of methane and air in a closed vessel. *J. Chem. Soc.*, 113:840–859, 1918.

[707] R. V. Wheeler. The inflammation of mixtures of ethane and air in a closed vessel - the effects of turbulence. *J. Chem. Soc.*, 115:81–94, 1919.

[708] F. M. White. *Viscous fluid flow*. McGraw-Hill, New-York, 1991.

[709] I. Wichman and G. Bruneaux. Head on quenching of a premixed flame by a cold wall. *Combust. Flame*, 103(4):296–310, 1995.

[710] F. A. Williams. *Combustion Theory*. Benjamin Cummings, Menlo Park, CA, 1985.

[711] F. A. Williams. The role of theory in combustion science. In *24th Symp. (Int.) on Combustion*, pages 1–18, Sydney, 1992. The Combustion Institute, Pittsburgh.

[712] P. Wolf, G. Staffelbach, A. Roux, L. Gicquel, T. Poinsot, and V. Moureau. Massively parallel LES of azimuthal thermo-acoustic instabilities in annular gas turbines. *C. R. Acad. Sci.Mécanique*, 337(6-7):385–394, 2009.

[713] P. Wolf, G. Staffelbach, R. Balakrishnan, A. Roux, and T. Poinsot. Azimuthal instabilities in annular combustion chambers. In NASA Ames/Stanford Univ. Center for Turbulence Research, editor, *Proc. of the Summer Program*, pages 259–269, 2010.

[714] X Wu, Z Huang, X Wang, C Jin, C Tang, L Wei, and C.K Law. Laminar burning velocities and flame instabilities of 2, 5-dimethylfuran-air mixtures at elevated pressures. *Combust. Flame*, 158(3):539–546, 2010.

[715] Y. Wu, D. C. Haworth, M. F. Modest, and B. Cuenot. Direct numerical simulation of turbulence/radiation interaction in premixed combustion systems. *Proc. Combust. Inst.*, 30:639–646, 2005.

[716] V. Yakhot, C. G. Orszag, S. Thangam, T. B. Gatski, and C. G. Speziale. Development of turbulence models for shear flows by a double expansion technique. *Phys. Fluids*, 4 (7):1510, 1992.

[717] I. Yamaoka and H. Tsuji. Determination of burning velocity using counterflow flames. In *20th Symp. (Int.) on Combustion*, pages 1883–1892. The Combustion Institute, Pittsburgh, 1984.

[718] H. Yamashita, M. Shimada, and T. Takeno. A numerical study on flame stability at the transition point of jet diffusion flame. In *26th Symp. (Int.) on Combustion*, pages 27 – 34. The Combustion Institute, Pittsburgh, 1996.

[719] B. Yang and S. B. Pope. Treating chemistry in combustion with detailed mechanisms - in situ adaptive tabulation in principal directions - premixed combustion. *Combust. Flame*, 112:85–112, 1998.

[720] V. Yang and F. E. C. Culick. Analysis of low-frequency combustion instabilities in a laboratory ramjet combustor. *Combust. Sci. Tech.*, 45:1–25, 1986.

[721] P. K. Yeung, S. S. Girimaji, and S. B. Pope. Straining and scalar dissipation on material surfaces in turbulence: implications for flamelets. *Combust. Flame*, 79:340–365, 1990.

[722] M. Yokokawa, K. Itakura, A. Uno, T. Ishihara, and Y. Kaneda. 16.4-Tflops direct numerical simulation of turbulence by a Fourier spectral method on the Earth Simulator. In *Conference on High Performance Networking and Computing archive*, Baltimore, Maryland, U.S.A., 2002.

[723] C. S. Yoo, R. Sankaran, and J. H. Chen. Three-dimensional direct numerical simulation of a turbulent lifted hydrogen jet flame in heated coflow: flame stabilization and structure. *J. Fluid Mech.*, 640(453-481), 2010.

[724] C. S. Yoo, E. S. Richardson, R. Sankaran, and J. H. Chen. A DNS study on the stabilization mechanism of a turbulent lifted ethylene jet flame in highly-heated coflow. *Proc. Combust. Inst.*, 33:1619–1627, 2011.

[725] C.S. Yoo and H.G. Im. Characteristic boundary conditions for simulations of compressible reacting flows with multi-dimensional, viscous, and reaction effects. *Combust. Theory and Modelling*, 11:259–286, 2007.

[726] A. Yoshizawa. Statistical theory for compressible turbulent shear flows, with the application to subgrid modeling. *Phys. Fluids*, 29(7):2152–2164, 1986.

[727] D. You and P. Moin. A dynamic global-coefficient subgrid-scale eddy-viscosity model for large-eddy simulation in complex geometries. *Phys. Fluids*, 19(6):065110, June 2007.

[728] D. You and P. Moin. A dynamic global-coefficient subgrid-scale model for large-eddy simulation of turbulent scalar transport in complex geometries. *Phys. Fluids*, 21(4): 045109, April 2009.

[729] Y. Zang, R. L. Street, and J. R. Koseff. A dynamic subgrid-scale model and its application to turbulent recirculating flows. *Phys. Fluids*, 5(12):3186–3196, 1993.

[730] O. Zeman. Dilatation dissipation: the concept and application in modeling compressible mixing layers. *Phys. Fluids*, 2:178–188, 1990.

[731] S. Zhang and C. Rutland. Premixed flame effects on turbulence and pressure related terms. *Combust. Flame*, 102:447–461, 1995.

[732] S. Zikikout, S. Candel, T. Poinsot, A. Trouvé, and E. Esposito. High frequency oscillations produced by mode selective acoustic excitation. In *21st Symp. (Int.) on Combustion*, pages 1427–1434, Munich, 1986. The Combustion Institute, Pittsburgh.

Index